The History of Accounting

This is a volume in the Arno Press collection

The History of Accounting

See last pages of this volume
for a complete list of titles

AUDITING
THEORY AND PRACTICE

BY

ROBERT H. MONTGOMERY

ARNO PRESS
A New York Times Company
New York — 1976

Editorial Supervision: SHEILA MEHLMAN

Reprint Edition 1976 by Arno Press Inc.

Reprinted from a copy in The American Institute
of Certified Public Accountants Library

THE HISTORY OF ACCOUNTING
ISBN for complete set: 0-405-07540-5
See last pages of this volume for titles.

Manufactured in the United States of America

Library of Congress Cataloging in Publication Data

Montgomery, Robert Hiester, 1872-1953.
Auditing theory and practice.

(The History of accounting)
Reprint of the ed. published by Ronald Press Co.,
New York.
1. Auditing. I. Title. II. Series.
HF5667.M7 1976 657'.45 75-18477
ISBN 0-405-07559-6

AUDITING
THEORY AND PRACTICE

BY

ROBERT H. MONTGOMERY, C.P.A.

of the firm of Lybrand, Ross Bros. & Montgomery. Editor Dicksee's "Auditing" (American Edition), Instructor in Accounting, Columbia University. Formerly Lecturer on Auditing, University of Pennsylvania and New York University. Attorney-at-Law.

NEW YORK

THE RONALD PRESS COMPANY

1912

TO

E. S. M.

WITHOUT WHOSE INSPIRATION
THIS BOOK WOULD NOT
HAVE BEEN WRITTEN

PREFACE

THERE is a demand for a practical book on auditing which up to this time has not been met. If my twenty-four years of continuous experience in professional accountancy work is a sufficient practical training, I trust I have established a *prima facie* excuse for the presentation of this book, which contains more of practice than of theory.

Auditing, in its broadest sense, is the most important branch of accountancy. During the early years of my clerkship in the office of Mr. John Heins, of Philadelphia (then President of the American Association of Public Accountants), and later, while acting as an instructor in the School of Accounts and Finance of the University of Pennsylvania, I strongly felt the need of a dependable textbook on the subject. My attention was all the more directed to the paucity of books on auditing and on other accounting and cognate subjects by contrast with the full and comprehensive literature of the legal profession which I had found of such great assistance in my studies preparatory to admission to the bar.

Mr. Dicksee's work on auditing was for many years an authority in American offices. In 1905 I published an American edition of his book, in which I omitted the statutes and other matter which related solely to British practice, and rewrote, or left unchanged, the parts applicable to American practice. The book met with such success that in 1909 a second edition was required.

During the last few years, however, I have noted in the profession a radical departure from the principles and procedure enunciated by Mr. Dicksee. More is now expected of the auditor, and, happily, many of the profession have met this broader demand and have shown that the services of the practitioner must extend over the whole field of business activity. In view of these recent and important developments, I feel justified in giving a subordinate place in this work to what were formerly regarded as the chief objects of an audit; and what I consider to be the major objects of a modern audit are discussed exhaustively.

It may be that I am too radical in some of my interpretations of the ideal procedure. Perhaps to follow strictly the rules laid down in this book would require more time than any auditor is willing to devote to a single engagement. The exigencies of a particular case may make the opportunities for investigation more limited than the auditor would wish them to be. But the student and the young practitioner particularly should, nevertheless, be careful not to restrict the scope of their theory and practice until they have considered the last safeguard which can be applied to business transactions and have followed up the slightest hint which may throw light upon any irregularity in a concern under audit.

I would not have the courage to present this book to the profession if it had not been for the commendatory assurances and helpful suggestions of my partners, William M. Lybrand, C. P. A., and Walter A. Staub, C. P. A., and my friend Joseph E. Sterrett, C. P. A., who read all my manuscript and to whom I am tremendously indebted. I am also indebted to John R. Wildman, C. P. A., of the New York University, who also read my manuscript and from whom I received many suggestions which I am sure will make the book more helpful to students.

The very comprehensive chapter on Municipal Auditing was (with very minor exceptions) prepared by U. L. Leonhauser, C. P. A., Secretary of the Metz Fund for Promoting Efficient Municipal Accounting and Reporting.

Other suggestions of value have come to me from my friends in the profession, among whom I must mention Herbert M. Temple, C. P. A., Waldron H. Rand, C. P. A., George T. Klink, C. P. A., E. G. Shorrock, C. P. A., Seymour Walton, C. P. A., Edward L. Suffern, C. P. A., and John B. Geijsbeek, C. P. A.

Necessarily much of my work was done at irregular intervals, which meant that my notes required careful revision and arrangement. This work was done for me by Gerald van Casteel, Esq., of the New York Bar, and I take this opportunity to express my appreciation of his able and conscientious work.

As my friends did not undertake to rewrite all of my manuscript, I am conscious of many imperfections in the present volume, and I shall gratefully receive any constructive criticism with which I may be favored by those who feel enough responsibility in connection with accountancy literature to contribute to another edition of this book, which I suppose will appear in the course of time.

ROBERT H. MONTGOMERY.

55 Liberty St., New York,
2d Sept., 1912.

TABLE OF CONTENTS

CHAPTER I. PURPOSE OF THIS BOOK

CHAPTER II. THE PURPOSES AND ADVANTAGES OF AN AUDIT

CHAPTER III. THE AUDITOR'S QUALIFICATIONS

CHAPTER IV. THE DUTIES OF AN AUDITOR

Audit of a Firm or Individual

How to Begin an Audit (Continued)

CHAPTER VII. BALANCE-SHEET AUDIT—ASSETS

General—Current Assets

Current Assets

Cash

Accounts Receivable

Certificates and Reports (Continued)

CHAPTER XVIII. THE DETAILED AUDIT (Continued)

Verification of Income

CHAPTER XIX. THE DETAILED AUDIT (Continued)

Purchases and Expenses

Purchases and Expenses (Continued)

CHAPTER XX. THE DETAILED AUDIT (Continued)

The Trial Balance

Asset and Liability Items

Office Methods

CHAPTER XXI. DEPRECIATION

Wasting Assets

Public Utility Companies

CHAPTER XXII. THE CORPORATION TAX LAW AND DEPRECIATION

CHAPTER XXIII. SPECIAL POINTS IN DIFFERENT CLASSES OF AUDITS

Building and Loan Associations (Continued)

CHAPTER XXIV. SPECIAL POINTS IN DIFFERENT CLASSES OF AUDITS (Continued)

Insurance Companies

Fire Insurance Companies

Life Insurance Companies

Casualty, Health, Surety, Title Guarantee, and Other Companies

Manufacturing

Publishers of Books

Publishers of Magazines and Newspapers

Breweries

Mining—Coal Mines

MUNICIPAL (Continued)

CHAPTER XXVII. SPECIAL POINTS IN DIFFERENT CLASSES OF AUDITS (Continued)

EXECUTORS AND TRUSTEES

CHAPTER XXXI. INTEREST

CHAPTER XXXII. THE LIABILITIES OF AUDITORS

CHAPTER XXXIII. THE LIABILITIES OF DIRECTORS

CHAPTER XXXIV. FEDERAL TAX ON CORPORATIONS

CHAPTER XXXV. CERTIFIED PUBLIC ACCOUNTANT LAWS AND EXAMINATIONS

CHAPTER I

PURPOSE OF THIS BOOK

The purpose of this book is to set forth the principles underlying the theory and practice of auditing and to outline the working program which must be followed in whole or in part in every audit.

An ideal audit cannot be made without a full perspective of the science of accounts, for many who have a good working knowledge of the details of practical accounting find it difficult to visualize, as it were, the records of business transactions.

The auditor who best accomplishes his task is the one who is able to put himself in the place of those for whom the accounts are intended, and he will not find this easy unless he has been trained to make the most of the figures which appear in a balance sheet or profit and loss statement. To present *correct* accounts is not enough, because correct accounts may not be clear to those for whom they are intended. A scientific system of accounts is a method whereby a graphic and intelligent record of facts may be assembled and by logical processes reduced to readable form.

Auditing is the analytical, as practical accounting is the constructive, branch of accountancy.

But the modern auditor is more than an analyst. The logical development of his profession and the increased appreciation of the value of his work have added to his former duties certain constructive functions which must be fulfilled in connection with a large proportion of his engagements.

The average business man has been trained from boyhood to read facts and figures from continuous printed pages. The trial balance of a ledger means nothing to him, except that part of it which contains the accounts receivable and payable, and these must not be called "Debit Balances" or "Credit Balances" if we would avoid the chance of being misunderstood.

Many intelligent people fail to grasp the usual and conventional hypothesis underlying the theory of double entry bookkeeping, and therefore facts or figures presented to them in a technical or formal shape may not accomplish the intended result.

Probably the majority of business men have been shown trial balances from their books which mean nothing to them, and this applies to the usual monthly balance as well as to the one made after closing the books. A balance sheet in conventional form is perfectly clear to the eye trained to read and understand figures and is perhaps as concise and satisfactory an exhibit as could be desired *for the person who understands figures*, but thousands of business men frankly acknowledge that they do not grasp the full import of a financial statement in the accepted form.

But if the man who is entitled to know all the facts contained in these balance sheets cannot or will not understand this method of presentation, is it not our duty to try another form and keep on trying until the results of his business become as interesting *reading* to him as the daily trade reports? If the client had his own way he would ask for a report on his business prepared so that he could read it.

This is the point of view to which every accountant must direct his attention until he can so connect figures and transactions that an audit will no longer mean a mere verification of the figures in the books, but will include a lively appreciation of every ramification of the business. In other words, the auditor must visualize the transactions themselves to see that their conversion into dollars and cents is reflected in the books of account.

The proprietor knows intuitively all of the possible functions of his business; the auditor may not know them intuitively, but he must ascertain how and why the proprietor looks at the business as he does, otherwise there will be no meeting of minds between the auditor and his client. Without a complete understanding of each other's point of view, ideal professional relations can never be maintained.

The following memorandum is submitted as suggestive only, but it is more than likely that it would be read through to the end by every man or woman who might have an interest in the enterprise in question.

Statement of Financial Condition of A and B at the Close of Business, December 31, 1911

The total assets of the firm on this date amounted to $213,333, consisting of the following items: Cash in bank, $9,465. This is somewhat less than is usually carried, but a number of bills were paid on December 31st, which reduced the bank balance accordingly. Bills Receivable, $8,450. These are notes not yet due, and are all believed to be good. They can, if necessary, be discounted at the bank and furnish additional funds. Accounts Receivable, $29,416. These were gone over carefully on December 31st, and an amount equal to all accounts long overdue was charged to Profit and Loss and carried to Reserve for Bad Debts account. They are also carried in a separate ledger and are being carefully looked after, and a fair amount will no doubt be realized therefrom. The sales for the month of December were nearly $20,000, and, as practically all sales are at thirty days' time, it is evident that collections are in fine shape.

Stock was taken on December 31st and amounted to $39,460. The market was somewhat lower on that date than when most of the goods were purchased, so, in order to be conservative, the inventory was priced at market. All obsolete and damaged stock was inventoried, but was not valued. It is proposed to dispose of all this dead stuff as soon as possible, as it is in the way, and is the source of constant expense and annoyance. The inventory sheets have been securely bound and placed in the safe.

The insurance on stock aggregates $45,000, which is about ten per cent in excess of the inventory. The rate, however, is only about forty cents since the installation of the sprinkler plant, and, as the amount fluctuates from day to day, it is considered advisable to cover a small margin above the estimated stock. The insurance question comes up automatically once a week so that we cannot be caught unawares, as was the case recently with the X Y Z Company.

In November, we paid the insurance for an entire year in advance, so that on December 31st the proportion prepaid amounted to $762, which is carried as an asset, because it should be charged against the operations of 1912. We also paid the discount on the notes at bank in advance to the extent of $412, and this is carried as an asset in the same way as the insurance.

On a conservative basis, the furniture and fixtures on hand on December 31st were worth over $6,000, but as liberal depreciation has been written off each year, this item now stands at $3,418. We are carrying insurance for $6,500, however, and in case of a fire there would be no trouble about adjusting the loss and proving our claim, as a carefully prepared schedule of each article, with date of purchase and cost price, is kept in the safe.

Our land and buildings are now carried at a net valuation of $84,710, made up as follows: Cost of land in 1897, $50,000; cost of buildings, $49,862. We have carried to our reserve account annual depreciation at the rate of four per cent per annum, reducing the accounts to $34,710. This rate is probably too high, as two and one half per cent per annum is stated to be the proper rate of depreciation on buildings like ours, but, as the depreciation is charged into the expenses every year, it keeps us on the safe side when figuring our costs, and, if it should ever be considered advisable to tear down some of our older buildings, the rate of depreciation charged will be justified. The machinery account now stands on our books at a net valuation of $37,240. The original cost of the machinery now installed in the plant was over $60,000, but depreciation at rates varying from ten to twenty per cent per annum has been charged on the same theory as with buildings. Much of our machinery is of a type which is subject to improvements and new inventions, and, as has been the case in the past, some so-called modern machines may become obsolete over night. If our machinery account were carried on our books at cost or nearly so, as is done by some of our competitors, we would no doubt be afraid to abandon it for fear of the resulting shrinkage in our assets, but the liberal depreciation charged and the consequent margin in this account permit us to keep absolutely up to date with our entire equipment. Unquestionably a fair share of our continued success as manufacturers is due to this policy.

Our auditors tell us that they have never examined the affairs of a single bankrupt concern where the machinery account was not inflated by reason of insufficient depreciation being written off, and they point out that the moral is obvious.

The depreciation on buildings and machinery is not deducted directly from the respective accounts, but is carried separately as a reserve. The reason for this is that in case of fire we can submit the cost of all the buildings and machinery to the adjusters and show them the accounts in the books. We have a subsidiary building and machinery ledger, which shows each building and each machine separately with cost of installation, etc. The aggregates of the detailed items in this ledger agree exactly with the totals in the general ledger.

If a fire occurred it would be a matter of negotiation as to the deductions for wear and tear, and, as the adjusters would be obliged to make their calculations on a basis of the life of the buildings and machines or their replacement cost, we ought to realize a much larger amount than that shown in the balance sheet. This conservative valuation not only means that we are not fooling ourselves, but our banks realize that we are not fooling them and compliment us on our method every time it is explained to them.

The President of the National Bank told us a short time ago that he believes we can borrow a larger amount on our statement as it is made up than some concerns whose plants may have cost far more, but whose methods are not as conservative. The distrust occasioned by lack of conservatism leads a banker to discount all the assets ruthlessly, while with us they feel perfectly safe in relying on our figures and "go the limit" when we ask for credit.

The assets referred to above aggregate at their reduced valuation $213,333. The total liabilities on December 31st amount to $74,493, leaving net capital invested in the business $138,840, of which there stands to the credit of Mr. A. $74,910, and to the credit of Mr. B. $63,930.

The liabilities in detail are as follows:

Bills payable, $18,500, consisting of three notes for $5,000 each, and one for $3,500. The former were discounted at the National Bank and are due January 25th, February 25th, and March 25th. The $3,500 note was discounted at the Citizens Bank and is due February 25th. As our purchases are increasing, due to the approach of the busy season, these notes will have to be renewed and additional funds secured. Our line at the National Bank is now $40,000, and at the Citizens Bank $25,000. This is more than sufficient to carry us through the season and will enable us to discount all our bills. The unpaid accounts payable for purchases on December 31st amounted to $24,218. No bills are overdue, and all invoices carrying cash discounts have been paid.

The collections which are sure, are not sufficient to meet all of our bills on our regular pay day (the 20th), so $10,000 should be borrowed, say on the 18th. The accrued wages up to the night of the 31st amounted to $1,340.

The taxes accrued to the same date amounted to $435. This represents a tax rate of two per cent, which is a decided advance over last year. We are unable to discern any additional benefits arising out of the increase, and it might be in order to suggest to the municipal authorities that it is up to them to establish efficiency and cost records and justify the enormous sums they are expending annually in an apparently aimless manner.

The only remaining liability is the mortgage for $30,000 on the real estate. As the interest rate is five per cent and as it is not due for three years, no action with respect to this debt is suggested.

The foregoing narrative is necessarily colorless and lacks the local flavor which might easily be woven about the balance sheet of a going business, so that as read *solely* by those connected with the particular undertaking, one item after another would awaken interest and stimulate action with respect to those figures which might appear to be unfavorable.

It is not hard to imagine a state of affairs different from that described, and it is quite within reason to prophesy that a cleverly written description of balance sheets in the manner described would excite decisive action on the part of an executive with respect to unfavorable items where previous efforts along routine lines had failed. In any event, it is well worth trying, particularly in connection with a profit and loss or trading statement where comparisons are important and instructive. An occasional witticism or business "story" would not be out of place, assuming always that a proper diagnosis has been made of the executive to whom the report is addressed.

There are many ramifications of business affairs which cannot be understood without more or less actual experience and technical training, and which therefore cannot be satisfactorily elucidated within the limits of one book; but it is the firm belief of the author that a common-sense knowledge of bookkeeping and a general acquaintance with business affairs are the most necessary foundation of the student of auditing.

It is not expected that a clerk with a little knowledge of accounts or a business man with no practical experience in other lines than his own can by a mere reading of these pages acquire at once the skill necessary for the professional accountant. Nevertheless, this book is intended for the instruction of those having but little experience as well as for the guidance of the qualified public accountant. Accountancy is a science, and it should be possible to present its underlying principles so that they may be comprehensible to the average mind. Theory alone, however, will never qualify anyone to practice as a public accountant any more than a medical student is qualified to practice medicine, no matter how thorough a knowledge of the science of medicine he may have acquired through lectures and books, unless he has had an opportunity to verify his book knowledge and demonstrate his skill in the hospital and the clinic.

If anyone who proposes to take up the study of auditing has not had a fairly thorough training in bookkeeping, and in addition has not had sufficient practical experience in business affairs to enable him to keep his poise when he is required to think and act quickly, he had better postpone his course until he has acquired enough experience to lay the necessary foundation.

It is absurd for any student to take it for granted that a good memory applied to a book on auditing will make him a good auditor.

The work of the auditor engaged in public practice is important enough to raise this work to the dignity of a profession. It has been called the profession of business advice. Some one has defined a profession as a calling which demands of its members a high order of intellectual attainment, which can be acquired only by long and arduous preliminary training.

CHAPTER II

THE PURPOSES AND ADVANTAGES OF AN AUDIT

THE average business man is not familiar with the purposes and advantages of an audit. A small minority have retained professional auditors and have gained their impressions of what an audit should be from the experiences growing out of such employment.

Where the auditor possessed a broad vision and had the advantage of long and varied experience, the result was a revelation to the business man. He found the value received so greatly exceeded the cost of the service that the relation became a continuing one. The client advised other business men to do likewise, and so the practice of the skillful auditor expanded.

But why is it that so many business men have never availed themselves of the opportunity to secure a service which has proved to be so valuable to their competitors, and why is it that many practitioners have not succeeded in enlarging their practice during the last few years, while a considerable number of auditors have built up large organizations and now have intrusted to them a very large volume of work? It must be that the business man who does not employ professional auditors is ignorant of the advantages of an audit, and that the would-be auditor who fails to secure enough engagements lacks the full conception of the objects of an audit, and therefore fails to create the proper impression upon the clients whom he does obtain. It follows that he will not be called upon for subsequent service, and naturally he is not recommended to the friends of his client.

The author has had nearly twenty-four years' experience in professional auditing in the United States. During this time there has been a vast development in commerce and finance and the science of auditing has made equal strides. But this latter fact is not known to all business men nor to all of those who have decided to enter the accountancy profession.

There will be further and rapid developments, but one can

hardly hope to keep pace with progress, much less be a factor therein, unless acquainted with its history.

The author has had the pleasure and privilege of knowing most of the successful practitioners in this country. He is familiar with their methods and he has watched the growth of their organizations.

The successful auditor is the best medium through which the business public will gain knowledge of the advantages of an audit. To be successful the auditor himself must have a thorough and definite grasp of the purposes of an audit.

The following observations and suggestions are based upon a careful study of actual conditions and may be relied upon by the student as representative of the accumulated experience of the auditors who head the profession at the present time.

THE PURPOSES OF AN AUDIT

In what might be called the formative days of auditing students were taught that the chief objects of an audit were:

(1) The detection or prevention of fraud;

(2) The detection or prevention of errors;

but in recent years there has been a decided change in the demand and in the service. That is to say, the financiers and business men who originally retained professional auditors to look for fraud or errors have enlarged their demands and now require a vastly broader and more important class of work, which those auditors who have advanced in skill and knowledge have been able to understand and perform. We must therefore relegate the former "chief objects" to a subordinate position without in any way depreciating their importance.

The relative position of the present-day purposes are:

(1) To ascertain the actual financial condition and earnings of an enterprise for

(*a*) Its proprietors (partners or stockholders);

(*b*) Its executives (managers, officers, or directors);

(*c*) Bankers or investors who are considering the purchase of securities;

(*d*) Bankers who are considering the discounting or purchasing of its promissory notes.

(2) The detection of fraud or errors as hereinafter explained.

The results secured by auditors are required for the following, among other purposes:

(*a*) In order that stock and bond holders or other owners may have submitted to them at regular intervals a comprehensive, even though a condensed, statement of the financial position and the net results of the operations of the business in which they have a proprietary interest, and that the fairness and accuracy in all essential particulars of the statement submitted may be attested by means of a certificate or report of a disinterested and competent authority.

(*b*) Upon a proposed sale or incorporation or other change in form or management, such as an attempt to bring in additional capital or the death of a partner or large stockholder. Matters of the highest importance arise in connection with the interests of partners in the event of death or other change in the partnership relations.

(*c*) To submit similar statements in more detail to banks and note brokers as a basis of credit.

(*d*) To submit certified statements to the mercantile agencies and to other organizations which call for periodical reports.

(*e*) To ascertain the true causes of fluctuations in profits or expenses.

(*f*) To state the facts in disputes or litigation, and to investigate the causes of bankruptcy for creditors or stockholders.

This is a partial list only of the manifold purposes for which audits or investigations are being demanded.

The nineteenth century auditor who looked chiefly for fraud or errors no doubt served a useful purpose, but his methods now illustrate the history rather than the modern practice of auditing.

Due consideration will now be given to the subject of fraud and errors. In subsequent chapters the present-day demands for "higher" auditing will be met with a full discussion of the more important work of the professional auditor.

THE MINOR OBJECTS OF AUDIT

The elementary or minor objects of an audit are:

(1) The detection of fraud.

(2) The detection of errors, and conversely the prevention of fraud and the prevention of errors, particularly of errors of principle.

The latter, of course, include the moral effect of an audit, which extends also to that very desirable result of keeping the work of the office staff sharply up to date. This might be classed as a constructive object.

(1) The Detection of Fraud: There can be no doubt but that the business public look upon the discovery of fraud as an important object to be attained by an audit, and experience has demonstrated that sufficient fraud has been so disclosed to warrant a continuance of the service of auditors who are retained to discover fraud if it exists.

Gradually, however, the business man is being educated to understand that the discovery of fraud is one, and only one, of the objects of an audit, and by no means the most valuable to him.

The detection of fraud is first in the logical presentation of the objects of an audit, as less experience is required to unearth it, and more definite suggestions can be made to the student in regard to it than is the case with the more important branches of the auditor's duties.

While an auditor who brings to bear all of his skill and resources, and who leaves no stone unturned in his search for fraud, but fails to discover a well-concealed defalcation, is legally exempt from liability therefor, yet he is, and properly should be, considered professionally responsible for such failure, and his practice suffers accordingly. Therefore particular attention must be paid to all possible avenues which are open for the dishonest clerk or official who has an opportunity to manipulate the records of business transactions.

Opportunities for wrong-doing vary, as a rule, with the size of the undertaking. In a small business the details are apt to be supervised by one or all of the proprietors, while in a large business much of the detail is necessarily left to subordinates. The auditor must be governed by the circumstances surrounding each engagement and then determine the amount of detail to be covered.

(a) Misappropriation of Money or Goods: Usually fraud

consists of defalcations involving the misappropriation of cash, either by the failure to account for cash receipts or by the entry of payments which are fictitious in part or whole.

In the following pages there will be outlined a procedure based on long experience which will disclose such practices in all ordinary cases.

With respect to the misappropriation of assets other than cash, a far more difficult task is at hand, but experience in such cases has also permitted the outlining of general rules which will materially assist the auditor.

(b) Manipulation of Accounts for Other Purposes: The abstraction of cash or goods is not the only reason for the manipulation of accounts. The auditor who has covered these two classes of frauds fully must, in addition, consider the possibility of other irregularities.

In many undertakings the sources of cash receipts and the disposition of cash expenditures are so carefully guarded that a misappropriation of cash is almost impossible.

It is hard to convince the business man whose accounts are so guarded, that an audit is of value, but relying again on experience, it has been demonstrated time and again that pecuniary profit in such cases may be obtained by the manipulation of records. Usually the fraud has been perpetrated by an official (frequently one who has the entire confidence of everyone) who has an interest in, or who receives a bonus based on, the net profits of a business or of a department thereof. In other cases the purpose is to deceive bankers, creditors, or stockholders.

The auditor must have all these purposes constantly in mind when determining his course of action. If he does not consider all the elements involved before commencing a given engagement, he may find at the end of a detailed audit that a balance sheet audit would have enabled him to secure satisfactory results in much less time.

In discussing hereafter the respective advantages of these two classes of audits, the author will endeavor to assist the practitioner in the selection of a proper line of procedure.

(2) The Detection of Errors: This object of an audit does not receive the attention which it deserves, and the auditor himself is probably to blame for the present condition of affairs in this respect.

During the time professional auditing was in a formative state in this country, auditors were frequently engaged to adjust accounts which had been badly kept by inefficient clerks. It was found that the books were not in balance, and that in order to adjust them a vast number of errors had to be located and corrected. In many cases this work consumed months of time and a correspondingly large fee followed. This was called "auditing," but in reality it was *accounting* work of the most elementary kind. A careful bookkeeper unacquainted with most of the principles of accountancy could have performed the service equally well and far more cheaply.

This practice cast more or less discredit on professional auditors, so that the tendency during recent years has been to belittle the importance of locating errors in books of accounts and to magnify the advantages of concentrating on the search for fraud and the verification of the balance sheet.

The author feels that this branch of auditing should be accorded its proper place in stating the objects of an audit, and the attention of the student is particularly called to the points of importance in the detection of errors.

For convenience the following classification is made, involving errors caused by ignorance, fraud, or mistake:

(*a*) Errors of Principle.
(*b*) Clerical Errors.
(*c*) Errors of Omission.
(*d*) Errors of Commission.
(*e*) Offsetting Errors.

(a) Errors of Principle: This is the most important class of errors and is one which the auditor must never overlook.

Errors of principle usually affect both the profit and loss account and the balance sheet. The most common error is to debit an asset instead of an expense account. For instance, an item of repairs will be charged to buildings account, or a payment covering expenses or services will be charged to the personal account of the payee and thus be included among the accounts receivable, instead of being charged to an expense account.

Other errors of principle do not affect the net profit or loss, but may seriously affect the conclusions which are drawn from the various revenue or expense accounts. For instance, an executive may have determined that the advertising appropriation shall be limited to five per cent of the sales. A large item of advertising expense may be charged to some other expense account in error, with the result that the executive, depending upon the ledger to give him the total expenditure, will authorize additional advertising and thus incur an unintentional and perhaps unnecessary expense.

Errors of principle are most easily detected by making an intelligent analysis of the accounts in connection with the preparation of the profit and loss account and the balance sheet.

(b) Clerical Errors: These are the most frequent errors which exist, and unfortunately few books of accounts are free from them. They consist of errors in the footings and forwardings of the books of original entry and ledgers; errors in postings other than those mentioned under (a), consisting of postings to wrong accounts in the same class, as to one customer or creditor instead of another, or the posting of an incorrect amount, posting to the wrong side of the ledger, or errors in drawing off the trial balance.

These errors are usually due to carelessness, but the auditor is not justified in assuming that accounts in which such errors exist are free from fraud. He must differentiate between clerical errors and intentional manipulation of the records. A careful examination must therefore be made of enough of these errors for the auditor to satisfy himself that they are bona fide. For instance, an excessive footing of a pay-roll or expense account might be carelessness or fraud; the posting of a greater amount to the credit of a customer's account than is shown in the cash book might be an honest error in posting or it might indicate an attempt to conceal a defalcation.

A fair test of these errors, however, is sufficient. It is no part of an auditor's duty (as such) to locate all clerical errors, and the auditor who devotes a considerable part of his time to this work lays himself open to just criticism.

Auditors lose sight of the fact that the closing of books and the resulting balance sheets are based on estimates only.

Some auditors spend many hours in adjusting balance sheet items in order to correct a few trifling errors, when there are valuations of hundreds of thousands of dollars in plant, merchandise, stocks, etc., all of which are necessarily estimates and which fluctuate from day to day—as must the value of all materials and goods. So long, therefore, as small errors in calculations, extensions, etc., do not, relatively speaking, actually affect the balance sheet, time should not be wasted on such adjustments.

(c) Errors of Omission: An auditor is justified in spending more time in looking for errors of omission than in connection with any other class of errors.

Where the internal check is not perfect, the utmost care must be taken to verify all possible sources of revenue to ascertain whether or not all such items are entered in the books. Errors of omission usually do not affect the trial balance and are, therefore, not detected automatically. They are distinguished from the class of errors where items are not posted at all, as with these (except where both sides of a journal entry are not posted) the trial balance is affected and the usual checking back of the postings would locate the differences.

Instances of errors of omission are as follows: Goods may be delivered but not billed; rent may not be charged or collected. On the other hand, purchases may be made and the goods received, but the invoices for same may not be entered in the books. In order to cover this class of errors, the auditor should locate all books of original entry, whether so-called memorandum books or other informal records, then a fair selection of items should be traced into the regular books of account. If the test does not disclose any material differences, it may be assumed that the records are accurate. If the test should disclose one or more errors of sufficient size to affect the results favorably or unfavorably, a more extensive test should be made. It might be well, however, before extending the verification to request authority for so doing from the client.

In an examination of the accounts of a publisher the auditor compared the advertisements appearing in one issue of a popular magazine with the book in which charges to advertisers were entered. It was found that an insertion of a full page had not been charged for. The item was billed and collected. Thereupon the other eleven issues were carefully checked, but no other omission was found.

If the auditor names a fixed fee for an audit, it is always well to state that tests only will be made. If an error is discovered in the test, the auditor has fufilled his agreement and need not go further unless an additional fee is arranged for. If he will broach the subject as soon as the test is completed there will probably be no difficulty in securing an extra allowance, but if no reference is made to his purpose to charge extra for additional work, he will usually have difficulty in collecting anything at all additional, no matter how many or how few errors are brought to light.

(d) Errors of Commission: These occur chiefly in connection with the books and records of original entry and consist of items which are incorrectly recorded, either in whole or in part.

For instance, an entry in the sales book may be incorrect as to quantities, or in the extension of the items. These errors do not affect the trial balance and frequently remain undetected.

The same tests as are recommended under (c) above should be followed, except that it is not usually necessary to cover as many items. Calculations of purchase and sales items are frequently verified by two persons in the offices where they originate, and almost invariably are checked in the offices to which they are sent.

The test, therefore, may be extremely limited, provided it is apparent that care is taken by the clerks in charge of such work.

(e) Offsetting Errors: These occur fairly often, and while they could be classed under the other headings mentioned, they are dangerous enough to deserve special mention.

An offsetting error is one which is counterbalanced by another error or errors. It is an annoying type. As one error may occur in an asset or liability account and the other in an expense or income account, an auditor is not justified in passing any accounts until satisfied that such errors do not exist. Of course, this does not mean the verification of every posting, but it does call for the tests or analyses described more fully hereafter.

Few executives realize the great number of clerical errors which are made every day. Perhaps these are most numerous in banks, brokers', and other offices where the accounts are balanced daily. An immense amount of work is accomplished in a short space of time. Clerks work at high pressure, and knowing that there will be a check on their work before they leave at night, they do not verify their entries as they go along, as is the case with many clerks who depend on the monthly trial balance to detect their errors. Consequently a great number of errors are made, and are located and corrected as soon as it is found that the day's work must be checked back. Many of these errors are of $10, $100, or $1,000. Therefore it is not strange if two errors of the same amount should be made in the same day in different departments, so that the accounts for that day actually balance in spite of the two errors.

Recently the author was called in by the senior partner of a large stock exchange house who was greatly troubled over the fact that two errors of $100 each had been made on a certain day and had remained undetected for three weeks. He felt that something was wrong with the system of accounts or with his clerks; he could not decide which. He was advised that the discovery and reporting of the mistake by the only clerk who could have benefited by it indicated that fraud was not intended, but that if a similar case arose soon again, a fuller investigation should be made.

The rule, therefore, is that an offsetting error may occur at any time, but that the law of averages would operate against much duplication.

The Auditor's Purpose: An auditor's duty is to discover and disclose the truth about accounts, but this is too general a designation of his duties to use when confronted with a specific case. Furthermore, the business world must, for many years to come, be educated up to a proper appreciation of an accountant's functions, so the present-day auditor must be a teacher as well as an adviser. He must be prepared to explain the *purpose* of his work and set forth clearly the *objects* to be attained as the result of his labors.

The professional auditor, therefore, must give the impression of having a scope and purpose far in advance of the old-time auditor, whose work was chiefly confined to ascertaining whether the accounting party had properly recorded all receipts and payments on behalf of his principal. In fact, the old-fashioned audit was a cash audit. A modern audit, however, although it includes the examination of cash transactions, has as its ultimate purpose the verification of the balance sheet.

An auditor should be prepared to state that he must make such an examination of the books and records of the undertaking as will enable him to satisfy himself whether or not the balance sheet is properly drawn up so as to exhibit a true and correct record of its financial affairs.

An auditor who has not himself a clear idea of the value or advantages of an audit can hardly expect to impress his client as to his purpose.

ADVANTAGES OF AN AUDIT

The chief advantages are, of course, identical with the main purposes of an audit. The minor objects, viz., that fraud will be disclosed if it exists; that technical errors, if any, will be discovered and corrected; that errors of principle, if they exist, will be detected, and the means of preventing their repetition in the future pointed out, have been discussed.

The major advantages which have been mentioned may now be enlarged upon.

(1) Condition of Affairs Accurately Shown: An accurate statement of affairs, together with a profit and loss account, showing how this position was reached, is prepared by a disinterested expert. In a vast number of cases this statement by the auditor is the first accurate information which the client has ever had as to his own condition.

Left alone, a business man seems to love to fool himself; so he goes along, year after year, overstating his assets, overlooking depreciation, and forgetting his liabilities. A correct balance sheet made up by a professional auditor brings him sharply to time. It will never be known how many enterprises have been saved from ultimate failure through the presentation of unwelcome facts by an auditor who cannot and will not be influenced by former inaccurate statements of condition.

(2) Bank Loans: Certified accounts are particularly valuable as a basis for bank loans. All leading bank managers recognize the assistance rendered to them in the course of their business by public accountants, and even if a business man is in the happy position of not requiring occasional aid from his banker, yet his financial rating is considerably higher if he is thoroughly up-to-date in the care of his books and accounts.

The extension of credit by a bank depends on the judgment of its officers as to the ability of the borrower to repay the loan when due. The auditor, by reason of his independence, is able to assist the banker in forming his judgment. The prospective borrower cannot view the condition of his own business without bias. The borrower expects to postpone the time of payment and therefore anticipates a future condition more satisfactory, doubtless, than is the case at the time of the application. The auditor must, in a measure, pass on the probability and the possibility of the future in the light of past results.

This does not excuse an auditor who estimates a definite profit in the future, out of which a bank loan will be paid, but it does support the recent statements of prominent bankers that the services of professional accountants are becoming of increasing value to them, largely because they are able to *report orally* the result of their "sizing up" of the borrower or the prospective borrower.

If an auditor refrains from expressing any oral opinion on the probabilities of the future of a business the accounts of which he has just subjected to the most thorough analysis and scrutiny, it is possibly because he relies upon the ancient fiction that an accountant deals with facts only, and that future results are not facts; or perhaps he is afraid to express his own convictions.

If he finds that he is usually right in his forecast of future business, it would seem only fair that his conclusions should be communicated to his client *at the time* they are formed.

It is an unquestioned advantage for any borrower to be able to comply with the requirements of the banker or note broker to whom he applies for a line of credit. The attention of a prospective client, may, therefore, be properly drawn to the official action of the supreme body of American bankers.

At the Convention of the American Bankers' Association,

held at Denver, Colo., in 1908, the Committee on Credit Information reported, urging "that every member exert his influence to have all paper purchased from note brokers presented with accompanying statements audited by Certified Public Accountants . . . ," and to that end asked that the Association, by the adoption of the Committee's report, "recommend that its members, in purchasing commercial paper from note brokers, give preference to such names as furnish accompanying statements audited by Certified Public Accountants."

Prominent bankers, from time to time, have urged their associates in conventions and elsewhere to require all prospective borrowers to furnish certified statements.

Unfortunately, competition in banking circles is still too keen to permit this rule to be adopted. Some recent large losses by banks, arising out of gross overvaluations of assets and understatements of liabilities on the part of borrowers, may incline them to require certified statements by impartial accountants.

(3) **Partnerships:** Partnership books should always be adjusted by a professional accountant if for no other reason than that he will act impartially and comply fully with the articles of copartnership. These accounts are peculiarly liable to disturbances by causes from which corporations on the whole are exempt. Disputes occur as to salaries, division of profits, partner's overdrawings, inattention to business, and many other things which would to a large extent be obviated if the books were regularly audited by a competent outsider. A partner dies and there is trouble with his administrator as to the division and withdrawal of the decedent's capital, in many cases resulting in expensive lawsuits and the permanent crippling of the business. A partnership goes into bankruptcy, perhaps through misconduct of a trusted partner. Had a continuous audit been in force the fraud might have been nipped in the bud. Again, for the protection of a limited or special partner and a silent or dormant partner a periodical independent audit is essential.

(4) **Fire Loss:** In the case of loss of merchandise by fire, a properly authenticated balance sheet prepared by a public accountant is a material aid in the adjustment of claims. This is not a theory; it has been demonstrated in practice. All business

men anticipate the possibility of a fire, but few of them consider just how they will collect their insurance.

During the progress of an audit the auditor will ascertain the methods of bookkeeping in force, and whether, in case of fire, the records would be properly protected. He will ascertain if a perpetual inventory be maintained, or whether it would be necessary to calculate the amount of the loss upon the usual basis, that is, to take the last recorded inventory, add purchases to date of fire and deduct cost of goods sold, the result being the stock on hand at time of fire.

The cost of goods sold is ascertained by deducting from the sales the average gross profit realized in prior periods. Fire insurance adjusters are shrewd and experienced and the business man whose records are in poor order is usually forced to settle upon a basis satisfactory to the adjuster. If the business man's accounts are in good shape and he can show that the last inventory had been certified to, he can decline to compromise and insist on the full amount of his claim being allowed.

(5) Bonding: A cashier whose books are audited regularly has little trouble in securing a good company to act as surety for him; in fact, several of the best companies insist, as part of the contract, that this be done periodically.

(6) Protection of Stockholders and the Public: The interests of the real proprietors of a business (the stockholders in the case of a corporation) should be protected in every feasible and reasonable manner. One way in which such an end might be served would be to conform to the English method. There stockholders elect at the annual meeting a professional accountant as the auditor of the company for the ensuing year, and his report is made to the stockholders and not to the officers and directors.

A corporation which has nothing to hide cheerfully sends its balance sheet out to its stockholders, and if the latter exhibit enough interest in the matter to request that the certificate of a professional auditor be attached, such request will probably be complied with. Therefore, in every possible and dignified way the auditor should impress upon stockholders the many advantages to themselves of such procedure.

The value of the publicity of audited accounts cannot be

overestimated. In a general way all corporations are believed to be making unreasonable profits, particularly all corporations which in any way attempt to serve the public.

For instance, in New York City, the taxicab companies have been attacked in the newspapers and one ordinance after another has been passed regulating fares, all, of course, reducing them. During the last four or five years at least two millions of dollars have been lost by three or four of these companies. During this time they have not made periodical statements to their stockholders nor to the public, setting forth these losses and the reason therefor. For some mysterious reason publicity has been shunned.

It is about as certain as anything can be that if certified statements of operations had been secured and sent to the newspapers annually, commencing, say, four years ago, a far different state of public opinion would have resulted.

Corporations which are secretive about their accounts or which issue statements not certified to, have only themselves to blame if they are made the victims of hostile legislation.

(7) **Sale of a Business:** The author has had several experiences in which it was demonstrated that if periodical statements of the results of operations duly certified to by responsible auditors had been available, large enterprises would have changed hands in a few days, but such statements not being promptly available, the sales were not made.

In one case the president of a corporation in which he owned a controlling interest was offered two and a half million dollars for control, subject to examination by accountants. He accepted. When an attempt was made to ascertain the earnings for a period of years it was found that no accurate records had ever been kept. Large profits had been realized, but the only reason this was known was because the money was in the bank. Physical inventories had never been taken and book inventories had not been kept. At the time of the proposed purchase the plant was operating on an extensive scale, but as no cost records were kept, it was impossible to determine the rate of profit on the current output. The deal was called off.

The president complained bitterly. He had paid enormous dividends, which he knew had been earned, but no one could determine just when they were realized, and the condition of the accounts cast suspicion on the whole enterprise.

Practically all business men look forward to retiring sooner or later. It is a kindness to them to indicate how much easier and more certain it will be for them to accomplish their purpose if they can produce correct certified accounts than to depend upon unaudited accounts, which may fail to meet the requirements of a prospective purchaser.

(8) Recovery for Negligence: The final advantage of an audit (and one upon which perhaps serious differences of opinion may exist as to the advisability of public discussion) is, that a client who may suffer loss through the dishonesty of an employee may recover an equivalent amount from the auditor, provided that the latter is shown to have performed his work in a grossly negligent manner, and provided, of course, that the defalcation occurred during the period covered by the audit and continued thereafter. For further discussion of this interesting, if not pleasant, topic, Chapter XXXII, "Liabilities of Auditors," should be consulted.

CHAPTER III

THE AUDITOR'S QUALIFICATIONS

Bookkeeping: The first important qualification of the professional auditor is a thorough knowledge of practical accounting, which necessarily embraces a complete mastery of bookkeeping. Bookkeeping is so readily learned by any one of ordinary intelligence that it is the most elementary step in the auditor's career.

Accounting: Accounting, however, is a science, and represents the highest development of bookkeeping. Accounting is not an exact science like mathematics; it is an applied or practical science.

Modern accounting must consider values as well as figures. The question of values enters so largely into every statement which exhibits the financial condition of a business enterprise that in the last analysis a balance sheet is an expression of opinion. The accountant as such is not a valuer or appraiser, but neither is he a copyist to transcribe figures from books, and without verification, hold them forth as dependable.

The majority of books of account do not represent the true financial position of their respective concerns, nor do they correctly show the current operations as they occur from day to day. Therefore the auditor must have such technical knowledge as will enable him to recognize and criticize accounts from a constructive point of view.

It is not enough that accounts are honest; in order to be correct they must include intelligent groupings of all cost and revenue factors, and they must indicate the true relations between the various groups.

Correct accounts are not necessarily complicated accounts. All depends upon the ability and experience of the designer, and as with all professional work, the greater the skill the greater the simplicity.

Accounts are merely the written expression of every-day commercial transactions. The written records, in order to be of real value, must be constructed along scientific lines, and in order to accomplish this, there must be a lively appreciation on the part of the accountant of the vital connection between the transactions themselves and the written records thereof.

Value of Theory: The degree of Certified Public Accountant, no matter from what State it is secured, cannot be deemed to be, in itself, a sufficient license to practice as a professional auditor. The qualifications already enlarged upon would be minimized to a hopeless degree if it were to be assumed that this degree can take the place of experience and training far broader than the examination papers will ever require.

It is a well-known fact that hundreds of bright bookkeepers have passed the C. P. A. examinations who never have had the opportunity of inspecting more than one or two sets of books and whose business experience has been limited to one or two special lines.

Nevertheless, the academic instruction and study of textbooks which forms a part of the C. P. A. courses will do much to help the student. Much of the accumulated experience of the profession has been preserved in books, and out of this experience has grown an approved general course of procedure that is of great value.

The majority of audits can be largely mapped out before the work is commenced, and in many instances before the books are inspected for the first time. Conditions may compel a change in procedure, but in few cases will there be any change in principles.

Therefore, in auditing, as in no other branch of accountancy, theory has a well-defined place, and the professional auditor who is unacquainted with all the developments of the science as improved and published by the other members of his profession will find himself as far behind the times as the physician would be who stopped purchasing medical books and reading medical periodicals. It is impossible for any one auditor to cover every ramification of accounting within the limits of his own practice.

He can secure the benefit of what others are doing provided only that the others will reduce their experiences to writing. The study of these writings serves as a basis for working theories which can be generally applied.

The auditor who scorns theory usually performs superfluous work and may be distinguished by his lack of clients. The following quotation from a recent address illustrates the importance placed upon theoretical training for a business career:

> Is it necessary to teach young business men theoretically, and if so, how is it to be done? The answer is found in the fact that in the last half century tremendous changes have taken place in the business world, and, while these are largely technical, they are connected with such an array of social, legal, political, and economic disturbances that the modern business man finds himself confronted with a host of problems of which his grandfather had barely an inkling, and which cannot be solved by rule of thumb. He needs understanding of political economy, of technology, of geography, of commercial law, and of various other things as an initial equipment.
>
> The aim is not to make a man a complete economist, a complete lawyer, a real chemist or an engineer, but to have him understand the elements of all these lines of activity. He must acquire a thorough knowledge of business management and of the goods that are handled, his mind must be awakened to a keen and intelligent interest in his occupation, he must be taught to think swiftly, accurately, and to a definite conclusion, and to grasp comprehensively all related matters; he must learn to read human nature and gain personal habits of order, exactness, and conscientiousness. The way is prepared for his uniting, in the actual business life which follows, theory and practice in comprehensive relation, the preliminary professional instruction making his thinking and his daily work harmonious and fruitful.

General Experience: The auditor conducting a general practice must be equipped to render service to every variety of business life. Without warning his first engagement may cover any one of many varieties of classes of accounts: municipal, public service, trading, manufacturing, banking, brokerage, insurance, professional, executors, institutional, and many more.

The professional auditor must have the benefit of what may be termed the equivalent of a clinic. No one careful of his health will consult a doctor who has not had the practical training which comes only from direct study of living patients.

Therefore the auditor must have a broad familiarity with general business customs and methods. It may be urged that it is difficult to acquire anything but the merest smattering of one business only, even by years of diligence, but this is incorrect. A working knowledge of the various classes of undertakings mentioned above can be attained by some years of application, but it may as well be admitted that the professional auditor can expect to be recognized as fully qualified only after he has had these years of experience in diversified lines.

As a matter of fact, there is only one satisfactory training ground, and that is the office of a public accountant. In no other way is it possible to secure the actual insight into a large number of business enterprises within a reasonable length of time.

But, it is not enough to see the practical side of business life; there is a vast quantity of general training which can be and should be acquired by study, reading, and observation.

The professional auditor is in a sense a specialized accountant. The corporation lawyer, the efficiency engineer, the business systematizer, the scientific manager, the cost-system installer, are specialists, as are surgeons and oculists. But professional men do not become skilled specialists until they have acquired the ground work of their professions, and this applies to the profession of accountancy as well as to law and medicine.

The auditor should have a fair knowledge of economic theories, labor questions, bonus and profit sharing plans of wages, banking principles and foreign exchange. He should study political economy, and follow the trend of public regulation of monopolies and trusts.

Federal control is a vital issue and the auditor's duty to himself and the future of his profession requires him to take an interest in all actual or prospective legislation affecting business interests.

In the past, too, many of the federal and state laws relating to corporate and other business undertakings have been framed and passed by those who have been lamentably lacking in knowledge and experience, with the result that the laws are not observed, or if an attempt is made to enforce them, unjustified annoyance and expense follows. If it is known that he is well-informed on legislation, the auditor will find that he will be consulted.

Special Faculties: In addition to the broadest kind of general training, the auditor who would be happy in his chosen profession requires certain faculties or talents which are inborn rather than acquired.

The most important of these are an imaginative and analytical mind. Of course his mental equipment must be of the highest type, but if he does not possess these two qualities the work of an auditor will be more or less burdensome and it will be practically impossible for him to get the most out of any accounts except those kept in the simplest form; even with these the man without a well-developed and vivid imagination is apt to take too much for granted and lose the opportunity to uncover fraud or carelessness.

The analytical faculty is perhaps the more important of the two. In many cases serious defalcations have been discovered and gross irregularities and extravagances have been disclosed by careful analyses of accounts, where a perfunctory audit consisting of routine checking of postings, footings, and vouchers would not have given rise to suspicion. The auditor who does not come naturally by the analytical faculty must cultivate it assiduously or success is impossible.

The analytical faculty will lead naturally to a proper grouping or synthesis of the results of the auditor's labors. As has been well said (Mr. Allen Ripley Foote, President of the International Tax Association, at the meeting of the American Association of Public Accountants at Denver, in October, 1909):

> A correct tabulation is not in itself a correct record. A record, to be correct, must be kept in a way to show, by proper grouping, the true relation between every factor involved in costs of living, costs of distribution, costs of doing business, and, in the final statement, showing the profit or loss for a fiscal year or for a period of years. Conclusions, or business and political policies based upon records that are not correct, must inevitably be unsound.
>
> *There is a wide difference between honest accounting and scientific accounting.* One may have a record that will honestly account for every dollar received and expended without having a record that will give any intelligent information regarding the true relation between all economic factors involved in statements of costs or of profits and losses.
>
> The records of all accounts should be intelligently grouped to show the economic effect of every factor essential to a true statement of costs or of profits and losses.

In a recent examination of the accounts of a brewery, an auditor had nearly completed the verification of the accounts without disclosing any hint of dishonesty; he then analyzed all costs and compared them with the results. In him the analytical faculty was developed to an uncommon degree, for he applied the knowledge of chemistry which he had acquired to the costs and decided that the results were not correct. A further and more detailed verification of the purchases disclosed the fact that the head maltster had diverted large quantities of materials to a plant owned by himself.

This, perhaps, is an extreme case, and it may not be reasonable to include chemistry among the auditor's qualifications, but it illustrates the value of a wide and liberal education. If the fraud had not been discovered, the auditor might have escaped censure, but his would not have been an enviable position, and the result justified the time involved in his study of chemistry.

Education: It is not intended to discuss the extent of the auditor's elementary studies, but it is obvious that the most complete course is the most desirable one. In other words, his preliminary education cannot be too extensive. Literature, languages, and history all have their value to the professional auditor, as do all subjects included in the education of a person of culture.

It is admitted by all that special knowledge and special mental training are required for success in business and professional life, and it is a tremendous advantage if this knowledge and training can be acquired without too much expenditure of time and effort. In business the tendency is toward too long an apprenticeship. A clerk may perform a certain function ten thousand times in spite of the fact that he has reached perfection after one hundred operations. The law or medical student, on the other hand, usually receives too little preliminary education.

It is to be hoped that the accountancy student will find the happy medium and acquire a maximum of useful knowledge with a minimum of effort.

This preliminary knowledge involves the study of the raw materials of industry, with the sources of their supply and the methods of their production; of the principles which underlie the financing of a business, the granting of credit, the sale of goods, the education of the consumer by means of advertising; the relation of the business man to transportation facilities; the principles of commercial law, of real estate values, and of insurance; of the institutions and agencies of commerce and finance.

A professional education demands of the student not merely

attendance at lectures and mastery of textbooks, but the working out of problems and cases and the investigation of questions involving the principles of the science which he is studying.

The accountancy student should at least read as much along the lines of his future work as is required of a law student along legal lines, and the latter covers tens of thousands of pages of textbooks, reports of cases, digests, etc., before and after his examination.

If at all possible, the accountancy student should acquire some knowledge of the law; the ideal training of a public accountant includes the study of all departments of the law, but if time does not permit, the student should endeavor to master the principles of at least the following branches: partnerships, contracts, corporations, evidence, surrogate or estate, real and personal property.

Moral Qualities: No matter how skillful and experienced an auditor may be, these qualities alone are insufficient to command the confidence of the public. The professional auditor must have a reputation for absolute integrity or his clientele will be limited and his chances for success very limited. He must have the ability to discover the truth and the courage to proclaim it without fear or favor in spite of the many temptations to be silent or equivocal. Frequently the telling of a blunt truth will be distasteful to the client and may threaten the loss of further engagements from the same source, but these instances, fortunately, are becoming rare, and the auditor who never deviates from the truth will never regret it, either from an ethical or financial standpoint.

As has been said by A. Lowes Dickinson, C. P. A.:

> The moral qualities called for are so high that it should place the profession at the head of all which come into contact with business affairs. The lawyer's duty is first of all to his client, and that duty frequently compels him to avail himself of technicalities and other means of enabling that client to evade the law and its penalties; but the public accountant has only one duty to his client and to the public, and that is to disclose to him or for him, "the truth, the whole truth, and nothing but the truth," so far as his abilities and special training to that end enable him to ascertain it. No legal quibble will save him from moral condemnation if he fails in this duty; no juggling with words and phrases will absolve him from responsibility, moral and often legal, for results which he has reason to know are not what they seem to be,

or which, having regard to his special training in business affairs and the accounts relating thereto, he ought to have known did not represent the facts. Errors there may be, and must be, and for errors made after full and proper precaution taken and due care exercised no responsibility will lie. But there is no profession in which the results of careless errors or misstatements will more certainly bring retribution.

Audit Clerks: It is assumed that every assistant in an accountant's office is a student and aspires to become a principal.

The discussion of the qualifications of the professional auditor will, therefore, apply to them as well as to all other students, but certain special qualifications may be mentioned which are desirable and necessary, provided the audit clerk, or assistant accountant, expects to advance in his chosen line. He must be trustworthy to an extraordinary degree, for he must observe all of the trust relations which exist between his employer and the client, and also perform the full measure of duty which every employee owes to his employer.

The most successful business men of to-day were at one time the most industrious and loyal employees. The man who does not serve well will not direct well. Nearly all of the professional accountants who are in the front rank to-day at one time occupied subordinate positions and did their work so well that promotion was inevitable.

The work of the junior is largely routine and is frequently uninteresting. The intelligent and honest clerk will follow directions implicitly, or else he will report to his senior that he wishes to know the purpose of what he is doing before he proceeds. The former is the wisest course, but if an audit clerk has had some experience, there can be no objection to his endeavoring to discover the relation of his work to the audit as a whole.

The clerk's attitude toward the client and the client's staff should be that of friendly interest: friendly because the relations are close and confidential and an attitude of utter indifference is not understood nor appreciated by the client. Obviously the clerk should not become so friendly with the client's staff that suspicion may arise as to his ability or willingness to criticize those of the staff who may require it.

If the clerk cherishes the hope that in time he will set up for himself, he should never allow himself to speculate on the chances of securing for clients in the future those upon whose accounts he is working. Simple loyalty and honesty to his employer should drive such thoughts out of his head; but for those who may not appreciate these qualities and who therefore do not observe them, it should be said that no successful practice has ever been built on such a foundation. Clients so gained expect to pay less and are more exacting; they usually have demanded certificates and reports which were not warranted by the facts, and they expect to find the younger auditor more complaisant.

In discussing the auditor's qualifications, great stress was laid on the value of imagination. This quality must, however, be kept under control on the part of an assistant.

Imagination is closely allied to curiosity, and the client cannot always distinguish between the two. The clerk should impart the results of his imaginings to his senior, so that what may be a "false alarm" will be withdrawn before being discussed with a client or his staff.

Qualifications Required by the Public: The profession is not yet well enough known to the general public to enable a prospective client to discriminate in every case between the qualified and the unqualified auditor. Happily this condition is improving daily, and it will not be very long before the properly trained practitioner will be preferred to the one who has neither the capacity nor the skill to undertake accounting work of any importance. The public point of view at the present time was well expressed by Frank W. Main, C. P. A., in the *Saturday Evening Post* of June 1, 1912. He said *inter alia:*

> That there is much confusion in the popular mind as to the real work of the accountant and as to the very important service which he is rendering in the business world, is not at all surprising.
>
> In the first place, jobless bookkeepers without number, auditors of individual companies, seeing other fields of advancement closed—and cost clerks, certain that their grasp of the one particular business with which they are familiar has given them a grasp of all businesses and a knowledge of all manufacturing problems—have started out in the professional field as full-fledged auditors, accountants, systematizers, and business experts, when, if experienced at all, their experience is confined to but one limited business. In some cases, at least, these "auditors" have about the same right to be known as professional accountants as a hospital orderly would have to palm himself off as a skilled physician.

Misfit Cost-Keeping Systems: The initial work which usually falls to the lot of the self-styled accountant on his first incursion into the professional field is usually in a line of business somewhat of the same nature as the one he has recently left. With the nerve which was necessary to start out in business for himself, and with his practical experience in that particular line, he is often able to render valuable service to his clients. As time goes on, however, and his business is extended into other lines, his difficulties increase; for unconsciously the effort is made to conform all business to the methods and the systems of the one concern with which he was most familiar. As a result, ludicrous situations usually arise, and the usual experience is that after heroic efforts of a few years he is glad to accept some permanent position at an assured salary with an established concern.

In his trail, however, are usually left scores of business men with the well-grounded belief that their own bookkeepers know all that any professional accountant does, and with the conviction that the paying to the accountant of the fees which he demands is only foolishness, as they are certain that the same services can be as well rendered by their own employees.

The second cause of confusion as to the real service which is being rendered by the professional accountant is the impression created by some auditing companies, with their more or less prominent boards of directors, that auditing, accounting, and systematizing constitute purely and solely a business; and that contracts for such work should be very largely placed in the same way that a contract for painting or brickwork would be, namely, to the lowest bidder.

Our profession now includes a large number of practitioners who are more interested in doing good work than in collecting large fees, or in building up what is known as a "large volume of business." They have the reward which accrues to those who follow the highest ideals, in addition to the pecuniary compensation which also accrues to the professional man who steadfastly adheres to the ethics of his profession and maintains high standards irrespective of present results.

CHAPTER IV

THE DUTIES OF AN AUDITOR

It has been pointed out that the disclosure of the truth "so far as his abilities and special training to that end enable him to ascertain it" is the first duty of the professional auditor.

An auditor's duties, however, are so diversified that some space may be properly devoted to a discussion of the more important responsibilities which are thrust upon him.

Non-professional Auditors: Until within a very few years a great deal of so-called auditing was done which was worse than useless, as it carried with it a sense of security which was wholly unwarranted, but which was substantial enough to deceive the very ones who might have been placed upon their guard if no such procedure had been followed. Many of the most serious defalcations which have come to light have occurred in banks, societies, and corporations, where the accounts were periodically submitted to audit committees or amateur auditors whose lack of skill and experience made it impossible for them to unearth clever fraud and manipulation.

Unfortunately, the loss in these instances usually falls upon the very class of persons who can least afford to lose. A number of institutions, societies, and clubs which exist for the purpose of conserving the savings of poor people fail to procure efficient auditors, but—supposedly to save expense—usually appoint one or more unqualified persons to conduct the audits.

Space does not permit any extended remarks upon the results of the work of these amateur auditors. A full review of the disastrous failures during recent years would alone exhibit the misery which has been caused thereby, and the neglect, ignorance, and carelessness of unqualified practitioners have been a large factor in these results, for in many cases the disaster could have been entirely prevented by the exposure of the guilty parties at the time the first so-called audit took place.

The number of nonprofessional auditors in England is said to be decreasing annually, but such does not appear to be the case in the United States. The aggregate membership in the British societies of professional accountants exceeds seven thousand, while that of The American Association of Public Accountants, in which all but a small percentage of the professional accountants in the United States are enrolled, is only slightly in excess of one thousand.

It is the universal practice of surety companies to renew bonds of employees only after certificates have been presented setting forth the fact that the accounts of the applicants for bond renewals have been audited and found correct. A great many corporations and societies of a more or less public nature, such as banks, trust companies, beneficial and loan societies, etc., have their accounts audited annually. Comparing the relatively small number of qualified accountants with the vast amount of auditing work done annually, it is readily seen that a great portion of the work is now being done by amateurs. The examinations made by stockholders' or members' committees and other amateur auditors are in nearly every instance incomplete, and defaulters whose accounts are being investigated by them are usually quick to realize the lack of thoroughness of the audit, with the natural result that large sums are abstracted with little chance of discovery. It has frequently been found, in instances where peculations have been unearthed by qualified auditors, that the accounts of the defaulter were audited by committees and other amateur auditors, and this latter kind of examination is responsible for many of the defalcations reported annually.

Many of these amateurs realize that they cannot make thorough examinations and would willingly turn the work over to qualified auditors; in fact, it is often the case that professional auditors are employed by, or are substituted for auditing committees and amateurs at the latter's request, and it is hoped that it is only a question of time before all of this important work is done by properly qualified auditors.

The by-laws of many corporations and associations contain a clause requiring that audits of their accounts and statements of their financial condition be made and certified to by Certified Public Accountants. Many of the largest corporations in the United States have adopted this course, and it is believed that the officers and a majority of the stockholders of corporations and members of societies generally are becoming impressed sufficiently with the necessity thereof to justify the expectation that before long the practice of having this work done by Certified Public Accountants will become general.

Official Auditors: "Official auditors" is the term used here to designate all who are engaged to audit the accounts of public officials, and such as are designated by State courts to examine and determine the correctness of the accounts of decedents' estates, etc. Lawyers are generally appointed for this last-mentioned work, and the records of the individual transactions are carefully examined by them usually to ascertain that they are not *ultra vires.*

Occasionally it has come to light that peculations had been carried on and that the accounts, incorrect in many important respects, remained uncorrected for some time. If the examinations of these accounts by these appointees were to be limited to the scrutiny of the individual transactions from a legal standpoint, and the actual auditing of the accounts were to be done by professional auditors, who are qualified by their training to discover accounting errors and defalcations, the accounts of estates would be more effectively audited.

The National and State Governments employ official auditors who are required to do much work which should be done by the professional auditor, and the lack of training of the appointees sometimes results in incomplete and inefficient work. Unquestionably it is only a matter of time before reforms will be demanded and much of this work and responsibility will devolve upon the Certified Public Accountant, or else the present incumbents will improve upon the quality of work performed by their predecessors and fit themselves for meritorious work.

Official auditors usually do not have at their disposal sufficient time to enable them to make complete audits and are generally limited as to the scope of their work, and it is also partly due to these facts that their examinations are not thorough, and therefore of questionable value.

The following are the most prominent official auditors employed by the National and State Governments:

Examiners for National and State Banks, Bankers, and Trust Companies; Auditors employed by the State Insurance and Charities Departments; Examiners in the Bureau of Corporations of the Department of Commerce and Labor of the National Government; Inspectors of the Bureau of Internal Revenue assigned to examine the accounts of corporations which report their net income as required by the Federal Corporation Tax Law. The supervision of corporations by the National and State Governments has increased considerably the number of official auditors, and with the extension of this supervision their number will be still further increased. The salaries paid to many of these officials are too low to attract men of proper training and ability, and, obviously, their work cannot be expected to be of the high efficiency of that required of qualified auditors.

The following news item which appeared in the *New York Times* of June 27, 1912, may be of interest in this connection:

ATTACKS FEDERAL BANK SUPERVISION

BINGHAMTON, N. Y., June 26.—The United States Grand Jury, in session here to-day, presented to the court a resolution advising that the revelations in the New Berlin Bank disclosed the fact that the present methods of National Bank examinations were faulty; that perfunctory examinations should be condemned; that the number of bank examiners is insufficient, and the method of compensation is certain to affect the character of the examination. Banker Arnold will be arraigned on indictments alleging bank wrecking to-morrow afternoon.

Staff Auditors: Another body of auditors, who cannot be included among any of the foregoing classes, consists of those who devote their entire time to one or a very few undertakings. This applies chiefly where the organization is large and the work diversified to such an extent that an officer can be profitably employed whose duties are supervisory only and who does not, or rather who is not supposed to perform any clerical duties or handle money, securities, etc.

In many of our largest corporations this officer is called the comptroller, and this is the correct title, but so many of these officers are and will be called auditors that it becomes necessary to classify them as such.

Experience has shown that these auditors gradually have thrust upon them executive duties which are in more or less conflict with the supervisory work which they usually are retained to perform.

A staff auditor cannot very well occupy two positions at the same time; he cannot originate or carry out a transaction which is administrative and later attempt independently to check the same operation.

There have been so many instances of defalcation and fraud by officers or clerks with the title of auditor that it makes the term a misnomer in the mind of the general public. No auditor should have such an opportunity, and if his duties are changed to such an extent that he has the same opportunity to defraud as a treasurer or cashier, then he should no longer be called an auditor. If he does retain the title, it is deceitful, whether willfully or unintentionally.

Professional Auditors: The professional auditor is one whose services are at the disposal of the public. He is charged with the responsibility of undertaking practically all of the work which may be tendered to him. He may, therefore, be said to owe a duty to the public to have a well-equipped office and a staff of specially trained assistants, otherwise he cannot conscientiously undertake work of any magnitude.

There are, however, a great many persons whose experience and ability qualify them as auditors of the highest rank, but whose services are not at the call of the general public, and who, therefore, cannot claim to be professional auditors.

Not an Insurer: In the exercise of his profession the auditor does not become an insurer, in spite of the desire on the part of many clients so to consider him. It is obviously his duty to provide such safeguards as are possible, based on his experience and familiarity with modern practice. He is assumed to have a full theoretical as well as a practical knowledge of the principles of auditing and to apply them skillfully to every case on which he is engaged. But this, fortunately, is the full measure of his responsibility.

The position is a reasonable one when examined from an equitable standpoint, particularly when compared with the premiums paid to liability insurance companies for protection against loss by fraud. The audit fee is not intended to and does not include insurance against loss by dishonesty.

Of course, circumstances may be such as to raise a presumption of negligence or lack of skill on the part of the auditor, but this does not alter the general rule. A full discussion of this subject will be found in Chapter XXXII, "Liabilities of Auditors."

Employees' Bonds: Irrespective of the question as to whether or not an auditor is an insurer, he should always include in his audit program the query: "Are all employees who handle funds under surety bonds?" If not, they should be. Some employers are lax in this respect, others will not incur the expense, and a fairly large class dislike to mention the matter to employees who have occupied positions of trust for a number of years.

The auditor should present the importance of such protection and point out that the expense is comparatively small, but that the risk is not an imaginary one. Of course the auditor has performed his full duty after his recommendation has been considered, and if nothing is done he cannot be blamed for subsequent loss.

It may be, however, that the matter should have consideration at each audit as conditions and employees change. It might not be difficult to persuade an employer to adopt a rule that every new employee should furnish a bond at the time of employment. This would mean that in time the entire staff would be bonded. In every case the employer should pay the premium.

Many employers find it valuable to insist on practically their entire force, including salesmen, furnishing a surety bond. The reason given is that all of them handle funds at one time or another. It makes it easier to demand bonds from cashiers when the rule is general, and a lower rate can be secured where several persons are covered by one bond. The chief value, however, in requiring bonds from salesmen is that the employer is assured that a most exhaustive inquiry is made into each applicant's character and reputation, extending back over a considerable period of years. This search is far more extensive than an employer can, or cares to, make himself, and as such a bond for, say, five hundred dollars does not cost more than two or three dollars, it is well worth a trial. Salesmen are usually intrusted with a traveling expense advance, and similar funds are placed at the disposal of other employees.

Several firms of accountants have enforced this rule for some years with a considerable measure of satisfaction. It is surprising sometimes to ascertain that an applicant whose credentials seem to be above criticism cannot qualify for a minimum amount bond.

This is considered a *prima facie* reason for nonemployment, or dismissal if taken on temporarily, and a good reason must be furnished to offset the effect of the refusal of the surety company.

It is obvious that a man who cannot furnish a five-hundred-dollar surety company bond is not a desirable audit clerk.

Employers sometimes think that placing an employee under bond in some way obviates the necessity for an audit. As a matter of fact, this precaution is all the more advisable in that a means is provided for recouping the amount misappropriated, if a defalcation does occur. The surety companies themselves advocate periodical audits. The National Surety Company of New York, one of the leading bonding companies in America, says:

> Frequent, regular, and thorough audits of cash and books of account by certified public accountants are unquestionably of the greatest benefit to the business man and institution, and should be universally adopted.
>
> We cannot put what we state above too emphatically, and it is deserving of the serious consideration of every business man.

The surety companies frequently quote their minimum rates where they find that the books are regularly audited by professional auditors in whom they have confidence, and this may represent a considerable saving to the assured.

AUDIT OF A FIRM OR AN INDIVIDUAL

The duty of an auditor to an individual or a firm is, of course, to disclose to his client, or clients, the facts as he finds them.

In audits of firms, the rights and liabilities of each partner must be considered. Usually one partner names or retains the auditor, and in many cases assumes an embarrassing proprietary interest over him. Nevertheless, the auditor must maintain the strictest neutrality, for partnerships too often end in litigation, and the auditor who has shown any signs of favoritism may find himself in an unpleasant position.

The partnership agreement should always be read carefully and any provisions as to the accounts noted and verified. Where there is no partnership agreement or where it is deficient in terms, the following guide may be profitably consulted, and where any material divergence exists between what a partner does and what he should do, the attention of each partner should be called to the infraction noted.

Partnership Agreements: Business men are beginning to appreciate the fact that professional accountants are able to advise them properly with respect to the accounts necessary to prevent disputes over partnership agreements. As accounts are the written record of the business, it follows that almost all differences of opinion between partners relate to the accounts. A lawyer does not foresee these differences and most of them do not understand accounts, therefore the accountant, whose experience fits him to point out in advance the various matters out of which misunderstandings arise, is the logical adviser and insurer against many of these points of difference.

The duties of the professional auditor are not always analytical; prevention is better than cure, so that when an opportunity presents itself whereby litigation and other unfortunate experiences may be avoided, it is his clear duty to point out the best course to pursue.

The following rules cover the more important points in partnership agreements, so far as the accounts are concerned.

(1) **Nature of Business:** The scope of the business and the relation of each partner to the business should be clearly stated, also whether a partner is permitted to engage in outside transactions and whether or not each partner is required to devote all of his time to the business.

(2) **Capital:** Specify amount to be contributed by each partner, and how it is to be paid. If partners agree to contribute equally, the agreement should state whether cash or its equivalent is to be provided and the penalty, if any, for the failure of one partner to contribute as much as another.

(3) **Changes in Capital:** If undrawn profits automatically increase and losses decrease the capital accounts of the partners, the agreement should cover the point fully, as the interest of the partners in capital and profits may not be the same.

(4) **Interest on Capital:** Unless provided for in the agreement, capital contributions do not bear interest. If interest is to be allowed, the rate should be fixed.

(5) **Withdrawals:** As this is frequently a matter of dispute, explicit provision should be made to cover the manner and extent of withdrawals and the penalty for overdrafts.

(6) **Undrawn Profits:** If profits are allowed to accumulate, the agreement should state whether such amounts are to be treated as loans or additional capital. This provision is important, as clause (8) may provide that profits are to be apportioned on the basis of capital.

(7) **Interest on Loans or Withdrawals:** If it is desired that interest should be allowed on loans, or charged on withdrawals, so state and specify the rate.

(8) **Distribution of Profits or Losses:** State the method of apportioning profits or losses and specify each partner's percentage, also any contingency which may affect the share of any one.

(9) **Approval of Accounts:** There should be some agreement as to the approval of the individual partner's accounts in respect to withdrawals as well as to the profit and loss and capital accounts. The best way is to require each partner to sign his respective ledger account.

(10) **Salaries of Partners:** If any partner is to receive a stated salary, specify the amount, when to be credited, whether or not interest is to be allowed thereon if undrawn, and whether the amount is to be charged as an expense of the business before ascertaining the profit or loss.

(11) **Dissolution:** State procedure if partner dies or withdraws; whether books shall be balanced at once or allowed to run on to end of month or other period; whether, in case of dissolution, partners are to share losses in same proportion as each one's capital bore to entire capital.

(12) **Special Causes for Dissolution:** If partnership can be dissolved for other reason than death, such as disability or intemperance, state complete details.

(13) **Settlement after Dissolution:** It is important not only to arrange the method of determining each partner's share upon dissolution, but it is equally important to fix the details of payment. The most equitable way is to provide for full payment

within a fixed period, or to pay a certain proportion annually or semiannually. State rate of interest on balance.

(14) **System of Accounts:** To obviate subsequent differences of opinion as to the system of accounts, the agreement should specify that double entry accounts be kept, that they be balanced regularly, and that they be audited annually or oftener by a professional accountant. It is desirable that the method of selecting the auditor be stated.

(15) **Disputes about Accounts:** An arbitration clause should be inserted to the effect that if any dispute arises involving the accounts, it is to be submitted for settlement to a Certified Public Accountant to be mutually agreed upon. As disputes occur with respect to other matters as well as to the accounts, in such cases the reference should be made to a Certified Public Accountant and a lawyer, with power lodged in them to select a third party in case of disagreement.

(16) **Firm Insurance:** If life insurance for the benefit of the firm is to be carried on the life of one or more partners, state how the premiums are to be paid, and the disposition of the proceeds if collected. Also state the disposition if the partnership is dissolved while the policy is in force.

The following argument advanced by an insurance solicitor has enough merit in it to commend it to the attention of every professional adviser:

> The alert intelligence of the American business man has discovered in life insurance a most valuable assistance in establishing his credit, and of late years the amount of insurance taken out for purely business reasons has increased enormously.
>
> Many partnerships have been crippled by the death of a partner at a crucial period in their existence. In every properly coordinated partnership each partner is a specialist in the department over which he has immediate charge. His death not only means a loss in efficiency which competition may render dangerous, but it may also mean the withdrawal of working capital at a time when the replacing of it would be difficult, if not impossible. There are, moreover, instances where it would be especially desirable to buy out the interest of the estate of the deceased and thus prevent the embarrassment of having this interest represented by a person ignorant of the business or antagonistic to the other partners. In fact, the more highly developed and successful the copartnership, the greater the possibility of loss through the death of a partner. The indemnity which life insurance offers against such a loss is well nigh perfect, inasmuch as upon the contingency of death

the policy is tantamount to a sight draft upon the company in favor of the surviving partners.

Partnership policies may be taken jointly upon the lives of a number of partners, providing upon the death of any member of the firm for the payment of the face of the policy to the surviving members. Should the partnership be dissolved, however, the policy could, if desired, be converted into separate insurances for equitable amounts upon the lives of the individuals who had composed the firm. Or individual policies may be taken in the first instance upon the lives of each partner. Upon the death of a partner the insurance upon his life would be paid to the surviving partners, the other policies remaining unaffected. Upon a dissolution of the partnership, a partner could purchase his own policy, having it released to such beneficiary as he might elect, and continue it as his own insurance. This privilege is especially valuable when the health of the insured has become sufficiently impaired to make it impossible for him to obtain new insurance.

(17) How to Avoid Litigation: In litigation between partners it has been held that where partnership books exhibit statements of account and entries of periodical settlement and partial divisions of assets, but there has been no final accounting, this will not constitute a settlement or account stated so as to preclude a revision of the accounts.

The auditor should therefore be careful in accepting statements of clerks or one partner that the accounts were settled up to a certain date. If at any time a final settlement had been made the words "final settlement to this point" would seem to be necessary to preclude the reopening of the accounts in the event that any subsequent dispute should arise.

"The binding force of an account stated will not be given to the mere furnishing of an account or other transaction which was not with a view to asserting a claim, establishing a balance due, or finally adjusting the matters of account between the parties." (Cyc. 1; 367.)

AUDIT OF CORPORATIONS

In the United States the auditor is usually appointed by the directors, although in most small corporations the directors and officers are identical and the appointment comes from one who acts in the capacity of an officer.

Officers and Directors: It is always a question as to how far a professional auditor should go in giving advice. Some accountants of long experience and large practice unqualifiedly recommend that an auditor's duty is to state facts, and facts only, and that inferences therefrom as applied to past or future are not to be drawn by professional auditors.

The author feels, however, that this is another point in practice where an auditor can frequently be of substantial assistance to his client by going somewhat beyond the facts and figures, and stating modestly and without prejudice the effect certain methods have had, or may have in the future.

This advice may be objected to occasionally and a client or two may be lost, but experience has demonstrated to the author that a great majority of business men feel so helpless about their accounts that they welcome any intelligent and constructive comments, criticisms, and advice which their auditor deems it wise to impart.

If the auditor does not have the full confidence of his client, the connection is not likely to be a permanent one; if confidence is reposed in him, it is considered entirely proper for business advice to be contained in a report.

Officers: Many officers of close corporations, holding all or nearly all of the capital stock, are apt to consider the business theirs, and run it as a partnership. Any bad consequences of this custom seem improbable, particularly so long as the corporation is making a profit, but as no one can foretell the future, and as so many prosperous corporations meet with reverses and subsequently go into bankruptcy, there is an obvious duty upon an auditor to advise the officers of close corporations that, for the sake of their own good names, all transactions of a corporate nature should be conducted with more formality than if no such restriction existed.

This applies particularly to the matter of compensation and dividends. In a vast number of corporations these items are handled without any formality whatever; it is considered too much trouble to have a meeting of the board of directors, so a verbal agreement is made; and once started, the practice continues. It should, therefore, be pointed out, in a tactful and friendly way, that strict observance of the law with respect to all matters in which the relation of the officers to the corporation is concerned is advisable from every standpoint.

As an example of this advice it should be noted that an officer cannot fix, nor participate in the fixing, of his own salary or other compensation.

In close corporations officers do not hesitate to loan money to carry on the business where the capital paid is insufficient. Frequently their personal accounts represent credit balances throughout a long period. Interest is usually credited thereon at six per cent unless a lower rate is arranged for. In the event of litigation with directors or stockholders who control or (as is often the case) who own one half the capital stock, and where control is divided, the status of these loans may be questioned.

In one case, not yet decided, two directors loaned large sums to a manufacturing corporation to enable it to produce a large quantity of machinery. The corporation consolidated with a competitor and received securities for its property. These securities were the sole asset of the old company and were valuable but not marketable. The directors who had loaned the money brought suit, alleging that the sums advanced were demand loans and were due and payable, and demanded that the securities be sold for what they would bring and their loans paid in whole or part out of the proceeds.

The other directors resisted the suit and claimed that it was understood that the loans were in the nature of additional capital, and while they were a first lien on the assets, yet a sale of unmarketable securities would be equivalent to a liquidation of the business, which was not contemplated and which would wipe out any equity the capital stock might have.

It may be a year or two before this case is decided. If an auditor had foreseen this result and had suggested that promissory notes be issued from time to time with definite due dates, the trouble would have been averted. This advice would have been bad for the lawyers but extremely valuable to the client.

The laws of the different States vary to such an extent in respect to the rights and duties of officers and directors that no attempt is made here to do more than suggest a starting point.

Directors: The foregoing remarks apply with particular force to directors who are also officers. Where a director receives no compensation, except perhaps a small attendance fee, the warning as to participation in meetings is not so pertinent, but it frequently happens that directors are interested in contracts and other transactions which are authorized or arranged at meetings in which they participate.

If the auditor discovers this state of affairs and is convinced of the bona fides of the transactions, he need not criticize, but he can point out the divergence from the law, state the proper procedure, and suggest that at the next meeting of stockholders all such questionable acts of the directors be ratified.

Under ordinary circumstances a director is held responsible for good faith only, but if the minutes are not full and clear and at some distant day a dissatisfied stockholder or creditor looks sharply for unlawful and unauthorized transactions, the director may find himself involved in annoying, if not expensive, litigation.

The auditor should, as far as possible, report to the board of directors individually, and it is not improper for him so to word his report as to invite personal conferences with any or all of them.

A director has an absolute right to inspect all of the books and papers of a company. This includes the auditor's report, and if an auditor has reason to believe that any director does not receive his report, he should investigate and at least ascertain whether the director is knowingly ignorant or whether he is kept in ignorance of the existence of the auditor's report because the officers or his colleagues have something to conceal. Many directors do not know that under certain conditions they are personally liable for all debts in excess of a certain amount. The auditor should post himself on this and other points so as to be able to make helpful suggestions.

Elsewhere in this book (p. 204) the liability of directors for payment of unearned dividends is fully discussed. It is unquestionably the duty of a professional auditor to warn the directors against any such action, and if it appears that his suggestion is unheeded, the auditor should seek legal advice in order to be sure that his own position is unassailable.

Successful business men might look with more favor upon directorships if they were sure that affairs of the corporation would have the periodical supervision of auditors who seek to broaden, rather than to narrow, their responsibilities.

Auditors are sometimes placed in an embarrassing position through their appointment by the very officer whose accounts they are supposed to audit and criticize. This is peculiarly a situation which requires tact. In view, however, of the clear duty of an auditor to be helpful, it need not be assumed that the work cannot be done as well as in the case of a more independent appointment.

If the auditor finds grounds for severe criticism, he must do his duty, but anything short of this can be adjusted quietly and amicably. It must be said to the credit of officers who are active in the selection of their own auditors that most of them are sincere in their efforts, and the frequent criticisms of their own acts which follow are as surprising to them as to anyone else.

Many corporations are run very carelessly, but an auditor should hesitate about reporting unimportant matters to a board of directors when a personal letter to the executive officers specifying what has been done which should not have been done, and what has not been done which should have been done, will be gratefully received and promptly acted upon.

On the other hand, where auditors have commented rather severely on the acts and omissions of the officers, the only result has been a dislike of all professional auditors and a failure to give consideration to the report.

Unless an officer is under suspicion he is apt to be much closer to and have the confidence of the board of directors to a greater extent than the auditor. Consequently, if the latter reports anything short of fraud, unless with the full coöperation of the officer, he loses prestige, and probably has lost the chance of being of value, and what is more serious, has hurt the whole profession.

Instances have been known where auditors have deemed it their duty to be so aggressive as to precipitate a crisis in the affairs of a corporation. The result of such interference might easily react on the owners of the corporation (the stockholders), whose interests the auditors should protect in every way. Let coöperation and helpfulness be the keynote of corporation audits whether the appointment come from an officer, the directors, or the stockholders.

Some slight advance has been made towards popularizing a

provision in corporation by-laws requiring the accounts to be audited by professional accountants, but such a provision has, so far, not been adopted by even one per cent of the corporations of the United States. The purchasers of the great majority of the bond and preferred stock issues of industrial corporations, however, are insisting on such a provision, and their action is having a marked influence on public opinion.

Auditors must educate the boards of directors, and as public opinion is demanding more and more actual supervision on the part of directors, a very large increase in corporation audits may be expected.

Stockholders, Directors, and Officers: The auditor must realize his responsibility in writing a certificate which will be circulated so widely that personal explanations or reservations cannot be made.

This is probably the greatest responsibility which the professional auditor faces.

The auditor of a corporation should at all times bear in mind that he has three parties to serve:

(1) Proprietors (stockholders), but stockholders have no separate or individual rights.

(2) Directors, who are the legal representatives of the stockholders and who must receive all due consideration as such.

(3) Officers, who are elected or appointed by the directors, and who are in possession of the property and charged with its proper administration; in effect, acting as trustees.

The present tendency is toward the fullest corporate publicity, and it is probable that few boards of directors will deliberately withhold material information from their stockholders. Nevertheless, the courts do not require full disclosure where the directors have a good reason for avoiding too much publicity of corporate affairs. The time is coming, no doubt, when this rule will be narrowed and any stockholder will be entitled to know far more about his company than he can now demand.

It is a happy omen that directors are becoming more sensitive to criticism than they used to be. A few years ago, if an auditor submitted a report that did not agree with the views of the board of directors, it was not uncommon to see it laid aside, and if any report at all went to the stockholders, it would be one made up to suit the directors themselves. The auditor was not displaced—he was ignored. Now an auditor is almost sure to get a full hearing before his report is disapproved, and a courageous auditor, who knows he is right, almost invariably wins his point.

Some auditors are still weak enough to be overpersuaded by an officer or director who wants to make a good showing, but they are digging their own pit. In the long run a subservient auditor will be despised by the clients he retains and shunned by all who are careful of their reputations.

AS AN EXPERT WITNESS

Few professional auditors escape their day in court as expert witnesses. The necessity usually arises out of investigations where fraud or disputes are known to exist, but experience teaches that fraud may be discovered in any audit, and in cases where it is least expected. Therefore, the auditor must look upon himself at all times as a potential witness. Neglect to give proper weight to this possibility has caused considerable embarrassment on more than one occasion where an auditor has placed someone in charge of an audit who is not qualified to make a creditable witness. Sometimes assistants, thoroughly equipped in other respects, are constitutionally unfitted to appear as expert witnesses.

Part of the program of an audit, consequently, is a provision for the substitution of an experienced senior or principal as soon as the work has gone far enough to warrant the assumption that an appearance as a witness is probable.

The author has testified as an expert witness scores of times, and submits the following suggestions based entirely on practical experience:

(1) Preparation Is always Essential: The average lawyer does not prepare his cases properly, because the majority are settled without suit, or when called are so frequently continued from time to time that he finds it fairly safe to take a chance of waiting until the trial or reference is on before going into the details of the accounts upon which he purposes to examine the accountant.

This makes it all the more necessary for the accountant to be ready. Unfortunately, the lawyer's excuses are received with less annoyance than the accountant's, and the latter must be ready to go into any or all phases of the matter on a moment's notice, or the lawyer, and through him the client, becomes impatient.

The section on working papers (p. 73) should be read at this point. Failure to make full and proper memoranda during the examination is as annoying subsequently as the failure to find data required, either because it is not properly arranged or filed, or because the query raised was not foreseen.

(2) A Witness Can Testify to His Own Work Only: While an expert witness is permitted to present synopses and summaries prepared from records offered in evidence, and is thus not compelled to produce his results item by item, yet he must testify that the results to which he testifies are his own preparation and not the work of others. The state of mind of the presiding judge usually decides this point where there is any dispute.

The author has found it valuable to have ready for inspection certain of the working papers written in his own handwriting. The attorney for the other side almost invariably raises this point when he thinks there is any likelihood of any of the work having been performed by others, and where the witness has a large practice, and is thought to be dependent largely on the work of assistants, or where the report indicates that one man could not possibly have compiled all of the data within a limited period of time. It is of the utmost importance, therefore, that the witness should be ready to state that the results to which he is testifying are his own work; that he brought the figures together; that if he did not perform all of the detail work, it was done under his supervision, and that he presents it as his work.

(3) Information Should Not Be Volunteered: As an accountant is supposed to testify to facts only, he will make the best impression when he answers questions explicitly and stops when he thinks the question has been answered.

If the attorney is not fully conversant with the details of the case, the accountant should, before the hearing or trial commences, prepare for the attorney written questions designed to bring out all of the matter favorable to his client's side of the case.

The auditor should never be asked to suppress facts within his knowledge, and cannot honestly do so, no matter how much pressure is brought to bear, but no code of ethics recommends, or as a matter of fact permits, a professional man to volunteer to outsiders, or to the opposing side in litigation, facts which would injure his client.

The accountant having, as a part of his duty, provided the means whereby favorable facts will be disclosed, must in every legitimate way guard against the disclosure of unfavorable facts. As intimated above, he must answer any pertinent question, no matter how much the answer may hurt his client, but if there is any possibility of such a question, in cross-examination, being irrelevant, or improper, he should give his own attorney plenty of time to object before replying, and if he is instructed to answer, his duty lies solely in telling the truth, and there should be no volunteering of information for which the question does not specifically call.

(4) Conclusions and Opinions: Practitioners differ as to how far an accountant is justified in testifying as to his opinions where the facts at hand may not be conclusive enough for him to state positively that his testimony is founded on conclusions based solely on facts and figures contained in the records offered in evidence.

Frequently the records are incomplete, but enough data may have been compiled to warrant a definite opinion as to certain results. Where the witness is acting in good faith, and is interested only in seeing that, as far as he is concerned, substantial justice is being done, it may be urged that his duty to his client requires the presentation of all the evidence possible, and that the other side can be depended upon to object to anything going in unless the ground work of relevancy has been laid.

On the other hand, it is contended that an accountant, as a witness, should be absolutely impartial and disinterested, that he should state the bare truth and be oblivious of which side it might affect. The author has heard this argument for many years, but in the course of his experience, which has brought him into contact, on one side or the other, with the leading accountants in this country, he has invariably found that the accountants are more or less interested in their side and the presentation of the facts favorable to their side, and he has failed to detect any signs of pure disinterestedness on the part of any one of them.

Furthermore, he has found in many instances that the accountants have been better advocates for their clients than the attorneys themselves, this being demonstrated not only by their testimony under oath, but by their skill in suggesting questions to the attorneys, and these questions have been directed to all witnesses, and not to those only who are examined on the accounts.

To sum up: the present practice seems to be for accountants to promote in all legitimate ways the success of the side of litigation on which they are retained, and they are not found to be unconcerned and oblivious of results; that the attorneys and parties to the cases know that this is the practice; that they are relying more and more on professional auditors to assist in the preparation of matters in litigation; and that the attorneys and others who have a first-hand knowledge of the present practice do not see any impropriety in it.

The author has no criticism to make of this procedure, but on the contrary believes that the accountants who have in many cases signally helped their clients by extra zeal would have fallen short of their full duty if they had maintained the attitude of a machine which shows final results, but which cannot make suggestions as to how those results may be used.

THE AUDITOR OF AN INSTITUTION OR SIMILAR ORGANIZATION

In recent years there has been a noteworthy advance in the practice of employing professional auditors for universities, schools, hospitals, clubs, churches, and many other quasi-public organizations.

Frequently one of the auditor's clients will be interested in the affairs of one of these enterprises and requests that an audit be made for his personal information. This is usually followed by formal appointment by the board of managers or directors and the auditor secures an opportunity to submit a certificate which finds its way into the annual printed report. Because such publicity is desirable and apt to increase his clientele, especially among those directly connected with that particular institution and because he feels under some obligation to his client, these audits are rarely remunerative. The auditor is sometimes forced seriously to consider the advisability of declining such engagements.

The investing public must be taught that corporations which do not publish certified statements of their condition and earnings should be looked upon with suspicion, and charitable or religious institutions should for the same reason be compelled to publish certified balance sheets and certified statements of their income and expenses. The giving public can then discriminate against the institution which does not fully disclose its affairs and so indicate that all of its financial transactions are beyond reproach.

During the last year the Chicago Association of Commerce considered this subject, and a committee appointed for the purpose arrived at the conclusion that all institutions inviting subscriptions from the public should submit to an annual audit. The Subscriptions Investigating Committee of the Association now gives its unqualified indorsement only to such institutions as, in addition to satisfactorily meeting all the other requirements of the Committee, have their accounts audited annually by public accountants. A plan was worked out under which a considerable number of public accountants in Chicago coöperate with this Committee by making audits of charitable and philanthropic institutions at a nominal rate per diem. The plan has now been in effect for a year; further details concerning it can be secured from Walter A. Staub, C. P. A., Secretary of the Accountants Association for the Audit of Local Charitable and Philanthropic Institutions, First National Bank Building, Chicago.

SPECIAL AUDITS

The professional auditor will find himself called upon for work of a special character, as, for instance, by a creditor's committee, or by a retiring partner, or by a dissatisfied beneficiary under a will. His duty under these varying circumstances is uniform, that is, his duty to himself and his profession is paramount, and he cannot avail himself of technicalities and evasion to conceal the true state of facts.

It is, however, not unprofessional to assure the payment of his fee, and as disputes frequently arise on this point in these special audits, a word of caution may be in order.

Where it is agreed by both sides of a dispute that an examination shall be made by an independent auditor, the latter is called upon, performs the services, and makes his report. But when he renders his bill, both sides disclaim it. This occurs so often that there is no excuse for an auditor getting caught twice, while those who have not so suffered can avail themselves of this warning.

CHAPTER V

ETHICAL DUTIES—LEGISLATION

The Auditor's Ethical Duties: Codes of ethics may be written or unwritten, but whether written or not they form a basis on which to judge the worthiness of the aspirant for professional standing. Just as a professional man is known by the ethics he observes, so is the profession itself known by the standard of ethics it sets up for the guidance of its members.

The medical profession has perhaps the most definite code, the observance of which has been made compulsory upon its members. It will probably be many years before accountancy ethics will reach the same degree of development, but the subject is receiving more and more consideration and careful study.

Following is that part of the by-laws of the American Association of Public Accountants prescribing a code of ethics for the profession, including the amendments submitted at the September, 1912, annual meeting in Chicago.

ARTICLE VI

Precepts of Professional Conduct

(*a*) A profession is an employment requiring a learned education, a vocation in which a professed knowledge of some department of science or learning is used by its practical application to the affairs of others in advising, guiding, or teaching them or in serving their interests or welfare in the practice of an art founded on it. Professed attainments and special knowledge as distinguished from mere skill; practical dealing with affairs as distinguished from mere study or investigation; the application of such knowledge to use for others as a vocation as distinguished from its pursuit for its own purposes.

(*b*) Professional conduct necessarily implies honorable conduct; and unprofessional, dishonorable.

(*c*) Public policy requires that certain occupations must be subject to legislative control due to the special scholarly and moral qualifications required of a practitioner and the injurious consequences likely to result from a lack thereof.

(*d*) The study of the sciences of higher accounting, finance, and industrial economics and the practical application of such acquired knowledge as a life career as such services may be demanded must be regarded as the practice of a profession.

(*e*) Every practitioner should aid in guarding the profession against the admission to the profession of candidates unfitted or unqualified because deficient in either education or moral stamina.

(*f*) A practitioner cannot offer his services for sale or vaunt his own abilities without violating the canons of good taste and professional ethics. No one invested with the dignity and prestige implied by such intimate relations with clients should be permitted to degrade it by mere cupidity. A wholesome regard for such dignity forbids an accountant advertising his talents or skill as a merchant does his wares.

(*g*) It is an undignified resort to low artifice to advertise under an actual or fictitious corporate name.

(*h*) An accountant should not speak slightingly or disparagingly of his profession, or pander to unjust prejudice on the part of the laity, and should scrupulously refrain from inciting or fostering such prejudice as a reflection upon a brother accountant.

Rules of Conduct

1. No member shall allow any person to practice in his name as a public accountant who is not a member of this association, in partnership with him or in his employ on a salary, nor shall he practice under an impersonal designation or corporate title.

2. No member shall directly or indirectly allow or agree to allow a commission, brokerage, or other participation by the laity in the fees or profits of his (the member's) professional work, nor shall he accept directly or indirectly from the laity any such commission or brokerage for professional or commercial business turned over to others as an incident of his service to clients, nor perform accountancy work payment for which is contingent upon the result of litigated or arbitrated issues.

3. No member shall engage in any business or occupation conjointly with that of a public accountant, which in the opinion of the Board of Trustees is incompatible or inconsistent therewith.

4. No member shall certify to exhibits, statements, schedules, or other form of accountancy work which have not been verified entirely under the supervision of himself, a member of his firm, one of his staff, a member of this association, or of a similar association of good standing in foreign countries.

5. No member shall in his business advertisements use any initials as an affix to his name that are not either authorized by statutory enactment of this country or by the well-known associations established for a similar purpose in the British empire, nor shall he affiliate with or substantially recognize any society that is designated or in any way sets itself out to be a so-called certified public accountant society unless the State in which such society is organized has the requisite statutory enactment in full force and effect.

6. No member shall take part in any effort to secure the enactment, alteration, or amendment of any State or Federal law affecting the profession

without giving immediate notice thereof to the secretary of the association, who in turn shall at once advise the secretary of the State or district society concerned.

LEGISLATION

The question of legislation looking to compulsory audits has been discussed frequently, chiefly by accountants, however, and as they are believed to be the chief beneficiaries, little progress has been made. But as soon as investors and stockholders, generally, come to realize that the protection is great and the expense small, legislation may be expected.

The following bill was introduced in a recent session of the Pennsylvania Legislature at the request of the then President of the Pennsylvania C. P. A. Board:

An Act

Requiring the certification of a certified public accountant of the State of Pennsylvania as to the correctness of any financial statement issued by any corporation of this State or by any foreign corporation or corporation of other States doing business in the State of Pennsylvania, for public information or for purposes of taxation, and to provide a punishment for the violation of this act.

SECTION 1. Be it enacted by the Senate and House of Representatives of the Commonwealth of Pennsylvania in General Assembly met, and it is hereby enacted by the authority of the same, that all corporations of the State of Pennsylvania or foreign corporations or corporations of other States doing business in the State of Pennsylvania, upon issuing any financial statement inviting the purchase of their stock or bonds, or in issuing any monthly, quarterly, semiannual, or annual statements of the condition or business of such corporations, or any financial statements given to the newspapers, financial agencies, or other financial statements for the purpose of public information in the State of Pennsylvania, or upon furnishing statements to the officials of the State of Pennsylvania for the purpose of taxation, shall be required to have such statements verified by a certified public accountant of the State of Pennsylvania.

SEC. 2. If any such corporation fails to have such certification made, it shall be deemed and held guilty of a misdemeanor, and upon conviction thereof shall be fined not more than one thousand dollars, nor less than five hundred dollars, and any officer, agent, or employee of such corporation furnishing a false statement, or any certified public accountant certifying to the correctness of a statement issued by any corporation, when it is vitally incorrect or misleading, the officer, agent, or employee making such false statement, and the certified public accountant certifying to such false statement, shall be deemed guilty of a misdemeanor, and, on conviction thereof, shall be sentenced to imprisonment for a term not exceeding two years and not less than one year, or a fine not exceeding five thousand dollars nor less than three thousand dollars, or both.

The bill, of course, did not pass, and is not referred to here as an ideal measure, but it is at least suggestive and should be of interest to all who contemplate legislation along similar lines.

It is suggested that a more desirable State law would compel all corporations to furnish *annual* reports to their stockholders, with a balance sheet and profit and loss statement duly certified to by recognized professional accountants. This suggestion brings up the question as to how much information should be furnished to stockholders.

The time-honored excuse for withholding information from stockholders is the expressed fear that competitors may take advantage of it. Many factors enter into the discussion, but it is becoming a well established custom that a corporation with a considerable number of stockholders is under an obligation to furnish such an annual report as will give the stockholders an opportunity to judge for themselves whether to hold their stock or sell it, and the report must be complete enough so that the opinion so formed will have a true basis.

Some of the most prosperous corporations in the country publish the most complete reports. They know that their competitors cannot get the slightest advantage from such statements, and they ignore the childish and silly excuses offered by corporations which do not publish reports.

The stockholder must be educated to discriminate between a report which is certified to and one which is not.

Legislation Proposed in New York State: Several years ago, in response to a demand for legislation which would afford greater security to investors, Dr. Jeremiah W. Jenks prepared a draft bill which was introduced in the New York Legislature but which did not pass. It was entitled "New York Business Companies Act." It is extremely suggestive, and portions thereof are inserted at this point as a reminder to professional auditors that constant agitation will ultimately result in favorable legislation, and any statute which safeguards the interests of the investing public will be even more beneficial to the profession. The auditor's duty to his clients happily includes missionary work along the line of compulsory audits.

The sections of the bill referred to which are of interest to the profession are as follows:

Officers[1]

Besides the usual officers, an auditor or auditors shall be chosen by ballot by the stockholders at their annual meeting, and no person or firm or corporation, a member, director, or officer of which is a director of the company to be audited, shall be eligible. Corporations organized under this act with a capital stock of one hundred thousand dollars or upward must select as auditor or auditors a person, firm, or corporation duly qualified and engaged in the practice of public accounting and auditing in this State. And the auditor or auditors selected by a corporation whose capital stock amounts in all to one million dollars or more must have his or their financial responsibility secured by a bond of fifty thousand dollars of some surety company authorized to do business under the insurance laws of this State; and for a corporation whose capital stock is less than one million dollars, by a bond amounting to at least five per centum of the capital stock and approved by the shareholders either at a meeting or through a committee selected for this purpose. The above provisions regarding bonds may be waived by the written consent of every shareholder.

Any stockholder shall be entitled, upon payment of cost of copying at not over ten cents a folio of one hundred words, to a statement at any time of all salaries paid to any officer or officers of the corporation, together with a statement of all contracts or agreements in which any officer of the corporation may be interested either as a contracting party with the corporation or as an officer or stockholder in any other corporation contracting with the company.

The salaries of the officers shall be fixed at the annual meeting unless the articles of incorporation provide otherwise. In case, however, salaries shall be increased at any time by the board of directors under provision of the articles of incorporation, report thereof must be made at the next annual meeting to the stockholders and laid before them for ratification. Their action shall be conclusive in all particulars.

If any certificate made, or any public notice given by the officers or directors of any corporation in pursuance of the provisions of this act, shall be false in any material representation, all the officers or directors who shall have signed the same, knowing it to be false, shall be jointly and severally liable for all the debts of the corporation contracted while they were directors or officers thereof, as a penalty enforceable in the courts of this State only.

Meetings

At the regular annual meeting, for which provision must be made in the certificate of incorporation or in the by-laws, the shareholders' balance sheet,

[1] The provisions regarding auditors are intended to protect shareholders against misuse of power by directors. Every effort is made to identify the interests of auditors and shareholders. The provisions regarding bonds of auditors will make their responsibility a real one. The further provisions regarding officers are likewise needed to hold them responsible to shareholders.

prepared and certified by the auditors as provided later, must be presented to the shareholders. If the directors or other officers of any corporation organized under this act shall fail or neglect to call, in the manner provided by law, the annual stockholders' meeting at the time appointed in the certificate of incorporation or in the by-laws and shall not hold the same accordingly, thereupon, from the time when said meeting was appointed to be held, until the meeting shall actually be held thereafter, all salaries of president, vice-presidents, secretary, treasurer, and directors shall cease and determine, and it shall be unlawful for any corporation or its officers or directors to pay directly or indirectly any salary or compensation to any of the above named officers or to any director for services rendered in the interim.

At the annual meeting any shareholder shall be entitled to require from the company and the directors shall be bound to furnish him with a copy of all or any parts of the directors' records of meetings.

Balance Sheet[1]

Every company and the directors and managers thereof

1. Shall cause to be kept proper books of account in which shall be kept full, true, and complete accounts of the affairs and transactions of the company; and

2. Shall once, at least, in each year cause the accounts of the company to be balanced and a balance sheet in this act referred to as the shareholders' balance sheet to be prepared, which balance sheet, after being duly audited, shall be laid before the members of the company in next general meeting; and

3. Shall cause a copy of such shareholders' balance sheet so audited to be sent to the registered address of every member of the company at least seven days before the meeting at which it is to be laid before the members of the company, and a copy to be deposited at the registered office of the company for the inspection of the members of the company during a period of at least seven days before that meeting, and every shareholder in the company or any person acting in his behalf shall be entitled to other copies thereof on payment of twenty-five cents each.

The shareholders' balance sheet shall be in such form as is directed by the certificate of incorporation, or the by-laws, or by a resolution of the company, and shall show in every case

1. The amount of share capital authorized, the amount issued, and the amount paid up thereon, distinguishing the amount of share capital paid up in money and the amount paid otherwise than in money, with a statement of nature of the consideration and the arrears of calls due, and the specific amounts issued during the two years next preceding;

2. The amount of debts due by the company, specifying the security, if any, allocated for each debt and distinguishing the amount of mortgages,

[1] It will be observed that this balance sheet is not published, but is given to the shareholders. Of course, in case of large companies whose stocks are on the stock market, this is equivalent to publication, while a small private corporation with but few members would be able to confine knowledge of its affairs to its few stockholders and the proper officers of the State.

debentures, and floating charges against the general assets of the company, the amount of the reserve fund, if any, and the amount of any contingent liabilities;

3. The amount of all current assets, after making a proper deduction for debts considered to be bad or doubtful. Any debts due from directors or other officers to be separately stated;

4. Whether the assets other than debts due to the company are taken at cost price or by valuation, or on what other basis they are reckoned, and whether any and if so what amount of percentage has been written off and what other provision, if any, has been made for depreciation;

5. The gross amount of the year's earnings, the deductions made from the same for fixed charges of interest and taxes and the surplus, if any, available for dividends;

6. The amount by which the gross value of the assets of the company has been increased since the last balance sheet in consequence of any increase in the valuation of real or personal property belonging to the company;

7. The amount of property, if any, for which shares were issued which has been sold since the last report, with a full disclosure of the consideration therefor in detail, the parties to the contract, and the real parties in interest.

The shareholders' balance sheet shall be accompanied by a certificate, signed by two or more of the directors on behalf of the board, stating that, in their opinion, the balance sheet is drawn up so as to exhibit a correct view of the state of the company's affairs and that, in their opinion, the statement is correct.

A copy of the balance sheet shall be sent to each director at least ten days before the annual meeting, and unless he formally at or before the meeting makes statement to the contrary, he shall be held to have also signed the report.

Duties of Auditors

The auditors of every company

1. Shall use reasonable diligence with the view of ascertaining that the books of the company have been properly kept and record correctly the affairs and transactions of the company;

2. Shall examine the shareholders' balance sheet and any accounts presented to the members of the company, and shall report in writing to the members of the company when the balance sheet is transmitted, that the balance sheet and accounts have been drawn up in accordance with the provisions of the New York Companies' Act, and when taken together, with any explanations attached thereto, present a correct view of the state of the company's affairs. Or, if the auditors are unable to make such a report, they shall report in writing when the balance sheet is transmitted in what respects the balance sheet and accounts fail to comply with these requirements, and shall sign a certificate at the foot of the balance sheet, stating whether or not all their requisitions as auditors, including their requisitions with regard to the private balance sheet hereinafter mentioned, have been complied with; and

3. Shall report in writing to the members all material information which they have observed or have become acquainted with with regard to the books, accounts, securities, vouchers, papers, writings, and documents examined by them, and for this purpose they shall at all times have access to all the books, accounts, and records of the company, and to the minute book, and shall be empowered to require from the directors and other officers such information and explanation as may be necessary for the performance of their duties.

If for any reason it prove impossible for the auditors to prepare their report before the date mentioned above, then they shall submit at the general meeting the reasons for their failure. The shareholders shall then take action and fix a later date at which a report shall be submitted either by the said auditors or by their successors in office.

If the auditors, or any one of them, think there is just cause to disapprove of any part of the said accounts presented to the members of the company, they, or any one of them, may disallow any part of the said accounts so disapproved of and shall report their or his disapproval in writing on the accounts and balance sheet.

Every such report and balance sheet shall be read before the company at the next general meeting.

Any auditor who shall willfully or through gross negligence certify that any false or fraudulent balance sheet or account is correct, shall be civilly responsible to any party injured.

Private Balance Sheet

The auditors of every company before making a report pursuant to the last preceding section shall require, and the directors and president of the company shall, without unnecessary delay, supply to the auditors a balance sheet, in this act referred to as the private balance sheet, giving the details on which the shareholders' balance sheet is founded and showing among other things the amount of deduction, if any, for debts considered to be bad or doubtful.

The private balance sheet must be signed by the president, treasurer, and by at least two of the directors of the company when there are not more than three directors, and by three, at least, when there are more than three directors.

The auditors may require the directors, treasurer, and president of the company to supply in writing, signed as hereinbefore provided, any further details or information affecting the balance sheet or any particular item comprised therein, and shall sign a certificate at the foot of the private balance sheet, stating whether or not all their requisitions as auditors have been complied with.

The private balance sheet shall not be issued to the members of the company, but shall, together with all such further details and information as aforesaid, be kept by the directors as part of the records of the company.

In this connection it may be interesting to note some of the provisions with respect to auditors which are contained in the

English Companies (Consolidation) Act, 1908 (8 Edw. VII, ch. 69).

SECTION 112. (1) Every company shall at each annual general meeting appoint an auditor or auditors to hold office until the next annual general meeting.

(2) If an appointment of auditors is not made at an annual general meeting, the Board of Trade may, on the application of any member of the company, appoint an auditor of the company for the current year and fix the remuneration to be paid to him by the company for his services.

(3) A director or officer of the company shall not be capable of being appointed auditor of the company.

(4) A person, other than a retiring auditor, shall not be capable of being appointed auditor at an annual general meeting unless notice of an intention to nominate that person to the office of auditor has been given by a shareholder to the company not less than fourteen days before the annual general meeting, and the company shall send a copy of any such notice to the retiring auditor and shall give notice thereof to the shareholders, either by advertisement or in any other mode allowed by the articles, not less than seven days before the annual general meeting;

Provided, that if, after notice of the intention to nominate an auditor has been so given, an annual general meeting is called for a date fourteen days or less after the notice has been given, the notice, though not given within the time required by this provision, shall be deemed to have been properly given for the purposes thereof, and the notice to be sent or given by the company may, instead of being sent or given within the time required by this provision, be sent or given at the same time as the notice of the annual general meeting.

(5) The first auditors of the company may be appointed by the directors before the statutory meeting, and, if so appointed, shall hold office until the first annual general meeting, unless previously removed by a resolution of the shareholders in general meeting, in which case the shareholders at that meeting may appoint auditors.

(6) The directors may fill any casual vacancy in the office of auditor, but while any such vacancy continues, the surviving or continuing auditor or auditors, if any, may act.

(7) The remuneration of the auditors of a company shall be fixed by the company in general meeting, except that the remuneration of any auditors appointed before the statutory meeting, or to fill any casual vacancy, may be fixed by the directors.

SECTION 113. (1) Every auditor of a company shall have a right of access at all times to the books and accounts and vouchers of the company, and shall be entitled to require from the directors and officers of the company such information and explanation as may be necessary for the performance of the duties of the auditors.

(2) The auditors shall make a report to the shareholders on the accounts examined by them, and on every balance sheet laid before the company in general meeting during their tenure of office and the report shall state

(*a*) Whether or not they have obtained all the information and explanation they have required; and

(*b*) Whether, in their opinion, the balance sheet referred to in the report is properly drawn up so as to exhibit a true and correct view of the state of the company's affairs according to the best of their information and the explanations given to them, and as shown by the books of the company.

(3) The balance sheet shall be signed on behalf of the board by two of the directors of the company, or, if there is only one director, by that director, and the auditors' report shall be attached to the balance sheet, or there shall be inserted at the foot of the balance sheet a reference to the report, and the report shall be read before the company in general meeting and shall be open to inspection by any shareholder.

Any shareholder shall be entitled to be furnished with a copy of the balance sheet and auditors' report at a charge not exceeding sixpence for every hundred words.

(4) If any copy of a balance sheet which has not been signed as required by this section is issued, circulated, or published, or if any copy of a balance sheet is issued, circulated, or published without either having a copy of the auditors' report attached thereto or containing such reference to that report as is required by this section, the company, and every director, manager, secretary, or other officer of the company who is knowingly a party to the default, shall, on conviction, be liable to a fine not exceeding fifty pounds.

(5) In the case of a banking company registered after the fifteenth day of August, eighteen hundred and seventy-nine

(*a*) If the company has branch banks beyond the limits of Europe, it shall be sufficient if the auditor is allowed access to such copies of and extracts from the books and accounts of any such branch as have been transmitted to the head office of the company in the United Kingdom; and

(*b*) The balance sheet must be signed by the secretary or manager (if any), and where there are more than three directors of the company by at least three or four of those directors; and where there are not more than three directors, by all directors.

SECTION 114. (1) Holders of preference shares and debentures of a company shall have the same right to receive and inspect the balance sheets of the company and the reports of the auditors and other reports as is possessed by the holders of ordinary shares in the company.

(2) This section shall not apply to a private company, nor to a company registered before the first day of July, nineteen hundred and eight.

CHAPTER VI

HOW TO BEGIN AN AUDIT

THE importance of knowing how to begin an audit cannot be overestimated. Until the business public is educated to a point where it knows just what is required and can ask for specific service, which in turn the auditor can perform without violating his rules of practice, his employment is more or less general in its nature and the scope of the work is left to the auditor.

For this reason many practitioners commence the work before they have a clearly defined line of procedure in their own minds.

Based on personal experiences of over twenty years, the author suggests the following preliminary program:

(1) As to the Client: Attention has been called to the uncertainty which sometimes exists as to the actual client whom the auditor is serving and to whom he is responsible. It may be a banker or a prospective borrower, a corporation or a dissatisfied stockholder, a trustee in bankruptcy or the petitioning creditors, or a creditors' committee, a municipality or an aldermanic committee, a State or an investigating committee of the Legislature. In all of these cases and many more, differences of opinion have arisen as to the *legal* status of the client; therefore, this word of caution addressed particularly to the beginner is in order:

Fix the legal responsibility of the client before work is commenced.

(2) Do not start until you are sure you will finish: Some auditing engagements have ended disastrously for the auditors because the work was undertaken blindly. It is not enough that some one should say, "Here are certain books and records; I want them audited and a report made to me of what they contain." The client may *think* he knows what he wants, he may be financially able to pay, and to a young practitioner the temptation to jump in and follow instructions is strong indeed. But the client may and does change his mind as the work progresses, and even if the instructions are in writing, he will find some excuse for his change of mind. He may still be able to pay, but he may not want to. There are several notable examples of work done along the lines indicated the bills for which have never been paid.

Therefore, spend some time with the client reviewing the work before it is commenced. Map out as definite a program as possible and overstate, rather than understate, the probable time which will be required. The client may have a vague knowledge of details, but he should know pretty well what the work should cover, and if the auditor cannot come to a fairly definite agreement with him as to the scope and extent of the work, the responsibility of making good is placed definitely on the auditor.

A few hours' talk of this nature may subsequently eliminate many days of useless work—useless because there may have been a mistaken idea as to the results wanted; or the results striven for might be very valuable and interesting *if* the work could be completed as originally planned.

In most cases the auditor's wide experience enables him to know better than the client just what should be done, and what may be safely omitted, but this does not relieve an auditor from his obligation to assure himself whether in the particular case before him the client's more intimate knowledge of the business does not justify him in indicating the general lines along which the audit should be made.

A full and frank talk with a client cannot do any possible harm and may insure coöperation and harmony, which might be lacking if the auditor shows too much of a disposition to run the whole job himself.

(3) Try to secure the friendly coöperation of the client's staff: A successful auditor told the author recently that in every audit he endeavored to attract, interest, instruct, and convert the office staff, and in so doing he not only made his own work pleasanter and more satisfactory in a professional way, but that he made them co-workers with him, and in many ways they aid the growth of a proper opinion of the value of the public accountant. Many instances are known where auditors have antagonized an office staff and sent them out to an extensive acquaintance charged with a desire to criticize most unfavorably not only the offending auditor (which would not be unfair), but also professional auditors as a class.

Some very large engagements have resulted directly from a word of commendation to others from a bookkeeper or clerk who has had a satisfactory experience with the auditor of his accounts.

All auditors of experience agree that the majority of men are honest—not a mere majority only, but *most* men are honest. Furthermore, most men are sensitive about having their honesty questioned even indirectly. The successful auditor does not conduct himself in such a manner as to indicate to *anyone* that suspicion exists. He *must* radiate his belief in the good faith and honesty of purpose of those whose accounts he is examining; but he will be none the less thorough and he will just as surely land any guilty man.

The honest man is also sensitive to criticism of his work. Here the auditor's task is harder, because the duty to one's client must be placed above everything else, and while it is sometimes unpleasant to condemn carelessness and mistakes on the part of the office staff, yet if it is evident that the client's business is suffering therefrom, failure to report actual conditions would be a breach of professional duty.

But the auditor who prepares his report and sends it in to the client without considering its effect on the office staff may be doing a positive injury to his client as well as to himself. The clerk whose work is criticized may be one of the most valuable on the staff. His merits may vastly outweigh his shortcomings, yet if he is sensitive he may resign forthwith, thus weakening the client's organization and subjecting the auditor to the wrath which he in a measure deserves.

Or again, the clerk or clerks whose work is criticized may not resign, but being in the confidence of the client and having his ear every day, may easily offset all of the good effect which the criticisms and suggestions might have, and, in addition, prejudice the client against the further employment of the auditor.

Naturally, the auditor is not informed as to what is taking place, and if his services are not called for when another audit is due, he is ignorant of the true reason for the decision against him.

Hundreds of business men have retained a professional auditor once as an experiment, because they had been told it was the proper thing to do, and would have become regular clients had the auditor been able to secure the sympathy and coöperation of the office staff.

Who can blame a busy man, necessarily dependent upon an organization of trusted employees, for heeding their opinion of an auditor?

All That is Required is Tact: The auditor need not stultify himself by failure to criticize. As a matter of fact, an honest staff resents gratuitous commendation if they know it is not deserved. All they want is a square deal. In practically all cases the methods in force were initiated by the client himself or by the predecessors of the present staff. They are simply following precedents or instructions and should not be personally blamed for unsatisfactory methods or results.

Let the auditor proclaim his gospel of helpfulness and ask for coöperation in the interest of the staff and in that of the client. Let him demonstrate quietly that he knows more than they do, but let it be done unobtrusively. Show them that failure to be up to date is detrimental to success, and that modern methods must justify themselves. Get them interested and ask their help in preparing an unbiased report on actual conditions, and obtain their approval of the suggested changes.

If this spirit prevails throughout the audit the client will be benefited, the office staff will be enthusiastic over the innovation, and the auditor will receive a unanimous invitation to come again.

(4) As to Fees: Compensation must depend on service rendered: The professional accountant offers his services to the business public as an adviser as well as an analyst or auditor; therefore it is obvious that the matter of compensation and status cannot be determined as it can in those occupations where the matter of output or results can be measured. You cannot gauge an output of brains as you can a stated amount of manual labor.

Great harm has been done to the profession by certain advertisers who, for the purpose of selling correspondence courses in accountancy, have exaggerated the compensation of professional accountants. There is no reason why the profession should be better paid than any other which serves the public to an equal degree. The implication in these advertisements that there is some fixed scale of fees which an accountant can charge is more or less correct, and it is unfortunate that such is the case, for it tends to place the profession on a par with day laborers.

If all accountants are to charge alike for their services, where is the incentive to excel and what kind of profession would it be if there were no premium on ability and experience? The best lawyers and the best doctors sometimes charge lower fees for the same service than less experienced and less competent practitioners, but such reduction is none the less professional.

So with accountants, as time goes on there will be less and less uniformity in charges, and the more skillful, capable, experienced accountant will not consider it necessary to place a fixed per diem rate on his services. Nevertheless, under present conditions per diem rates yield the greatest compensation. Where flat fees are charged it almost always means that some concession has been or will be made in the per diem rate, so that the auditor who can always command liberal day rates will reap the greatest financial reward.

The one good argument for a stated fee (and it is a strong one) is that the client prefers it in perhaps nine cases out of ten. Professional men should place the adherence to the ethics of their profession and the satisfaction of their clients above pecuniary gain. Therefore, if the work is fully and properly performed and the client is satisfied, the method or rate of compensation should be secondary, and a round fee, under such circumstances, is quite as ethical as a per diem rate.

If the fee has not been arranged beforehand and litigation is necessary, the auditor will receive the usual professional fee, provided, of course, that witnesses can be obtained to testify that the work measures up to the usual standard of professional work and that the fee is a reasonable one.

Juries, however, are apt to be more unreasonable than clients with respect to professional charges, and the rule of arranging fees beforehand should not be deviated from except in special cases.

Several years ago an inquiry into the actual rates charged by accountants was conducted in New York City. There was, of course, a wide divergence between the fees named by well-established firms having a large clientele and the accountant just starting in practice. The result of the inquiry is mentioned here for what it is worth, and without any attempt to set it up as a standard for other parts of the country, nor even for accountants practicing in New York City.

The questions and answers, with slight modifications in the form, were as follows:

Q. What is the maximum rate received per day, and for what class of work?

A. $100 per diem was the maximum rate received, and that only for a special class of work, such as an investigation calling for particularly expert knowledge. In one case, however, $250 per day was charged for a few days' service.

Q. What is the minimum rate per day received?

A. $10 per day.

Q. What is a fair average rate for accountants of the highest class?

A. $50 per day.

Q. What is a fair average rate for accountants who might be considered as not of the highest class?

A. $25 per day.

Q. What, in your opinion, would be a standard rate for investigations requiring first-class ability as a minimum?

A. $25 per day.

Q. What, in your opinion, should be the rate for ordinary audits and examinations not requiring the highest ability, as a minimum?

A. $15 per day.

Q. If you were establishing standard rates, taking all circumstances fairly into consideration, what rates would you advise?

A. For standard rates the minimum fee for the man in charge should be $25 per day; for ordinary assistants, $15; and for juniors used in clerical checking, $10 per day; but the restriction of this compensation is not advocated, especially for those in charge of work, to $25 per day.

Q. To what extent are assistants used?

A. Probably 90 per cent of accountants in active practice use assistants.

Q. What are the maximum and minimum per diem rates received for the services of

(*a*) Senior assistants?

(*b*) Junior assistants?

A. Senior: maximum, $25; minimum, $15. Junior: maximum, $15; minimum, $10.

Contingent Fees: One of the proposed amendments to the

by-laws of the American Association of Public Accountants provides that:

> No member shall agree to perform accountancy work payment for which is contingent upon the result of litigated or arbitrated issues.

It is proper that the auditor should avoid even the appearance of evil, but it is a debatable question as to whether this rule is not so strict that literal compliance therewith is impracticable. If this is the case, the rule should be reframed in order to properly express the thought that it is always wrong for an auditor to undertake work which he cannot conscientiously certify to, or to submit figures which may reflect his prejudices rather than his honest convictions.

As a matter of fact, auditing work may be performed upon the basis of a contingent fee, the propriety or honesty of which can no more be questioned than if it were undertaken upon a basis of per diem rates.

An actual experience will illustrate the point. A cashier who had access to the books of a corporation forged the indorsements on certain customers' cheques and misappropriated the proceeds. The president discovered the fraud and attempted to locate the items in order to recover from the banks which cashed the cheques, but he was unfamiliar with bookkeeping methods and was only partially successful. He suggested to a professional auditor that the books be carefully audited and that the full amount for which the banks could be held responsible be ascertained. He had an unreasonable fear that the work might be very expensive and the results unfruitful, so he suggested to the auditor that the latter should receive one half of the net amount recovered in full payment for his services. The auditor accepted the proposition, unearthed claims aggregating several thousand dollars, and received for his services something in excess of his regular per diem rates.

The banks did not pay willingly and required the most complete proof before making settlement. The auditor could not in any possible way have improperly influenced the results, so that if he had refused the engagement because his compensation depended upon a contingency, he would have suffered an unnecessary pecuniary loss and his client might have lost an equal amount.

In the opinion of the author, the auditor should subject each engagement to scrutiny to discover any possible reasons why he should not undertake it. Work which involves his integrity should *always* be declined. But if he can conscientiously accept work where his fee depends upon a contingency, he should not refuse the required service.

(5) As to Where the Work is Done: This question receives but little consideration in the usual audit *until it is too late to make a change.* Most audits are made in the office where the general books of account are written up. Provided there are ample space, adequate light, satisfactory and sanitary working conditions such as pure air, etc., and reasonable freedom from interruption by unauthorized persons, this is the ideal place.

When the audit is being arranged for, all of these points can be discussed, and few clients will hesitate to modify or improve existing conditions in order that the audit work may be performed under favorable auspices. But if this matter is left in abeyance until the audit is actually commenced, changes are almost impossible to effect, or if not impossible, the auditor usually deems it inadvisable to open up the subject.

Therefore, stipulate for the best possible working conditions *before work is commenced.*

(6) Working Papers: It may sound paradoxical, but the time to arrange working papers is *before* the actual work of the audit begins.

The most important point to emphasize is that the more inexperienced an auditor is, the more working papers he produces, so that the student or practitioner who aspires to a high place in his profession will avoid all unnecessary compilations and comments; he will try to settle his doubts relative to questionable transactions immediately, for the majority of his questions will be answered satisfactorily; he will eliminate the copying of trial balances, statements, etc., unless he has a clear idea as to their ultimate use, and he will ruthlessly destroy his papers as soon as their value is questionable.

It is a pity that the limits of this book make it impracticable to include detailed illustrations of how things should be done and how they should *not* be done. Perhaps the assertion that the skill of an accountant can always be ascertained by an inspection of his working papers is too sweeping, but it will hold good in so many cases that it may as well be called a general rule, and therefore prospective auditors should take notice that some day they may be so judged.

If the professional man were as careful with his tools as is the mechanic, he would do better work and he would save himself many hours of duplicated labor. The average lawyer, for instance, makes his notes on scraps of paper and in such an unsystematic way that an orderly filing of them is impossible. Subsequently (in many cases) the notes cannot be found, or if found, they cannot be understood. Fortunately for the lawyer, his notes are, in a majority of cases, not required later, which accounts perhaps for his carelessness.

But an accountant must be the personification of order and system; his business is to criticize careless methods in others and construct proper systems for those who have none. Therefore he must convey the impression that he appreciates order and good methods and be able to demonstrate this by an exhibition of the highest degree of perfection in his own working papers.

Stationery is cheap, far cheaper in proportion than the implements used by mechanics, yet many accountants will use a scrap of paper or the back of an envelope to make a record in connection with an audit, when the items so noted are important enough to be set down in an orderly way on a whole sheet of specially ruled paper. It really seems absurd to devote much space to this matter, and it is only because there is such a widely prevalent looseness in this respect that emphasis is given to the use of good stationery and importance placed on plenty of stationery always being available.

An accountant or a bookkeeper should have on hand at all times a complete assortment of specially ruled paper of all sizes. Let him consider this as part of his plant, if need be, for a very small expenditure will secure a large supply of paper. The special rulings should cover every form for which there may be the slightest call.

With respect to money columns, paper should be ruled having from three to eighteen columns. The former will be the most used, but there is a constant call for the latter. Then, of course, ledger-ruled paper will frequently be used, and it is very desirable to have ledger paper with two money columns on both sides. The paper should be put up in pads of fifty sheets each.

In commencing an audit, a full assortment of paper, together with various colored pencils or ink, etc., will be gathered together and carried preferably in a stout leather portfolio with a first-class lock on it and containing convenient pockets for papers, pencils, rubber stamps, etc. Is it not obvious that a client or a client's clerk will have more respect for an auditor who is fully equipped than for a man who is compelled to borrow first a sheet of paper and next a pencil in order to record details of the petty cash as counted?

It is no excuse to urge that many offices of comparatively wealthy concerns are woefully lacking in good stationery and that a little pile of carefully cut used envelopes for making memoranda is still in evidence in many offices. In most cases such a supply is sufficient for the bookkeeper who is not in possession of ruled paper, and who probably does not see any necessity for having it on hand. He is so blissfully unconscious that there are scores of uses to which he might put some well-ruled paper for the edification and financial benefit of his employer, and which would almost surely result in an increase in his own salary, that it is not fair to the wide-awake man to say too much about it. The benighted user of old scrap paper will simply make way some day for a more competent successor.

The professional auditor, however, cannot afford to start wrong, for he does not have the same opportunity for concealing his incompetency. Stock up, therefore, and keep stocked up, for a few extra dollars invested in a big supply of stationery will be the greatest possible help to the young practitioner. Having the paper, use it. That is, don't even try to economize, for it is not safe to temporize and think that a particular memorandum is unimportant and, therefore, just as well recorded on a scrap as on a whole sheet which may have cost a quarter of a cent.

It will be a great convenience to head up several sheets of paper at the commencement of an audit along the following lines:

Cash Vouchers lacking.
Errors in footings—Cash Book.

Errors in footings—Sales Book.

Errors in postings—Private Ledger, etc., etc., etc.

There should be an absolute rule strictly adhered to, forbidding the writing of more than one class of errors on the same sheet of paper. If, for instance, an audit develops but three errors in footings and postings, one being in the cash book, one in the journal, and one in the sales ledger, there should be three sheets of paper submitted at the close of the work, one error appearing on each. The reason for this is evident. The work covered is assumed to be a test only, and no one can tell how many errors may develop if additional verification is required.

It is almost criminal for an accountant to write and rewrite and classify and reclassify his memoranda during the course of an audit, when every bit of the rewriting and reclassification could have been avoided by using one sheet of paper for each class of errors or queries.

There is a general habit to minimize the importance of working papers, and while the client suffers most because his affairs are not properly looked after, yet the auditor who starts in wrong does himself positive harm by not getting the most out of each engagement.

An auditor who is careless about his working papers has taken up an audit, and having forgotten to supply himself with stationery, calls on the client's supply. Irregular pieces of scrap paper are supplied to him, and on these he makes his various notes and comments. He dislikes to ask too often for paper, and so economizes by using both sides of some pieces and fills others to the limit. By the time the audit is completed he has a veritable mess of scraps. He then vainly attempts to make sense out of a lot of notes which were considered of great importance when made and which would have been written out properly if the means had been at hand. How is it possible for such a man to write a report of the greatest possible value to his client? Even if he finally deciphers all of his notes and does not forget to look on the back of every scrap, he has made so much trouble for himself that in consequence thereof he has written a report in a troubled and irritated frame of mind and his careless style has, of course, permeated the text.

Consider the case of an auditor who takes the trouble to provide himself with an ample supply of paper; who uses a separate sheet for each class of error, suggestion, or comment. When he is ready to write the report he merely sorts his working papers, and with full notes before him, with no irrelevant matters constantly interrupting his train of thought, has simply to proceed in an orderly manner to the close.

Is it worth while? Who has the better chance for another engagement from the client so served?

Permanent Filing: After a report has been written great care must be taken to file working papers intelligently and according to a well-laid-out and thoroughly understood plan, or serious inconvenience may be sustained on subsequent occasions when a particular schedule or reconciliation sheet is required in a hurry.

A plan which has been followed with success is the following:

Commencing with the balance sheet submitted to the client each item thereon is assigned a letter. For instance, if Plant is the first item among the assets, the letter A is assigned thereto. Each schedule relating to Plant would be marked A1, A2, A3, etc., and all papers containing information bearing thereon are grouped accordingly.

The same plan applies to the Profit and Loss statement, and to any other schedules where the supporting papers are numerous.

When the single letters are exhausted, double letters may be used as AA, BB, etc. Variations of this plan will suggest themselves to the auditor who has had difficulty in locating working papers.

(7) Familiarity With System in Use: In considering the auditor's qualifications, stress was laid on the importance of a knowledge of different classes of businesses. During his early training he will have had an opportunity to acquire special knowledge with respect to many lines of commercial activity, so that many of his engagements will cover undertakings, the special features of which will be familiar to him. It is impossible, however, for any auditor to have experience in every line of business, and engagements will have to be made to audit accounts of which he has no technical or special knowledge.

An admission as to his unfamiliarity will win greater respect than an attempt to conceal his ignorance; progress cannot be made without asking many questions, and it will not take a client long to discover the ignorance if an attempt is made to conceal it. In any event, and despite long experience with the same class of business, the auditor should ask questions about the personnel and the special features of the business under review.

Local conditions and peculiarities may sometimes produce strange results, and the auditor will find it easy to acquire a broad knowledge of many things during his preliminary conferences which would later take far more time to acquire. The client and his staff expect to be asked a lot of questions (intelligent and tactful ones, of course) at first, and the wise auditor will make copious notes of the information so derived. The client will probably volunteer the history of his life and the progress of his business in great detail, and advantage should be taken of such an opportunity to grasp the technical points of the business. Later on it may be difficult to catch the client in the same frame of mind.

(8) Schedules of Books, Records, and Names of Clerks: A mastery of the general system in use includes a comprehensive knowledge of the books and records which contain the transactions of the business under audit. Books of account are the histories of business enterprises. As a history is not complete unless it records an unbroken narrative of facts, the auditor must determine whether or not he will find such a continuous record of the transactions of the business in the books submitted to him.

The time to determine this is *before the audit begins,* and at the time of the inquiry a full description of the records should be made and the names of the clerks responsible therefor carefully noted.

In England, it is customary in most cases, and compulsory in others, for the auditor to be supplied with a list of the books in use. In this country the advantage of this precaution is strangely neglected.

No book should be listed until its use, or abuse, is fully comprehended. This is a favorable opportunity to fill out any gaps in the complete survey of the business which the auditor must possess.

The answers to the preliminary questions and a detailed schedule of all the books in use should form the basis for an intelligent study of *how to begin.*

(9) Procedure where Previous Audits have been Made: A prominent accountant estimates that not more than ten per cent of the business concerns of this country have their accounts audited. But as most of the work that is done is satisfactory, it is only in rare cases that one auditor replaces another.

It is not considered ethical for one auditor to supplant another where the only reason for the change is that of remuneration. If a client expresses dissatisfaction with the work of one auditor and announces his intention of retaining another, there can be no objection to the appointment.

Wherever feasible, the auditor should receive a copy of his predecessor's report, but if it cannot be had, his inspection of the books, and the unsolicited remarks of the client's staff, will probably indicate the extent of the previous audit.

Of course, no auditor could be held responsible for the acts or omissions of another auditor, but he would have no justification for blindly following the procedure of a previous audit, even though the client requested it. Therefore the auditor should regard all that he learns of his predecessor's work as information purely supplemental to that already pointed out as important, and weighing all together, he will proceed as his own best judgment dictates.

Sometimes, from a feeling of delicacy, the auditor will not insist on a full explanation as to why the previous auditor's services have been dispensed with. In view, however, of the fact that auditors have been displaced for failure to discover specific weak spots, it is obvious that the succeeding auditor would be at a disadvantage without this knowledge, so that in all cases insistence on an explanation can do no harm and may be very useful.

Shortly stated, a safe general rule is to proceed as if no previous audit had been made, unless complete reports of another auditor, in whom the fullest confidence is placed, are in evidence, and unless there is no question as to the reason for the former auditor's displacement.

(10) Final Considerations: Detailed or Balance-Sheet Audit?

It might be inferred that having studied the matter from so many standpoints, and particularly after having had a final interview with the client, there would remain nothing to do but to commence the actual work.

This, however, is not the case. Now is the most important time for calm reflection. Up to this point many features were more or less uncertain. The client's understanding of the state of his books and the detail therein and the explanations of the clerks, together with a survey of the books themselves, all affect the final decision as to what should be done.

Frequently a client will make the broad assertion that he wants a complete and detailed examination of his books. Subsequent inquiry may develop the fact that a first-class system of internal check exists, or that the transactions are so numerous that a detailed examination is quite out of the question. Therefore the auditor should reserve final decision as to the scope of his work until he has inspected the books and interviewed those in charge thereof.

The final point to be decided is: Shall a detailed or a balance sheet audit be made? These two classes of audits are discussed fully in subsequent chapters, but it is desirable that a brief survey of each be made at this point in order that we may now completely cover every phase of preparation up to the actual physical work of the audit itself.

The Detailed Audit: In all cases where a complete examination is desired or desirable a detailed audit should be made. In those undertakings where there is no satisfactory internal check, the detailed audit is the only one which will cover the income and expenditures for the period under audit. This applies, therefore, chiefly to small enterprises, but as the organizations which have a complete system of internal check are very much in the minority, the auditor will most frequently have to undertake a detailed audit. But a detailed audit in the sense in which it is used here does not contemplate the verification of every item in the books.

Not many years ago one of the principal features of every audit was the inspection and verification of vouchers for cash payments. In many instances certificates stated without reserve that the "accounts have been audited and found to be correct," when, as a matter of fact, absolutely nothing else was done but to compare certain receipts purporting to represent payments of cash and acknowledgments thereof, with the payment side of the cash book. The certificates appearing at the end of treasurers' statements in most published reports of charitable and religious institutions show just such a state of affairs.

It seemed conclusive to many people that if a cashier or a treasurer could furnish a voucher for every item of cash disbursement, there simply could not be anything wrong about the accounts as a whole. As the science of accounts developed, some auditors were not satisfied with this, and they supplemented the examination of the vouchers by a complete verification of the footings and postings. Having done this, they were content, and felt that great strides had been made in the art. Add to the above the checking of the trial balance and you will have the full program of a large percentage of audits—certainly up to ten or fifteen years ago. Sad to relate, a considerable number of present-day audits vary little from this procedure, in spite of the fact that professional auditors now have an opportunity to profit by the mistakes of their predecessors and to use more scientific methods in their work. Some auditors, however, do all their thinking after they start to work, and will not take the time and trouble to plan ahead.

Careful consideration of a large number of defalcations reveals the fact that most of them would *not* have been discovered by a verification of the vouchers, footings, postings, or trial balances. This fact does not eliminate the necessity for proper attention to such work, but it does emphasize the greater necessity for attention to the work which experience shows is productive of the most satisfactory results.

An auditor must at all times study and think and must appreciate the need of preparing all his plans on a *relative* scale. Conceding the obvious conclusion that no audit can or should embrace a complete verification of all the transactions of the period under review, then the cutting-out process must proceed along the lines of *greatest* resistance, and the points covered will then coincide with the weak spots.

In the succeeding chapters the author will outline the procedure for a detailed audit in which proper weight is given to the verification of the routine bookkeeping, but laying more stress on other phases of the accounts which have proven to be those most susceptible to fraud, carelessness, and ignorance.

Where there is a satisfactory system of internal check, the auditor is not expected, and should not attempt, to make a detailed audit. The word "satisfactory," however, is used advisedly, for more than one large corporation with a comptroller and a force of staff auditors lacks a complete system of internal check.

When the staff auditor is also an official in the business, he is seriously handicapped when he endeavors to check the records of other departments of the organization. There are so many opportunities to impose administrative functions upon him that within a short time his supervisory and auditing duties are hopelessly entangled. Proof of the frequent existence of this condition of affairs is seen in the discovery of defalcations on the part of officials who were not supposed to have access to funds or securities.

If the staff auditor is a clerk, his position is still more difficult to maintain. If his superiors are dishonest, he soon has to choose between dismissal or silence. Therefore the mere statement that an auditing department exists is not enough evidence in itself to obviate the necessity for a detailed audit.

Balance-Sheet Audit: If the auditor has satisfied himself that the system of internal check *is* adequate, he will not attempt to duplicate work which has been properly performed by some one else. His duty will then be to verify the assets and liabilities, and to make such an analysis of the Profit and Loss Account as will enable him to certify that it has been properly stated.

But there is a much wider field for balance-sheet auditing than this. Bankers are awakening to the value of certified statements from borrowers or prospective borrowers, and there are vast possibilities in this class of work. The auditor who can undertake these engagements with a clear outline of what is to be covered, and more important still, what may be omitted, has a tremendous advantage over the auditor who does not appreciate the peculiar circumstances which surround this class of work. Balance-sheet audits are also required in many other cases. The author will, in another chapter, attempt to set forth as concisely as possible what, in his opinion, *should* be done in a balance-sheet audit, and what *need not* be done, and what *should not* be done.

System of Internal Check: Reference has several times been made to the fact that the question of whether a detailed audit should be made, or whether a balance sheet will accomplish the desired end just as well, depends to a considerable extent on the existence or lack of a satisfactory system of internal check.

Such a system consists in the accounting records, methods, and system generally of an establishment being laid out in such a way that no part of the accounts will be under the absolute and independent control of any one person; that, on the contrary, the work of one employee will be complementary to that of another; that safeguards are thrown about the handling of all moneys, particularly with regard to such transactions as cash sales, payrolls, freights, etc.; that the method of handling and recording incoming and outgoing goods, especially the latter, is such as to insure all goods paid for being actually received and charges being made to customers for all goods shipped; and in general to have in effect a continuous audit of the details of the business.

While the details of a system of internal check vary somewhat in different cases, the following general points usually require to be covered:

(1) The Cashier: All cash payments shall be made by cheque, signed by one of the principals, and supported by a duly authorized voucher.

All cash received, whether it is in the form of cheques or cash, shall be deposited in bank daily.

Small payments that must be made in currency shall be made from a petty cash fund set aside for that purpose. The petty cashier shall take receipts or vouchers for all payments and shall record them in a petty cash book or on a report form. Monthly, or more frequently if necessary, he shall rule off his book or sheets, certify to their correctness, and surrender them together with the vouchers in exchange for a cheque for the same amount. This should also be done at the close of every fiscal period.

The cashier shall have no access to any of the individual ledgers nor to the statements sent to customers.

The bank pass-book shall be balanced, or a statement of account secured from the bank, at least monthly; the outstanding cheques shall be listed and the balance shown to be in bank shall be reconciled with the balance called for by the cash book.

(2) **Vouchers:** All goods purchased or expenses incurred shall be evidenced by an invoice from the vendor or creditor. Such invoices shall be checked as to extensions and additions, shall be duly approved as to quantity and quality by the persons receiving the goods, and as to price by the person authorizing the purchase. They shall then be approved for payment by the executive in charge of the accounting department and turned over to the treasurer for payment.

(3) **Sales:** The extensions and additions of all sales invoices shall be checked at least once before the invoices are sent out.

When possible the duplicate copy method of writing the salesbook should be used, the first carbon copy of the invoice becoming the sales record. This gives in the sales book an exact copy of the invoice sent out, and is admissible as such in court.

(4) **Ledgers:** The general ledger shall contain a controlling account with each subsidiary ledger, and each individual ledger shall be balanced monthly.

The trial balances from the sales ledgers shall indicate the age of all overdue accounts.

Accounts considered uncollectible which have been written off shall be recorded in a Bad Debts register and followed up just as persistently as if they were still on the books.

(5) **Other Considerations:** Even though stock accounts are kept—and this is, of course, very desirable—physical inventories shall be taken at proper intervals to verify the balances appearing on the stock accounts.

An adequate method of following up collections must be provided.

Equally necessary is some provision for safeguarding the incoming mail so that cash received shall reach the cashier.

Such a pay-roll system shall be devised as will render it most difficult to "pad" the roll and will insure the detection of errors in time, rates, or extensions.

Every member of the office staff shall be required to take a vacation each year.

Suggestions to Clients' Staff before Commencing Work: In the great majority of audits which are made for the first time the client will have informed his entire staff as to his intentions, so that there is no possible chance of gaining any advantage by surprising them.

Then, too, it may be that the audit is being made at the request or on the suggestion of one or more of the staff. This occurs very frequently where ambitious bookkeepers and cashiers realize that the methods in use in the office are obsolete.

If the auditor desires full coöperation, he should seek an opportunity to ascertain the condition of the books and records as soon as possible after the engagement has been made. He will gain nothing whatever by jumping in before the books are written up or balanced.

As he will probably be asked what he desires in the way of vouchers, etc., the following memorandum has been prepared. It is, of course, only suggestive, as the auditor must be governed by local conditions:

(1) A correct trial balance, as of the date the audit is to be made, should be prepared. If not ready by the time the audit is to be commenced, the auditor should have a conference with the client and the bookkeeper and determine (a) if the work is to proceed at once; (b) if it is to be postponed until the differences are located; (c) if the auditor, acting as an accountant, is to locate the errors.

(2) Controlling accounts in the general ledger should be in agreement with the subsidiary records; if not in agreement, the matter should be discussed with the client and an understanding reached as to whether the errors are to be located or allowed to stand.

(3) Schedules of Notes Receivable (whether or not discounted), Notes Payable, Bonds, Stocks, etc., should be prepared.

(4) Monthly statements from creditors should be preserved.

(5) Paid bank cheques and all other vouchers should be taken from the files and arranged *as requested* by the auditor.

The auditor should not disclose the use he proposes to make of the vouchers.

(6) If an inventory has been taken, the auditor will state to what extent he desires the certification of those responsible therefor, and he will insist on the original sheets being preserved and submitted.

(7) If there are many accounts receivable, it may be wise to request that they be divided into groups, showing all those overdue, etc., so that an estimate of the reserve for bad debts may readily be made.

CHAPTER VII

BALANCE-SHEET AUDIT—ASSETS GENERAL—CURRENT ASSETS

General Principles. The underlying principles of a balance-sheet audit may be reduced to writing and are not subject to change to fit particular businesses or special systems of account. They are few in number and can be applied generally.

The principles upon which all balance-sheet audits are based are as follows:

(1) The auditor must ascertain that all of the assets shown by the books to have been on hand at a certain date were actually on hand.

(2) He must ascertain whether any other assets, not on the books, *should* have been on hand.

(3) He must ascertain that the liabilities shown by the books to be owing at a certain date were *actual* liabilities.

(4) He must ascertain whether or not *all* liabilities were in fact shown by the books.

(5) He must ascertain whether or not the liabilities so shown were *properly* incurred.

In the following pages these theories will be discussed and the work incident to a balance-sheet audit will be explained.

Limitations of Balance-Sheet Audits Must be Understood: In arranging for a balance-sheet audit, the distinction between an audit of that character and a detailed audit should be pointed out to the client.

It sometimes happens that after a balance-sheet audit, specifically provided for in writing, has been made and the report rendered it is discovered that petty defalcations have been going on for a long time. It is natural for the client, in such event, to criticize the auditor, but if the latter has a written offer, to which he can refer, it can be clearly shown that the detection of the small theft was not within the scope of the engagement. If, however, the auditor has been careless about the preliminary arrangements and has not explained, nor put in writing, the limitations of a balance-sheet audit, he will find himself in an embarrassing position and is fortunate if the worst that happens is the loss of that client.

While an auditor cannot be held liable in money damages unless negligence is proved, yet a jury might find that a client who instructed a professional auditor to "make an audit," without any limitations being mentioned, could reasonably expect the details of his accounts to be fully covered. For instance, an auditor making a balance-sheet audit would rarely prove the footings of the petty cash book; but if it were afterwards found that these footings had been systematically overstated and the client defrauded, an auditor's freedom from, or liability for, negligence might rest entirely on the conditions of his employment.

Assets. One definite point to be kept in mind in a balance-sheet audit is that an entry on the books which purports to record an asset is *nothing more* than a *book* record, and there can be no good excuse for accepting such entry as final. The data supporting the entry may be in order, but it is the auditor's duty to verify independently, as far as possible, the fact that the asset still exists, or did exist at the date of the balance sheet.

CURRENT ASSETS

The current assets will be discussed first. These are called "quick," or "floating," or "liquid." The author prefers the term "current" as applied to all of those assets which are for sale. If any doubt exists, it can be settled by the answer to the question: Is it the purpose of the business to convert these assets into cash at the earliest practicable moment?

If the audit occurs some time after the closing date, numerous changes are apt to have been made in the current assets and the subsequent entries and changes will have to be carefully scrutinized.

At the outset the auditor should carefully read the schedule of assets to be verified and outline a specific plan which has for its basis the connection between the entries supporting the asset accounts and the *things themselves*. In other words, all of the assets which *should be on hand* must be accounted for, including those on the books and those which may have been omitted from the books.

Liens and Hypothecations: Throughout the verification of the current assets the auditor should be vigilant in his endeavor to ascertain whether the title to the accounts, the stock-in-trade, the machinery and other items is free and clear, or whether a lien exists thereon which is not fully disclosed on the books and in the financial statements.

Insurance policies are often good guides to title. The holder of a lien on merchandise or the owner of a chattel mortgage is usually careful to protect his security, and wherever an insurance policy is payable to more than one party "as their interests may appear," the auditor is put on notice that the property insured is not free and clear.

Any information secured relative to liens or encumbrances must be reflected in the report on the audit, or on the face of the balance sheet if no report is made.

Proportion of Current Assets to Other Liabilities and Capital: The rules call for a verification of the assets which *are* on hand and those which *should be* on hand, but the latter term applies to physical existence only and does not mean that the auditor must necessarily pass upon the *propriety* of the aggregates of the various classes of assets. At the same time, in order to be as valuable as possible to a client, whether a borrower or a banker, the auditor should endeavor to determine whether or not the *relative* proportions of cash, accounts, and stock compare favorably with those of the most successful concerns in the same line of business.

This thought is admirably expressed by the eminent banker Mr. Joseph B. Martindale, President of the Chemical National Bank of New York, who said at the last Bankers' Convention:

> I have always claimed that under normal business conditions a stated amount of capital (borrowed as well as invested) should allow a concern in any line of business to carry a certain amount of merchandise. This merchandise later is converted into bills and accounts receivable; later on into cash; and upon these transactions, subject to the charges of conducting the business, there should be realized a certain amount of net profit. All of these items in a well-organized and well-conducted business should be in

relative proportion one to the other. And if the best results are to be attained, the management of any concern will see to it that each dollar of its capital carries its proportion of merchandise, and will also see to it that the merchandise is moved rapidly and converted into a bill or account receivable, and that its outstanding debts are promptly collected, and that its cash is used to reduce materially, or entirely liquidate, its indebtedness, thereby saving interest and expense. We have in a number of instances followed this natural sequence in business and have found any number of instances where each dollar of capital (invested or borrowed) was not performing its full duty, and following the matter still further, we found it due to either extraordinary expenses, or losses, or due to indolence and a lack of an aggressive policy in handling the affairs of the concern. These are "earmarks" which will denote a condition of this kind, and we believe that it is our duty to examine these conditions thoroughly.

As an illustration of this, some years ago, a certain firm reported in their statement an invested capital almost equal to the amount of their annual sales. At the same time their statement showed a substantial liability for borrowed money. It seemed incredible that a working capital invested and borrowed of more than the amount of the annual sales could be correct, but that is what this report showed. Upon closer analysis and further information, it was found that in the accounts receivable of the firm there were many old accounts running years back, which they were carrying as good accounts, and also substantial sums due the firm from the partners, which were, in other words, overdrafts. When the statement was all boiled down, it was found that their actual capital was less than one half that reported in their statement. These are the "earmarks" which, upon close observation and the knowledge of credit, prove invaluable to one's institution.

It is vitally important in examining and passing upon a statement that one should be thoroughly familiar with the conditions surrounding the business during the year. Conditions may have made it impossible for any concern to make money, and where a concern reports a gain in its capital, one owes it to himself and to his institution to inquire thoroughly and closely as to the causes which produced such a result when all the conditions were adverse.

As an example, we have the accounts of a number of houses in the same interior city in identically the same line of business, and while the amount of their capital varies (and, consequently, their volume of business), we can each year, by working out the percentages, see which concern is obtaining the best results upon its volume of business and the amount of its capital.

From the standpoint of good banking it is not in the province of any bank to furnish permanent working capital for any one of its depositors. A bank whose liabilities are all payable on demand should observe closely the well-established rule that its borrowers should at some time during each twelve months liquidate their indebtedness to the bank for a reasonable period of time. In my opinion, this is neither unjust nor arbitrary, and is dictated by well-demonstrated and sound banking and business logic.

I have always believed that an independent audit by a firm of certified public accountants is desirable. And from the standpoints both of the borrower and the lender, it is wise at least once a year to have the affairs of a firm or corporation examined and audited by a high-class firm of auditors.

It is obvious that no concern can have a "clean up" annually or oftener unless its current assets are susceptible of being turned into cash within a reasonable time. Therefore, before the auditor commences his verification of the current assets, he should ascertain as accurately as possible the normal proportion of each class of such assets in the average concern in the same line of business as that under audit.

With this as a starting point he will be able to determine, as his work progresses, how far from normal the concern may be, and an opinion so formed should be of the greatest possible value to his client.

CASH

Cash in Bank: If no notice has been given to the client's staff, the cash should be balanced immediately, the bank balances being verified by independent confirmation. The cash transactions since the date of the balance sheet should be scrutinized and the footings proved in order that the balance on hand as stated therein may be shown to be correct.

When the audit occurs a considerable time after the date of the balance sheet, it is customary to secure certificates from the banks covering the balances as of the closing date. These are reconciled with the books, accepting as a basis the schedule of outstanding cheques shown by the books.

Many auditors accept bank pass-books as conclusive evidence, but the author has encountered several cases of fictitious pass-books and two cases where the genuine pass-books were very cleverly altered. Therefore, to be safe the auditor should have one of his own staff secure the pass-books or statements from the bank, or preferably have the confirmation of the balances mailed direct to him by the banks.

The auditor should satisfy himself that the cash in banks is free from any liens or offsets and may be withdrawn on demand.

The auditor may very properly inquire into the average balance carried, as it is possible that the concern is overconservative and maintains a cash balance in excess of its requirements. If all purchases are discounted and nothing is borrowed, it may not be worth while to criticize, but instances are known where large borrowers have carried cash balances considerably in excess of the requirements of sound business financing. The cost in such cases is large enough to attract attention, and the auditor should tactfully investigate the circumstances leading up to the custom. It may be found that those in charge of the finances are ignorant of the general usage, in which case the auditor can suggest what, in his opinion, would represent an adequate average balance to be maintained throughout a given period.

Auditors of broad experience frequently suggest that where the balances in commercial banks are larger than necessary to secure the maximum line of credit, some funds be transferred to trust companies where interest is allowed on inactive accounts. Some of the largest trust companies now accept active commercial accounts and even allow interest on daily balances. The rule with National and State Banks is by no means uniform, but many of them allow interest to desirable depositors.

Cash on Hand: Where the petty cash balance or fund called for by the balance sheet is small, it may be unnecessary to attempt to account for it, as it might require considerable time to inspect and prove all of the entries between the closing date and the time of the audit. Usually a scrutiny of the subsequent entries will be sufficient.

If the balance is, say, over $100, it had better be verified by actual count and proof. In an English case an auditor who failed to verify a petty cash balance of nearly $4,000 was held to have committed a breach of duty. The actual balance was $150.

The balance should consist of actual cash, not memoranda or "cash items." A cashier who is carrying questionable items as a part of his cash balance may borrow money enough on the closing date to enable him to pay the entire balance into bank, or to exhibit the cash to an executive; after doing so the cashier will immediately put the items back into the cash drawer and again withdraw the cash. If there is any suspicion that this is being done, a second count of the cash on hand should be made toward the close of the audit.

It depends on the auditor whether this part of the work proves pleasant and satisfactory. It is quite possible that an auditor will, in his desire to jump in without notice, really upset a cashier who has certain routine methods of handling the cash and cash records. First impressions are very important, and it never pays to disarrange the work of a single person in a client's office unless a definite reason exists for proceeding offhand and without giving notice. Where the client does not inform his staff that the accounts are about to be audited, it is, of course, desirable for the auditor to take advantage of the chance to surprise the man in charge of the cash. Probably more petty frauds are disclosed in this manner than in any other, for too many men are unable to distinguish between their personal funds and those of their employers. Many of these discrepancies are under one hundred dollars, and if the cashier were given time to put his cash drawer in order, the shortage would disappear. It may be argued that in such a case no great harm would ensue, as there would be no actual money loss to the client. No greater mistake could be made, however, for a man whose moral sense is so blunted that he will pilfer a few dollars is on the highway to further frauds and needs only a good chance to misappropriate anything of larger value on which he can lay his hands.

In practice the auditor's appearance is usually expected. If the audit is a periodical one, an approximate time of commencing is known in advance, and if it is a special engagement, in most cases the negotiations with the auditor are known to all in the client's office. Here the auditor can exercise a little tact or diplomacy. The cashier may, for instance, balance his cash late in the day, and if it is much of a task he will be anxious to hurry off home upon the striking of a balance. The wise auditor will make it a point to tackle him first thing in the morning at a time when the memoranda of the day have not commenced to accumulate and when the cash book is written up and the footings shown.

Very often slips of paper, tickets, and so-called vouchers will make up a large portion of the "cash" in the drawer. In all cases count the actual money first and then list the memoranda. This record should be full and complete, for there may be some delay before it is used again, and cases have been known where unauthorized tickets carried as cash have mysteriously disappeared immediately after an auditor's count of the drawer.

If there is a difference between the amount on hand and the balance called for by the cash book or the round sum carried in the ledger as a petty cash fund, it is not wise to assume at once that there is something wrong. The auditor should note the cash-book footings, and with this information in his possession, together with his count of the cash drawer, he can afford to give the cashier a chance to hunt for the difference. If the cashier balanced the night before, the error may be in the auditor's own figures. If a shortage exists, it should develop at this point.

When the cash balance consists of several bank accounts or funds, care must be taken to see that the entire balance is verified simultaneously. Instances are known where auditors have been deceived through one balance, after being inspected, having been transferred and used on a later day in connection with another balance.

ACCOUNTS RECEIVABLE

Trade Debtors: In a long-established business where the sales are fairly constant, the accounts can be valued on a basis of past results. Ascertain the percentage of bad debts in past years and apply this percentage to all sales up to the closing date. The sales, for, say, the last month, should be scrutinized (not footed) in order to ascertain whether or not there is any evidence of predating, billing to fictitious customers, or including consigned goods or goods sent on approval as sales at full prices.

Consigned goods may be included among the current sales in good faith, if it has been the custom of the concern to do so, but this, of course, does not justify the practice, which results in anticipating profits that have not been earned.

Accounts current should be obtained for all consignment accounts, and any unsold goods at time of closing should be added to the inventory and priced at cost or market, whichever is the lower. If the goods are salable and practically sure to be sold, accrued charges thereon may be added to the inventory prices.

If past experience is not available the outstandings will have to be valued on their merits, because the auditor cannot hope to have reliable statistics of other concerns or for a series of years upon which to base his conclusions. The auditor of experience will have a general familiarity with the normal volume of outstandings which various classes of business may be expected to carry, and he should, for his own information, compare the relative outstandings of each business to the gross sales, and of different concerns in the same line of business. The value of such a comparison may be apparent at a glance, and negligence and laxity may stand revealed which might not be apparent in a routine audit. The best method of collating such data is to compile statistics covering gross and net figures and the percentages produced thereby, at the close of each audit. In the course of time a vast quantity of information will be at hand and available at a moment's notice for comparative purposes.

When the list of open balances is compared with the sales ledgers it should be noted that the balances are represented by specific invoices of a recent date; otherwise, the balances should be analyzed. An old item in a running account or a bill partly paid, followed by others fully paid, usually means that an allowance has been or will be made.

Schedules should be made of all overdue accounts classified according to age. Those quite old cannot be considered as worth anything unless a very strong argument is presented, supported by *documentary evidence.*

It is a rule of law that assent to the correctness of a balance may be inferred from retaining an account rendered without objection within a reasonable time, and the burden of impeaching the accuracy of the account, for fraud or mistake, is cast upon the party complaining of the balance, but the only proper test of ability to pay is *payment,* and where this is delayed an unreasonable length of time, the inference is that "ability to pay" is lacking.

Accounts ranging from long overdue to those just over the "net" period should be depreciated as may be determined after proper inquiry has been made.

The auditor must ascertain whether any accounts have been pledged or assigned. This is frequently done without any record being made in the books.

The following suggestions will be found useful in fixing a valuation upon trade accounts which are overdue:

(1) Have the terms of credit been habitually ignored? Even so, the debtors may be perfectly good, but such accounts should have special attention from the credit manager.

(2) If payments on account are being made, is the balance being increased or decreased? If the former, this is *prima facie* evidence that debtor is approaching the time when all payments will stop. This is a class of account which deserves more attention than it receives. The auditor should keep this point in mind, and a word of advice from him may save ultimate loss. Salesmen relinquish these accounts very reluctantly, but they are not the best authorities on the ability of a debtor to pay.

(3) If credit has been stopped and no recent collections appear, ascertain if account has been placed with attorneys for collection.

(4) If in hands of attorneys, ask for correspondence. Accounts are frequently placed with lawyers who are not equipped for collection business and who do not keep after the debtors. Unless frequently checked up, the debtor will not pay. So long as his money lasts, or he desires to preserve his credit, a debtor will pay those who press him the hardest.

(5) If a debtor who has paid cash commences to give notes, ascertain if a sound reason therefor has been offered and whether the change has been approved by some one in authority.

In all, except the rarest cases, those in charge of the outstandings will be found to be optimistic to an unreasonable and undependable degree. Nevertheless, their knowledge must be utilized by the auditor, who can discount their estimates as much as seems necessary and finally draw his own conclusions.

A certificate as to outstandings ought not to be given unless the schedules of accounts have been compared in detail with the customers' ledgers, and the footings of the schedules verified. The procedure in this case should be the same whether or not a controlling account is kept, except that this rule may be modified in the case of a concern having a very large number of open accounts which are subject to internal check.

Discounts which will be deducted by customers and which, while called cash discounts, are greater than a concern would pay for the use of money, must be allowed for. In a stable business it is usually possible to deduct a fixed percentage from all the outstandings. Where special discounts are given, it may be necessary to classify the balances before determining the deductions to be made. If freight allowances are permitted, care must be taken to see that adequate provision is made therefor.

Rents, etc., Receivable: The foregoing comments refer to what are known as trade debtors and apply chiefly to mercantile and manufacturing concerns. The same principles govern the verification of the outstandings in enterprises which are not generally classified as mercantile or manufacturing.

For instance, real estate agents, as well as manufacturing establishments, may show on their balance sheets large items which represent real estate rentals uncollected. Likewise, stockbrokers carry very large items of assets which represent balances due by customers. The balance sheets of financial institutions, and of enterprises where investment securities are owned, will contain items of interest and dividends due but not collected. The balance sheets of commission houses will show commission and other charges as accounts receivable.

In all cases the auditor must satisfy himself:

(*a*) That the items constituting the balances are bona fide and

(*b*) That the balances have not been liquidated in part or in whole.

The means of verifying these requirements do not differ in principle from the rules enumerated for testing the accuracy of balances due from trade debtors.

In the chapters on different classes of business concerns the reader will find suggestions bearing on the special attention, if any, demanded by circumstances which are peculiar to a particular business.

Miscellaneous: In many balance sheets, accounts receivable from customers are mingled with other debit balances. The latter may include advances to salesmen and others; overdrafts of officers; claims against railroads, creditors, or the government for alleged overcharge of duties; prepayments on purchase contracts; guarantees; etc. Not infrequently considerable amounts will be included which represent charges to vendors for goods returned. Such balances are rarely settled in cash. Where the open items consist of cash debits, it may be assumed that purchase invoices exist which have not yet been credited to the account. The distinction to be drawn here is that instead of dealing with the accounts in groups, each individual account must be scrutinized and valued on its merits.

Sometimes these so-called accounts receivable are not "receivable" at all, but are merely advances under contracts where the goods or materials purchased were not delivered at the date of the balance sheet. One experience of the author's will illustrate this point.

An iron company was under contract to purchase large quantities of ore and to make periodical payments irrespective of actual deliveries, except that the ore was all to be delivered within one year. After the payments commenced and before any ore was received, its books were closed. The payments were included among the regular accounts receivable in the balance sheet. The author separated the items and set up a new balance sheet showing the advances under their proper caption.

The balance sheet was to be used as a basis of credit, and a banker or creditor would have been grossly deceived if the adjustment had not been made, as the item "accounts receivable" in a balance sheet, stated without modification, indicates one of the best quick assets, whereas in this case not one cent could be realized on this item until the ore was shipped and received, converted into iron, the iron sold, and the proceeds collected. In other words, it was a deferred asset of the most extreme kind.

The president of the company strenuously objected to the restatement of the balance sheet, saying that it had always been done in the old way and that the change, if made, would attract unfavorable attention.

While changes in the form of annual statements due to previous erroneous practices are always to be regretted, nevertheless it is clear that the facts must be shown when they are known. In this instance the balance sheet was restated in correct form, and has been so stated from that time.

In another instance a silk merchant had made advances to a manufacturer. These advances amounted to several hundred thousand dollars and were included in the aggregate of his accounts receivable without any explanation. He had secured a large line of credit based chiefly on his outstandings.

Investigation disclosed the fact that the advances carried with them the ownership of several mills which were being conducted at a loss, so that the accounts, instead of being current accounts receivable worth their face value, represented real estate, machinery, raw material, manufactured and finished goods, the highest total value of which fell far short of the aggregate advances.

The caption "Accounts Receivable" is sometimes used to cover deferred charges to operating, such as rents paid in advance and similar items. In no sense of the word are these accounts receivable. The test is: Will the balances be liquidated in cash in due course? Of course nothing will be realized by a going concern from such accounts, and in the case of a liquidation no funds arising therefrom will be available for the payment of debts.

Deposits: Another class of items sometimes mingled with the current assets is that of cash deposits put up as security under a lease for the faithful performance of a contract; as security for costs, etc., in an appeal to a higher court; by agents who have ordered goods in advance, such as automobiles; with public utility companies, etc., etc.

In all of these cases and many others the proprietors of a going business feel that the cash so paid out is a good asset. Frequently they either count on getting back the cash itself or they know that the deposits will be applied on purchases.

In the former case the cash may be returned, but the period of realization is most uncertain and cannot be depended upon as a source of funds available for other purposes than the special one for which the deposit was made. The landlord who holds a cash deposit as security under a lease will probably require the same or a larger amount upon renewal. If there is no renewal, he may hold deposits for several years pending the settlement of a claim for injury to the premises.

In the latter case it is true that the deposits will be applied on purchase contracts, but this is in effect a prepayment and no cash will be returned which can be paid to other creditors.

For all practical purposes, therefore, these items are a part of the fixed or deferred assets and furnish very poor security for unsecured creditors.

Verification of Outstandings by Correspondence: There is but one absolute method of ascertaining the accuracy of the aggregates shown on the balance sheet as due from trade and other debtors, and that is to procure an acknowledgment of the debt from the debtor. This, of course, is impracticable in most cases, but wherever the opportunity affords, the auditor should verify the correctness of the outstandings by requesting confirmations by direct correspondence with the debtors.

This subject is discussed more fully on page 263 hereof.

CHAPTER VIII

BALANCE-SHEET AUDIT—ASSETS (Continued)

CURRENT ASSETS (Continued)

Notes Receivable: This account ought to include unmatured notes only, free from liens.

In almost all respects the valuation of notes receivable should be made along the lines indicated for accounts receivable.

In some trades notes are given by concerns of the very highest standing, as for instance, in the silk and jewelry trades. In other lines, as for instance, the automobile and grocery trades, notes are considered a sign of weakness. The first consideration, therefore, must be as to the custom of the particular business under review. If it is usual to accept notes from first-class debtors, the notes will be valued in the same manner as book accounts. (See page 94.)

If notes have been accepted from other than trade debtors, or if it is not the general custom of the trade to give notes, then each individual note must be valued on its merits. The examination should, of course, cover notes under discount as well as those on hand. The former should be verified by correspondence with the bankers, or by inspection of the discount records, and the latter by actual inspection.

The balance sheet should show the notes under discount, as a contingent liability therefor exists. They represent an asset, hypothecated as it were, against which a loan has been secured from the bank, therefore the aggregate under discount should appear as a footnote on the liability side of the balance sheet.

Instances have been known where notes for large sums, but with makers of little responsibility, have been discounted and renewed as long as the banks would take them. Where the facts are not known and several bank accounts are kept, it is comparatively easy to shift discounts from one bank to another.

It is obvious that such notes are in reality *notes payable.*

The auditor is not justified in certifying to the balance-sheet item of notes receivable unless he believes that all of the notes will be paid when due, or unless a sufficient reserve is created to cover probable losses in realization.

Where notes have not been paid at maturity, they should, as stated above, be taken out of the notes receivable account, as the latter account should represent unmatured notes only. It might be feasible to carry dishonored notes in a separate account, but it is considered proper accounting practice to debit the personal account of the debtor with the amount of the note and the protest fees and include the debt among those of the class to which it belonged before it was converted from an account into a note receivable.

Thus if a grocer sold sugar to a customer, took a note for the amount of the sale, was unable to collect when due and charged the note and protest fees back to the customer's account, then he would include the new balance among other trade debtors. This is the proper way to handle the transaction. The auditor, in valuing the accounts, will estimate the actual worth of this account, taking into consideration the facts as shown on its face.

Protested notes are frequently paid thereafter, but they cannot be classed with accounts not due, nor with those overdue from chronic slow payers. The maker of a note who fails to meet his obligation at maturity is never a desirable customer, and in the long run subsequent credit extended to such customers invites ultimate loss.

There are exceptions to this rule in the case of such concerns as agricultural implement manufacturers where it is the custom to take notes for a large part of the sales, and many are not paid during years of crop failures. These overdue notes are considered almost as collectible (so far as ultimate realization is concerned) as the unmatured ones, and, as it is more convenient for the collection department to handle them as notes than as part of open accounts, they are not charged back to the customer's accounts.

Under such circumstances in stating the item "Notes Receivable" in the balance sheet, the auditor may not consider it necessary to separate the overdue and not due notes, but he should be sure that one class is as good as the other, or that a sufficient reserve has been created for the probable loss.

Stock Subscriptions: The uncollected balances due from stockholders in respect to their subscriptions to the capital stock of a corporation are undoubtedly accounts receivable, but it is not considered proper to include such balances with the receivables of any other class. The reason for this is obvious. If the subscriptions are overdue, the fact of their noncollection indicates poor management or undesirable stockholders. If not due, it affords those who use the balance sheet an opportunity to inquire into the financial standing of the debtors. If good, it not only means that a certain amount of liquid capital will be forthcoming at a certain date, but it furnishes evidence that the capital stock is being paid for in cash, and is reassuring as to the future, because the connection of financially responsible stockholders with a company usually means that they are prepared to stand by it and protect their interests.

Installment Contracts: In several lines of business sales are made or contracts are executed under conditions which require time to consummate, or which are payable in installments. It is customary to charge the total contract to the debtor and credit the collections on account as they are made. Experience has demonstrated that many of these contracts are not carried out, in which case balances due are uncollectible. If a business has been established for a number of years, past results can be used as a guide in valuing the outstandings, but where the business has been recently established, great care must be taken. The first point to consider is the character of the contract and description of the subject matter.

In the case of piano contracts where a material first payment is collected, and where the piano can be taken back without excessive cost, the loss would be small; but the reverse is the case with the class of contracts for correspondence courses and books. It is not usually considered worth while to attempt to reclaim books and lesson papers, although title does not pass until the final payment is made, nor is it usually worth while to enter suit for collection of the balance due. Therefore, in all cases where this class of contracts is entered at the full purchase price, a considerable reserve must be provided for bad debts.

INVENTORIES

Raw Materials, and Stock Purchased to be Resold in the Same Form: Under this caption should be included only stocks of goods owned and under the control of the owner. Stocks are often hypothecated, and if this is the case, the fact should be stated on the face of the balance sheet.

The basis of value should be cost or market, whichever is the lower. If purchases have been made on a falling market, it is not conservative to place a higher value on an inventory item than the price at which the same thing can be duplicated in the open market. It deceives the banker, creditor, and stockholder, who have a right to believe that the values stated are real values as of the date of the balance sheet.

It may seem inconsistent to advocate a somewhat different principle when purchases have been made on a rising market and where the goods cannot be duplicated, except at a higher price. In this case, however, the conservative course is to carry the items at cost and thus do away with the objectionable practice of anticipating a profit.

In this connection raw materials are dealt with as being the first stage of a manufacturing process. If bought and sold without alteration in form, there is some merit in the contention that the difference between cost and market is a loss or gain properly applicable to the period preceding the closing of the books, but the fact, nevertheless, remains that the goods in the inventory have not been sold and no profit has been earned.

The safest rule is the better one to follow, and this is unquestionably cost *or* market, whichever is the lower. If the market is higher than cost, and cost is used, it is quite in order to indicate this fact (if it is important) in a footnote on the balance sheet, and no criticism will follow, whereas bankers are never pleased to learn that an inventory has been marked up and a profit taken which is not yet realized.

The physical condition and salability of the stock must also be considered. If there is deterioration or if part of the stock is out of date, or otherwise unsalable, the asset loses its most important aspect, availability. This is a most difficult fact for the auditor to determine, but he must depend upon his own intuition and inquiries to determine whether or not the stock is in good condition or merchantable, supplementing this, of course, by certificates from those in charge of the departments concerned covering this point fully.

The price placed upon raw materials can be checked in nearly all cases by recent purchase invoices, while with all staple goods reports as to current values are readily obtainable.

The extensions should be tested and all large items scrutinized. Exceptionally large quantities of particular items deserve special inquiry, and some general familiarity with the normal stock, which any well-conducted concern in the same line of business *should* carry, is very desirable.

The footings, too, should be verified, or at least be thoroughly tested. Many instances have been found where serious errors have existed in both calculations and footings, so that an auditor who fails to cover this point fully is open to criticism.

In a celebrated English case it was held by the Court that an auditor is not a valuer; that it is not his duty to take stock; that in the absence of suspicious circumstances he is entitled to rely upon the representations of responsible officials; and that he is not guilty of negligence if he accepts the certificate of such persons to the value of the stock-in-trade.

The auditor's course, therefore, is to secure all the evidence within his power to demand, and lacking any part of the proof which he deems necessary, his only course is to qualify his certificate accordingly.

The author thinks the accountants in England rely too much on the decision of a Lord Chief Justice that the auditor "is not called upon to be suspicious, nor even to make inquiry, provided that nothing comes to his notice to cause him to think that there is need." This may be law, but it is a poor rule to insert in an audit program.

It may be that the borrowers and debtors in the United States overstate their inventories and deceive their creditors to a greater extent than is the case in England, in which case an auditor there may be justified in accepting the certificate of some one else as the sole check on the stock, but the auditor here who would acquire a reputation for dependability will not be content with this measure of his duty.

Is it not true that the stockholder or banker is being taught to look on the professional auditor as a sort of watchdog, one who will detect all irregularities, insist on businesslike methods, see that the accounts are stated clearly and correctly, and prevent unsatisfactory conditions generally?

Now what more important element of business is there than "stock-taking"? Is it not the most important of all? On it may depend financial success or failure; on it dividends may be paid or passed. Is it not then, in every sense of the word, a financial transaction to be audited?

The English law says that the auditor is using reasonable care and skill when he accepts the certificate of a responsible official. The profession will not advance in usefulness and standing if this is to be the standard on this side of the Atlantic.

The author differs from those who maintain that an auditor, *not* being a valuer, has no right to attempt to pass upon physical valuations, including stock-in-trade and plant; his opinion is that an auditor's duty is not properly performed unless he does all that his experience and skill enable him to do.

Numerous instances might be cited where professional auditors, without any special knowledge whatever in particular lines of business, have detected overvaluations, excessive statements of quantities, and misstatements as to the condition of the stocks, some of these discoveries being of sufficient importance to stop the sale of a business or the extension of a line of credit by a banker.

In many of these cases the inclusion in the certificate by the auditor of a statement to the effect that he has accepted the inventory valuations without verification would have been acceptable to his client at the time, but subsequent events would have demonstrated the worthlessness of the report from a practical point of view.

Looking at it from another angle, it may be asked: Why not as well accept a certificate from the cashier that the cash balance is duly accounted for as to accept the certificate of the stock-keeper that the materials and goods under *his* care are on hand?

The author has compiled some simple directions for use by those who desire to make a real test of what is frequently the largest item on a balance sheet. If these are followed with care, the auditor need have no hesitancy in certifying to the accuracy of the inventory item in the balance sheet.

These rules rest upon the assumption that, since an auditor is not a valuer, he is not charged with a special or technical knowledge of the elements surrounding stock-in-trade, so that if he exercises due care and skill he may feel that he has conscientiously discharged the duties imposed upon him. They are submitted as a guide to the auditor who desires to do all that he can do to inform his clients as to the exact conditions of the business under examination.

RULES FOR VERIFYING INVENTORIES

(1) Secure original stock sheets, no matter how rough or soiled they may be. Decline to accept "fair" copies unless originals have been destroyed, in which case consider that a *prima facie* case of concealment has been made out and require strong affirmative proof to account for the missing records.

(2) If not certified to or initialed by the persons who took the stock, by the persons who made the calculations and the footings, and by those who fixed the prices, have this information supplied and see to it that the persons who made the certificates or who supply the information are dependable and take the matter seriously. Insist on a clear and detailed statement in writing as to the method followed in taking and pricing the stock.

(3) Test the calculations, including all large items, and prove the footings. If the inventory is a very extensive one and made up largely of small items, prove the footings by sight, i. e., foot a page or two and use the totals of those pages as a mental guide in looking over the other pages.

(4) Where stock records of prices and quantities, or either one, are kept, compare the totals of the physical inventory with the book figures and trace any material discrepancy.

(5) Where stock records are kept and no physical inventory has been taken, the former must be very carefully investigated as to the method in use, the care taken in carrying out the system, and all other features connected therewith which will assist in forming a conclusion. Ascertain when the last physical inventory was taken and compare same with book records. If no recent comparison is possible, select a few book items of impor-

tance and personally compare with the things themselves. If discrepancies are found, do not assume, without further proof, that they are clerical errors only. Large thefts of goods have been discovered by tests of this kind.

(6) Ascertain that purchase invoices for all stock included in the inventory have been entered on the books. Look for postdated invoices and give special attention to goods in transit.

(7) Ascertain that nothing is included in the inventory which is not owned, but which is on consignment from others. If goods consigned to others are included, see that cost prices are placed thereon, less a proper allowance for loss, damage, or expenses of possible subsequent return. This does not include goods at branches, as the valuing of such stocks will be governed by the same principles as apply to the head office. Ascertain that nothing is included which has been sold, billed, and is simply awaiting shipment.

(8) If duties, freight, insurance, and other direct charges have been added, test same to ascertain that no error has been made. Duties and freight are legitimate additions to the cost price of goods, but no other items should be added except under unusual circumstances.

(9) Select a fair number of items and compare the inventory *prices* with the most recent purchase invoices for the same kind of goods. If the prices vary, ascertain the average cost of recent purchases.

(10) Make an independent inspection of the inventory sheets to determine whether or not the *quantities* are reasonable, and whether they accord in particular instances with the average consumption and average purchases over a fixed period.

In re Kingston Cotton Mill Company: In an English case, the judge's opinion, which will be found in Chapter XIX hereof, the auditor had failed to discover inflation of some years' standing of both quantities and values in the inventories of cotton and yarn on hand. It appears to have been admitted that a comparison of the quantities of cotton purchased and of yarn sold with the quantities in the inventories certified to the auditors by the managing director would have disclosed the fact that the quantities as stated in the inventories could not be correct, yet, despite this, the court held that the auditors were not guilty of negligence. The inventories were entered in the balance sheets "as per manager's certificate," and the court appears to have taken the view that there was no obligation on the auditors to go back of the manager's statement. Most prominent American accountants would now, however, probably agree that such a failure to discover the true state of affairs when the means for doing so were available is inexcusable.

Remember that in many classes of goods of which full stocks must be kept the sale of a few articles at a large gross profit is depended upon to offset the probable loss on the goods unsold in the same class. The residual stock of such classes may have little or no value.

Always attempt to check the totals by the "gross profit test" and compare the percentage of gross profit shown with that of previous years. In a business where the average gross profit remains fairly constant this test is a dependable one, because, if the rate of gross profit is apparently not maintained and the discrepancy cannot be satisfactorily accounted for by a rise or fall in the cost of production or of the selling price, the cause of difference will usually be due to errors in stock-taking or to the improper inflation of values.

(11) Compare the inventory sheets in a general way with those of the previous period for the purpose of noting any variation in the prices at which similar classes of stock are taken.

(12) After this is completed and other parts of the examination about concluded, apply the knowledge so acquired to answering the following questions:

(*a*) Is any of the stock damaged, depreciated in quality, or have the styles or shapes changed?

(*b*) Is any of the stock obsolete, out of date, of a size or quality no longer used? Have purchases been made in gross or dozen lots to secure a low price, leaving many odds and ends of broken lots?

(13) Scrutinize sales since inventory date and compare some of the items to determine whether there is ample margin between the two prices to cover all expenses of sale and handling, plus a profit. Otherwise it may be inferred that the inventory was padded, and that just cause exists for a more comprehensive examination

These suggestions may seem unduly extended and not applicable to a small business, or in the case of a quick examination to ascertain the condition of the business. Close study and slight modification to meet particular circumstances will, however, prove their practicability.

Goods in Process: If an adequate cost system is in use, and is accurately kept, it will be found that monthly, or more frequent, book inventories can be consulted. Comparisons should be made of some of the items with actual physical inventories, and if any material discrepancies exist, they should be investigated.

Where a good cost system is not in force it is almost impossible for an auditor to verify the goods-in-process section of the inventory to his satisfaction. Where applicable, the rules cited above for inventories should be followed, but most of the items will have lost their identity. The difficulty of the task must not excuse the auditor from further inquiry. He will find in nearly every case some information bearing on the most important thing he wishes to know, viz., is the inventory fairly priced, or is it overstated?

The financial standing and profits of the undertaking must also be taken into consideration. The concern which realizes good profits is not so apt to overstate its inventories as the one which is hard pressed for capital or which is unprofitable. In the latter cases nearly every one connected with them may be depended on to bolster up a weak statement as much as possible, and no item in the inventory is easier to juggle with than that of partly manufactured merchandise. The most practical test is an examination and test of such cost records as may exist. No matter how crude the accounting system may be, no concern of any size will be without some sort of cost records. It may be difficult to get access to them, as many so-called practical superintendents are strangely noncommunicative as to how they arrive at their costs. They will support, with much vigor, the contention that modern cost systems are complicated and no good, and that they can calculate their costs exactly without so much detail, but they rarely consent, voluntarily, to open up their records. But there must be some one who makes up the costs, and the production of these records should be insisted upon. The cost sheets should show the successive steps of each article manufactured, and some of the stages may be identified with the inventory items.

The auditor should probably leave this part of the audit until the last. If the valuations of raw materials, manufactured goods, plant and machinery, accounts receivable, etc., are conservative, he is not called on to make an exhaustive inquiry into goods in process. On the other hand, if other items are overvalued, the chances are that this item will be even more so, and he can be governed accordingly in making his recommendations as to reductions in inventory valuations.

It is urged by some accountants, where goods are being made to order, or under contract, and are therefore practically sold, that in addition to direct costs and a proportion of such general expenses as heat, light and power, depreciation and rent, there should be added administration and selling expenses. The author does not agree with this view and believes that in no event will conservative methods admit of any part of administration and selling expenses being added to the cost of goods.

It seems hardly necessary to add, that in passing upon the valuations of all stocks of partly finished goods it should be definitely ascertained that all of the stock will be completed within a reasonable time.

Finished Goods: If a good system of cost accounts is not in force, difficulty will be experienced in passing upon the prices placed upon stock-in-trade which has been manufactured or partly manufactured. Where the cost system is accurate and dependable, care must be taken to ascertain that the results shown thereby are used as the basis for the inventory. A practice which deserves condemnation is that of pricing finished goods at *sales* prices, less an estimated cost of delivery and similar charges. This, of course, anticipates the entire profit on such sales, for it cannot be said that a profit is ever earned until delivery has been made and a cause of action established against a solvent debtor. The fact that goods may be made up on the order of a responsible purchaser in no way alters the principle. Until delivery has been made and the goods accepted, the sales contract is not complete. It is not uncommon for orders to be canceled or goods refused for so many reasons that they cannot be enumerated here, therefore no conservative manufacturer considers that any profit is earned on undelivered goods.

Some cost systems include ordinary overhead charges and others go so far as to include rent and interest. No definite rule can be laid down on this point, because special circumstances must always be considered, and the purpose of the audit has a direct bearing upon the subject. The auditor, therefore, must be governed by his best judgment in passing the principle upon which the prices are based.

The author suggests, however, that in verifying a balance sheet which is to be used as a basis of credit, the item of interest should not be considered as a part of the cost of the goods unsold, and that other items nearly as questionable, such as rent, administrative salaries, etc., be excluded, unless he is fully convinced that their inclusion is in order. In other words, do not certify to an "inventory at cost" item in the balance sheet unless assured that "cost" in that particular case carries with it its own explanation, and that subsequent criticism cannot arise. "Cost" may include all expenses incurred in manufacturing, except selling and managerial expenses, but no profit may be included. The selling and administrative expenses continue after the inventory date, and profit should never be anticipated.

It is obvious that the "inventory at cost" item should be so certified only where the cost price is below the net selling price, allowing for *all* expenses of sale and carrying, and where similar goods cannot be duplicated in the market at a less cost. This may be a difficult point to pass upon, but it must nevertheless be dealt with. One test is the general result of the business. If conducted at a loss, it might easily be true that costs are excessive, so that to use such figures would be to overvalue the assets to that extent. If a factory is running on part time only or if it is a new enterprise, the actual cost of production may be in excess of the market value of similar goods. In such cases the stock should be marked down to the market price.

In other respects the procedure in verifying the inventory of finished goods is the same as that suggested for "raw materials." (See pages 104 to 107.)

The Turnover: While the inventory is being verified, the auditor should ascertain the aggregate sales for the last year.

If the turnover has not been rapid, it may be due to a poor stock of goods. Some business men dislike to sell below cost and would rather accumulate a big stock of old goods than dispose of the old and unseasonable stock at a sacrifice. The usual outcome is that the stock becomes unwieldy and funds are lacking to purchase new goods. The inventory and the gross sales may, therefore, have a direct connection.

An auditor should always seize an opportunity to compile data with respect to the number of times various stocks of goods are or should be turned over in a year.

Supplies, Stores, etc.: In addition to the regular stock-in-trade, other supplies are usually on hand and should, of course, appear in the inventory, unless the total value is very small.

These items should be separated from the merchandise stock, as one class represents an asset which it is expected will be converted directly into the equivalent of cash; whereas such items as fuel, office and factory supplies, repair parts, and similar materials and stores, represent expenditures about to be made for maintenance, and therefore not to be included in a calculation as to how much can be realized within a given time to pay debts.

The general rule of valuation also applies, i. e., cost or market, whichever is the lower. Care must be taken that nothing is included except usable items. The auditor should demand the original stock sheets and test their accuracy sufficiently to satisfy himself that the item is a genuine one.

It is sometimes found that articles partly used are included under this caption, but it is not proper to include anything except new and usable materials, which would have to be duplicated at the same or a greater cost if they were not on hand.

Investment Securities: As we are now discussing current or quick assets, it must be understood that the term "investment securities" does not include any securities the sale of which would affect the normal operation of a business.

Where stocks or bonds represent control or a material interest in other enterprises, the ownership of which carries more or less value to the holder outside of the direct return thereon, they should be designated as fixed and not current assets.

Securities, as Stock-in-trade: Where the purchase and sale of securities is part of the regular business of the firm or corporation, an inventory thereof should be taken as with the stock-in-trade of other concerns.

It is usually easier to ascertain market values than is the case with other inventories, but greater care must be taken with the individual items. The rule of cost or market, whichever is the lower, also applies and governs each item rather than the aggregate. That is, any security which has depreciated in value should be written down to the market, but an apparent rise in value should not be taken advantage of unless the securities are in active demand and the market continues in an equally satisfactory condition after the date of the balance sheet and up to the time of the report.

It frequently happens that a few sales of an inactive security may appear to fix a higher valuation than that at which they are carried, but these sales and quotations are exceedingly uncertain. The auditor, in pricing securities, must be sure of his evidence.

The securities must be examined by the auditor in person or he must secure confirmations of their existence from those who hold them. It is needless to say that the securities should be counted as soon as possible after the audit starts, and that all should be submitted to the auditor at one time. If this is not practicable, the auditor should place one of his assistants in a position where all changes between the commencement of the audit and the completion of the verification of the securities can be noted.

Certificates out for transfer should be verified by correspondence.

As coupons due at future dates may be detached and sold, the careful auditor will note that bonds have all unmatured coupons attached. Where investments are supposed to remain unchanged, it is suggested that the auditor note the serial numbers of a few representative stocks and bonds and check these numbers on subsequent visits. Instances have been known where securities have been sold immediately after an audit and replaced before the commencement of another.

A director of a bank told the author that in examining securities the same lot of bonds had been handed to him four or five times at each examination during a period of some years. If ordinary precautions had been taken and all the securities ordered into the directors' room at one time—a feasible and simple plan in this instance—a large defalcation would have been prevented or discovered at an early stage.

Temporary Investments: Considerable publicity has been given in recent years to the desirability of trading and manufacturing concerns purchasing and carrying a reasonable line of marketable securities to provide for unforeseen contingencies, or for extensions of the business or other extraordinary needs which require funds on short notice.

The theory is that many businesses which have expanded rapidly, and which are apparently prosperous, have invested all of their available capital and surplus in extensions of their plant, etc., and a sudden call for cash finds them in a vulnerable position. This argument is sound enough from a conservative point of view, but it may be urged that the merchant who is too conservative will never buy, for fear he cannot sell, and that he may as well invest his surplus earnings in his own business and thus earn a much higher return than is realized from securities.

This is peculiarly a question to be decided on its merits in each case, but it may be remarked in passing that the principal exponents of this plan for business men are periodicals, the success of whose financial advice departments depends on the advertising patronage they receive from bond houses.

These investment securities, to fulfill their function properly, should be on hand (not hypothecated) and be presented to the auditor for his inspection.

As the whole theory of these security holdings lies in their availability, they should be priced at their fair market valuation as on the balance-sheet date, irrespective of cost. Otherwise, they cannot be considered as the equivalent of cash. This, however, is not a hard-and-fast rule. Where the variations in market prices are slight and the tendency is upward, no adjustment in values need be made. Where the tendency is downward the auditor should insist on a revaluation unless the variation is so small that the difference is trifling.

A further test of the availability of this class of securities is the existence of a firm market and stable quotations. If not listed on the stock exchange the bankers who make a specialty of the particular issues should be asked for a "bid and asked" quotation as of the date of the balance sheet.

Postage and Other Stamps: In most audits this item will be unimportant, but in some classes of business the stamps on hand will be sufficiently large to require attention. This is particularly the case with stockbrokers in New York, who usually carry large quantities of transfer stamps.

The principal reason for presenting the matter at this point is that it gives an auditor an opportunity to inquire about the stock of stamps on hand and to look into the method of handling them. So much carelessness exists in this matter that it is well worth investigating.

Deferred Charges to Operation: In nearly all balance sheets items will appear which can be classified under this caption, although in many cases where there are only one or two accounts such as prepaid insurance, rents, etc., there is no grouping, but the items are stated in detail.

The auditor cannot verify the accuracy of the book figures unless an analysis is made of the charges to the various accounts. As this subject is discussed fully in the chapter on the detailed audit (page 241), no comment is here required.

CHAPTER IX

BALANCE-SHEET AUDIT—ASSETS (Continued)

FIXED ASSETS

As distinguished from current assets, those more or less permanent *with* which the business is carried on are generally known as fixed assets. Instead of being offered for sale they are maintained, or renewed, and their *use* provides the means of carrying on the business.

Period to be Covered: Where an audit covers several years, or the entire life of the undertaking, an analysis of the items of fixed plant will be made in due course and the auditor will have before him all of the facts upon which to base an opinion as to whether or not the accounts represent fair cost of the *existing* assets. In a balance-sheet audit, however, the period to be covered usually rests with the auditor, and a serious question arises as to how far the book valuations may be accepted as a basis for actual values, assuming that the concern is to be valued as a going business, and that cost, less proper depreciation, is the result desired.

The auditor may as well accept the position here, as with inventories, that he is expected to report the facts about the plant account; where he cannot secure reliable information with respect to plant values he should state in his report that real estate, machinery, and similar assets are stated at book valuations. He should, however, attempt to ascertain whether these book valuations honestly reflect present conditions. His services are of little real value if such items are grossly overvalued and a net worth is shown which should be corrected by an intelligent use of evidence easily available by the auditor.

The auditor is charged with the duty of attempting to analyze the items of fixed assets as shown by the books to ascertain the principles upon which they have been created. In a few large enterprises an item of "plant" will appear which represents an aggregate valuation covering the purchase price of perhaps the entire fixed property. It may be largely overvalued to offset common capital stock issued in payment therefor. In such cases, and in the absence of an appraisal of actual physical values, the problem is difficult and requires more detailed attention than can be devoted to it in a general treatise of this nature. The auditor, of course, cannot intelligently criticize such a valuation, even if it is absurdly excessive, unless he can secure an appraisal, approximate or actual. A statement that the plant is obviously greatly overvalued might lead bankers or others interested to call for an appraisement.

Auditors whose practice is chiefly with large corporations meet this problem frequently. Mergers and reorganizations lead to "lump" sums among fixed assets and any analysis thereof is out of the question. The records are not, as a rule, available, and if they were there would be so many changes in the principal items that the auditor would not be much better off. The property of large corporations is apt to depreciate or appreciate to a considerable extent; it rarely stands still. In the case of railroads the Interstate Commerce Commission desired an analysis of the property accounts of all roads reporting to it, but frankly gave up the problem and finally settled on the requirement that all additions subsequent to July 1, 1907, be analyzed in detail.

This course may be followed to advantage in industrial corporations. The lack of past data is no excuse for a continuance of poor bookkeeping, and the auditor who has any influence in the matter should request that intelligent analyses of all capital expenditures be preserved.

In many corporations the property accounts represent merely the securities issued and their actual value is not of prime importance to the auditor. He is greatly interested, however, in the operation and development of the enterprises and must assume the responsibility of classifying subsequent expenditure between capital and income.

In a great many balance-sheet audits data can be secured without much trouble which will show the component elements of the values, viz., the book cost of the various divisions of the plant and equipment accounts, whether the charges appear to include only items of additions and betterments, and if depreciation has been provided for.

In brief, in all balance-sheet audits the auditor must, if possible, secure an analysis of the existing book valuations, even if it is necessary to go back over the transactions of many years.

The borrowers whose books do not lend themselves readily to an audit by professional accountants are usually the ones whose financial statements need serious scrutiny on the part of prospective lenders and creditors.

Value as a Going Concern: We are dealing with enterprises which are continuing in business, and of which a forced sale or liquidation is not contemplated, so that in attempting to fix the net value to a concern of its fixed assets we may say that, as a general rule, the correct basis is cost, less adequate depreciation for wear and tear and obsolescence.

It need not be considered that the dismantling of a plant or a forced sale under unfavorable circumstances would seriously disarrange the book values, provided the latter were based on the foregoing rule. This aspect of the case is well known to all who are interested, but no one, not even a banker, would contend that the balance sheet of a live enterprise should exhibit its assets at a "scrap" valuation.

Land and Buildings: Many auditors are too apt to take it for granted that real estate, a record of which appears in the books of accounts as owned, is actually the property of the business under audit, and that it is free and clear unless a mortgage also appears on the books. As a matter of fact, serious flaws have developed in the title to real estate which has been carried on balance sheets as an asset and which has been relied upon as a basis for credit.

This is not a difficult matter to cover, much easier, in fact, than many of the other items on the balance sheet of considerably smaller amount. The most practicable method, and one on which an auditor is entitled to rely, is to secure from the regular attorney or a title company a letter or certificate, properly signed, stating:

(1) Whether the title to the real estate as it appears, or is described, on the books is in the name of the individual, firm, or corporation whose name appears at the top of the balance sheet or in the auditor's certificate.

(2) That the said real estate is free and clear of any liens whatever, including the following:

(*a*) Mortgages.

(*b*) Judgments.

(*c*) Taxes, water rent, and other municipal liens.

While the foregoing liens, if disclosed, would appear among the liabilities, yet the place in an audit to cover this point is in connection with the verification of the asset side of the balance sheet.

It may be urged that an auditor should not depend upon the certificate of an attorney when there is no special difficulty in having a search of the public records made by his own staff, or by some one not connected with the enterprise, but in practically all cases the result would not be any more satisfactory, and in most cases difficulties present themselves which make it inadvisable for the auditor to attempt to assume the work of a lawyer.

An important distinction which must not be lost sight of is the classification of the real estate. A balance sheet should always show

(1) Real estate used in the business.

(2) Other real estate (if any).

This segregation applies to all concerns except those in which real estate is dealt in as a commodity. Taken in connection with the profit and loss account it shows at a glance whether the outside real estate is producing enough revenue to warrant holding it, and taken into consideration with respect to the indebtedness, it will afford an opportunity to decide whether it is wise to hold it indefinitely.

(1) Land: Land should appear in the balance sheet at cost, and should not be written up, although it may be clearly established that values have increased. As a matter of fact, an increment in the value of land usually means higher taxes, with no increase in earning power, so that the increased valuation is a detriment so far as current operations are concerned. The business does not receive any benefit therefrom except in case of a sale or a liquidation, and an adjustment of the book value need not be considered till these actually occur.

Similarly, if the land has apparently depreciated in value,

custom justifies the carrying of this item at cost until realization, at which time only can the actual value be determined.

A distinction must be made between improved and unimproved property. With the latter taxes and other carrying charges are sometimes added to the cost. The auditor should make a careful analysis of the items for use in his report. The facts speak for themselves so strongly that the auditor need do no more than refer to the items. All carrying charges, including interest, should be treated as revenue expenditures unless it is obvious that there is a continuous increase in the actual value of the property. When this is affirmatively shown, the carrying charges may be capitalized.

The largest realty company in the United States observes the following rule, as stated in its last annual report:

> The company's real estate is carried on its books at its original cost. The entire expense of carrying the unproductive real estate is charged out of income, but in order to show the amount which the respective properties have actually cost us, this expense has been added to book value and a like amount has been set aside as a reserve.

This is conservative practice and is to be commended.

Where the auditor finds that an adjustment has been made increasing the book value of land, the fact should be noted on the balance sheet. Otherwise, a situation like the following may arise:

A corporation had accumulated an operating loss of about two hundred thousand dollars. Its land was within the limits of a large city and had obviously increased greatly in value, but no adjustment of the same had been made in the books. The company was at times a borrower up to about a million dollars, and the banks required periodical financial statements. The banks did not, however, require, and the corporation did not furnish, the certified statements furnished by the auditors (which exhibited the land at cost and the deficit mentioned above), but did furnish a balance sheet in which the land value was marked up several hundred thousand dollars—enough to wipe out the deficit and produce a surplus. As the land valuations were not excessive, the banks were not put upon notice that the company was losing money and that the books showed a deficit.

Property may be situated in or near a city and as time goes on may appreciate greatly in value based on transfers or appraisements of land similarly located. It must be remembered, however, that it is a fallacy to assume that the value of land available for any kind of improvement can be directly compared with the value of land upon which a manufacturing plant has been erected. The value of the plant cannot be separated from the value of the land itself, because, based upon the assumption that the land could be sold for general purposes, in ninety-nine cases out of one hundred the buildings (being adapted for one purpose only) would have to be demolished and the capital loss thus sustained would more than offset the appreciation in the value of the land.

Therefore an apparent rise in the value of the land is not the equivalent of an increase in assets unless the proportion the improvements bear to the entire investment is a small one. The auditor can readily test the propriety of such a statement of increased land value by asking the question: Is the land available for sale aside from the improvements?

Bankers are strangely negligent in accepting such statements, when they could without cost just as well have the facts. No borrower could afford to refuse to furnish a certified statement when called upon to do so by the lender.

(2) Buildings: The valuation of buildings opens up the question of depreciation, which is discussed fully in Chapter XXI. Following the suggestions there made, buildings should appear on the balance sheet at cost and a reserve should be created sufficient to cover the wear and tear and obsolescence thereof, *accrued* to the date of the balance sheet.

As an aid to forming an opinion upon the value of buildings, the auditor should personally inspect the plant and note whether it appears to be in good condition.

Leaseholds: Very few manufacturing plants in the United States are built on leased premises, but inquiry as to this should be made, however, in *every* audit where real estate appears as an asset. In a surprisingly large number of cases hotels, theaters, office and "loft" skyscrapers, and other business buildings are erected on land which is leased for a definite term of years.

So far as the author has been able to discover, it is not customary for the owners of such buildings to provide a sinking fund to take care of the diminishing value of their property, nor even to charge depreciation as one of their expenses. There are two reasons for this: first, the term is usually a long one, running from twenty-one to ninety-nine years. In this age of startling changes such a long term, or one of sixty-three or eighty-four years—the latter being the most popular in New York City—is equivalent in the minds of real estate operators, to a freehold, and no provision for the far distant future seems necessary. The second reason is that in the great majority of cases land has appreciated in value faster than the buildings thereon have depreciated. For instance, a building on upper Fifth Avenue, New York, built twenty years ago on leased ground, with, say forty-three years to run before the lease expires, could be demolished and the vacant land sub-let for a great deal more than the building was worth, in addition to the rental under the original lease. With similar experiences in other cities it is difficult to persuade the builder that a sinking fund should be created, although he will probably admit that the building is depreciating in value.

The auditor should use this admission as a basis for the argument that the depreciation in value of a building, computed on its life and on the expiration of the lease, is an annual charge against the revenue which the building produces; that, unless and until the leasehold is sold or parted with, the only *facts* at hand are that the building is diminishing in value, slowly but surely, from the two causes stated.

An auditor should not set off one against the other without so stating the fact in his certificate or showing it on the balance sheet, otherwise he is guilty of conniving at a practice shunned by all conservative men, viz., taking credit in a current period for a prospective profit. Nevertheless, he must not ignore the question of a rise in value, as it may have an important bearing on the borrowing capacity of the concern. Therefore, whenever an auditor is met with a claim that the unexpired portion of a leasehold is of great value, he should secure an appraisal thereof from a reliable and disinterested real estate agent.

If a lease has been purchased, and the purchase price appears on the books as an asset, the expired portion should be written off periodically. If an appraisal should establish the fact that the price paid was too high, it would be wise and conservative to increase the installments to such an extent that the cost would be written off before the expiration of the lease. But if this is not satisfactory to the lessee, the auditor would not be justified in insisting upon it any more than he would be in requiring a tenant who, under a long lease, is paying more rent than similar space could be secured for later, to set up a reserve for excessive rent.

Machinery and Equipment: As with buildings, machinery should be valued at cost and a sufficient reserve provided to cover depreciation. In determining the sufficiency of the machinery reserve, consideration should be given to the question of obsolescence. No general rule can be found which will govern the rates of depreciation applicable to any particular plant. Much depends upon the way the machinery is used and cared for. The life of a lathe in one plant may be twenty years; in another the same lathe will be out of commission in ten years.

The auditor must apply the general principles of depreciation to the item of machinery and then bring to bear the special knowledge he has gained of the plant under review before expressing his opinion as to the accuracy, or otherwise, of the book values.

The auditor should not fail to inquire whether a detailed record is available showing the particulars of the cost, etc., of the machinery. In many factories such a record exists, being kept for insurance purposes or as a check on depreciation charges. This record is found usually on cards or in a loose-leaf book, and as it is not considered one of the regular books of account, it will not be submitted to the auditor unless he asks for it. If accurate, it is an invaluable aid in determining the value of the machinery. The record should show how and when acquired; cost, including installation; amount reserved each year for depreciation; position in factory, etc.

Strange as it may seem, there is a tendency towards excessive depreciation reserves, particularly with respect to certain machinery the important parts of which can be and are renewed from time to time and where the cost of such renewal is not charged to the reserve. A manufacturer who wants to be conservative will allow, say, fifteen per cent per annum on machinery. He may set aside this rate for three or four years and make no charges for renewals against it. Now when it is applied to any particular machine it will be apparent at once that it is impossible for the machine, so long as it is not obsolete, to depreciate more than, say, thirty per cent. In other words, the machine could not be operated properly if it were allowed to deteriorate below seventy per cent of its normal condition. There is a standard below which it cannot go or it could not be operated at all.

There is some basis of reason in a factory manager's contention that his plant is as good as new. He knows that every machine is working to its effective capacity, and that any considerable depreciation thereof is a physical impossibility or he could not produce a normal output.

There is, of course, accrued depreciation on every machine, and this is usually admitted, sometimes after a strenuous argument, but the auditor who argues that a five-year-old plant has depreciated, say, fifty per cent, fails to obtain a respectful hearing, because, if it were true, the plant could not be running, and that fact is stronger than his theories.

The real point at issue is that a considerable reserve for obsolescence is necessary in every plant where machine tools and similar equipment are used. Depreciation, as such, cannot exceed a definite limit, but a machine which would never require more than thirty per cent or forty per cent reserve for depreciation, no matter what its age may be, should have an obsolescence reserve of perhaps as much or more.

Constant changes are being made in factories and mills. Machinery which is comparatively new is set aside or discarded for improved models, and this possibility should influence the auditor who passes upon the value of such assets.

In some cases the argument is advanced that the superseded machinery is as good as ever and is always available in case of emergency or a sudden demand for an increased output. This sounds plausible, but does not work out well in practice. The proper value to place upon such discarded machinery, designated as "reserve plant," is the nominal sum of $1.

Small Tools: As a rule the practice of depreciating this item by way of a percentage cannot be followed satisfactorily. So many small tools are used up, or lost, or stolen, that an inventory should be made at periodical intervals and all the tools on hand revalued for balance-sheet purposes.

If this has not been done, the auditor can fix his valuation only from the best evidence available, but he should insist on a material writing-off from the book values unless liberal depreciation has been provided for.

Furniture and Fixtures: This is an asset which has little residual value, and conservative concerns charge off the larger proportion of the cost.

In most establishments many items, such as partitions, special shelving, etc., are charged to the fixture account, and frequent alterations and changes are made. For this reason most of such expenditure is in the nature of repairs and should be charged off at the time. If charged to an asset account, it should be distributed ratably over one or more years' operations.

Where alterations are made in leased premises, the auditor must be careful to see that if the lease is about to expire nothing is carried as an asset except movable fittings, etc., and that if removable, ample allowance is made for deterioration.

The auditor should not pass the item of furniture and fixtures without giving some thought to its physical condition. His experience should furnish data as to the actual value of this item and it should be impossible to induce him to certify to an overvaluation.

Packages: In certain lines of business, such as breweries, milk depots, spring-water dealers, bakers, etc., a considerable number of packages, such as casks, kegs, bottles, cases, cracker tins, etc., are owned, which are used for convenience of transportation only and are supposed to be returned when empty. At balancing time an accurate inventory should be taken, if possible, but if not practicable, the auditor will be under the necessity of making his own calculations as to the number required for the normal operation of the business. He should then inspect the reserve supply and decline to certify to a greater number than is thus disclosed, unless furnished with unquestioned proof as to such larger quantity.

In many cases concerns go on the assumption that all such

packages are in possession of some one who will in due course return them, but experience proves that a considerable percentage are lost, broken, or stolen, and that to carry purchases as stock on hand is a misstatement of fact.

Deposits of cash are frequently received as security for the return of packages, and the aggregate of such deposits may be large. If so, the auditor should note the relation of this liability to the cash on hand. The deposits constitute a trust fund and should not be used for working capital, although it is hardly necessary to keep a separate bank account therefor. The customers of a large cracker company returned empty tins in such numbers during the panic of 1907 that the cash required to return their deposits seriously affected the financial condition of the company!

Horses: Horses not only become less valuable through age, but depreciate according to the manner in which they are worked. A revaluation on the basis of the age of the horses and the nature of the business is more satisfactory than the writing off of a fixed percentage annually. The auditor should, if feasible, count the horses called for by the inventory, although he may be unable to pass upon their condition.

Wagons, Automobiles, etc.: While these depreciate rapidly, and in the case of automobiles the apparent life is short, yet it must be realized that the nature of the items permits repairs to be made which largely take the place of renewals. In an automobile, for instance, tires are renewed, the motor may be replaced, and taxicab companies entirely rebuild the bodies. Depreciation, therefore, as distinct from repairs and renewals may be a smaller factor than is apparent at first glance. Of course, full allowance may be made for "accrued" wear and tear, but any such rate of depreciation for taxicabs as has been advocated, viz., three years, is manifestly excessive in view of the fact that many cabs are in daily use which are four or five years old.

Patterns, Drawings, Lasts, etc.: These items frequently represent large outlays by manufacturing concerns and form a difficult class to value. Where they are used for stock or regular output, their value depends upon their life and upon the probability of renewed use. Where acquired or made for special jobs, the residual value is small, and the book value should have been a charge against the jobs themselves. In every case these items should be looked upon with suspicion and overwhelming proof must be adduced before passing any material sum on their account as an asset. The auditor may meet with strong opposition in his efforts to reduce this item to a reasonable basis, for it represents the skill and often the affections of the proprietors, who dislike to hear its value depreciated.

The auditor must, however, be firm and decline to set up sentimental values as tangible assets. The auditor of considerable experience will, upon reflection, recall the small actual value which this item represents.

The facts are not difficult to ascertain. The public demands change, and patterns, etc., must be made to suit the changing taste. Likewise, what appear to be standard patterns for stable businesses change rapidly. Engineers make about as many alterations in their "styles" as do milliners. As soon as demand ceases most of the old patterns may as well be scrapped, and this rule applies to hardware designs as well as to patterns for ladies' dresses. More than one balance sheet of a hardware manufacturer or a maker of dress patterns shows a valuation placed on designs entirely out of favor.

The charges against this account are usually cumulative, i. e., they follow the output almost automatically, whereas, if any considerable percentage of the old patterns, etc., were available for use, the additions to the account would not keep pace proportionately with the production, but would increase very slowly. It is incumbent upon the auditor to apply these tests before accepting the book valuations.

Wherever feasible he should advise a conservative course such as writing down the book value to $1.

Electrotypes, Woodcuts, etc.: The arguments just urged as to patterns apply with equal force to these items. Conservative publishers charge almost the entire cost of plates as a direct cost of a first edition, and are careful to revalue the balance of the account at frequent intervals. If a book or other publication is successful, the cost of plates, etc., can be readily absorbed in its cost, while if it is not successful, no reorders can be looked for and it would be folly to carry the plates in the balance sheet at *any* valuation except as scrap metal.

A number of bankruptcies have occurred in the publishing business through a disregard of this fact.

Patents: Patents are granted in this country for seventeen years, so that a proportionate part of their cost should be charged off periodically to provide for the writing off of the entire cost by the expiration date.

In many cases a residual value remains through the building up of good will in connection with the handling of the patent, but this is a different class of asset, and the auditor is not justified in ignoring the diminishing period. Other instances of depreciation affecting patents are obsolescence, the impossibility of producing the article as a commercial or workable success, or failure to induce the public to buy the patented article. It by no means follows, therefore, that a patent remains of value during its whole life, and consequently revaluation in such cases should be resorted to.

In no event should the value be written up, even though it appears to be much in excess of the cost price.

The auditor should see the patent papers, or secure a certificate from the patent attorneys to support the item.

The ledger caption of the "Patents" account sometimes is the nearest approach to evidence which is called for or submitted. If the ledger account has been arbitrarily so named to offset an issue of capital stock, and is not represented by actual patents of any value, the auditor should insist on a renaming to accord with the facts.

He has no more right to certify to a large asset item of "Patents," where the value is not substantiated, than of any other item the meaning of which is reasonably clear to the public, or which they think is clear to them.

As a matter of fact, an auditor can form a fairly close opinion on the value of a patent. From a commercial point of view, if it is an old one, past results have a distinct bearing on the point. Pending litigation furnishes another clue. If it is a new patent, an auditor is as well qualified as anyone else to guess the outcome of the future. This is not an argument to place anything but facts in the written report, but this good rule does not bar an auditor from discussing the matter with his client, and, if requested, stating his experience in connection with the subject.

Copyrights: The same considerations apply to copyrights as to patents, except that the term is forty-two years or fifty years after author's death. As most copyrights diminish steadily in value, depreciation should not be based on their life.

Revaluation of each one is the only satisfactory solution. In all cases the auditor should be furnished with a list of copyrights owned, and inquiry based on this list will develop evidence as to the actual worth of the asset.

CHAPTER X

BALANCE-SHEET AUDIT—ASSETS

FIXED ASSETS (Continued)

Good Will: This asset is in a class by itself. The question of depreciation certainly cannot be applied to it as to other items. If earnings decline for any reason, the value of good will declines correspondingly, because by its very nature its value depends on earnings of a certain amount being maintained. Good will, however, always appears, or should appear, on the balance sheet as a separate item, and well-established practice permits it to appear at cost, irrespective of fluctuations which affect its value. As a matter of fact, its actual value changes from day to day, and there would be so much uncertainty in any attempt to adjust its book value that by common consent it is left alone, except in cases where earnings are unusually large, and it is considered advisable to write it off. In such cases the very fact of there being sufficient earnings to write it off would justify its retention, whereas earnings not up to expectations, and insufficient to enable a concern to write it off, would indicate that its book value is inflated. As good will does not suffer wear and tear, does not become obsolescent, is not used up in the operation of the business, depreciation, as such, cannot be charged against it.

When it is written off, a secret reserve may be created, so that no criticism can be sustained where it is permitted to stand at cost.

The intangible nature of good will has made this item an easy excuse for manipulation. Not long ago an able judge held that the use of the term "good will" to describe overvaluations had been sadly overdone. In the particular case then before him stocks and bonds had been issued to owners for their several enterprises and it was obvious that such payments included all the good will which could possibly be ascribed thereto, and that further, large blocks of stocks and bonds handed to the promoters for "services" constituted overissues thereof. He also said that the dummy directors who solemnly voted that the properties acquired were worth the price fixed by the promoters were neither competent to pass thereon nor independent enough to make their decision binding.

Computation of Good Will: The following comments and the charts appearing on page 133 are reproduced by permission from *System* for January, 1912:

Despite all the sound reasoning of advertising experts and accountants, despite all the beating of tomtoms by underwriters and passionate promoters, good will is still the fourth dimension of business. It is there, but the difficulty lies in making another see it where you see it and in making him see it as large as you see it. For, like the fourth dimension, you can't feel it with your hands. The courts protect it, declare it to be as tangible an asset as real estate; hard-headed business men, as well as luminous theorists, insist that it be regarded as so much property. It is. It should be. But how many business men have any that they can sell for cash in hand? Proportionately, very few. Negotiable good will is the exception rather than the rule in business. Every man is positive he has some until he tries to exchange it for cash. Then the majority discover that either they have much less than they dreamed or none that is salable.

Lately, the proprietor of a big New York department store suffered a shock. He had an excellent location, he had been a heavy advertiser, but he paid his bills in four or five months. Consequently, he paid more for standard stock than did his competitors; manufacturers and jobbers came to him with only riffraff and odds and ends not to be placed elsewhere, and the public tired of his goods. In short, the good will bought and paid for in location and advertising foundered and sank on a sea of ill-favored goods. He had to choose between selling out at the precise cost value of his stock and bankruptcy. He sold.

Can the value of good will be anything more than each man's guess? Yes, there are rules for estimating it, and these are coming more and more into use. First, however, it is not unwise to make sure that you have some negotiable good will, for this depends upon varying contingencies: upon the degree to which it can be transferred, upon the public favor of each individual business, upon numberless other factors whose vital value may change with the moon. The most significant of these other factors which go to make up good will can be listed. They are trade marks, trade names, competition, advertising, merit of goods, location, franchises, patents. Location sometimes counts for more than all these other factors put together—and, again, is dwarfed to insignificance by a single one of them.

These, then, are the props upon which good will is reared. But how can its value be determined in dollars and cents?

The first steps are as sound and firm as those in a government building. The net earnings of the business must be learned.

One normal year may be taken by itself or from three to five years of

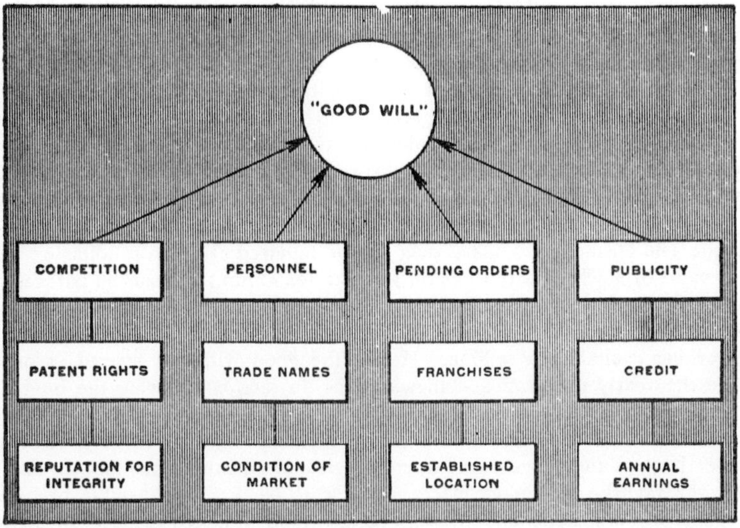

Some of the factors that enter into a computation of the "good will" of a business. For obvious reasons these factors vary greatly in importance, dependent upon the peculiar conditions that affect the business that enters into the transaction.

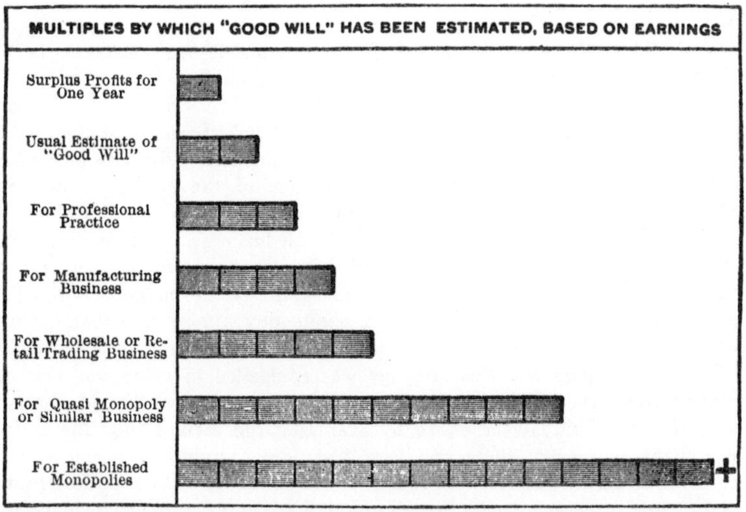

The first in computing "good will" is determine net earnings of a bulsiness, from which sum is deducted the interest on capital actually employed and the value of the owner's services. The result multiplied ordinary by two, but sometimes by many times that amount, has been accepted as the Value of the "good will."

uneven earnings may be averaged. It matters not so long as the probable net earnings for the forthcoming year are at hand to serve as a basis. From these, all authorities agree, two deductions should now be made: one is the interest at six or seven per cent upon capital actually employed, the other, a sum equivalent to the owner's services to the business.

Here we have the actual surplus profits of the business, and right here we have to take to the ladder of theory. How many times these surplus profits is good will worth?

In the case of a large retail dry goods store this is what actually happened: The business was taken over at one hundred cents on a dollar of the cost value of stock, at fifty cents on a dollar for fixtures. Then the purchaser agreed to pay $50,000 annually for the next five years for the good will. This $250,000 may loom large to you, but the business netted $125,000 annually on a working capital of a million. Hence, the good will was figured at only twice the yearly net profits—somewhat less, in fact, considering the interest lost through partial payments.

At the risk of disappointing many who are figuring their good will higher because they have never attempted its sale, I must state that, in practice, the favorite multiplier in use appears to be 2. The business brokers, accountants, adjusters, and lawyers with whom I talked seemed to settle upon this figure, regardless of the nature of the business, provided only it were not a monopoly. One New York lawyer whose firm formerly negotiated the sale of many large businesses said: "Most people figure their good will at twice the annual profits. If their stock is worth $40,000 and they net $20,000, they want $80,000 for their businesses."

The good will of many a business is computed at twice its earnings without making the prescribed deductions for interest on capital and for owner's services. Thus the accredited rules for computing it are constantly being broken and exceptions discovered. An investigation of the actual value of good will is largely, at best, a study of exceptions. Average sales of good will at normal prices take place all the time, but nobody hears of them; the abnormal ones alone are reported and serve to mislead. Business men hear of these exceptional prices, have no knowledge of the average ones, and tend to make their own estimates too high. This increases the difficulties of a subject of itself easily the most difficult in all business. Last summer one of the leading members of the New York bar served as referee on a case in which it was necessary to set a dollars-and-cents' value on good will. He reported to the court: "Sales of such a commodity are so rare that the inquiries that were addressed on the trial to the experts who testified brought no help." The good will this attorney was compelled to value was that of a firm of architects who had planned, among other structures, the Manhattan Opera House. This lawyer ended by averaging the earnings for the entire five and one half years these architects had been carrying on business, and then multiplying these average yearly earnings by 2. It is indicative to observe how often one finds this figure 2 used in practice, particularly in nearly all the varied forms of retail business.

Most buyers of small stores are paying, through ignorance, a higher price for good will than they perhaps realize. When they neglect to deduct for owner's services and interest on working capital, it amounts to multiplying the actual profits by a larger number than two. But these small stores are generally taken over by men untrained in these lines, by men eager to invest their small capital where it will earn them a living, and, hence, willing to pay a premium for the good will. But in pursuits for which a special training is necessary, the market is narrow and the owner usually has to sell to a competitor, thoroughly informed and not likely to overvalue any one's good will except his own.

Just what is good will?

No one definition has ever been fashioned fully to clothe it in all its varying forms—not since advertising became the pacemaker in this age of speed and guided business to new and quicker thoroughfares. One knows that it exists. In special instances one can determine definitely just what caused it to be, but whim as well as habit sometimes has a hand in its making. You may catch it or you may lose it with a slogan. One candy manufacturer may gain it by advertising; another without. This storekeeper may secure it by manifesting a partiality and personal interest in the affairs of his customers; that one may achieve the same end by caring for nothing except the merit of and the satisfaction given by his goods.

Usually, good will represents the industry, judgment, tact, and courage of the man at the top as reflected in his clerks, salesmen, or workmen. As Emerson put it: "Every successful business is the lengthened shadow of some one man." Long after the Fifth Avenue Hotel was left hopelessly downtown by the mad race north of hotels and theaters in New York, it held its own because its courteous clerks had made so many warm and personal friends. These thought little of the increasing inconvenience of the hotel's location.

In many respects good will is the life insurance of business. Annually the shrewd merchant or manufacturer invests in this form his extra energies and convictions. As a result, in the event of his own sudden death, sometimes something passes on to his heirs more highly valuable than his mere store or plant. And on the other hand, if he lives to that ripe age when he begins to think of retiring, he finds coming to him, as with an endowment policy, the cash surrender value of his good will.

Sinking Funds: The caption "Sinking Fund," or any other fund, should always represent an asset, and inquiry should always be made (whenever the nature of the undertaking raises the question) as to the disposition of this account. In many mortgages, especially when secured by coal, ore, lumber, etc., it is provided that a certain amount, based on the production, shall be paid to trustees for the purpose of extinguishing the debt at or before maturity. These amounts properly appear on the balance sheet as assets, and it should be clearly shown what investments have been made and the cash, if any, which remains uninvested.

This principle is not affected in theory by the fact that some sinking funds instead of being actual assets, are deductions from liabilities. For instance, a sinking fund may be used in buying up a corporation's own bonds. The actual facts are better expressed if the bonds so held (and which may be canceled) are deducted from the total outstanding, rather than shown as an asset.

A certificate from the trustees as to the state of the fund is sufficient evidence for the auditor, so far as the examination of the cash and securities is concerned.

If the bonds have been surrendered to the company, the auditor should examine them and note whether proper safeguards are provided to prevent improper use thereof.

The creation of sinking funds and other points in connection therewith is discussed on page 177.

Fund and Other Permanent Investments: In this class are included the securities, held for income purposes, or as investments of sinking, reserve, and other special funds.

The element of permanency consists in the purpose of the investments, i. e., they are not bought and sold with a view to a profit in the turnover, nor are they held as a temporary reserve to be instantly converted into cash.

In many instances the market price at a particular date may be fixed by a few small transactions which have little bearing on actual values, owing to the limited demands, and perhaps an urgent necessity to sell on the part of an unfortunate investor. The plan of valuing bonds which have been purchased for permanent investment advocated by leading authorities on the subject is to compute their value on the basis of the effective, or actual rate of interest, if held to maturity as determined by the prices at which they were originally purchased.

Bonds are rarely purchased at par or face value. To make the amount of the purchase equal the par value at maturity requires an adjustment of accounts. The scientific method of adjustment is known as amortization or accumulation and involves a debit or credit to interest account at each periodical adjustment of the book value, in accordance with the effective rate of interest, on the basis of which the investment was made.

The corporations in whose balance sheets marketable investments play a leading part are insurance companies, banks (more particularly savings banks), and trust companies. State laws require that the solvency of insurance companies be tested by the sufficiency of the assets (valuing stocks and bonds at the market prices) to meet the present value of policy contracts in force and sundry other liabilities. Owing to the abnormal decline in the market values of securities in the fall of 1907, the statements of almost all the life insurance companies at December 31, 1907, showed a startling decrease in surplus as compared with the close of the preceding year. This shrinkage attracted considerable attention, and as the corporate bonds owned (the fall in whose market quotations was largely responsible therefor) were yielding the same rate of income as when purchased, and as there was no serious question as to the security of the principal of most of them, emphasis was given to the question of whether the basis of so-called market value was not an erroneous one. This rather startling object lesson resulted in a more general appreciation of the advantages of amortization. A professional auditor should be fully conversant with the principles of amortization and recommend its adoption wherever possible.

In preparing a balance sheet which shows investment securities at their amortized values, it is interesting and advisable to mention, in a footnote or other suitable place, the market values at the date of the balance sheet.

Where securities are purchased for a definite purpose, such as the creation of a fund to retire maturing obligations, the questions of income and of amortization are both important. The auditor should in all cases secure a copy of the board minutes or trust deed provisions which govern the setting aside and handling of the fund. Any variation therefrom may be important and should be fully investigated.

If the balance sheet does not disclose the fund properly, the auditor must insist on its being corrected. Many corporate officers neglect sinking fund and similar requirements where the trustee fails to inquire periodically into the transactions of the corporation, and when their omissions are called to their attention they in turn point out the excellent financial condition of the company and argue that the provisions are intended merely to safeguard the bondholders from loss in case the company were unsuccessful, and as the contrary is the case, there is no necessity for bothering with the setting aside and investment of a sinking fund.

Many bonds are secured by mortgages on personal property. Failure to observe trust deed requirements occurs most frequently where there is a sale of a part of the property pledged under a mortgage. When obsolete or worn-out property is sold, all proceeds of such sales are the property of the trustee, and any use thereof by the corporation is conversion.

Therefore, wherever an auditor finds that there has been an issue of bonds he should secure a copy of the mortgage securing the same, examine its provisions, and note any apparent failure to observe them.

It may be that resolutions will be found in the board minutes requiring the investment of part or all of the surplus in specific securities. The latter part of the requirement will not be difficult to verify.

Treasury Stock: When stock has been issued fully paid and has been returned to the treasury of the company which issued it through purchase or gift, it is known as "treasury stock" and should appear on the books as an asset. It represents property of more or less value and is not a deduction from the outstanding capital stock unless it is retired by due process.

If purchased by the corporation, cost price is the correct basis of book entry; if acquired by gift, opinions differ as to the form of entry. The best authorities sanction the setting up of the stock as an asset at par value, offsetting this entry by the creation of a reserve or surplus account which is designated as a capital item, and is clearly differentiated from the surplus which arises out of profits or which is available for dividends.

As treasury stock is sold or otherwise disposed of, the asset account is credited and an adjustment made between this account and the reserve or surplus account for the difference between the book value and the proceeds of the sale.

For the purposes of a balance sheet the auditor should use

his discretion and place such a value upon the stock as in his opinion reflects its actual value. So long as the item is separately and fully stated there is no good objection to using the book figures. It is never proper to include among the current profits or as a part of the surplus available for dividends any part of the book value of treasury stock. This would not, however, apply where stock had been resold at a profit and the profit realized in cash.

In verifying the existence and location of the stock the same rules should be observed as with other securities.

Unissued Capital Stock: This is to be distinguished from treasury stock, and good accounting practice does not require any entry therefor in the books of account until it has been subscribed for.

WASTING ASSETS

Certain assets, such as mines, lumber, etc., are in a sense both current and fixed in their nature, but almost invariably a considerable degree of permanence attaches to them and as their conversion into cash is a very gradual process, such assets should appear as a subdivision of those which are known as "fixed."

Values to be Written Down: It is obvious that a mine or a tract of timber from which ore is being taken or timber removed is worth less at the end of a fiscal period than at its commencement. Consequently the balance-sheet valuation should be reduced in direct proportion to the depletion of the mine or the cutting of the timber. The usual reserve for depreciation is, or should be, superseded by a sinking or extinguishment fund account.

There is, however, a decided difference between the necessity for providing for the renewal of plant and making good the diminishing value of a mine. In one case it must not and cannot be assumed that there will be no new machinery to buy, whereas the owners of a mine expect that the produce thereof will be converted into cash and become available for distribution as dividends, unless they as owners have decided to retain the proceeds and invest it in other ways.

In such cases the law will not prevent the payment of dividends out of capital, but the by-laws of the board of directors of a corporation may make it illegal. The auditor must acquaint himself with the facts relating to the phases of each particular case.

Mines: The auditor should follow the suggestions relating to land (page 119) so far as title and encumbrances are concerned.

In verifying the accuracy of the value placed upon the mining property the auditor as a rule will not have much to guide him. He must, however, keep in mind the fact that as operations proceed the value decreases. An analysis of the original cost, taken into consideration with the engineer's estimates of total contents, will be a valuable check on the allowance for depletion. It may not be customary to submit the engineer's records to the auditor, but the latter is on notice that no well-managed mining company attempts operation on a large scale unless fortified by the scientific calculations of skilled engineers. With these before him and with the records of production as shown by the books, an auditor can arrive at a reasonable conclusion as to how the book valuations have been estimated. If his own figures vary to any great extent from the books, the auditor should decide that the matter demands further investigation.

Timber Land: It will be assumed that all timber propositions which have arrived at a stage where an audit is in order are conducted on a well-thought-out plan. The quantity of standing timber will have been estimated and verified (cruised) and, with this as a starting point, the auditor can estimate the average depletion charge which should be provided for.

It is obvious that an attempt to certify to results based on an examination of money values only would be hazardous to an extreme. The books should show quantities as well. If they do not, the auditor is warranted in having his suspicions aroused.

Contingent Assets: The auditor rarely discovers any trace of assets which have been omitted from the books, but occasionally he is fortunate enough to disclose tangible assets which, when properly applied, increase the net worth of the business under audit.

In addition to the assets discussed in the foregoing pages, the auditor should consider the possibility of the indebtedness to a corporation of any person or persons.

Capital Stock Calls and Assessments: In some states there is a statutory liability on the part of stockholders in business corporations for an amount additional and equal to the par value of the shares. This corresponds with the liability of stockholders in all National banks and some State banks and trust companies. The possibility of such recovery is an asset which should be taken into consideration wherever it exists; the credit of a company incorporated in a State having such a law should be strengthened thereby, particularly if some or all of its stockholders are of recognized financial standing.

In other cases the auditor may find that the capital stock has been only partly paid and that the uncalled installments are not charged to the stockholders in the books, nor mentioned in the statements. This occurs where the corporation is a close one and the officers and directors are identical. The amount callable should be ascertained and the probability of collection duly considered.

Liabilities of Directors: In another chapter (page 45) attention is called to the liabilities of directors for various shortcomings. In many States directors are personally responsible for debts contracted under certain circumstances and in excess of certain sums. Where there is any possibility of this contingency, the auditor should refresh his memory as to the laws governing corporations of the State in which the company is incorporated, or in which it has its principal office, and ascertain whether or not the directors have automatically made themselves responsible for any part of the indebtedness. This is especially important if an examination is being made for creditors.

SECRET RESERVES

After all recorded assets have been dealt with, and after due consideration has been given to any assets which have been inadvertently or fraudulently omitted from the records, it may be necessary to investigate the authority under which assets have been intentionally omitted from the books or the balance sheet, or both.

It may be perfectly obvious to everyone connected with the concern under audit that certain assets exist and are known to be the sole property of the enterprise, yet acting under instructions from an executive source, these assets are never mentioned in the published reports of the concern's financial standing. Or there may be obvious undervaluations which, after being so carried for a number of years, are suddenly written up to their actual value.

As a matter of fact, the auditor will not find a great many instances of secret reserves, but wherever he represents stockholders or others who are interested in knowing the full value of the assets, he should consider the possibility of the following improper treatment of accounts or assets:

(1) *Systematic concealment of additions to plant or equipment by charging the cost thereof to maintenance instead of to asset accounts.*

This practice must be clearly proven, as it is not intended to unreservedly condemn the occasional charging off of plant additions where the obvious purpose is to be conservative, and where the cost is not a material factor in the operations of the period. But if it is evident that a considerable sum has been expended in improvements and there is no reflection thereof in the accounts, then the auditor should insist on restating the accounts and bring out clearly the actual earnings of the period.

(2) *The creation of excessive reserves for depreciation, bad debts, or similar items, unless the fact that the reserves are excessive is expressed on the face of the balance sheet.*

This is, perhaps, the favorite method of deceiving minority stockholders when the directors or other insiders wish temporarily to understate the earnings as well as the assets.

It is not intended to condemn at this point the practice of setting aside what may appear to be excessive reserves in order to keep down taxes. In many instances during recent years corporations have provided heavy depreciation reserves in order to avoid the payment of State and Federal taxes on earnings and assets. Usually this is done in close corporations and each stockholder is fully informed as to what is being done. In such cases, where the reserves are officially created, the auditor can hardly object to the statement of the accounts as they appear on the books.

In the natural course of events the State and National taxes will be paid because the understatement of profits is temporary and the profits of future years may be expected to reflect the working out of the reserves.

The auditor is so accustomed to these reserves being insufficient that he feels reluctant to criticize liberal allowances, unless there is an apparent desire to defraud innocent stockholders. Otherwise, he commends the disposition to be conservative, and watches with interest the final outcome of the reserves.

The taxing powers are prone to exact their pound of flesh and rarely provide the means whereby an overpayment for one year may be applied in reduction of subsequent assessments.

Until our systems of taxation are founded on reason and some knowledge of business and accounting procedure, attempts to avoid overpayments may naturally be expected, and if such attempts produce underpayments the fault may fairly be charged jointly to those responsible for the tax legislation and to those entrusted with the enforcement of the laws.

(3) *Inventories should reflect fair values, as explained in Chapter VI, but there is a limit beyond which valuations cannot be reduced, unless the circumstances of the reduction are stated on the face of the balance sheet.*

This rule is of somewhat greater importance than the preceding one, because reserves stand out to a certain extent and grossly excessive reserves are apparent, but if an inventory is undervalued, anyone unacquainted with the fact is not able to detect the fraud, no matter how carefully the balance sheet might be analyzed. If there is an honest desire to be ultra-conservative and write something off the inventory after it has been properly valued, it should be accomplished by creating a "reserve for possible loss on realization of inventory" and setting up this reserve on the balance sheet, with a footnote stating that the inventory itself is not excessive.

If those responsible for the balance-sheet valuations wish to write down the inventory, but do not want the fact reflected in the balance sheet, the auditor is put on notice that an attempt is being made to deceive some one. The lack of a good reason for concealing the truth is *prima facie* evidence of dishonesty and the auditor should act accordingly.

(4) *The circumstances surrounding the writing down of assets must be carefully looked into.*

So many assets are overvalued that it is usually refreshing for an auditor to discover a willingness to write down overvaluations out of profits. Instances are known, however, where such adjustments have been so stated as to conceal their true import and minority stockholders have lost thereby.

In all cases the full earnings of a period should be shown, and if it is desirable to write off assets, such as good will, or write down overvaluations, such items must appear as extraordinary deductions and not applicable solely to the period under review. If the accounts are so stated, no fault can be found therewith. A stockholder who does not understand accounts may look at the final figures and form an erroneous conclusion as to the actual profit of the period, but if there is no attempt to deceive and if the accounts are clearly set forth, the stockholder is simply suffering the penalty of his ignorance.

There does not appear to be, from an accounting standpoint, any justification for flagrant undervaluations under any circumstances, but as the practice has supporters among some very reputable financiers, it is at least in order to examine the arguments used in support of secret reserves. The principal argument is that stockholders are notoriously hungry for dividends, and a surplus available (in their opinion) for dividends, but not so distributed, reflects no credit whatever on the management, but quite the contrary. On the other hand, if the profits of the good years are all divided so that when the inevitable poor year arrives the dividend must be passed, there is bitter criticism. Some boards of directors think that stockholders as a class must not have full information for their own good, therefore, in order to avoid criticism, the profits of the good years are not fully disclosed and dividends are continued through the unprofitable periods.

Banks and trust companies assume this patriarchal attitude more frequently than is the case with industrial corporations. Perhaps there is some justification for this practice on the part of banks whose stockholders rarely change and where dividends are largely depended upon for living expenses.

With respect to the banking house and equipment, there can be little, if any, objection to writing down their value to a nominal amount. Except in a few localities, bank buildings and bank furniture are not assets which can be realized upon to pay depositors. The building occupied by a failed bank is not an attractive place for another bank to start business in, and such buildings are rarely suitable for anything else. It may be proper, therefore, for a bank to write down its property account to the actual value of the land and the auction value of its furniture, vaults, etc. This is a secret reserve on the basis of a going business, but as banks publish frequent statements of their assets, no one who owns stock and who desires to ascertain the book value of the stock need be deceived.

Of course, if a bank's premises are also occupied by tenants who pay remunerative rentals, this fact should be taken into consideration in writing down the book valuations. It might be fair to assume that if a sudden demand for funds were made and it became necessary to sell the building, a price could be immediately realized which would represent the capitalized valuation of the property, assuming that the bank's own quarters would not yield any return.

There are few, if any, other classes of enterprises where there is any justification for writing down the cost or value of assets in order to provide a secret reserve to be held in abeyance for the purpose of continuing dividends on a constant basis. The stockholders of industrial corporations do not have as good an opportunity of forming an opinion upon published balance sheets as the stockholders of banks. They must rely on the accuracy of the amount which is reported as the net profit for the period. Such stock changes hands more frequently than bank stock.

It is apparent that a stockholder who desires to sell and who fixes a price upon his stock based upon the reported earnings of the last period is at a great disadvantage with a prospective purchaser of his stock, who may know that the full earnings were not disclosed by the report but that a part of the profit was diverted to a secret fund which it was proposed to use subsequently to bolster up an unusually unprofitable period.

It has been argued that good faith on the part of the management should be the sole test of whether or not such transactions be acceptable enough to a professional auditor to warrant his certifying to a balance sheet and profit and loss account in which they appear.

An auditor can give advice, but he cannot control the action of a board of directors, nor in this country does he communicate directly with the stockholders of a corporation. What should he do when he is asked to certify to a statement which he believes contains all of the facts and figures which the board of directors, acting for the stockholders and for their interests, think they should have, but which conveys a false impression in that the profits are understated owing to the creation of a secret reserve?

The auditor who finds himself in such an uncomfortable situation has but one course to pursue; he should send in his report setting out the true facts as he has found them, and commenting upon the asset valuations of which he cannot approve. The directors cannot publish the report unless the existence of the secret reserve is disclosed. If they do not publish the auditor's report, but put out an uncertified balance sheet, the auditor can do nothing.

It might not be a bad idea to urge every stockholder proposing to sell his stock to call for a professional auditor's report upon the accounts and affairs of the corporation before the sale is consummated, but, unfortunately for professional auditors, the value of their certificates is not yet appreciated by the majority of investors. When a man buys a horse he wants it examined by an expert on horses; so he calls in a veterinarian. He knows less about accounts and values than he does about horses, but he does not think of calling in an expert on values or accounts when he buys or sells a share of stock. He has heard about the value of the services of a veterinary since his childhood, but he does not know that the absence of an auditor's certificate from a balance sheet may indicate that the assets shown therein are improperly stated, and that if he decides to sell because the business does not appear to be as prosperous as he thought it would be, his action is exactly in line with the intention of the insiders, who promptly buy out all those who have become discouraged.

The fact of the matter is that an auditor is taking big chances when he passes a balance sheet which conceals or understates assets. Good faith may be only apparent, the real purpose of the management being to buy the interests of the misinformed.

In no event, however, should an auditor certify to a balance sheet from which any asset has been omitted entirely. The arguments in favor of an undervaluation are weak enough, supported as they are by the general assertion that the item speaks for itself in the balance sheet, but there can be no argument at all to support the complete omission from the asset side of the balance sheet of any item of property, tangible or intangible, which has or may have a market value.

The auditor who knowingly certifies to such a statement can be held responsible, and money damages recovered, by any stockholder parting with his stock on the basis of the balance-sheet figures. Such an action would be founded on a charge of deceit or fraud depending upon the circumstances of each case.

Ernest Reckitt, C. P. A., has said on this point:

The shareholders of a corporation have certainly a right to know the real value of the tangible assets, the estimated value of the good will, and how much "water" there is in the stock, and any statement which does not separate these items should be looked upon with suspicion. A shareholder is entitled to his pro rata share of the whole profit between regular fiscal periods during the time he is a shareholder. He may not receive his profit entirely in the form of dividends, but that portion of the corporation's profits which is not paid out in dividends, but left in surplus, should be so presented to the public that, *other things being equal,* the selling price of the stock will correspondingly increase, and the shareholder will receive the balance of his profits upon the sale of his stock. It is for these reasons that, in my opinion, the public accountant should refuse to countenance the "secret reserve" or any other action which makes it difficult for the layman to determine the true financial condition of the company in which his funds are invested.

The shareholder has too frequently been considered as a child, from whom it might be advisable to keep certain facts. I believe this condition of affairs is fast disappearing, and that the best coöperation is attained by the directors taking their shareholders into their confidence, and if there is "water" in the stock, let them separate it from the rest of the assets, and then, at the close of the year, the total additions to the plant should be charged to plant account, and an entry of like amount could be made crediting good will or franchise account and charging surplus, instead of charging the additions of the year direct to surplus, and thus clouding the issue.

CHAPTER XI

BALANCE-SHEET AUDIT—LIABILITIES

In a balance-sheet audit nothing is more important than to ascertain whether or not all the liabilities of any nature whatsoever appear and are properly stated.

At the outset of this chapter it may be proper to illustrate this point in order that the auditor will realize the importance of placing himself in the position of the one who will read the balance sheet later.

Bankers extend credit to trading concerns, not to furnish additional capital, but to assist them to carry stock-in-trade, or accounts receivable, at their busy season, and they expect to have the borrowings repaid or materially reduced *during* the dull season. Therefore the balance sheet of a trading concern is always scanned closely by the banker to determine the proportion of current assets to current liabilities, and he calculates the time within which the stock-in-trade should be realized upon. Now it may be that the concern has contracted to purchase large quantities of goods which have not been received, and these contracts may call for large cash payments within a comparatively short time. Furthermore, the contracts may have been made on a declining market, and the goods to arrive may cost more than would have been the case if not contracted for in advance. This information would not appear on the regular books of account, but is it not the kind of information which the banker requires to make up his mind in passing upon the desirability of the risk, and is it not the kind of information which an auditor should seek in order to be of substantial value to his client?

The auditor who limits himself to an examination of the formal books of account in making an audit is preventing himself, in many cases, from being of constructive value, and in other cases he is approaching the limits of liability in money damages for negligence in not doing all that a skillful and experienced auditor should do. It is conceded that when an auditor assumes to pass on matters which are not in the books he is opening up a wide field, and perhaps a troublesome one to cover, but it may as well be admitted that the ordinary so-called checking of books, and the subsequent balance sheet prepared therefrom, are about as valuable to the banker or other creditor as the information which the borrower can and does furnish himself.

Accounts Payable: The ideal course by which to satisfy oneself that all obligations to trade creditors appear in the books at the balance sheet date would be to read all the incoming mail for some days before and after such date. The period prior would yield information as to the original invoices for purchases, and during the subsequent days ordinary monthly statements, followed later by polite requests to pay, would show practically all of the class of debts mentioned. The mail would likewise bring notices of maturities of promissory notes.

Unfortunately, the auditor rarely has an opportunity to open the mail of his clients, although it might shed light on more items than accounts and notes payable. In the absence of this short cut an auditor must first see to it that all the accounts payable shown on, or indicated by, the books are reflected in the balance sheet, and, second, he must conduct a proper investigation to ascertain whether any accounts payable actually due by the concern under audit, and not shown on the books, should be included among the liabilities.

The auditor cannot foresee the use to which a balance sheet may be put, so that it is always his duty to use plain terms and classify the liabilities so that any pertinent question which arises in the mind of an interested person may be answered without the necessity of a special examination for each question. It is not enough to state the aggregate of the debts of a firm or corporation, unless it is desired that it shall be understood that all consist of open accounts payable, incurred in the regular course of business, not due, and for which value has been received. If various classes of debts, incurred in other than the regular course of business, are included in one sum, it has been made impossible for anyone not familiar with the facts to express a reliable opinion upon the financial position of the concern.

For instance, it might appear that a firm had assets of $100,000, consisting chiefly of accounts and stock-in-trade, and accounts payable of $25,000. If the latter were not due it would be a fair inference that the accounts receivable and merchandise stock would be liquidated quickly enough to pay the obligations as they matured. But suppose it were shown that some of the accounts payable were long overdue; that the accounts receivable were very slow; that the merchandise stock was selling poorly; and that cash receipts were being used to pay wages and similar expenses. Would this make a favorable showing in the eyes of a banker who might be considering the advisability of extending a line of credit?

Of course a firm in such a condition might deserve the confidence of a banker, and there might be ample security for a reasonable line of credit, but no auditor would be justified in merely stating the bald facts as shown. If the auditor does not feel warranted in adding a few words of comment to convey unequivocally that the assets were not readily realizable and that the accounts payable were long overdue, then his point of view is too far apart from the author's. The latter can be of but scant service to one whose conception of an auditor's duty is that it requires him to state so-called facts only. The principal reason why some business men feel that professional auditors cannot help them is that they have been unfortunate enough to hear the words and see the figures which emanated from an auditor who felt that he exceeded the limits of propriety if he ventured an opinion upon any important item of the balance sheet.

It is a reasonable assumption that no balance sheet prepared within, say, twenty days of a certain date, exhibits every liability. No exception is made for those concerns which maintain an inflexible order system and where the books are not closed until every order issued is represented by a purchase invoice. It is always found that some one has ignored the rules and ordered something for which a liability exists, or it may be for an expense which does not require an order, such as long distance telephone calls or lawyers' bills. Taxes of which little is known may be accruing, or goods may not have been delivered to a customer who has refused to accept them, and return freight charges and storage may have accrued. The best the auditor can do is to schedule all of the liabilities to which he can find the slightest clue.

So many balance sheets have been issued which have failed to include all of the liabilities that the author feels justified in discussing the matter fully, in order that the student may have the benefit of accumulated experience.

Trade Creditors: This may not be the largest item of the liabilities, but it is clearly the most important to verify. The notes payable outstanding may be larger in amount, but the proceeds thereof were presumably used to discharge trade debts, so that the latter item loses none of its importance because the balance is small.

As already stated, an auditor might ascertain the total amount of the debts by examining all of the mail over a sufficiently long period, but as this procedure is perhaps out of the question, he must do the next best thing.

Statements from creditors are valuable in verifying the amount due or claimed to be due, and if the time permitted (which it usually does not) the auditor could do no better than to request a statement from everyone with whom the concern might be expected to do business. Even then some one from whom a purchase had been made might be forgotten, the invoice might be omitted from the books, and the fact concealed from the auditor.

Most concerns keep order and receiving records of some description. The auditor should compare the entries in this record during the period immediately preceding the balance-sheet date with the purchase journal or voucher record to ascertain if the purchases indicated are entered. Every entry need not be checked. It is necessary to test only enough of the work to be satisfied that no invoices have knowingly or unknowingly been suppressed.

Where an audit is not completed until more than a month has elapsed after the closing date, the voucher record should be scrutinized to ascertain whether invoices entered subsequently belong to the prior period.

The open accounts on the ledger should be compared with the schedule of accounts payable. It should be ascertained that the balances represent specific and recent items only. If not, why not? Where any account does not look regular in every way the statement from the creditor should be asked for. If it cannot be found, request a duplicate. If told that the creditor does not send statements, *demand* that one be procured. The latter excuse is often made, but almost invariably it follows an inquiry relative to a disputed account and where the ledger shows a less amount to be due than is claimed. Nearly all business houses do send statements either on a fixed day each month or as bills fall due. The author has never heard of a refusal to furnish a duplicate, or to furnish a memorandum of the amount due at any stated time.

As a test, call for certain statements in every case, even if none of the accounts appear irregular. Disputes occur so frequently over discounts, allowances, returns, etc., that it may be the auditor's only chance to test the reliability of the purchase records.

The inspection of the order and receiving books is also important in that it may disclose receipts of goods at or before inventory time the invoices of which are not entered, the reason given for the omission being that as the goods were received late it was not considered worth while to add them to the inventories, or to pass the invoices through the books until after the closing date. If this practice involves a few items of small amount only it is not worth condemning, but if the quantities and amounts are relatively large the auditor must add the goods to the inventory and the amounts of the invoices to the accounts payable.

When examining the receiving and other records for evidence of purchases not represented by entries in the books, it should be remembered that the date of an invoice may not represent the date of its shipment, the practice of "dating" (i. e., dating an invoice forward to some future time) being not at all uncommon.

It is assumed that the ledger balances represent the amounts due after trade discounts have been deducted but before cash discounts are taken into consideration. Trade discounts should not appear on the books of account, being direct deductions from list prices. In respect to cash discounts, however, the practice is not uniform. Some concerns take advantage of every cash discount and make the deduction immediately upon receipt of the invoice and before it is entered. Where this has been done the auditor need not hesitate to pass the accounts as they stand, but where the deductions have not been made the auditor should be governed by the size of the discounts. Where the allowance is one per cent for payment within ten days, or where the rate is lower, the amounts due should be taken at their face. This gives the period following the balance-sheet date the benefit of the earning, but it is not out of proportion to the cash required and the expense of salaries, postage, etc., incurred. On the other hand, if the allowance is more than one per cent for prepayment, and if the concern has ample funds to pay all maturing accounts, it may reasonably be urged that the earning belongs to the period preceding the closing of the books. For instance, an invoice for $1,000 may be dated June 23rd, "thirty days net, two per cent ten days." It could hardly be urged that on June 30th the liability would be more than $980, provided that the cash balance indicated that the discount would be taken advantage of.

If the auditor desires to adjust the accounts in accordance with this suggestion, it will be necessary only to note the actual deductions, per cash book, during, say, the first half month succeeding the balance-sheet date, allowing for any possible items arising out of new transactions. This would obviate the necessity of calculating the amount in detail.

As a matter of general practice an auditor will not care to take advantage of this opportunity to reduce the liabilities, as there are possible deductions from assets which usually more than offset this amount, but in the event that the greatest exactness is required, or if there is any evidence of a desire to understate the net worth of a concern by undervaluing the assets, it may be necessary to apply the same principles to the liabilities. Or again, a concern doing a very large business, such as a department store, may allow no cash discounts to customers but may exact them from its creditors. In such a case the adjustment suggested may make a material change in the balance sheet.

Consignments: If the business under audit is one where there is any possibility of goods having been received on consignment, and part or all of such goods having been sold without a liability therefor having been created in the books, the auditor must use all due diligence to cover the point fully. Instances have been known where concerns have sold and collected for consigned goods without making any record of the liability until payment is made. This may occur where there is no intention to deceive, as consignment accounts are usually treated as memoranda only.

If inquiry develops the fact that goods have been received on consignment, all records in connection therewith should be called for. If the goods have all been sold, the consignor's account should show the full amount due and, if the debt is a current one, the amount will appear among those due to trade creditors.

If it appears that the consigned goods are partly sold and partly on hand, a memorandum or "pro forma" account sale should be made up for the part of each lot disposed of but not yet accounted for. The net proceeds due to the consignors should be entered as a liability in an account called "Accounts Payable Consignors." As some time may elapse before payment, it is not necessary to include the aggregate among the trade creditors, except as a liability accrued, but not due. When the books are reopened, the entries for the uncompleted consignments should be reversed.

Notes Payable: It is usual and desirable to divide the aggregate of notes payable into:

(1) Notes issued for merchandise.
(2) Notes discounted by own banks.
(3) Notes sold through brokers.
(4) Demand loans.

And a further separation which is not often seen, but which is most desirable, is:

(*a*) Notes accompanied by collateral.
(*b*) Notes with which no collateral is given.

There is not much to say with reference to the procedure involved in verifying the existence of outstanding, unpaid promissory notes except to warn the auditor that a great many instances have been known where outstanding notes have not appeared as liabilities on books of account.

It may safely be said that if deception is intended so far as the concealment of liabilities is concerned, there is a greater likelihood of its existing in connection with notes payable than with accounts payable. The latter are usually evidenced by invoices, and any attempt to hold them out would attract suspicion on the part of the office staff. With notes, however, it is comparatively easy to secure discounts, secrete the proceeds, and make no entry therefor on the books at all. This omission is more difficult to detect in, and probably occurs more frequently in connection with, single-entry than with double-entry books.

The point is of special importance where audits are made for the benefit of prospective lenders of money. The borrower tries to increase his assets and decrease his liabilities to the greatest possible extent. He also may attempt to conceal the fact that he has issued notes and may be carrying open accounts on the books, while in reality notes have been issued therefor which are falling due or which are overdue and unpaid.

In a recent bankruptcy case it was disclosed that a large number of notes had been given to creditors without any record thereof appearing in the books. The notes bore interest and several creditors had secured judgment for nonpayment. As the interest and costs amounted to a considerable sum, the liabilities were increased accordingly.

A more dangerous type of concealment exists wherein notes are issued in a firm or corporate name for money borrowed by individuals and which pass into the hands of innocent holders, who, of course, can collect if a concern is solvent. Notes of this description are sometimes renewed time and time again before discovery. An auditor who examines the books of account in the meantime is hardly likely to find any trace thereof.

If the notes are discounted by one of the regular banks, it would seem that the auditor, as well as the office staff, would be put on notice. This point is usually covered by a statement to the staff that the discount is a personal loan to a partner or officer. The auditor might secure a clue, or at least grounds for suspicion, if he would trace back to its source every credit of cash to the credit of a partner or officer of a corporation. As a matter of fact so many so-called loans of this nature have been made that an auditor may with propriety ask the question in connection with every such loan: "Where did you get it?" In other words, the credits to the individual accounts of partners or officers might represent items which are in fact liabilities of the firm or corporation.

Mortgages: As a mortgage derives its chief value from the fact that upon registry it becomes a lien, the auditor would seem to have an opportunity to verify the existence of such an obligation by inspecting the public records. Auditors admit the value of the knowledge which such an inspection discloses, but very properly urge that special training is necessary to undertake the task.

It is admitted by all that a well-equipped auditor must have some knowledge of law, and an important branch of such necessary knowledge is that pertaining to negotiable and non-negotiable instruments, mortgages, deeds, contracts, etc. The author suggests that a reasonably intelligent auditor or audit clerk can ascertain the procedure of the public registry office in less than an hour, and that a search for unsatisfied mortgages or judgments can be made in less time than it takes to verify the footings of a voucher register, and is an immeasurably more important thing to do. If the auditor is timid about undertaking the job, it might be worth while to arrange with a local lawyer or title company whereby, for a small fee, any mortgages or judgments entered against his clients would be reported to him.

So much for a purely independent search. If the auditor feels justified in accepting the book record as to the existence of a mortgage, he should at least endeavor to verify the amount, the rate, the due date, and the property secured thereby. All of these points are of interest to those who may desire to refer to the balance sheet of the mortgagor.

It should be borne in mind that a payment on account of a mortgage must be recorded or the entire amount will remain as an encumbrance on the property. Therefore, if payments on account appear, the auditor should ascertain if the principal has been legally reduced; if not, the fact should appear on the balance sheet.

Bonds: So many different classes of bonds have been evolved by the fertile brains of needy financiers that no attempt will be made here to differentiate except in a general way.

Bonds secured by a mortgage upon real estate are, of course, the most popular with investors. At one time all bonds, when they were not otherwise designated, were supposed to be secured by real property, but to-day many issues of bonds are mere promissory notes, differing only from the usual form of the latter in that they are larger, have coupons attached, are sealed, and are also less valuable because they do not fall due for a considerable period. From the auditor's point of view the security is important because of its bearing on other obligations and the equity, if any, which may exist for a subsequent lender or creditor.

Balance sheets are, as a rule, deficient in the information which they impart with reference to the real estate or personal property which is pledged with an issue of bonds. Sometimes a bond is a first lien on certain assets and a second lien on others. When considering the matter of liens it should be noted that interest unpaid is a lien as well as unpaid principal.

If it is feasible to have a balance sheet disclose the position which a bond bears to the assets, it is the auditor's duty so to state it. In any event he should determine as nearly as possible the position, if it is not so disclosed.

The corporation which issues bonds should, and in most cases does, keep a copy or sample thereof. The auditor should read this carefully in connection with the mortgage or deed of trust, make an abstract of these documents, and note all references to interest rate (or rates, as changes are sometimes made), due date or dates (installments of principal are frequently provided for), property pledged, sinking fund or similar provisions, and in fact anything which relates to the accounts or financial transactions of the maker.

Judgments: It frequently happens that a prosperous concern will dispute a claim, litigate it, and have judgment entered against them. If the case is appealed the judgment may be allowed to stand or a bond may be given pending a final decision. In rare instances are these debts entered on the books. Most business men consider that the entry of an invoice is an admission of liability, and, of course, will not permit the entry of a claim which they propose to fight.

What position must the auditor take? If a balance sheet is being constructed, the amount of the judgment should be included as a liability or a reserve set up to cover the estimated liability under the claim. If a balance sheet has been completed, the auditor should call attention thereto in a footnote.

How is the auditor to be informed as to the existence of

judgments? As mentioned under mortgages (page 155), he should be able to examine the public record himself. If he is not willing to do this, he should make such inquiry or investigation as is feasible. An inspection of lawyers' bills is a good way to secure a clue. If a concern is able to pay, but does not do so on principle, the auditor will have no difficulty in learning the facts. If a concern is obviously hard up, the auditor is charged with constructive knowledge that judgments *have* been obtained, and he is not safe unless he secures a report based on a search. Even if the search costs a few dollars the expense will be well worth while. If the audit is made for a banker, the latter may have had a search made, or, if not, will do so through his own attorney.

Interest Payable: Many of the liabilities which appear on a balance sheet carry interest, therefore the calculation of accrued interest to the date of the balance sheet is an important matter. The auditor should consider the possibility of an accrual upon the accounts as well as notes payable, bonds, etc. Enough book accounts bear interest to warrant an inquiry being made into its possibility.

Loan accounts of partners and officers of corporations almost invariably bear interest, but it is not always calculated up to the date of closing the books. Judgments, overdue taxes, and other liens, bear interest sometimes at an extremely high rate.

Legally, the interest on a bond is secured by the same property as the principal and in effect becomes part of the principal, but the latter is a long-term obligation, while interest is payable at frequent intervals and should therefore appear as a current liability.

Taxes: The balance sheet of a commercial enterprise not owning real estate rarely shows a liability for accrued taxes, yet probably ninety-nine out of every one hundred are liable therefor. Under the Federal Corporation Tax Law a tax of one per cent is imposed upon the net profits of a corporation in excess of five thousand dollars. This tax must be paid even if a corporation is dissolved before the end of the year during which the tax is imposed. As the tax is specifically based on the net profits of a particular period, although payable some months thereafter, the tax accrues throughout the specified period, and if a net rofit in excess of five thousand dollars is disclosed upon the losing of the books, a reserve of one per cent thereof should e made.

Bond interest which accrues from July 1st to December 31st, nd which is payable on January 1st, always appears among the abilities on December 31st, assuming, of course, that a proper ystem of accounts is in force. The Federal tax has accrued, and payable thereafter, just as surely as any other item.

The uncertainty as to the constitutionality of the law may ave justified the omission of this liability from balance sheets rior to 1911, but there is no longer any doubt about the necesity for a strict compliance, and auditors cannot certify to the alance sheet of a prosperous corporation which has not given roper consideration to this subject.

A corporation which had made a large temporary profit was issolved in July. A balance sheet was prepared and on its howing, a distribution of capital and profits was made. In the ollowing February the government demanded a report and one er cent of the profit realized. One of the directors had to pay he assessment.

The matter of taxes is of extreme importance in all audits of ublic service corporations, but the auditor should consider the ossible liability for taxes before finally passing upon any alance sheet.

Water Rates, etc.: There are certain expenses, such as gas nd water, the bills for which are frequently rendered at long ntervals. The auditor should provide for all accrued expenses f this class.

Wages: The date of the balance sheet does not always coinide with the date to which a payroll has been calculated. Unless the amount is trifling the amount accrued should be ascerained and entered as a liability.

Where there is little fluctuation in the number of men emloyed, it will be sufficient to take the proportion of the full veek's payroll; i. e., if the next succeeding payroll amounts to 1,000, and three days accrue in each period, the liability can be tated as $500, although each day's total might vary a few lollars from the others. The difference would not be large nough to pay for the work involved in making the calculations.

Rent: Rent is usually payable in advance, but this is not always the case. If any is accrued and not paid, it should be shown.

Freight: Sales are frequently made on a basis of free delivery to destination, and current freight bills are sometimes permitted to run, if the concern is well known.

An allowance of freight to a customer should be treated as a deduction from amounts due from trade debtors.

Goods may have been shipped, refused, and returned, in which case freight charges will have accrued.

Traveling Expenses and Commissions: It is important to note whether the accounts of all traveling salesmen have been received and entered before the books are closed. The auditor should secure a list and, if any report was not so entered, provision therefor should be made.

Ample provision should be made for all commissions eventually payable on sales which have been billed to customers. As commissions are frequently not payable to salesmen until the sales have been collected from the customers, accrued commissions are often omitted from the books. As they must, however, be paid out of the proceeds of the sales on which the full profit has already been taken into the accounts, they should clearly be set up as a liability.

Legal Expenses: All concerns have more or less litigation. Lawyers are usually expensive, but they have the merit, if it can be so termed, of waiting for their money. Before the books are closed the lawyers should be requested to send in a bill. If one is not found, the auditor should ascertain the amount due, if any.

Audit Fees: In line with the theory that all accrued expenses must be included among the liabilities, it might be assumed that the expense incurred for an audit to, say, June 30th, would be a proper charge to the period prior thereto. In practice, however, it is not usual to include the audit fee as an outstanding liability as of the date of the balance sheet. If the auditor has not performed any work on the accounts until after the closing date, it is certain that no legal liability exists at that time.

Under ordinary conditions the amount of the fee is not

known until after the report is written and submitted, so that no more than an estimate could be included.

Ordinarily the fee is not such a liability as should be provided for, provided that the audit commences after the closing date. An exception should be made, however, in the case of a partnership or a close corporation where a partner or stockholder is about to retire. The audit being partly for the benefit of the retiring party, and he being entitled to a copy of the report, it is proper that a sufficient reserve should be set aside, prior to the closing of the books, to provide therefor.

Damages: It is customary to insure against liability for damages claimed by employees or the public, but few insurance policies, if any, assume an unlimited liability. Then all concerns do not carry such insurance, although it is a reflection on a man's business ability to omit such protection. Furthermore, claims for damages may arise out of alleged breach of contract, or failure to deliver goods, or for any one of many other reasons.

The auditor should inquire as to this possible liability and should also request that a letter be procured from the concern's attorneys stating any pending claims or suits.

It may be that claims have arisen which have not been referred to the attorney. It often happens that a salesman claims commissions in excess of those paid to him, or an employee who has been dismissed claims salary or other compensation for an uncompleted term of service, or claim is made for a part of profits, which has not been paid. It is true that these are unusual items, but it is equally true that tens of thousands of dollars have been paid out in liquidation of disputed claims.

If an auditor finds any evidence which leads him to suspect that there may be a possible liability of this nature, he should insist on being informed as to all of the facts. He can then form an opinion as to the reserve, if any, which should be made on the books and balance sheet to provide therefor.

Coupons, Unused Tickets, etc.: The auditor of a railway company will expect to (but may not) find a reserve account for the outstanding liability in respect to unused tickets, but the point receives little or no attention in other cases. Many kinds of enterprises sell tickets, or issue coupons at a discount for cas which are a charge on the subsequent operation of the busines Tickets or coupons are issued by taxicab companies, sprin water dealers, restaurants, amusement parks, and shows. Tel phone companies formerly issued stamps good for long-distan calls.

Not all of the unused tickets, etc., will be presented, but s long as they are outstanding, provision must be made f redemption. The auditor will not attempt to verify the ou standing liability in detail, but he should carefully examine th system followed, because if the proper principles are observe the outstanding book liability will be in excess of the actu redemption which may be expected. Many tickets, coupons, etc are lost or destroyed, and it is obviously impossible to issu duplicates.

Deposits: Reference is not made to the deposits received b banks, bankers, and saving funds, but to the funds which ar deposited as a guarantee of good faith, or as part paymen on a purchase, or as security for an unliquidated or possib debt.

If the concern is operating under a public franchise, as a ga or electric company, it may have the power to require deposit and in many instances it will be charged with the payment o interest thereon. Interest is not usually paid until the receipt fo the original deposit is surrendered, and this may be many year afterward. Large numbers of the receipts are lost or destroye and demand is never made. Nevertheless, the company shoul carry all of the deposits as a liability and reserve the interes accruing thereon until a sufficient time has elapsed to warran writing off such deposits as may have been uncalled for so lon that the chances of payment are remote.

The custom of receiving deposits of money from employee is well enough established to warrant the inclusion of the captio "Deposits" as one of the liabilities to be reported by prospectiv borrowers to banks.

The auditor should investigate the procedure followed fron the time a deposit is accepted to the time it is withdrawn. Ther should be ample safeguards surrounding the handling of suc funds, as the deposits are frequently offered by ignorant person and foreigners who are not familiar with business methods and who might be induced to accept irregular receipts from clerks not authorized to handle the money. It is important that the books and stationery used should be specially prepared for the purpose, and the utmost care should be taken in writing up the records. The clerk in charge of the books should not be allowed to receive or pay money.

If pass-books are furnished to depositors, the auditor should call in as many as possible and compare the entries and balances with the books. There are so many different methods in force that the auditor must rely on his general experience in order to satisfy himself that the aggregate deposits appearing on the balance sheet as a liability represent the actual amount due to depositors. The rate of interest paid should be verified and the calculations tested. Accrued interest at the date of the balance sheet not credited to depositors should be added to the total deposits shown by the books.

For various methods of calculating interest see Chap. XXXI.

In clubs and similar organizations it is customary for members to deposit a small sum as security against the loss of keys, etc. To avoid bookkeeping in connection therewith, a very loose method may be in force. Frequently the cash received is placed in a drawer or box without any record being made. Subsequent payments are likewise made without record. Theoretically the balance on hand represents the liability for outstanding keys, etc. Practically it is known that part of the cash will never be called for. This permits unauthorized payments to be made from the fund, or part may be fraudulently abstracted. The matter is unimportant except that such laxity places temptation in the way of junior clerks and may be responsible for starting them on a criminal career.

The auditor should call attention to the importance of a careful record being made of *all* receipts and payments, no matter how small, primarily for the purpose of facilitating an audit, but in reality to inculcate in every employee handling cash the greatest care and accuracy in connection with the handling of money.

Unclaimed Dividends: The proper way of dealing with dividend accounts is to set aside in a separate fund or bank account the full amount of each dividend declared, charging against it all payments.

It sometimes happens that stockholders cannot be reached, and dividend checks are withheld or, if issued, are not cashed within a reasonable time. This may leave an outstanding liability which may remain undischarged indefinitely. Where such a state of affairs exists, any payments out of the regular order should be noted, as it may be found that unauthorized payments are being charged thereto.

CHAPTER XII

BALANCE-SHEET AUDIT—LIABILITIES (Continued)

CONTINGENT LIABILITIES AND CAPITAL

It is not enough that a balance sheet shows what *must* be paid; it should set forth with as much particularity as possible what *may* have to be paid. More than one apparently prosperous business house and many corporations have been wrecked through the necessity of having to meet obligations which did not arise out of the operation of ordinary business transactions. Nevertheless, the obligations were real ones, no matter how unlikely they appeared to be when contracted, and a true statement of the financial affairs of such concerns, prepared at any time after the obligations had been entered into, would have set them out. Accountants experienced in bankruptcy affairs well know that rarely, if ever, do contingent liabilities appear on the books of account.

It is the duty of an auditor who makes a balance-sheet audit to discover and report upon liabilities of every description—not only liquidated debts, but possible debts. It is true that contingent liabilities are at best difficult to locate, and almost impossible of discovery when an attempt is made to conceal their existence, but a professional auditor is supposed to undertake difficult tasks, and if he cannot report on anything except the entries which he finds in the books, he had better retire from the profession.

Notes Discounted: As shown under "Notes Receivable" (page 101) an apparent asset may represent an actual liability. For instance, a trade debtor may give a note for $1,000 which closes his account. The note is discounted, which closes the Notes Receivable account. The debtor finds he cannot pay and renews the note when due. This may be repeated several times, but at last a renewal cannot be secured and the note must be paid by the indorser. After it is known that the note will not be paid at maturity by the maker, the liability of the indorser is more than contingent—it is actual.

Of course, if the reserve for bad debts includes a provision for the full amount of the note, it would be duplication to set up a further reserve against the payment of the note. Usually the bad debts reserve is *not* large enough to take care of the contingent liability on notes discounted, so that the auditor should investigate the status of all notes under discount, and if it appears probable that any will not be met when due, the liability therefor should be shown. In cases where the auditor is satisfied that notes will neither be paid nor renewed he should include the amounts under current liabilities stating the date when due.

Indorsements: In addition to the contingent liability upon notes discounted for the benefit of the indorser, there may exist a liability based on indorsements for the benefit of others, usually known as accommodation indorsements.

It is not proposed to discuss this subject exhaustively, as the question of *ultra vires* at once arises, but from a practical point of view it may be assumed that every indorsement, whether by an individual, firm, or corporation, *may* become an ultimate actual liability of the indorser. Promissory notes are negotiable instruments, and, in order that they may circulate freely, an innocent purchaser for value, without notice of a lack of consideration on the part of a maker or indorser, may sue and recover from any or all, in turn.

The assumption that the maker will pay, or that the notes will not be used, or will not find their way into the hands of outsiders, has been dissipated in so many thousands of cases that the auditor who fails to include accommodation indorsements as liabilities because he is advised that there is no possibility of payment being demanded is assuming a risk for which there is no professional, legal, or moral justification.

It is possible that circumstances may exist where such indorsements are not liabilities, as would be the case if a note were overdue and the holder had notice, but the vital point to bear in mind is that solvent, straightforward concerns do not as a rule request nor secure indorsements unless under stress of necessity, or upon the payment of a consideration. If the maker of the note is "hard up," the indorser should expect to pay (as he usually is obliged to do). If consideration has passed, the indorser is still likely to have to pay, but having received compensation, his statement should show the amount thereof among the liabilities to indicate the risk which has been assumed. The full amount of the note, less the compensation received, is a contingent liability.

Naturally the auditor will not include indorsements among the liabilities on the balance sheet unless he gives due consideration to the possibility of an asset to offset. The offset will usually consist of a claim against the maker or prior indorser who has failed to meet an obligation, which at once is *prima facie* evidence that the asset is not in satisfactory shape. In the majority of cases it is merely a question of sizing up a bad debt.

The foregoing remarks apply to cases where the auditor is informed or readily ascertains that indorsements are outstanding. We have now to consider the procedure where no such information is volunteered, nor apparent on the records. The author was about to state that the auditor is justified in assuming that the practice does not exist, in view of the fact that the great bulk of concerns have a strict rule which forbids indorsements or guarantees, and that there must be special cause for suspicion before special inquiry need be made, but reflection brings to his mind so many instances of contingent liabilities of this nature that the suggestion is made that all audit programs contain some reference thereto.

The financial "atmosphere" of a concern is a fairly dependable index as to possible obligations or entanglements which may find expression in commitments leading to future embarrassment. The most common cause is overextension of business affairs, and this is more likely to occur with a prosperous man than with an impecunious one. The latter has little opportunity for expansion, while the former is fairly besieged by promoters and others who know by long experience that the most likely investor in a new and untried enterprise is a man who knows nothing at all about it. All over the country men who have made fortunes in their own businesses are squandering their capital in outside ventures.

If an auditor's report went no further than his client's office it would not be necessary for him to concern himself with the relation of outside ventures to the balance sheet of the business under audit, but now that banks are demanding certified balance sheets, the auditor must always proceed on the assumption that the balance sheet prepared by him will go into general circulation. The auditor who is observant, therefore, will be able to determine by what he sees *in* an office what has probably taken place outside.

If a partner, or officer, has withdrawn considerable sums of money for investment in outside enterprises, there will probably be some reference thereto in the books. Many corporations are partnerships under another form of organization, and the officers, who are usually identical with the large stockholders, keep personal accounts in the corporation books. The charges to these accounts will indicate, in some degree, the interests in outside affairs.

Let us consider the usual effect on the finances of a firm or corporation where its owners are connected with other enterprises. The firm or corporation may have good assets of $200,000 and total liabilities of $100,000. Suppose one or more of the partners or officers becomes interested in another business or in a flotation of doubtful merit. It may be urged that so long as the balance sheet of the firm or corporation is true and reflects its actual financial condition, the action of its partners or officers cannot affect it. But soon the outside venture requires more cash than can be supplied, so the partner or officer gives his note for $25,000, which is discounted. The auditor comes in at this point, discovers the interest in the outside deal, makes inquiry, and is informed as to the note. He finds further that there is not the slightest prospect of the note being met by the outside business.

Is it not apparent that the cash account of the firm or corporation will be called on to meet that note? This has happened in thousands of actual cases; is it not likely to happen every time? Should the auditor state the assets as $200,000, the liabilities at $100,000, and a contingent liability of $25,000? Legally, no, but if he can find a way to do it, he should not hesitate. Banks, creditors, and investors would have saved millions of dollars in the past if auditors had so stated the affairs of corporations. Is it not possible to protect the innocent investor or creditor when facts of this nature are disclosed, and where a reasonable interpretation makes them relevant?

If there is nothing in the books to indicate any connection on the part of the concern itself, a partner or an officer with outside ventures, and there is no apparent reason for suspecting any possible indorsement of another's paper, the auditor may not feel it necessary to carry his inquiries further. In fact, it might be impracticable even if it were desirable. Nevertheless, it must always be borne in mind that the indorsement of notes for outside ventures has resulted disastrously, and in cases where it was least expected, consequently it is a possibility of importance.

Guarantees: Almost all of the remarks under indorsements apply with equal force to guarantees. In one case the liability is fixed and definite by reason of the indorsements of negotiable paper, whereas a guarantee may be less definite so far as legal liability is concerned, and the amount of the obligation may be uncertain. Otherwise there is the same likelihood of being required to pay ultimately, and if the guarantee covers an obligation incurred in connection with an outside venture, there also exists a strong probability that the funds necessary to discharge the obligation will be withdrawn from the concern under audit.

The proprietor of a successful business reported to the mercantile agencies a net worth of about one million dollars. His statement indicated that his assets were not readily realizable, but his reported liabilities were small and his credit was rated first class. He was induced to invest in the stock of a distillery and was elected a director. The distillery needed money and he was induced to indorse some of its paper and guarantee other loans.

The president of the distilling company was found to be a defaulter to a large extent, and the company went into bankruptcy. The indorser and guarantor was called upon to meet obligations aggregating over one hundred thousand dollars, and he was unable to pay all of his debts as they became due. He is still struggling and may eventually pay in full, but it has meant the ruin of his own business.

If an auditor had stated the accounts of the guarantor's business, it is not likely that any mention would have been made of the outside liabilities, as the business was incorporated and the indorsements would have been *ultra vires* for the corporation. But when the notes came due and the guarantor started to pay, the only funds available were the resources of his own company, and these funds were used. Therefore his balance sheet to the agencies was misleading, because there were contingent liabilities affecting it *in fact* if not in law.

An auditor could have readily ascertained the existence of the directorship, and inquiry no doubt would have brought to light the indorsements and guarantee. If so, would he have been justified in mentioning the matter on the balance sheet? The author is of opinion that it would have been desirable for him to do so. Whether or not it would have been his clear duty could have been determined only in connection with the circumstances of his employment. In a serious matter of this nature an auditor should consult his attorney before disclosing damaging information, as it is possible that the scope of his employment might be limited and that his only course would be to withdraw from the engagement.

Unfulfilled Contracts: It has been mentioned that liabilities not on the books, in the form of contracts to accept delivery of goods contracted for before the date of the balance sheet, may call for the payment of large sums of money within a short space of time. It may be urged that on the face of this statement there would be no change in the net result shown by the balance sheet, as an asset would be received to offset the liability.

A banker, however, might look upon this condition in a far different light. The balance sheet, for instance, might show stock on hand large enough or too large for the normal requirements of the business, and any unfulfilled contracts outstanding at balance-sheet time which called for the receipt of additional stock, which might not be readily salable, would mean an actual liability, whereas the offset would be an asset of doubtful value.

In every audit, therefore, the auditor should call for copies of all orders for future delivery, and if such orders call for stock in excess of the current and reasonable prospective demand, mention thereof should be made in the balance sheet. The details reported would depend on the circumstances of each particular case.

The Minute Book: Experience has demonstrated to auditors hat the examination of the minute book is a most prolific source of information relative to contingent liabilities.

Recently one of the largest corporations in this country ssued its annual report. Included therein was the auditor's cerificate, which said in effect: "The balance sheet is correct, subect to any adjustments which might have been indicated by the minute books, which we were requested not to read." What did this mean?

If the minute books contained evidences of liabilities or changes in assets, as might be inferred from the refusal to submit same to the auditors, how much dependence could the directors expect to have placed upon their report by the stockholders and the public? On the other hand, if the contents of the minute book were harmless, why should the auditors be refused access thereto and thus give rise to unfavorable comment.

The auditor should always insist on an inspection of the minutes of a board of directors, and of the executive or any other committee of the board. If permission is withheld, his certificate should be written along lines indicated above, except that the refusal would be notice to the auditor that special care should be taken in passing upon balance-sheet items which might be affected by the action of a board of directors.

The following points might be involved: contracts for additions to or for additional plant equipment; purchase of other corporations or large interests therein; contracts for future deliveries of goods and materials in unusual quantities; payments of bonuses and special compensation to officers and others out of past profits, but actual payment to be made at a future date; settlement of pending litigation for a sum in excess of the liability, if any, carried therefor in the books; possibility of litigation such as alleged infringement of patents, which might seriously affect the value of assets; contracts or agreements which might tend to increase the assets or reduce the liabilities. These are only a few of the matters which the reading of corporate minutes reveals to the auditor.

Usually the disposition is to conceal from an auditor evidence of contingent liabilities, the thought being that he might feel it his duty to provide therefor in the balance sheet. Less frequently good news is withheld in order that the balance sheet may show up as badly as possible and thus give the directors time to acquire stock below its value.

The author once insisted on reading the minute book of a street railway company. The president's reluctance to produce the book was explained when it was found that at a meeting attended by the president he agreed to accept common stock of the company at par for his services. He had, however, directed the treasurer to pay it in cash. As the stock was worth only a few dollars a share, his disinclination to carry out his agreement was natural, perhaps, but illegal and dishonest. He was obliged to adjust the matter.

RESERVES

The matter of reserve accounts is in an unsatisfactory condition from the point of view of a professional auditor chiefly because the term is indiscriminately applied to items which are essentially different. For instance, an inspection of balance sheets will disclose that the following accounts are called "Reserves": provision for probable losses in respect to accounts or notes receivable; accounts set up to cover depreciation of plant and other assets such as patents, trade marks, etc.; discounts which it is expected will be deducted by trade debtors; arbitrary charges against surplus to provide a book account for "working capital"; sinking fund accounts to take care of depletion of mines, or to retire bonds at maturity.

It will be noted that some of the so-called reserves are actual deductions from assets and should be so treated, thus having the effect of liabilities, while others are not liabilities at all. The distinction lies in the creation of the accounts. If the debit or offsetting entries are proper charges against income, then the accounts should be deducted from the assets to which they relate, or else they should be set up as liabilities and should never be grouped with the surplus account. On the other hand, if the accounts represent sums set aside after the net profit of an enterprise is determined upon a proper accounting basis, for the purpose of conserving its financial interests by reducing the surplus available for dividends, and thus in reality form part of the general surplus of the business, then the accounts should be stated as a section of the surplus account.

This line of reasoning may be tested by setting up on one side the assets at what the auditor believes to be a fair net valuation; from the total so ascertained, the liabilities actual and contingent, should be deducted; the balance will represent what may be termed the net worth of the business. If a corporation, the capital stock may now be considered, leaving the balance, if any, to represent surplus.

It cannot be maintained that a sum set aside to provide additional working capital could be treated as a liability in any sense of the word. To whom is it to be paid? A liability, from a balance sheet point of view, is an obligation or a debt to the public, i. e., something which must or may have to be *paid* before partners or stockholders can receive a dividend or a distribution.

In actual practice reserves are usually shown between the definite liabilities and the surplus, but wherever it is possible to state actual assets and actual liabilities apart from capital, surplus, and surplus reserves, it should be done. Some reserves represent unliquidated liabilities to the public, but others, such as depreciation reserves, are, strictly speaking, direct deductions from assets and are not liabilities.

If a necessity seems to exist for stating the gross amount of the assets on one side and the reserves against such assets on the other, then the reserves must be included among the liabilities in order that the aggregate of one side may be deducted from the other in order to determine net worth. This procedure must not be confused with the criticism which is applied to the balance-sheet form which shows on one side or the other, items which are not assets nor liabilities nor deductions from either class. Any amount which directly relates to an actual asset or liability may be grouped therewith without violating the rule against the misuse of these two terms.

The author's test, therefore, is that a reserve account, to properly appear among the liabilities on a balance sheet, must represent:

(1) Estimated amounts which are believed to have accrued and which, when liquidated, will be actual liabilities;

(2) Items which are deductible from assets to reduce the latter to their true value;

(3) Contingent liabilities;

(4) "Reserve" of an insurance company.

Under these will appear:

(1) Accruals such as interest, wages, taxes, etc.;

(2) Depreciation and obsolescence of plant, exhaustion of mines, estimated loss on accounts receivable, etc.;

(3) Provision for the contingencies discussed in these pages, but the reserve should be based on evidence more tangible than a mere desire to be conservative. A vague feeling that something might have been overlooked which would decrease the assets or increase the liabilities is not the proper subject for a reserve. Conservative management "reserves" part of its surplus for such contingencies, but it appears as surplus and not as a liability.

(4) The reserve of an insurance company is usually an actual liability, i. e., income has been received and treated as income, whereas part only has been earned, as in the case of fire insurance and similar companies where premiums are paid in advance, and the unearned portion should be carried as a liability. Theoretically, the aggregate of this unearned income forms a reserve for reinsurance, the theory being that if a company desired to suspend business, it could reinsure all of its risks out of the reserve and leave its capital and surplus intact. Likewise, life insurance companies not only collect premiums in advance, but they also collect more than is sufficient to pay for the insurance carried. The excess is returnable to the assured under the contract, and is therefore a liability rather than part of the accumulated surplus of the company. Under some policies the excess is rebated annually, under others no distribution is made until the policy expires. From an accounting point of view a mutual insurance company would have no surplus, because as it agrees to insure at cost, all excess premiums received are the property of the assured. Of course a life insurance company should be conservative to the last degree, and it may be that it would not be safe to allocate all of the estimated excess income to specific policy holders.

All of the classes of reserves just enumerated have been or

will be fully discussed under their respective heads. The so-called reserves which are not charges against income, but which are set aside after net profits are determined, and which therefore are in reality divisions of surplus account, will be discussed under the general title of "Surplus."

CAPITAL AND SURPLUS

Having discussed the asset side of the balance sheet, and having enumerated all of the obligations, certain and uncertain, which should appear on the opposite side thereof, the auditor should devote particular attention to the treatment of what may be termed the net worth of a firm or corporation. By this is meant the excess of assets over liabilities. This forces some comments which the author would prefer to omit, but as the form of a balance sheet is of the utmost importance, they cannot be avoided.

Primarily a balance sheet is prepared for the information of the proprietors whose assets and liabilities are therein set forth. In practice this is true as to firms, small corporations and large corporations, where there are but few stockholders. In the case of corporations with numerous stockholders, however, it is well known that the balance sheet is made up for the directors or those who control, rather than for those who own.

If a balance sheet were always intended to reach the owners of the business, whose sole interest therein is to ascertain the net worth of their property, the logical form of a balance sheet would be to show the net worth clearly. But this is not done when assets are shown on one side, and on the other, under the general heading "Liabilities," there appear in this order: capital stock (not a liability), accounts, and notes payable, etc., reserves (some being liabilities, some not), then surplus, the total exactly agreeing with the total of the assets.

The average investor does not understand accounts. How is he to determine the net worth of the business of which he is a part owner? The proper way to enlighten him is to classify the balance-sheet items. The assets should be shown, then the liabilities; the excess of assets over liabilities (if any) should appear next; finally the capital or capital stock and surplus representing such excess. If it is desired to set aside part of the surplus for other purposes, the segregation should be shown on the balance sheet.

This grouping can be used where it is desired to state the assets and liabilities in parallel columns with the totals of the two columns in agreement (see page 220), as well as where the assets are first stated; then the liabilities thereunder, followed by the capital plus surplus, or capital less deficit, as the case may be. (See page 217.) In both cases it will be noticed that the only variation of any consequence from the form criticized is in the captions and the groupings. But these are read seriously by many business men, so that care should be taken to use terms as nearly descriptive of the items to which they apply as possible.

There is really very little defense for the form of balance sheet which shows capital and surplus as liabilities, and deficit as an asset. It is true that it enables an accountant to set down two sets of figures which exactly balance, and the author freely admits that the best corporations and the best firms of accountants use the form under condemnation, but in his opinion the practice is merely the outgrowth of custom and expediency and will be changed in time.

Capital Stock: The auditor should examine the charter or certificate of incorporation of the corporation, the by-laws and the board minutes for information relative to the authorized capital, the method of payment, and all other provisions governing its issuance. He should ascertain that there has been no overissue by examining the certificate books and stock ledgers, and he should verify the proceeds of its sale. In most States capital stock cannot be issued for a consideration less than its par value.

Our lax laws, however, permit almost any kind and quantity of tangible or intangible property to be solemnly valued at any conceivable sum, and while an auditor is not supposed to certify to anything which he knows is not true, yet we have not yet reached the point where an auditor is justified in volunteering an opinion that capital stock issued in payment for property acquired is not full paid because in his opinion the property is not worth the amount of stock at par issued therefor. Of course, in a special investigation, an auditor may be asked to investigate points of this kind, but in an ordinary audit where stock has been issued for property, and the records are in satisfactory shape, the auditor is not called upon to challenge the good faith of the directors.

Of late years it has become popular to adopt by-laws which call for certain amounts of current assets to be maintained, for certain reserves to be created, etc. The auditor will need to verify all of these requirements.

If stock has been sold .on the installment plan, the auditor will ascertain that the calls have been promptly met and whether any are in arrears. If special terms have been extended to any stockholder, approval of the board is necessary.

Premiums on Capital Stock: Where stock has been sold at a premium, the auditor will see that all premiums have been collected. The funds so realized should be credited to Premiums on Capital Stock account, which should remain open, and appear on the balance sheet as a special surplus account. In no event, however, should the account be transferred to general surplus and thus be looked upon as available for dividends. It would probably be legal to declare a dividend out of funds so raised, but it would be so improper as to sustain a charge of dishonesty against the director who voted therefor.

Sinking-Fund Accounts: The author contends that reserves for depreciation, when calculated scientifically, should be deducted from the assets which are affected thereby or else be shown as liabilities. If it should happen that compulsory sinking-fund requirements exactly agree with the exhaustion of mines or depletion of other wasting assets, the amounts thereof will likewise appear as liabilities and depreciation reserves are unnecessary. As a matter of fact, however, sinking-fund requirements are usually in excess of actual depreciation or exhaustion reserves, so that the point to be settled is the proper method of showing that the sinking-fund requirements have been legally complied with and at the same time exhibiting the assets and liabilities as they actually exist.

For illustration, a mortgage covering coal lands may require the payment to the trustee of a sum equal to ten cents per ton mined. The exhaustion charge based on engineers' estimates may be five cents per ton. The reason for the difference is obvious. The holder of a bond would not care to take the chance of waiting for the last ton to be removed before receiving the last of his principal.

In order to sell bonds the security must be ample and a considerable margin must be allowed for errors in estimates. No doubt the mortgage will require that the sinking fund shall be a charge against earnings, and this is reasonable, as it serves to prevent excessive dividends until the bonds are all retired. In the meantime, however, there is no reason why the stockholders should be kept in ignorance as to the true earnings realized, even if they are not entirely available for dividends so long as the bonds remain unpaid.

Therefore, the only way to show the exact (or as nearly exact as possible) earnings would be to carry a reserve-for-exhaustion account among the liabilities equal to five cents per ton, and a reserve-for-sinking-fund account equal to an additional five cents per ton as a segregated part of the surplus. After all of the bonds are retired this reserve account would be closed into the general surplus account.

The reserve-for-exhaustion account should be sufficient to equal the book value of the property account by the time the coal is practically exhausted. This rule applies irrespective of any special requirements for sinking-fund installments, and irrespective of a trust deed provision that such installments are a charge against income. All fixed or wasting assets must be kept intact, either in their original form or by creating an equivalent in cash or some other satisfactory asset. The amounts required to maintain this equilibrium are charges against income, but as soon as the installments are in excess of such requirements, the excess forms a part of the surplus of the business and should be shown as such. The question as to how much, if any, of the surplus is available for dividends is another matter.

Reserve for Working Capital: It has been held to be legal to set aside annually or at other periods out of the earnings of a company a reasonable amount as a reserve for additional working capital, which is therefore not distributable in the shape of dividends. This reserve may be temporary or permanent, as the directors may determine, and corresponds with the surplus of a bank or trust company, which is never used for the purpose of dividends unless some extraordinary occasion arises. The account is a discretionary one and is almost entirely a matter of bookkeeping, or rather it is a sort of notice to stockholders that the amounts so set aside will not be distributed.

To treat such an account as a liability is a fallacy, because at any time the directors can transfer the entire balance to general surplus and pay out all or any part of it in dividends. Therefore the account should always appear on the balance sheet as a section of surplus, and never among the liabilities. An auditor should never set up an account of this nature in the books nor show it on the balance sheet unless it has been formally authorized by the board of directors. It is a most commendable practice to accumulate a substantial surplus, and if the directors believe that the temptation to declare dividends will be less if the surplus account proper is diminished and some other account with a different name is increased, the auditor cannot object. But no such diversion of profits should be attempted by an officer of a company on his own initiative.

Preferred Stock Accumulated Dividends: Capital stock is not a liability, nor can a dividend thereon be a liability unless action has been taken and the funds set aside for the purpose. When this is once done the action of the directors cannot be rescinded and the dividend becomes a liability.

But a situation sometimes exists with respect to unpaid dividends on preferred stock which are entitled to accumulate in favor of the preferred stock until paid or otherwise disposed of. This preference, however, is a factor only as against the common stock. It does not accumulate as a liability and is not deductible from the surplus, if any, which exists. In other words, a corporation may have a book surplus more than sufficient to pay accumulated preferred stock dividends, but so long as no dividend is declared by the directors no book entry is permissible. The balance sheet will not reflect the aggregate of the unpaid dividends unless it is noted thereon as a memorandum.

Common stockholders usually have a keen interest in the value of their shares, and it is not only permissible, but desirable, that any arrears which may exist with respect to accumulated dividends should appear as a footnote or memorandum on the balance sheet.

Surplus: This should be the last word on the balance sheet, and it should have as specific a meaning as any item of assets or liabilities. This is rarely the case, however, and auditors are as much to blame for this condition as anyone else.

The "surplus" of a corporation should represent an actual surplus, that is, a balance of net profits after all reserves have been provided, including the reserves *out of* surplus, such as working capital, etc., leaving an amount safely distributable as dividends.

This does not mean that there must be cash on hand sufficient to pay the whole amount of surplus in dividends, but that if at any time there should be surplus funds, the directors may rely on the integrity of the surplus account and not lay themselves open to an action for paying dividends out of capital, or before reserves for compulsory sinking funds, etc., have been created.

CHAPTER XIII

PROFIT AND LOSS ACCOUNT

At least nine tenths of all of the enterprises with which a professional auditor has to deal are conducted with the expectation of realizing a profit. Certainly more than half, and probably three-fourths, of these enterprises have their accounts stated and results shown in a form to which a professional auditor cannot certify without modification or adjustment. That is to say, most concerns state their profit and loss accounts incorrectly.

There are frequent differences of opinion with respect to a balance sheet, but, after all, it is not usually so difficult to reach an agreement as to the amount at which the assets and liabilities shall be stated when they are compiled from the books and adjusted to meet known conditions, including valuations of disinterested persons and the scheduling of all known liabilities. Reliable appraisal companies will place valuations upon all the physical property. As to other assets and liabilities, there is rarely any serious question of the amounts stated by the auditor. But as soon as an attempt is made to state a definite and final amount which represents the net profit of any concern for a given period, there arises the most difficult and unsatisfactory problem which an auditor must solve.

In view of the fact that there is scarcely any likelihood that two professional auditors to-day would, with respect to the accounts of an undertaking of any considerable magnitude, show the same net result of profit, it is not surprising that the usual profit and loss account is prepared upon a basis which admits of criticism. It is extremely important that an effort be made to establish standards which will appeal to those responsible for the stating of accounts as scientific and reasonable. The latter term may seem out of place, but it must be understood that rules which are purely theoretical will not be observed.

It is not difficult to write out a memorandum of the items which appear on the debit and credit side of the profit and loss account, but unfortunately in actual practice the items assume so many different aspects that all of the rules heretofore published have failed to furnish a practical method of handling them. It is the purpose of this chapter to discuss theories, both legal and professional, and follow up the theories by illustrations which, while they may not establish a standard upon which all will agree, may nevertheless assist those who desire to study the suggestions of others as a means of arriving at their own conclusions.

A balance-sheet audit is only partially completed with the verification of the assets and liabilities. There will be shown thereon a deficit or a surplus, and it is absolutely impossible to form any intelligent conclusion as to the operations of a business unless an analysis in the form of a profit and loss statement accompanies the balance sheet. It is not enough to know that the balance sheet shows a substantial surplus; the preceding balance sheet may have shown a much larger one!

It is not enough to know that the profit or loss for a particular period is a certain sum. All who are interested in the enterprise desire to know the particulars of the net result, and the auditor who states the transactions in an intelligent, scientific, readable way is the one who finds favor with business men.

The form of the statement and related subjects are fully discussed in the chapter on certificates and reports (page 207).

It is proper to mention at this point, however, that the auditor who familiarizes himself with the legal as well as the economic aspects of income and expense accounts is best prepared to analyze accounts properly and to present the results so that the relation of certain figures or groups of figures will convey all that they should convey.

Legal Definition of Profits: The courts in different jurisdictions have defined profits, net profits and profits available for dividends, in so many different ways that an auditor or corporate officer who desires authority for any position which he desires to assume can usually find it in the law reports.

It has been held in judicial decisions that a dividend may be declared out of the profits of one year although there is a large deficit carried over from previous years, and that "past due floating debt should be paid or funded before a dividend is declared."

Nearly every conceivable situation between these two extremes has been held to be legal or illegal, depending on the judge deciding the case.

In many of the decisions profits are defined and the ludicrous definitions and comments in themselves explain why it is that the courts vary to such a great extent in settling disputes which involve accounts. The fact is that judges, who are trained as lawyers, understand as little about accounts as the members of the bar. The adage "A little knowledge is a dangerous thing" has its exemplification in the treatment by lawyers of questions of accounting. They have the temerity to settle matters of the greatest importance, involving complicated accounts, without any evidence that anyone who understands accounts has been consulted in the settlement. Occasionally an instance is found where the departure from the usual legal comment is so great that it is worth placing on record. The court said in one case in point:

If at the end of the first year the line of railway is still in so good a state of repair that it requires nothing to be laid out on it for repairs in that year, still, *before you can ascertain the net profits,* a sum of money ought to be set aside as representing the amount in which the wear and tear of the line has, I may say, so far depreciated it in value as that that sum will be required for the next year or next two years. I should think no commercial man would doubt that this is the right course—that he must not calculate *net profits* until he has provided for all the ordinary repairs and wear and tear occasioned by his business. That being so, it appears to me that you can have no net profits unless this sum has been set aside. When you come to the next year, or the third or fourth year, what happens is this: as the line gets older the amount for repairs increases. If you had done what you ought to have done, that is, set aside every year the sum necessary to make good the wear and tear in that year, then in the following years you would have a sum sufficient to meet the extra cost.

Another legal definition of net profits is the following:

Theoretically all profits are "net," but as the expression "gross profits" is sometimes used to describe the mere excess of present value over former value, or of returns from sales over prime cost, the phrase "net profits" is appropriate to describe the gain which remains after the further deduction of all expenses, charges, costs, allowance for depreciation, etc.

Economic Definition of Profits: In discussing the subject of profits the "Encyclopedia of Accounting" states that from an economist's point of view profit consists of the surplus remaining over from the employment of capital after defraying all the necessary expenses and outlays incurred in its employment, and after the capital has been replaced or provision made for its replacement. If there are not sufficient assets left to replace the capital, the result of the venture or employment is a loss and the amount by which the capital is diminished is the measure of this loss. Profits are arrived at by means of balance sheets showing the true financial position of the concern, supplemented, where the books are properly kept, by a profit and loss account.

For example, the profit of a company for the first year would be the excess of assets over liabilities (including in the latter the paid up capital), while there would be exhibited in the profit and loss account the sources from which the profits have arisen. The profit for any period is the difference between the surplus of assets over liabilities at the beginning of the year and the surplus as shown at the close.

Accountant's Definition of Profits: If a public accountant were asked to define the term "net profit" he would probably reply: "The net profit of a business is the surplus remaining from the earnings after providing for all costs, expenses, and reserves for accrued or probable losses."

But there are capital profits and revenue profits, as for instance, part of a tract of land upon which a factory has been erected may be sold for an amount equal to the original cost of the entire undertaking. This is a realized profit, but not one which falls within the ordinary definition, therefore it is not wise to rely exclusively upon any one definition.

As stated on page 180, the author believes that the word "surplus" should be used only to designate an amount available for dividends. The term net profits should be used only to designate the amount arrived at by stating the income actually accrued during a stated period, collected or collectible, less the cost thereof, and after provision is made for further costs accrued but not paid, such as depreciation, obsolescence, taxes, and other charges apportioned against the income, such as reserves for strikes, workmen's pensions, etc., but before any reserve is created for working capital, unknown contingencies, etc. If an absolutely accurate balance sheet could be prepared at the beginning and end of a period, the difference would represent the net profit or net loss for the term, but the valuation and revaluation of capital assets involves too much speculation to permit such a practice being recognized as satisfactory. This, in effect, is the method used in arriving at results in a single-entry business, and its utter failure to justify itself is reason enough for abandoning it.

A business man wants to know his gross earnings for the year, together with all of the costs and expenses which are properly chargeable thereto. Naturally the net result, be it a profit or a loss, will coincide with the changes in the balance sheet at the beginning and the end, exclusive of capital receipts or expenditures during the period. But the business man does not always think that; sometimes he wants to have the gross earnings stated and as few deductions therefrom as possible made, in order that a favorable result may be shown. He may be willing to create a reserve for depreciation on the books, and in the corporation tax returns, but he does not always want it to appear in the statement which he shows his banker. He does not consider that the profit and loss account as he would state it, taken in connection with his balance sheets, would be inaccurate on its face. The professional auditor, however, is under a much greater responsibility. He cannot afford to prepare a profit and loss account which omits any material item. Just what should be included and what excluded will now have our attention

EARNINGS

Gross Earnings: It is customary ana desirable to show the gross business transacted, whether arising from sales of goods, services rendered by professional men and others, or by public service corporations or similar enterprises.

Returns: Where earnings arise from the delivery of goods and for any reason the goods are returned, the aggregate thereof is usually deducted from the gross sales before stating same. The reason for this is that if the goods are returned and credited at the same price at which charged, and are available for resale, then it would be improper to augment the sales by transactions never consummated, and thus render less valuable, calculations of gross profits, etc. This is the general rule, but if anyone for whom a statement is being prepared desires to have the returns shown as a deduction from the gross sales, there is no objection to complying with the request. It may be of interest as a means of showing whether the proportion of returns to the total volume of business is proper or otherwise.

Ordinary Transactions Only to be Included: It should be noted here that in the first division of the profit and loss account the only earnings which should be shown are those which are incident to the normal operation of the business. All other earnings should be excluded at this point. The reason for this is that the relation of one account to another, for immediate observation as well as for future comparative purposes, must be expressed in percentages and amounts and the inclusion of any item out of the ordinary scope of the enterprise would affect the percentages and thus diminish the value of the comparisons.

Allowances and Rebates: These are the next deductions and will also be direct, except that separate ledger accounts should be kept therefor, unless the items are few in number and amount. Wherever the aggregate is a material percentage of the gross sales, and therefore subject to comment and possible criticism, it should be shown on the statement.

Bad Debts: The earnings just referred to are gross and are so stated whether or not realized in cash or its equivalent. The question arises as to whether an allowance, or reserve, for bad debts should be considered at this stage and be deducted direct from the gross earnings, or be treated as an expense of administration or selling and be included under one of these groups. The proper place is that group which reflects the cost of collecting the proceeds of the sales.

One concern may decide to take its chances on the acumen of its salesmen and maintain no credit department. The proportion of bad debts may be fairly large, but may not be sufficient to warrant the expense of a competent credit force. Another concern in the same line of business may have a well-equipped credit department and its losses from bad debts may be very small, but there will be two items of expense to be grouped if an intelligent comparison with the other concern is desired. For these and other reasons the provision for bad debts should not be deducted directly from the earnings.

The reserve created, however, is a deduction from the item of trade debtors or accounts receivable on a balance sheet. It is not a liability and should never be placed among liabilities or on the liability side of the balance sheet.

The inspectors sent out by the Bureau of Internal Revenue to verify corporation tax returns claim that a charge to the profit and loss account representing a provision for bad debts cannot be accepted as a proper charge unless specific accounts are designated. This attitude is substantially borne out by an official ruling of the Commissioner, viz:

> Bad debts, if so charged off the company's books during the year, are proper deductions. But such debts, if subsequently collected, must be treated as income.

This position is on a par with other and equally absurd decisions of the Bureau referred to elsewhere. Take, for instance, a department store manager whose experience has extended over a great number of years. He may have discovered that the loss from bad debts is one per cent of the gross sales and, based on this experience, a monthly charge is made to profit and loss and a corresponding reserve is created. When debtors' accounts are eventually beyond hope of recovery, they are debited to the reserve. This is an expense of the business and no ruling of the Treasury Department can make it anything else. For a full discussion of bad debts refer to page 297.

Work in Progress: So far as the books of account are concerned a clear line must be drawn between earnings which are represented by completed transactions with trade debtors and those which are only partially completed. In any case no profit must be taken unless a cause of action has arisen which can be enforced against the debtor. In other words, where work in progress cannot be earmarked as for a definite customer, or where it has not proceeded far enough to base an action, it must be taken into the inventory at cost and no profit thereon will appear in the profit and loss account. But if work is undertaken "on order" and is proceeding satisfactorily, and it is apparent that the estimated profit thereon will be realized, more or less, then it is permissible to take credit for the proportion of profit earned to the date of the account.

Ordinarily, on the theory that profits must not be anticipated, this principle would not be considered a conservative one. In trading concerns orders are frequently taken far in advance, and goods in an inventory may have been sold and be simply awaiting delivery. Accounting authorities agree that the profit on such sales should be deferred to the period during which delivery is made.

It may therefore be pertinent to inquire why it is that a profit may be taken on a contract only partially completed and with many contingencies to face, any one of which might delay or prevent the contract being fulfilled according to its terms. Perhaps the best and frankest answer to this argument is that expediency governs one case, while the other is subject to ordinary commercial practice.

Most concerns which sell ahead have a fairly constant and uniform business and no statistical problem is affected by charging sales expenses to one period while the following period reaps the benefit thereof. But a shipbuilder may have at the end of one fiscal period a dozen jobs under way, while at the end of the next period he may have six or eighteen. If he were to take in the profit on completed jobs only his books might show a state of affairs vastly different from the facts, that is, his most prosperous year might easily show up the worst. The same condition exists with contractors in the building and other trades.

It may be urged that the taking of a profit on uncompleted work is an extreme case of anticipating earnings, a practice which is condemned throughout this book. This is admitted. It should be borne in mind, however, that in all cases where there are inventories and similar assets the closing of books is necessarily based on estimates, and many instances are known of serious mistakes in fixing valuations on real estate and stock-in-trade.

The necessity of closing at a fixed date each year may be supported by careful estimates, and it will be found over a period of years that a contractor who has carefully estimated the value of work in progress, and who has conservatively estimated his profits thereon, will have arrived at figures quite as dependable as is the case in a business where the units of production are smaller and where it is not the practice to anticipate profits.

Experience in dealing with contractors' accounts soon enables the auditor to verify, at least approximately, the accuracy of the figures submitted in connection with work in progress.

Recently the practice of having work done at a maximum profit or upon a fixed percentage has been extended to much work which formerly was undertaken for a round sum. In such a case the profit is determined by the extent of the work completed and may be taken into account in the same manner as with professional earnings.

Where the units of production are smaller and the time of completion is comparatively short, there is no sanction for including any profit whatever in the inventory prices of unfinished goods. Under a very accurate and carefully kept cost system it may be possible to arrive at the cost price of work in progress. The auditor should ascertain that the principles upon which the costs have been calculated are correct and should also satisfy himself that the quantities have been checked and certified to by responsible parties.

Departmental Profits: It has been held by some accounting authorities that when the product of one department of a business has been completed and is turned over to another department, the originating department may take credit for its production at the market price, and if the market price is in excess of its cost, then a profit is earned and may be taken into account immediately.

In support of this view it is pointed out that in some concerns there may be, say, four distinct stages between raw product and finished goods. Other and competing concerns may deal only with one, two, or three of these stages, so that what may be an intermediary stage for one will represent raw materials for another.

For instance, a steel plant may mine its own ore and manufacture its own pig iron. A competitor may purchase all of its pig iron. The former's iron may cost $10 per ton; the latter, having to buy on the market, may not be able to secure any iron under $12 per ton.

The iron may be used to manufacture identical products. At what price should the former concern charge the department to which the iron is delivered? If at $10 per ton, the manager will be credited with a lower cost on his production than his competitor, although the latter may, as a matter of fact, be more efficient.

So far the argument is a strong one, and the point can be conceded if the interdepartmental profits are suspended until the product is finally disposed of. Otherwise a concern manufacturing its goods from the first stage to the last might find itself with a large inventory of manufactured goods and a large apparent profit and yet be wholly unable to convert the book profit into cash.

For comparative purposes and in order to determine the efficiency of different departments, it may therefore be permissible to adjust costs to market prices provided that in all cases such intermediate profits be held in reserve until there has been a conversion into cash or its equivalent.

A complete answer to the demand for an earlier disposition of these profits is that the purpose of organizing an enterprise which includes various stages of manufacture may be assumed to be the expectation of producing a given article in complete form for market at the lowest possible price, and it is expected that the larger the number of stages which are covered the lower will such cost be. This would not be the case if it were planned to take credit for a series of profits throughout the process of manufacture, as this would obscure the actual cost of the finished article.

Profits of Subsidiary Companies: In recent years there has been a tendency toward concentration of production, and the same problem arises with respect to intercompany profits as with interdepartmental profits. This subject was discussed by William M. Lybrand, C. P. A., in his paper on "The Accounting of Industrial Enterprises," read before the American Association of Public Accountants at Atlantic City in 1908. He said *inter alia:*

> Some of the industrial enterprises of the present day begin their ownership with the raw materials and manufacture their output all the way from the first stage to the last. Necessarily this manufacturing cannot, in every instance, be performed in one continuous operation or by one plant, and there will be constant transfers from one company to another of product finished up to a certain point, but subject to further manipulation in order that it may be disposed of in a different form. At the end of the fiscal year or other balance-sheet period there will doubtless be a quantity of such merchandise

in the inventories of the several subsidiary companies, purchased by one company from another at a price greater than the actual cost of manufacturing. As the companies are entirely distinct from each other, it may be argued that the purchasing company will be justified in including such merchandise in its inventory at the price paid to the company from which it was acquired. The purchase, however, having been made by one subsidiary company from another, is in effect merely a transfer from department to department of virtually the same corporation and not a sale on which profit can be said to have been realized. The principle that profits must not be anticipated would seem therefore to be applicable in such instances, and it would follow that a reserve should be provided equal to the amount by which such merchandise at intercompany prices exceeds its actual manufacturing cost.

In the annual report of the United States Steel Corporation for 1911 it is stated that these intercompany profits, which formerly were segregated as part of the surplus account, but included among the inventories, had been eliminated from the surplus account and the inventories correspondingly reduced. The report stated that:

Inventory valuations as stated are on the basis of the actual purchase or production cost of the materials to the respective subsidiary companies holding the same, unless such cost was above the market value on December 31, 1911, in which case the market price was used. But as stated in previous annual reports, the valuations on the basis indicated include, in respect of such commodities in stock at the close of the year as had been purchased by one subsidiary company from another, an amount of profits accrued thereon to the subsidiaries selling the same or furnishing service in connection therewith. These profits are not, however, carried into the currently reported earnings of the entire organization until converted into cash or a cash asset to it, being meanwhile segregated and carried in a specific surplus account which is practically a guarantee fund for these profits so locked up in inventories pending their realization in cash. In order to present the accounts on even a more conservative basis than heretofore observed, it was decided in this year's consolidated general balance sheet to state the amount of the specific surplus account referred to as a reduction in the total valuation at which all inventories are carried in current assets. Accordingly, in the subjoined table the surplus account in question is likewise shown. This plan results in there being carried in the combined assets for all of the companies the inventories of those materials and products on hand which have been transferred and sold from one subsidiary company to another, at net values which are substantially the production cost to the respective subsidiary companies furnishing the same. The net valuation thus obtained and shown for the total inventories of all materials and products is largely below the market value of the same.

This is sound and conservative accounting and should be

followed by every corporation which desires to allow the future to reap the benefit, if any, of future transactions, rather than to sell goods to itself at a profit.

Sales for Future Delivery: As mentioned under "Work in Progress," it is customary in many lines of business to solicit and accept orders for future delivery. Where the expenses of taking the orders have been incurred and where the goods themselves are on hand ready for delivery, it may seem ultra-conservative to advocate waiting for actual shipments before taking credit for the profit thereon. Nevertheless, this practice is generally followed by successful concerns, whereas the unsuccessful business man, in his attempts to bolster up a tottering business, usually anticipates every profit in sight and forgets the accrued expenses.

Theoretically if goods have been sold and are ready for shipment and the terms of the order permit immediate shipment, it may be assumed that a cause of action has so nearly arisen that no great harm could follow if the goods were entered as a sale, accounts receivable were debited, and the profit and loss account increased by the profit. But every business man knows that up to the instant of shipment, and sometimes afterwards, cancellations are received and accepted, or a fire or some other unexpected occurrence may operate to prevent the consummation of what appeared to be a sure thing.

In the annual report of the International Harvester Company for 1911 appears the following comment on this point:

> Assuming a continuance of present credit methods and the same proportion of forward sales, it is considered advisable to gradually establish a contingent reserve for deferred profits on forward sales. Theoretically and technically, a profit is earned when the sale is made, but when the actual realization of the profit on certain sales is deferred a considerable time beyond the close of the fiscal year, it is obviously a conservative and sensible policy to establish a contingent reserve to meet this condition inherent in the business. This policy prevents the misleading transfer of book earnings to surplus, where a long period of time elapses between the date of the sale and the realization of the profit in cash.

The balance sheet of the company shows a reserve for unrealized profits of $2,500,000 which has been accumulating for some years.

The conservative business man does not and will not anticipate the profits on goods ordered but not shipped; the conservative auditor will not certify to accounts which are prepared on any such basis. For a legal discussion of this question see the American Malting decision (page 595).

Participations and Underwritings: During recent years bankers have extended the privilege of participating with themselves in underwritings and purchases to a considerable number of investors and others. It is, therefore, not an unusual occurrence to see some reference to such participation in books of account.

Perhaps a majority of underwritings yield a net profit to participants, but many wind up with a loss. Interim accounts are reports of progress only and may be founded on the quotation of a supported market, so that it is most unsafe to take into account any profit at all until it is realized in cash.

This rule applies with equal force where securities of a new corporation are distributed as a bonus. There may be a market price in effect which would insure a handsome profit, but such quotations may be nominal only. The sale of a part of the participation at a profit on the purchase price should be applied against the entire purchase in order to write down its book cost. This is based on the same general principle, viz., that the market may be a fictitious one and not to be depended upon.

Profit on Sale of Assets: It may be that a profit has been realized on the sale of a portion of the fixed assets of a concern. Legally this profit may be carried to surplus and distributed as a dividend, but such a course is apt to create a false impression on stockholders. It is much better to carry such an item to an account whose caption indicates the character of the entries therein, and which may be carried on a balance sheet as a separate section of the surplus account. Under such circumstances it will not appear to be applicable to dividend distributions and can be held as a contingent reserve against possible losses on other capital adjustments.

Appreciation in Value of Assets: It has been intimated elsewhere in this book that appraisal companies are apt to certify to valuations in excess of book figures. It must be said in favor of these companies that they seem to carry on their appraisals in a careful and conscientious manner and it may be that the rise in the prices of materials and labor during the last ten or fifteen years justifies their apparent overvaluations.

Unfortunately many business men who secure an appraisal which sets forth that their buildings and machinery are, on the basis of a replaceable valuation less depreciation, worth more than they cost originally, wish to set up on their books and statements this diagnosis, and do not like to be told that they are making trouble for themselves. They have a larger valuation to wipe out by depreciation reserves, and thus, in a sense, they are increasing their cost of production. After a credit to surplus account is once made it is most unlikely that any part thereof will be used except for dividends.

The law on the subject of profits is not well settled and will not be, so long as the majority of lawyers retain their profound ignorance of accounts, but it is quite likely that no legal obstacle would prevent a corporation from revaluing part of its assets and applying the excess so raised to surplus available for dividends. With the law in such an unsatisfactory condition it remains for the professional auditor to educate the business public to the principle that it is not only foolhardy but unscientific to write up the value of an asset which is not for sale and which therefore cannot be represented by cash or its equivalent. Funds for dividends should be realized from the earnings, otherwise the working capital of the company is permanently depleted if a cash dividend is declared out of surplus created in the manner stated.

There may be in exceptional cases an obvious rise in value of an item of fixed assets, but a footnote on the balance sheet is all that is required to secure the benefit of an increased credit rating, and any adjustment of the account in the books by increasing the asset and crediting surplus is rarely permitted by good accounting practice.

Professional auditors should interest themselves in the corporation laws of their respective States and assist in the enactment of statutes comprehensive enough to cover the points just discussed.

CHAPTER XIV

PROFIT AND LOSS ACCOUNT (Continued)

EXPENSES AND LOSSES

THE several accounts which include in more or less detail the charges against or deductions from the earnings of an enterprise are fully described in Chapter XIX, "The Detailed Audit of Expenses." There are, however, some accounts which do not arise out of cash transactions and others about which more can be said. These accounts will now have our attention.

Reserves: We have discussed on other pages the following reserve accounts:

Bad Debts, page 297.
Accrued Expenses, page 200.
Depreciation, Exhaustion, etc., Chapter XXI.
Obsolescence, page 199.
Contingencies, page 165.
Sinking-Fund Accounts, pages 135, 177.

The question now arises as to how and when these charges should appear in a current profit and loss account. The fact is that they do not as a rule appear in the current profit and loss account at all.

A fair proportion of the ten per cent of the business enterprises of this country who do consult professional accountants heed the advice given and include among their expenses, or deductions from income, *all* of the costs of doing business, and the words "net profit" are not used except after full allowance has been made for keeping the capital intact. Most of the remaining ninety per cent, and those who consult but who do not heed the professional auditor, however, include among their earnings every dollar of possible income, but from such earnings are deducted only such costs and expenses as are apparent and easily ascertained, the balance being designated as "net profit." This balance is carried to surplus and is thereafter referred to as the profit earned during the period stated. Subsequently (but only if the period has been a prosperous one) various deductions are made from surplus, covering depreciation, adjustment of inventories, writing off of accounts receivable, etc.

This practice seems hopeless to the auditor who is familiar with actual conditions and who knows that about ninety-nine per cent of such deductions were direct charges against earnings and that most of the items could have been included in the current profit and loss statements. But business men will fool themselves, and corporation officers and directors will fool their stockholders, and attempt to fool the public. However, a slight, but perceptible, progress is being made, and it is inevitable that some day the words "net profit" will have the same meaning as the word "sterling" on silver. Laws and custom will decree that the issuing of false statements such as are now spread broadcast will be a punishable offense.

It is regrettable but true that many financial writers of ability who should, and perhaps do, know better, are responsible for much of the present unsatisfactory state of affairs in this respect. Just as surely as a corporation does issue a carefully prepared balance sheet and profit and loss statement, probably one certified to by reputable auditors, in which proper deductions are made to cover the items heretofore referred to, one or more of these writers will learnedly analyze its contents for the edification of the investing public. *Almost invariably* they will ignore the deductions for depreciation, etc., and solemnly state that during the period the corporation "earned" a given per cent on the capital—carrying out the rate to several decimal places. They may mention incidentally that *from the profits* there were certain deductions, thus emphasizing their own opinion that the actual profit was the one used as a basis for calculating the rate earned, and that the deductions were purely voluntary.

When legislative investigations are instituted, these figures are also the ones used, and the fallacy has been carried so far that some corporations that have not and never can earn a dividend on their common stocks are cited as having realized large earnings. In the case of the United States Steel Corporation nearly all of the financial writers, and certainly all of the statesmen (?), who have investigated its affairs state its net earnings over a period of years as many millions of dollars greater than the accounts of the corporation itself show.

What is the real trouble? Surely accurate accounts are desired. Is it because the tendency to overstate profits and understate losses is so general among business men that no standard exists?

Perhaps public accountants are themselves somewhat to blame for present conditions. Have they always been keen to make all the deductions of which they have any knowledge from earnings before designating any one sum as "net profit"?

The fact is that, because some of the reserves for depreciation, etc., are more or less difficult to ascertain, it has been fairly general to omit them entirely, or qualify the account by stating that the profits are so and so exclusive of some very large costs and expenses. Is it not peculiar that this action on the part of the auditor exactly fits in with the wishes of the client who knowingly overstates his profits? Candidly, is it not possible to estimate more closely on an allowance for depreciation than on the valuations of fixed assets or current inventories to which the auditor so cheerfully certifies?

Depreciation: The question of depreciation is important enough to require an entire chapter for its discussion (see Chapter XXI), but at this point it is in order to consider whether or not depreciation is to be included among the cost and expense items in the current profit and loss account.

In the preceding section attention was called to the general practice of omitting this and other items from ordinary operating accounts. Accountants of experience defend this practice on the ground that where depreciation has not been calculated at all, or where an arbitrary amount has been set aside, the task of determining a fair allowance—one that can be included among operating costs without detracting from the value of the entire statement—is too onerous to handle, with the result that costs are compiled without any allowance for depreciation. It is, of course, assumed that mention is made of the omission before any final figures are certified to.

It will always be admitted that wear and tear, and perhaps obsolescence, is going on all the time. If not admitted in so many words, the repairs and maintenance accounts speak for themselves. The usual and time-worn argument against provision for deterioration is that constant attention is given to the upkeep of the plant and renewals and repairs are looked after as soon as, or before, occasion demands.

Disregarding for the moment the fact that there is always a considerable amount of *accrued* wear and tear not apparent enough to necessitate immediate attention, there is to be considered the question whether the renewals and repairs which will be imperative, and which are always included among the expenses or costs, recur regularly enough to be charged up as incurred without upsetting the equilibrium of the accounts, or whether in the ordinary course of affairs the amounts fluctuate so greatly that factory managers are justified in leaving the items out of consideration in self-defense, as otherwise their costs would vary to such an extent that comparative records would be ludicrous.

In the case of fuel, for example, no such difficulty arises. Purchases and consumption run along regularly and no one would think of omitting the cost thereof. Now wherein lies the essential difference between the cost of fuel consumed under a boiler and the accruing loss on the purchase price of the boiler itself? Both are consumed in the process of manufacturing. The cost of both must be reimbursed from the proceeds of the sale of the product manufactured, or the capital of the concern will be depleted. Capital depletion is exactly what happens in thousands of cases. The cost of fuel is made a part of the cost of the product, but for some mysterious reason the cost of the boilers is provided in some other way, or at least that is the effect of the accounting system followed.

The most flagrant fallacy is found in connection with the accounts of the first year's operations of a new plant. The management, if sane, must know that the buildings and machinery will not last forever and that into every unit of production there has gone some part of the entire cost of the plant. It would be ridiculous to charge the total cost of buildings and machinery into the operations of the first year, but is it not equally unsound to make no charge whatever thereto merely because the exact amount of the charge is somewhat difficult to ascertain?

Accounting difficulties are comparative only, and accurate

accounts always require careful and intelligent attention. If the same thought were given to calculating the proper proportion of the cost of a boiler, which forms a part of the cost of operation, as is given to determining the basic costs of other elements which enter into the manufacturing operations of a modern plant, the amount arrived at would be quite close enough to form a dependable item of prime cost.

Professional auditors fail in their duty whenever they allow an opportunity to pass which might permit them to elucidate the foregoing principle. Thousands of enterprises have gone into bankruptcy solely because their accounts never exhibited the full cost of their product. As soon as accounting practice and procedure and commercial common sense are developed to the point where an allowance for depreciation is made just as much a part of prime cost as labor or materials, a considerable number of business failures will be prevented.

Obsolescence: The author is not prepared at this time to support the contention that an allowance for obsolescence is an item of prime cost as is the case with depreciation. The latter is certain and cannot be avoided any more than taxes or death.

Obsolescence is never certain. It is true that most of our modern machinery has superseded other machinery which was not worn out, and the plant of ten years ago which counted on a twenty-year life for its equipment and set up a depreciation reserve on that basis has not been able to renew that machinery out of the reserve.

Take the case of a machine costing $1,000 in 1903 with an estimated life of fifteen years and a scrap value of $100. There would have been $900 to charge to operations and a depreciation reserve based on the expected life would be conservative accounting. In 1910 it is found that the machine is obsolete and a new one costing $1,500 is purchased, but the new one has twice the capacity of the old. Here we find our answer to a large extent. An old machine will not be superseded by a new one unless the latter has greater efficiency or capacity, and this supplies authority for capitalizing part of the cost of the new machine.

It is obvious that obsolescence cannot be foreseen, and any attempt to reduce the contingency to a definite allowance to form part of current operating costs would defeat its own purpose. In view of the rapid strides in all of the mechanical sciences, obsolescence is likely to continue to be a serious factor in the ultimate cost of producing manufactured goods. Therefore, wherever possible, a reserve should be created to meet the possibility, but the reserve should be provided for out of profits before stating the surplus applicable to dividends and never as an item of prime cost.

Accrued Expenses, etc.: It is perhaps superfluous to mention that the items of expenses in a profit and loss account embrace those which have accrued during the period, whether paid for or not. At the closing date all accrued expenses, rents, taxes, interest, and similar items should be ascertained and entered as liabilities on one side and charged to their respective expense accounts on the other.

As many of these expenses are more or less unusual in their nature, it seems unavoidable that some are omitted. The question then arises in subsequent audits as to whether the items applying to prior periods should be charged to surplus or included among the current expenses of the period in which paid. There are two reasons in favor of the latter practice and no good reason in favor of the former. In the first place, where charges are made against an old book surplus it simply means that so far as published accounts go they are never in evidence. That is, the items were not known at the time and were therefore omitted from the period in which they belonged, and being eliminated from the period in which paid they practically disappear.

The most valuable records compiled are comparative schedules of earnings and expenses, and where these are carried along from year to year it is practically impossible to adjust reports which are perhaps a year old and of which frequent use has been made. Therefore proper accounting practice permits the inclusion of such items in the current profit and loss account, without calling special attention to the matter, unless the items are large enough to alter materially the results. Where the items are comparatively small it may be assumed that corresponding items are omitted from the current accounts and will have to be taken care of in the subsequent period.

This must not be construed as an excuse for closing accounts before every known liability is taken into consideration. The auditor who does not satisfy himself that all known liabilities and those which should be known are included in a balance sheet is guilty of negligence and deserves any consequence which may ensue.

Cash Discounts: Where it is customary to permit trade debtors to deduct a discount for cash within a limited period these deductions are entered in a separate column of the cash book. The discount allowed up to the date of the closing will, of course, appear in the books, preferably in a separate ledger account.

The aggregate of such allowances should be entered among the expenses of the business and not as a direct deduction from gross earnings. The theory is that the discount allowed represents a premium paid for prompt attention and for the use of the money at an earlier date than it would be received if no inducement were made for prepayment. Where the items are strictly cash discounts, and are not permitted if the debtor does not pay within the limit, then the total allowance is clearly an expense and should not be charged against sales as if it represented an abatement of the purchase price of the goods.

Trade Discounts: The author, in common with most practitioners, has always stated that trade discounts were direct deductions from invoices and should not appear in the books of account of the seller or the purchaser.

It is true, however, that in some trades considerable importance is placed upon the variations in trade discounts, and it would seem to be in order that the accountancy student should be given an opportunity to decide for himself whether trade discounts have any place in books of account. This point assumes importance in auditing because the auditor cannot very well report the amount of trade discounts given or received unless the items have been separated throughout the period covered by the profit and loss account.

At the request of the author the "case" for trade discounts was stated by John R. Wildman, C. P. A., as follows:

The general practice is to deduct trade discounts from the face of the purchase and sales invoices. It is claimed, however, that in large organizations, where the fixing of prices is delegated by the administrative officers to the respective heads of purchasing and sales departments, the recording of the data in question facilitates the compilation of statistics which will show the average discounts and thus serve somewhat as an index to the efficiency of the heads of the respective departments as well as to serve as a guide to the administrative officers in reaching conclusions and formulating policies concerning these phases of the business.

Theoretically, it appears to have some scientific foundation. Practically, it is questionable whether the amount of work involved is warranted by the purpose for which the data are used.

Accounting instruction, in my opinion, should be as broad as possible. Every phase of a subject should be discussed. All the facts should be presented. The relative advantages and disadvantages of various methods should be explained. After discussion the instructor should state the preference dictated by the general practice so far as it can be ascertained. Further, the relation of trade discounts to cash discounts, and the relation of both to the purchase and sales prices, seem worthy of discussion.

Disposition of Profit after Being Determined: When an auditor has determined the amount which he is willing to certify represents "net profit," the difficult part of his task is completed. Probably he will not be asked whether the amount shown should be paid out in dividends or transferred to surplus, and as a matter of principle he is not concerned. It may be, however, that his opinion will be asked, in which event he may be able to suggest such a disposition of the profit as will conserve the best interests of the concern.

Whether to declare a cash or a stock dividend is a question which may very properly be referred to the auditor. There should be no transfer of profits to general surplus account unless the entire amount is applicable to dividends when and if declared. The net profit for the period is first shown, then any transfers which have been authorized by the board are deducted, the balance being carried to surplus. This practice has been followed by some of our best-managed corporations for a number of years, and has the sanction of law in that the courts have repeatedly held that the directors of a corporation need not declare dividends unless they so desire, provided they can show that the funds which would be required for dividend disbursements can be used to better advantage in the business.

It is carrying this discretion to an extreme which stockholders never contemplate when they purchase stock, for the directors to invest the surplus in securities the control of which is not a necessary incident to the carrying on of the business for which the corporation was organized.

In England the law is as follows:

English Companies (Consolidation) Act 1908. Table A. Section 99. The directors may, before recommending any dividend, set aside out of the profits of the company such sums as they think proper as a reserve or reserves which shall, at the discretion of the directors, be applicable for meeting contingencies, or for equalizing dividends, or for any other purpose to which the profits of the company may be properly applied, and, pending such application, may, at the like discretion, either be employed in the business of the company or be invested in such investments (other than shares of the company) as the directors may from time to time think fit.

An auditor will recommend the setting aside of reserves for contingencies or for the equalization of dividends or other reasonable purposes so long as the financial condition of a corporation demands conservative financing, but when it finds itself so well off that it can not only pay all of its debts, but has cash enough to purchase investment securities, then the auditor had better allow the board itself to take all the responsibility. The practice savors too much of paternalism. Stockholders are said to forget dividends quickly, and it is therefore not thought safe to pay out big dividends in good years and small or no dividends in poor years. But some stockholders are quite as well qualified as the directors to invest their earnings and prefer some variation in the dividend rate to an attempt to build up a big surplus and indefinitely postpone the distribution of the earnings of a particularly prosperous period.

PRINCIPAL AND INCOME

It has been pointed out in other chapters of this book that the distinction between principal and income (or capital and revenue) must ever be in the auditor's mind. It affects the balance sheet as well as the profit and loss account and is a fact to be faced rather than a theory to be played with.

As the matter is discussed fully under various headings, it is not necessary here to review the attitude of the auditor with respect to determining whether a given item belongs to principal or to income, because by reason of his training and experience he will decide each question according to its merits, with sound accounting principles to guide him. It is at present doubtful, however, whether the courts can be depended upon to decide as equitably.

Dividends Must Not Be Paid from Capital: While questions with respect to capital and revenue arise in every branch of accounts, many of them are not met squarely, but are passed over undecided. Issue is not usually joined until the question of a dividend arises. Directors and managers who will not admit that depreciation is an operating expense will nevertheless hesitate before voting for or advocating the payment of a dividend before there have been set aside sufficient reserves to maintain the capital intact.

Section 23 of the New York Stock Corporation Law provides:

> The directors of a stock corporation shall not make dividends, except from the surplus profits arising from the business of such corporation; nor divide, withdraw, or in any way pay to the stockholders, or any of them, any part of the capital of such corporation, or reduce its capital stock, except as authorized by law. In case of any violation of the provisions of this section, the directors under whose administration the same may have happened, except those who may have caused their dissent therefrom to be entered at large upon the minutes of such directors at the time, or were not present when the same happened, shall jointly and severally be liable to such corporation and to the creditors thereof to the full amount of the capital of such corporation so divided, withdrawn, paid out, or reduced.

The English Companies (Consolidation) Act, 1908, contains the following provisions relative to dividends:

> Table A. Section 95. The company in general meeting may declare dividends, but no dividend shall exceed the amount recommended by the directors.
>
> Section 96. The directors may from time to time pay to the members such interim dividends as appear to the directors to be justified by the profits of the company.
>
> Section 97. No dividend shall be paid otherwise than out of profits.

There is no practical difference between this law and that of New York State. In neither jurisdiction is it permissible to pay a dividend unless the capital is unimpaired. Where the assets *have* depreciated in value and the depreciation is not provided for out of earnings, the capital is impaired.

There are undoubtedly many corporations in existence today whose dividends are being or have been paid out of capital. If stockholders appreciated their rights, many directors would be called to account for this.

The most notable case in the United States wherein it was shown that dividends were paid out of capital instead of net profits or surplus is the American Malting case, which is fully reported on page 595. If an auditor finds himself in disagreement with a board of directors over the allocation of items to capital or revenue he may find it salutary to request them to read extracts from this case.

Decedents' Estates: The distinction between principal and income assumes more importance in some trust estates than in ordinary commercial practice, because while with the latter the result of a misapplication of an item may affect the ultimate solvency of an enterprise, in respect to an estate the decision of a court as to a dividend being principal or income may actually deprive a dependent of the necessities of life.

Wasting Assets: It is permissible for a mining company to pay out in dividends all realizations from its operations, but its stockholders are on notice that the capital of the company is being dissipated. On the other hand, if a steel company owns ore lands it must not treat the entire net income from ore sales as profit, but is obliged to allocate the realizations into principal and income. The principal must be kept intact in order that the capital may not be depleted. The income may be distributed in dividends.

In an estate the practice (in the absence of testamentary or statutory provisions to the contrary) is similar to that of mining companies, that is, the tenant for life may work a mine or a quarry or cut down timber and is not required to make good the depletion. In the case of buildings, etc., the rule is different; they must be maintained, ordinary wear and tear excepted.

Interest: Interest and similar income is said to accrue from day to day so that the full amount accrued to the date of the decedent's death becomes principal.

It has been held in at least one State that where the interest is represented by a coupon the amount thereof is not apportionable, but represents a separate contract to pay a definite amount at a certain time. The distinction between such a contract and a registered bond, where the interest is paid by check and is not represented by coupons, is a fine one, rather beyond the comprehension of a layman.

Dividends: The date of the declaration of a dividend fixes its standing as principal or income; if declared before the decedent's death it is principal, even though it is payable after the date of death. It accrues wholly on the date of declaration, i. e., there is no apportionment based on the period it covers.

Stock, and Extraordinary Cash Dividends: The foregoing rule does not always apply to dividends which are declared out of the regular order. It is rather popular for corporations and banks to accumulate their excess earnings for a long period of years and then make an extraordinary distribution at one time, in cash or in stock. In most cases, and in all cases where full and correct accounts have been published periodically, these hoarded earnings become identified with the capital of the undertaking, and furthermore are reflected in the market price of the stock.

From an accountant's point of view it seems absurd that a life tenant, to whom there is devised the income for life on, say, ten shares of stock, should receive as *income,* say, ninety shares of the same stock, thus vitally depreciating the estate left for the remainderman. But the courts have so held in spite of the injustice of the result. In some jurisdictions, however, the decisions have been to the effect that extraordinary dividends are distributions of principal.

Space does not permit a lengthy discussion of this subject. Any one interested and seeking further particulars is referred to a very able and interesting paper on the subject by William F. Weiss, C. P. A., of New York.

CHAPTER XV

CERTIFICATES AND REPORTS

WHAT shall it benefit an auditor if he perform the highest grade of professional work and be unable to present his results in a form acceptable to and understandable by his client? Yet this happens every day, chiefly because some auditors apparently prepare reports for themselves rather than for those they are supposed to enlighten. An engineer builds a bridge for others to use. It is useless unless it is safe and convenient. The man who rides across it does not care how many difficult problems were encountered in the building, nor how they were solved; he is content to judge the engineer by results. So with a banker or a business man. He employs an auditor because he wants results, and he wants results which he can use without having to follow in the auditor's footsteps and traverse the same jungles of figures and grapple with the same problems through which the results were accomplished.

As pointed out in Chapter VI, the auditor should prepare for the termination before he starts, and as the consummation of an audit must include a report on his work, this fact must be kept in view during the progress of the work.

If feasible, the auditor should picture himself in his client's position and reason out what he would want if the other man were doing the work. The examination may have started under most favorable auspices; it may have been executed in an unexcelled manner, but if it is not delivered properly the first two factors go for naught.

It hardly seems necessary to state that reports should be typewritten and an office copy preserved, yet auditors are frequently induced to submit manuscripts of which no copy has been retained. Subsequent embarrassment has followed this unwise practice, through loss of the original, unauthorized alterations therein, etc. It is better to keep a client waiting than to run such a risk. Promises to return for rewriting are not kept, as a rule, and the auditor who relies on these and similar promises ignores a precaution which experience has demonstrated to be valuable.

Something More Than Figures are Wanted in a Report: A prominent banker recently said to the author that most of the reports submitted to him were lacking in information which the auditor was peculiarly able to furnish. He said that auditors who are retained to investigate earnings, expenses, assets, and liabilities, frequently going back over a long series of years, have an unusually good opportunity, for instance, to size up the personnel of an organization, particularly the office staff, but also to a certain extent the other departments.

A banker is obliged to vouch for an enterprise as a whole when he offers its securities to his customers. He wants the assets and liabilities and net profits stated in proper form for publication, and requires a certificate attached which reads well, but he wants a supplemental report for his own use expressing the auditor's opinions on just as many points as the latter can comment on intelligently. He does *not* want trial balances and lists of debtors and creditors and memoranda of errors in postings and similar bookkeeping data. He will read only what is of interest to him and these things are not.

The same principle applies to the client whose own accounts are being reported upon by an auditor. The auditor secures access to records which the usual executive does not see, and has a chance to observe the staff under conditions which do not exist when the boss is around. This does not contemplate that the auditor will report trivial matters which will make the staff hostile without being of any real benefit to the client.

Elsewhere in this book it has been pointed out that the successful auditor must secure and retain the hearty coöperation of the office staff, and this fact is here reiterated as a reminder that a report should be a constructive document and helpful to the client's staff as well as to the client. Occasions may arise where the auditor cannot prevent his report from arousing hostility on the part of the staff. If this must be, let it be because vital defects are criticized and not trivial ones.

Terminology: It is most important that an auditor express his findings and opinions in good simple English. His aim must be to write so clearly that his report cannot possibly be misunderstood. He will not err if he follows the simple language of the Bible or of Lincoln rather than the involved style of Henry James.

It has been said that accounts are the language in which business transactions are written. It is incumbent on the auditor to exemplify the fact that this language is a simple one, and readily understood. Classics may be read in dead languages, but commonplace business history is better understood if written in a live tongue.

Figures in themselves are of no value, but correctly arranged and properly interpreted, the accounts of a business organization furnish a basis for knowledge which is indispensable in the successful conduct of any enterprise.

The truth *may* exist in a report poorly written, but if it is not evident to any interested party, then the language used is not well chosen.

Scope of Report: Certificates and reports, if true, must be founded on the work which has been done. A report should be a narrative of facts. It may include a short history of the enterprise under audit, particularly where it is intended for the perusal of those whose information on this point is limited.

A certificate should be brief and to the point and embody conclusions based solely on the auditor's investigations.

A report is for the edification of others, and it is the duty of the auditor to make it interesting. The most successful auditors pay much attention to this aspect of their work, so that clients are glad to get their reports and read them.

How much space should be given to the detailed work done by the auditor? The average client does not care how the auditor arrived at his results—all he wants is information. He asks: "Are the accounts correct, or, if not correct, wherein are they inaccurate, and how shall they be improved?"

Some auditors who have not verified every item on the books think that they escape responsibility by detailing all of the ground covered. If work is omitted which should have been performed, a carefully worded report pointing out that other work was done and omitting any mention of the work in question cannot be used to escape liability.

Reports must be founded on facts discovered, verified, or compiled by the auditor, but it is neither desirable nor necessary to comment on immaterial matters and furnish superfluous schedules.

The purpose for which the report is to be used must in every case be carefully considered before it is written. For instance, a prospective borrower does not want an auditor to submit a balance sheet which is accompanied by comments on the system of accounts, nor does he want long schedules of clerical errors. On the other hand, it is quite in order to submit a balance sheet accompanied by qualifying comments, provided the changes which the auditor thinks should be made in the balance sheet figures are not permissible in the books, or where balance-sheet items are not sufficiently self-explanatory.

Where balance sheets are not designed for publication the most satisfactory report consists of the following:

Certificate of Audit.

Comments on Audit and on Balance Sheet.

Balance Sheet, supported by detailed schedules wherever they are necessary or deemed to be of practical use.

Profit and Loss statement, divided into sections or groups and supported by schedules if required.

Special Schedules.

Certificate of Audit: The certificate should be as short and concise as possible. Attempts to qualify a certificate are not looked on with favor, and unless an auditor has been greatly restricted in the scope of the audit, it is his duty to conform as nearly as possible to the "audited and found correct" style. Of course, where qualifications are necessary they must go in without fear or favor, but the point the author has in mind is the evident fear of many accountants that their certificates will be taken seriously and acted upon, and in this fear they hedge them about with all sorts of ambiguous qualifications. Sometimes they sound like arguments, i. e., the certificate will read in effect that if so and so were done, so and so would be the result. Most business men will listen to sound arguments *before* the report is written, and the changes recommended might as well be made in the balance sheet and thus permit the giving of an unqualified certificate, which is always the most desirable.

A form, variations of which are used by leading auditors, is as follows:

THE BOARD OF DIRECTORS,
A B C COMPANY.

We have audited the accounts of the A B C Company for the year ended December 31, 1912.

We verified the Cash, the Inventories of Raw Materials and Supplies, Work in Progress, and Finished Product, and the other current assets as of December 31, 1912.

The Raw Materials and Supplies on hand and in process of manufacture were priced at cost, except that where market values at December 31, 1912, were less than cost, the inventories were reduced to market values. Sufficient reserves have been made for probable losses on notes and accounts receivable.

We examined the charges to capital accounts and find them to represent actual additions to the Company's property. Ample allowances have been made for depreciation of plants. All known liabilities have been included in the accounts.

WE HEREBY CERTIFY that in our opinion the accompanying balance sheet and profit and loss statement correctly presents the financial condition of the Company as of December 31, 1912, and its operations for the year ended with that date.

(Signed) X Y Z,
Certified Public Accountants.

If qualifications are necessary, the above form can be used as a basis and the qualifications mentioned in their proper place.

Where a shorter form is wanted for a certificate which is to be appended to the condensed balance sheet used by note brokers and others, the following is acceptable:

We have audited the accounts of the D E F Company for the year ended November 30, 1912, and

WE CERTIFY that the above balance sheet is in our opinion a correct statement of the financial condition of the Company as of November 30, 1912, and that the accompanying profit and loss statement is correct.

(Signed) R S T,
Certified Public Accountants.

The question sometimes arises as to how to submit a balance sheet and report thereon when the audit is made so long after the balance sheet date that adjustments cannot be made as of that date, and the auditor cannot certify that the balance sheet "agrees with the books and is correct." The best way is to have the entries journalized before the report is written, and no matter how long after the date, the entries should read "as of" the date of the balance sheet, and when posted to the ledger the items should be connected with the closing date by a star, or asterisk. Subsequent trial balances and any subsequent references will then find the accounts in order, and there can be no difficulty if the necessity arises for their being reconciled with the balance sheet.

Wherever the auditor's recommendations as to adjustments of asset or liability items are not or cannot be adopted and recorded "as of" the date of the balance sheet, the most satisfactory form of report thereon is to submit the balance sheet as shown by the books and precede this with comments which will be bound with and permanently attached to the balance sheet, so that improper use cannot be made of the balance sheet by removing the qualifying comments.

Clients do not always appreciate the position of an auditor with respect to the use of balance sheets. Experience has shown that they frequently hope for a more favorable statement than they receive, and as the audit may be for the purpose of securing credit, an unfavorable statement places the client in an embarrassing position. Auditors must always be on their guard, therefore, that balance sheets made up by them and subject to qualification are not submitted in such form as will admit of their being separated from the qualifications.

Based on long experience of his own and other firms, the author believes that the only safe method of reporting is to use paper bearing one's own watermark. This is not very expensive when a considerable quantity of paper is used.

Where an auditor is able to construct his own balance sheet and can certify thereon that it is correct, it does not make any difference whether or not it is separated from the comments. In fact, it is usually preferable to submit such a balance sheet complete in itself.

Form of Balance Sheet: Many tiresome pages have been written explaining, or trying to explain, why it is that universal American custom decrees that assets shall be placed on the left hand side of the balance sheet and liabilities on the right hand side. The explanation is no more satisfactory than the reasons advanced by English authorities to support their custom of placing the liabilities on the left and the assets on the right.

The author ventures the following:

The English practice is purely the outcome of custom. A long time ago some one started that way and every one since has followed, until now the form has the sanction of law. (See forms prescribed under the English Companies Act.)

The only sound reason the author can think of for the custom is that a conservative Englishman looks for his liabilities first and then looks to see if he has enough assets to discharge them.

In the United States, accountancy has developed more scientifically than in England. If a short cut is logical we take it. When it was found that loose leaves were far more convenient and economical to handle than leaves bound permanently together, we adopted them. So with balance sheets. It was observed by accountants that the average American looks for his assets first and subsequently glances at his liabilities in order to assure himself that his excess of assets is as much as he believes it to be.

Furthermore, it is common sense for a man who decides to record his financial condition to place his possessions first. Frequently a man has few or no liabilities, so that the practice of stating the assets first, then the liabilities, if any, as a deduction therefrom, thus arriving at the surplus, is the logical presentation applicable to the great majority of business enterprises in the United States.

What may be styled the account form of balance sheet is one with the assets on the left and the liabilities and net worth on the right, this permitting an agreement between the totals of the two sides. Sometimes a deficit exists and the bookkeeper's passion for making things balance is so strong that the deficit is included among the assets! The almost incredible result is that practically all published balance sheets consist of a confusion of figures on both sides which exactly agree in total. The reader thereof who is not trained in accounts does not comprehend the details, but he is reassured in some mysterious way when he finally discovers that the liabilities at least do not exceed the assets.

The author's conception of an ideal balance sheet is one which will set forth:

(1) The assets, properly valued and grouped, and arranged in the order of their availability.

English law and custom may be against this form, but nevertheless it is the most readable and the most understandable to the average business man. Furthermore, it has the sanction of the bankers and credit men of this country, who use balance sheets oftener than any other class. (See official forms, pages 217-223.)

(2) The liabilities also properly grouped and arranged in the order they will, or should, be discharged.

(3) If possible the excess of the assets or the liabilities should now be shown in order that there may be clearly apparent to anyone interested the net worth, or capital and surplus, of the enterprise.

(4) A statement showing to whom the excess belongs or by whom it is due. That is, if a corporation, there should be shown the capital stock issued, the addition thereto if a surplus of assets exists, or the deduction therefrom if there is a deficiency.

ASSETS			
Current Assets:			
Cash		$0.	$
Notes and Accounts Receivable		0.	
Inventories		0.	0.
Deferred Charges to Operation:			
Prepaid Insurance, etc.			0.
Plant Assets:			
Real Estate		0.	
Machinery, Fixtures, etc.		0.	0.
Good Will, Patents, etc.			0.
LIABILITIES			
Notes Payable	$0.		
Accounts Payable	0.		
Accrued Wages	0.	0.	
Bonded Debt		0.	
Reserves		0.	0.
EXCESS OF ASSETS (OR NET WORTH)			
Represented by:			
Capital Stock		0.	
Surplus (or Deficit)		0.	0.

The most popular form among large industrial corporations which publish their balance sheet is as follows:

ASSETS		LIABILITIES		
Plant Assets:		Capital Stock		$o.
Including Real Estate, Machinery, Patents, Good Will, etc. . . .	$o.	Bonded Debt		o.
		Current Liabilities:		
		Notes Payable .	o.	
		Accounts Payable	o.	
		Accrued Wages, etc.	o.	
				o.
Deferred Charges to Operations:		Reserves		o.
Insurance, Interest, etc., prepaid	o.	Surplus		o.
Current Assets:				
Inventories	o.			
Accounts and Notes Receivable	o.			
Cash	o.			
	oo.			oo.

But the above arrangement is not easy reading for one unaccustomed to accounts, and it presupposes that the reader can discriminate between actual liabilities and surplus. So long as it is unnecessary, it is unfortunate that the surplus must be included under a caption which is misleading.

The following form is preferable:

ASSETS			LIABILITIES AND CAPITAL		
Current Assets:			Current Liabilities:		
Cash	$o.		Notes and Accounts Payable		$o.
Notes and Accounts Receivable . .	o.	o.	Bonded Debt		o.
			Reserves		o.
Inventories . . .		o.			
Deferred Charges to Operation		o.	Total Liabilities . . .		o.
			Excess of Assets made up as follows:		
Plant Assets:			Capital Stock . .	o.	
Real Estate, etc. . .		o.	Surplus (or deficit)	o.	o.
Good Will, etc. . . .		o.			
Total Assets . . .		oo.	Total Liabilities and Capital . . .		oo.

It is asserted that there is a demand for the form of balance sheet at top of this page from those whose chief desire is to see the relation of the fixed assets to the capital stock. But this information could be more readily secured from the second form, because where fixed items appear first it is usual to place the capital stock first among the liabilities and the surplus last. As the surplus may be as large as or larger than the capital, it is very necessary to have these figures nearer together, as provided in the second form.

It is, of course, impossible to mention by name the assets and liabilities which are found in different enterprises, therefore these outline forms must be suggestive only. It is hoped that other chapters of this book in which is pointed out the importance of the auditor's placing himself as far as possible in the position of the one who is to use the accounts will be more helpful in framing a balance sheet than a set form, which might apply in a few cases, but which would be restrictive and therefore of little value in others.

One general principle which should be observed in all balance sheets is that the matter of the arrangement of the groups is not of so much importance as the relation of one to the other. That is, it does not greatly matter whether the fixed assets are first or last, but it is important that the balance sheet shall indicate, if at all possible, the relation of the fixed assets to the other assets and to the liabilities. For instance, a concern owning a million dollars of fixed assets should have a capital and surplus, or funded debt, of at least as much, otherwise the current liabilities would be excessive.

Statement Required by Banks: For some years bankers have required borrowers to furnish statements of their assets and liabilities. At first a uniform statement was not insisted on, but it was found that some borrowers were disinclined to submit full reports and others did not know what details the banker wanted. Individual banks thereupon compiled their own forms and furnished blanks to their customers. These blanks were by no means uniform, and as many borrowers used more than one bank, the diversity became a nuisance to both banks and borrowers. The former, in exchanging credit information with other banks, found comparisons difficult, and the latter were put to unnecessary trouble in arranging and rearranging their statements.

Finally an attempt was made through the various bankers' associations to formulate a uniform or standard blank which would embody the information most useful to banks. This plan was entirely successful and resulted in the present standard form of borrowers' statement. The form which is reproduced herewith is that officially adopted by the New York State Bankers' Association:

STANDARD FORM OF BORROWERS' STATEMENT

TO THE.....................BANK:

For the purpose of procuring credit from time to time with you for our negotiable paper or otherwise, we furnish the following as a true and accurate statement of our financial condition on....191..., which we may hereafter be considered as representing to be a true statement of our financial condition unless notice of change is given you.

ASSETS				
CASH on hand and in bank				
NOTES RECEIVABLE of customers (not transferred) .				
ACCOUNTS RECEIVABLE of customers (not transferred)				
NOTES AND ACCOUNTS RECEIVABLE of officers (not transferred)				
MERCHANDISE finished (how valued.......) .				
" unfinished (how valued.......) .				
" raw material (how valued.......) .				
LAND owned by corporation, used for this business .				
BUILDINGS owned by corporation, used for this business				
MACHINERY owned by corporation, used for this business				
....				
....				
....				
TOTAL				

LIABILITIES				
NOTES PAYABLE given for merchandise				
NOTES PAYABLE negotiated to own banks				
NOTES PAYABLE otherwise disposed of				
ACCOUNTS PAYABLE				
DEPOSITS OF MONEY WITH US				
....				
....				
BONDED DEBT (when due)				
MORTGAGE DEBT				
CHATTEL MORTGAGES				
....				
....				
....				
TOTAL LIABILITIES				
CAPITAL				
SURPLUS including UNDIVIDED PROFITS				
TOTAL				

STANDARD FORM OF BORROWERS' STATEMENT—Continued

CONTINGENT LIABILITY: Notes Receivable of customers Discounted or Sold and not included in assets enumerated above $..................

Other contingent liability......................... $...............

We Have Not Pledged or Assigned any of the above Accounts Receivable; our Assigned Accounts Receivable amount to....... $...............

Other assets used as collateral...

INSURANCE: on merchandise $...............buildings $............... machinery $................Total Insurance

BUSINESS and RESULTS: Annual Sales for the year ended..........191.. or from..........191..to..........191..

Gross Profits on Sales	for the same period $...........
Expense of Conducting Business	" " " "
Net Profit	" " " "
Other Income including investments	" " " "
Combined Profit	" " " "

DIVIDENDS PAID for the period.......191..to.........191..$..........

BAD DEBTS for the period.............191..to.........191..$..........

CAPITAL: Authorized $...............Issued $......................

Par Value $......per share

BANK ACCOUNTS: where kept...

MORTGAGES and BONDS on what assets a lien..........................

Average TERMS on which we SELL....................................

Average TERMS on which we BUY.....................................

TIME OF YEAR when NOTES and ACCOUNTS RECEIVABLE of CUSTOMERS, Uncollected, are generally maximum...................... minimum......................

TIME OF YEAR when STOCKS of MERCHANDISE on hand are generally maximum.............minimum................

TIME OF YEAR when LIABILITIES are maximum.......................... minimum................

STATEMENT: is it based on actual inventory?.......................... if so, Date................................

VERIFICATION: have the books been audited by a Certified Public Accountant?...............if so, Name and Date of Audit.............

(Sign corporation name)

....

Date Signed............191..

This form is more explicit and desirable than that officially recommended by the American Bankers' Association. In the New York State form the matter of hypothecations is brought prominently to the attention of the prospective borrower. In the light of many unfortunate experiences where liens on accounts and stock-in-trade have been concealed, the importance of this possibility is unquestioned.

Furthermore, in the American Bankers' form there is danger in the arrangement of the Assets and Liabilities in that Reserves are not deducted from the former nor included among the latter, thus permitting the inference that by deducting the liabilities *as shown* from the assets *as shown* the net worth of the corporation may be ascertained.

It is true that reserves are not liabilities, but where they are created in order to provide for depreciation, bad debts, etc., the aggregate thereof is a direct deduction from the assets, and borrowers should not be encouraged in the belief that a banker considers that the "total" assets and the "total" liabilities may be stated before consideration is given to items which are in fact directly related thereto.

The following is the "short form" recommended by the American Bankers' Association:

ASSETS					LIABILITIES				
Cash	....	......	......	....	Notes Payable	....	......	......	....
Bills Receivable (net)	....	......	......	....	Accounts Payable	....	......	......	....
Accounts Receivable (net)	....	......	......	....	Deposits	....	......	......	....
Merchandise	....	......	......	....	Bonded Debt	....	......	......	....
Land	....	......	......	....	Mortgages	....	......	......	....
Buildings	....	......	......	....	Accrued Liabilities	....	......	......	....
Machinery—Fixtures	....	......	......	....	TOTAL	....	......	......	....
....	....	......	......	....	Capital	....	......	......	....
....	....	......	......	....	Surplus—Profits	....	......	......	....
....	....	......	......	....	Reserves	....	......	......	....
TOTAL					TOTAL				

CONTINGENT LIABILITIES. On bills receivable discounted............................Other............................

CASH. On hand and in bank, $..................................Names of banks..................................

BILLS RECEIVABLE. Any overdue or doubtful?........Any from officers, directors, sub-companies, or similar sources?........

ACCOUNTS RECEIVABLE. State amount doubtful, not from customers or in any way not realizable within immediate future....

MERCHANDISE. Finished.........Unfinished.........Raw.........Valued at cost or market?.........Is all salable?........

LAND. Describe briefly...................................Assessed value................Market value................

BUILDINGS. Cost $..........................Age...............................Depreciation............................

MACHINERY AND FIXTURES. Cost $..................Depreciation...................Condition...................

OTHER ASSETS.

Are any of assets unavailable for paying debts?...................Losses....................

INSURANCE. State what kind and amount...

NOTES PAYABLE. To own banks.....................Through brokers....................Otherwise....................

ACCOUNTS PAYABLE. Terms of purchase?...........................Do you discount and anticipate?........................

DEPOSITS. Time or demand?........................From whom?........................Interest........................

BONDED DEBT AND MORTGAGES. Due?................Rate.................On what assets a lien?................

ACCRUED LIABILITIES. Itemize...

CAPITAL. Preferred Authorized $.....Issued $.....Dividends.....Common Authorized $.....Issued $.....Dividends $.....

RESERVES. Itemize...

NET SALES.

Last fiscal year		....
Cost of sales		———
Gross profit		
Interest, taxes, depreciation, etc.	....	
Dividends paid	....	———
Surplus for year		═══

Have the books been audited by a Certified Public Accountant?....If so, give name of firm and date of audit...........

CORPORATE NAME...

By...
(State officer's title)

Date signed...

Office address.......................................Nature of Business.......................................

Location of plants and branch offices...

To a professional auditor the question, "Have the books been audited by a Certified Public Accountant?" is of particular interest. This question was suggested by James G. Cannon, President of the Fourth National Bank of New York City, one of the foremost bankers of the country, who has for many years advised bankers to use professional auditors more generally.

Unfortunately for both bankers and auditors, the former have not had the nerve to take this advice except to a limited extent. There have, however, been some "horrible examples" where the calling in of auditors previous to making loans would have saved the banks millions of dollars.

It will be noticed that the bankers wish to read the statements just reproduced along the lines advocated on page 214 hereof; that is, they want to know about the assets in the order of their availability, and want to ascertain the liabilities in the order they must be discharged.

In order that there may here be a full presentation of the forms in general use throughout the United States, we will next consider the ones issued by the mercantile agencies. These forms are supplied to practically every business concern in existence, and are therefore more familiar to the average business man than any other. The arrangement is not ideal by any means and the information which may be gathered from it falls far short of that supplied by the bankers' and credit men's associations. It is possible that the agencies do not feel at liberty to request as full a statement as the others, but it is obvious that their forms might be improved without seriously affecting their chances of securing information. The corporation forms in use by the two large agencies are as follows:

FIRST FORM

STATEMENT OF FINANCIAL CONDITION

Name..

Engaged in the business of...

Located at..

From Inventory of..............19.. *Dated*.....................19..

Under what State laws incorporated?...............When?...............

Authorized Capital?................Subscribed Capital?.................

Preferred Stock?...................Common Stock?......................

Bonded Debt......................Bearing interest at..........per cent.

ASSETS

Stock on hand, raw and finished	$...............
Amount of book accounts considered good	....
Amount of notes considered good	....
Cash in Bank	....
Cash on hand	....
Machinery and fix ures	....
Any other assets, exclusive of patent rights.............	
....	
REAL ESTATE, consisting of......................	
....	....
Total Assets	$...............

LIABILITIES

For merchandise	$...............	
For machinery and fixtures . .	....	
For borrowed money . . .	....	
For mortgage on real estate . .	....	
For all other liabilities . . .	....	
Total Liabilities		$...............
Total Assets over Liabilities		$...............

Is the surplus at the risk of the business?..................................

Do you keep books of account of the business?...............................

If so, what books?...

Do you borrow on accounts receivable?..

Date last dividend declared......................How much..............

INSURANCE ON STOCK, $.............ON BUILDINGS, $...........

Annual rent, $...................Annual business, $...................

SECOND FORM

ASSETS..................19

Cash in banks	$................
Cash on hand	....
Notes receivable, actual value	....
Accounts receivable, actual value	....
Merchandise (finished and unfinished)	....
Raw material	....
Machinery and fixtures	....
Real Estate	....
Other investments (not including patents, trade-marks, patterns, etc.)	....
TOTAL ASSETS	$................

How much, if any, of above Accounts Receivable have been assigned or pledged for loans . . $...........

LIABILITIES...........................19

Capital stock paid in	$................
Surplus and undivided profits	....
Bills payable	....
Accounts payable	....
Bonded debt	....
Mortgage on real estate (not included as Bonded debt)	....
Chattel mortgage on all kinds of property	....
Borrowed money from banks (not included above)	....
" " " individuals (not included above)	....
All other liabilities	....
TOTAL LIABILITIES	$................

How much, if any, of the above indebtedness is past due . . . . $...............

CAPITAL

	Authorized	*Subscribed*	*Paid in*
Common Stock	$.............	$.............	$.............
Preferred Stock	$.............	$.............	$.............

HOW PAID IN:

In cash	$.............	
Patents, trade-marks, patterns, etc.	$.............	
In other property	$.............	$.............

Give particulars and the value of each kind of property......................

....

Amount of annual business	$.............
Amount of annual expense	$.............

Annual dividend...

Surplus (not including undivided profits) . . . . . $.............

Indebtedness of company to stockholders included in liabilities..............

Amount of insurance on merchandise . . . . . . $.............

Amount of insurance on buildings and plant . . . . $.............

Ever had a fire; if so, give particulars...

Other interests of *principal* directors..

CHAPTER XVI

CERTIFICATES AND REPORTS (Continued)

Statements Requested by Credit Managers: The scientific granting of credit requires a high degree of ability, and this is possessed by the modern credit manager, or he would not occupy the important position which he fills to-day. Nevertheless, he does not depend solely on the data he can secure from the mercantile agencies and similar sources, and many concerns have adopted their own system of credit reports from customers and prospective customers.

The form recommended and indorsed by the National Association of Credit Men does not differ materially from that used by bankers, but it is believed that the exact form will be of interest to those who are anxious to ascertain the point of view of men *to whom* reports are frequently addressed. As stated elsewhere, the auditor who prepares his reports in a form easily read and easily understood by those for whom they are intended will be the most successful.

Preceding the form is the following pertinent observation:

> Large assets are not always necessary to the creation of credit. What is most desirable is, that credit be in relative proportion to the actual assets. The giver of credit is a contributor of capital, and becomes, in a certain sense, a partner of the debtor, and, as such, has a perfect right to complete information of the debtor's condition at all times.

Those accountants who call a deficit an asset and classify capital stock and surplus as liabilities will be shocked to see the informality of the following form. It brings out in strong relief, almost brutally, the "total active business assets," and the "total business liabilities"; and it is evident from the spaces provided that the difference between the two must be the "net worth."

It is a corporation blank, but the intelligent mind that devised the form was not hampered by the fetish of trying to make the two sides balance, but went straight to the point and asked for the information which a credit manager, or a business man, or a banker wants. Too much emphasis cannot be placed upon this. Clients assume that their own bookkeepers can prepare trial balances; that is, if they think about the matter of balancing at all. Professional auditors must get away from the delusion that every item in a trial balance must be transferred to a balance sheet.

The author does not advocate a change in the present system merely because it has been demonstrated time and time again that bankers and business men want some other form of statement than that which has been thrust upon them by accountants who are still only bookkeepers, but because the *scientific* manner of presentation is that which reduces figures to readable form and which discloses facts rather than book balances.

This form of statement may be considered crude by the technical auditor, but the author ventures the opinion that if it is presented to one hundred business men, side by side with the usual debit and credit form of balance sheet, ninety-nine will express an immediate and emphatic preference for the one now shown:

CREDIT STATEMENT RECOMMENDED BY NATIONAL ASSOCIATION OF CREDIT MEN

To..............................

For the purpose of obtaining credit now and hereafter for goods purchased, we herewith submit to you the following statement of our resources and liabilities, and will immediately notify you of any material change in our financial condition.

In consideration of your granting credit to the undersigned, we agree that in case of our failure or insolvency, or in case we shall make any assignment for the benefit of creditors, bill of sale, mortgage, or other transfer of our property, or shall have our stock or plant attached, receiver appointed, or should any judgment be entered against us, then all and every of the claims which you have against us shall at your option become immediately due and payable, even though the term of credit has not expired. All goods hereafter purchased from you shall be taken to be purchased subject to the foregoing conditions as a part of the terms of sale.

ACTIVE BUSINESS ASSETS	Dollars	Cents
Value of merchandise on hand at cost.		
If manufacturing, raw material, $.		
finished, $. . . . . unfinished, $.		
Notes and accounts, cash value.		
Cash in hand.		
Cash in bank.		
Bills or accounts receivable, due from officers.		
Patents and patterns.		
Fixtures and machinery.		
Total real estate, cash value. . . . . .$.		
Total encumbrances on real estate, $.		
Equity.		
Total Active Business Assets.		

BUSINESS LIABILITIES	Dollars	Cents
Owe for merchandise, open acct., of which $. . . . . . .is past due		
Owe for notes for merchandise. .		
Owe banks.		
Owe for bills for paper sold.		
Owe others for borrowed money		
Owe taxes and rent.		
Mortgages on fixtures & mach'y		

Total Business Liabilities. . . . .

Net Worth in Business. . . . .

OFFICERS

	Name in Full	Address
President	. . . .	. . . .
Vice-President	. . . .	. . . .
Secretary	. . . .	. . . .
Treasurer	. . . .	. . . .

DIRECTORS

. . . .

. . . .

The above statement, both printed and written, has been carefully read by the undersigned, and is a full and correct statement of our financial condition as of. . . . . 191. . .

Dated. . . . . 191. . Corporation Signature. . . . .

Town. . . . . .State. . . . . By. . . . .

Contingent Liability {
Accommodation Indorsements. . . . .
Indorsed Bills Receivable and Outstanding. . . . .
. . . .

Authorized Capital. . . . .

Subscribed. . . . . .Paid in. . . . .

How paid in: Cash, $. . . . .

Other property. . . . .

Incorporated in what State and under what General Laws or Special Act?. . . . . .

. . . .

Nature of business?..
Date of charter?..
Suits pending, and of what nature?................................
....
Are any merchandise creditors secured in any way?.................
Amount of annual business...
Annual expenses....................Annual dividends..................
When was last dividend declared?..................................
Rate.................Insurance carried on merchandise..................
On fixtures and machinery...............On real estate................
Regular time of taking inventory..................................
Keep bank account with..
....
....
Keep the following books of account...............................
....
If you have pledged or transferred outstanding accounts or property remaining under your control, state amount thereof and amount received, or to be received, on account of such pledge or transfer..........................
REMARKS...

Liens and Hypothecations: Instances have been known where certified balance sheets have gone out wherein accounts receivable and merchandise inventories, included among the assets without any qualification, have, as a matter of fact, been pledged as security for loans, and thus were not assets in the sense which anyone making use of the balance sheets had a right to assume.

A concern might have accounts receivable of $10,000 and stock-in-trade of $10,000, with accounts and bills payable of $15,000. If the latter were entirely unsecured, a prospective creditor might extend further credit if the concern's standing were good, on the theory that in the event of bankruptcy there could be a shrinkage in the assets of twenty-five per cent before a creditor would lose anything.

But suppose it were found that all of the accounts receivable had been assigned to, and a chattel mortgage on the stock taken by, a creditor for $10,000. This would mean that in bankruptcy the unsecured creditors would probably receive nothing.

The professional auditor must never certify to a balance sheet without fully considering the possibilities of liens upon the assets, and if any are discovered, such liens must be plainly indicated on the face of the balance sheet or mentioned in the certificate, otherwise he is guilty of suppressing material information and can probably be held responsible in damages to any one relying thereon who suffers loss in consequence.

If there is any difficulty in securing information of this nature, the auditor may have to ask the question shown in the credit men's standard form. If he finds no trace of liens, and the officers or partners state in writing that there are none, then he could not be held guilty of negligence. It would not do, however, to rely on not finding any evidence; there should be affirmative proof that no liens exist.

PROFIT AND LOSS STATEMENT

A profit and loss statement is one which assembles all of the income and expenses, or gains and losses, for a stated period. It is synonymous with the "Revenue" statement sometimes presented, but as the term "Revenue" is more frequently used to designate one side only of a profit and loss account, the term is not properly applicable to a statement which includes expenses as well as income.

The profit and loss statement may be divided into as many sections as are desirable or necessary. The student of accountancy is usually taught to prepare the profit and loss statement in two sections, the first being a trading or a manufacturing account, the second section being called the general profit and loss account. This illustrates the principles of grouping and enables percentages to be calculated which are extremely valuable for comparative purposes. The trading or manufacturing account usually shows on one side net sales, and on the other prime costs of sales; i. e., materials used, labor, and other direct expenses. In some cases other expenses are included, such as rent, interest, taxes, etc.

In modern practice it is not customary to submit a trading or a manufacturing account under these captions. The experienced auditor or accountant compiles a profit and loss account suited to the requirements of each enterprise upon which he is reporting, and in a form understandable to those who are to use the report.

The following condensed form of Profit and Loss statement was submitted to the St. Louis Congress of Accountants in 1904 by A. Lowes Dickinson, C. P. A.:

Gross Earnings (whether sales of products, transportation earnings, professional earnings, etc.)		$.............
Deduct—Cost of Manufacture or Operation:		
(*a*) Manufacture (for a manufacturing concern)·		
Labor	$.............	
Material	....	
General Manufacturing Expenses	....	
(*b*) Cost of Operation (for concerns not manufacturing):		
(Under suitable headings according to the nature of the business)	....	
		....
Gross Profits		$.............
Other Earnings		....
		$.............
Deduct—		
Expenses of Sale (Manufacturing business only)	$.............	
Expenses of management (if distinct from operation)	....	
		....
Net Profits from operations		$.............
Deduct—		
Interest on Bonds	$.............	
Other fixed Charges	....	
		....
Surplus for the year		$.............
Extraordinary Profits (detailed)		....
Surplus brought forward from preceding year		....
		$.............
Deduct—		
Extraordinary charges not applicable to the operations of the year . . .	$.............	
Interest and Dividend on Stocks . .	....	
		....
Surplus carried forward		$.............

Where further information is required the condensed statement is supported by schedules or exhibits which go into as much detail as may be necessary.

The auditor should strive so to arrange the accounts as to show a comparison with previous periods; also, wherever the nature of the business permits, unit costs or earnings should be shown. For instance, the accounts of a taxicab company, if properly set up, will show the average gross earnings of cabs per day. They will also show the operating cost per mile. Perhaps the simplest illustration is a blast furnace. Here it is relatively easy to determine the cost of producing a ton of pig iron, but the figures would be of little value unless the output were shown with the average cost. The production for one week might be 10,000 tons and the average cost $8 per ton; the next week if the production were 15,000 tons and the cost $8 per ton, the natural inquiry would be: Why is the cost not proportionately less upon the greater output? If the cost per ton were reported separately from the production, attention might not be called to the possibility of lower costs being in order.

The relation which each class of expense bears to the total value of business is always interesting. In dull times it may be expected that certain so-called fixed charges will not vary, but there are other classes of expenses which should fluctuate ratably with the volume of business.

The auditor who states the accounts of a number of concerns in the same line of business can readily acquire a knowledge of income and costs which he may impart for the benefit of all at the expense of none. He must not divulge to one client the affairs of another, but if he ascertains that the office staff of one wholesale grocer costs one per cent per annum of the sales, while another costs one half of one per cent and is equally or more efficient, he certainly is justified in making a special investigation into the matter, and cannot be criticized for reporting that one per cent is excessive.

Use of Charts: The use of charts by engineers probably dates back to the early days of that profession; likewise, the use of charts by accountants can be traced back many years. Their use, however, is by no means general, although there are occasions when a chart can portray a situation far more graphically than columns of figures, particularly to a man who is more used to blue prints than to accounts. When accountants can visualize figures as an architect can a building, their reports will be more popular.

Sales Charts. An effective use of charts can be made in a wholesale or retail trading concern where the question of comparisons is of great importance. A chart can be prepared at the commencement of a fiscal year showing the comparative

SALES

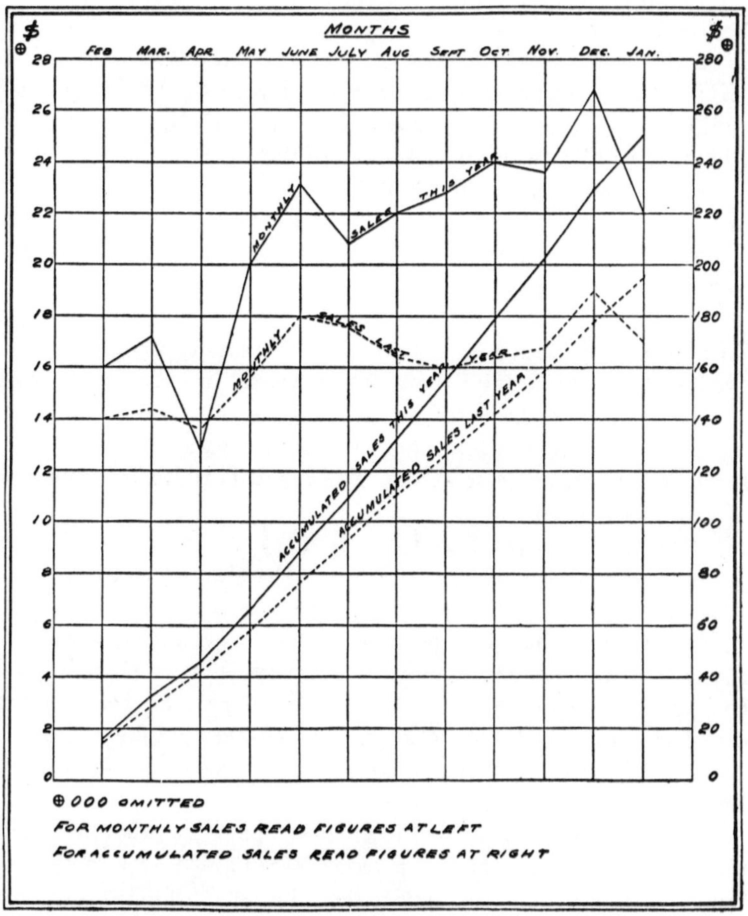

sales by months and the cumulative totals for the preceding year, e. g.:

It will be noted from the above that during the preceding year the monthly sales in February were $14,000, going up to $18,000 in June, down to $16,000 in September, up to $19,000 in December, and down to $17,000 in January. These figures are shown by the dotted black line. The new year (solid line) commences with $16,000, a gain over the previous year as clearly shown by the chart. In May the increase is not only maintained, but the rate of gain is increased.

In other words, a chart will show a trend which columns of figures fail to emphasize. The best place for a chart of this kind is on the wall of an office or on a map holder. It may be kept private by having a cover over it, or it may be rolled up. The auditor may submit a sample chart, based on past experience, which will indicate the possibilities of the plan.

Gross and Net Profit Charts: It is sometimes difficult for a business man to calculate how much gross profit he must make to cover his general expenses. The use of a chart will assist him to solve his problem.

The chart opposite illustrates the fact that in any business there is a point above which increases in sales return a net profit greater proportionately than the increase in sales. In other words, above a certain point any increase in sales occasions an increase in direct cost, but does not necessarily increase the overhead or indirect expense at all. The result is that the percentage of profit is greater.

The chart shows that from January to June cost and expenses were increasing, and that when the slump in sales came in July and August, the expenses were not reduced in proportion. The result was that in September the sales were just enough to cover cost and expenses. Had the expenses been kept down to the point at which they started in January, the reduction in direct cost due to the decrease in sales would have kept the total cost well below the low point reached by the sales. The lower line represents the net profit realized.

It will be noticed from the chart on page 233 that whenever the gross sales are above $10,000 per month, the net profit increases rapidly, and below $10,000, the net profit drops at once.

After a little experience the business man will be able to *see* the danger mark.

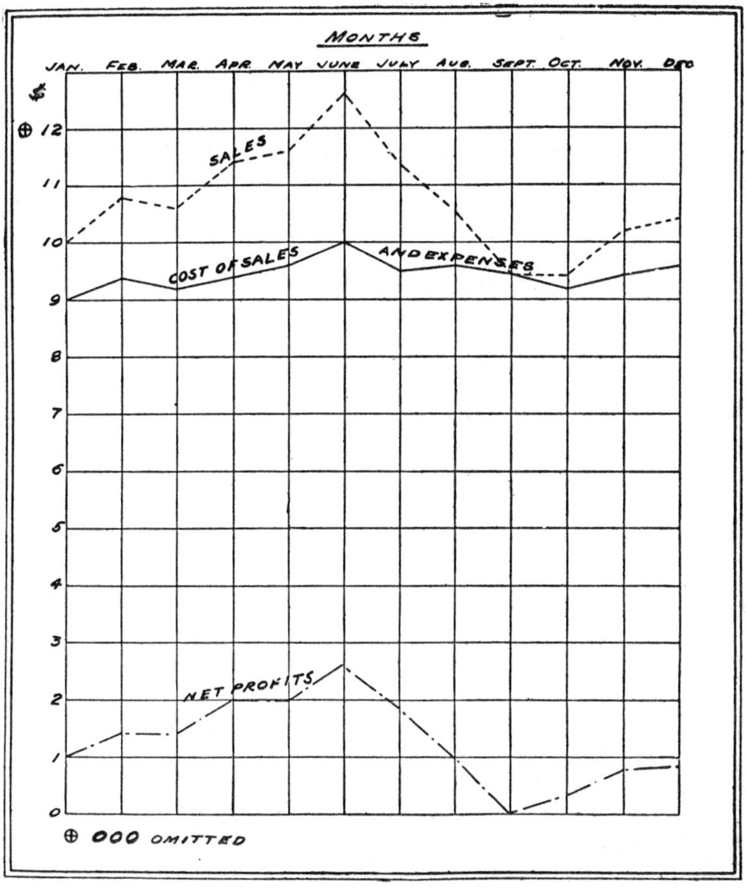

Combined Purchase and Sales Charts: If business is not good purchases may represent an unnecessary risk as compared with sales. A chart would show the sales and purchases month by month, thus giving instant expression to an expansion of one against a contraction of the other, as shown on page 234.

It will be noted that in June the sales fell off, but that the purchases kept up the regular advance, and that by November the sales were actually less than the purchases, indicating an enormous increase in the inventory. If the chart had been kept up to date the proprietor would have noticed the trend in July and purchases might have been cut down at once.

It may be objected that a good business man always keeps in touch with such important matters and that while such a chart might be of interest to him it would have no practical value. This is true of many men, but it is not true of the many who have

COMPARATIVE CHART OF SALES & PURCHASES

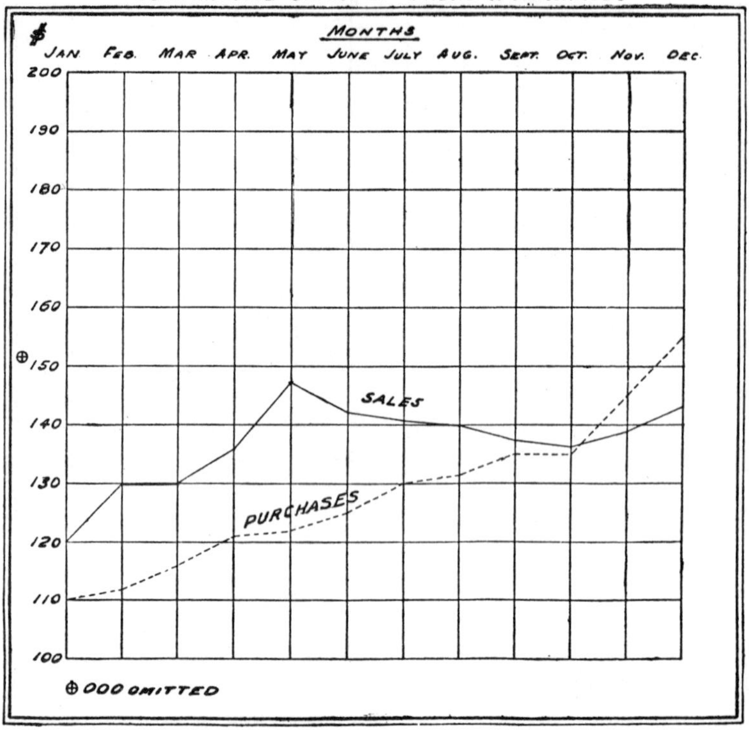

such a poor clerical staff that they cannot depend on their results, or those who ignore book figures because they are not able to understand the monthly "trial balances" which they receive.

Charts like the above can be kept up day by day so far as sales are concerned. As to purchases, all depends on the method of entering invoices. If compiled monthly only, of course the chart can be posted only once a month, but if it is looked after, say, by the 10th of each month, it will be up-to-date enough to be of substantial value.

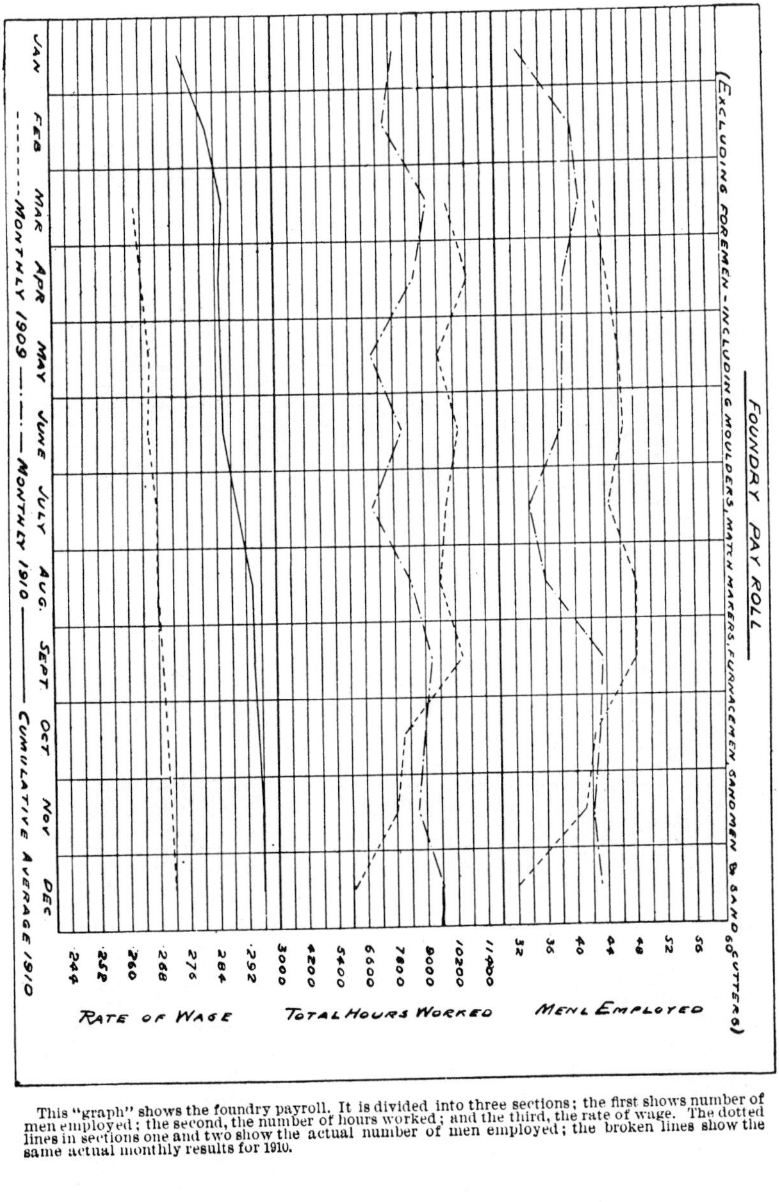

This "graph" shows the foundry payroll. It is divided into three sections; the first shows number of men employed; the second, the number of hours worked; and the third, the rate of wage. The dotted lines in sections one and two show the actual number of men employed; the broken lines show the same actual monthly results for 1910.

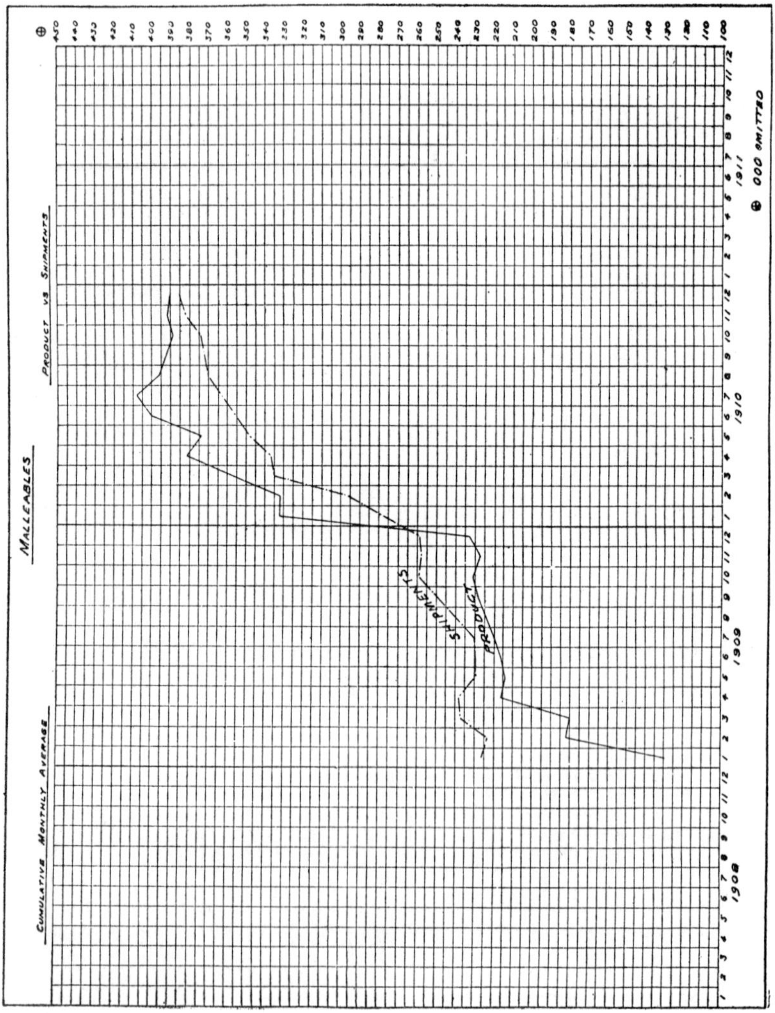

This "graph" shows the product in the foundry and the shipments of malleables—cumulative monthly averages in each. This tells, at a glance, that the manufacturer was guarding against over-production and against producing less goods than he sold. So long as the graphic line "shipments" topped that of "product," all was well, but when the lines came together, as in December, 1909, it was time to investigate.

The illustrations shown on pages 235 and 236 are taken from *System* and are illustrative of the use of charts in relation to labor and production statistics.

Value of Comparative Statistics: The head of the fidelity department of one of the large surety companies states that a great many irregularities and defalcations, especially through the padding of pay rolls, would be uncovered in their infancy if the managements of factories and commercial business houses would pay more attention to their accounts and have compiled by their accounting department comparative statistics of their business —and then study them. He cites the case of a cashier of a manufacturing concern who had been padding the pay roll for years. It was the practice of this concern to have the pay roll approved by the foreman, the superintendent, and the general manager. It would then be sent to the cashier, who made alterations in the total figures, drew a cheque for the raised amount, cashed it, and paid off the men. The pay roll did not leave the cashier after it was given to him to draw the cheques, he making the distribution for posting. This went on for years, the cashier each week pocketing from two to nine hundred dollars, until a change of executives brought in a manager who had been accustomed to getting his accounts down so as to show the economic condition of his business in statistical form. He had been in the same line before and he knew that the price of raw material, the rates for wages, and the various expenses were about the same as in his former place, but the profit and loss account showed a much smaller net profit. It was soon found that this was due to the high charge for labor, and upon analysis of this charge the stealings were discovered.

This is but one instance, but it is not hard to see that in showing the results of a business in graphic form so that the relation of the various elements, one to another, is easily seen, abnormal conditions are at once detected.. Some men will say that those things are interesting and all very well if one had the time and money to get them up. They do not realize the cost of not getting them up. Statistics compiled by one of the large bonding companies show that during the last three weeks of March and the month of April, 1911, shortages amounting to more than one half million dollars were discovered in mercantile houses alone.

What Not to Report: As heretofore stated, it is not wise to report unimportant errors, etc., first, because it accomplishes no useful purpose, if true. In any event criticisms of this nature should never be made without confirmation from the office staff, as they might be able to come back with proof that the errors or omissions were apparent only.

Likewise, long schedules of trade debtors and creditors are superfluous. For some years public accountants made it a rule to furnish their clients with detailed schedules of accounts receivable and payable, believing that such information was desired by them and would be of value. They found, however, that in nine cases out of ten these schedules were not referred to, and in the one case remaining the schedules desired were the *latest* ones rather than the ones submitted by the auditors, which were usually one or two months old. The practice was, therefore, quite generally abandoned, and these schedules are now furnished only on request.

In reports where special circumstances govern, such as changes in partnership, it may be necessary to submit detailed schedules. But the above remarks refer to the ordinary periodical audit.

A schedule of vouchers and paid cheques not submitted is sometimes of importance, but, as a rule, it is more desirable to prepare such a list before the end of the audit and hand a duplicate to the bookkeeper, so that the missing vouchers may be located. After as many as possible are located, the corrected list should be handed to the proprietor with a request that he look over it. If further inquiry or search is requested, it should be made *before the audit is completed.* If no further attention is required, the schedule is not important enough to put in a report.

The auditor should scan the list of outstanding unpaid bank cheques. A cheque is sometimes issued to close a disputed account, etc., which renders it desirable from both the client's and the auditor's point of view that it be used. The inspection would apply only to those outstanding an unreasonable length of time. If any doubt arises the matter should have attention at once, and no mention need be made in the report unless some irregularity is discovered.

Restrictions on Client's Use of Reports: Mention has been made of attempted unauthorized use of auditors' reports and certificates. This is obviated by a judicious selection of clients, but it may happen that a client who has paid for a report will feel at liberty to use part of the contents without disclosing the context. Anticipating this possibility, experienced auditors bind and fasten their reports securely together, and page them in such a way that a part cannot be used without revealing the fact that it is not complete.

It does not seem feasible to suggest any plan whereby clients or others may be prevented from *quoting* from a report. So long as the statement is not made that the quotation represents conclusions of fact to which an auditor has certified, it may not be objectionable, but it is remarkable how critical business men are with respect to the connection, or alleged connection, of a professional auditor with men or enterprises of a doubtful character.

In one case a well-known firm of auditors had for many years audited and certified to the accounts of a small and prosperous corporation. A large concern bought the small company and consolidated it with a number of others. The bankers who marketed the stock stated in their circulars that the accounts of the small company had been audited by one firm and the accounts of all the others, and of the holding company, had been audited by an audit (stationery) company. The latter continued the audit until the holding company went into hopeless bankruptcy. The firm was not connected with the enterprise after its clients sold out, but after the bankruptcy a large banking house intimated that the mention of the firm's name on a circular relative to a company with such an objectionable history might seriously affect their own attitude in employing the firm for accountancy work.

This is an extreme case, but it illustrates the great importance to an auditor of restricting the use of his name to professional work which is creditable to him in every way, and in connection with clients or promoters who are beyond suspicion.

Misleading Advertisements: Auditors are sometimes requested to compile data or statistics, or prepare calculations for use in new enterprises. Great care must be taken to restrict the use of the reports submitted for such purposes.

Recently an issue of preferred stock was advertised and a large bonus of common stock was offered as an inducement to purchase. The following statement was made *inter alia:*

> Based on reports of A & B, certified public accountants, on manufacturing costs and selling price from six months operation at part capacity of plant at Blank City, EARNINGS AT FULL CAPACITY ARE ESTIMATED AT OVER THIRTY-FIVE PER CENT ON THE COMMON STOCK AFTER PAYMENT OF SEVEN PER CENT DIVIDENDS ON PREFERRED STOCK.

The intention of the foregoing was clearly to deceive. It was so printed that everyone gathered the impression that the auditors had made a report, based on which earnings equal to thirty-five per cent on the common stock could be expected.

It may become necessary for auditors to print on their stationery some form of notice to the effect that no public use can be made of the information conveyed unless a memorandum setting forth the form of the proposed use is submitted for inspection.

Compulsory Reports: Compared with our lack of legal requirements, it is of interest to note the reports which must be prepared in England.

The following is an extract from Table A of the English Companies Act of 1908:

> Section 106. Once at least in every year the directors shall lay before the company in general meeting a profit and loss account for the period since the preceding account or (in the case of the first account) since the incorporation of the company, made up to a date not more than six months before such meeting.
>
> Section 107. A balance sheet shall be made out in every year and laid before the company in general meeting, made up to a date not more than six months before such meeting. The balance sheet shall be accompanied by a report of the directors as to the state of the company's affairs, and the amount which they recommend to be paid by way of dividend, and the amount, if any, which they propose to carry to a reserve fund.
>
> Section 108. A copy of the balance sheet and report shall, seven days previously to the meeting, be sent to the persons entitled to receive notices of general meetings in the manner in which notices are to be given hereunder.
>
> *Audit:* Section 109. Auditors shall be appointed and their duties regulated in accordance with sections 112 and 113 of the Companies (Consolidation) Act, 1908, or any statutory modification thereof for the time being in force.

CHAPTER XVII

THE DETAILED AUDIT

GENERAL PRINCIPLES

Completed Audit: It was stated in Chapter V that before commencing an audit the auditor should be furnished with a correct trial balance as of the closing date. This applies to what is known as a *completed audit,* which is the term usually employed to designate the audit where a complete fiscal or interim period has elapsed and where a final report is to be made on the work accomplished. The procedure outlined in this and succeeding chapters is designed to cover such a completed audit.

Continuous Audit is the term applied to the supervision by an auditor who attends at intervals *during* a period, and makes a report of progress rather than a report which embodies a balance sheet and a profit and loss account. In modern practice this distinction receives little consideration. Up-to-date concerns demand monthly reports of operations, and monthly balance sheets follow as a matter of course.

The auditor who is retained to audit the accounts, and pass on or prepare these monthly reports may be said to make a completed audit, although in some cases part of the audit work is left until the end of the fiscal period.

In large enterprises where a detailed audit is made the auditor may arrange to perform part of the work during the term in order to forestall congestion towards the end of the period. Sometimes the client requests that frequent visits be made so that if errors of principle or clerical errors are being made they can be detected and corrected before very much damage has been done. It is important, too, that if fraud is being practiced it should be discovered at the earliest possible date. Furthermore, frequent and unexpected visits tend to keep the client's staff up-to-date in their work, and carelessness as well as actual errors may be disclosed. The moral effect is also valuable.

If a large amount of detail work is to be verified, it is important that it be completed as soon after the closing date as possible in order that the auditor's report may be submitted within the shortest possible time thereafter.

Where interim audits are made and the auditor relies in subsequent audits on the work of previous visits, there is a possibility of the figures which he has passed being tampered with in order to conceal fraud. The author is not, however, prepared to offer suggestions for the detection of manipulation of accounts after they have been audited. In the preparation of a balance sheet and profit and loss account, if analyses of the accounts are made, unauthorized alterations, if any, will probably be revealed. As a matter of fact, experience has demonstrated that such a contingency is a remote one and its possibility is best guarded against by the intuition of the auditor rather than by his attempting to follow certain set rules.

Completed audits are fast supplanting continuous audits and it is deemed to be of more importance here to describe the former fully. The auditor who masters all the essentials of a completed audit can readily prepare a program for a continuous audit.

AUDIT NOTEBOOKS

Theoretically there is a great advantage in having available a formal program or memorandum book, which maps out the general procedure to be followed in a detailed audit, together with such additional information as will indicate any special points which are applicable to the particular audit to which the notebook relates. Based on a somewhat extensive inquiry, it appears that nearly all of the leading professional auditors of this country have used some form of audit notebook at one time or another. In most cases the books were used during the early years of practice, but have been abandoned.

The reasons for discontinuing their use are not uniform. The value of a more or less complete program is admitted by all, and some firms have compiled a set of instructions and furnish all of their assistants with printed copies. It is not believed, however, that the use of printed audit notebooks is as general to-day as it was a few years ago.

This is an indication of progress, because the old-style audit, which comprised a verification of footings, postings, and vouchers, has been found to be of little practical value, and as the printed audit notebook was specially adapted for these operations, the change in method naturally made them obsolete.

The intelligent auditor makes a study of each engagement and outlines a program the use of which will produce the results which he decides beforehand are necessary. The program will be reduced to writing, but it will vary to such an extent in different audits that it is not considered practicable nor desirable to attempt to use the same program for more than one client, but it is available for subsequent audits of the same accounts, in which case memoranda and suggestions occurring during the progress of one audit will be embodied in the program for the next.

The author does not recommend the use of printed instructions, because it is impossible to make them comprehensive enough to cover all of the work necessary in any one audit and it follows that they are not adapted for general use. The student who is attempting to gain a knowledge of the principles of auditing has no use for an audit notebook, and the practitioner whose experience is limited and who feels the need of a complete program should seek to obtain the benefit of the knowledge of more experienced practitioners (particularly the successful ones) before writing out a memorandum for himself or instructions for an assistant.

The audit notebook had one advantage which must not be overlooked, viz., spaces were always provided for a record of work done and the initials or marks of the one who was responsible therefor. This record is valuable in case of subsequent questions as to errors made or work not fully covered. It is important, therefore, that in the special program which the auditor compiles for his engagements, spaces be provided to permit of the fixing of responsibility for the carrying out of each item of the instructions.

As much has been said and written in favor of audit notebooks, and in order that the student may judge for himself the question of the desirability of their use, permission has been secured to reprint several specimen pages from "The American Audit Record," designed and published by Morgan L. Cooley, C. P. A., which is the most satisfactory form in use.

AUDIT MEMORANDA

An inspection of this record will quickly indicate its very great value both to the accountants doing the detail work, especially on a second visit, and to the home office.

The schedules are designed to cover usual operations; in some cases options are provided; for unusual operations space will be found. Each book will contain Notes for four periods or examinations, and will not only supply information regarding matters relating to past work, but will save much time and duplication in preliminary investigation, arrangement of operations, etc., for future audits. This is of utmost importance when it becomes necessary to rotate accountants, and in consideration of the large number of contracts taken upon the basis of a fixed fee.

With this record completely written up, the office is provided with full information regarding the detail operation of the work and is in a strong position to administer the same.

The records should be returned with working papers, carefully written up, at the close of each audit. Data should be required relating to each operation performed and carefully compared with the information submitted by another accountant upon auditing a subsequent period. A card index may be kept showing the disposition of all books, and it would be advisable to retain in the office copies of all books in the hands of accountants.

NOTES MADE IN THE FOLLOWING PAGES REGARDING

Hours Consumed 1	2	3	4	Periods	1 From To	2 From To	3 From To	4 From To
				1 General Organization and System of Internal Check	By			
				2 Method of Taking and Pricing Inventory	By			
				3 General Condition and Usefulness of Books	By			
				4 Recommendations for Improvement	By			
				5 Sufficiency of Depreciation	By			
				6 Sufficiency of Reserve	By			
				7 Sufficiency of Working Capital as Shown by Interest Paid, Discount Neglected, etc.	By			
				8 Each Item of Balance Sheet	By			
				9 Accruals	By			
				10 Deferred Charges	By			
				11 Contingent Assets and Liabilities	By			
				12 Allocation of Charges and Credits re Capital vs. Operation and Maintenance	By			

CAPITAL STOCK, DIVIDENDS, BONDS AND INTEREST

Hours Consumed 1	2	3	4	Periods	1 From To	2 From To	3 From To	4 From To	Remarks
				CAPITAL STOCK					
				1 Scheduled from Certificate Book by					
				2 Compared with Stock Ledger by					
				3 Compared with Private Ledger by					
				4 Certified by Transfer Agent Certificate Received by					
				5 Dividends Vouched by					
				6 Authority Verified by					
				BONDS					
				1 Certificate from Registrar Received by					
				2 Interest Checked by					

PRIVATE LEDGER

Hours Consumed 1	2	3	4	Periods	1 From To	2 From To	3 From To	4 From To	Remarks
				1 Trial Balance at Beginning by					
				2 Footings Verified by					
				3 Examined to Note If All Postings Have Been Checked by					
				4 Trial Balance Before Closing by					
				5 Trial Balance After Closing by					
				6 Prepaid Items Checked by					
				7 Accruals Verified by					
				8 Reserves Noted by					
				9 Remaining Assets Verified by					
				10 Remaining Liabilities Verified by					

INVENTORIES

Hours Consumed 1 | 2 | 3 | 4	Periods	From To 1	From To 2	From To 3	From To 4	Remar
	1 Physical Items Verified by					
	2 Appraisal Made by					
	3 Prices Checked by					
	4 Extensions Checked by					
	5 Footings Verified by					
	6 Compared with Ledger by					
	7 Reserve for Depreciation Computed by					Basis
	8 Officials' Figures Accepted by					

If tests are made, state exact extent in each case.

ACCOUNTS RECEIVABLE LEDGER

Hours Consumed 1 | 2 | 3 | 4	Periods	From To 1	From To 2	From To 3	From To 4	Remarks
	1 Footings Verified by					
	2 Balances Agreed with Controlling Account by					
	3 Balances Verified by Construction of Controlling Account by					
	4 Over-due Accounts Scheduled by					
	5 Reserve for Bad Debts Computed by					
	6 Reserve for Discounts Computed by					
	7 Customers Asked to Confirm Balances by					By means of
	8 Personal Accounts Scheduled by					

ACCOUNTS PAYABLE LEDGER

Hours Consumed 1 | 2 | 3 | 4	Period	From To 1	From To 2	From To 3	From To 4	Remarks
	1 Footings Verified by					
	2 Balances Agreed with Controlling Account by					
	3 Balance Verified by Construction of Controlling Account by					
	4 Personal Accounts Scheduled by					
	5 Receiving Records Compared with Invoices Recorded by					

THE AUDIT OF INCOME AND EXPENSES

General Principles: There are two underlying principles which govern the procedure in the detailed audit of income and expenses.

(1) The auditor must ascertain whether the earnings shown by the books are properly accounted for, and whether any of the earnings are omitted therefrom.

(2) He must ascertain whether or not the expenses and losses are properly stated and supported.

At the commencement of a detailed audit it is important for an auditor to investigate thoroughly the relation of the clerical staff to the work and to each other. Auditors are fond of stating that a cashier should never have access to the ledgers, and that a ledger clerk should have no access to the cash.

Theoretically this is an ideal condition and exists in most large concerns, not because the proprietors realize that it is a proper safeguard, but because there is enough of each class of work to warrant the employment of an individual clerk for each class. But in a small business where the cashier's duties are not extensive enough to keep him busy all the time, he is required to assist with other duties, and naturally he is expected to undertake the work for which he is best qualified—the postings to the ledgers. So long as there are business enterprises the proprietors of which consider that a bookkeeper's duties include the functions of a cashier as well as those of a ledger clerk, it will be necessary to exercise special vigilance in the audit thereof, for fraud is so easily concealed that many clerks yield to temptation, knowing that their defalcation will not be disclosed unless a professional auditor is employed.

And in many instances where professional auditors have been expected, the clerks have used most ingenious means to conceal their fraud, so that an auditor should have a knowledge of as many of these subterfuges as possible in order to detect irregularities of any nature.

Prior Periods: In a detailed audit covering, say, a year, the question frequently arises as to the auditor's responsibility for the period prior to the commencement date. He will of course, have it definitely understood that the commencing date should be definitely fixed and be supported by a balance sheet which is assumed to be correct.

As a matter of fact, there is little danger in this procedure. A proper audit for a year must of necessity shed a clear light on the operations of the period immediately preceding, and if nothing in the current work has given rise to suspicion, the former accounts may be left undisturbed. Of course, if any special reason exists, or a client insists on going back for two or more years, the auditor must comply, but he should make the suggestion that the last year should be audited and *reported upon* first, so that there will be a chance for reflection before incurring the expense incident to a long engagement.

Verification of Footings and Postings: The least important part of the audit is the verification of footings and postings, but the subject demands attention and will then be dismissed. It will have to be a very small business indeed where there can be any justification for verifying every posting and every footing. In past years about half of the auditing which was done consisted of the laborious work of checking postings in detail and verifying the footings of all books, including the ledgers. An analysis of various defalcations which have occurred in recent years demonstrates the fact that the percentage of frauds which have been concealed by false postings and incorrect footings is small. This small percentage may be covered just as well in what may be called a "test" audit as in a so-called detailed audit. Where books are out of balance there is a distinct value in checking over as many postings and footings as possible, for it not only gives the auditor a chance to see at first hand the sort of errors which the bookkeepers have been making and thus furnishes data for his report, but it helps along the current work, and if all the differences are located, he will earn the good will of the bookkeeper, which is also an important matter. The undertaking of this sort of work is dangerous, however, unless it has been definitely arranged with the client and he is convinced that part of the work being done is that of an accountant and part that of an auditor.

Some auditors are fond of testing the ledger postings by making up their own controlling accounts, or else reversing the process and by analyzing each ledger account, extracting the totals of each source of original entry. There are very exceptional cases where this plan may be followed, principally where the ledger is not in balance. It is an old-fashioned scheme, however, and has no place under modern methods in a well-ordered plan. Great advantages accrue to the auditor who knows enough to be able to prove such work by tests and thus gain valuable time which can be devoted to other and more important work—more important because the largest number of frauds occur in other places than footings and postings. Therefore, in that vast number of audits where there has been no fraud, but where the auditor wishes to justify his employment, *all* the constructive or labor-saving suggestions will arise from the other portions of the work.

Many cases are known of audits ocupying, say, four weeks, where the verification of footings and postings has taken three weeks and all the rest of the audit has taken one week. There can be no hard-and-fast rule as to the time each class of work should take, and it is not worth while to attempt to approximate one, but it must be obvious that unless there is some specific justification for this division, it would be far better to spend one week on postings and footings and three weeks on work which afterward will mean something to the clients.

The question arises: Is it not possible that in thus cutting down the work by two-thirds too much has been taken for granted and that an auditor would not be excused who neglected such a material part of the work as that of verifying the footings and postings? The latter part of the question is answered by the statement that no auditor can be excused who *neglects any* part of the work. We must, however, be sure in each case which is presented that we take nothing for granted until we have made such intelligent and exhaustive tests as will assure us that the accounts as a whole are, in our judgment, correct. Note the expression "in our judgment"; for the moment you deprive the auditor of the free exercise of his judgment, you are reducing him to the position of an automaton, and the title of *professional* auditor becomes a misnomer. What is an intelligent and exhaustive test of postings and footings? In seeking an answer, first direct your attention to the four general groups into which they can be divided. These are: (1) the records of the purchase of goods or materials as reflected in purchase or invoice books, voucher registers, etc.; (2) the records of sales as found in sales books or binders or in any one of the various good and bad forms used; (3) the receipt of cash; (4) the payment of cash.

The majority of postings and footings occur with respect to the records mentioned, so that if we can agree on what constitutes a fair test of these groups or divisions, we can safely leave the remaining records to be dealt with on their merits.

The following suggestions are grounded upon the fundamental principle that no audit is complete unless the trial balances of all the ledgers have been proved. There may be exceptions, as, for instance, a department store where there are one hundred individual ledgers, in which case an exhaustive test would be sufficient.

(1) Purchase Records: If fraud exists with respect to purchases, it usually will be found in overcharges or fictitious vendors, and very seldom, if ever, will there be any concealment of fraud through manipulations of footings or postings. The auditor does not seek to locate clerical errors in trial balances, but is concerned with the possibility of the trial balance, which is ostensibly in agreement, being *forced.* As this occurs not only in cases where fraud exists, but also where there is a lazy or incompetent bookkeeper, the auditor should always be on the lookout for evidence of forced balances. As a rule, however, where a trial balance *is* forced there will be no alteration in the current postings and footings. The usual and popular expedient is to alter in the ledger the last posting during the period to one of the large nominal accounts, such as sales or expenses.

These remarks as to the trial balance have a bearing on purchase records to the extent that, no matter what other detail work is omitted, the verification of the postings of the monthly or periodical aggregates must not be forgotten. By this is meant the debit side of the purchase accounts. Usually the checking of the credit postings can be omitted.

As to the footings, in a fairly large concern, prove the footings of about every tenth or twelfth page in addition to the last page of each month, where the audit covers a period of one year. In a smaller concern, prove, say, every fifth or sixth page, including always the last page of each month. It is hard to imagine, and wide experience has not developed, a case where such a percentage would not have been just as effective in any given audit as the verification of the footing of *every page*. That is, the verification of every page did not disclose any discrepancies (except as hereafter noted), so that, naturally, the work could have been cut down eleven-twelfths with equal results (except as to cost to the client). The last page in every case is mentioned particularly, because instances are known where such figures have been altered.

(2) **Sales Records:** The monthly or other aggregates of the sales postings should be checked.

Controlling Account: If there is a controlling account in the general ledger with customers, it will not be necessary to verify in detail the postings of the customers' ledgers. If there is no controlling account, the auditor should construct one, so in neither case is it worth while to prove the debit postings.

The controlling account is a compilation of the aggregates of the postings to the individual customers' accounts. They may be classified as follows.

DEBITS	CREDITS
Total of opening balances, as per last trial balance.	Cash.
Sales.	Discounts.
Protested or returned cheques, notes, etc.	Returns and Allowances.
Interest, etc.	Notes.
	Accounts charged off, etc.
	Total of closing balances.

In some sets of books it may take as much work to construct the controlling account as to verify every posting; but even so, the time spent in the preparation of the account is not lost, because the data secured thereby will be useful in stating the results of the business.

There is more fraud in connection with accounts receivable than in any other department of a business, but the fraud does not consist in a failure to post the sales which are recorded *in the sales books* to the ledgers. The fraud is in omitting the sales from the sales records entirely or in the failure to enter cash collections.

It is, however, important to know that all the sales appearing in the sales record have been posted. As stated above, this can be, and should be, covered by use of a controlling account as the items are of such a nature that they are grouped in the original records, and where the posting of a thousand entries in one can be proved by one operation, time is saved. This method assumes, of course, that there will be a verified trial balance of the customers' ledgers to support the controlling account. The question of accounts which have been collected, but which do not show the collections, will be considered later.

As to the footings, verification is somewhat more important than with purchase records. In a large concern, prove, say, every eighth page, and in a small concern, say, every third or fourth page, always including the last and sometimes the next to last page of each month.

Cheques Received must be Deposited: In those corporations where the capital stock is all, or nearly all, owned by its officers or directors, the latter frequently handle the funds of the corporation as if no corporate responsibility existed. Usually they act honestly and no harm is done, but an auditor cannot afford to pass over illegal acts which come to his knowledge, although so far as can be foreseen no one will be injured thereby.

The practice of an officer using cheques drawn to the order of the corporation for his private use cannot be condemned too severely, and yet it is not uncommon. All cheques should be deposited, and the officer can withdraw a similar sum if the corporation is indebted to him.

In a New York case, decided by the Court of Appeals in 1908, where the president of a corporation (the stock of which was all owned by himself and the secretary-treasurer) used a cheque drawn to the order of the corporation and indorsed by it to pay his personal debt, the creditors of the corporation upon its being declared insolvent compelled the trust company that cashed the cheque to refund the money.

Periodical Verification of Bank Balances: The auditor should ascertain by personal investigation whether the bank balances have been verified at frequent intervals throughout the period covered by the audit. It frequently happens that clerks are careless about reconciling the bank balances with those shown by the books. In some cases the pass books are not left for settlement for many months; in other cases the pass books are balanced by the banks and delivered to the depositors, but are not verified by the latter.

In the middle and far West, the banks have quite generally adopted the plan of sending monthly statements to all depositors, accompanied by the paid cheques. There is a growing tendency on the part of the banks in the East to follow this plan. This is to be commended, as it leads naturally to more frequent reconciliations between the parties.

But the bank statements may be filed away without examination unless some one in authority insists on prompt attention. Instances have been known where junior clerks have forged signatures to cheques, and owing to carelessness in inspecting the bank settlements, the fraud was not discovered for a long time.

The law is that the writing up of a bank pass book, with a return of paid cheques, or a statement of account, is not conclusive upon the parties so as to preclude an ascertainment of the true state of the accounts in a case where cheques are included in the balance which are subsequently discovered to be forged. But where the depositor is under a duty from the usages of business or otherwise to examine the account within a reasonable time and to give timely notice of any objections he may have, an omission to perform this duty, leaving the bank to rely upon the presumption that the account is acquiesced in, whereby it is misled to its prejudice, will make the account conclusive. The law is not unreasonable in holding that where bank settlements lie around untouched for long periods those in control of the business should know that a risk is being run for which there is no excuse.

The auditor may sympathize with the clerk who is overworked and who omits the reconciliation of the bank balances for what he considers more important duties, but nevertheless, such neglect may be costly and should be reported.

(3) **Cash Receipts:** In all well-regulated concerns *all* cash receipts are deposited in bank and all payments, therefore, must be made from the bank account. This almost disposes of the question of verifying the footings of the cash book. Where the bank account is proved and the cash receipts and payments are traced into and out of bank, it would seem logical that the footings of the cash book could be automatically proved at the same

time. If this does not seem to be complete verification, in a large business, the proving of every third or fourth page will be a complete check.

In many small concerns the cashier handles the receipts, writes up the cash book, and makes the deposits. He might retain a portion of the receipts, force the footings of the column to agree with the actual deposit, and increase the footings of the discount column. The cash book would then balance across, the cash balance agree with the amount shown by the pass book, and as the discount column would be posted in total by the bookkeeper, the ledger would be in balance without any falsification being made therein. If there were special columns provided for cash sales or similar earnings, the footings of such columns could be reduced by the amount of the shortage and thus afford additional facilities for covering up the amounts taken.

The postings of the nominal accounts should usually be verified, not because there is any great danger of fraud lurking therein, but for the purpose of locating any possible posting to a wrong account. For instance, it frequently happens that part of a plant or old machinery may be sold. Sometimes such items are posted to an earning account instead of to a capital or a reserve account. These postings are, as a rule, few in number and are important enough to be verified *in extenso*.

The postings to the credit of customers should be proved in totals through the controlling accounts. If there is no controlling account and one cannot be constructed readily, a fair test should be made of the individual ledger credits, working, of course, from the ledger back to the cash book and not *vice versa*. The reason for this is obvious; if a customer has been credited with an amount which purports to have been posted from the cash book, but which, as a matter of fact, is not entered there at all, the discrepancy would not be discovered by using the cash book as a basis, and it would not be safe to depend on looking through the ledger subsequently to see that all items are ticked. It is sometimes suggested that the chief danger in such practice lies in the possibility that the ledger clerk can, where the work is not finished at a sitting, supply the ledger tick marks himself. There is not much basis for this fear, but it would be foolish to expose one's self to it where no necessity exists.

If it is thought wise to verify the individual postings to the customers' accounts, do not check every one unless some very good ground for suspicion exists. If the audit is a periodical one, say, for six months, cover about half the letters of the alphabet only. Six months later cover the other half, or one-fourth only at each audit, and take two years to the entire list. It is not an infrequent fraud wherein ledger credits do not appear as cash debits, but it is hard to imagine one case where a good test would not have disclosed the fraud. Very few men would confine their peculations to customers whose names commenced with X Y Z only. The auditor can afford to take the chance that the defaulter will inadvertently manipulate the account of an A customer, in which case he would not escape the first time, and if he used only one or two letters, he would still be detected in a reasonable time.

(4) Cash Payments: On the payment side there is also a possible opportunity for fraud being covered by erroneous footings. In most cash books there are columns for different expenses which are posted in total at the end of the month. If the cashier were to take an unnumbered cheque from the back of the book, or one of a style similar to the ones in current use, and have it drawn to his order or to some name representing himself and did not enter the amount in the cash book, the footings could be falsified to that extent. The cheque could be numbered to correspond with those in use at the time. When the bank settlement was received and the balance verified, the cheque could be destroyed.

Instances are known where cheques were marked as void on the stubs and the two halves of one cheque pasted on two stubs (one of the portions, of course, being without a number), thus providing a cheque which was used by the cashier to obtain money fraudulently.

These manipulations are not likely to occur more than once in an auditor's experience, but all of the possibilities mentioned are based on actual experience, so that an auditor cannot afford to neglect all reasonable precautions to ascertain if such fraud exists.

The auditor should insist, wherever feasible, on having *all* payments represented by cheques. It reduces the possibility of manipulation of cash-book footings to a minimum, and for this reason alone is worth all the trouble which may be occasioned by the necessity of depositing all currency receipts. If the footings cannot be proved by the bank account, verify, say, every third or fourth page.

If the cash book is properly columned and a controlling account is kept with accounts payable, most of the postings will consist of monthly aggregates, which should be checked to see that they do not get into the wrong ledger account. Here, however, it is important to avoid duplication. In many audits it is desirable to make full analyses of the various expense and purchase accounts for use in the reports. If feasible and convenient this work should be done at the time of the verification of the postings, for it may be found that the details in the ledger are not sufficient and the cash book pages must be consulted again.

Postings to the individual accounts need not be verified unless some special reason appears. The payments are supposed to be vouched to establish their authenticity, and it is not necessary to trace the payments to the debits of the accounts. A controlling account supported by a trial balance of the subsidiary ledger is a good proof, but even where this is *not* in evidence the checking of the debit postings is usually superfluous.

Summary: As against the practice—fairly common—of checking all postings and footings, the above course will seem radical. It is not radical, however, if it is approved after full discussion and thought, and if it will stand the additional test of each particular audit. Where the slightest cause for suspicion exists, there must be a careful study of every phase of the situation.

But if suspicion has been aroused and there is a probability of something being wrong, the most foolish thing an auditor can do is to jump in blindly and tick every entry in the books. This has been done more than once, but the practice cannot be condemned too strongly.

Other Records: In many lines of business the books of account bear distinctive titles, and it may be that in the foregoing pages these books have not been called by their technical names. For instance, in a magazine publishing business a sales book, so called, may not be found, but a subscription record and an advertising register will usually be kept.

With these books, as to footings and postings, about the same procedure should be followed as with a regulation sales book—as a matter of fact, that is exactly what these two records represent—sales of advertising space and sales of copies of the publication for a stated period (subscriptions). It is far more satisfactory to have an illuminating title like this for a book than to attempt to cut down the number of account books in use and perhaps journalize every transaction. Aside from the saving of labor to a bookkeeper through the use of books for special purposes, is the more important function of keeping the records clear to one who does not understand bookkeeping. Most business men are at sea when they try to understand an ordinary journal, but if a book is labeled "subscription record," or "advertising register," anyone with ordinary intelligence knows exactly what to look for within its pages.

CHAPTER XVIII

THE DETAILED AUDIT (Continued)

VERIFICATION OF INCOME

It is obvious that a dependable analysis of frauds can never be compiled from accurate data, but an estimate prepared from long experience supports the assertion that nearly, if not quite, seventy-five per cent of defalcations and frauds are connected directly with a failure to account for income or cash receipts, and less than twenty-five per cent with methods of improperly diverting cash after it has found its way into the treasury.

We will discuss as of the more importance the seventy-five per cent division. This, in turn, can be divided into two groups: the first embracing that class of frauds which consists in a failure to enter in the books, or at least in the books which form a part of the double-entry system, any record whatever of the sale or delivery of goods or materials; the second class includes those cases where there is a record of the original sale or delivery, but where the subsequent collection is omitted entirely or where the entry of collection is postponed until a later date. Obviously, the former methods will be the ones most easily concealed, and the auditor must, therefore, be especially vigilant in this part of the audit.

It is assumed that the auditor has secured a list of all books in use. This list should include not only the books which form part of the double-entry system, but also all those usually termed "memorandum" books, which contain original data, and from which the formal entries are compiled.

When the audit is completed the auditor should be able to certify that, in his opinion, all revenue or earnings have been properly accounted for. This does not mean that the cash which was duly entered in the cash book and the sales which were in due course entered in the sales records were assumed to be *all* the cash receipts and all the sales without further investigation.

A careful inquiry should be made, or personal watch kept, to see who opens the mail, and what record, if any, is made by such person.

Sales: It is important to ascertain that all cash sales are accounted for. In nearly every business some sales are collected for at once and are not passed through the customers' ledgers. If the general ledger shows few such transactions, this should not influence the auditor unless he has made inquiry from some one other than the cashier. One instance may be cited where the auditor found that there were practically no cash sales accounted for. He inquired as to this and was informed that it was not the custom to make such sales. Further investigation, however, developed the fact that the cash sales had been quite large, but that his first informant had pocketed the whole proceeds. In this case a rough memorandum was discovered which enabled the auditor to locate the entire shortage. It will be found the rule rather than the exception that there is some sort of record which can be compared with the cash book. The formal original records, which are nicely written up and which agree exactly with the other books, are not the ones the auditor wants. If he can find the first "originals," in rough form, perhaps, and very dirty and almost illegible, there is no doubt about the advisability of using such records in preference to the fair copies, because the latter are frequently written up by the same men who write up the final cash records. Professional auditors agree that original records corresponding closely to the above description have revealed to them perhaps more instances of fraud than any other source. The importance placed upon them cannot, therefore, be overestimated.

The list of memorandum books required should include the original records of sales and the original records of shipments. Rarely are the order books or shipment or delivery books considered as formal books of account, and it is perhaps fortunate for the auditor that this is so, because in many cases where the examination of these records has revealed fraud there has been great astonishment and usually indignation that an auditor should ask to see "memorandum" books. In most of these cases if the defaulters had suspected that the books mentioned would be called for, they could readily have been destroyed or altered before examination.

It is the auditor's duty to verify the income from sales as evidenced by the records or papers covering the transactions from the time an order is received until the goods have been delivered. Wherever possible, therefore, he secures the order books and compares some of them with the ledgers to see that the orders were filled. If not, why not? It may be that through carelessness an order was not filled and that it was not reported. Here is a good chance to be of positive value to the client.

Orders may have been filled and the proceeds collected and not accounted for. This should be discovered by comparing the shipping or delivery books with the sales records. Tests here are all that are necessary, because any system of fraud in this channel has been, in practically all known cases, continuous, so that a complete comparison for a few weeks or a month would cover the point quite as well as a more exhaustive comparison.

A fruitful source of inspiration in the effort to ascertain whether or not all the income has been accounted for is the balance sheet—or the trial balance after closing, which may state the various items of assets in greater detail than the balance sheet. Proper thought should be devoted to each item to determine the possibility of the income therefrom being omitted from the books. For instance, a mining company's balance sheet may show that it owns workmen's houses. The auditor will then have to find out if all of the rents of *all* the houses have been accounted for. Furthermore, where there are tenants he will usually find sales to them of coal or other fuel and all sorts of supplies. If he does not find any record of such sales, he should inquire why from some one "higher up." He should not take the cashier's word for it.

These comments are merely suggestive and serve to illustrate the idea that the auditor must not use the receipt side of the cash book as a basis for verifying the actual income or receipts. He must work from every outside source he can find *to* the cash book, and he will then be reasonably safe.

There is not the same difficulty with the cases in which there has been some record in one of the original books of account of a sale, the subsequent collection of the proceeds of which has not been accounted for, or in which although the sales have been debited in due course to customers, the collections have not been credited.

The former class will be disclosed by a good test of the footings of the sales records, and the proof of the postings of same to the customers' ledgers. This has been fully covered. The instances where credits have been arbitrarily made to customers' accounts, but without corresponding entry in the cash book, have also been covered.

Cash Discounts: The auditor should secure from the principals an authoritative statement of cash discounts allowed to customers, and with this as a basis a fairly exhaustive test should be made of the discount deductions or allowances as stated in the cash book. In rare cases the cash book will show net receipts only, in which event discounts are credited through an allowance book or journal, but as the latter method involves writing customers' names twice, no up-to-date concern would permit it. The discounts should appear in a column on the *receipt* side of the cash book, and next to the column containing the gross or net collections from customers.

For convenience in posting, the gross amount is sometimes entered in the "Accounts Receivable" column. The total of the discount column must then be deducted therefrom in order to arrive at the cash balance. The better practice, however, is to enter the net cash collection in one column and the amount of the discount in the next. In posting, the two amounts should be entered "in short" on the credit side of the customer's account and the gross amount extended to the money column.

Instances are known where cashiers have systematically overstated the discount allowance either by increasing the amount actually deducted or by entering a discount where none was claimed or allowed. This is a matter to which little attention is directed in an establishment where the work of cashier and bookkeeper is performed by the same person, or where the posting clerks are mere machines, and can be depended upon to overlook fraud of this nature. In view of this probable freedom from detection and the numerous frauds which have thus occurred, the auditor must make a test thorough enough to satisfy himself fully. It is not likely that if there is anything wrong it will appear only occasionally, so that the test, while exhaustive as to the period covered, need extend over only a few days or weeks, depending on the volume of collections.

Collections not Accounted for: We now come to what is believed to be the most prolific source of fraud practiced, viz., the failure to enter in any book the collections from customers. The detection of such fraud is difficult and it will pay, therefore, to devote considerable time and space to the subject.

The most common irregularity can be illustrated as follows: Customer A on January 2nd pays $112.53, say, by cheque; the cashier fails to enter the collection in his books. If he has made other collections in currency exceeding $112.53, he will deposit the cheque and take the equivalent in currency from the drawer, thus obviating the necessity of forging the indorsement and having the cheque cashed, although the latter method is more common than is generally supposed. In the first case the fraud might be discovered by comparing the details of the cash receipts with the details of the bank deposits as listed in the cheque stubs or copy books, but this record is not always available and auditors frequently find that where such a fraudulent practice exists the record of the bank deposit has been altered or made up to correspond with the cash book, which makes the comparison of no value.

In most such cases the thief does not consider it safe to hold out collections too long for fear some one in the office will discover that customer A has not paid and go after him. Therefore, on January 31st he decides that it will not be wise to hold up A's credit any longer, and accordingly credits him with $112.53 in the cash book, and the amount finds its way to the ledger in due course. By this time the cashier is further in trouble: the customer B having on January 31st paid $250 (also by cheque) the cashier fails to enter the amount and thus creates a cash "over" of $137.47, which he removes from the cash drawer as soon as he can accumulate that amount of currency. Here again may be urged the importance of recommending to clients the daily deposit of all receipts—currency and cheques. There will then be far less opportunity for fraud afforded to a clerk dishonestly inclined.

So it continues. The defaulter must soon credit B with $250, and he therefore calls on C's account, or by this time A may have paid again. In all cases it will be found that the amount grows larger and larger until in many cases the discovery is forced without the aid of an outside auditor. In more cases, however, it goes on for years and unfortunately more than once such a practice has been in full force during, prior, and subsequent to, periodical audits by public accountants.

Confirmations of Outstandings: The best way to detect such a defalcation is for the auditor to send out statements to all customers, requesting them to confirm the accuracy of the balance on a blank inclosed for the purpose, which in turn is returned direct to the auditor's office. This is the practice followed by many leading auditors, and where the client does not or will not consent to such a course, the responsibility for the integrity of the customers' balances is squarely up to him. Every year the objections to this practice grow less, and no doubt within a few years the verification of customers' outstanding balances by correspondence with the auditor will be the rule rather than the exception.

The old form was substantially as follows:

Dear Sirs:

In making our periodical audit of the accounts of.................... we desire to verify the accounts receivable by direct correspondence with each customer, and we are therefore sending you (attached below) a memorandum of your balance, which we would ask you to kindly compare with your books, advising us as to its correctness or otherwise.

If the balance does not agree, please inform us fully as to the reason and amount of the differences.

A stamped envelope is inclosed for use in replying.

Very truly yours,

————————,

Certified Public Accountants.

.................Perforations here...................

No................. 191

The balance of $ .... under date of .... charged against my account on the books of..................is correct.

Very truly yours,

The above form, or some variation of it, was used extensively for several years, but it was found to be expensive and not entirely satisfactory. The fact is that where balances are correct there is no necessity for an acknowledgment.

The most popular form at present is as follows:

PLEASE EXAMINE
this Statement carefully. If it is not correct, please communicate DIRECT with our Auditors,
LYBRAND, ROSS BROS. & MONTGOMERY,
55 LIBERTY STREET, NEW YORK,
giving full details of any differences.

It consists merely of a rubber stamp used on the regular statement forms of the concern under audit and is more effective than any other method.

The statements are of course prepared in the client's office in the usual manner—not by the auditor. The latter, however, should compare balances with ledger accounts before mailing and the mailing should be done by the auditor. For some accounts no statements are sent and a list thereof should be prepared and approved by the proper authority. Some auditors object to this procedure on the ground that customers who are in the habit of visiting the client's place of business are apt to disregard the request to take up differences direct with the auditor and in most cases will report direct to the bookkeeper any discrepancies. Even where customers are not accustomed to calling at the client's office they still insist on writing direct in connection with anything which concerns their accounts, as they do not or will not appreciate the value of an independent check. The auditor, therefore, cannot depend on having reported to him all discrepancies in customers' accounts through the plan suggested above. As a practical matter, however, the scheme will bring to light any systematic fraud, because all customers do not object to communicating direct with an auditor and if a bookkeeper has been systematically manipulating customers' accounts, one or more can be depended upon to so advise the auditor, in which case the latter is put on notice and other instances of fraud should be looked for.

It has been found that this independent check is of value not only in the disclosure of fraud, but also in the insight which it gives as to the condition of the accounts with respect to unadjusted items, allowances, etc. It is needless to say that some bookkeepers are careless and others lazy, and where this is so it is important for the auditor to find it out. In all classes of business various claims and errors crop out from time to time. Where these affect customers' accounts, adjusting entries should be made at once, otherwise the outstanding balances do not reflect the true state of the accounts. If a bookkeeper *is* lazy or careless it will soon develop in the replies from customers to the requests for confirmations. In several instances this inquiry has demonstrated a very unsatisfactory condition where the cause was carelessness and not fraud. In many instances, however, carelessness leads to fraud. The very nature of a business will suggest to an intelligent auditor practically every source of revenue, special and ordinary.

Where the auditor can check loose methods he may really be preventing fraud, and the auditor who prevents fraud is a very useful person.

It is, of course, impossible in a limited space to suggest more than a bare outline of the procedure to be followed in ascertaining that all income has been accounted for.

Income from Investments: As mentioned elsewhere, it is now a frequent practice for mercantile and manufacturing firms and corporations to invest a part of their surplus in income-bearing securities. By reason of the fact that these investments are outside the usual transactions, the income therefrom is not usually subjected to internal audit.

The auditor will obtain a schedule of all securities held during the period of the audit and will ascertain that all dividends or interest accruing thereon is properly accounted for. If any of the investments are in inactive stocks and the dividends thereon are irregular and cannot be verified through the usual channels, a schedule of collections should be compiled and submitted for approval to some one in authority.

Where the investments are all grouped in one account, attention should be called to the desirability of opening a separate account with each one, and noting at the top of the page full particulars as to the serial numbers of the bonds or stock certificates, together with interest or dividend dates and similar information. If numerous, it would be best to have a subsidiary ledger or record for these details.

Interest Receivable: Attention is called to remarks under "Interest Payable" (page 158) and to Chapter XVIII, where it is shown that considerable carelessness exists with respect to the collection and payment of interest, and to the danger of accepting bankers' figures as infallible.

Interest on mortgage investments should be verified, as shown under "Income from Investments" (page 265).

Interest on other loans where the interest rate and other conditions are not always fixed in advance demands more attention. Few businesses exist, particularly those conducted by firms and individuals, where private loans or advances do not appear. These may be to friends, or business associates, or to employees, or to customers who request temporary accommodations. More frequently they will represent investments entirely outside the business and in connection with enterprises about which little is known.

Any auditor who has had long experience can recall innumerable instances where men have made fortunes in their own business and have squandered their entire surplus, and often most of their capital, in mines, plantations, patents, and all sorts of industrial flotations about which they had no technical knowledge whatever.

Frequently these outside ventures commence with small loans, and it is here that the auditor can sometimes be of real service to his client. The client should be impressed with the necessity of keeping his own capital intact, and should not have so-called investments in loans to others while borrowing himself. The auditor should point out to the client that he is not a banker, but that if loans or advances are made to others, interest thereon at current rates should be paid promptly and that the loans should be cleaned up or materially reduced periodically—just as is required by a banker. Considerable space is devoted to this matter here because borrowers of this class are not, as a rule, prompt in paying interest, so that the failure to discover such collections will give an auditor a good opportunity to criticize unbusinesslike practices.

Interest on bank deposits is not often inquired into, yet it may be that credit is being given at two per cent when two and one half or three per cent may have been arranged. Therefore the auditor should always verify the rate actually in force. A rough calculation can usually be made with respect to the amount credited on balances. Cheques issued follow a well-defined course, except in special cases, so that the test of a month or two, based on average daily balances, will disclose whether or not the amount received is approximately correct. The auditor can often have one of the office staff compile these figures and thus reduce his own time thereon to a minimum.

Discount for Prepayment: There is some difference between interest received on notes receivable from customers and cash discounts allowed by creditors for prompt or anticipated cash payments, although theoretically they both represent a profit or return upon the capital invested in the business. In one case the amount collected is almost invariably calculated at the legal rate of interest and is in effect an offset to the interest paid upon money borrowed. This will be apparent if the possibility of discounting the notes receivable is taken into consideration, in which case the interest on the notes is added to the face of the notes and the bank discount is deducted therefrom. It is not customary or necessary to credit the interest to one account and charge the discount to another account.

The rate of interest allowed for prepayments is purely arbitrary and fluctuates to a considerable extent. Most concerns wish to know the amount realized from this source and a separate ledger account should be kept for it.

Trade Discounts: Trade discounts are direct deductions from the purchases on one hand and from the sales on the other. That is, no ledger account should be kept for trade discounts, and the term itself rarely appears in books of account.

The test of a trade discount is the rate. In some lines of business a discount of seven per cent is allowed for payment within thirty days. This is not a cash discount, as no business house would pay the rate for money which is implied by the rate of discount. Therefore, the concern which receives the discount cannot credit it as an interest earning. As a matter of fact, it is a common occurrence for notes to be given, in which case the seven per cent is deducted from the face of the bill and interest at the rate of six per cent per annum added to the balance for the term of the note. This clearly establishes the fact that the deduction represents a trade and not a cash discount.

The distinction, therefore, is based on the answer to the query: Is the rate one which is obviously granted for anticipation of obligations not due? For instance, the strict enforcement of the terms "two per cent ten days, net thirty days" indicates that the two per cent is an earning and not a deduction from the purchase price. As a general rule any discount in excess of the terms just mentioned may be treated as a trade discount.

For an argument in favor of entering trade discounts in the books of account, see page ~~000~~ 201.

Rents Receivable: Where the item of income from rentals is inconsiderable the records relating thereto are not apt to be in good condition for auditing. If the item is a considerable one, reference should be had to the suggestions under the audit of "Real Estate Accounts" (page ~~000~~ 492).

In the first place a complete list of all rentable property is essential, and next in importance is a schedule of rentals which should be received therefrom. With these two points covered the auditor can make a satisfactory audit. The premises should be inspected and note made of vacancies, if any. Vacancies during the period should be listed and verification secured from some source independent of the clerk in charge of the collections.

The author had nearly completed the audit of a small railroad company when this question arose. The balance sheet disclosed the ownership of some rentable buildings. When asked for the records relating thereto, the treasurer attempted to defer the inquiry, but after a list was secured and the possible income calculated, he confessed that he had misappropriated most of the rent collections. The amount was comparatively small—a few hundred dollars out of total income of several millions—but the ordinary income was controlled and checked by other departments and he seized the only opportunity for fraud which seemed safe.

Where collections are in the hands of reputable agents, who

render periodical statements, it will not be necessary to check the income in so much detail, but careful inquiry should be made to satisfy the auditor that the agent has charge of *all* the property, and that the statements, when received, are checked both as to collections and deductions. It is obvious that the auditor will trace into the cash receipts the total amount turned over by the agent for the entire period, and if there is the slightest doubt as to the genuineness of the statements submitted, the auditor should request the agent to hand him a memorandum of payments for the period.

Realizations from Items Previously Charged to Profit and Loss: Among the miscellaneous items of income which may be found in almost any business, and to which the auditor should pay particular attention (chiefly because it may not be expected), are subsequent realizations from assets which had been charged off to Profit and Loss as uncollectible. The procedure is not so difficult as it appears at first sight, because the number of debits to Profit and Loss over a period of years is not usually very great, and as only a small proportion of these items can, in any event, admit a subsequent realization, it will not be much of a task for an auditor to analyze the "possible" items and scrutinize them with the sole object in view of probable or possible collections.

Customers' accounts are the most prolific source of delayed realization, as they are often written off after bankruptcy proceedings have been instituted, and before the final dividend has been paid.

Some bankruptcies extend over a long period of years, so that every such account written off should show beyond any doubt that a *final* dividend has been received. Where accounts have been written off without any evidence that bankruptcy proceedings were ever started, the written authority for such action should be submitted to the auditor.

Stocks, bonds, loans receivable, and similar items are sometimes written off before the properties or persons represented thereby have finally been adjudicated bankrupt or otherwise definitely declared to be hopeless. This line of inquiry does not require much time, but experience has proved its worth.

Consignments and Goods Out on "Memorandum": As carelessness is apt to exist in connection with all transactions which are out of the regular routine, the auditor should carefully inspect the records relating to charging out, keeping track of and collecting the proceeds of goods sent out on "memorandum" or "on sale," both of which are trade terms for consignments.

If not charged to the regular ledger account of the consignee (which may be inadvisable), the record of outstandings should be kept in a substantial loose-leaf binder in form and in dignity equal to the ordinary customers' ledgers.

It is necessary to create an impression of permanence about the records in an office, or the data which are considered to be temporary will be kept in an unsatisfactory and careless manner.

The record should be looked upon as a running account and all freights, drayages, insurance, and other charges posted thereto as incurred. In support of the memorandum or temporary records which are closed, the auditor should be furnished with evidence that the terms and conditions are in order. Usually the correspondence relating thereto will be sufficient, provided it carries the authority of one competent to fix such terms. A careful test of the accounting for the net proceeds as shown to be due by the record just described will then be made. If the test proves that no loss is likely to have occurred, there is no necessity for a complete verification.

Where consigned goods have not been accounted for when the books are closed, the consignee should be asked for an account current up to the date of closing. Based on this, credit may be taken for the proceeds of sales actually made. The balance will be treated as stock-in-trade and valued on the basis described on page 000. Goods which have been charged out at selling prices and appear as accounts receivable will likewise have to be treated as stock-in-trade and the valuation adjusted to the proper basis for balance-sheet purposes.

Goods Received for Sale: Where the concern under audit is the consignee, the accounts will be handled differently. If the goods received are to be sold on commission for account of the consignor, then the income will consist of a commission on the selling price, or perhaps the gross amount realized above a certain fixed price, or some one of the many other understandings upon which consignments are received.

The auditor must have access to the exact contract between the parties in order to test the accuracy of this income. In many cases the agreements are verbal or are based on correspondence more or less conflicting as to definite terms. Misunderstandings frequently arise between the consignor and the consignee, due principally to the failure of the minds to meet before the contractual relations commence. The auditor will usually have an opportunity to urge the desirability of an explicit contract being entered into at the outset and the furnishing of a copy to the client's office, so that the terms and conditions of each consignment may be noted in the books. Where a consignment is only partially disposed of when the books are closed, care must be taken that the unsold goods are not included in the inventory. A record of the quantities on hand should be made, but the values should be entered "in short" and a memorandum made that the items belong to the consignor.

Inquiry should be made as to whether such goods are insured, and if so, in whose name. If in the name of the consignee, the policies must contain a stipulation covering the facts of title.

On lots partly disposed of, credit may be taken for the proportionate commission or profit on goods sold and delivered, but no income should be taken credit for on unsold or undelivered goods. In order to satisfy himself that the accounts are in order the auditor should request that *pro forma* account sales be made up for all open consignments. The quantities not yet disposed of should be checked with the inventories and the accrued earnings can also be verified.

The account sales should be scrutinized in order to see that all legitimate charges are made to the consignor. Commissions and freights are not usually forgotten, but careless clerks do not always include insurance, cartage, allowances, and similar items which may be permissible. Other items, such as extra charges for special services, postage, etc., may not be thought of, but as items of this nature are charged by some commission houses, it is always pertinent to inquire whether the matter has had full consideration.

Sales not Delivered: In closing books there seems to be a temptation on the part of most concerns to anticipate all profits in sight. Therefore, where sales have been made for future delivery, the tendency is to charge the goods and create an account receivable or make some adjustment of the profit and loss account to include the profit which it is expected will be realized. Conservative business men do not follow this course, but experience proves that it is followed often enough to compel an auditor to be constantly on his guard.

In the automobile trade, for instance, sales are effected and substantial deposits or part payments received long before the cars are delivered. But no profit has been realized and may never be realized, so that the inclusion of this hoped-for profit in a profit and loss account is absolutely wrong.

Thousands of such sales are never consummated by reason of the failure of the factories to build the cars. The sales have been canceled and the deposits returned, and all expenses incurred thereby have not been compensated for.

In other cases the goods may be on hand or in process of manufacture, so that the expectation of being able to deliver is based on a sounder hypothesis, but the rule is precisely the same. No profit must be taken until a delivery or a tender has been made and the sale is converted into a valid claim against a solvent debtor.

There is some merit in the contention that where sales for future delivery have been made, and the goods are on hand ready to ship, the goods may be inventoried at something more than manufacturing cost. That is, the expenses of sale having been incurred to this extent, the period in which delivery is made should be forced to bear its share of the burden, and such expenses should be carried forward as an asset under the caption "Deferred Charges to Operations." These expenses may include sales expenses such as commissions, traveling, salaries, advertising, etc., but must not include any part of fixed charges such as rent, administration expenses, etc.

Where part of the sales price has been collected in advance or deposits have been received, such items should be separately stated on the balance sheets, as they do not constitute trade liabilities, but on the contrary are evidences of prospective profits. But as already stated, the prospective profit must not be anticipated, and if sales not delivered have been charged to customers, the auditor should eliminate such items from the accounts receivable and the sales account and add the goods to the inventory at their cost.

There may be many a slip between the order and the profitable closing of the transaction, as Judge Clark said in the American Malting case (see page 595):

> These contracts were to deliver at a future time a product not yet made, from raw material, not yet purchased, with the aid of labor not yet expended. The price agreed to be paid at that future time had to cover all the possible contingencies of the market in the meanwhile and might show a profit, and ran the chance of showing a loss.

Sales of Building Lots: In the audit of a land or real estate company it would at once occur to the auditor that he must look carefully for receipts from sales of building lots. Now the last places to look at are the receipt side of the cash book and the sales book or other record of the sales, although when he asks for a record of sales, that is the point to which he will be directed, and at least nine out of ten times the client will expect him to take these records as starting points rather than to consider such a record as a goal *toward* which he is working.

There probably never has been a land company which did not issue a map of its property nicely marked off into lots with a number and block for every lot. What could be simpler than for the auditor to take a map and one of the printed pricelists usually available and proceed to account for every lot? All lots sold for less than list price should pass inspection by a duly authorized officer. All lots not accounted for as sold should be on the "for sale" list or else specified as being set apart for particular purposes, these purposes to be evidenced by resolutions of the board of directors or other authority properly expressed.

As most lots are sold on installments, the auditor will then look for collections of interest on the deferred installments and will require that every such item be accounted for.

And so through the rather simple processes of most business enterprises it will be possible to *think* out the sources of revenue instead of using the books as a guide, for by so doing the auditor will avoid the danger of being influenced by the entries which are shown therein and thus lose sight of the fact that those entries are not all which *should* appear.

CHAPTER XIX

THE DETAILED AUDIT (Continued)

PURCHASES AND EXPENSES

Vouchers: It must be admitted that the examination of vouchers is necessary and valuable, but with respect to *relative* importance, such work will be classified down toward the end of the list. If a careful comparison of vouchers with cash books would disclose improper or extravagant purchases or expenses, the very considerable work involved would be justified, but, unfortunately, the ordinary voucher, so-called, is usually little more than a receipt for a given sum of money and is usually of so little practical use that many concerns never insist on vouchers nor do they preserve them when they are furnished.

Of course, this is a matter which should not be discussed with anyone whose accounts are being audited. Where vouchers are taken, an auditor should call for vouchers covering all payments and require that they be arranged in order to correspond with the cash-book entries. He should not allow it to be known that there is any probability of his not checking any part of the vouchers, or it will be difficult to secure them properly and have them arranged in order. If a cheque bears on its face or back any indication of its purpose, it is the best receipt for money paid that can be secured. If it bears no evidence as to its purpose, but can be readily identified with a particular bill or invoice, it still is a better voucher than a receipted bill. The comparison of vouchers with a cash book without the identification of the entries in the cash book with the cheques is worse than negligence, for the sole purpose of vouching cash is to ascertain, as nearly as possible, that the payments represent an equivalent in value to the payers and that the equivalent—that is, the discharge of a like liability—is received when the cash is paid. A mere receipt for so much money, which can readily be forged, is poor evidence of a legitimate payment, but a paid cheque, properly indorsed and otherwise identified as representing a definite liability, is pretty fair proof that the money has reached a creditor; and if the auditor follows it up by a careful scrutiny of the documents supporting the cheque, he is on the right track.

It must be remembered, however, that a paid cheque unsupported by other documents is not conclusive evidence of the propriety of a payment. This is well illustrated by the following instance in the author's experience:

The accounts of a district school board which had passed out of existence were to be audited. Only a small amount of funds was handled, the total collection of taxes for district school purposes being about $15,000 per annum. The records submitted to the auditors were fairly complete, with the exception that no paid bills were turned over to the new board. The paid cheques, however, were intact, the cash book had been well kept, with some attempt at classification of expenditures, and the minute book contained complete lists of all the bills approved for payment by the board at its meetings.

Every disbursement recorded in the cash book was found to be supported by a paid cheque, and all the payments had been duly authorized by the board. Most of the payments were of very moderate amounts, and thus far everything appeared to be in order. Practically nothing had been seen to arouse the auditor's suspicions. Several payments, each for a little less than $150, had, however, been made to a wholesale drug house and a pharmacist respectively. The auditors could not think what articles aside from sponges would be purchased from these sources, and concluded to obtain duplicate bills so as to ascertain the nature of the articles purchased. The request for such bills was in both cases met with the reply that no payment of the amount mentioned had been received from the school board. Further investigation developed the fact that the indorsements on the cheques had been forged, which fact the auditor could not know from an examination of the cheques themselves, as they bore evidence of having passed through bank in the usual way. It finally developed that the indorsements had been forged by a member of the school board.

Furthermore, even a bill certified as to receipt of the articles shown thereon, approved for payment by the authorized officials, and evidenced as to actual payment by an indorsed cheque which has passed through bank in the regular manner, may not be conclusive evidence of the honesty of a transaction. Another school board (not the one mentioned in the preceding paragraphs) had purchased a piano for $450. The documents supporting the payment were all in regular order, and the piano itself was in existence as proof of the fact that the article charged for on the bill had actually been received. The auditors, however, made a personal visit to the store where the piano had been purchased and without revealing their identity made inquiries as to the prices of various styles of pianos. They were offered exactly the same style of piano for which the school board had paid $450 for $275, and this without any "haggling" over the price. The piano concern later admitted that when it received the school board's cheque for $450, it (the piano concern) paid $200 in currency to the bearer of the cheque. Of course, the "refund" never found its way back into the school board treasury.

In small concerns many items of payments will be posted direct to expense and other general ledger accounts. The vouchers for such items should include complete evidence of being genuine. The best vouchers for payments posted direct to personal accounts are the paid indorsed cheques, because the credit side of the personal ledger accounts will have been compared with the original invoices, so that very little evidence of the discharge of the obligation is required.

An auditor can be of great assistance to his client by looking into the various operations surrounding a payment as well as passing on the question as to whether or not it is a *bona fide* transaction.

Purchase Invoices: The bill or invoice should bear on its face all the proper marks or initials to indicate that the goods or materials were received in proper order as to quality and quantity; that they were as ordered, which includes an approval of the price, provided it was recorded at the time the order was given, or an approval by a responsible and authorized official where the price was not fixed in advance; that if the quotation was "delivery free," freight was not paid, or, if paid, has been charged back to the vendor; that where custom permits or any other indication appears of a cash discount being in order, it was deducted;

that in all other respects the purchase was in order, including the checking of the calculations, the notations as to the department or account to be charged, etc.

Inquiry should be made as to whether the receiving clerks keep an independent record of all goods received irrespective of invoices to cover, and whether the subsequent comparison of these records is carried out intelligently and completely.

As stated above, these invoices should be thoroughly tested to ascertain the internal method of checking their accuracy, but the auditor should never, as a matter of course, attempt to verify the whole of the purchase vouchers unless he has a further purpose in view than to "audit the books." In a large concern the auditor does not think of examining every purchase invoice. He makes copious tests and if nothing suspicious is discovered, is willing to certify that the accounts are correct. An auditor should not inspect every voucher even in a small establishment unless there is some special reason for doing so.

There are many more important things to do in an audit, and the time spent on vouchers must bear a proper relation to the other time and to the fee, if it is to be fair to the auditor and to the client.

It is true that some books and articles on auditing recommend the examination of all vouchers, but these are not based on successful experience nor upon a proper realization of the service which the client is entitled to receive.

Where a system of internal check is in force, it will not be necessary to inspect every invoice; a complete test should be made to see that there is a strict compliance with the rule heretofore mentioned, but this test will be complete by taking, say, three or four months out of twelve and examining each item, alwavs including the last month of the period. The auditor should then look over the cash book very carefully for the other eight or nine months, and in connection with his analysis of the ledger accounts he can note any unusual or suspicious-looking item and call for the voucher covering it. This will obviate the necessity of checking over the mass of documents which he has satisfied himself by his general test to represent purchases for the proper and ordinary purposes of his client. The analysis of the ledger accounts is important wherever charges have been made to plant accounts. These must always be supported by proper vouchers.

In making the test care must be taken to ascertain that bills are made out to the concern under audit and not to its officers or clerks. Of course, where the disposition of the things purchased is checked such an irregularity would be disclosed.

It is important to know not only that the entries purporting to represent purchases made are proper, but that all invoices for purchases actually made have been entered previous to closing the books. This can be quite satisfactorily tested where there is an adequate system of recording purchase orders issued, of keeping record of incoming goods, and of checking invoices against order and receiving records. The comparison of creditors' statements with the accounts payable record should under ordinary circumstances also enable the auditor to detect the omission of purchase invoices.

In the case of Irish Woolen Mill Company, Lim. v. Tyson and others, which is more fully referred to in the chapter on Liabilities of Auditors, the auditor was held liable for negligence in having failed to detect the intentional omission of purchase invoices when the books were closed and the subsequent entry of the invoices in the following fiscal period. The purpose of the company's secretary was to make a better showing than its operations and financial condition justified. The court held that the auditor, who had made monthly audits for a number of years, should have had his suspicions aroused by the fact that invoices were charged into each period which, according to their date, belonged in a previous period, and that had he then made the investigation which this suspicious circumstance called for, the fraud would have been detected.

Missing Vouchers: These are a source of much needless work to many auditors. If an audit is being made and no evidence whatever of fraud is found, and if the payments for which vouchers are not submitted appear in every way to be regular, it is usually a waste of time to list them in detail and consume a lot of time in having them located. In most cases they will not be found, as many vouchers are never returned or are mislaid or lost in the mails.

No specific rule can be formulated with respect to missing

vouchers, but the author wishes to go on record as opposed to the contention of some auditors who regard this point as a very serious one in every audit. The experience of the author has been that where a cashier enters an irregular or wholly fictitious payment, he will always be sure to have a voucher to cover.

Vouchers for Petty Cash Payments, Pay Roll, etc.: Where payments are made covering expenses and wages, and for similar purposes, and where there is no ledger account with the payee, great care must be taken to ascertain that the amounts have not been overstated, either by fraudulently raising the figures on the bill or memorandum or by entering a larger amount in the cash book than the voucher represents.

Petty Cash: Vouchers are often altered and petty cash payments are frequently the subject of manipulation. Junior clerks see how easy it is to hand in a memorandum calling for $10 postage when $5 is all that is necessary, or, in fact, used, and they gradually extend their field of operation until large sums are abstracted. Postage or mail books are in general use in England, and if more generally adopted here would save many a boy from the penitentiary. It is a grave responsibility for any employer to permit, or any auditor to approve, a loose or inefficient system for handling petty cash, postage, etc.

A large percentage of young boys who are employed in the business districts of our large cities and who have access to or can draw from petty cash funds, are constantly following the races through the worthless afternoon papers, through poolrooms, or in other ways. Conversations in large offices often indicate the keenest interest in the results of the races not only near New York, but throughout the country. Professional auditors should take a firm stand on all questions, public or private, which affect gambling.

Coming back to petty cash vouchers, in view of the informality of many of them, the auditor's best protection is to have some responsible person scrutinize the payments, rather than the vouchers themselves, and indicate his approval by initialing each page or each month of the petty cash book. The whole question of petty cash vouchers is one which calls for the exercise of good judgment rather than the application of fixed rules, and the auditor should take this view of it rather than feel that it is merely a matter of comparing pieces of paper with certain entries on the payment side of a cash book.

There is no great objection to examining every voucher where the concern is not too large, and where the auditor has plenty of time, and where he does it properly, but he should relegate the inspection of vouchers to its proper place and, if pressed for time, he should attend first to more important matters.

Where a test is considered sufficient the auditor may verify all of the vouchers for a certain period, or all vouchers exceeding a certain amount for the entire period.

There are numerous ways of handling petty cash, but unfortunately most of them provide little or no check upon the cashier and furnish afterward no evidence of the faithful discharge of his trust.

The method of charging all petty expenditures in a lump sum to an expense account known as "petty expenses" is a most common one, and one that is highly undesirable. The older method of paying such expenses out of incoming cash or of cash received from cash sales, and oftentimes of not making any entry whatever, is still worse.

The most satisfactory method is that known as the "imprest" system. The petty cashier is provided with a fund of $100 or $500, or whatever amount is necessary to meet the average expenses of two weeks or a month. This amount, when paid to him, is charged to an account in the general ledger known as "Petty Cash Fund" and stands undisturbed from month to month.

The petty cashier keeps a cash book provided with a column for each of the principal expense items, such as Office Supplies, Factory Supplies, Postage, Stationery, and Printing, etc. He continues to pay from his cash fund until the balance gets low, or until the end of the month, when he rules off his book, presents it to the cashier together with his vouchers, and receives in exchange a cheque for the exact amount of his expenses. This and whatever cash balance he had left make up the original petty cash fund. The general cashier in recording the cheque on his records does not charge "petty cash," but he charges the various expense accounts direct, posting from the footings of the columns in the petty cash book.

In some instances a loose summary sheet is used to which the vouchers are attached and on which they are entered in detail. This system does away entirely with the petty cash book, and the summary sheet and supporting vouchers become the authority for the issuance of a refunding cheque to the petty cashier.

Organization and Similar Expenses Which Affect More Than One Year's Operation: If the expenses incurred in the organization of the company, such as incorporation fees, legal, engineering, and other expenses, engraving bonds and stock certificates, transfer fees and stamps, etc., are more than can fairly be charged into current expenses, it is permissible to spread the charges over a term of years, preferably three, and not more than five. But it should be ascertained whether or not the promoters (if the enterprise was "promoted") agreed to pay any part of these expenses. This is a matter of increasing importance, as a number of corporations are being organized where this obligation is assumed by the organizers.

Other items, such as advertising and exploitation expenditures which are intended to produce future business, may not appear to be a proper charge against income which could hardly have received the benefit of such payments. An auditor may pass the carrying forward of any legitimate expenditure which has been incurred solely for the benefit of future business, provided that in his judgment the setting up of the deferred charge, and its consequent inclusion as an asset, is justified by its probable value to the future business.

But it is not enough that the expenditure has been made. For instance, a large number of circular letters calling attention to a special sale in January may be sent out in December. If the auditor commences work in February and finds that the campaign was a total failure, it would be rather misleading for him to certify to the accuracy of a balance sheet as of December 31st showing the entire expenditure as an asset.

An auditor should be willing to back up his opinion by his certificate. If in his opinion expenditures of this nature are actually deferred assets, he should so certify. It should, however, be noted that the most successful concerns carry on selling campaigns all the time, and there must be some limit to the postponement of the actual charges to current operating.

In the discussion of a paper presented at the 1908 meeting of the American Association of Public Accountants in which the matter of deferred charges was mentioned, George O. May, C. P. A., said:

> A further point raised by one of the speakers was as to the carrying forward of expenses on seasonal business. I think this is a dangerous practice, especially where there is a big asset of good will. I think the more conservative view to take is that the expenses necessary to keep up the next season's business are effectively an expense for preserving the good will of the business. As regards the buying expenses of a department store, I do not think any valid objection can be taken to these being included. In my experience it has often been found, in fact generally, that department stores do not take into account discounts on purchases on the one hand, or buying expenses on the other, and that these about offset each other.

If the business is not successful there will be no future profits to which the deferred items can be charged. Therefore, the auditor should use every argument he can muster to induce his client to absorb these expenses as soon as possible, and never carry them forward unless it would be improper, from every point of view, to include them among the current expenses.

More than one enterprise has been wrecked by the failure to look preliminary or establishment expenses squarely in the face. The temptation to state the current operations in such a way as to show a profit has been too strong, and so they have gone along from year to year, the burden increasing instead of diminishing, with an inevitable day of reckoning when it is realized that liabilities cannot be liquidated with capitalized expenses.

The recent report of an automobile business stated that the auditors had insisted on charging off all of the expenses of establishing branches which previously had been carried as an asset. The monthly reports had shown big profits, which had been largely paid out in dividends, with the result that the working capital had been reduced to an amount below the safety line.

If auditors with the courage of their convictions had been consulted earlier and had called attention to the overstatement of profits, the company's credit would probably not have been impaired to the extent it was,

Extraordinary expenditures, such as repairs and renewals incident to accidents or storms, are sometimes capitalized at the time with the expressed intention of spreading the loss over several years. The same situation arises where accident insurance is not carried, a certain percentage of the gross receipts being set aside to a reserve account to pay losses, and the payments being in excess of the reserve. Quite frequently the debit balances so created are carried forward as an asset until subsequent accruals wipe out the deficit.

This practice is not sound, because in the last analysis it simply results in setting up on the balance sheet accounts which are in no sense of the word assets. If the word "assets" means anything at all, there can be no justification for the inclusion of items of maintenance, expended because of necessity, and which do not tend to improve the physical or financial position of the enterprise.

It may be that these charges, if incorporated among the costs and expenses of a current period, tend to hide the normal operations, but if the unusual item is clearly set forth this procedure is preferable to making direct charges to surplus. It may be hard to resist the temptation, but the practice is to be condemned. It may not sound well or look well, but it has the advantage of portraying the actual state of affairs, which is not the case when an attempt is made to designate an expense account as an asset. Directors who realize their personal responsibility for dividends paid out of capital will not vote for a distribution of earnings which does not take into account expenses actually incurred.

All payments for insurance, bank discount, rent, taxes, dues, subscriptions, and similar items should be scrutinized in order to determine the proportion, if any, which applies to a subsequent period and thus constitutes an asset when the books are closed, in the form of a deferred charge to the future operations of the business. In order to save the auditor's time he may request one of the client's clerks or the insurance broker to calculate the prepaid items, in all cases testing the accuracy of their work.

Where discount on bonds is carried as a deferred charge to operations, the auditor should verify the amortization calculations. If this provision is not in order, an adjustment should be made before the balance sheet is certified to.

Legal Expenses and "Graft": If charges to legal expenses consisted merely of current bills from attorneys, no special mention would be necessary, but the account is such an elastic one that it requires special and careful attention.

In some lines of business secret commissions are paid to the purchasing agents of customers. In spite of the publicity which such practices have received during the last few years, "graft" still exists and no doubt will flourish for years to come. Where the recipients are unusually sensitive it is customary to charge the amounts paid to legal expenses or some other account which serves to screen the true purpose of the payments. From an accounting point of view this is, of course, highly objectionable, because it permits sales to go through with what are almost invariably excessive gross profits without the chance of charging against such sales one of the direct expenses connected therewith. Legal expense is not usually regarded as one of the items of selling costs, and the auditor who suspects the truth can hardly restate the accounts to accord with his suspicion. The vouchers for such payments will be signed by some responsible officer of the corporation or a member of the firm, so that the honesty of the disposition of the funds can hardly be questioned.

Some years ago an auditor of high standing discovered in the audit of one business that a commission had been paid to the superintendent of the plant owned by another client. He informed the latter, but was not profusely thanked for his information. The other corporation learned of the fact, called it a gross breach of trust, and declined to pay the auditor's bill.

If an auditor feels that the morals of his client are to be judged along with the accounts, he should have the courage of his convictions and so inform the client before the work is started. He will not then have to charge off his bill to bad debts.

Repairs and Renewals: In the audit of a large manufacturing establishment this will be the most troublesome account upon which the auditor will be called to pass.

The underlying purpose of the audit of expenses is to ascertain as far as possible that an equivalent was received for the liability assumed, but the improper application in the books of the expenditure for repairs and maintenance may upset the accuracy of a balance sheet in spite of the fact that value was received for the liability assumed. That is, the expenditure for repairs or for renewals may be charged to plant or some other asset account instead of to current operating expense, thus inflating the assets on one hand and the profits on the other. It must be kept in mind constantly that tacit conspiracy usually exists to bring about this very result, and the auditor will be apt to find strong forces arrayed against him as soon as an accurate accounting for maintenance items is begun.

The ordinary manager, superintendent, or foreman seems to feel that it is a reflection on him individually or on his department to incur any considerable expense on renewals and repairs which he knows will increase his cost of operating. He knows that an item charged to an asset account will not be charged against him, so it is no wonder that an analysis of plant accounts sometimes discloses remarkable items which are in no sense of the word betterments, but current maintenance.

In order to make a complete audit of items which should be charged to repairs, the charges to plant accounts must be analyzed.

Allowances and Returns: There are two very good reasons for a careful scrutiny of all credits to customers, the first being that by means of unauthorized credits fraud may be concealed. That is, cash collected from a customer is not accounted for, and subsequently, to avoid discovery, the ledger account is closed by an entry which indicates that goods have been returned or that an allowance has been made.

The second reason is that in the absence of fraud there may be carelessness both in the manner of granting credit for allowances and returns and in the record thereof. For instance, some automobile dealers deduct freight from credits for returned defective parts; others do not. To a dealer doing a large business this makes a difference of several hundred dollars a year.

In some concerns full credit is not given where goods are returned simply on account of an overstock. In others, there is little or no check on the returns and full credit is allowed.

The auditor should, therefore, examine the record which has been kept and see to it that so far as possible the entries are approved by some responsible official and that no abuse has been made of the return privilege. In order to test the integrity of the entries, it may be desirable to call for the correspondence in connection with a certain number of items.

Goods returned are not purchases, but deductions from sales, but so far as stock records are concerned they should be treated as purchases and tests should be made to see that the entries in the return book are posted to the stock sheets as regularly as those in the purchase records. Otherwise an opportunity might be afforded to a stock clerk to ship goods without accounting therefor.

Separate columns should be kept in the allowance and return book, as allowances may or may not be posted to a separate ledger account, while returns are always deductible from sales.

The newspapers recently reported a case wherein it appeared that the bookkeeper of a baking company had manipulated his books by crediting customers with excessive returns. The following is the police account, in part:

> He (the bookkeeper) left the firm the early part of this month, and when his books were examined, the firm found a shortage of more than $1,500. He admitted entering in the books to the credit of customers a greater number of loaves of bread daily than were actually returned by the firm's drivers.

Empties: In many lines of business shipments are made in bottles, boxes, barrels, or other form of package, which have a residual value, the test of the latter being the cost, durability, and expense of return. When no charge is made for the package and credit is allowed for returns, there is the equivalent of a purchase, provided the allowance is not more than the open market price. If the credit is at a higher price than the market, the excess is clearly a deduction from sales. If credit is passed only upon return and the allowance is not more than cost, no record need be kept of those outstanding, as it makes no difference whether or not they are returned. If a separate charge for packages appears on the invoices, there is no difficulty in keeping track of the aggregate charged for and the aggregate returned, if the information is of value.

In the case of kegs, crates, syphons, etc., for which no charge s made, but which must be returned, the most common, and probably the most satisfactory, method of handling is to note the quantities in the sales book and post the items to the customers' ledger, in which a special column should be provided on both debit and credit sides. If this system has not been in force, a very careful test of the records should be made, as errors usually exist, and they may be unnecessary as well as expensive.

The method of inspection and of passing credit should have the auditor's attention. If the receiving clerk is careless or inefficient, the number of packages returned may not be verified and damaged or broken packages may be passed as in good condition. The clerk in charge of the credits should not be allowed to settle the custom of the house with respect to prices to be allowed, freight payments, etc.

If packages are charged to customers at a substantial increase over cost, and if permission is granted for return at the same price, the auditor must provide a reserve to cover outstandings when the books are closed.

Where packages are furnished free with an obligation to return, it must be assumed that customers treat the obligation lightly and that a considerable proportion will not be accounted for, in addition to the usual losses and breakages. If feasible, an attempt should be made at some convenient time to secure an actual inventory of packages on hand and within reach that are positively known to be recoverable. A comparison of these figures with the book inventory would form a sound basis for a depreciation or expense rate.

Salaries: In all cases a pay-roll book showing names, positions, and salary rates of all employees should be kept. This does not include workmen and others whose compensation is referred to throughout this book as wages.

The book should be arranged with thirteen columns, to cover three months' time. Each column should be initialed by an executive. The cashier should have written authority for each change in rate and for each name added. If one cheque is drawn for an entire pay roll, the auditor should verify the footings of, say, every third week.

Salesmen's Commissions: Examine contracts and note provisions as to percentage, territory, and particularly as to whether commissions are payable on delivery of goods or on collection c accounts; also whether based on gross sales or on net proceed after deductions for cash discounts, freight, etc.

Traveling Expenses, Entertaining, etc.: Examine contract of salesmen, if any, to see if limit has been placed on travelin and other expenses. If contracts are not required, inquire o manager if any understanding of this nature is in force.

In many concerns the utmost liberality prevails in suc allowances, but sentiment along these lines is changing and sales men are being held to a stricter accountability than was formerl the case. The auditor, therefore, should take pains to mak inquiries on this point at each audit.

Vouchers for traveling and similar expenses should be ap proved by some one in authority.

The auditor is interested in seeing that railroad mileage i properly accounted for. Mileage may be carried as a separat account on the ledger, if it is large, or it may be regarded as cas and included in the cash figures.

When it is given out, the full amount in the book is charge at cost against the Traveling Advance account of the one who i using it. When it is returned, credit is given just as if cash wer received.

Wages: In the audit of a business where many employees ar found it will be necessary to devote some time to a consideratio of the system in force, with respect to time records and wage payments. It is a well-known fact that receipts are worthless sc far as being a check on the amount paid. It may be valuable tc a concern to have a receipt from each man to guard against sub sequent disputes, but these receipts are of little real value to ar auditor who is attempting to prove to his own satisfaction tha the aggregate amounts of the pay-roll payments have reached th hands of those entitled thereto. The auditor must think this ou for himself in each audit, but it is suggested that the best check on wages payments is to use as many people as possible during the various stages from the point where the time is recorded tc the final handing out of the envelopes. If the latter, for instance is done by an employee who has no access to the rolls or to the cash, it makes a good check. If an auditor is on hand when the men are being paid off, he should supervise the operation or take a more active part, if feasible. Obviously, this procedure would be of no value unless it was done without notice to *anyone*.

A few large corporations have tried the experiment of paying exclusively by cheque, but it is believed that the plan has been abandoned by most of them.

The auditor must direct his attention to two main points, viz., the records which may be kept accurately, or inaccurately, and the clerical force in charge of the records, who may be honest or dishonest.

Fortunately for employers, most of the records now in general use are, or should be, mechanical or automatic. The time clock registers the time in and out, and other devices stamp the time actually employed on various jobs. In the office these records in turn are checked and proved by mechanical means.

The audit of wages earned therefore resolves itself into a critical inspection of the system in use. Before making this inspection, the auditor should acquaint himself with the particulars of all the latest devices on the market. He can then evince a familiarity with any system he finds and note any lack of efficiency, and is also in a better position to make suggestions where unsatisfactory methods are found.

The author feels that the scope of this book is too limited to contain directions as to the best system, except to suggest that, since scientific management has taken hold of the labor question so seriously, and has been more or less successful, the auditor who has to deal with the audit of wages paid, and who is expected to criticize the records relating thereto, owes to himself and his profession the duty of at least reading the best-known books on factory management, and glancing over the descriptive circulars of some of the really wonderful mechanical appliances designed especially by experts familiar with the practical side of the question. So much for the system.

The personnel and extent of the clerical force are important from the auditor's point of view. He should be especially vigilant in small establishments where the office force is small and where the same clerk keeps or assists with the original records, makes up or assists with the envelopes, and distributes them or has some connection with the distribution thereof.

Concrete instances may serve better than theory in pointing

out the course the auditor should take to satisfy himself that the pay rolls are correct.

The auditor should ascertain that the names of discharged men are removed from the pay roll as of the proper date. In a large factory the foreman handed in to a clerk in the office who had access to the pay rolls, slips bearing the names of men discharged. He destroyed the slips and recorded full time to the credit of the men discharged. In paying off he secured the envelopes and retained the money. The fraud was not discovered for a long time.

In a factory where time books were kept by the foreman, the assistant cashier transferred the time therein to the pay-roll book In addition, he entered several fictitious names. The cashier himself made up the envelopes and superintended the paying off Each week a number of envelopes were left over, as is nearly always the case in a large plant, on account of sickness, etc Most of them are called for within a short time. In this case the dishonest clerk always had an opportunity to secure the envelopes covering the fictitious names. The fraud was discovered by the auditor calling in the time books and comparing them with the pay roll.

Duties: The vouching of duties is one requiring great care, because, until recently, collectors of internal revenue would not accept cheques in payment, but insisted on legal tender. Where such payments are few in number, they are usually made through a custom-house broker, and his invoices, if properly checked and approved, will be sufficient evidence of the propriety of the payments.

In any event, the auditor should inquire into the procedure in force and satisfy himself that the matter is properly handled. Instances have been known where everything was left to clerks who did not have skill enough to discover errors if they did exist

Interest and Collection Charges: Too much confidence is placed in the accuracy of bank clerks; therefore it will usually be found that interest charged on loans and credited on balances, discount deducted, and collection fees charged are, in nine cases out of ten, accepted as final without being checked by the client's staff. Auditors whose experience includes much bank work are familiar with the numerous errors made by bank clerks in their own records, and while perhaps a majority of bank officers insist on these errors being located and corrected, yet it is obvious that in calculations involving interest and collection charges or credits, there is not the same likelihood of correction of errors as exists with those items which enter into the regular double-entry system of the bank.

It follows that many errors will be made and will remain undetected unless the auditor tests the items. But the auditor should not stop with the verification of the calculations. Banks will charge as high an interest rate on loans and discounts as they think the traffic will bear, and if an auditor finds that a concern with first-class credit is being charged six per cent, when he knows that other concerns of equal or inferior standing are paying four and one-half or five per cent, it will certainly be in order to mention the matter when a good opportunity arises. The successful auditor will not lose any good chance to render a service which falls within the scope of a business adviser.

Insurance Premiums: Experience shows that the bills of insurance agents are rarely scrutinized unless the item of premiums is a very large one and the bill is in charge of some one especially designated to keep track of the insurance in force and the rates charged for insurance. For this reason a careful audit of the premium bills and a careful analysis of the total insurance carried is a fruitful field of inquiry for the auditor, and particularly advisable in audits where great care is taken with other classes of expenses.

In one case an auditor noticed that a policy had been canceled and another company substituted. He looked for a credit to cover the return premium on the canceled policy, but failed to find it. This started a complete investigation into insurance matters, and it was found that for several years back one or more policies had been canceled each month, due to the undesirability of the risk, but that no credit therefor had been issued by the agent. The total amount recovered amounted to several hundred dollars and the discovery greatly enhanced the auditor's reputation.

Sufficient attention is not paid to the amount of insurance carried. If overinsured, a useless expense is incurred, and if underinsured, an unjustifiable risk is assumed. The matter is one requiring comparatively little time, perhaps not so much as to verify the footings or postings for a short period, and is of very much more importance.

As stated elsewhere, the unexpired portion of premiums prepaid at the date of the balance sheet is a deferred asset. In a going business it is proper to set up the full unexpired proportion of the premiums paid in advance, but in a statement of affairs, such as is required in the event of proposed or forced liquidation, it may be necessary to base the calculations upon the "short" rates which are used in the cancellation of policies.

Freight and Express: Freight is another class of expense which is passed by many auditors on the assumption that the amounts paid are sure to be accurate, and that it is a waste of time to attempt to go into detail. As a matter of fact, transportation companies, and particularly express companies, are chronic overchargers, and every bill must be checked most carefully.

An auditor need not go into tariff details, but he should inquire closely into the method of check in use, and if he finds that the freight and express bills are not approved as to weights and rates by an intelligent clerk who uses all possible sources of information to secure the lowest quotations, he will probably find an opportunity to make a constructive report on the situation.

Many trades have a central association with a traffic bureau, which furnishes full and free information when requested to do so by its members. The Interstate Commerce Commission will also assist a shipper who feels aggrieved.

In one very large manufacturing company being audited for the first time by the author's firm, it was found that practically no attention was given to the inspection of freight bills, it being assumed that the charges were always in order. A careful test disclosed the fact that many purchases had been made on a basis of freight being prepaid by the shipper. Now it is the custom in such cases for the consignee to pay the freight and deduct same from the invoices. The company under audit had paid the freight in every case, but had charged it to purchases account instead of to the shipper. The investigation was carried back several years and many thousands of dollars were actually recovered.

Postage: Vouchers should be secured for all purchases of stamps. Postmasters will always sign receipts when requested to do so.

Defalcations of small sums are frequently found in connection with postage accounts, so that an auditor should not only scrutinize such payments very carefully, but should suggest safeguards which will reduce future possibilities of loss, and more important still, remove a serious source of temptation to junior clerks.

There should be some relation between the total cost of postage and other expense accounts, such as stationery and printing, advertising circulars, etc.

A daily mail book showing the total postage used on outgoing mail requires very little time to compile and is valuable for several reasons. It affords an opportunity to apportion the cost to various accounts and has a most excellent moral effect on those who handle the stamps, as some one in authority from each department should initial the charges to such department at least weekly.

Inquiry should be made to ascertain if postage is paid on outgoing shipments of goods in small quantities. Many concerns add postage to such shipments, and custom permits it unless quotations are made "prepaid." If not so made and a considerable number of shipments are made by mail, it will be in order for the auditor to suggest that the cost of the postage be added to the invoice.

In one instance, where quotations distinctly stated that postage would be added where small lots were sent by mail, the shipping department was extremely careless and few such charges were made. The auditor who discovered the laxity received warm commendation for his vigilance and was requested to make the most comprehensive investigation into all the other departments of the business.

Journal Vouchers: Vouchers should be submitted for all journal entries and the auditor need not announce in advance how many of them he intends to inspect. If formal vouchers have not been taken, the journal should be read over carefully and all entries for which authority should have been secured pointed out as requiring proof.

The journal can be used fraudulently by fictitious or irregular credits to customers or other personal accounts to conceal the misappropriation of cash collected therefrom. To detect this, all credits to customers for allowances, returns, etc., and all accounts charged off as bad should be approved by some authorized official. If no such approval appears, the auditor should ask that the journal entries themselves be initialed. Other credits to personal accounts are made for salesmen's expenses, etc. These should be verified in the same manner as cash vouchers.

Well-managed concerns now supply their salesmen with a fixed fund, and payments for expenses cover the exact expenditures during a given period. This obviates the necessity for paying out round sums after the first item. Subsequent payments can be charged direct to the proper expense account and journal entries are done away with.

Transfers from one account to another may be for the purpose of fraudulently increasing one account or decreasing another.

The experienced auditor need not spend very much time on the journal, as a careful glance over the pages will develop any entries which require explanation. The inexperienced auditor should examine the entries carefully and call for documentary evidence to support an item which by any chance might be irregular.

There is a tendency on the part of bookkeepers to use a printed form for journal vouchers which serves in most cases as a memorandum from which the actual book entry is made, the result being that every entry is duplicated. One, however, is called a voucher, although it may not be approved nor have attached any evidence of its authenticity. If such a form is used, any papers or documents relating thereto, such as original correspondence from attorneys stating that an account is worthless, etc., should be attached. Where founded on the action of a committee or board of directors, reference should be made to the page of the minute book where recorded. If reference is made to a contract or agreement, the file or location of the original document should be stated.

Purchase Returns: It is no part of the normal conduct of a business to return goods which have been purchased and received. For this reason, when goods are returned because they are defective or unsatisfactory, or because they were not ordered, etc., the record of such returns is not always a permanent or satisfactory one.

In most cases dependence is placed on a memorandum on the original invoice, and if made before the invoice is entered on the books, it is practically sure to prevent payment. But sometimes the invoice will have been entered, and if care is not taken, the account will be paid in due course without making any deduction.

The best preventive is to have a good-sized book labeled plainly "Returned Purchases," in which shall be entered a memorandum covering every return. This book should be compared with the purchase books regularly to prevent errors in payments.

Cancellation of Vouchers: Instances are known where dishonest clerks have used old vouchers to support fictitious, duplicate payments, altering the dates thereof. It is always important for an auditor to mark a voucher in such a way that there can be no possibility of its being presented or used again.

The best method of cancellation is to use a rubber stamp bearing the name of the auditor and the initial or number of the clerk in charge of the audit. Some auditors use a conductor's punch.

The book entries should be marked in some distinctive way to indicate that a voucher therefor has been compared with the entry, and as the voucher may be more or less incomplete, it is wise to use different marks or initials to indicate the kind of voucher submitted.

Each auditor should select his own marks. It is advisable to change them from time to time as the client's clerks become familiar with the marks, as well as the procedure of a routine audit.

CHAPTER XX

THE DETAILED AUDIT (Continued)

THE TRIAL BALANCE

One of the most important matters in any audit is the verification of the trial balance. By this is not meant the routine checking of the ledger footings and extraction of the balances merely to test its arithmetical accuracy, but that careful examination or study of it which will throw light on the entire and detailed working of the whole system. Every ledger caption should mean something. After some experience, an auditor, by simply looking at the various accounts scheduled on the trial balance, will be able to discuss the whole system, and without further data suggest improvements therein. Of course, no sane practitioner would commit himself after such a cursory glance, but he will have gained sufficient insight into the affairs of his client to suggest the next and succeeding steps in the audit. He must not spend too much time on trifling errors in a trial balance, but should take enough time to satisfy himself that the trial balance honestly represents the face of the ledgers and that it may be relied on as a basis for a report or balance sheet.

The auditor should secure a copy of the last trial balance at the earliest possible moment. Usually, if he will ask for it at the commencement of an audit, it will be copied for him by an office clerk. He need not ask for the customers' balances in detail, as he will wish to compile these himself, as explained hereafter. As to the other accounts, however, the trial balance is of great importance. Subsequent analyses of accounts will lead up to the trial balance, and any alteration of figures in the ledger would probably be disclosed thereby.

If the trial balance is not correct, it is no part of an auditor's duties to locate the error or errors therein. He should insist on the client's staff securing an exact balance, or, if this is impracticable, the matter should be referred to the client and an understanding reached as to further procedure.

The best plan is for the audit to proceed as if no difference exists. The various tests suggested should be made, but no more, unless numerous errors are discovered, in which case permission should be secured from the client to verify all the work and secure a correct balance. Where the errors are few in number and the accounts are reasonably correct, the auditor should not attempt to hunt for clerical errors. He would better postpone the audit until they are located, even if an additional clerk is required. Any one who spends his time in such work is not, and is not developing into, a professional auditor. Such elementary bookkeeping work should be left to clerks.

Outstanding Accounts: A schedule of accounts receivable should be compiled as part of the trial balance. It is a waste of time to prepare or verify a trial balance and subsequently duplicate the larger part of it in the form of customers' balances.

The balance due from each customer should represent specific invoices unpaid, or else it should be clear that the debtor is making partial payments. Where the credits indicate that the latter is not the case, yet the balance due cannot be identified with the most recent invoices, then it is apparent that a discrepancy exists which requires explanation. In all such cases the auditor should require one of the office staff to show the composition of the balance. It may develop that in order to furnish this information the entire account will have to be analyzed, but this, of course, is the best possible reason for insistence on the part of the auditor.

Income from sales cannot be completely verified until all debits to customers are ascertained to be collectible; charges known to be uncollectible, but remaining open in the accounts of solvent debtors, may be difficult to locate, but are none the less important.

If the balances used in the final trial balances are not brought down, then they should be noted on the ledger pages in ink. Preferably, this should be done by the office staff, but, if necessary, the auditor should do it himself.

Bad or Doubtful Accounts: The schedule just referred to, in addition to showing that the balances due from solvent debtors are composed of collectible items, should indicate each account that is overdue, stating the number of months past due, so that a subsequent classification can be made to determine the amount required to be reserved to bring the aggregate due from trade debtors to an amount which will be realized in cash.

It is not always desirable to close a doubtful account to profit and loss, nor is it desirable to carry an account long overdue among the current accounts. The best practice, therefore, is to transfer the account (or the sheet, if the ledger is in loose-leaf form) to a doubtful accounts ledger, at the same time creating a reserve therefor. The balances in this supplemental ledger will not be lost sight of, as they form part of the trial balance.

As soon as an account is known to be irretrievably bad, it should be written off entirely. In the meantime a record of the progress of collection, such as commencement of suit, etc., should be noted on the account.

Provision for bad debts in the form of a reserve should be made each month, based on a percentage of the total sales. This fixes in the minds of all concerned that losses may be expected and stimulates the credit and collection departments to keep down the losses and "make a profit on the reserve." Where this course is not followed, the auditor will have to make the reserve large enough to cover the losses which his experience teaches will be incurred.

In this respect managers and others sometimes mislead the auditor because they will not admit the full amount of bad debts. After some years of experience an auditor finds that his opinion on this point is better than any one else's and he will use his own judgment in stating the probable losses. This applies especially where the business is comparatively old and actual losses for a series of years can be ascertained.

ASSET AND LIABILITY ITEMS

From the standpoint of clients' relations to their employees, the audit of income and expenses is more important than the audit of the balance sheet, but the accuracy or inaccuracy of the balance sheet affects proprietors, whether partners or stockholders, also the public as represented by bankers, creditors, prospective investors, or as a basis of transfer from one partner to another.

The detailed audit naturally includes a verification of the assets and liabilities, and in order to avoid repetition, the chapters on balance-sheet audits (page 87) should be referred to as indicating a part of the program of a detailed audit. Some balance-sheet items are more fully covered in a detailed audit than in a balance-sheet audit. They will be discussed at this point.

Notes Receivable: The record of notes received should be examined, and if comparatively few notes have been received, the disposition of each note should be followed from the account to which credited until collected or returned unpaid. If a large number of notes have been received, the auditor should test the accuracy of the record by selecting a few months at random out of the year and verifying in detail the transactions appearing in those months.

Notes Receivable Protested: See that they are charged back to the individual account of debtor, and that a subsequent attempt is made to collect. The protested note should be submitted as a voucher or otherwise accounted for in all cases where the item is still open. It would be possible for a dishonest cashier to charge back as unpaid, items actually collected, and subsequently write off the account to bad debts; but in such a case, as no voucher could be produced, the fraud would be disclosed. It is a small matter, but the auditor should ascertain whether or not all protest fees and accrued interest are charged to debtors, as well as the face of the notes. In many cases collection can be made subsequently and the omission to charge all proper items direct to debtors' accounts means a loss thereof.

Inventories: In a detailed audit this item in the balance sheet should be the first to be examined if there are collateral indications that the business has been profitable, even though the books show a loss. Inventories are frequently taken hurriedly, materials in transit are often omitted, or included when the bills therefor have not been entered. An inventory at the beginning of a period might be overvalued, and at the end undervalued, and numerous other causes might be cited to suggest errors which, if not detected, result in misleading profit and loss statements. In a case of this nature an auditor will find the inventories a most fruitful source of error.

Here also an auditor will have to use good judgment in passing values, for each increase or decrease in an inventory affects the profit and loss account correspondingly. It is about as bad to pass undervalues as overvalues where the result may be used in an ulterior matter. The most flagrant cases, however, are overvaluations, and with these an auditor must deal without fear or favor.

Premiums and Discounts on Bonds to be Amortized: Where bonds are sold at a premium, the amount received in excess of the par value represents the equivalent of interest collected in advance, and must be held in reserve and distributed over the years to which it applies as a reduction in bond interest account. For instance, a corporation may sell its five per cent 10-year bonds at 105, indicating that its credit is rated on a basis of about four and one-half per cent, that is, if a four and one-half per cent bond had been issued, the corporation should have realized about par. Therefore, the bond interest, when paid, is subject to a deduction of one-half of one per cent annually. The excess received at the time of sale should not be applied to income or to surplus, but, as stated above, must be carried as a deferred credit and reduced annually.

Likewise when bonds are sold at a discount it is because the rate of interest the bonds bear is less than the effective rate at which the corporation's credit is rated. For instance, if five per cent 10-year bonds are sold at 90, it means that the corporation's borrowing strength is rated at about six per cent, and in order to reflect the actual rate each year as interest is paid, it will be necessary to carry the discount as a deferred charge among the assets and write off to interest account one per cent annually. This, added to the amount paid in cash, will adjust the interest account to the proper cost.

Premiums on Capital Stock: With respect to premiums received on capital stock, the principle is different. There is no liability on account thereof, and no distribution to the income of future years.

The amount received is clearly a capital receipt and is not available as a fund out of which to pay dividends; that is, from an accounting point of view. There may be no legal obstacle in the way of crediting the premiums to surplus, and paying out the entire surplus as dividends, but in effect a board of directors might as well attempt to pay out the remaining portion of the amount paid for stock. Let us suppose that stock is issued at $110 per share, $100 being credited to capital stock, and $10 to surplus. If the latter amount is distributable, why not $10 more, leaving $90 to be credited to capital? The answer would probably be made that the law will not permit capital stock to be issued at a discount, but as property of all kinds may be turned in as payment for stock, the theory of stock being issued for actual value is a dead letter.

Premiums received on capital stock should be credited to an account so entitled or to capital surplus, and should not be absorbed in the regular surplus account.

Branch Accounts: The extent of the examination of branch accounts will depend on the system of accounts employed. Where local collections are made, the accounts receivable will require the same attention as described on page 258; where shipments are reported to the head office, and collections are not made locally, there will still be the necessity of testing the delivery records to ascertain that all have been reported, and that cash sales, if any, have been duly accounted for. At the same time the stock accounts will require attention, both from the point of view of theft or loss and overvaluation.

Nearly all branch managers have an interest in the profits derived from their own territory, and in consequence nearly all branch managers place the highest possible valuation on their stock-in-trade. It may seem difficult to manipulate the stock record valuations where prices are fixed at the head office, but opportunities usually arise in connection with shopworn or obsolete stock, etc., and in some cases quantities are deliberately overstated.

Local expenses and purchases are usually reported to the head office in detail, so that outstanding liabilities should be comparatively easy to verify. If paid locally, the usual precautions will have to be taken to ascertain that no omissions are made. (See page 148.)

In some cases where time does not permit an auditor to visit all branches personally, local auditors can be employed to advantage. Uniform instructions should be sent out and adhered to strictly, so that the auditor in charge will feel safe in using the figures so verified. Where this procedure is necessary the certificate should be modified as follows:

"We have audited (head office accounts) . . . and have compared the returns from the several branches therewith (the latter having been audited locally and the certified returns submitted to us), and in our opinion they are correct, etc."

Capital Expenditure: Throughout the audit of expenditure the distinction between capital and income must be borne in mind. It is sometimes believed that so long as expenditure for capital outlay, as well as for current maintenance, is charged to income and not capitalized, no fault can be found with such a conservative course, but that the reverse of this practice cannot be justified under any circumstances. Theoretically this position is wrong, the proper rule being to ascertain the correct application of each payment and to charge the account to which the item belongs. Practically, much can be said in support of what is known as the conservative method.

The great difficulty in ascertaining the exact effect of alterations, betterments, and new construction, and the prevailing tendency of managers and others to emphasize the propriety of capitalizing the payments, inevitably educate accountants and business men who do not want to deceive themselves, to the determination to charge to maintenance every item about which there is the slightest doubt. In other words, a practice which is objectionable in theory becomes a virtue in practice, and a substantial reason therefor is that the business always gains thereby and never loses.

The audit of capital expenditure is rarely satisfactory when made by items, as one item may be chargeable to capital, while another item of exactly the same nature may be chargeable to income, the distinction depending entirely on the purpose for which used.

All well-regulated concerns have a storeroom system, which means that most debits to plant accounts originate in storeroom charges. It is simply impossible to determine long afterward, by a mere inspection of the voucher, whether it should be charged to one account or another.

The most satisfactory verification is to secure a dependable memorandum of the additions and improvements which have been undertaken or completed in order to increase the earning power or efficiency of the plant. That is, if a new building has been erected or a new power plant installed, assemble all of the items applicable thereto and compare the expenditure as a whole with the estimated value of the improvement, or the official authorization, ascertain what it replaced, if anything, and what additional capacity or economies are effected thereby.

Odds and ends should not be charged to capital, so that the increase in plant accounts for a given period should be reducible to definite grouping as indicated above. If it is found that the total capacity of the plant is not materially increased by the outlay, it may be inferred that the changes were necessary to renew or replace worn-out or obsolete buildings or equipment.

Cash Discounts on Capital Payments: It is held by some that the cash discounts deducted from payments on account of capital outlay should be credited to interest or discount account and be treated as an earning. This, however, is a fallacy, as will be shown by a concrete example. Suppose a fund of $10,000 is set aside to buy machinery; the invoices may aggregate exactly $10,000 and are subject to a discount of two per cent if paid within ten days. Advantage is taken of the discount and $9,800 is paid out. It cannot be contended that the cost is $10,000 and an earning of $200 is realized, because such is not the fact. The machinery cost $9,800 in cash, and the cash balance which remained is simply an unexpended fund. It has not been used and is now available for other purposes. This is parallel with the treatment of cash discounts on merchandise purchases, the net result being the same because the purchases account is ultimately reduced by the amount of the discount through the profit and loss account.

Real Estate: In any business other than that of real estate operators there will be very few items of payment in connection with the purchase of land or improved real estate. More frequently it will be found that bonds or stocks are issued in payment therefor. Usually these items can be vouched from the minutes of boards of directors, the contracts themselves and the acknowledgments of the payees.

An instance is known of a promoter who was made the president of a holding company who paid himself, as representing one of the subsidiaries, a larger number of bonds than he was entitled to. The records of the holding company were altered to fit the transaction and the auditors were deceived. If the books of the subsidiary company had been examined, the fraud would have been discovered.

Buildings: Where a considerable amount is being expended on new or old buildings, the payments should be carefully vouched. Individual payments, however, will probably be supported by genuine-looking vouchers and will not reveal irregularity, which may be going on, either on the part of the client's staff or on the part of the contractor. Therefore, the operations as a whole should be checked with the authorizations of the board of directors, or executives in charge of the work, and with the bids or estimates submitted before work was commenced.

Unfortunately architects' certificates as to partly completed work are not always reliable, on account of the connection which sometimes exists between contractors and architects, and in rare cases only can an auditor go behind these certificates.

It is permissible to charge all expenses and outlays in connection with these operations, such as permits, architects' and engineers' fees, clerical salaries when clearly applicable to new work, and similar items to the work itself. It may seem more conservative to charge part of this expenditure to revenue, but in all cases it is preferable to assemble all costs into one account, then if it appears desirable to write off a part of the cost, it can be done at any time. The whole cost, however, having once appeared in one account, will subsequently be available for any desired information.

Where new buildings are erected in whole, or in part, by the concern itself, it is important to ascertain that no profit is included. Auditors frequently find this state of affairs and are met with the argument that if the contract had been awarded to an outside concern, a contractor's profit would have been added. A concern not in the contracting business cannot always, however, erect a building, or, in fact, perform any work outside of its usual operations, at the same cost as one whose sole efforts are devoted to this class of work and who may be depended upon to have discovered economies in purchasing, planning, and executing not possible except after long experience. If an actual saving has been effected, it is not a realized profit and should not be treated as such. The asset account should represent cost and no more.

Machinery, etc.: The important point to keep in mind in connection with purchases of machinery, tools, fixtures, etc., is whether they represent actual additions to plant and equipment, or whether they are renewals. This point is covered in Chapter XXI, "Depreciation." The cost of installation, including freight, labor, and other items, is as much a part of the cost as the price of the machinery itself.

Where machines, etc., are built by the concern itself, the remarks found above under Buildings will also apply.

Notes Payable: All notes paid during the period under audit should be submitted as vouchers. If notes are issued from a stub book, or if a special form is used, all should be accounted for. Spoiled notes should be pasted on their respective stubs as is done with cheques.

If careful consideration is given to the notes issued during the period, it will assist the auditor to determine whether all notes outstanding at the date of the balance sheet appear thereon.

Partners' Withdrawals: If payments are made in currency, partners should approve their accounts as they appear in the ledger.

The practice, so prevalent, of drawing comparatively small amounts at a time and initialing a voucher, or declining to give one at all, is a direct temptation to dishonesty on the part of the cashier. Auditors should criticize the practice vigorously and suggest to partners that their withdrawals be by cheque only, and that they pay their personal bills through their own bank accounts.

Dividends: The audit of dividend payments is simple. Authorization must always be found in the board minutes, and any dividend declared, if paid, must be paid to all stockholders of record at the date named. Dividends cannot be declared as of a past date, but may be dated ahead as far as may be desired.

In the case of Jones v. Terre Haute & Richmond R. R. Co., (57 N. Y. 196), Commissioner Reynolds said:

It is certainly true, as a general rule, that a stockholder in a corporation has an interest in proportion to his stock in all the corporate property and has a right to share in any surplus of profits arising from its use and employment in the business of the company; and this legal right does not depend upon the question whether he is a stockholder of long standing or of recent date. The moment a person becomes stockholder in a corporation, all the incidents of interest or quasi-ownership in the corporate property attach.

In another New York case the court refused to order the directors to pay additional dividends, although the corporation had a very large surplus, part of which was in bank and represented a sum far in excess of that actually required for current purposes, and part of which was invested in outside securities. The court said, "The discretion of the directors in regard to declaring dividends will not be interfered with in the absence of fraud or an abuse of discretion."

Stock Dividends: Dividends are supposed to be distributions of earnings and accrue to the stockholder only at the time of declaration. A stockholder in a corporation having a large surplus and earning several times the amount of its dividends is no more justified in taking a proportionate part of an expected dividend into his accounts as income than he would be in assuming that the entire surplus would be divided. When the dividend is actually declared and becomes an obligation of the corporation, it becomes, in turn, income receivable to the stockholder.

In the case of a stock dividend the rule also applies, the only exception being where the dividend is an extraordinary one and where the distribution includes the surplus of two or more years which, as a matter of fact, has been capitalized.

Not long ago the Standard Oil Company of Indiana declared a stock dividend of 2,900 per cent, that is, the holder of $100 in stock received additional stock amounting to $2,900. Suppose the owner of one share died shortly before the declaration of the dividend, leaving the income of his estate to his wife for life and the principal to his children, the stock would have been appraised at perhaps $2,000, based on earnings of, say, ten per cent per annum on that price. If the principle that dividends are income were applied, the widow would receive the $2,900 per share in new stock, and at her death, if no other change took place, the children would receive the original share, worth now only $100 and yielding perhaps seven per cent per annum. This would be so inequitable and so at variance with the testator's intentions that most of the States would permit the dividend to be treated as a distribution of principal and not of income.

Precisely the same rule should apply where stocks are carried on balance sheets at very high figures and are reduced in price per share through the distribution of large stock dividends. Unless it is very clear that the declaration consists of the earnings of a recent period, the whole dividend should be treated as capital. If it can be apportioned, it would be proper to apply that part of it representing a distribution of the earnings of the last year or period to current income. Where State laws govern the matter the laws must be observed. The auditor should be thoroughly informed as to the provisions of the law in this respect in his own State and in any others where he practices.

Capital Stock: A trial balance should be taken of the stock ledger to see that the aggregate outstanding is in agreement with the general ledger account. It should be noted if there is any account in the name of the company or its treasurer, which was intended to represent treasury stock, but which may or may not be such.

The stock certificate books should be examined and reconciled with the stock ledger. All canceled certificates should be inspected or accounted for. As stated on page 353 under "Banks," fraud has been practiced by raising certificates.

Bonds: A proof should be taken of the bond ledger or register to ascertain that the aggregate outstanding is correct and is in agreement with the general ledger. Canceled bonds should be inspected or accounted for. The bond agreement should be read, and if it contains any provisions as to sinking funds, etc., it should be seen that these are carried out or report made thereon.

It should be determined whether or not the amount of interest accrued has been set up in the accounts and whether the amount due has been paid.

Careful methods should be in force relative to coupons. They should be canceled effectively immediately upon receipt, and kept on file, not destroyed. The auditor should see that the canceled coupons are accounted for.

Taxes: Corporations are subject to special taxes, such as the Federal Corporation Tax, State Franchise Tax, etc. The auditor should see that these, as well as the usual taxes on property, are provided for.

In New York State there is a tax of two cents per hundred dollars of par value or fraction thereof, imposed on all transfers of stock. The seller of the stock, or his broker, pays this tax by affixing revenue stamps to the certificate surrendered. The officer of the corporation, however, who transfers the stock or causes it to be transferred is liable to the penalty for failure to pay the tax.

OFFICE METHODS

In nearly every audit where no previous work had been done for the client the auditor was formerly asked to note any improvements or changes which might occur to him during the progress of the audit. It did not seem incongruous that a professional accountant whose whole time was spent in examining and criticizing accounts should in the course of an extensive practice acquire experience of great value, and that he should be able to give to new clients the benefit of such experience. At the present time there is somewhat of a feeling that the auditor is not a specialist in system work and that in order to be up-to-date an "efficiency engineer" must be employed. But suppose we compare present conditions with those of about ten years ago. At that time stationery houses, which carried an "auditing department" as a side line, were making a great stir through advertising and traveling solicitors, and were offering to produce wonderful results, including daily balance sheets and profit and loss statements, the only requirement being the installation of their patented stationery. Offices were turned inside out and new books and blanks were installed by the ton, but for some reason the service did not measure up to the promises, and hundreds of offices discarded much of the "junk" which had been thrust upon them and went back to saner methods.

For a short time the auditor was back in favor. He had no cut-and-dried system, nor did he know before he entered an office how its system should be mapped out, but out of long experience he was able to make suggestions which cut out unnecessary work and proposed changes which embraced the use of all the latest labor-saving devices. Then came the "efficiency engineer," who again modestly affirmed that the auditor was not a specialist in systems and that he could not be expected to keep his clients up-to-date. The crop of over-charged and dissatisfied patrons of the "efficiency engineer" is commencing to be heard from, and it is believed by some who have studied the situation that before long the auditor will be back in his former position as a recognized authority on business systems.

The auditor should keep fully informed on the latest devices, mechanical and other kinds, for saving labor or rendering it more efficient; he should understand and be prepared to explain the relation of one department of a business to another and the advantages of coördination; he should study cost systems and be ready to install any required accounting system; he should acquire and follow up a knowledge of the means of imparting information by means of charts and other visual methods.

It might be urged that an auditor cannot hope to cover more than a small part of the field of auditing within a considerable period of practice, and that to expect him to add the work of a system specialist is unreasonable. The answer to this is that no one can be a good auditor without picking up all of the rudiments of systematizing, and that in any event system is a matter of evolution.

Ready-made systems have been popular, but never successful. No system will work out well unless a good man studies the concern and becomes acquainted with its personnel before he starts, and then "lives with the job" until its completion. The auditor may not be able to handle many such engagements, but he should not allow the so-called system experts to bluff him out of the remunerative work. He is probably better qualified to perform it than anyone else.

Styles of Books and Records: The auditor will note by actual inspection whether the records are kept economically and efficiently or otherwise. If the old-fashioned bound books are in use and loose-leaf records would be an improvement, he should recommend a change. On the other hand, it may be that some records are being kept on cards or loose leaves which could be written up more readily and referred to more easily in bound books. In such a case the latter would be recommended.

In view of the elasticity and convenience of cards and loose-leaf records, these systems are becoming more and more popular. In the early stages it was feared that the leaf or card might be lost, destroyed, or easily altered, but after a number of years of experience this fear has practically disappeared.

Filing Systems: With the unit system of records has come the unit system of filing. Press copy books are becoming a rarity and have been discarded by most modern offices. Documents, correspondence, etc., are now filed in vertical files and in such a form as to be readily accessible.

In many modern offices the method is in force of making a carbon copy of each letter, and in the mailing department a press copy in a letter book. The carbon copy takes the place of a "tickler" and is filed so that it will come up for further attention on the day decided upon. The letter book impression is taken just before the letter is put in the envelope and records the signatures and other identifying marks. It is properly indexed, and becomes a safeguard against the loss of the carbon or the unwarranted alteration of the letter.

The essential features of a filing system are:

1. Certainty of obtaining any paper or all papers on a particular subject.
2. Rapidity of obtaining filed papers.
3. Rapidity of filing papers.
4. Cheapness of operation.
5. Simplicity.
6. Small space required.
7. Cross-reference, numbering, etc.

In a report on the handling and filing of correspondence, President Taft's Commission on Economy and Efficiency makes the following suggestions, which apply with as great force to the average business corporation as to the government service:

1. That all correspondence shall be filed flat in vertical files.
2. That all correspondence should be filed by subjects arranged upon a self-indexing basis.
3. No book or card record of correspondence is desirable.
4. That carbon copies should supplant press copying.
5. That the employment of the dictation machine (phonograph) for dictating should be extended widely.
6. That transparency or "window" envelopes should be used.

7. That forms that must be filled in on the typewriter should be so arranged as to facilitate the work.

8. That on internal correspondence no salutation or complimentary closing should be used and that the initials of the person addressed and the writer should be used instead of full names.

Copying: Where large quantities of copies are desired, there are the multigraph, the revolving duplicator, and the old-fashioned flat duplicator. The revolving duplicator is perhaps the most popular, requiring only the typewriting of a waxed-paper stencil. For work requiring more than a thousand impressions, the multigraph or one of the several makes of printing machines is preferable.

Mailing Department: The handling of mail is important and has come to be a separate department. Incoming mail usually contains remittances in cheques and cash, and has proven in more cases than one a simple source of illegitimate wealth to enterprising but ill-paid clerks and cashiers. Some responsible person—preferably an officer of the company—should have charge of the incoming mail. As it is opened it should be distributed to baskets designated for the various departments, and should be delivered with as much care as is used in opening it.

Outgoing mail must be handled differently. It is desirable to have the stenographers who write letters address the envelopes at the same time, and then, instead of delivering them both to the executive, the letter only should be delivered, and the envelope (together with any inclosures) sent to the mailing department. When the letter has been signed it is sent to the mailing department, where it is put in the envelope, with the inclosures, and is sealed, stamped, and mailed. It is the duty of the mailing department to keep posted on changes in closing hours for the various domestic and foreign mails.

Stock on Hand: In many cases the auditor will find it practicable to introduce a perpetual inventory of stock on hand. He may base his suggestions on the following general recommendations quoted from "The Accountant's Manual," Vol. II:

(1) Debit and credit accounts should be opened, as far as possible, for each description of stores used. On one side of the accounts the receipts would be entered, showing the date, weight, quantity, or number, and other particulars; and, on the other side, the stores issued from time to time would be entered, with such particulars as were necessary or suitable, the difference

representing what ought to be in hand, or thereabouts, as, in accounts of this kind, the balance shown upon the accounts can hardly be depended upon exactly.

(2) It is the opinion of practical mill owners and managers that in many cases a really efficient and exact check on stores is not practicable. It could, no doubt, be devised, but the detailed work in connection with it, and consequent labor and expense, put it out of the range of every-day business, whatever theorists may say. But many useful rules may be laid down preventive of fraud and waste, amongst others the following, taken from actual experience:

(*a*) Where stores are distributed for use upon a specific job, the job should be stated, with the weight, quantity, etc.

(*b*) If material of the same kind is distributed to various men for the same purpose, a comparison should be made between the results produced by each. If discrepancies are found, inquiries should be made, and doubtless in some cases a good explanation could be given: e. g., use of old machinery or appliances, etc.

(*c*) The storeroom should be situated in a convenient place, and be in charge of a competent man who combines practical knowledge of the stores with sufficient bookkeeping experience to appreciate the importance of account keeping.

(*d*) The principal, or manager, should make a point of examining at times the stock ledgers and exercising general supervision of the department. Frequent and unnotified visits should be made, and the store keeper, if possible (it is not always possible), changed (occasionally).

(*e*) Some kinds of stores should never be given out unless the used-up stores are returned. For example, a workman making requisitions for files, brushes, and like things, should be supplied only on his giving up the old articles. This is a very good check when the nature of the stores will allow of its application.

Stock accounts should show quantities as well as values, the one forming a good check upon the other.

The forms used should provide for an opening balance or inventory, to which are added daily the quantity and value of the material purchased or manufactured. There should be provision for totaling these debits and for deducting therefrom the quantity sold and the *cost value* of same. The balance should agree with an actual inventory.

A more detailed form used by many concerns provides columns to show not only the balance and purchases daily, but also the sales and the new balance. Noted at the top of the sheet or card is the minimum quantity of stock to be carried, as well as the maximum quantity. Whenever the stock reaches a low point, the records are checked by comparison with an actual inventory. Thus the taking of inventory is not left until the end of the period, but is taken continuously.

Business to-day is so varied in its nature that some lines will not permit of a regular system of stock accounts—nor is it especially necessary, as in the case of traders dealing in small articles broken from bulk. While different methods of check must be employed in such cases, there are some general forms which may be adopted and will be found practicable for ordinary lines of business.

Every trade is supposed to earn a certain percentage of gross profit, which should be based on the cost price of goods and not on the selling price. If, therefore, a stock account is started with the actual stock on hand valued at the purchase price, and there are added to it the total quantity purchased from time to time (say monthly), and also the estimated gross profits referred to, this amount, less the total sales, should show the stock on hand, assuming that the gross profit named has been exactly earned. By deducting the gross profit from the sales and then crediting the stock account, the same result would be secured. This book-figure can easily be verified or corrected at the time of actual inventory.

Another common and often useful practice in testing the accuracy of the stock at any time is to make a comparison between the stock and sales for a particular period and a corresponding period of prior years, though this is only a rough test and not definite.

The accounts of an establishment handling various kinds of goods should be so kept that the position of the various departments as to purchases, sales, etc., may readily be secured. Such a system serves two most useful purposes. (1) Attention is directed to any discrepancy between actual and estimated gross profits by means of a like difference between a physical and the book inventory. (2) Needed information is furnished from month to month as to the probable amount of stock in each department, and this knowledge serves as a guide to and check upon the various departmental managers, as well as affording material for an interim balance sheet, if one is desired.

Where a more accurate check on the various departments is

desired, the following method is employed: All goods ar charged to departments at the selling price, this having been de termined in advance. Any changes in value are recorded an when the inventory is taken it is priced both at cost, for th private office, and also at selling price, for the purpose of verifi cation, and the account is supposed to balance exactly. House whose business reaches a large volume find this system give satisfactory results with but slight discrepancies. It can b extended, too, with advantage to other trades, such as retai branch stores selling cigars, groceries, men's furnishing goods and similar lines.

To furnish conclusive information relative to gross profit made in various retail lines is, of course, impossible. Situation nature of the business, policy of the management, local condi tions—all enter into the result so that any attempt to outlin even approximate figures would be unwise and misleading However, any auditor might compile a table out of his own expe rience that would prove of value.

If it becomes necessary for the auditor to design stock ac counts for any particular business, he may well take advantage of whatever practical experience is possessed by his clients o their managers, supplementing such knowledge by his own expe rience, and if he should be so fortunate as to have an intimate acquaintance with the special business in hand, he will undoubtedly find it of the greatest assistance.

Controlling Subsidiary Ledgers: There will be found in nearly every concern some device adopted by the individual bookkeepers for balancing their ledgers. This is usually in the shape of a large "proofsheet," on which are recorded the totals of the various books or columns from which the details were posted. Where there are a number of ledgers, each dependent upon all the others for its balance, even such a makeshift is helpful in locating the ledger that is out of balance.

But a much more practical and a more scientific method employs in the general ledger a controlling account with each subsidiary ledger. From the various books of original record the details are posted to the subsidiary ledgers, but the totals are posted to the respective controlling accounts in the general ledger, keeping that ledger in balance. For instance, there may be two sales ledgers (A-M and N-Z) to which the details of the sales book are posted. In the general ledger "Sales" account would be credited as usual, but in addition each of the sales ledger controlling accounts would be debited with its part of the total sales.

Ledger A-M Controlling Account ....
Ledger N-Z Controlling Account ....
To Sales Account ....

Columnar Ledgers: Another form of ledger, to which the term "self-balancing" is fully as applicable, is the columnar ledger. Its advantage lies in the fact that a large number of customers or accounts can be carried in a comparatively small space and can be referred to with a minimum of effort. It can be used, however, only when the number of transactions with each customer is small.

The ledger gives a line or a double line to each account and provides columns for posting the debits and the credits once each month or at other intervals. The totals in each column are carried forward from page to page or are recapitulated, and the final totals should agree with the totals in the controlling accounts in the general ledger.

Another use of the tabular ledger is as a summary of charges where customers have a very large number of transactions monthly. The details are kept in a subsidiary ledger and are posted in total to the tabular ledger. It then becomes a ledger of controlling accounts, and is in turn controlled by an account in the general ledger.

Efficiency of Organization: An auditor is peculiarly fitted, upon the completion of an audit, to comment intelligently upon the efficiency of the organization. He has had access to all the records and has seen the performance of the staff under a variety of conditions. The average client to-day wants suggestions relative to the perfection of his organization, and it is only right that he should have them. The auditor should be able to judge whether the staff is too large, whether the arrangement of the office and the layout of the work is capable of improvement, and whether there is needless repetition of records in different departments.

Many times it is possible to show laziness or pure inability on the part of employees by the application of the efficiency theory that for any task there is a determinable standard. Suppose it had been demonstrated that a clerk under favorable condition should be able to post three hundred items per day. A little investigation shows that because of the use of the old-fashioned index and awkward books he is able to post but two hundred items, therefore the work is only 66⅔ per cent efficient. The book of original entry is being used by two people, so he has to lose 10 per cent of the time waiting for it. That brings the efficiency of the work down to only 90 per cent of 66⅔ per cent, or 60 per cent. He is fifteen minutes late in the morning, begins to put his books away fifteen minutes before closing time at night, and reads the paper for half an hour after lunch. Another 12½ per cent of the 66⅔ per cent is gone! His efficiency, then, would be 51⅓ per cent. But he has so little faith in the accuracy of his work that he checks every posting back to the original record, losing at least one-third of the possible 100 per cent, and bringing his net efficiency to 18 per cent.

If he were paid $18 per week and another man were obtained who could perform the work according to the standard set, or 100 per cent, it would be profitable to pay the efficient man even $50 per week and still receive from him twice the service-value of the inefficient man.

CHAPTER XXI

DEPRECIATION

With the modern development of business and industry and the enormous additions to the value of property, plant, appliances, and stock in trade, the question of depreciation or allowance for loss of value has naturally gained much in importance.

Indeed, the settlement of the question of what shall be allowed for depreciation is one of the most important which accountants are called upon to discuss. The auditor must always consider the adequacy or inadequacy of the provision made, before he can determine the form of the certificate or report which he can give.

It is important at the outset to distinguish between fluctuation and depreciation. The former may be a change for the better or the worse in the value of the assets and is attributable to causes apart from the business itself. Entirely extraneous influences may cause fluctuation in the value of assets and, therefore, it is generally admitted that as the actual manufacturing profits are not affected thereby one way or the other, these fluctuations in value need not be considered in the current accounts.

Depreciation, however, is a decline in the value of property such as may reasonably be expected to occur as a result of wear and tear and gradual obsolescence. It is due to the possession and use of the assets, and therefore is a part of the cost of operation. A concise definition of depreciation which has been widely used is that it is the deterioration of anything by time or use. P. D. Leake's definition, "expired outlay upon productive plant," is a good one, as is also "accrued renewals."

Before leaving the subject of fluctuation it may be well to consider for a moment what treatment may be accorded to a favorable fluctuation in the value of fixed assets and current assets. In the former case it is generally conceded that the increase may be treated as a secret reserve. In the latter case it is temporarily a secret reserve which will be included in trading profits when the assets affected are realized. An unfavorable fluctuation, if apparently of a temporary character, may be disregarded, but when it is probable that the unfavorable conditions will remain until the time of realization of the assets affected, provision should be made for the loss; in other words, an unfavorable fluctuation should be charged against the period in which it occurred (as an extraordinary item) instead of against the period of realization.

In general it is not necessary from a legal standpoint to charge an unfavorable fluctuation in fixed assets against revenue before the declaration of dividends from current profits. While these fluctuations may be disregarded in accounts, it may be desirable, however, to present the true state of affairs to stockholders by means of a note attached to the balance sheet or included in the auditor's report.

The New York Court of Appeals, in one of its decisions, stated the theory of a depreciation reserve in a most lucid manner, as follows:

> Judicial notice may be taken of the fact that in the conduct of many industrial enterprises there is a constant deterioration of the plant which is not made good by ordinary repairs and which, of course, operates continually to lessen the value of the tangible property which it affects. The amount of this depreciation differs in different enterprises, but the annual rate is usually capable of estimate and proof by skilled witnesses. No corporation would be regarded as well conducted which did not make some provision for the necessity of ultimately replacing the property thus suffering deterioration; and we cannot see why an allowance for this purpose should not be made out of the gross earnings in order to ascertain the true earning capacity.

Although the charge for depreciation is recognized by the law, and provision is made therefor in the forms supplied by the Treasury Department in connection with the Federal Corporation Tax Law, there is a wide difference of opinion as to the amount of the allowance to be made from time to time. Many company officials—particularly railway officials—prefer to regard depreciation charges as flexible. They adjust them to meet the conditions of different years, so that in time of large profits the allowance shall be large, and during bad years the allowance small, or none.

This, however, is entirely opposed to sound accounting principles, and the Treasury Department in this instance agrees with e opinion of the accounting profession. It is important that ere should be some fixity in regard to the rate of depreciation be allowed. Under the system of varying charges for depreation it would be impossible to fix an intelligent basis of rates, id comparisons with other years would be practically worthss. If the business man, whether in the railroad world or elsehere, is to pass over one year without making any allowance r depreciation, it will result in a misrepresentation of condions at the end of that year, and it is unjust and incorrect in very way to expect a good year to bear the burden of depreation which has occurred in one or more bad years.

Causes for Depreciation: The various elements of depreciaion have been very clearly described by Professor M. E. Cooley:

(1) *Depreciation Due to Wear and Tear and Exposure to the Elements.* his is continuous. All elements have a wearing life varying with the element self. No element can be completely worn out; it can be worn only to a oint below which it becomes unsafe or no longer serves its original funcion. In practice the average condition of all elements must be maintained at high percentage of the original cost if the property is to serve its purpose roperly. This percentage varies from seventy-five per cent to eighty-five er cent of the cost new of the property. The difference between this perentage of from seventy-five to eighty-five and the original one hundred is a lepreciation which is inherent in the property and cannot be dispensed with. t must be met by a sinking fund, or its equivalent, otherwise this part of the riginal investment becomes lost.

(2) *Depreciation Due to Accidents; a Sudden Depreciation.* An engine r a boiler may be wrecked, and with it, other machinery. This might, and robably would, involve a considerable expense for repairs or replacement esides possibly crippling the plant in part. Cars may collide or a car may drop through a bridge. A bridge itself may fall or be carried away by floods. A storm, as a cyclone, may work havoc, entailing costs in excess of those proper to be charged to ordinary maintenance of property.

(3) *Depreciation Due to Inadequacy.* Cars suitable in the past had already been superseded several times by larger and better cars. This has rendered the track, structure, and bridges inadequate, and as more power is required to propel the larger cars, the power plants have become inadequate. The public demand is largely responsible for this depreciation due to inadequacy.

(4) *Depreciation Due to Obsolescence.* This, while closely allied to the depreciation due to inadequacy, is different in that it embraces changes due to advance in the art. More efficient and effective machinery has appeared which must be substituted for the old to keep abreast of the times. For example, in steam-engine practice the turbine has come into general use during the past five years and the art of steam turbines is at the beginning. Generators

adapted to piston-engine practice are not adapted to steam-turbine practi and must also be changed. Boilers adapted to piston-engine practice must b replaced to carry the higher pressures required. Condensers must also b changed to secure the better vacuum required to realize the full advantage the steam turbine. Owing to the rapid disappearance of coal beds, the pric of fuel must advance, and this presumably will before many years forc the adoption of the gas producer and the producer gas engine. Water power are wisely being developed, but to utilize them requires the scrapping o large parts of the machinery in use at present.

Repairs and Maintenance: It is an accepted rule that repair and all other expenses of maintenance should be charged agains profit and loss, but the auditor should not decide on the amoun required for depreciation until he has scrutinized the repair account, as in this account he may find that charges have bee made for renewals and replacements which, as far as they go apply in lieu of a depreciation reserve.

If a machine could be built like the "one-hoss shay," this question would not arise and a depreciation reserve would work out exactly, but under modern conditions it invariably happens that a machine wears out one part at a time, and if the parts are replaceable, the life of the machine as a whole may be extended almost indefinitely. Obsolescence and inadequacy are the practical factors which operate against a fair test of the possible life of present-day plant and equipment.

Mr. Henry Floy, the eminent engineer, cites the following instance:

> For example, the life of the ordinary steam engine may be taken at twenty years, but it is not uncommon to find engines still in use that are very much older than this. The writer noted, within a few months, that a vertical engine installed in England in 1856 had recently been equipped with condenser, supplied with superheated steam, and was still in use at fifty-five years of age, giving economical and satisfactory results.

Methods of Applying Depreciation in the Books: (1) The FIXED PERCENTAGE BASIS is the most popular and is the one in general use. It is applied:

(*a*) On a flat basis, e. g., if the life of a machine is ten years, one-tenth, or ten per cent, is charged off annually.

(*b*) On a reducing scale basis, i. e., a rate is ascertained which, when applied to the original cost and on the diminished value thereof as periodically determined, will reduce the book value to scrap value at the end of its estimated life.

Method (*a*) is more generally followed than (*b*), although there is in use a method which is a cross between the two and which is not scientific. It consists in charging the rate as determined under (*a*), but in applying it to the reducing value instead of to the original cost. For instance, if the life of a boiler is estimated at ten years, ten per cent per annum is set aside, but on the diminishing value. If the table on page 326 were calculated on this basis, the book value would be $348.68 at the end of the tenth year, instead of $100 as under the other methods.

Nevertheless, this is a popular method and must be reckoned with. The fact of the matter is that when an executive directs a clerk to "charge off ten per cent for depreciation," he does not stop to consider whether it means off the original cost or the reduced value.

The theory of and advantage claimed for (*b*) is that repairs and maintenance are very light during the early years of a machine and very heavy during the later years. In both (*a*) and (*b*) it is contemplated that all maintenance costs are to be charged off in addition to the depreciation.

Roughly speaking, with (*b*) the aggregate of depreciation and maintenance would be the same each year, whereas under (*a*) the aggregate during the first years would be light and during the last years heavy.

(2) SINKING FUND METHOD: If it is proposed to set aside such a sum periodically as will equal the original cost of a machine (less scrap value) at the end of its estimated life, it is customary, after taking into consideration the average rate of interest which can be secured, to pay into a fund a fixed amount periodically. The aggregate thereof, together with the accumulated interest, will equal the amount required to renew the machine in question. This method is seldom followed.

There is good authority, however, for its use where a single, large piece of property is being operated.

This point is well expressed by Mr. Floy:

> In all cases involving a consideration of the expenses of keeping a property in operation, there should invariably be included allowances to cover all ultimate depreciation and replacement. For a small company or where

relatively large proportions of the invested capital are locked up in a f or single pieces of property, it is preferable to accumulate, in advance out operating income, reserve funds from which to provide for all classes depreciation. But such method may be unnecessary and possibly an ine pedient accounting complexity with large corporations, where the inve ments in any single piece of physical property are small, relative to the to investment. The truth of the above will be at once recognized from t following illustration. If the company which erected the Metropolitan Li Insurance building had only that property, it would be essential that fun should be laid aside annually in amounts sufficient to replace the original i vestment at the end of the useful life of said building.

The unsettled conflict between the Third Avenue Railwa Company and the New York Public Service Commission wit reference to the actual setting aside of an amortization fund an a depreciation fund is of considerable interest. The Thir Avenue Railway Company had gone through a receivership an the par value of the securities of the reorganized company ex ceeded by a considerable amount the value of the physical prop erty owned by the company. The Commission directed that fund be created into which the Company pay annual installment out of its income, so that at maturity of the outstanding secur ities an amount would have been accumulated which, togethe with the company's other property, would equal the par value o the outstanding securities.

The Commission also directed that there be set aside annu ally at least 20 per cent of the earnings for current maintenanc and future replacements (depreciation), the unexpended portion of this amount to be "credited" to a separate depreciation fund at the end of each year.

The opinion of the Commission is of sufficient importance and interest to warrant the reproduction in full of that part dealing particularly with the amortization and depreciation funds.

Amortization of Discounts. The requirement that discounts shall be amortized is a generally recognized principle. The unanimous conclusion of the Railroad Securities Commission in its recent report to the President of the United States was to this effect: "It seems to be generally agreed that no limitation should be placed on the price at which bonds can be sold, but any discount should be canceled or amortized during the life of the bonds by the appropriation each year out of annual income or surplus accumulated after the issue of the bonds of not less than the proportionate amount of the discount." The Securities Commission also said, regarding the issue of stock below par, that the difference between par value and cash received should be amortized within a short term of years, thus:

> If a document says one hundred dollars has been paid, one hundred dollars ought to be paid. The most that can properly be done is to allow companies which cannot sell such stock at par to arrange for the "amortization," or gradual cancellation, of any necessary discount by appropriating, out of future income or surplus which may accrue subsequent to the issue of such stock an annual sum having precedence over dividend-payment, to be so applied on capital account as to make the deficiency good in a period of no very great length.

The Public Service Commission has approved the issue of approximately $100,000,000 par value of bonds exclusive of the securities of the reorganized Third Avenue and Metropolitan Street Railway companies. Probably 90 per cent of these securities have been 3½, 4, or 5 per cent bonds, issued at less than their par value. It has been the invariable practice of the Commission to require the difference between the cash proceeds of the bonds and their par value to be treated the same as bank discount or interest paid in advance and to be amortized within the term of the obligations. The propriety of this requirement has never been contested by any of the corporations affected. This procedure is in accordance with well-established principles of accounting and with the rules of accounting prescribed by the Interstate Commerce Commission and the two Public Service Commissions of New York and other regulatory bodies.

In the previous opinions in this case the Commission found the total liabilities of the entire Third Avenue system, after eliminating book entries, intercompany accounts, etc., to be approximately:

Receiver's certificate and notes	$3,755,000.00
Funded debt of Third Avenue Company	5,000,000.00
Funded debt of underlying companies	5,892,000.00
Funded debt—other liens	1,240,000.00
Real estate mortgage	12,000.00
Other current liabilities—estimated	2,811,744.34
New refunding bonds	15,790,000.00
New income bonds	22,536,000.00
New stock	16,590,000.00
Total	$73,626,744.34

Upon the other side of the account the Commission found the following assets and funds to be paid over:

Physical property estimated to have a value at that time of about	$35,100,000.00
Current assets	1,746,637.72
Cash assessment	7,200,000.00
Total	$44,046,637.72

The excess of liabilities over assets is thus seen to be nearly $30,000,000. If the revisions in current liabilities and assets requested at a former hearing were allowed, the excess would be nearly $29,000,000. Even assuming that the current liabilities unfunded would be paid out of operating expenses, there would still remain an excess of upwards of $26,000,000.

The Bondholders' Committee estimated that the 4 per cent bonds might sell for about 80, which is equivalent to a yield of slightly more than 5 per cent per annum when account is taken of the fact that a bond now bought for $800 will be redeemed by the company at its maturity for $1,000. The market value of the income bonds was estimated at 70, and the stock at about 30. Thus, upon the Committee's own estimate, the par value of the new securities exceeded the cash by $21,500,000, shown as follows:

Par value			*Cash value*
$15,790,000	4% refunding bonds	@ 80	$12,632,000
22,536,000	5% income "	@ 70	15,775,200
16,590,000	Stock	@ 30	4,977,000
$54,916,000		Total	$33,384,200

(From the letters of Henry Floy, engineer, and Guthrie, Bangs & Van Sinderen, counsel to the Bondholders' Committee, printed in the proceedings of the directors of the Third Avenue Railway Company and filed as Exhibit F with the petition of the company, May 26, 1910.)

Assuming that the property is maintained by annual cash expenditures and a depreciation fund, it would follow that in 1960, when the bonds become due, there would still be a difference between the total capitalization and the value of the property (assuming that the amount of cash now paid in will be used to increase the value of the property) of approximately $25,000,000.

In order that this difference, which is in the nature of a discount upon securities, may be eliminated during the life of the bonds, it is necessary that an amount should be set aside annually out of income before dividends and interest on the income bonds may properly be paid. It is evident that the annual amount is determined by the rate at which the fund will accumulate. It is certainly not less than four per cent, and upon this basis the annual payment would be $180,000, plus four per cent upon previous payments and accumulations. If this course is followed, the company in 1960 will have a fund which, together with its other property, assuming it to be maintained as above stated, will be equivalent to the par value of the securities then outstanding.

It is apparent that if the company is able to earn only four per cent upon this fund, either through investments in securities or in its own property, the net deduction will be $180,000 per annum. If, however, the company is able to earn even more than four per cent per annum, the income above four per cent will work to reduce the net annual charge against income by the precise amount which the actual earnings exceed four per cent. If, for example, the company should be able to earn six per cent per annum, the net amount would be less than $100,000.

Unless some such plan is followed, the company will not be able in 1960, in refunding the bonds then due, to present as the basis for such refunding property which is equal to the par value of the securities. They will be represented in part by discounts upon issues of 1912, fifty years before.

DEPRECIATION. The foregoing requirement has reference only to the *present* impairment of capital. This impairment of capital has resulted to a considerable extent from the neglect of the old campany to make proper provision for depreciation. If the company does not reserve a sufficient portion of its revenue to replace capital consumed during the year but not requiring replacement within the year, and then proceeds to treat the entire surplus as divisible profits, it is actually violating the corporation law against the declaration of dividends out of capital just as effectually as though it sold stock and distributed the proceeds immediately in the form of dividends. Unless, therefore, careful provision is made for the creation of a depreciation reserve, there may be another repetition of the financial collapses that have been so conspicuous in the history of the street railways in Manhattan.

Under the Third Article of the first refunding mortgage and the Fifth Article of the income mortgage, the company agrees and covenants to maintain property by making needful repairs, renewals, and replacements, and under the Second Article of the refunding mortgage it further agrees that no bonds shall be issued for replacements or operating expenses. To provide for such replacements, however, there ought to be some definite provision for a depreciation reserve. The matter assumes a special importance in view of the fact that the declaration of interest upon the income bonds will depend upon a precise definition of expenses and other deductions that may be made from revenue. Without clear definitions there is an almost certain likelihood of disputes between the income bondholders and the stockholders as to the true amount of the profits. The Second Article, Sub. a, of the income mortgage enumerates the various items of expense to be deducted from revenue and specifies depreciation or obsolescence, but leaves the amount of such charge to be determined entirely by the discretion of the Board of Directors. When it is recalled that in one case where it was the object of the company to show small earnings Receiver Whitridge testified before the Commission that the total annual depreciation amounted to $600,000, and that in a second case, where it was the object of the company to show large earnings, the same Receiver testified that depreciation amounted only to $300,000, one will realize the necessity of a more specific definition of depreciation.

In the opinion of the Commission, there should be reserved out of revenue for the upkeep of the property, including both current maintenance and future replacements, in accordance with the accounting rules of the Commission, at least twenty per cent of the operating revenue of the Third Avenue Railway. This minimum rate has been used in other mortgages and contracts, is practically the standard percentage used by engineers in appraising street railways, and more especially is the rate estimated by the Chairman of the Reorganization Committee of the Metropolitan Street Railway Company.

The Commission does not fix twenty per cent as the maximum rate or as the rate applicable to all cases. Further, if this rate should prove to be too high after a number of years, the facts may be presented upon application to the Commission for a modification of this order. But it is of prime importance that the situation into which the street railways of Manhattan drifted a few years ago be not repeated. Therefore, the Commission directs the company to provide and maintain two reserve funds, one for depreciation and one for the amortization of excessive capitalization so that the bondholders may have property of some sort wherewith to reimburse the holders of securities.

February 7, 1912.

The President (formerly the Receiver) of the Third Avenue Railway Company has taken decided exceptions to the rulings of the Public Service Commission and the matter will probably be settled only after protracted litigation.

The following table shows the results of different methods of calculating depreciation over a period of ten years upon an article costing $1,000 with a break-up value of $100 at the close of the decade.

Year	Fixed Percentage Method. 10% on Original Value	Fixed Percentage Method. 20.57% on Diminishing Value	Sinking Fund Method. At 5% Compound Interest
1	$90.00	$205.70	$71.55
2	90.00	163.38	71.55
3	90.00	129.78	71.55
4	90.00	103.08	71.55
5	90.00	81.88	71.55
6	90.00	65.03	71.55
7	90.00	51.66	71.55
8	90.00	41.03	71.55
9	90.00	32.59	71.55
10	90.00	25.87	71.55
			$715.50
Compound Interest at 5%..			184.50
TOTALS	$900.00	$900.00	$900.00

(3) PRODUCTION METHOD: A method of making depreciation allowances which has its advantages under certain conditions is that of charging an established rate per unit of output. This is especially applicable in the case of, say, a blast furnace where the frequency with which the linings will need to be renewed depends on the extent to which the furnace is being used. If it is being run at full capacity night and day, the wear on the linings is obviously much greater than if the furnace had not been in continual use during the entire fiscal period.

Another species of depreciation which may be said to come

under the above caption is that caused in a plant by the exhaustion of the mines or timber lands in connection with which the plant was constructed. Most of the value of coke ovens, for instance, is gone when the mines for which they were constructed are worked out. Consequently, in determining the amount to be written off for depreciation of mining and lumbering plants, the factor of the probable future output of the mines or lands will be an important one and it will frequently be found advisable to base the plant depreciation charge on the output. Certainly this should be done where it is evident that the plant will outlive the exhaustion of the mines or lands. In such cases the depreciation charges should be sufficient to absorb the entire cost of the plant, less residual value, by the time the mines or lands are exhausted, even though at that time the plant might still be in good operating condition.

Sinking Fund Requirements to Retire Bonds, etc., Must Not be Confused with Depreciation Allowances: The trained accountant or engineer recognizes the distinction between depreciation and sinking funds and never confuses the two terms. Not so, however, with lawyers and business men. The modern industrial bond is not popular unless a provision is inserted in the trust deed requiring that a sufficient sum be set aside annually, or otherwise, to retire the bonds before or at maturity.

It is usual to provide that the installments must be provided out of earnings, and this is a wise course to follow, as it serves to keep down dividend declarations during the life of the bonds. Nevertheless, the sinking fund installments are capital expenditure and do not properly appear among operating expenses, but should be stated as deductions from the net profits when ascertained. This course fulfills the obligation imposed in the trust deed and yet does not permit the surplus to be overstated.

Now the sinking fund provision may be greater or less than the amount required for depreciation, aside from the fact that one is an operating expense and the other is a discharge of a capital obligation. Therefore, depreciation should be calculated and charged against earnings before the net profit is determined irrespective of the existence or nonexistence of sinking fund requirements.

The common misconception of the proper treatment of compulsory sinking funds can be explained by an illustration taken from actual practice. A manufacturing corporation handling a patented device issued bonds aggregating $375,000, payable in installments of $25,000 annually for fifteen years. Having in mind possible competition and obsolescence of its property, it was provided that the sinking fund installments be charged against earnings. The president of the company had a contract under which he was to receive a bonus of five per cent of the net profits in addition to his salary, but it was specifically provided that as to him the charges against earnings should not include the sinking fund installments. In making up the first year's accounts the auditors decided that the depreciation reserve, as nearly as could be determined, should be stated as $25,000, and this amount was included among the operating expenses.

When their report was submitted to the directors, the president referred to his contract and stated that the sinking fund provision and depreciation were synonymous and that he was entitled to five per cent of the earnings before any deduction was made for depreciation. The majority of the directors agreed with him, with the result that the company has overpaid the president $1,250 per annum for several years.

Perhaps the time will arrive when depreciation will be generally considered as a prime operating cost. If it is so treated throughout the accounts, no such misunderstanding as that above cited could occur.

Depreciation Is an Operating Expense: We often see a statement in published reports that a corporation has realized net profits amounting to a certain sum, and that out of these profits an allowance for depreciation has been made. It would be just as logical to state that a candy manufacturer had earned a net profit of one hundred thousand dollars and that out of said one hundred thousand dollars there had been set aside twenty thousand dollars to pay for the sugar consumed in the manufacture of the product.

The use of that which is consumed is a loss or expense. Machinery is consumed; sugar is consumed. You cannot say that one is an operating expense and the other is an item which need not be ascertained nor taken into account until the net profit is shown. Net profit means only one thing in the vocabulary of the professional auditor, and that is the excess of income over operating costs, expenses, and losses. It cannot be determined by taking into account *all* of the income and a part only of the charges against income. If the provision for depreciation is not such an item as can be included among the costs of operation, then it is a misnomer.

This view of depreciation is well expressed by Professor Henry C. Adams, writing with respect to railroad accounts, but the principle enunciated applies with equal force to industrial accounts.

> When carried to its final analysis the question of formal depreciation charges to operating expenses is simply a question of what constitutes cost of operation, and the time when such cost shall be acknowledged in the accounts. The position which the Interstate Commerce Commission's system of accounts assumes on this point is, that the depletion of an asset which represents an investment through the use of that asset in operation creates an item of cost of operation which should be reflected in the accounts when the fact of such depletion takes place, and that a statement of net revenue made without including this element of cost in operation expenses is an erroneous statement.

Depreciation a Local Issue: The auditor must use his own judgment in passing on rates of depreciation just as much as he does when he inspects purchase vouchers. In one locality steam coal may be two dollars a ton, in another four dollars. The variation may be entirely legitimate. In one locality boilers may depreciate 7½ per cent annually, in another the rate may be 15 per cent.

It is not merely a question of the life of the boilers, because no experienced engineer or boiler manufacturer would answer the question unless he knew the use to which the boiler would be subjected, the climate, the water, the class of labor, the probabilities of shut-downs, etc. And similarly with almost all other classes of property which depreciate by wear and tear. Therefore, wherever rates of depreciation are mentioned in this chapter, they must be taken as suggestive only and in a relative sense. The student without other experience can thus broadly acquaint himself with general observations and modify his views later on as he gains experience.

Investment of Depreciation Reserves: It has been urged that unless an amount corresponding to the reserve for depreciation is invested in marketable securities, it is not a *de facto* reserve, but merely a book account. This is a matter of secondary importance. The principal point to consider is whether or not there has been charged to income a sufficient sum to cover the loss by wear and tear and obsolescence. So long as this is done there is no possibility of the amount thereof being paid out in dividends. It is left in the business in the form of cash or any other undivided asset. The question of its investment is immaterial.

The concern that can and does purchase securities equal to its depreciation reserve and retain such securities until the proceeds are needed for the purchase of machinery, etc., could certainly be depended upon to renew its machinery when necessary even though its depreciation reserve was represented among its current or fixed assets.

The life of plant and equipment is too uncertain to warrant the purchase of bonds which are to be sold to finance renewals. A well-managed plant is attended to daily as to its up-keep, and renewals and changes are made as needed.

Importance of Provision for Obsolescence: It has been pointed out that actual depreciation is ascertainable. That is to say, machinery, for instance, cannot be operated efficiently if it falls below, say, 70 per cent of its condition when new. If its theoretical life is ten years and 30 per cent has been set aside during the first three years, the question then arises as to what to do at the end of the fourth year. If the shop is properly managed, it is probable that the machine is worth 70 per cent of its cost and will remain so until superseded. But no manufacturer can depend on keeping up his equipment by renewing old machines in whole or in part. It is inevitable that improvements will come so long as the times produce inventors and men of initiative. Therefore the manufacturer who is willing that the product of a machine shall bear the cost of the machine continues to charge operating and credit reserve for depreciation with such an amount as will enable him to discard his old machine as soon as a better one appears.

One of the foremost efficiency engineers in this country told the author that the tendency to scrap old machines and buy new ones had often been carried to an extreme; that in some cases a new machine of twice the capacity of an old one costs much more than twice as much, and that the interest, depreciation, and other charges against the new machine more than offset the saving in time or increase in production.

Nevertheless, the tendency to discard is strong, and the auditor who endeavors to charge out the cost of a machine against its product must set up a reserve for obsolescence or he will find the reserve for depreciation insufficient.

It is not advisable to separate the accounts in the books nor on financial statements. No manufacturer cares to publish his estimate of that part of his equipment which is getting out of date.

Depreciation of Different Classes of Property: Passing from a general discussion of the rules which have the approval of competent authorities, it is desirable to study their application to various classes of assets. For the sake of convenience we will take up the depreciation of fixed assets as they appear in Chapter IX (page 117).

Land: It is usual to dismiss this item with the statement that land does not depreciate. Nothing could be further from the fact. The great bulk of land in the United States is depreciating through use just as much as depreciation occurs in machinery through use.

The land on which buildings are erected or which is used for storage purposes, etc., may not depreciate, and the aggregate of such holdings is very large, but the auditor must inquire into the purpose for which land is used, its location, etc., before he can decide offhand that the land has not depreciated.

Land used for agricultural purposes may depreciate through use and does depreciate unless a certain rotation of crops is followed or unless fertilizers are used. The latter is equivalent to the cost of maintenance and repairs in a factory.

The price of flax seed has increased enormously because during the early years of farming in the West the vitality of the land was exhausted by raising a crop which impoverished the soil to such an extent that the farmers were obliged to discontinue the raising of flax. During the period when this crop was using up the value of the land the farmers should have set up a reserve for depreciation, and it would have been apparent that the net price realized from the flax crop was not nearly so high as it seemed, and that wheat, while bringing in less cash per acre, would hav been more profitable.

This illustration may not seem pertinent enough to warran its inclusion in a book which is intended to be practical, but th author wishes students in particular to use their imagination o every possible occasion, and this is a convenient place to reiterate the advice. Heretofore textbooks on auditing have state without qualification that land does not depreciate. If it is a fac that three-fourths of the land in the United States is depreciatin through use, these statements should not have been allowed t go unchallenged so long.

Land fluctuates in value, sometimes violently, but such variations are not to be confused with depreciation.

Buildings: It is difficult to foretell at what rate building will depreciate, and it is practically impossible to set a standar common to all the different classes of buildings which may b found among the assets of different enterprises. When th ledger account includes land with buildings, the depreciatio usually must be confined to the buildings only. As a genera plan, if the allowances for depreciation take the form of th installment plan, the annual rate of deduction will range fron one per cent to five per cent of the original amount, the rate varying according to the workmanship, material, service to whic the building is put, climate, and any other factor which may influence the life of the building. By the sinking-fund system th sum to be set aside must be such as will accumulate to the cos of the building during the probable life of the building. Repair will have to be borne by the income, in addition to the item o depreciation.

It must be remembered that no building will last forever and this statement is made in the face of the claims of the advocates of concrete construction. Possible appreciation in lan should not be used as an offset against the depreciation of buildings unless the former is set out clearly on the income side o the accounts and the charge for depreciation included among th expenses. It will then be apparent that an anticipated profit i being used to offset an actual expense.

The following rates of depreciation on buildings are take from different authorities.

J. S. Government Allowance			Per Cent Per Annum
3rick buildings:	Occupied by	Owner	1 to 1¼
	Do.	Tenant	1¼ " 1½
'rame buildings:	Do.	Owner	2 " 2½
	Do.	Tenant	2½ " 3

Wisconsin Commissions	Years of Life
First-class stone and brick (office buildings)	75
Second-class shops, car-barns, and power stations	50
Brick gas retort houses	30
Frame dwellings	35
Frame stables and coal sheds	20 to 25

Public Service Commission, New York	
Brick buildings	2%

Chicago Traction Co. Valuation	
Brick buildings	1½%

Leaseholds: Premiums paid for leases may be considered as he price of a terminable annuity of an amount equal to the difference between the annual value and the annual charges. In the case of short-term leases it will be found most convenient to charge a proportionate part against each year's revenue, but this method would not be desirable in the case of longer leases, as it s not sufficiently accurate. The annuity method would be more desirable where long leases are concerned, as it is not proper that he early years should bear the carrying charges on the full purchase price in addition to a prorated installment of the principal.

It sometimes happens that at the end of a lease there is a claim for damages based on the condition of the premises. It is not usually possible to restrict the use under a long lease to ordinary wear and tear. The amount thereof will vary according to circumstances, and the possibility of this contingency must be taken into consideration in making the calculation. When there is an agreement in a lease calling for the restoration of premises to the original condition at the termination of the lease, the estimated expense may be accumulated and spread over he years of the life of the lease.

In England, where leaseholds are far more common than here, the annuity system is usually applied and the interest on he investment is charged each year on the diminishing value of he lease. The amount of depreciation is fixed, but as the reserve grows larger the interest charged decreases.

When new buildings are erected on leased land the full cost thereof will have to be provided for during the term unless there is a provision for revaluation at the expiration. In any event the amount which will disappear from the assets at the end of the lease must be absorbed equitably during the period. The annuity system is suggested as the plan most suitable.

Machinery and Equipment: The rate of depreciation to be allowed in the case of machinery has been the subject of more discussion than any other allowance of this nature. So many factors enter into the life of machinery that it is absolutely necessary for each machine to carry its own individual rate, and this can be determined solely by experience. In the case of two machines exactly alike in the beginning used in different factories, there may be a considerable difference in length of life and service; consequently no hard-and-fast rule can be laid down. But in addition to charging all repairs and part renewals to operating, from 7½ to 12½ per cent should be written off annually from the original cost to provide for normal depreciation by wear and tear and obsolescence.

It is invariably desirable that a subsidiary ledger should be kept containing details of the machinery accounts in the general ledger. This assists in arriving at rates of depreciation and is of great value in case of fire or in determining the amount to be written off in case of sale.

A considerable part of the ordinary wear and tear for which depreciation reserves are created is usually charged to operating expenses in the form of repairs and maintenance. Small parts of machines are wearing out or breaking and are being constantly renewed. In some cases nearly every part of a machine may be renewable, and it is quite conceivable that at the end of five or six years a machine may be largely renewed and be about as good as new. If in the meantime depreciation at the rate of 10 per cent per annum has been reserved without any adjustment for new parts supplied it is evident that the reserve is too large.

It is not intended to advocate any reduction in ordinary depreciation rates, but it is suggested that the careful auditor should study the relation between the depreciation reserve and the physical condition of the machine. Reference to Professor Cooley's description on page 319 herein will remind us that machinery to serve its purpose properly must be maintained at from 75 per cent to 85 per cent of its original condition, therefore there is no necessity for providing the cost of maintenance plus the wear and tear element of depreciation if the latter is fully covered by the former.

The following tables compiled by Mr. George A. Cravens and published in the Electrical Review, April 23, 1910, are of interest. Rates of depreciation on various kinds of equipment as estimated in connection with litigation and by recognized authorities are shown.

Table II indicates the variation caused by light or heavy use.

TABLE I

Items	Chicago Traction Commission	Chicago Union Traction Co.	Milwaukee Electric Railway & Light Co.	Wisconsin Railroad Commission	Average English	Average Scotch Practice	Philip Dawson	Stone & Webster	Industrial Power Plants	Professor G. F. Gebhardt	Miscellaneous Sources
Boilers	3.5–10	6.6	7.5	6.6–8.5	5	5	8–10	5	2.5–3.3	4–6.6	7.5
Steam Piping	3.5	6.6	7.5	5	5	5	8–10	5	2.5–3.3	5–8	5
Auxiliaries	5–10	6.6	5	6.6–8.5	5	5	8–10	5	4–6.6	3–5	7.5
Steam Engines	3–10	6.6	5	5–6.6	5	5	4–6	5	2.5–5	4–6.6	5
Steam Turbines			5		5	5	7–9	5	2.5–5	4	4
Belted Generators	5–10	6.6	7.5	5	5	5	5–10	5	6.6	3.3–4	7.5
Wires and Cables	2	6.6	5	2	5	3	3–5	5	4–6.6	5	5
Switchboards, etc.	2	6.6	5	2	7.5	5	8–10	5	2–5		5
Motors	5–10	6.6	5	5	5	5	5–8	5	4–6.6	5	5
Storage Batteries		6.6	10		5	5	9–11	5	5–10	6.6	10
Shop Equipment	3–10	5	7.5	3.3–10	7.5	7.5	12–15	5	4–10		7.5

TABLE II

Items of Equipment	Light or Intermittent Service	Heavy or Continuous Service
Boilers, Water Tube	4–6.6	5–8.3
Boilers, Fire Tube	5–6.6	6.6–10
Piping, Steam, and Water	4–5.5	5.5–8.3
Auxiliaries, Steam	3–5	4–6.6
Engines, Steam	4–5	5–6.6
Turbines, Steam	3–4	4–5
Generators, Belted	4–6.6	5–8.3
Wires and Cables	3–5	4–6.6
Switchboards and Instruments	2–5	5–8.3
Motors (A. C. and D. C.)	4–6.6	5–8.3
Storage Batteries	5–6.6	6.6–10
Shop Equipment, Tools, etc.	5–10	7.5–15

Small Tools: Small tools should be revalued periodically thus fixing accurately the rate of depreciation. If this plan is followed for several years and a dependable rate is secured, it may be feasible to omit the revaluation for a year or two, applying the rate previously ascertained.

Furniture and Fixtures: Many concerns write down this item to $1, and the practice is to be commended unless stockholders, partners, or other interested parties are being deceived. Where the asset is a large one such a course is not so feasible, but there is no doubt that this item is usually overvalued so far as any possibility of realization is concerned.

Usually in a going business, assets are not treated on the basis of realization values, but in the case of furniture and fixtures so many changes are made to suit the convenience and whims of executives and clerks, and offices are moved so often from one place to another, that furniture and fixtures have a most uncertain value.

Office partitions are frequently built at the expense of tenants and are worthless at the end of the lease. In the meantime changes are often made, and if the auditor is careful he may find duplications in the account.

If it is important to write off actual depreciation only, it will be found that 15 per cent per annum will represent a fair average allowance.

Landlord's Fixtures: Leaving out of consideration the complex question as to what are and what are not landlord's fixtures, it may be laid down as a general rule that the minimum rate of depreciation upon machinery and fittings erected upon leasehold property should be written off at a rate at least sufficient to wipe off the book value before the expiration of the lease.

In the case of machinery, etc., which will not become landlord's fixtures, a less rate may be permitted, but it is imperative that in such a case it should be clearly understood and agreed what are to be the landlord's fixtures and what are not.

Horses: It will be readily seen that the depreciation of horses and other animals is rapid and inevitable. The rate of allowance may be from 15 to 25 per cent of the cost. By means of revaluation, which can be more accurately done in the case of horses than with most other assets, it should soon become possible to letermine the actual rate of depreciation. These revaluations should be fairly frequent.

Wagons, Automobiles, etc.: In the case of wagons it will be ound that 8 to 10 per cent per annum is an ample allowance, provided that all repairs, renewals of parts and maintenance are charged to operating expenses.

As with wagons, most of the parts of an automobile can be eplaced. Under ordinary conditions the rate of depreciation on automobiles should be fixed at from 15 to 20 per cent per annum. The most expensive parts, such as tires, motors, and bodies, may be easily replaced, and if charged to operating will leave unprovided for only accrued depreciation and obsolescence.

Ships: Although the depreciation of ships is invariably great and must be the subject of allowance, it is a difficult matter to ay down any fixed rate to be written off. The amount of depreciation should be certified by an engineer, and unless there appears to be some reason to doubt the correctness of his report, he auditor is not responsible. The auditor's certificate should state clearly that inadequate allowance for depreciation has been made unless an amount has been provided which in his opinion s ample.

Patents: Although it is true that some value may attach to a patented article even though the patent has run out, it is generally conceded that it is well to write off the entire cost of a patent during the period of protection. The patent derives its value in great measure from the fact that it is a monopoly, and he moment the monopoly has ceased by the termination of patent rights, the value is seriously affected, if not entirely wiped out. In the case of a patent which has been leased and not purchased, the item should not be treated as an asset except to the extent of its actual cost in fees, etc. To capitalize a patent lease at any sum in excess thereof would be as incorrect as to capitalize good will, although both are latent assets in every paying concern.

Copyrights may be treated in a similar manner, except that their commercial value generally expires long before the termination of the copyright. (See also "Publishers' Accounts.")

The original life of a patent is seventeen years, and renewals are dependent upon the introduction of some essential novelty.

Good Will: While good will does not depreciate, it is constantly liable to fluctuations. Good will is not usually written off, and the question of the amount at which it shall stand in the balance sheet was not formerly deemed to be within the scope of the auditor's work, but the present range of an auditor's duties compels him to give serious thought to this item. The various points connected with the valuation of good will are fully discussed on pages 131-135 and should be referred to in case a question arises as to writing off all or any part of the amount at which good will is carried.

WASTING ASSETS

Mines: Depreciation of mines is equivalent to a depletion of mineral wealth. The value of the mine to the owner or lessee has decreased at the end of a year by exactly the amount of ore extracted. But on account of the uncertainty in the total amount of ore, its quality and grade and the expense which may be involved in mining, it is a difficult matter to set such a rate of depreciation as will represent the average depletion during the life of the mine or the term of the lease, as the case may be. The only way in which this can be done is by estimation, which is naturally inaccurate and may be misleading.

Under most State laws a mining company is not compelled to write off any depreciation before declaring a dividend, but it is generally considered better finance to write off annually such proportion of the total cost less residual value of plant as the output bears to the estimated content of the mine, or, in case of a leased mine, such proportion of the total cost as the output bears to the output estimated for the duration of the lease.

On account of the great uncertainty of mining, and the fact that stockholders object to the accumulation of large reserve funds, which would earn only a low rate of interest and might just as well be distributed as dividends, it may be better policy that mines should be regarded as non-permanent undertakings in which excesses of current revenue might be distributed without regard to the value of the remaining assets in their relation to the amount of paid-up capital.

Timber Lands: In just the same way that the removal of a ton of ore or coal reduces by so much the value of the mine, so the cutting of each thousand feet of timber likewise reduces the value of the land on which it stood. It is obvious that there should be written off from year to year such proportion of the cost of the lands as the quantity of timber cut during the year bears to the quantity standing on the entire tract at the time of its purchase.

In some cases allowance for the value of the cut-over lands may be made in determining the amount which should be charged off for depletion of the timber. Very frequently, however, the cut-over land has but little value.

Inasmuch as the total quantity of timber standing on a tract of land can be determined with much greater certainty than is the case with the contents of a mine, it follows that the depletion charge per thousand feet of timber cut can be more accurately fixed than is true of the depletion charges for mining operations.

PUBLIC UTILITY COMPANIES

Out of the agitation for municipal ownership and regulation, and the litigation resulting therefrom, has arisen a considerable amount of information bearing on the depreciation of such properties.

The following quotation and rates of depreciation are taken from Foster's Valuation of Public Utilities, page 198.

In the Milwaukee Three-Cent Fare Case a number of engineers testified as to rates of depreciation, and these have been tabulated in comparison with rates specified by other engineers and companies.

	Cooley–Beegs–Starret–Pence				Chicago		Officials
	Milwaukee Three-Cent Case				Union T. Co. Case	U. T. Co. Stone & Webster	M. E. R. & L. Co.
Improvements	4 & 2		2	2	2	2	3
Track Main	8	8.5	8		7.75	7.2	7.5
Special Work				12.5–7	7.75	7.2	12
Paving	10	8.5	8		10–4	10–4	10
Cars, Bodies, and Trucks	8	6.66	6	6.66–5	5	5	7.5
Electrical Equipment		8.5			8.5–$6\frac{2}{3}$	8.5–$6\frac{2}{3}$	6
Electrical Distribution	8	8.5	7				7.5
Poles—Iron				2.5	5	5	
Poles—Wood				$8\frac{1}{3}$–$6\frac{2}{3}$			7.5
Wiring, etc.					14–10	14–10	
Feeders and Cables				4			5

CHAPTER XXII

THE CORPORATION TAX LAW AND DEPRECIATION

UNTIL recently judicial decisions on the subject of depreciation were rare, arising chiefly in those cases where the point at issue was the payment of dividends out of capital. With the passage of the Federal Corporation Tax on August 5, 1909, there arose the necessity on the part of every corporation of considering whether or not there had been any loss during the period covered by the returns which might be included among the deductions permitted by the Treasury Department. The law provides:

> Such net income shall be ascertained by deducting from the gross amount of the income received within the year ****** (2) all losses actually sustained within the year **** including a reasonable allowance for depreciation of property, if any.

In the regulations subsequently issued by the Treasury Department it was ingeniously argued that "received within the year" meant exactly the same as "accrued within the year," and that "actually paid" meant the same as "accrued," which accounts for the use of the word "accrued" in the following official explanation of the clause relating to depreciation.

> Depreciation. The deduction for depreciation should be the estimated amount of the loss, accrued during the year to which the return relates, in the value of the property in respect of which such deduction is claimed that arises from exhaustion, wear, and tear, or obsolescence out of the uses to which the property is put, and which loss has not been made good by payments for ordinary maintenance and of repairs deducted under the heading of expenses and maintenance and operation or in the ascertainment of gross income. This estimate should be formed upon the assumed life of the property, its cost value, and its use. Expenses paid in any one year in making good exhaustion, wear, and tear, or obsolescence in respect of which any deduction for depreciation is claimed, must not be included in the deduction for expense of maintenance and operation of the property or in the ascertainment of gross income, but must be made out of accumulative allowances deducted for depreciation in current and previous years.

Immediately after the returns for the first year were filed, the inspectors of the department (evidently inspired in their rulings, as all of those of whom the author has heard disagree with the instructions) commenced to pass arbitrarily on the allowances for depreciation which many corporations claimed in the returns. The statement was made that the Government proposed to decide every doubtful point against the corporations, relying on the latter to litigate the particularly unjust rulings and thus provide the Department with precedents which they could use subsequently if they so desired. Unfortunately for the corporations, the rulings against them individually usually aggregate a few hundred or a few thousands of dollars only, and they have hesitated to proceed against the Treasury Department and the Department of Justice combined. A vast number of these decisions are unjust and indefensible from an accounting or any other point of view. It is believed that if corporations would refuse to pay the additional amounts assessed against them by irresponsible and unqualified inspectors, the courts would not sustain the Treasury Department.

Recently the Nipissing Mines Company was assessed some thousands of dollars of additional tax on the ground that the depreciation claimed by it and deducted from its gross income was not entered on its books. The company resisted the payment and was sued by the government. The case was tried before a jury and a verdict rendered for the company.

The opinion of the court is interesting, as an evidence of what may be expected if other unjust suits are brought by the government.

United States District Court

Southern District of New York.

The United States

v

The Nipissing Mines Company.

Lacombe, C. J. (charging jury.)

This statute provides for a deduction of all losses actually sustained within the year, including reasonable allowances for depreciation of property, if any. That is within the second subdivision of Section 38. The circumstance that in the third subdivision of Section 38, where the form of making the return is provided for, the same words are repeated, with a slight modification requiring a separate statement of any amounts *allowed* for depreciation of property, does not, in my opinion, change the meaning of the words used in the second subdivision of the paragraph. The word "allowed" refers to an allowance by the Commissioner of Internal Revenue and his allowance or disallowance ends the matter unless some case is made out upon the strength of which a party may come into court to test the reasonableness of the allowance or disallowance by the Commissioner. The suggestion that there can be no allowance for depreciation unless such depreciation is entered in the books of the company, recorded from time to time, seems to me without force. The books may be very badly kept; kept in such a way as will in the end bring them into trouble and difficulty, but this act doesn't provide any penalty for bad bookkeeping. It simply provides that one per cent of the net profit of the various corporations shall be turned over to the Government, and provides that in finding out that net profit there shall be a reasonable allowance for depreciation. Now, the testimony here seems to me entirely reasonable, and certainly it is not contradicted, that the value of the ore as it lies in the ore beds is, as stated by the witness to be, 31.1 cents. The Government does not controvert the testimony by other witnesses, nor does it dispute the expert's method of calculating. This unit of value 31.1 cents multiplied by the total amount of ore that was removed during the year, indicates in dollars the amount by which the total assets of this company were depleted through the operation of the mine during that year. It seems to me to be a reasonable allowance for depreciation within the meaning of the statute. Certainly so much value has been eliminated from the property of the company forever. Granting the proposition that such is a reasonable allowance for the depreciation, upon the figures here there is no net profit remaining, which would indicate that the Government's claim for $8,534.68 should be dismissed, and that a verdict should be directed in favor of the defendant for the counterclaim, being the amount taxed, which it paid, $5,188.62, with an exception to the Government on each of these rulings.

If the evidence had shown that the unit value 31.1 cents is too high, there would be some net profit despite the depreciation, but the case must be determined on the testimony. It makes no difference that in filling up the form of return under the direction of the Revenue Officers this claimed allowance was called "return of capital," which it certainly is *not,* instead of "depreciation of deposits," which it clearly is.

If the known value of an ore bed were exactly $2,000,000 and exactly $500,000 were taken out of it each year, in four years there would be nothing left. It is difficult to say why it may not reasonably be said that the ore bed suffers each year a depreciation of $500,000, just as a $10,000 piece of machinery with a life of ten years suffers a depreciation of $1,000 each year. As I read the statute, Congress intended to allow all reasonable depreciations to be deducted from the gross profits to find the net, and the reasonableness of any deduction asked for depends upon the nature of the claim on which it is based, not upon the amount of dollars it may aggregate. Nor is it apparent why it should make any difference that one cannot tell with reasonable certainty the total value of the deposit so long as the value of the amount removed in any one year can be ascertained with sufficient accuracy. Nor is it apparent why the problem is altered in any way by the circumstance that the property was bought at a very high or at a very low price, or that the capitalization of the company which owns it is large or small.

Verdict directed for defendant for $5,188.62.

The official decisions bearing on the subject are quoted in full, as it is probable that many corporations have followed them blindly, not knowing that they are subject to judicial review, and that if an additional assessment is made which is not warranted by commercial or accounting practice, the courts will not permit the collection of such assessment.

It may be noted that the first official ruling quoted is very neatly disposed of by Judge Lacombe:

> The suggestion that there can be no allowance for depreciation unless such depreciation is entered in the books of the company, recorded from time to time, seems to me without force.

The author does not advocate the practice of omitting depreciation charges from the books of account. On the contrary, he urges the entry of depreciation allowances wherever such a loss is accruing, but this need not deter an auditor from advising a client that depreciation may be claimed as a deduction in the corporation tax reports, even though it has not been entered in the books. In this case the only point at issue is whether the depreciation allowance can be sustained.

The client can very properly be warned that if the charge does not appear in his books, the burden of establishing its propriety is cast upon him, whereas if entered in the books in due course, the burden of eliminating or cutting down the item is upon the government.

It will be observed by those familiar with the terms of the corporation tax law that many of the decisions of the Treasury Department are somewhat at variance with the exact letter of the law. Indeed, it has become impracticable to follow strictly along the lines of the act and the Bureau of Internal Revenue has been obliged to reconcile a not altogether workable law with existing conditions.

In Treasury Decision 1742, paragraphs 83-94 inclusive and 96-105 inclusive, we find the following decisions:

83 Depreciation to be an allowable deduction in the return of annual net income of a corporation must be charged off on the ledger of the corporation, so as to show a reduction in the capital assets of the corporation to the extent of the depreciation claimed.

Note. On May 9, 1912, a letter of instruction was sent to Internal Revenue agents in which this arbitrary rule was reversed, it being found that the corporations whose accounts were in the best order were those who maintained depreciation reserves. In other words, the Treasury Department was not powerful enough to order corporations to depart from proper standards.

The Commissioner's letter follows:

Referring to Item 83 in T. D. No. 1742, and the various letters written from this office in which it has been stated that such depreciation to be allowable must show an actual shrinkage in the value of the capital assets with respect to which the depreciation is claimed, you are informed that it appears that the interpretation placed upon this in some cases has been that there must be an actual change in the figures representing the value of the capital assets against which the depreciation charge has been claimed. It is desired to modify this to meet the needs of corporations whose books are kept in various ways, but which in the main are kept in accordance with the principles laid down by the highest authorities among public accountants, and it is requested that hereafter when the depreciation account of a corporation is entered as such on the books of the corporation so as to constitute an actual charge against the property account affected thereby, the charge so made may be accepted as a sufficient compliance with the requirements of the rules of this office with respect to claims for depreciation made in returns of annual net income for the special excise tax on corporations.

Attention, however, is called to the fact that no part of the funds set aside for depreciation may be diverted for any purpose other than making good the depreciation in the property affected without actually reducing the valuation of the property against which the same was charged, if the same shall be desired to be claimed as a deduction in the return of annual net income.

84. Deduction on account of depreciation of property must be based on lifetime of property, its cost, value, and use, and must be evidenced by a ledger entry and a like reduction in the plant and property account with respect to which the depreciation is claimed.

85. In the case of corporations owning stocks and bonds or other securities, if an annual adjustment of the value of such securities is made and the adjusted values made a matter of ledger entry, the appreciation of such securities as so entered must be accounted for as income, and the depreciation may be deducted from gross income. If no annual adjustment is made and the securities are carried from year to year as a permanent investment there will be neither gain nor loss, as to the principal of such securities until the same shall have been disposed of, when the gain or loss as com-

ared with the original cost shall be prorated, and the amount of such gain r loss apportioned to the years since the incidence of the tax, to wit, Janu- ry 1, 1909, shall be added to or deducted from the gross income of the year n which the securities were so disposed of.

86. Where increase or decrease during the year in the value of real state acquired in previous years, sold or held for sale, is taken upon the ooks and the rate cannot be accurately determined with respect to individual ears, such increase or decrease may be prorated as provided by regulations n cases of sale of capital assets.

87. Premiums on stocks and bonds arbitrarily charged off on the books f a corporation do not constitute a proper deduction on account of depre- iation, unless there shall have been an actual shrinkage in value of such tocks and bonds to the extent of the deduction claimed during the year for which the return is made.

88. Net income on uncompleted contracts may be estimated on the basis f the percentage of the work completed as compared with the contract price f the whole work.

89. Cost of drilling new wells by oil corporations is considered better- nents and additions to the capital assets of the corporation. The expense f drilling dry wells may, however, be charged to profit and loss.

90. Discounts, other than bank discounts on notes executed by a cor- oration, should be segregated from the interest item on the return, and hould be included under expenses, item 4.

91. The mere removal of timber by cutting from timber lands, unless he timber is otherwise disposed of through sales or plant operations, is con- idered simply a change in form of assets. If said timber is disposed of hrough sales or otherwise, it is to be accounted for in accordance with egulations governing disposition of capital and other assets.

92. Deduction on account of depreciation of property must be based on fetime of property, its cost, value, and use.

93. Loss due to voluntary removal of buildings, etc., incident to im- rovements, is either a proper charge to the cost of the new additions or to epreciation already provided, as the facts may indicate, but in no case is it proper deduction in determining net income, except as it may be reflected n the reasonable amount allowable as a deduction for depreciation.

94. Depreciation of company's stock is a loss to the stockholders, but ot a loss to the company issuing the same, and therefore not a proper de- uction.

DEPRECIATION IN MINERALS, OILS, ETC.

96. In case of corporations whose business consists in part or wholly f mining, producing, and disposing of deposits of nature (ores, coals, gas, etroleum, and sundry minerals), the conduct of such business will be nderstood to comprehend two classes of gains or losses, viz.:

(*a*) The gain or loss resulting from the sale of capital assets, i. e., either he increment or the loss, arising through possessing over a period of time he investment in the same.

(*b*) The trading or commercial gain attached to the conduct of the industry, the employment of working capital, the effort and risk involved.

97. In the ascertainment of net income deduction will be allowed for depreciation arising from exhaustion of deposits of ore, mineral, etc., and for depreciation and obsolescence of improvements, in accordance with general regulations respecting depreciation allowances, on the basis of the original capital investment cost of the properties concerned to the company reporting.

98. A further deduction will also be allowed, through not including the same at all in the item of gross income (item 3, Form 637), for the unearned increment represented in such properties as at January 1, 1909, which will be determined in general as follows:

99. An estimate should be made as of January 1, 1909, of the fair market value at that date of the minerals, etc., in deposit. This estimate should be formed on the basis of the disposal value of the minerals *in total* and exclusive of value of improvements and development work. This valuation should also be reduced to a unit value per ton, barrel, etc.

NOTE. Values, as aforesaid, should not be estimated on the basis of the assumed salable value of the output under current operative conditions, less the actual cost of production, because, as hereinbefore stated, the selling price under such conditions comprehends a profit both for carrying the investment in minerals, improvements, and working capital, and for conducting operations in respect of production and disposal of product. The value to be determined as stated must be on the basis of the salable value of the entire deposit of the aggregate units of minerals considered *en bloc* if disposed of in that form. Nor must such valuation comprehend any speculative value which might attach to a sale of the minerals *en bloc;* i. e., a value which might be obtained on the ground that the future would develop a much greater reserve of mineral deposits than were believed to exist at the time the estimate as of January 1, 1909, was formed. Any value of this latter character would attach obviously to such additional reserves when developed in future.

100. The unit value as of January 1, 1909, ascertained as above outlined, would indicate the value to be attached at that date to the capital assets disposed of during any calendar year succeeding, and should be used in determining the unearned increment at January 1, 1909, which may be excluded entirely from the item of gross income, as before explained, in the following manner, viz.:

Value at January 1, 1909, determined in manner outlined, of minerals, etc., which may be removed and disposed of in any year subsequent thereto .... $————

Less the following:

(*a*) Proportion of depreciation charge applying to exhaustion of minerals disposed of, ascertained as first explained herein on basis of original cost........$————

(*b*) Royalty paid, if any, on minerals disposed of......$————

Balance, being unearned increment at January 1, 1909, to be excluded from gross-income item..........$————

101. The precise detailed manner in which the estimate of value of minerals, etc., as at January 1, 1909, shall be formed, must naturally be determined upon by each corporation interested, but formal record of such estimates, together with all sustaining information, should be carefully filed so as to be readily accessible for reference. Values as stated, as determined at January 1, 1909, should be used in compilation in all subsequent years' excise tax returns. The question as to whether it subsequently develops the property possessed a greater quantity of mineral, etc., reserve than was in the aggregate estimated as of January 1, 1909, is immaterial. Any excess which may be developed will be considered as possessing the same value at January 1, 1909, as that which then may have been known to be in the property.

102. Each excise tax return (Form 637) should be accompanied with memorandum setting forth the extent in amount of the exclusion made from the item gross income for unearned increment realized during the year, as above outlined.

103. As the amount to be deducted for depreciation (paragraph 2 preceding) is to be formed on basis of the estimated reserve of minerals, etc., it follows that if it develops such estimate is understated, the cost investment in the capital asset may be wholly extinguished before all mineral reserves are removed. When this is reached, further deductions for exhaustion of minerals should be discontinued, but in such event, it will be noted, the allowance for unearned increment which is to be excluded entirely from gross income will be correspondingly increased.

104. In case of corporations leasing mines and paying royalties on minerals, etc., removed, the royalties paid are to be treated as expenses and deducted in ascertaining net income, as provided in general regulations. Any leasehold investment which the operating corporation may have in such properties, either through a payment originally made for acquirement thereof or for improvements made upon the property, to be accounted for in accordance with regulations governing depreciation allowances and disposition of capital assets.

105. In respect to properties of the character in question which may be acquired by a corporation after January 1, 1909, a deduction will be allowed only as to depreciation arising from exhaustion based on original cost. No exclusion from gross income can be made for unearned increment, as profit arising in sale of such capital assets applies wholly to the period subsequent to January 1, 1909.

CHAPTER XXIII

SPECIAL POINTS IN DIFFERENT CLASSES OF AUDITS

FINANCIAL

Introductory: It is impracticable to discuss in one book all the special points which arise in the audit of various enterprises. The general principles which underlie all audits have received full consideration and the rules which have been formulated will serve as a working program for the audit of any concern. Nevertheless, it is of great value to a practitioner to acquire special knowledge of as many kinds of business as is feasible.

The knowledge of the possible weak spots and the points of greatest importance in any given audit enables an auditor to make a better start than if his equipment consists solely of a knowledge of general principles.

Human activity, so far as the relation of one person to another is concerned, finds expression in the universal medium of exchange—money; and the records of any or all of these activities, no matter how well or poorly kept they may be, constitute the field of the professional auditor.

The various classes of accounts with which an auditor has to deal are:

Financial.
Insurance.
Manufacturing.
Mining.
Trading.
Transportation.
Public Utilities.
Governmental.
Executors and Trustees.
Professional.
Institutional.
Miscellaneous.

The foregoing groups will be considered with reference to those points only in which peculiar conditions exist or where special emphasis is required. No attempt will be made to cover any class of business in detail.

NATIONAL AND STATE BANKS

In recent years the subject of bank examinations has received much more attention than formerly. This is largely due to the passing away of the opinion once held by many bank directors that the examinations made by Government examiners for the Comptroller of the Currency and for the Banking Commissioners of the various States covered all that was necessary in the way of inspection of a bank's condition and accounts.

Despite these Governmental examinations, reports of bank failures and defalcations are frequent, and subsequent investigation has often brought out the fact that the defalcations had been more or less cleverly concealed for a period of years.

Government examiners should not be too sharply criticized for their failure to detect such conditions, as the time allowed for separate examinations is limited, and it is physically impossible for them to make thorough audits within the time available. Again, it must be remembered that the chief object of these examinations is to ascertain that the banks are solvent and are complying with the law. Some degree of protection is afforded depositors by these examinations, but the examiners do not represent the stockholders or the directors, and the directors should not regard the work of the examiners as being done for their benefit.

Official examiners recognize this state of affairs and are making a determined effort to improve the unsatisfactory conditions which exist.

The *New York Times* reported a meeting of the official examiners in its issue of July 9, 1912, as follows:

LOW PAY ENDANGERS BANK EXAMINATIONS

Paltry Fees for Inspection of Country National Banks Result in Slurring of Work

Dishonesty Is Undetected

The subject that received the most attention in the meetings was the low rate of pay of the National Examiner working in the country, both from the standpoint of its inadequacy and from that of the corresponding menace to depositors, caused by the hurried way in which he must complete his task and get on to the next town, if he is to make enough to pay for his keep and traveling expenses. It seems that the rate of compensation was fixed in 1875 and has never been changed.

For examining a bank with less than $100,000 capital the Examiner gets $20. At least two days, it was declared yesterday, should be devoted to a thorough examination, and sometimes it is necessary to employ an assistant. All this comes out of the $20, including the assistant and his expenses. The rate advances with the size of the bank, but never gets up very high. For a bank capitalized at $100,000 to $300,000 the fee is $25; for a $300,000 bank, $35; for a $400,000 bank, $40; for a $500,000 bank, $50, and for a bank capitalized at $600,000 or over, $75.

A recent defalcation in this State was cited as an instance of what may happen under a system where the National Bank Examiner has not time and cannot afford to take time to make much more than a superficial inspection. One of the officers had been robbing this bank for years, his peculations aggregating some $350,000. It had been examined by three or four different men in that time, but none of them had found anything wrong, and one of the examiners said yesterday that this affair was the worst black eye the Government examining system had received in many years.

Because of the agitation for Government guarantee of bank deposits, in which case losses would probably be paid from a fund sustained by a tax levied against the banks, the latter have in some large cities made a determined effort to allay public feeling by decreasing the number and size of bank failures. The outcome of these efforts has been that in some cities all of the local banks clearing their cheques through the Clearing House are now examined periodically by a salaried examiner appointed by the Clearing House Association.

Clearing House examiners have been appointed in comparatively few cities, and in some quarters much opposition has been shown toward the movement, as it is argued that so long as a bank is solvent and is permitted by the government to continue business, it should have the privilege of naming its own independent auditor, and that the information received and reports rendered by such auditors should not be in the hands of anyone with discretionary power to discuss the bank's affairs with competitors who are members of the Clearing House Association committee.

While the examinations made by Clearing House examiners

are usually quite thorough, they will in all probability be limited to a few of the larger cities, as in small cities and rural communities no Clearing House Associations exist.

Some States require semiannual examinations to be made by committees of directors of each bank, with liberty to the committee to employ professional accountants for the purpose, the latter to report to the committees and the committees to report to the State.

The following quotation from an address by James B. Forgan, President of the First National Bank of Chicago, delivered on September 17, 1909, at the Convention of the American Bankers' Association, at Chicago, is of especial interest, as it refers to the responsibility of bank directors and the necessity for the employment by them of competent auditors to make investigations:

> The same ordinary prudence which men exercise in their own affairs is required of bank directors. The application of it differs with the varying circumstances of the banks. Just as men of small or moderate affairs can undertake the personal management in detail of their own businesses, while those of large affairs must of necessity employ others to manage for them and must relieve themselves of details, so bank directors, under similar circumstances, may assume the details of management or appoint others to do so. Their delegating authority to others does not, however, relieve them of responsibility for the direction and supervision of the management or of keeping in touch with what is done. In banks of moderate size this can be accomplished by committees. In the largest banks, however, it becomes necessary for the directors to delegate even the details of their supervisory duties to experts and to rely on their investigations and reports for an intelligent knowledge of what is being done and of their bank's condition. Systematic organization is necessary, whether a bank is small or large, and directors must see to it that one of its results is that they are kept fully posted as to the bank's operations and condition. This can be accomplished quite as effectively in large as in small banks through the employment of competent auditors, either permanently or when they are wanted. Such auditors, in their investigations, should represent the directors and should report direct to them, uninfluenced by any of the executive officers. But, however it may be accomplished, it is up to the directors to keep themselves posted as to their bank's operations to the extent of enabling them to form a correct opinion of actual conditions in them and to judge of the integrity and ability of the management, as it is conducted by the officers to whom they have delegated managerial powers. Only thus can they intelligently exercise their control of the management, a responsibility from which there can be no escape.

The auditor engaged to examine the affairs and accounts of a bank should procure a copy of the statement published by it in response to the latest call of the Comptroller of the Currency or the State Banking Commissioner. A careful scrutiny of this statement will give him a good idea of the volume of the work and nature of the assets and liabilities which will shortly demand his attention.

The audit should be started without notice to either officers or employees of the bank, and a large staff should be available so that all the changeable assets can be examined on the first day.

Cash and Securities: The verification of the balance-sheet items should receive attention first. This involves the actual count and examination of such assets as may be actually on hand, and comparison thereof with the general ledger accounts; the independent outside confirmation by correspondence of such of the assets as admit of such verification; and a thorough test of the integrity of every other account in the general ledger.

If there is a large quantity of cash on hand and the entire staff must be used to count it, the other changeable assets, such as securities owned by the bank, notes discounted, notes for secured loans and the collaterals therefor, etc., should be locked up in a safe and the latter sealed, and access thereto refused, except with approval of the auditor, until they have been examined.

All of one class of the assets above mentioned should be brought to the auditor before the examination of each is begun so as to prevent duplication in counting; e. g., all cash should either be brought from the vaults and tellers' cages to one point, or the auditing staff should be so distributed that counting of the cash at all points will begin simultaneously; transfer of cash between the cages and the vault should be prohibited until all of the cash has been counted and the aggregate amount is proved with the general ledger account therefor.

It is important that the genuineness of the cheques on hand, which are to be sent to the Clearing House, be verified. The only safe method to accomplish this is for the auditor to insert in each Clearing House envelope a confirmation slip (and stamped envelope addressed to himself) requesting verification of the aggregate amount of the inclosed cheques and detailed advices as to any which may be returned as unpaid. The failure to do this may be serious, as forged or "fake" cheques may be returned to the bank without being brought to the auditor's attention. In addition to this, it is desirable that the source of cheques of large amount to be sent either to the Clearing House or to out-of-town correspondents, or to be collected by runner on the following day, be ascertained, and that examination be made to see that the depositor has received credit therefor.

Correspondents' Accounts: Accounts current should at once be requested (to be sent direct to auditor) from reserve agents and out-of-town correspondents with which the client carries deposit accounts. It is also important to make note of the last deposits made and the number of the last draft drawn by the client against these banks for use in later reconciling the accounts current with the client's records. The auditor should examine these draft books carefully to ascertain that none have been used out of consecutive order or from the back of the book, as missing drafts may have been cashed and the proceeds counted as cash, or the cheque may have been included that very day with other cheques and sent to another out-of-town correspondent and charged to the latter as a deposit. Defalcations have been cleverly concealed for some time by this method, as the account with the bank on which the draft was drawn was not reduced on the client's books until after the date of the audit, and the item did not appear on the account current of the depository until the end of the month.

Confirmation of Demand Notes, etc.: All borrowers on unsecured demand notes should be requested by mail to confirm the amounts of their loans direct to the auditor. If any payments on account have been misappropriated and not indorsed on the notes, these confirmations should reveal that fact. Similar confirmations, showing the collateral as well as the amount of the loans, should be secured from borrowers on time or demand collateral notes.

All securities owned by the bank or deposited by customers as collateral for loans should be carefully examined. Denominations of stock certificates have in the past been so cleverly raised as to deceive bank officials, who accepted them as collateral for loans.

Correspondents who may hold notes or securities for the

bank's account should be requested to confirm the amounts thereof direct to the auditor.

In the case of a National Bank the Treasurer of the United States should be requested to confirm the amount of bonds held by him to secure circulation and Government deposits, and the amounts of the circulation redemption fund, outstanding circulation, Government deposits, and any balances which may be due by him to the bank.

Certificates of Deposit and Certified Cheques: The balances in the cashier's cheques, certificates of deposit, and certified-cheque accounts should each agree with the aggregate of the respective classes of items outstanding. In this connection the canceled items should be inspected and compared with the stubs or original records in order that the auditor may assure himself that none posted on the ledger as paid are outstanding.

Capital Stock: The capital stock certificate book and stock ledger should be examined and the aggregate of the outstanding stock proved with the general ledger account. Recently in New York the vice-president of a National Bank was arrested, convicted, and sentenced for forgery and fraud in connection with the misuse of his bank's stock certificates. He had torn certificates from the stock book, forged the cashier's name thereto, added his own name, and had deposited them as collateral for a personal loan from a large trust company.

Depositors' Accounts: Opinions differ as to the responsibility of an auditor in connection with the verification of depositors' accounts. As these form the largest portion of the liabilities, he should make some effort to verify their correctness, in addition to merely taking a trial balance from the depositors' ledgers. He should ascertain that trial balances are taken off regularly, that the ledger clerks are transferred occasionally from one ledger to another, that some one other than the ledger clerks compares the balances in the ledgers with the pass books when the latter are "settled" and delivered to the depositors, and that the clerk initials the pass books and ledgers as to correctness. In addition to this the bank should insert in the pass books a form of confirmation of the depositors' balance, which should be carefully filed when signed and returned by the depositors.

The auditor should mail statements of their balances to all

depositors with inactive accounts, should verify the settlements of all pass books in the bank, send out request for pass books of all other active accounts and verify the settlements of the latter when received and balanced. It is hardly to be expected that every depositor will send in his confirmation or pass book promptly, and it will be necessary for the auditor to keep a list of all depositors on which to make note of those accounts which have been verified, and which may be used as a guide at future dates for the confirmation of all accounts.

In comparing pass books with the ledgers it is important not only that the balances be compared, but that the deposit entries in the pass books for some time prior to the settlement date be examined. This will disclose any ledger cross entries which may have been made and which should be especially investigated. They should not be permitted, except upon officially signed debit or credit slips, as defalcations have been cleverly concealed through the use of such cross entries.

In banks where the practice of balancing pass books has been superseded by the system of rendering monthly accounts current to depositors and returning to them at the same time all paid cheques, the auditor should compare the statements with the ledgers, inclose his confirmation form, and mail them himself.

Verification of Income: Tests should be made to ascertain that the bank is receiving at proper times and in correct amounts the income on its securities and interest on the loans it has made or notes it has discounted. Almost all banks include discounts among their earnings as soon as the notes are discounted, and the conservative and proper method of carrying reserve for unearned discounts is not generally followed. In the middle West, however, a number of large institutions now show such a reserve in their balance sheets, and it is to be hoped that in time the practice will become general.

Expenses: The details of the charges to expense accounts should be scrutinized, the unusual items thoroughly investigated, and tests made of the correctness of the usual ones. The salary rolls should be checked and thorough tests should be made of the correctness of interest paid on deposits. Postage-stamp payments are usually large and should receive careful attention.

Secret Reserves: If these are found they should be noted i the auditor's report if the audit is made for the first time. Suc reserves are hidden in various ways, generally in understating o the books the value of the banking house or in carrying an ac count in the depositors' ledgers. This latter method should b discouraged, as only *bona fide* depositors' accounts should appea in these ledgers.

Internal Checks: The auditor should carefully investigate a of the bank's methods of conducting its affairs for the purpos of ascertaining that the work is so divided and carried out as t reduce to a minimum the opportunity for fraud, and that in s far as possible the system in use provides for internal check o the integrity of the accounts.

Employees handling cash, securities, notes, or cheques shoul not have access to or assist in writing up or proving the genera bookkeeping records, nor should bookkeepers have access to th records of the tellers. Clerks making original entries should no see the records, which are a check on those entries, and so fa as possible the clerks should occasionally be transferred fron one set of records to another, so that if fraud be committed, i cannot remain concealed for any length of time. Ledger trans fers and other unusual entries should not be permitted excep upon written order bearing official signature.

Scope of Report: The auditor's report should be very com plete, including not only statements of the bank's condition an income and expense accounts for the period under review, bu also detailed statements of the securities owned, collateral loan and value of collateral, single name and indorsed paper, and tota liability of each borrower. He should also call particular atten tion to any memoranda which may have been carried as cash, a overdue notes, insufficiently secured collateral loans, loans t officers and employees, overdue interest, and uncollected incom on securities.

The auditor should bear in mind, when examining the affair and accounts of banks and financial institutions generally, tha his certificate will be regarded as an assurance of the reliabilit of the statement so certified, and that while he does not guar antee the security of the deposits made by the public, the latte will, and justly so, severely criticize him if subsequent develop nents show that at the time of his examination the bank was nsolvent, but that his report did not reveal the fact.

Instances of Fraud: Defalcations are especially to be guarded against in financial institutions. The following are some of the chemes which have been used by defaulters.

A note teller in a bank, in order to cover up cash abstracted, would increase the amount of total of loans made for the day. He would turn in to the general bookkeeper, accompanying his voucher, an adding-machine list which, if it had been footed, would have been found not to be the same as the total shown by he adding-machine list. Later on, at such times as the accounts were examined and the notes proved either by a bank examiner or others, he would put in forged notes to cover the amount short, using the name of some concern which had a good line of credit with the bank.

A note teller started in this way by taking about $200 and was finally short $7,000. He made no false entries in the books, outside of the adding-machine list and the total of the daily ticket which he turned in to the general bookkeeper. The defalcation was not discovered until the bank was merged with another bank. If the notes had ever been checked back with the original discount register, it would have been found that the forged notes were not entered therein.

Another note teller, among whose duties it was to send out items for collection, would abstract cash and enter in his accounts certain items as being out for collection. These items he represented to be notes deposited for collection for which he had paid cash, and the record was made to show that the notes were on some distant point which would take several days for return. In doing this he always used the name of some good customer whose line of credit was unquestionable. This practice went on for a long time until a bank examiner, who had been over the accounts several times before, happened to question the teller about one of these particular items at a time when the teller had just returned after a few days' absence from the bank. The teller became nervous and somewhat evasive in his answers. The examiner then wrote to the firm whose name was used in connection with these items and found they had deposited no such items for collection.

In this connection the auditor would have discovered the true condition if he had verified the outstanding items for collection, either by correspondence with the bank to which the collection was sent, or by writing to the individual or firm who it was claimed had deposited the item.

Another bank teller in a large bank opened an account with a small bank in another part of the city. He would draw cheques on the bank in which he worked, using some fictitious name, and deposit them in the bank in which he had an account. When those cheques came in through the Clearing House to the bank in which he worked, they came to him and he would promptly tear them up. At the end of the day his department would be short and this shortage would be charged to an "over and short" account, as would other items, until such time as the errors would be discovered, when they would be taken out of this account.

He continued this practice over a long period, taking small amounts, till he was finally discovered, when the bank's "over and short" account amounted to some $40,000, a part of which represented the stealings of this teller; but it was not known just how much. It was extreme carelessness on the part of the bank to allow such an account to assume large proportions. The bank stated that there were certain losses which it could not guard against, and it estimated that these losses would amount to several thousand dollars a year, no matter what precautions it might take.

The following extract from the (New York) National City Bank's, July, 1912, circular is of particular interest in that it states the latest suggestions made by the Comptroller of the Currency to examining committees of national banks:

Bank Examinations by Directors: On June 1 the Comptroller of the Currency requested the boards of directors of National Banks to send to his office a copy of the reports of the annual or semiannual examinations made by the examining committees or by other parties at the instance of the directors, and not a single bank has declined to comply with such request.

A review of the reports that have been received shows that many of these examinations are deficient in their scope and that many features essential to a thorough understanding of the bank's affairs are not covered. As heretofore pointed out in this circular, a number of States have provided by law for reports by the examining committees of State banks to their State

Banking Departments, and in these States a form of report has been prepared for that purpose. At the beginning, however, the Comptroller of the Currency does not intend to prescribe a form for the directors to use in making reports to his office, or to require examinations of a technical character, but rather to offer such suggestions as will lead to really effective examinations. The following list of general points to be covered has been drafted by the Comptroller with a view to sending the same to those banks where the report of the examining committee shows the examination to be superficial:

1. The cash should be counted and the total compared with the books of the bank. Cash items should be carefully scrutinized, and any improper items, such as unposted cheques held for the purpose of not showing overdrafts, and any other items that cannot be readily converted into cash should be reported.

2. The bonds and other securities of the bank should be examined and those not on hand should be verified by reference to the receipts of the parties with whom they are deposited. The market value and the amount at which carried on the books in the aggregate should be shown, and any stocks held by the bank should be listed with a statement showing the reasons the securities were taken by the bank.

3. The notes should be carefully checked and their total compared with the general ledger. The genuineness, value, and security of each note, and of any collateral thereto, should be carefully determined, and any losses ascertained, or probable, in the judgment of the committee, should be noted. The liabilities of each of the larger borrowers, and loans to affiliated interests, should be aggregated and carefully considered. The report should also show the general character of the loans; whether well distributed; the general character of the collaterals; whether corporations in which officers or directors are interested borrow to an undue extent; also any large liabilities of the officers or directors. It should also be shown whether all paper claimed by the bank as its own property, including collaterals, is properly indorsed or assigned to it, and all mortgages recorded. Any loans exceeding ten per cent of the capital and surplus of the bank should be reported. The signatures of all note makers and indorsers should be carefully scrutinized and any erasures and alterations or any indications of manipulation should be carefully investigated and reported to the full board. All overdue paper should be listed and comment made as to its collectibility.

4. The certificates of deposit and the cashier's cheques should be verified by totaling those outstanding and as shown by the register and comparing with the general ledger, and also by comparing the canceled certificates and cheques with the register and checking them against the stubs.

5. The copy retained by the bank of the report of condition made to the Comptroller at the last call should be compared with the bank's books at that date, particularly with reference to the excessive loans and directors' and officers' liabilities reported to the board of directors.

6. The bank's last reconcilements of accounts with correspondents should be compared with the bank's books and a transcript of the bank's account

from the date of the last reconcilement to the date of the examination sent to the corresponding bank, with a request for verification.

7. Individual ledger balances should be verified in such manner as the directors may deem advisable, by calling in pass books, by sending out reconcilements of certain accounts selected by the directors, or in some other suitable way. A trial balance of the ledger should be taken by some member of the committee, or at least by some person other than the clerk engaged on the ledger.

8. Overdrafts should be totaled and carefully considered and the report should show any estimated losses.

9. The committee should consider carefully the Profit and Loss and the Expense account, with a view of determining whether the charges against those accounts are proper and whether the earnings of the bank warrant the expense charges, and the bank is making a legitimate profit.

10. The examining committee should inquire carefully into the arrangement of the working affairs of the bank and ascertain whether any employee who keeps the individual ledger receives deposits or balances pass books, and whether the employees are properly bonded and in whose custody the bonds are lodged.

11. Any liability of the bank for borrowed money should be listed and the proper authority and the necessity for such borrowing ascertained. The total amount of the present liabilities of that nature should be reported to the board, including money borrowed from other banks on certificates of deposit.

The Comptroller desires that the report of the directors or the examining committee should show that the above points have been covered and that it should recite any deficiencies discovered. The report will also be expected to contain a complete statement of the total assets and liabilities of the bank, with any additions or deductions that in the judgment of the directors should be made as a result of their investigation; and a detailed statement of the loans which the directors estimate as worthless, doubtful, or insufficiently secured, giving reasons therefor, and as nearly as possible the real value. It is furthermore desired that the report contain a statement of any matters which in the opinion of the committee affect in any way the bank's solvency, stability, or prosperity.

The Comptroller believes that there are few instances where the examining committee cannot, if they will take the necessary time, cover these points fully and satisfactorily, and that an examination twice a year, along the above lines, by a committee of the directors who will give sufficient time to the work to make it thorough and complete, cannot fail to be of great benefit to all concerned, especially to the shareholders who have placed them in their positions of trust.

SAVINGS BANKS

The general procedure in auditing a savings bank is more or less similar to that necessary in auditing a National or State bank. Savings banks are limited by the laws of most States to certain classes of investments and are not permitted to discount notes or to make unsecured loans. For this reason most of their assets consist of bonds, mortgages, and other long term investments. At the time of examining the mortgages the auditor should ascertain that in those cases where the mortgage covers improved property, sufficient insurance is carried (payable to the bank as mortgagee), to protect it in case the improvements are destroyed by fire.

Some trouble will probably be experienced in procuring the addresses of all the depositors for the purpose of sending out requests for confirmations of their accounts. Any neglect on the part of the employees to make every effort to get these addresses and keep them up to date should be mentioned in the auditor's report. Defalcations in savings banks are more often concealed through manipulation of depositors' inactive accounts than in any other way.

It will be found to be just as effective and less expensive to mail to depositors such a form of confirmation as will require the depositor to communicate with the auditor only in case of a difference rather than to send a form which every depositor must sign and return. As a great many savings bank depositors are of the working class, usually a smaller percentage of the confirmations of the last-mentioned kind are returned to the auditor than in the case of depositors in National and State banks. In sending the suggested form of confirmation it is desirable for the auditor to insert an unstamped envelope for the depositor's use in case he finds it necessary to communicate with the auditor.

TRUST COMPANIES

The name "Trust Company" indicates that it was the original object of such institutions to act in a fiduciary capacity and exercise trust functions only. A few companies still limit themselves to these purposes, but most of them now conduct a banking business in addition thereto. Their charters are usually very liberal. While they may not issue circulating notes, and in some States are forbidden to discount commercial paper, they are, on the other hand, allowed to make loans on real estate, which privilege is denied National banks.

The audit of the banking department of a trust company should be conducted along lines similar to that followed in the audit of a National or State bank. The audit should, however, also embrace such other departments as the trust company may be operating. These departments usually are the trust fund, safe deposit, bond, real estate, and corporate trust departments.

None of these departments should carry any cash on hand, as all necessary funds should be deposited with the banking department. All securities which should be on hand must be accounted for, and the general records of each department should be carefully checked. Such tests of the detailed work should also be made as will satisfy the auditor that the trust company is properly accounting to the beneficiaries of all trusts, and to the principals for whom it may be acting as agents, of the income collected by it.

The collection of the trust company's income from these departments, such as commissions on the transactions of the trust and real estate departments, income and profits on bonds handled by the bond department, income from safe-deposit boxes and silver-storage vaults, and fees from corporations whose securities are handled by the corporate trust department, should be thoroughly tested. The expenses of the various departments should also be given careful attention.

It is physically impossible, as well as unnecessary, in the audit of a large trust company for the auditor to check in detail all of the transactions during the audit period, and the efficacy of the internal check provided by the system in use should guide him in determining to what extent to carry the tests of the detailed work.

INVESTMENT COMPANIES

The theory on which investment companies are formed and operate is that by merging the capital of many investors and distributing it over a large number of investments the proportionate risk of loss incurred by any one investor is very small. The operation of the law of average also permits of investing in securities yielding a somewhat higher rate of income without the probability of the total capital being lost, which latter is not infrequently the case with an individual investor who may have but a small amount to invest and hence cannot distribute it over a number of investments. Aside from holding companies which are organized more for the purpose of practically merging a group of companies than for trading in their securities, investment companies are much more common in Europe than in the United States.

Purchases and sales of securities should be verified by the brokers' memoranda therefor. Especially important is it in this connection to see that accrued interest on bonds and dividends on stocks bought or sold ex-dividend are properly treated. Entries for purchases and sales of securities made at a flat price should be made so as to apportion the cost of sale between the interest or dividend accrued to date of purchase or sale and the net capital cost or realization.

Income accruing from all investments held during the audit period should be accounted for. The securities held at the date of the balance sheet will, of course, need to be examined.

If the net result of the year's changes in investments is a profit, it may be paid out in dividends; if the net result is a loss, it must be charged against surplus, unless a reserve already exists against which the loss may be charged. The most conservative policy for the treatment of profits realized from changes of investments would be not to credit them at all to the current income account, but to a special reserve or surplus account to provide for possible future losses on investments owned which cannot be foreseen at the present time. When profits on investments are treated as income, they should be separately shown in stating the income account.

The complexion of the balance sheet will necessarily depend very largely on the valuations at which the investments held are entered therein. Consequently the verification of the investment valuations may well be said to be the most important single feature of the audit.

Should investments have been acquired in exchange for the company's own stock and be carried on the books at values which are obviously in excess of their real values, even though the latter may not be definitely ascertainable from market quotations, it is clearly the duty of the auditor to call attention to the fact that such investments are not being carried at their actual value.

Each individual investment need not be written down to market value when there has been a fall in price. If the aggregate market values of all the investments equal the total cost thereof, that is sufficient. Should the aggregate market values, however, be less than cost, it is preferable to credit the net difference to a Fluctuation Reserve rather than to adjust the book value of each individual investment. It is also preferable to show the Fluctuation Reserve as a deduction ("in short") from the total value of the investments in the balance sheet rather than as an item among the liabilities. This reserve is not an actual liability, but exists solely for the purpose of bringing the book value of the investments down to market value. It is quite in order to readjust the reserve from year to year to accord with changed market conditions. Care should be taken, however, that reserves for losses or decreases in market values are not treated as an extraordinary charge in the Profit and Loss account of the year in which the reserves are made, and then when prices go up again, that part of the reserve which is no longer needed, be treated as ordinary income.

The book value of investments should not be increased when market prices exceed cost. The same reasons which are effectively urged against the increasing of plant or merchandise values above cost apply in valuing the investments held by an investment company—in a sense they form both its plant and stock-in-trade. Should it be desired to show the investments at market values which are in excess of cost, the excess should not be credited to the ordinary income or surplus account from which dividends are paid, but should be credited to a special reserve or surplus account.

A distinction should be made between *bona fide* investment companies and speculative securities companies. The former's income is derived principally from the income received from investments owned, whereas the latter's chief source of income is the profit realized from purchases and sales of securities. It follows that the investments of a real investment company are to a certain extent fixed assets, and that this may be taken into consideration in treating them in the accounts, but that the investments of a speculative finance company are its stock-in-trade and should be valued in the same way as stock on hand is valued in the case of mercantile undertakings, viz., "cost or market, whichever is the lower."

A difficulty which will frequently be encountered is that of ascertaining the real value of the investments. Nominal stock exchange quotations for securities with a restricted market do not always indicate the realizable value of a large block of stocks or bonds. As already stated in the case of *bona fide* investment companies, the book values of the individual investments need not be varied to conform to changes in market values. The object in view, viz., to reduce the aggregate book value of the investments to the aggregate market value thereof, is just as effectively accomplished by setting up a reserve for the difference between total cost and total market value.

Apparent increases in investment values by reason of rising market prices should not be treated as income until they have actually been realized by sale of the securities. It is important for the auditor to see that all profits on sales of investments which may be shown were actually realized, and that they have not been brought into the books by placing a higher value on securities received in making exchanges. So far as possible, the auditor should also satisfy himself that no part of the profit shown is the result of "wash sales" or other transactions of a similar character.

The valuation of marketable investments was well treated in Mr. Dickinson's admirable paper on "The Profits of a Corporation" (Proceedings of the Congress of Accountants, 1904, pages 183-184).

In conclusion, it may be stated that, even though under certain circumstances the payment of dividends by investment companies without first making good decreases in the value of investments may not conflict with existing laws, such a procedure is so at variance with the canons of sound finance that the auditor should be certain that the published reports, and particularly his certificate, clearly show the actual condition of affairs.

STOCKBROKERS

Without doubt a practical knowledge of the "inner workings" of a stockbroker's office is valuable to the auditor engaged to make an audit of accounts of this nature, but the lack of such special knowledge is not an insuperable obstacle to a competent accountant. From good articles which quite often appear in financial magazines, and from talks with stockbrokers, a good idea of the methods in use can be obtained. It is, however, important that prior to beginning an audit of such accounts, the auditor have a knowledge of the books used. It often occurs that stockbrokers require special accounting work done at busy periods, and such work affords the future auditor a good opportunity to familiarize himself with the books of account.

Brokers buy and sell securities for customers and, at times, for their own account. The customers may pay for such purchases in full and request the delivery to them of the securities purchased, or they may be carried "on margin" by brokers for the customers' accounts. Customers may desire brokers to remit the entire proceeds of sales of securities or may leave the proceeds on deposit with the brokers for future use in purchasing other securities.

Brokers therefore not only handle cash, but securities as well. Usually the values of the securities carried by brokers are many times larger than the cash on hand and in bank. Brokers find it necessary to borrow large sums of money from banks as collateral for which they are required to deposit securities, which in most cases are those which are being carried "on margin" by the brokers for their customers. At times, brokers must borrow securities from other brokers, or may find it desirable to lend them securities. It is also necessary to send securities to the transfer offices of various companies to have certificates transferred to customers' names, and securities are at times deposited with stockholders' or bondholders' committees, or for other reasons may not be in the office of a broker at the time the audit is begun.

Obviously brokers' books must account for all securities, as well as for all cash, and for this reason they are radically different in form and nature from the books of account usually found in other lines of business. The books generally used in stockbrokers' offices in New York City are the following:

Cash Book: For recording the cash receipts and payments, and the securities received and delivered.

Clearing House Blotter: For recording the purchases and sales on the floor of the Stock Exchange of securities listed on the Exchange. Settlement of the net difference between the value of the securities purchased and sold each day is made direct with the Stock Exchange Clearing House on the following day, instead of with each broker with whom the transaction was made.

Ex-Clearing-House Blotter: For recording the purchases and sales of securities not listed on the Exchange. Settlements are usually made for such transactions direct with the party from whom the securities are purchased or to whom sold.

In both of the blotters above mentioned columns are provided for entering the commission charged for executing the customers' orders, the value of revenue tax stamps required by the New York law to be attached to certificates when sold, the amounts to be paid to or received from other brokers, and the amounts to be charged or credited to customers for the purchases or sales of securities.

General Ledger: This ledger contains the various asset, liability, income, and expense accounts of the business. The customers' and stock and money loan accounts are usually carried in this ledger in total by the use of controlling accounts.

Customers' Ledger: Separate accounts are kept herein for each customer, which show not only the customers' transactions and cash balance due by or to them, but also the stocks "long" and "short" in their accounts.

Stock Record: Under accounts with each security are recorded on the "long" side the customers who are "long" of the securities, from whom securities are borrowed, or the investment accounts in which are carried the securities owned by the brokers; and on the "short" side the securities on hand (usually termed "in the box"), the customers who are "short" of the securities, the brokers to whom securities are loaned, the banks or others holding securities as collateral for loans, and the securities in transfer. The accounts with stocks are kept in shares, and those with bonds are kept in their par value and the aggregate of the "long" and "short" sides must agree. Numerous vertical columns are provided for rebalancing at the close of each day those securities in which transactions were made.

Margin Record: The status of each customer's money balance and the shares of stocks and par of bonds held as security for his account, and the market value thereof, are recorded herein, and this information is kept up to date (to the minute) at all times. It is the indicator of weak margins and a most important book. In large offices it is necessary to have several such records. Margin clerks must be alert and thoroughly familiar with each account under their supervision. Laxity or neglect in this department may result in large losses if the market is active.

Record of Money Loans: Entries are made herein of money loaned or borrowed, and the collateral received or deposited therefor. Separate accounts are kept with each loan and the aggregate of all the loans must agree with the controlling accounts for "Money Loaned" or "Money Borrowed" in the General Ledger.

Record of Stock Loans: For recording the securities borrowed from or loaned to other brokers and the amounts of money deposited or received as security for their return. The aggregate of these loans must agree with their respective controlling accounts in the General Ledger. Securities sold or bought ostensibly for cash, but which are not delivered or received for various reasons on the day following the transactions, but which non-deliveries are not intended to act as "loans," are termed "Failed to Deliver" and "Failed to Receive" items respectively, and are usually covered by controlling accounts in the General Ledger and the details entered in a separate portion of the Record of Stock Loans.

Other Books: In addition to the books specifically referred to, there are daily records of stocks in box, bank pass books, cheque books, petty cash books, order books, register of securities received and delivered, customers' press-copy books for copying notices of purchases and sales and customers' statements, pay rolls, and other subsidiary expense and memorandum records.

Use of Abbreviations: In most brokers' offices the names of securities are rarely written out in full in the books. The Stock Exchange initials are generally used in referring to listed securities, while the names of unlisted stocks are abbreviated. It is, therefore, essential that the auditor be familiar with these customary abbreviations.

Program of Audit: A large and competent staff should be used on the audit of a broker's office, as the work must be done rapidly and accurately. The cash and revenue stamps on hand must be counted and the balances checked with the general ledger accounts. The securities on hand must be examined and scheduled, and confirmation forms prepared of all money and securities borrowed and loaned and the collateral therefor, which should be sent at once to the proper parties, and the aggregate of each class of transactions proved with the controlling accounts in the General Ledger. Confirmation forms should also be sent to the transfer offices of companies holding securities for transfer.

The Stock Record should be checked from the schedule prepared of the securities on hand, and from the duplicates of the confirmations covering money and stocks loaned and borrowed and the collateral therefor, and of the securities in transfer. The stocks "long" and "short" in customers' accounts should be checked to the Stock Record from the statements to be sent to the customers. The securities "long" and "short" in the client's own investment accounts may be checked from the General Ledger.

It is extremely important that the stocks be balanced quickly, as in an active market numerous changes are made and the investigation of differences is very troublesome.

The customers' statements referred to are copies of their ledger accounts, which are usually written up daily and press-copied at the end of the month and sent to them. The balances at the beginning of the month, the transactions during the month, and the balances at the end of the month, as well as the calculations of interest on each transaction, are shown on these statements. The securities received and delivered and "long" and "short" at the beginning and end of the month are also shown thereon.

These customers' statements should be press-copied before being turned over to the auditor, who should mail them, after checking the stocks "long" or "short" at the time of the audit, and scheduling the customers' names and money balances, for checking with the trial balance of the customers' ledgers to be verified later. When mailing them, a form for confirming the balances and securities in their accounts at the date of the audit should be sent to all customers, as well as return envelopes, so as to insure the confirmations being sent direct to the auditor's office. Accounts for which no statements are sent should be particularly investigated and called to the client's attention, as they may prove to be "blind" accounts which are being used for improper purposes.

Accounts of the client with other brokers, usually in other cities, are termed "Our Accounts" (with others); statements are usually sent monthly to the client of the monthly transactions, together with the money balance, and the stocks "long" and "short" at the end of the month. These statements from other brokers should be compared with the corresponding accounts on the client's ledgers, and the genuineness of the statements received should be verified by confirming the money balance and securities in the account by correspondence.

The margins in the customers' accounts should be carefully scrutinized, and accounts with weak or no margins called to the client's attention.

The bank accounts should be reconciled with the general books and the trial balances of all ledgers verified. No nominal accounts should be kept in the Customers' Ledger, and all of the accounts in the General Ledger should be carefully scrutinized, and such as are not covered by the work usually done in an audit of brokers' accounts should be carefully investigated and their correctness determined.

The correctness of the interest charged customers and paid to banks and brokers, and of the commissions charged for executing customers' orders and paid to floor brokers for executing orders, should be thoroughly tested.

The collection of income due during the audit period on securities owned by the client should be verified, and all of the charges to the various expense accounts should be carefully scrutinized, and vouchers and pay rolls examined and compared with these entries.

The most satisfactory audit of brokers' accounts is the continuous audit, in which the auditor makes frequent visits and detailed examinations into various departments of the business at different times, in addition to verifying completely the cash, customers' accounts, money and stock loans and collaterals, and balancing the securities at least twice annually.

Brokers collect considerable sums in dividends for their customers, a part thereof being in turn paid to the latter, but the larger part credited to their ledger accounts. The collections made are credited to one or more dividend accounts. These accounts are debited with the payments to customers (or to other brokers who hold stock certificates which still stand in the name of the broker who sold them some time before) and with the amounts transferred to the credit of customers whose accounts are "long," the stock on which the dividend has been collected. The dividend account is also credited with the amounts charged to customers who are "short" of the stock on which a dividend has been paid. Theoretically the nature of the dividend account is such that it needs little or no inspection, but as dividends are sometimes not called for until long after their declaration, it is necessary to verify the entries in the account to make certain that advantage has not been taken of the condition mentioned to abstract dividends which may not be called for or which should have been credited to some customer's account, but on which a "chance is taken" that the customer will not detect the failure to credit the dividend to his account.

Instance of Fraud: A recent case of fraud discovered in a stock broker's office was accomplished in the following manner:

The cashier was allowed to do part of the work on the ledgers. The footings of the receipts entered in the Ex-Clearing-House Blotter were reduced to the extent of the amounts to be taken or already obtained. Cheques were taken from the back of the cheque book and given the same numbers as current cheques. Money was obtained thereon and the cheques destroyed when they were returned by the bank, when the pass book was balanced. No entry was made in the blotter for these items, but the items posted in the ledger or the footings of different accounts were falsified in order to show a correct trial balance. Most of the erroneous entries were made in the interest account, which, for the most part, showed only totals of the interest for the month as entered in the different customers' accounts. The totals were ascertained from a detail sheet, which was later destroyed, and the amount actually entered was not in accordance with the aggregate of the items for the month. At other times payments were charged to personal accounts for which no statements were sent out. The charges were sometimes fictitious entries entered in the ledger account only or a posting made from an item in the blotter which was not covered by one of the regular cheques.

BUILDING AND LOAN ASSOCIATIONS

Building and loan associations are usually organized on the mutual plan, and the by-laws of most, if not all of them call for an annual audit of the association's accounts. Unfortunately for the stockholders, however, this requirement is most frequently complied with by the appointment of an auditing committee composed of two or three members of the board of directors, and, as is usual in the case of amateur audits, examinations made under such circumstances and by such agencies are not always to be relied upon. When it is considered how much power, as far as the finances and accounts are concerned, is exercised by one man (usually the secretary) in these associations, it would certainly pay them in the end to have the accounts periodically audited by public accountants.

The fact that the accounts are as a rule so completely in the hands of one person renders it obligatory on the auditor to make a thorough and detailed examination. In an audit under such circumstances tests of the work are not usually sufficient.

The audit of a building and loan association differs from that of most financial institutions in that it has to deal with an organization the capital stock of which is not fixed in amount, and that the borrowers are, for the most part, stockholders as well, and both interest and principal of the loans are paid in small installments, such payments being made either monthly or weekly at the same time that dues, i. e., payments on account of capital stock, are paid.

The capital stock consists of a number of series, a new series being started each year, each six months, or in some few cases even as often as every three months. A fixed amount, usually one dollar, though sometimes fifty cents or twenty-five cents (the latter very infrequently), is paid, say, monthly, on each share of stock held, and when these periodical contributions, together with the accrued profits, reach a specified amount, say, $200, the series of stock is paid off. In this way there is a constant contributing and withdrawing of capital going on, one or more new series of stock being started each year, and one or more series maturing in each year. In addition to matured stock, withdrawals are made by the stockholders who for one reason or another cannot or do not care to continue until the maturity of their series. In the case of such withdrawals a penalty is imposed by paying somewhat less than the full amount of the profits accrued on the stock. In a well-managed association, the by-laws of which call for monthly payments of $1 per share and fix the full value of a share at $200, a series usually matures about eleven or twelve years after its inception.

Verification of Income: The dues paid in by members are not, of course, income or earnings. They are contributions of capital, and a very careful accounting thereof is essential. By ascertaining the total shares outstanding in each series at the beginning of the year and allowing for withdrawals during the year (after the year in which a series has its inception no additional shares can be issued), the receipts from dues can be proven as a whole.

The interest on loans will need to be carefully verified. Much of the interest is paid in monthly installments, and as many of the loans are made on a six per cent basis, the interest can be quickly verified. In connection with loans to stockholders the item of premiums must not be overlooked. The by-laws of many associations provide for what practically amounts to competitive bidding by the stockholders for the funds in the treasury. When the applications for loans exceed the available funds, a premium is paid by the successful applicants. The granting of these loans should be recorded in the minutes, and the premiums to be accounted for should be ascertainable from this source.

Fines on delinquent dues and interest are other items of income. They are usually fixed at a high rate, e. g., two per cent per month, to compel promptness in making payments, but do not usually form a large item of income.

In the case of associations which charge admission fees (usually twenty-five cents per share) these are readily verified in total on the total number of shares in the new series issued during the year.

Building and loan associations do not invest in real estate except when compelled to buy it in to protect an investment in a mortgage loan which is foreclosed. When real estate is owned, the income therefrom should be verified. A comparison of the net income with the book value of the properties should be made so as to be sure that real estate is not being carried at excessive figures.

The best verification of the dues and interest appearing as unpaid on the books is to publish a list of the account numbers and amounts of such arrearages in the association's published annual statement. A good verification of the capital stock outstanding would be for the auditor to be present at the meeting next following the commencement of the audit and to examine each stockholder's pass book as it is presented at the time of paying dues. The numbering of all stockholders' accounts and the consecutive numbering of the pass books by the printer, all pass books to be accounted for, is also a safeguard.

Expenses: These are verified in the usual manner. To the credit of these associations it must be said that most of them are economically conducted and the direct outlays for salaries, etc., are seldom excessive.

Inspection of Securities: A very important feature of the audit is naturally the examination of the securities owned. Mortgages, insurance policies, and other documents pertaining to real estate loans, assigned capital stock certificates, notes for loans on stock collateral, and real estate deeds are all to be carefully scrutinized.

Distribution of Profits: An important part of the audit is the verification of the annual statement. Most associations publish, in addition to a balance sheet, a statement of cash receipts and payments, and not the profit and loss account, although it is on the basis of the results shown by the latter that the apportionment of profits among the various series of stock is made. There are several plans of profit distribution in use, not all of equal merit.

The most equitable and accurate plan is to treat as the capital for the year the dues paid in and the profits accrued thereon up to the beginning of the fiscal year under review, plus the equivalent sum for one year of the installments paid in during the year, and less the entire dues paid in and the accrued profits to the beginning of the fiscal year on stock withdrawn during the year. On the average working capital for the year so determined, the percentage of the year's earnings as shown by the balance of the profit and loss account is ascertained. The calculation of the average working capital is made by separate series as well as in total, and the percentage earned added to each series. The total earnings for the year are thus apportioned among the various series. The accrued profits in excess of the amounts actually paid to withdrawing stockholders are included as a part of the year's earnings.

A plan which is in use by many associations, but which is misleading, in that the apparent percentage of earnings to capital is higher than is actually the case, is that by which accrued profits are not treated as a part of the capital, the profits being calculated and apportioned simply on the basis of the dues paid in. As this constitutes a smaller amount on which to calculate the percentage which the earnings are of the capital stock, the apparent rate of earnings is higher than the actual rate.

Some associations even go so far as to reapportion each year all the profit earned, not only in the current year, but in preceding years, on all unmatured series of stock. This is clearly wrong and inequitable. Each year, which usually marks the entrance of a new series of stockholders, should witness the apportionment of its earnings in accordance with the actual earnings, which apportionment should remain undisturbed in the remaining years which the various series have yet to run.

It should be stated, however, that in many cases the by-laws of the association prescribe the basis on which profits shall be apportioned among the various series, and in such an event the auditor cannot do otherwise than comply with them. Even in such cases, however, it would seem desirable to call the attention of the directors or the stockholders to the desirability of adopting the most accurate method.

Most associations publish balance sheets, statements of receipts and payments, and statements of capital stock more or less like the following forms:

BUILDING AND LOAN ASSOCIATION

BALANCE SHEET........................191

Assets		Liabilities	
LOANS:		Loans Payable (if any)	$..........
Real Estate Loans with Stock Collateral	$..........	Unearned Premiums	....
Real Estate Loans without Stock Collateral	....	Dues, etc., Paid in Advance	....
Stock Loans	....	Accrued Taxes (if any)	....
	$..........		$..........
Real Estate	....	CAPITAL STOCK:	
Other Investments (if any; state nature)	....	Dues Paid In and Accrued Profits Thereon, Per Schedule of Series and Values Annexed	....
Dues, Interest, etc., Delinquent	....		
Prepaid Insurance and Taxes	....		
Cash	....		
	$..........		$

RECEIPTS AND PAYMENTS

YEAR ENDED......................191

Balance (Beginning of Year)		$..........	PAYMENTS:	
RECEIPTS:			Loans	$..........
Dues	$..........		Matured Stock	....
Interest, Premiums, and Fines	....		Stock Withdrawals	....
Admission and other Fees	....		Salaries	....
Rents	....		Rent, Printing, Stationery, and Sundry Expenses	....
Loans Repaid	....		Real Estate Expenses	....
Sales of Real Estate	....		Borrowed Money	....
Money Borrowed	....	....	Interest	....
				$..........
			Balance (End of Year)	....
		$..........		$..........

STATEMENT OF CAPITAL STOCK

..........................19

		Shares			Value per Share				
Series No.	Date of Issue	Bor-rowed on	Free	Total	Dues	Profits	Total	Value of Series	With-drawal Value per Share
....	....	....	....	....	$.......	$.......	$.......	$.......	$.......
....	....	....	....	....	....	....	....	....	....
....	....	....	....	....	....	....	....	....	....
		....	....	....				$.......*	

* This amount should agree with the item of "Capital Stock" shown in the balance sheet.

Fewer associations publish the Profit and Loss Account, though all ought to do so. The following is a form thereof:

PROFIT AND LOSS ACCOUNT

Year ended..............................191

Earnings		
Interest		$..........
Premiums		....
Fines		....
Admission and Transfer Fees		....
Rents of Real Estate	$..........	
Less—Insurance, Taxes, etc.	....	....
Profits on Stock Withdrawals		....
		$..........
Expenses		
Interest on Stock Withdrawn	$..........	
Interest on Borrowed Money	....	
Administration Expenses	....	....
Net Profit for Apportionment Among Stock Series		$..........

A few associations publish statements of capital stock showing the dues paid in and the profits earned in each year on each series of stock outstanding. This makes a very complete and informing exhibit of an association's experience for a period of years.

Being chartered by the States, building and loan associations are usually subject to the supervision of the State banking departments. The forms of report required vary in different States. The foregoing have been selected and adapted from the best ones in use.

CHAPTER XXIV

SPECIAL POINTS IN DIFFERENT CLASSES OF AUDITS (Continued)

INSURANCE COMPANIES

IN almost all States insurance companies cannot organize under the general corporation laws, but must incorporate under special laws. These laws usually provide *inter alia* that the companies shall be subject to inspection by the Insurance Commissioner of the State. Furthermore, such examinations are not limited to the State in which a company is incorporated, but it is subject to examination by the Insurance Commissioner of every State in which it is registered to do business.

The examinations made by State Insurance Commissioners are similar in purpose to examinations of banking institutions made by the National and State Governments. The chief ends sought in these examinations are to ascertain whether or not the company is solvent and to prevent any violation of the insurance laws. While these are most important objects—even preëminently so—they by no means embrace all the duties of the professional auditor.

As is to be expected, the State examinations vary considerably as to the efficiency with which they are conducted. It is not to be wondered at if the staff of a department, whose members may have been recruited largely through the medium of political appointments, does not possess technical ability or experience of a very high order. In this connection it may also be mentioned that the abuses which were revealed by the investigation of a number of the large New York life insurance companies had been going on for years in spite of the fact that the companies were supposed to be periodically examined by the New York Insurance Department, and were reporting regularly to that Department. It is a significant fact that in recent years quite a number of the large life insurance companies have adopted the plan of having their accounts audited by public accountants.

FIRE INSURANCE COMPANIES

Naturally the auditor will need to inform himself as to the meaning of various technical terms and expressions. Aside from this, the audit of a fire insurance company will offer no serious difficulty, as the accounts are not very complicated.

Premiums form the largest item of income. The initial record of the premium income appears in the agents' reports. Enough of these should be traced into the books to satisfy the auditor of the correctness of the books in this respect.

Balances due from agents at the close of the fiscal period should be thoroughly verified. This may be done by analyzing the agents' accounts and taking up with some one in authority such balances as are in arrears. The balances should also be verified by comparison with the closing balance on the agent's last monthly statement.

Income from investments is another considerable item; this can and should be completely verified. The securities themselves must also be examined; this will be done in the same manner as in the case of banks or other financial institutions.

Unless the audit is specifically limited to the verification of the balance sheet, the payments for losses and expenses will need to be vouched. The vouchers for losses paid, expenses, and other items of outgo, should be properly approved. Insurance policies on which losses have been paid should be traced into the premium income record to see that the company actually received a consideration for the risk on which payment was made to the insured. Irregularities in the accounting for premiums may perchance be brought to light by this plan. In connection with losses, steps should also be taken to see that collection has been made for such part of the loss as had been reinsured. The system of recording reinsurances should be such as to insure the collection of the pro rata part of losses payable by other companies. Credits to agents for return premiums, rebates, and commissions should also receive attention.

The importance of safeguarding the payments for premium refunds and rebates from the standpoint of establishing an effective internal check, as well as the importance of the professional auditor's covering the matter thoroughly, is forcibly brought out by the following extract from a newspaper account of the embezzlement of $13,000 in a little over three years by two clerks who asserted that they were not in collusion, but who were both "operating" at the same time in the New York office of a large British fire insurance company:

Walker and Bradford, as their depositions state, were employed in the auditing department of the insurance company. . . . Their method of obtaining money was to cause cheques to be issued which appeared to be in payment of premium rebates on canceled policies. Both Walker and Bradford prepared these cheques in the regular course of their day's work and presented them to the cashier for his signature. Then they were supposed to be sent to persons who had canceled policies. The accountants discovered that no account was taken of the cheques thus issued and that the returned vouchers were never examined.

Bradford said the idea of drawing cheques to fictitious persons, or of duplicating cheques already issued and then forging the indorsements, came to him through the suggestions of a fellow employee, who, however, had no idea of operating it himself.

"I went broke one night," says Bradford in substance in his deposition. "I think I had been shooting craps in Dey Street. At any rate, the family were all away. I had sent my wife to the country, and there was no one at home. I was at my wits' end to raise money the next day.

"I went out to lunch with a fellow employee and in the course of the meal he suggested how easy it would be to raise money by duplicating cheques sent to policy holders who were withdrawing, or even by sending cheques to purely fictitious persons. The fact of the sending of a cheque was entered in a register, but when the cheque was returned from the bank it was never examined beyond seeing if it bore the proper indorsement. It was never compared with the policy which occasioned its issuance, and so the company never knew whether a rebated premium had been paid more than once or not. That started me thinking.

"I didn't have to make a study of it. It came just as naturally as taking a drink. The cheques all went through. I got various persons to cash them, and the company always paid without question. By this time I had got to the point of drawing cheques for any name at all and then indorsing them properly. Then it occurred to me once that if an investigation were made of the register it would be found that the name of the person who actually had received the proper cheque for his rebate wouldn't agree with the indorsement on my cheque, which corresponded in number to the good cheque, always supposing that it was my cheque which chanced to be looked up. I never felt in any fear of their finding both cheques.

"To cover myself I began erasing names from the register and substituting the names for which I had made out my cheques. These erasures finally attracted the attention of the auditors, but they couldn't catch onto the scheme then until I told them how it was worked."

Walker stumbled on the plan because he happened to notice once that in eight years only one thorough examination of the canceled policies and payments of rebated premiums was made by the auditors of the company. As soon as he found how easily the scheme worked, he began to pay his bills with cheques drawn on the insurance company.

He bought a piano with one of his early cheques, making the cheque payable to the piano salesman from whom he made his purchase. In the insurance company's office, had any one looked it up, it would have appeared that this salesman was receiving a rebated premium on a canceled policy. To the salesman himself it appeared merely that Walker had asked his employer to make out a cheque for his convenience.

Walker said he paid his rent regularly each month with one of the company's cheques, making it out in favor of his landlord. Walker said that while Bradford never suspected him, he had known for six months before their arrest that Bradford was doing the same thing, but said he never had spoken to him about it until they met in police headquarters as prisoners.

Most of the cheques which Bradford and Walker drew were for amounts less than $50, so that it required more than 200 falsified cheques for them to obtain the $13,208.

Liabilities: By far the largest, as well as the most important, item among the liabilities is the reinsurance reserve. The basis on which this must be calculated is usually fixed by State law. The plan most generally followed is to reserve one-half of the gross premiums (net of reinsurance) on all unexpired one-year policies and pro rata parts of the gross premiums on unexpired policies written for a longer term than one year, allowance being made for the full number of years of the term which have already expired. The deposits reclaimable by the assured are taken as the liability on perpetual policies.

The liabilities should include full provision for losses adjusted, but not yet paid, and for all unadjusted or disputed losses. Unpaid expenses, accrued taxes, etc., should also be allowed for in stating the liabilities.

An excellent article on "Auditing Insurance Accounts," by George Wilkinson, C. P. A., is to be found in the May and June, 1910, numbers of *The Business World*. The article confines itself to the auditing of fire company accounts.

LIFE INSURANCE COMPANIES

In many respects the audit of a life insurance company will follow the same lines as the audit of a fire insurance company. There are, however, some points of difference, as will presently be seen.

The investments of even a moderate-sized life company will be found to be very numerous, and their examination will require considerable time and care. In addition to verifying the fact of their being in the possession of the company or deposited with properly constituted authorities, such as the State insurance departments (when the latter is the case, the fact should be verified by correspondence), the income which should have been received from the investments is to be verified.

The auditor will do well to inform himself as to what securities are legal investments under the laws of the State in which the company is incorporated. The valuation of the investments is of great importance, and is considered somewhat at length in another part of this book.

Loans to policyholders secured by an assignment of the policies now form an item of considerable size in the assets of most large companies. Inasmuch as the loan never exceeds the amount of the reserve accumulated on the policy, such loans are a very good asset. The notes and assigned policies should be examined as a means of verifying the policy loans.

The laws of most States prohibit insurance companies from investing in real estate except for their own use. These laws have, however, been interpreted as permitting the ownership of large office buildings, of which a company may use but a small part for itself. The companies must also buy in real estate occasionally to protect their investments in mortgages. Consequently, real estate may form another asset of considerable amount. This necessitates a verification of the income from rentals. Receipts from sales of real estate should also receive attention, as it is usually the aim to dispose of foreclosed property as soon as it can be done without loss. The valuations at which the real estate appears in the balance sheet should be supported by independent appraisals.

The insurance reserve of life insurance companies is calculated on an entirely different basis from that of a fire insurance company. The calculations are made by the company's actuary and the auditor is not ordinarily expected to do more than see that the reserve as stated in the balance sheet agrees with the actuary's figures. Sometimes, however, the auditor is instructed to make a test of the actuary's calculations. In such instances it may be desirable for him to engage the services of an actuary to do this work. On the other hand, the accountant who has a good grasp of the underlying principles of life insurance can, himself, by the use of tables which are prepared for the purpose, test the calculations of the reserve and satisfy himself that it has been properly summarized, and that it includes reserves for all classes of outstanding policies which require them.

It is rather surprising that, with the magnitude which the insurance business has attained, the companies are, or at least until recently were, content to put up with the primitive accounting systems in use by most companies. This may have been due in part to the fact that the forms of reports prescribed by State insurance departments encouraged unscientific accounting methods. While the forms of report have been somewhat improved in recent years, they still leave much to be desired.

A few years ago a committee of the American Association of Public Accountants, acting jointly with a committee of the New York State Society of Certified Public Accountants, appeared before the Armstrong Committee of the New York Legislature. In addition to forcefully presenting the necessity for reform in insurance accounting methods (see the April, 1906, *Journal of Accountancy* for a report of the Committee's criticisms and suggestions), the Committee submitted a number of model forms, which are reproduced herein.

It is a matter of regret that the insurance authorities did not see fit to adopt the forms. They would have been a great improvement over the present forms. They give in a concise manner the information which is of value to the policy- or stockholder, and by means of supplementary schedules they can be amplified as much as may be desired.

The model forms, while designed primarily for life companies, could easily be adapted to the needs of fire and other insurance companies.

THE IDEAL LIFE INSURANCE COMPANY
BALANCE SHEET, DECEMBER 31, 19...

ASSETS

REAL ESTATE—(Appraised Value):			
Office Buildings:			
Home Office	$........		
Domestic Branches	....		
Foreign Branches	....	$........	
Other Real Estate		....	
SECURED LOANS:			$........
On Mortgage		$........	
On Policies		....	
On Other Collateral		....	$........
BONDS, STOCKS AND OTHER MARKETABLE SECURITIES —(Market Value):			
Bonds:			
Government, State and Municipal of the United States and Canada	$........		
Railroad and Traction Companies in the United States and Canada	....		
Foreign—Held Chiefly to Comply with Statutory Requirements	....		
Miscellaneous	....	$........	
Stocks:			
Railroad and Traction Companies in the United States and Canada	$........		
Financial and Insurance Companies in the United States and Canada	....		
Miscellaneous	....	$........	
Syndicate Subscriptions		....	$........
CASH:			
In Banks and Trust Companies:			
Home Office, Subject to Cheque	$........		
Branches and Agencies, Subject to Cheque . .	....		
On Deposit on Special Terms	....	$........	
Deposits with Foreign Governments		....	
In Transit		....	
On Hand—At Home Office, Branches and Agencies		....	$........
PREMIUMS IN COURSE OF COLLECTION OR COLLECTED AND NOT REPORTED:			
First Year Premiums		$........	
Renewal Premiums		....	
Annuities		....	$........
AGENTS' BALANCES AND MISCELLANEOUS ADVANCES .			$........
INTEREST AND RENTALS DUE OR ACCRUED:			
Interest:			
On Bonds and Dividends on Stocks	$........		
On Secured Loans	....		
On Agents' Advances and Balances	....		
Miscellaneous	....	$........	
Rentals		....	$........
			$........

THE IDEAL INSURANCE COMPANY
BALANCE SHEET, DECEMBER 31, 19...

LIABILITIES

GENERAL INSURANCE RESERVE:			
(Describing Basis)			$........
CURRENT LIABILITIES:			
Under Policies and Policy Contracts:			
Death Claims—Due and Unpaid	$........		
Matured Endowments	....		
Annuities—Due and Unpaid	....		
Dividends—Due and Unpaid	....	$........	
Commissions and Current Expenses:			
Commissions on Premiums in Course of Collection	$........		
Current Expenses	....	$........	$........
Premiums, Interest and Rents Prepaid, and Sundry Deposits			$........
CAPITAL STOCK			$........
SURPLUS AND RESERVES:			
Contingency Fund		$........	
Investment Fluctuation Reserve Fund		....	
Deferred Dividend Funds		....	
Annual Dividend Funds		....	
Unappropriated Surplus		....	$........
			$........

THE IDEAL LIFE INSURANCE COMPANY

ASSURANCE ACCOUNT FOR THE YEAR ENDED DECEMBER 31, 19...

PREMIUMS FALLING DUE WITHIN THE YEAR:			BENEFITS UNDER POLICIES:		
First Year	$..........		Claims on death or maturity after deduction of $ applied to purchase Annuities and Instalments	$..........	
Renewal	....		Annuities and Instalments	....	
Annuities	....	$..........	Surrender Values after deduction of $ applied to purchase Paid-up Insurance	....	$..........
EARNINGS ON INVESTMENTS AFTER DEDUCTION OF TAXES AND OTHER EXPENSES DIRECTLY APPLICABLE THERETO:			EXPENSE OF CONDUCTING BUSINESS:		
Interest and Dividends	$..........		Commissions	$..........	
Rents, less Expenses	....		Agency Expenses (Abstract A)	....	
Profits on Sales of Bonds and Stocks, Net	....		Administration, General Expenses (Abstract B)	....	
Gain in Market Values	....	....	Insurance Taxes	....	....
Total Income		$..........	Total Outgo		$..........
DIVIDENDS APPLIED TO PURCHASE PAID-UP INSURANCE AND ANNUITIES		....	RESERVE ON POLICIES IN FORCE DECEMBER 31, 19...		....
RESERVE ON POLICIES IN FORCE, JANUARY 1, 19...		....	SURPLUS FOR THE YEAR		....
		$..........			$..........

SURPLUS ACCOUNT

19... Jan. 1.	SURPLUS AS PER PREVIOUS ACCOUNT	$..........	19... Dec. 31.	APPROPRIATIONS:		
				For Contingency Fund	$..........	
Dec. 31.	SURPLUS FOR THE YEAR AS PER ASSURANCE ACCOUNT	....		For Investments Fluctuation Reserve Fund	....	$..........
				DIVIDENDS TO STOCKHOLDERS		....
				DIVIDENDS TO POLICY HOLDERS		....
				BALANCE—Being Surplus at December 31, 19.., as per Balance Sheet		....
		$..........				$..........

THE IDEAL LIFE INSURANCE COMPANY

ABSTRACT "A"

AGENCY EXPENSES FOR THE YEAR ENDED DECEMBER 31, 19...

	State or Country	Total Expense			Rents	Salaries	Allow-ances	Bonuses and Prizes	Printing and Sta-tionery	Postage and Exchange	Traveling Expenses	Office and Sundry Expenses	Furni-ture
		Total	Apportioned to										
			New Business	Renewal									
DOMESTIC..............													
Total Domestic.............													
FOREIGN................													
Total Foreign....													
Total Domestic and Foreign...													

THE IDEAL LIFE INSURANCE COMPANY

ABSTRACT "B"

ADMINISTRATION AND GENERAL EXPENSES FOR THE YEAR ENDED DECEMBER 31, 19..

Departments	Total Cost			Rent	Salaries and Pensions	Directors' and Committees' Fees	Traveling Expenses	Banquets and Conventions	Advertising	Printing and Stationery	Postage Cables and Telephones	Legal Expenses	Furniture and Fixtures	Audit of Accounts	Sundry Office Expenses
	Total	Apportioned to													
		New Business	Renewal												
Executive															
Secretary															
Financial															
Supplies															
Real Estate															
Supplies															
Cashier															
Accounting															
Actuarial															
Auditing—Domestic															
Auditing—Foreign															
Agency—Domestic															
Agency—Foreign															
Issue of Insurance															
Policy Loans															
Claims															
Surrender Values															
Advertising															
Medical															
Legal															

CASUALTY, HEALTH, SURETY, TITLE GUARANTEE AND OTHER COMPANIES

In the main, the accounts of these companies will be similar to those of fire companies. The most important difference is that the basis of determining the reinsurance reserve is not always the same as for fire companies. For instance, it is customary to include the full amount of the gross premiums on unexpired risks in the reserve of marine and inland navigation companies. Health companies resemble life companies somewhat and their reserve may be based on actuarial principles.

Insurance Companies and the Corporation Tax: In auditing the accounts of an insurance company the question of the correct amount to pay under the Federal Corporation Tax will probably arise. A decision bearing on insurance reserves and sums set aside for amortization of bonds was rendered by the Commissioner of Internal Revenue, August 25, 1911, as follows:

First. The net addition to reserves required by law to be made within the year to reserve funds may be the highest amount required by any State in which the insurance corporation actually does business. In the case of assessment insurance companies the law provides that the actual deposit of sums with State or Territorial officers, pursuant to law, as additions to guaranty or reserve fund, shall be treated as being payments required by law to reserve funds.

Second. The reserves carried by various insurance corporations to provide for taxes due and payable within the year for which the return is made cannot be accepted as taxes paid unless such taxes were actually so paid. The second paragraph of section 38 of the Act of August 5, 1909, referring to deductions from gross income, provides, "(fourth) all sums paid by it within the year for taxes imposed under the authority of the United States, or of any State or Territory thereof, or imposed by the Government of any foreign country as a condition to carrying on business therein." You will note that the language of the statute is "all sums paid by it within the year for taxes," etc.

Third. Relative to amortization of bonds, where a corporation holds bonds which were purchased at a rate above par and said corporation shall proportionately reduce the value of those bonds on its books each year so that the book value shall be the redemption value of the bonds when such bonds become due and payable, the return of annual net income of the corporation holding such bonds may show the depreciation on account of amortization of such bonds. The requirement is, however, that the amount carried to the amortization account each year shall be practically proportioned with respect to the difference between the purchase price and the maturing value and the number of years to elapse until the bonds become due and payable. With respect to bond issues where such bonds are disposed of for a price less than par and are redeemable at par, it is also held that because of the fact that such bonds must be redeemed at their face value, the loss sustained by reason of their sale for less than their face value may be prorated by the issuing corporation in accordance with the life of the bond.

With respect to depreciation on real estate, it appears to be difficult to say more than is set forth in the regulations. The depreciation must have actually occurred before it can be allowed. Where it is necessary to estimate the depreciation, such estimate must be in accordance with the best data obtainable with respect to properties similar to that on which the depreciation may be claimed. It is understood, of course, that such depreciation should be charged off on the books of the corporation claiming the same.

With respect to the last sentence see Chapter XXII. The commissioner's ruling on this point has been reversed by a court decision.

MANUFACTURING

The accounts of manufacturers are submitted to the auditor probably as often as any one other class of accounts. Consequently he should be well informed on such matters as are especially pertinent to manufacturing accounts.

Expenditures for wages should be thoroughly verified. It is well for the auditor to be present at the paying off of a roll so that he may observe the methods used; in fact, he should follow the system of handling the pay roll through from the initial steps in making it up to the final paying out of the wages to the workmen.

The system of receiving materials and checking the invoices therefor, both as to quantity and quality, should also be made the subject of careful observation. An especially important matter is to see that freights which are chargeable to shippers are duly deducted from the payments for purchasers. Similarly, the freights on outgoing shipments should be examined to make certain that none which are prepayments on sales made f. o. b. factory, and which are consequently chargeable to customers, have been absorbed in the manufacturing expense accounts.

Depreciation of plant is an item which, while not peculiar to manufacturing industries, is of especial importance in that connection. The basis on which the allowances therefor are made varies in different industries. For textile mills, machine shops, etc., it is customary to base the depreciation allowances on percentages of the plant values, the percentages being in turn based on the estimated useful life of the plant or different parts thereof. In industries like blast furnaces and coke works the allowance is frequently based on a certain rate per unit of production, the amount of the allowance for different fiscal periods varying in direct proportion to the fluctuation in the output of pig iron or coke respectively. A legitimate reason for such a basis is that in industries such as those named, a very large output imposes a correspondingly heavy strain on the plant, whereas when the production is light, the wear and tear on furnace and oven linings, etc., is much less.

Miscellaneous income needs to be carefully looked for and verified. One such item which is quite frequently encountered is the income from houses owned by manufacturers who are located at a distance from cities and towns, and who rent these houses to their employees. Most frequently, though not invariably, the rents are deducted from wages payable to the employee tenants.

As often as not, the record of rents is in crude form. A suitable form of rent roll should be suggested. The record should be based on the rents accruing, not merely on the collections when made.

In stating the operations of the undertaking, the taxes, repairs, and other expenses which can be allocated to the houses owned should be applied against the rents (though preferably showing the gross of both rents and expenses), and the net income or expense extended.

When the buildings used for manufacturing are leased and a portion of the space is sublet, it is desirable that both the gross amount of rent paid and the amount received for the space sublet be shown so that any fluctuations in the net amount of rent paid which are due to the sublet premises becoming vacant may carry their own explanation with them.

A comprehensive system of cost and stock accounts is very desirable. In the absence of such a system the inventory valuations contain an element of guesswork and the auditor cannot be certain that they represent actual manufacturing cost. Correct cost and stock accounts are also of vital importance for the aid

MODEL MANUFACTURING COMPANY

BALANCE SHEET........................19...

Assets

Property Account:			
Balance at....................19		$..........	
Construction and Purchases of Additional Property During Year		....	
		$..........	
Less Charged off to Following Accounts:			
Reserve for Depreciation	$..........		
	....	....	$..........
Good Will			....
Deferred Charges to Operations:			
(Prepaid Insurance, Taxes, etc.; Advanced Mining Royalties and Similar Expenses Chargeable to Future Operations)			....
Investments:			
Outside Real Estate and Other Property		$..........	
Stocks of Other Companies		....	
Bonds of Other Companies		....	....
Current Assets:			
Inventories		$..........	
Bills Receivable		....	
Accounts Receivable		....	
Cash		....	....
Sinking and Special Fund Assets:			
(State Nature of Assets and Funds for which held)		$..........	
		....	....
			$..........

Liabilities

Bonded Debt:		
(State Nature, Rate of Interest, and Due Date of Various Issues and Show Deduction of any Unsold Bonds)	$..........	
	....	$..........
Current Liabilities:		
Bills Payable	$..........	
Accounts Payable	....	
Accrued Taxes	....	
Accrued Interest	....	
Miscellaneous	....	....
		$..........
Reserves and Special Funds:		
(State Purpose and Amount of Each Reserve or Fund)		....
		....
		....
Capital Stock:		
(If more than One Class state accordingly)	$..........	
Sinking Fund Accounts	....	
Surplus, As Annexed	....	....
		$..........

FORM PRESCRIBED BY THE ENGLISH COMPANIES ACT

BALANCE SHEET OF THE..........CO., MADE UP TO.....19..

PROPERTY AND ASSETS

PROPERTY HELD BY COMPANY:		
Showing:		
Immovable Property, distinguishing:		
(a) Freehold Land	$	$
(b) Freehold Buildings		
(c) Leasehold Buildings		
Movable Property, distinguishing:		
(d) Stock-in-Trade		
(e) Plant		
The cost to be stated with deductions for deterioration in value as charged to the Reserve Fund or Profit and Loss		
DEBTS OWING TO THE COMPANY:		
Showing:		
Debts considered good for which the Company holds Bills or other Securities		
Debts considered good for which the Company holds no Security		
Debts considered doubtful and bad		
Any Debt Due from a Director or Other Officer of the Company to be separately stated		
CASH AND INVESTMENTS:		
Showing:		
The nature of Investment and Rate of Interest . . .		
The Amount of Cash, where Lodged, and if Bearing Interest		
	$	$

CAPITAL AND LIABILITIES

CAPITAL:		
Showing:		
The Number of Shares	$	
The Amount Paid per Share		
If any Arrears of Calls, the nature of the Arrears, and the Names of the Defaulters		
The Particulars of any Forfeited Shares		
DEBTS AND LIABILITIES OF THE COMPANY:		
Showing:		
The Amount of Loans on Mortgages or Debenture Bonds		
The Amount of Debts Owing by the Company distinguishing:		
(a) Debts for which Acceptances have been given .		
(b) Debts to Tradesmen for Supplies of Stock-in-Trade or Other Articles		
(c) Debts for Law Expenses		
(d) Debts for Interest on Debentures or Other Loans		
(e) Unclaimed Dividends		
(f) Debts not enumerated above		
RESERVE FUND:		
Showing:		
The Amount set aside from Profits to meet Contingencies		
PROFIT AND LOSS:		
Showing:		
The Disposable Balance for Payment of Dividends, etc.		
	$	$

CONTINGENT LIABILITIES:

Claims Against the Company not Acknowledged as Debts

Moneys for which the Company is Contingently Liable .

which they give in carrying on the manufacturing operations to the best advantage.

In those industries in which there is but a single unit of production—such as tons, pounds, barrels, or gallons—at least the sales accounts should be kept not only as to values, but also in quantities. Under such conditions it will occasionally be possible to lay out the accounts on the general books in such a manner as to show therein the average manufacturing cost per unit of production. Keeping cumulative records of quantities in connection with the values, not only of sales, but also of materials purchased and used, will enable the auditor to make a comparison of the quantity of materials used with the resulting quantity of finished product, and ascertain whether the ratio of one to the other is within a reasonable range of the average experienced in the particular industry.

Uniformity of detail in the financial statements of manufacturing concerns is not to be expected. It will doubtless be of interest to students, however, to see forms of statements which are actually in use. On page 392 is shown the general form of balance sheet which is used by quite a number of American manufacturing corporations, following which is the form prescribed by the English Companies Act.

PUBLISHERS OF BOOKS

Publishers who do not do their own printing and binding are in the position of merchants who have goods manufactured for them according to their special pattern and design. Those who, in addition, have their own printing plants are both manufacturers and merchants. In practically all cases, even if there is not a retail store connected with the business, there is a department for filling retail mail orders.

There are several considerations more or less special to publishers' accounts, and reference will be made to these. Royalties paid to authors, while not exclusively found in publishers' accounts, are in point of proportion a more important item here than in most businesses. Royalty accounts with authors should be carefully checked. The credits thereto should be thoroughly tested to see that they are for quantities actually sold and that the rate per copy is in accordance with the contract between publisher and author. Sometimes the contract will be on a profit-sharing basis, and in such cases the auditor will need to satisfy himself that all costs have been taken into account.

Advance payments on account of royalty should not be included among the accounts receivable from customers, but should be set out separately in the balance sheet. The matter of royalties also raises an important question regarding the valuation of unsold books at inventory dates. If authors are credited with royalties only as their works are actually sold, care should be taken to see that the cost of production at which the books in the inventory are valued does not include the item of royalty. Of course, if authors are credited with royalties as books are bound, even though they are not yet sold (there are some publishers who pursue this plan, though they are in the minority), it is quite proper to value the books at a figure which includes the royalty.

Another very important question in connection with the valuation of sheet stock and bound books is that of salability. Cost is far too high a valuation of books for which the demand has died out, or for which there may never have been a demand.

The best way to determine the strength of the demand for books of which large quantities are on hand is to ascertain the number sold during the last fiscal period. The ratio of the quantity on hand to the quantity sold will furnish data for determining whether or not the stock should be valued at full cost or only a fraction thereof, or, if quite unsalable, at the price of waste paper. Even in applying this test, however, care must be taken not to be misled by large sales early in the period which may have dwindled away in the latter part of the period; the facts in such a case probably being that the demand has died out.

Still another consideration in connection with inventories—and this affects accounts receivable as well—is to see that the latter do not include consigned stock in agents' hands. Such stock should appear in the inventory at cost or less and not among the accounts receivable at selling prices.

Such stock on hand as paper, ink, binding materials, and other supplies presents no unusual problems. With regard to the quantities of stock, books are an article of which the auditor can readily verify the quantities stated in the inventory by making an actual count. It is very desirable to make some such tests, especially of the larger quantities.

The overvaluing of artists' drawings (for illustrations), if indeed, any value whatever is to be allowed for them, must be guarded against. Such values are sometimes based on sentiment rather than on what would be realized if the articles were sold.

Whether or not the values placed on the book plates are reasonable, demands careful inquiry on the part of the auditor. "Circumstances alter cases," and this adage is true of book plates as well as of other things. Obviously, it would be quite proper to carry the plates of an edition of the Encyclopedia Britannica or of some standard scientific work at a considerable part of their cost long after the entire cost of the plates for a more ephemeral piece of literature, like a novel, should have been written off *in toto.* The plates for a novel should be written off entirely as a part of the cost of the first edition—there may never be another the great majority of novels don't run through more than one As already indicated, the plates of a work which will be standard for a number of years may be written off more gradually particularly as the greater initial cost frequently includes large expenditures for contributions and editorial work which take the place of royalties payable over a period.

The fact that the effective demand for such a work is realized over a long period of time is another justification for charging off the cost of such plates more gradually.

At the same time, the world moves so rapidly and new discoveries are so frequent that works which are standard to-day are out-of-date to-morrow, and an issue of an encyclopedia or other reference work is not authoritative for as long a period as was formerly the case.

Some large failures in the publishing business are traceable to the omission to charge against the cost of books a proper proportion of the cost of plates. In view of the large profits which were apparently being earned, liberal amounts of cash were withdrawn from the business. The actual facts were that the liquid assets or working capital of the business were being replaced by a growing fictitious investment in plates and copyrights. The only safe plan is to charge off liberally.

As a parting word on the subject it may be said that the value of plates and copyrights should never be increased above cost. Even though there is every indication that the demand for certain publications will continue, or even increase, and result in large profits in the future, that is no reason for anticipating such profits and capitalizing them by raising the book value of the plates, and correspondingly crediting current income or even surplus account.

Accounts receivable require especially close scrutiny in a publishing business. One pitfall has already been referred to, viz., that accounts will frequently be found among the receivables which are in reality consignment accounts. Where books are sold on the installment plan the balances on such accounts also require careful examination. The right to reclaim such books if they are not paid for in full does not put the accounts in the secured class, as it usually costs about as much to recover books sold on the installment plan as they are worth.

An especially liberal reserve for losses on installment accounts should be made, as there is a large margin of profit in installment sales to offset the losses which may confidently be expected. The condition of the other customers' accounts as to promptness of payment will naturally be an important element in the determination of how large the reserve for possible losses thereon should be.

Large amounts of postage are used in a publishing business. A record of the purchases of stamps and of the quantities issued for use on requisitions of the shipping, advertising, correspondence, and other departments should be kept as a means of preventing abuses which may otherwise occur.

There are quite a few sources of miscellaneous receipts in the publishing business, particularly in the printing end, such as waste print paper, cuttings, ink barrels, boxes, gilt sweepings, etc. So far as possible all such items should be carefully accounted for.

PUBLISHERS OF MAGAZINES AND NEWSPAPERS

These accounts present some problems quite different from those of book publishers' accounts. Finished stock is usually a minor item, consisting of back numbers and bound volumes of magazines. Past issues of newspapers are never given any value in the inventory other than as waste paper.

Plates also are not a vital factor. Their value should be limited strictly to that of the metal as such excepting, perhaps, for the small amount of plates for advertisements under long contracts and similar standing matter, on which a somewhat higher value may be placed.

Two of the most important items which are peculiar to magazines and newspapers are the revenues derived from advertising and "circulation" respectively. A century ago newspapers may have been published on the basis of the income from subscriptions furnishing the bulk of the wherewithal to pay the cost of publication, but that day has past long since, and the same thing may be said of magazines. Ordinarily, the subscription or circulation revenue does not cover the cost of production and distribution, and the only inducement to extend the circulation is because of the higher rates for advertising space which the larger circulation commands.

In the case of a monthly magazine, all the advertisements in several numbers out of the year's issues should be compared with the charges for advertising recorded in the books. Proper authority should be shown for such advertisements as have been inserted without charge. Some of the contracts should also be consulted for the purpose of testing the correctness of the rates charged. If the accounts of a newspaper are being audited, the charges for the advertisement in one or two days' issues of each month should be verified. More difficulty is likely to be encountered in verifying the revenue from classified advertising than in verifying the income from display advertising, particularly if the system of recording the classified advertisements is of the happy-go-lucky kind which not infrequently obtains. The importance of examining the commission accounts of advertising agents and solicitors should not be overlooked.

Subscription income is difficult to verify. On account of the immense volume of detail it is out of the question to check it with any approach to completeness. The best that can be done, in addition to making tests of the clerical work, is to assure oneself that the system is the best that can be devised to safeguard the integrity of the subscription, or—as it is usually termed in the case of newspapers—cash circulation, and to compare the total circulation revenue with the approximate amount which it would seem that the number of copies printed, after making due allowance for unsold and returned copies, should have yielded.

Data for making the latter test will be obtained from the press run record, the circulation manager's statement of the disposition of the number of copies printed (sold, exchanged, returned, distributed free, etc.) and the news agency's reports. That part of a magazine's circulation which goes directly to subscribers by mail may be approximately verified by dividing the weight per copy (including wrapper) into the total weight shown by the post office receipts for second-class postage paid. This must be done separately for each issue, as the number of pages will probably vary from one issue to another, and this will in turn change the weight per copy. Knowing the circulation of a magazine, some idea can be formed of the approximate amount of subscription revenue which should have been received.

Precautions should also be taken to prevent abuses of the free list. Names should be entered thereon only with the approval of some one in authority.

While on the subject of verifying circulation, it may not be amiss to refer to so-called "circulation audits" which are at times made on behalf of advertisers' associations or directly for newspapers which desire to substantiate their claims of having a certain circulation.

There are a number of ways of manipulating newspaper circulation records which can be detected only by an audit of the general accounts. For example, the cash sales (office sales and mail subscriptions) may be inflated, making them, say, $100 or $200, or more, larger than the amount actually collected and then charging off the inflated amount monthly, quarterly, or at irregular intervals, to some expense account, no details accompanying the entry therefor in the general cash book. Another method which has been used is to overcharge news-agents' accounts or to charge to fictitious agents papers which were never actually delivered. Eventually such charges, which served the purpose of inflating the circulation earnings when they were made, are written off as bad debts or to some expense account (really an offset against the circulation earnings account and frequently sc treated in preparing the confidential statements for the manage- ment). In the circulation accounts receivable ledger these credits may be entered as cash instead of as allowances or as bac debts written off.

From the foregoing it is obvious that a circulation audi which is restricted to an examination of the circulation records and during which the auditor does not have access to the genera books, is absolutely worthless. It proves nothing except, per haps, that the circulation records may have been very cleverly manipulated. A verification of the revenue purporting to have accrued from circulation can be conclusive only when the dis position of the cash represented to have been received is traced and the outstanding accounts receivable are satisfactorily veri fied. Other means, or rather partial means, of verifying the cir culation are the press-run book, which is a record of the numbe of papers indicated by the automatic counters on the presses to have been printed, and the quantity of paper used, the latte being ascertained by referring to the purchase invoices and applying the quantity of paper on hand at the beginning and end of the period. The auditor must, of course, take steps to assure himself that the press-run book which is submitted to him ha not been "faked" for his especial benefit. From either of thes sources only the gross circulation printed is obtained. It wil still be necessary to ascertain the number of copies spoiled, un sold, returned, sent to exchanges, etc., and deduct the tota thereof from the number printed before the net paid circulation can be determined.

The subscription earnings account of a magazine should include only that part of the subscriptions received which ha actually been earned during the period. That portion of sub scriptions received previous to the period under review, bu which has been earned during the period, should, of course, also be included therein. The unexpired pro rata of subscriptions in force at the close of the period should appear in an unearned sub scriptions account and be entered among the liabilities in the balance sheet as unearned or deferred income. There are severa methods for determining the actual subscription earnings of th period and the unexpired amount at the end of the period

Under either plan the subscription receipts are credited to an account termed, say, unearned subscriptions, and periodically, usually monthly, the amount earned during the period is transferred to a subscription earnings account. One way of determining the amount of the monthly earnings is to classify the subscription receipts according to expiration dates, from which the actual earnings for a given month can readily be determined. Another way is to ascertain the average annual realization per subscription and then multiply the number of copies mailed by one-twelfth of the average annual rate. While the second plan can be safely followed if the data used in making the calculations is carefully verified, the first mentioned plan is, perhaps, less liable to give rise to inaccuracies.

With many newspapers the annual or semiannual subscriptions form such a small part of the total circulation that a reserve for unexpired subscriptions is almost or quite unnecessary. Others again have a very large mailing list of individual subscribers, and in such cases a reserve for unexpired subscriptions should, of course, be created.

A reserve for returns should also be made in the case of both magazines and newspapers. A very few of the magazines do not permit agents to return unsold copies, but the great majority do. Almost all newspapers accept from newsboys unsold copies of the previous day's issue in exchange for the current day's papers. In the case of regular news agents credit is allowed in the monthly settlement for copies charged, but not sold by the agents. The reserve should be based on past experience as to the ratio of returns to gross circulation, and, if set up only at the end of the fiscal period, will be determined by applying the percentage decided upon to the circulation accounts receivable.

Not all magazine publishers print the magazines themselves. The printing and mailing is sometimes done by contract, the publisher supplying the paper, which he buys direct to eliminate the printer's profit thereon. Frequently, however, a newspaper publisher will have his own printing plant. The accounts pertaining to this end of the business will naturally call for much the same general treatment as those of other printers.

Publishers who have their own printing plant frequently do job printing. Even if there is not a regular job department, special work like circulars of newspaper-sheet size may occasionally be run off. This, as well as other sources of miscellaneous receipts, which are often quite numerous, should not be overlooked.

Magazine and book publishing is very frequently combined in one business, but this fact of itself does not introduce any complications except in the apportionment of general charges. The magazine and book departments will ordinarily be found to be quite distinct.

BREWERIES

In breweries there is probably a greater opportunity for theft of supplies or product and misapplication of collections than in almost any other business. The containers—boxes, bottles, kegs, and barrels—are never sold, but remain the property of the brewer. The value of these should not be set up in the balance sheet as accounts receivable if they are charged against customers. This is sometimes done. It is easily seen that the loss in such stock is considerable, and that the value set upon it should be investigated carefully. The auditor should see that adequate accounting methods are in force, not only for the containers, but for all other stock, and, if not, report should be made thereon.

The fact that collections are frequently made by the drivers is a weak point, requiring special attention and necessitating close scrutiny of all allowances and discounts.

Usually a large amount of money is invested in saloons either owned or controlled by reason of loans made. Frequently the brewery pays for the license and collects on same from the saloon keeper in monthly installments. The auditor should see that the income from these sources is properly taken up, and at the same time see that adequate provision is made for bad and doubtful accounts, as the loss on these advances is considerable and is looked upon as being an expense of keeping the product before the public. In addition to amounts actually loaned to customers, the brewery frequently guarantees loans made to customers by others. Such guarantees constitute a large contingent liability and should be set up as such in a balance sheet or indicated in a footnote.

MINING—COAL MINES

A practitioner engaged to audit the accounts of a mining enterprise for the first time will do well to make an inspection of the entire mine workings and equipment, accompanied by the client's engineer or mine superintendent. Careful observation will give him some idea of the condition of the equipment and scope of the undertaking, which should be of assistance to him when auditing the books and preparing the financial statements.

As the largest source of income is from the sale of coal, the inventories and the sales tonnages should be proved with the production records. Deductions from miners' wages for "blacksmithing" (dressing their tools) are frequently made on the basis of production; when so, the collection of this income can be verified in total. Arrangements are usually made with companies operating general stores at the mines (unless the mining company operates its own store, which will, in that case, be audited separately) to allow the miners to make purchases on credit, the amounts due therefor being deducted from the wages of the mining company's employees. Commissions on these collections are generally charged by the mining companies. The collection of rents from houses occupied by employees and owned by the mining company should also be checked.

Some coal companies own railroad cars, for the use of which income should be received from the railroad companies on a mileage basis.

The matter of royalties on coal mined from leased lands requires careful attention. They are based upon tonnage of production or cubic yards or acreage of the seams worked, and the royalty agreements usually provide for a minimum annual payment, in the event of the production being so small that the regular royalty rate would not require payments equal to the fixed minimum.

In the case of comparatively new mines, the minimum royalties will usually be paid during the sinking of shafts and period of development work. If the lease agreement allows a lessee to recoup himself subsequently for the proportion of the minimum royalty paid in excess of the amount earned (calculated on a tonnage basis), such excess is usually carried among the assets as a deferred charge. As the production increases to a point beyond that at which the royalty, calculated on a tonnage basis, equals the fixed minimum, and the lessee begins to recoup himself for the advance royalties, the amounts of such retained royalties should be applied in reduction of the deferred charge above mentioned.

It is important that all royalty agreements be carefully examined, and if they do not provide that the lessee may recoup himself for advance royalties, the latter should be charged against revenue. It sometimes occurs, where a mine is being operated under several leases, that only a portion of the leased lands are being mined, and that portions thereof will never be worked. Obviously, any minimum royalties paid under terms of leases covering lands in that class should not be carried as deferred charges, and for that reason the advance royalties account should be analyzed and such charges eliminated if included therein.

If a time limit is set in which the lessee must recoup himself for advance royalties, any portion still carried as a deferred charge at the time the limit expires should be at once charged off.

All lands, plants, and equipment accounts should be scrutinized, and only such charges should be included as represent the cost of lands which add to the area of coal available for future mining, or which cover expenditures for development, construction, and equipment which will result in increased production.

Provision should be made for reduction of equipment, development, and construction accounts to the amount of the residual value of the machinery included therein by the time the mines are exhausted. This is usually done by charging mining costs at a certain rate per ton of production. The depreciation of railroad cars, if any are owned, and of live stock, should not be taken care of on such a basis, however, but on the basis of probable length of service.

While it is desirable to provide for depreciation in value of lands by reason of the depletion of the coal thereunder, it is not certain that mining companies are legally required to replace such wasting capital by reserving any portion of their earnings therefor. In instances where this is not done, the auditor can only call attention to the advisability of such a course, which, when followed, is usually based on the number of tons produced. The following extract from a paper prepared by A. Lowes Dickinson, C. P. A., and read at the St. Louis Congress of Accountants in 1904, is of interest in this connection:

In the case of minerals, the product taken out of the land becomes the stock-in-trade of a corporation as soon as it is extracted, and whatever the land was worth before its extraction, it is clearly worth an appreciable amount less thereafter. The provision to be made should be on the basis of the number of tons extracted, having regard to the total tonnage available and to the realizable value of the property after the minerals have all been extracted. The same principle would also apply to timber lands where no provision is made for reforesting. The contention is sometimes made that no provision need be made for exhaustion of minerals where the amount of mineral known to be in a definite tract at the end of any period is largely in excess of that which had been discovered at the beginning of the period. This argument cannot, however, for a moment be admitted, except as a reason for reducing the tonnage rate to be provided. As a general principle, whatever there was in the land, whether known or unknown, has been reduced during the period under consideration by whatever amount has been extracted; and while the new discoveries may be accepted as reducing the necessary rate of provision for extinction from, say, one dollar to one cent per ton, the original principle that provision must be made holds good on the smaller figure, whatever it is. It may be, of course, that the provisions made in earlier years have been sufficient to cover a number of future years on the basis, from the commencement, of the rate subsequently found to be sufficient in view of the new discoveries, and in this case there is obviously no necessity to provide further for extinction until the total production at the new rate is equal to the total amount written off.

Mortgages upon coal and ore lands usually provide for the establishment of a sinking fund from which to pay off the mortgage, either in installments or in full on a specified date. The auditor should read carefully all the mortgages of the property of his client and call attention to any unpaid sinking fund charges.

Some mortgages require payments to be made into the sinking funds on the basis of the entire tonnage mined (which would include all coal consumed in the company's operations), while others base the charge only on commercial production, which would be only that actually sold.

The cash held by trustees of sinking funds is to be used for retiring mortgage obligations only, and therefore should be shown separately on the balance sheet and not mingled with current cash accounts.

GOLD MINES

Accountants are often engaged by committees of dissatisfied creditors or stockholders to investigate the disposition of the cash capital invested in gold, silver, copper, and other mining enterprises. In instances where the ore is found in profitable quantities, the auditor should not feel compelled to accept the periodical cash, production, and shipping statements received from the mine office, unless accompanied by original vouchers, ore records, assay reports, and shipping data.

Not only should the shipping memoranda be compared with the sales reports, the vouchers for expenditures at the mines compared with the cash statements, and all of the mine reports carefully checked and compared with the general books, but every effort should be made to account for the entire production. Where the product is sent to outside smelters for reduction, tests should be made, using the client's assay reports of values shipped as a basis, to ascertain that the smelter returns are correct.

The correctness of the distribution of expenditures between capital and operating accounts should be certified to by the mine manager. He should be requested to furnish a certificate setting forth in detail the local current assets and liabilities or the fact that none exist.

A report from the mine manager upon the efficiency of the plant and equipment, and upon the age and condition of the buildings and other more or less permanent local assets, is necessary in order to properly consider the question of depreciation which should be allowed for in the accounts.

A large portion of the mine employees' wages is based on production, and tests of the correctness thereof can readily be made. The balance of the wages should be carefully scrutinized and portions of the pay rolls compared with timekeepers' records.

Often mining companies own and operate stamping mills, smelters, short connecting railroads, and other enterprises, the accounts of which should also be carefully examined.

As the accounts and the conditions under which various mining enterprises are carried on differ widely, no set instructions for auditing them can be laid down; the audit should, however, be thorough and detailed enough to cover all possible sources of income, to reveal operating waste, if any exists, and to enable the auditor to satisfy himself that no operating expenses are charged to capital accounts. It is also desirable that the scope of the examination be definitely stated in the auditor's report.

TRADING—WHOLESALE MERCHANTS

The audit of accounts of wholesale merchants demands extreme vigilance on the part of the auditor, because unless the system is complete, not only as to financial transactions, but also as to accounting for the actual stock received and delivered, the discovery of loss by error or fraud, if any exists, is exceedingly difficult.

Comparisons should be made of the stock records with the details of the sales and purchases entered in the general books. These should reveal any payments charged as purchases which are not *bona fide* or for which all the goods were not received. Theft of stock or of the proceeds of such as may have been sold for cash, as well as the shipment of stock without charging customers therefor, should also be discovered by such comparisons.

Additional to the possibilities of fraud above mentioned are those in which attempts at concealment are made by making false entries on the financial records only, such as the theft of customers' remittances, in whole or in part, and allowing their accounts to remain open in the ledger, or writing them off through the journal ostensibly as bad accounts, or as having been closed by discounts, allowances, or return of goods; by erroneously reporting the aggregate of cash sales, raising the amounts of vouchers covering cash paid for freight and expressage, etc.

Particular care must be exercised (to avoid misstating the business results) to ascertain that the mathematical calculations of inventory are correct, that the unsold stock has been priced at either cost or market price—whichever is the lower—and that sufficient allowance has been made for probable discounts on customers' accounts not yet due in addition to the usual reserve for uncollectible accounts, depreciation of fixtures, etc.

In establishments doing an export or import business, accounts with foreign houses are usually kept in both foreign and

United States currencies. As many of such accounts are settled in foreign currency, it is necessary to calculate at the current rate of exchange the equivalent in American money of the foreign balances, and to take up in the profit and loss account the differences between these equivalents and the balances in the accounts kept in American money. Differences between balances in foreign banks and the equivalent in American money should be similarly adjusted.

In stating the results from trading, the total sales, the cost of sales, and the gross profit should be shown separately, so that the auditor may judge if the percentage of the latter is up to the rate which may reasonably be expected to have been realized. The subject of gross profits on sales is treated in further detail under the caption of "Retail Merchants."

RETAIL MERCHANTS

The volume of detail in a retail business of any size, particularly if credit is extended to customers, is so great that it is difficult to make a satisfactory audit for a moderate-sized fee It is obvious that a complete audit of all the details is out of the question, but the tests of the correctness of the different sections of the accounts should be sufficiently varied and comprehensive to disclose any systematic manipulation of the accounts.

If the business is a large one, some system of internal sales audit will probably be in use. The auditor should trace the daily totals into the general books and also test the make-up of the daily totals. It may also be possible for him to suggest additional safeguards for the prevention of irregularities in the handling of cash sales.

If the work in connection with the customers' charge accounts is properly systematized, the auditor can verify the accounts receivable with some degree of assurance. The sales returns, and allowances and cash totals should all be traced into the controlling accounts and the trial balances of the customers ledger verified. A good verification of the outstanding balance is for the auditor to compare the monthly statements at the close of the period, either with the trial balance, or if that has not yet been prepared, then with the ledger itself, before the statement are sent out.

It is customary to allow employees of the store a special discount on their purchases and also to permit their accounts to run until pay day, when settlement is made. If these accounts are numerous, they should be segregated either in a separate ledger or in a section of one of the customers' ledgers. The auditor should see that none of these accounts has been permitted to run past pay day without settlement being made, and particularly that no balances are standing against persons who have left the employ of the store.

In some businesses, particularly those handling small articles broken from original packages, it is not feasible to keep complete stock accounts and some other check on the accounting, for the wares handled must be used. This is found to some extent in a comparison of the rate of gross profit earned in one period as compared with prior periods. Decided variations should be susceptible of definite explanation as being due to specific causes; a decrease in the percentage of gross profit which cannot be satisfactorily explained raises at least a presumption that the proceeds of sales are not being fully accounted for, or that payments are being made for goods which are not actually being received by the house.

Percentages of gross profit are by almost all merchants calculated on the sales, and not on the cost of the goods sold.

In some lines of retail trade, such as cigars, men's furnishing goods, etc., it is possible to apply a check on the accounting for sales which is also used in some department stores. The plan is to charge all goods purchased to a stock account at their selling values; credits are made on the account for any changes in selling prices; the inventories at beginning and end of the period are priced at both cost and selling value, and the latter values applied in stock account mentioned. The crediting of the actual sales of the period should balance the account. There will naturally be some differences, but if they are not very large, the sales can be considered to have been fully accounted for.

Some method of determining the approximate stock on hand, even if calculated only on the basis of an estimated rate of gross profits on sales, is needed by all merchants for the purpose of determining the proper amount of insurance to be carried on the stock, as well as to prevent overbuying.

Whenever several different lines of goods are handled, both sales and purchases should, as far as possible, be kept separate for each line. The rates of gross profits on the different lines will probably vary, and the information as to the results of the business done in each class of goods will be valuable to the manager.

In a business conducted entirely on a cash basis the number of customers' accounts is greatly reduced, but they are not in all cases entirely eliminated, as regular customers often leave deposits to avoid the inconvenience of paying separately for each purchase. The auditor should see that deposit accounts are not overdrawn, and that if interest is credited, it is at the proper rate.

A quite general practice is to issue a credit memorandum to customers returning goods, which memorandum may be either applied in payment of subsequent purchases or cashed on presentation to the cashier. It is desirable that these credit memoranda be controlled by an account on the general ledger. If this is done, it is possible for the auditor to satisfy himself by testing entries for credit memoranda issued and paid, and by reconciling the aggregate of the outstanding memoranda with the balance of the controlling account, that the credit memoranda have been properly handled.

DEPARTMENT STORES

A department store is really a group of retail stores in different lines of business with one general management and with the accounting centralized in one department.

Practically all department stores have a more or less efficient staff auditing department. This department pays particular attention to the continuous auditing of the sales. The volume of detail in connection with the cash and charge sales is so great that the professional auditor is not expected to go back of the summaries prepared by the auditing department. He should, however, see that the various totals on the summaries are properly carried into the general books.

The auditor should also satisfy himself by careful investigation that the system of internal audit is such as to insure an accounting for all sales. It is particularly important to see that the system of handling C. O. D.'s and "will calls" (similar to C. O. D.'s, excepting that the customer will pay for the goods on calling for them at the store, instead of having them delivered) is such as to reduce the possibility of fraud or error to a minimum. Controlling accounts for these classes of transient items are of decided assistance in this respect.

The volume of merchandise purchases in a department store is very large, and it is out of the question under ordinary circumstances for the auditor to examine all or even a considerable part of the purchase invoices. Tests should be made, however, and especial care should be given to see that a proper plan of verifying and approving each invoice is in use and that it is actually carried out. It is important that the plan be such as will guard against the failure to deduct freight when the goods are bought on a delivered basis, shortages in weight or count, and allowances for defects or inferior quality. Frequently goods are paid for before they are actually received in order to obtain the cash discount obtainable for early payment. The system of approving invoices should insure such purchases being verified on receipt of the purchased goods and insure that claims, if any be in order, are made.

As discounts on purchases form no small part of the net income of department stores, it is desirable that this subject receive attention during the course of the audit. Almost all department stores are wide-awake to the importance of having all invoices approved as quickly after receipt thereof as possible, so that the discount day may not pass before the approved invoice reaches the treasurer's department for payment. Should the auditor, however, discover any deficiency or weakness in this respect, he may rest assured that his client will very much appreciate having his attention called to the matter.

Salaries and wages form the largest single item in the expenses, and the verification of the expenditure therefor is of prime importance. The padding of pay rolls as far as sales clerks are concerned can usually be detected by comparing the pay roll with the auditing department's analysis of sales by sales clerks. Vice versa, this is also somewhat of a check on the statements of sales. The payments for expenses will be found to be very voluminous, and it would not be practicable to vouch them with any approach to completeness. A study of the comparisons shown by the departmental accounts for different periods will, however, indicate such of the expenses as should be specially investigated.

Almost without exception, some form of departmental accounts, i. e., accounts showing the operations of each department separately, will be found to be in use in every store. Their accuracy and completeness vary: in some cases they are very complete and are controlled by accounts in the general ledger; in other stores they are on a single-entry basis, arbitrary charges for rent, interest on stock, and similar items are made of which no cognizance is taken in the general books, and no attempt is made to bring the aggregate of the results shown in the departmental accounts into agreement with the final results shown on the general books. It is certainly most desirable that the departmental accounts be controlled by the general ledger, and if the system of accounts be well laid out, it is entirely feasible.

While daily statements of sales and weekly or monthly statements of profits (based on estimated inventories) are furnished to the management, most stores close their books and state the final results of their business operations twice a year, the closing dates being either the end of January and July or of June and December. The first half of the year is called the spring season and the latter half the fall season. In comparing the operations of a department for different periods, the comparison should always be made between the same season in different years and not between the two seasons in the one year. The volume and character of the business done in the spring season varies considerably from that of the fall season.

In studying the operations of the various departments, one of the most important things to be considered is the rate of gross profit on sales. Any undue fluctuation therein from one year to another should be thoroughly investigated. Fluctuations in the ratio of selling expenses to sales should also receive careful attention. The volume of business done exerts, of course, a more noticeable influence on the percentage which the expenses are of the gross sales than should be the case with the gross profit.

The basis of the apportionment among the various departments of such expenses as delivery service, wrapping desks, insurance, general administration, etc., ought to be investigated. A rough and ready way of distributing such general charges may work serious injustice to some departments, undue advantage to others, and result in misleading showings generally.

In verifying the assets and liabilities, no unusual questions of principle are encountered. The principal assets are accounts receivable and merchandise inventory. Customers' accounts receivable should be analyzed as to date; this will furnish a basis for the determination of a proper amount to be reserved for uncollectible accounts. Notes receivable held by a department store may ordinarily be viewed with some suspicion as to the financial strength of the makers. Goods sold at retail are usually purchased by the customer for consumption and not for resale; consequently the account should be paid at maturity and the giving of a note therefor is a confession of the customer's having purchased in excess of his ability to pay.

The important questions in connection with the inventory are the correctness of quantities, prices, arithmetical work, and salability of the stock. For the correctness of the quantities the auditor will be dependent largely on the certification of those who took the inventory and of the "buyer" (department manager). The investigation of large increases or decreases in the inventory as compared with prior dates will sometimes result in the detection of errors in quantities. Prices may be tested by reference to the purchase invoices. Goods which are still in original packages should be inventoried by reference to the purchase invoice therefor, and verification thereof is comparatively simple. Sufficient tests of the extensions and footings should be made to assure the correctness of this element. Goods should be so indicated on the inventory that those purchased prior to the current season can be readily identified and allowance made for eventual loss thereon owing to the necessity for price reductions to close them out. (See page 104, "Inventories.")

Some department stores, in fact quite a number of them, also have a wholesale department. Whenever this is the case, the audit of the accounts pertaining to the wholesale department will follow the lines laid down under "Wholesale Merchants."

AUTOMOBILE DEALERS

It is important that the auditor thoroughly familiarize himself with the terms of the dealer's contract with the manufacturers. Deposits with the latter are not accounts receivable, but payments on account of cars to be purchased during the contract period, and the amounts so deposited may be deducted pro rata from the price to be paid for each car or from the last shipments. The unapplied balance of such deposits should be confirmed by correspondence with the manufacturers. Interest on these deposits is sometimes paid by the manufacturers, and where this is the case its collection should be verified.

Deposits by customers with the dealer should appear in separate accounts, as they are not current accounts payable. If any interest is to be allowed on such deposits, the auditor should ascertain that proper entries for the accrued portion thereof have been made.

Cars on hand should be physically examined and their numbers compared with the daily car record. The ownership of cars in the possession of others for alterations or other purposes should be confirmed by correspondence. The invoices for unsold new cars should be used to verify the prices at which they are taken into the inventory and the second-hand cars should be appraised, but in no case should the appraised values exceed the allowances made to the customers for the cars plus the cost of overhauling them. Usually the dealer incurs a loss on the sale of second-hand cars, and this fact must be considered in passing upon their value for balance-sheet purposes.

Statements of accounts receivable balances, after being stamped with request to communicate directly with the auditors if not correct, should be sent to all customers. Liberal allowance should be made for the probable loss on any old or disputed accounts.

All accounts with manufacturers should be checked against statements received from them. This is important, as allowances are often made to satisfy customers and charged to the manufacturers, but for which the latter will not pass credit to the dealer.

The inventories should be carefully examined, all obsolete parts eliminated, and allowance made for probable loss by falling off in demand for parts of cars manufactured prior to the audit year. In some cases manufacturers agree to keep a certain quantity of parts on hand at the dealers' repair shops. The value of such consignments should either be deducted from the inventory or be shown in a separate ledger account.

The correctness of the cost of work in progress in the dealer's repair shop should be tested by examination of the shop cards. All of the cars, both new and second-hand, on hand at the beginning of and purchased during the audit period should be accounted for as charged against some customer or as still on hand at the close of the period.

Tests should be made of the deliveries from stock to ascertain that parts and supplies are paid for in cash, charged to customers either directly or on shop or road repair cards, or are properly used to repair demonstrating cars and second-hand cars taken in exchange. Charges for shop and road repair work should also be checked.

Time reports of workmen in repair shop and the preparation of pay rolls should be investigated to ascertain that actual work only is paid for, and that it is charged on shop or road repair cards. Office, demonstrating, and general expenses should be vouched and compared with prior periods. Contracts with salesmen should be examined and commissions paid to them verified.

A liberal reserve should be made for free repairs to sold cars, which are usually necessary during the year subsequent to car sales in order to retain the good will of customers, but the cost of which will probably not be collected from the manufacturers.

BRANCH ACCOUNTS

The close relation which exists between a branch house and the parent concern presupposes the existence of complete records or reports at the head office; but it will be necessary for the auditor to ascertain definitely how complete the branch records are and by what system they are reflected in the general books.

Some branches keep a full set of books and furnish regular returns as required by the home office. In such case the latter will have but a current account with the branch in the general books, which will be a controlling account, and will represent the branch's capital, composed of the assets at the branch less the liabilities. Usually such assets will be represented by cash, stock on hand, and accounts receivable, and in preparing the final or consolidated balance sheet, the branch balances must be divided into the various classes of assets of which they are made up. They should never be treated simply as an account receivable. Where a branch is not visited by the auditor, complete reports or returns should be furnished him, properly certified, and so far as may be necessary he should check them into the head office books. All cash remittances included in the branch report, as well as all cash sent from the head office, should be vouched in the general books. A reconciliation of the account between the branch and the head office should be made, either at a particular date during the audit or as of some date within the period under review. The only items affecting such reconciliation will be the cash or invoices in transit, and these should subsequently be vouched to determine the absolute harmony between the two sets of books.

Some concerns allot a permanent cash fund to each branch, and require that all receipts be deposited to the credit of the home office. In such cases it will be necessary to see that the moneys received at the branch appear on the bank statement or pass books as deposited.

When an auditor accepts the certificate of officials or other persons for the verification of assets at branches, he should limit his responsibility by a statement to that effect in his report. He should, however, satisfy himself that all questions of principle, such as valuation of stocks, depreciation, reserve for bad debts, etc., have been properly considered.

Some head offices now have on file duplicates of all records prepared by the branch houses. The latter are able to furnish these by the use of typewriters or other mechanical bookkeeping devices adapted for the purpose. By one operation customers' ledgers are posted, customers' monthly statements are written, and duplicate ledger sheets are prepared for the head office, while duplicate records of cash receipts and disbursements form a cash book with which it is possible to keep in close touch. The facilities thus afforded, whereby instant reference can be had to branch transactions, make possible a most satisfactory branch-house internal audit at the home office.

Goods billed to retail branches by the head office are charged either at cost price, at cost price plus a percentage, or at selling price, inventories in each case being taken on a similar basis. For balance-sheet purposes the auditor should see that the values of the stocks in the last two cases have been reduced to cost or market price.

Schedules of debtors at the branch should be submitted duly certified and the auditor should make certain that all branch liabilities not already shown in the head office books have been taken into account.

In making up a balance sheet of the concern as a whole, the auditor must not overlook the fact that accounts between branches and the home office included in controlling accounts with the ordinary receivables and payables are to be eliminated.

In addition to the points mentioned above, the audit of foreign branches involves the question of exchange, and this requires that the conversion of the various items into domestic currency should be checked and that the difference in exchange ascertained to have been properly handled. In the case of English or French currency, the rate of exchange is sufficiently stable to warrant the accounts being converted on a fixed basis, and the only difference will then be in connection with remittances. Where exchange fluctuates, the value of the fixed assets should be converted into domestic currency at the rate at which actually purchased, the current assets and liabilities at the rate prevailing at the close of the fiscal period, and remittances during the period at the actual rate at which made. If the conversion results in a loss, it should be charged off; if a profit, it is proper and is sometimes considered desirable to carry it forward as a reserve against possible losses in a succeeding period.

CHAPTER XXV

SPECIAL POINTS IN DIFFERENT CLASSES OF AUDITS
(Continued)

PUBLIC UTILITIES

For a number of years there has been a growing tendency toward strict regulation of public service corporations. Wisconsin, the pioneer State in this movement, has for some years had a commission which has done very effective and progressive work in this respect, and New York's Public Service Commissions (there being two, one for the counties of New York, Kings, Queens, and Richmond, and the other for the other counties in the State), which were created in 1907, have also performed good service. Some other States have also created similar commissions or have conferred real power on formerly ineffective governmental bodies which were nominally charged with the duty of regulation, but which were without authority in law to enforce their mandates.

The powers of the various commissions vary. In some States they have large powers, such as the right to grant or deny franchises, to regulate the issue of stocks, bonds, and other evidences of corporate indebtedness, to regulate rates, to issue mandatory orders with reference to operation, etc. One of the powers with which practically all these newer commissions are vested is that of prescribing uniform systems of accounts for the various classes of public service corporations coming under their jurisdiction. This is rightly regarded as an important element in the proper regulation of the conduct of public utilities. Classifications of accounts have been promulgated by the commissions of a number of States for electric railways, gas companies, and electric light, heat, and power companies. These classifications have frequently been prepared after consultation with representatives of such bodies as the American Street and Interurban Railway Accountants' Association and with prominent public accountants and conferences between the commissioners of various States, so that the variations between the classifications prescribed by different States and by the Interstate Commerce Commission (which also exercises jurisdiction over certain classes of public service corporations other than steam railroads) are not material. The principal feature of these classifications which might call for criticism is a tendency toward too minute a subdivision of the operating expenses. To relieve small companies of the burden which would be imposed by requiring them to use in complete detail the prescribed classifications, the classifications have been condensed somewhat for moderate-sized companies, only the very large companies being required to use the classifications in their entirety. The distinction is drawn by making each grade of classification obligatory on companies having gross annual revenues within certain limits.

The earliest, and still most important, instance of governmental regulation of public utilities was the creation of the Interstate Commerce Commission in 1887 to supervise steam railroads transacting an interstate business. The Commission early in its existence began to require the submission by the railroads of annual reports prepared on uniform lines. In 1906, a number of very important amendments were made to the Interstate Commerce Act. The jurisdiction and powers of the Commission were greatly extended. In addition to steam railroads, all electric railways, express companies, sleeping-car companies, carriers by water (as described in the act), pipe lines (excepting water and gas), and telephone companies whose business activities are not confined within the limits of one State, are subject to the Commission's authority. The Commission now has the power to fix maximum rates, a power most far-reaching in its effects, not only on the corporations subject to its authority, but also on the communities whose ability to maintain their commercial supremacy or equality of advantage is dependent on the fixing of fair rates as compared with those enjoyed by competitive points. Another notable broadening of its powers was the conferring of the right to prescribe a uniform system of accounts for each class of corporations subject to its authority, and the enforcement thereof by making deviation therefrom a penal offense. This was an important development of the limited power formerly enjoyed of calling for uniform reports.

A most important feature of the new classification of accounts for steam railroads promulgated after the enactment of the amendments of 1906 is the requirement that periodically entries be made for depreciation of equipment. It may well be expected that in time depreciation charges will also be required to be made for all other parts of the physical property which are subject to depreciation or gradual exhaustion. This recognition by a governmental body of a fundamental accounting principle is gratifying to accountants, who stood for years practically alone in their advocacy of the need for depreciation charges in the accounts of railroads and all other public utilities.

State Legislatures can, and in some cases already have, enacted laws delegating to commissions or municipalities the power to fix the rates to be charged by public service corporations operating within the State. Under these circumstances the auditor has responsibilities additional to those which simply consider the stockholders. In a sense he stands between the company and the public. Should depreciation allowances and other necessary reserves be omitted from the accounts, the apparent profits shown will be larger than is actually the case and may result in an agitation for a reduction in rates charged to consumers which the real facts in the case do not justify. In the ensuing litigation it will probably be very difficult to convince either judge or jury that depreciation charges, etc., which were not made at the proper time should now be allowed as an element in the cost of operation. On the other hand, if the reserves for depreciation and the like are excessive, the profits will be shown at less than their real figures and the public will be deceived.

The importance of this subject was recognized at a national gathering of public accountants as long ago as 1904, when a paper on the subject was read and a special committee was appointed to consider the matter. This committee later reported as follows:

> The committee appointed at the Congress of Accountants, held at St. Louis, U. S. A., in September, 1904, to review the paper by Robert H. Montgomery, C. P. A., upon "The Importance of Uniform Practice in Determining the Profits of Public Service Corporations Where Municipalities Have the Power to Regulate Rates," having taken the paper into consideration, have come to the following conclusions, and now beg to state the same as their opinion upon the questions raised:
>
> I. A distinction must be made between the profits of an undertaking

rom the point of view of the general community and the profits available 'or dividends from the point of view of a corporation owning such under-aking. The former would be the net earnings from the operation of the undertaking, after providing for all waste or depreciation of capital assets arising directly out of such operation; while the latter would be arrived at only after providing also for any possible loss on capital assets arising from causes not directly incident to such operation and for interest on borrowed money.

II. The net earnings of a public utility with which the general community is concerned are determined by the excess of gross earnings over expenses, defining the latter terms as follows: Gross earnings consist of the charges for all services rendered during the period as distinguished from mere receipts, but would exclude incidental earnings not arising out of the operation of the utility, such as interest on investments.

Expenses consist of: (1) The direct cost of operation and of maintenance (ordinary repairs), expenses of management and provisions for bad debts, damage claims and rebates, as well as extraordinary expenses incurred during the period, such as legal charges, etc., but they should not include interest on borrowed money, discounts on bonds issued, or other charges in connection with the promotion or financing of the undertaking. (2) Depreciation: (a) On plant—physical—covering wear and tear, including direct requirements for renewals, etc., arising both from known and probable causes, such as electrolysis, etc. (b) On plant—indirect—due to obsolescence and the like, but not that due to a fall in value from general causes. (c) On other capital assets which are diminishing in value as a direct result of the operation of the property, such as moneys properly expended in acquiring from the local authorities the franchise under which the utility is operated where such franchise is, as is usually the case, terminable after a certain number of years; or cost of mines, quarries, or other similar properties which are being used up continuously for the purpose of operating the utility. But there should not be included any provision for recouping promoters' profit or other watered capital, or for possible loss by reason of a general fall in values, etc., on the purchase at the end of the franchise of the whole undertaking by the public authorities, i. e., the State or municipality.

III. In dealing with the private accounts of a corporation operating the utility, earnings will also embrace miscellaneous receipts, if any, not connected with the actual operations of the undertaking, and the following additional expenses should be allowed for before arriving at a balance available for distribution:

(1) Depreciation: An additional amount to cover any excess of the book value of good will, franchise, and plant over that provided for under section 2, subsection (c) above, or over the sum it may be expected to realize on the expiry of the franchise.

(2) Interest: On bonds or other funded or floating debt.

IV. In determining the rates which should be charged to the public, regard must be had (a) to the profit ascertainable under section II, and (b) to further charges specified under section III, which would have to be borne by the corporation out of such profits. For instance, if eight per cent per annum on the capital invested is considered a reasonable rate for a corporation to earn, taking into consideration the risks in section III, then the rates should be fixed so as to allow of a profit of eight per cent calculated as laid down in section II, and out of this profit the corporation would have to provide for the risks and expenses stated in section III.

A. Lowes Dickinson, Ernest Reckitt,
Elijah W. Sells, John B. Niven,
Harvey S. Chase, Robert H. Montgomery, *Chairman.*

One of the most vital questions confronting the auditor of public utility accounts is the separation of all expenditures into the two classes of capital and revenue, or—as they are more often termed in practice—construction and maintenance. Frequently expenditures are of such a nature that it is open to debate as to whether they belong in the one class or the other.

A factor which contributes to make the distinction difficult is that most public service corporations, particularly railways and light and power plants, do not have any but very extensive additions to plant made by outside contractors. The work is done, under the direction of their own engineers, by their own workmen. As these same forces also do the current maintenance work and use the same kinds of materials for construction as for maintenance purposes, it is practically impossible to determine merely from the nature of the labor and material expenditures whether they are capital or revenue charges.

The only satisfactory solution of the problem is for the company to keep such cost accounts of its construction work as will relate the expenditures to the thing done or accomplished. It is then possible for the auditor to satisfy himself by conference with the company's engineer, as well as by his experience with other engagements in the same field, whether or not the capital charges are proper. Unfortunately, many companies do not keep such construction cost records, though all should. Where they are lacking, one of the best things for the auditor to do is to have the engineering department submit a statement of the construction work done during the period under review and the legitimate cost of each part thereof. Such a statement will usually be of material assistance in passing on expenditures which have been charged to capital account. The best managed companies have a system of "Construction Authorizations" which are prepared by the engineering staff and approved by the board of directors or executive committee. These authorizations form the best basis for construction cost accounts.

Charges for additional equipment are usually more easily traced, and there is not, as a rule, much difficulty in coming to a conclusion as to whether the charges should go to capital or revenue.

While it is advisable that in cases of doubt the decision be in favor of the conservative policy of charging the items in doubt to maintenance, yet excessively conservative practice must also be avoided, as it increases the apparent cost of service rendered and consequently is unjust to the consumers.

There is no question but that the cost of the original plant and all extensions and additions are proper capital charges. Reconstruction expenditures frequently give occasion to much doubt as to their proper apportionment. If the reconstruction has resulted in increased capacity, some portion thereof is properly chargeable to capital. The most equitable plan is to charge to capital the reconstruction cost and eliminate therefrom the cost of the construction work or equipment which has been replaced. The result is that the plant always stands on the books at the last cost, i. e., the cost of the plant as it stands at the present time. In cases involving the determination of rates which are equitable to the consumers and yet at the same time yield a fair return on the actual investment, it is certainly most satisfactory to have the investment in plant appearing at the cost of the present plant, and not at the cost of the plant as it was at some earlier date.

In considering the question of a proper charge for depreciation of plant, which is an element in the cost of service rendered (see Section II, subsection 2 (a) of the report supra), it would seem that it should be based on the cost of the plant in operation. This would necessarily include the last cost of any parts of the plant which might have been reconstructed or replaced since its original construction.

While there is necessarily a different classification of accounts for each of the various classes of public utilities, the general principles underlying all of them are the same. A committee of the American Association of Public Accountants submitted to the 1907 convention of the Association the following:

STANDARD SCHEDULE OF REVENUE AND EXPENSE

(Income and Expenditure)

For Municipal Industries and Public Service Corporations

Revenue from Operating		
Gross Earnings from Public Services		$..........
Gross Earnings from Private Consumers		....
Gross Earnings from By-Products, etc.		....
Total		$..........
Deduct Rebates, Refunds, Discounts, etc.		....
Total Revenue from Operating		$..........
Expense of Operating		
1. Expense of Manufacture:		
Operation	$..........	
Maintenance	....	
Product Purchased (Gas, etc.)	....	
2. Expense of Distribution:		
Operation	....	
Maintenance	....	
3. General Expense (Salaries, Office Supplies and Expenses)	....	
Total (1, 2, and 3)	$..........	
4. Taxes (Real Estate and Other)	....	
5. Franchise Taxes (paid or accrued annually or otherwise)	....	
6. Rentals (Leaseholds, etc.)	....	
7. Insurance (Fire, Accident, and Fiduciary)	....	
8. Damages (including Extraordinary Legal and Other Expenses and Losses)	....	
9. Guaranty (Bad Debts Written Off and Reserve for Doubtful Accounts)	....	
10. Depreciation (Deterioration Written Off and Reserve for Estimated Depreciation)	....	
Total Expense of Operating		$..........
a. Net Revenue from Operating (or Deficiency)		$..........
b. Other Revenue or Income, net (from Sources Other Than Operating)		....
c. Appropriations for Operating, Provided by the Municipality from General Funds		....
Total Available Income		$..........
Disposition of Available Income		
11. Interest on Funded and Floating Debts		....
Remainder of Available Income		$..........
12. Reserved for Sinking Funds	$..........	
13. Reserved for Amortization Funds	....	
14. Reserved for Other Funds	....	
Total Reserves	$..........	
15. Dividends (Private Plants)	....	
16. Appropriation to General City Funds (Public Plants)	....	
Total disposition of Available Income		$..........
Credit (or Debit) balance transferable to "Surplus"		$ ....

NOTE.—The various items in this condensed statement (particularly expense items 1, 2, and 3) should be supported by detailed schedules.

This is a condensed form suitable for any form of public utility—railway, gas, electric light and power, water works, or telephone—and would be accompanied by schedules giving the details pertaining to the particular utility for which used. It would be especially useful in comparing the operations of different undertakings, as it brings out quite distinctly those items whose treatment is a matter of judgment, such as depreciation, or which for any other reason may be considered as "variables."

The exhaustive report of the National Civic Federation on "Municipal and Private Operation of Public Utilities," issued in 1907, will be of both interest and value to the accountant who wishes to devote especial attention to the accounts of public service corporations.

The tendency of legislation for the regulation of rates to be charged by public service corporations is to limit them to such rates as will not yield more than a moderate return on the capital actually invested. As the accounts of but very few companies have been kept in such a way as to exhibit clearly or conclusively the cost of the plant, not to mention proper allowances for depreciation, one of the first steps when fixing of rates, renewal of franchises, or similar negotiations are under consideration, is to have the property appraised. The following suggestions for the making of such an appraisal are quoted from Mr. Henry Floy's recent book on "The Valuation of Public Utility Properties."

APPRAISALS OF PUBLIC UTILITIES

Suggested Procedure: A valuation, to be complete in the fullest sense, must take into consideration not alone the original cost, present value, or cost of reproduction of the physical plant, but also the intangible and non-physical values, the limitations of franchise, as well as the market quotation of securities. To complete a valuation of such broad scope, the following method of procedure is suggested:

(*a*) Obtain from the proper officials of the company data, drawings, and specifications covering original construction as well as later additions, also lists of material and supplies, and if available, a complete inventory of all existing physical property. Where inventories are incomplete, as is usually the case, they must be completed by field inspection, and in every case verified and checked. How thoroughly and with what detail inspection may be necessary depends on the thoroughness of the appraisal being made. For example, test holes may have to be sunk in order to verify information as to excavation, foundations, buried pipes, duct lines, or other subsurface structures. The size, quantity, and condition of all physical property must be determined.

(*b*) Obtain available data as to costs and prices by examination of corporation vouchers, not only for the period in which the appraisal is being made, but covering also original cost. Classify the cost of different materials and labor, in accordance with that method which will enable a convenient and easy comparison for the appraisal work in hand. Particular attention should be given to expenditures during the early history of the company covering items that may properly be qualified as "Development Expenses," such as interest, taxes, and similar expenses during construction, checking the cost as ascertained from vouchers with the book cost. The two are not likely to agree, due to destruction of old records, accidentally or otherwise, and the fact that expenditures may have been made and no vouchers received therefor.

(*c*) Examine the record books of the corporation, ascertaining therefrom all information as to the issuance of stocks, bonds, or other forms of indebtedness, the cash received therefrom, records of transactions of the officials in authorizing contracts, and the prices thereof.

(*d*) A personal inspection and examination must be made of a physical property by the individual in charge of the appraisal work, and a more or less detailed acquaintance had with the plant and the conditions under which it is operating, even though the working out of detailed information is left to one's subordinates.

(*e*) Determine the unit prices to be used and the percentages to be allowed in connection therewith; the fixing of unit prices and percentages to be added depends upon the basis adopted for the prices themselves.

(*f*) Using the completed inventory, the unit prices determined upon are to be applied and the work carefully checked to avoid errors. Two inventories and two sets of unit prices may be necessary if both the original cost and the cost of reproduction are being determined. To the totals obtained from applying the unit prices to the inventory should be added the percentages for engineering, contingencies, and administration or superintendence during construction, etc., in order to obtain the cost of the physical plant.

(*g*) If the depreciated or present value is desired, the amount of depreciation must be determined in accordance with the principles laid down in the chapter on "Depreciation" and this sum deducted from the cost, giving the present value of the physical plant.

(*h*) Investigate the actual operating conditions, method of serving the public, rates charged, system of providing for depreciation, and maintenance of the property.

(*i*) Ascertain the limiting conditions in the Articles of Incorporation, charters, franchises, municipal contracts, or other governing obligations, determine whether local conditions are such as to promise fair treatment and a bright future for the corporation, or whether its business is likely to be interfered with, either through competition or popular opposition.

(*j*) Development expenses are determined from a consideration of the time necessarily consumed in building the plant under consideration, the rate of interest, taxes, and other such expenses, with proper allowance for remuneration to the original promoters of the enterprise.

(*k*) Consideration should be had as to whether good will, franchise, or going value should be allowed for, and if so, the amount may be determined from a consideration of the matters set forth in another chapter.

(*l*) The sum of the physical plant value plus the development expenses, plus the value of franchise, good will, going value, or contracts, if any, will result in a sum representing one fair value.

The items to be determined in making a valuation to ascertain the total fair value of a utility property may be diagrammatically summarized as follows:

Net cost of physical plant. Contractor's profit. Engineering. Contingencies, etc.	**Structural value.**	
Expenses preliminary to beginning plant construction. Overhead expenses during construction. Working capital. Superseded plant.	Development expenses.	**Total value.**
Franchises. Good will. Going value. Contracts.	Intangible value	

STEAM RAILROADS

Taken as a whole, railroad accounting has probably reached a higher degree of standardization of accounting than any other branch of industry or commerce. The uniform reports called for by the Interstate Commerce Commission for the past twenty-five years, and the authority which the Commission has exercised for the past five years of not only prescribing uniform reports, but the accounts to be kept, and forbidding any deviation from the prescribed classifications, have undoubtedly contributed to a considerable extent to this result. On the other hand, it is to be noted that some of the Commission's instructions have not been based on sound accounting principles. For instance, the classification of construction expenditures which was in effect for many years permitted bond discount to be capitalized and charged to construction. The latest classification, however, recognizes the force of the accountant's contention that discount is nothing else than interest paid in advance and consequently cannot properly be permanently capitalized, and the present classification forbids the capitalizing of discount on bonds. It is generally admitted that the classifications now in force are based on sound accounting principles.

In England one requirement of the Railways Act is that before a dividend can be paid auditors must certify the semiannual accounts. In recent years the number of American railroads having their accounts audited by public accountants has considerably increased. In time, no doubt, stockholders will insist more firmly on an independent verification of the accounts submitted by the management.

As with all public service corporations, one of the most vital points in auditing railroad accounts is to establish the correctness, or otherwise, of the apportionment of expenditures as between capital and income, or, as it is also termed, construction and maintenance. The true condition of a company's operations and finances has probably been more often concealed by either manipulation or lack of good judgment in making charges to capital accounts than in any other one way. In the case of many large railroads the auditor's problem of satisfying himself that the apportionment of expenditures as between construction and maintenance has been correctly made, while by no means entirely solved, is somewhat simplified by the fact that construction work is usually done under a department other than the one charged with ordinary maintenance work.

The prime consideration in connection with the verification of income, and the one in which an audit of railroad accounts differs from an ordinary audit, is the audit of the traffic earnings. These fall into two general classes, viz., freight and passenger. The principal data from which the traffic earning accounts are built up are the periodical reports from station agents of freight received and forwarded, tickets sold, etc. Also of importance are reports from "foreign" (other) roads, train conductors' reports of cash fares collected, car records showing the movement of cars out on foreign lines or foreign cars on the company's own lines. From the last-named records are calculated the charge against or credits accruing to foreign roads for equipment "away from home." An important item of indirect income, i. e., a refund of expenses paid out, consists of the charges to other roads for repairs made to their cars while in temporary use by the company whose accounts are being audited. Shop reports are the usual basis for these charges.

In the case of large railroad systems it is manifestly impossible for the professional auditor to examine in any reasonable length of time all the original reports and other data which form the basis of the traffic earning accounts. Also in view of the fact that almost every road has a highly organized auditing department whose duty it is to conduct a continuous internal audit, it is not necessary or even desirable that he should attempt to do so. The system in force should be carefully studied to make sure that by its use an effective check on the station agents, ticket offices, and others handling funds for the company's account is maintained. Sufficient tests should also be made by comparison of original reports with the summaries into which their various totals are carried, etc., to assure the auditor that the system is being faithfully carried out.

Reports from station agents, in addition to forming the basis of the traffic earning accounts, are of service in certifying that asset appearing in the balance sheet as "Due from Agents." Every agent makes a report, at least monthly, of the account between the company and himself, showing thereon *inter alia* the uncollected freight bills and the balance due the company for collections made, but not yet remitted. The balance due from each agent per the company's books should be verified by reference to the agent's last report. Frequently the two will not be in exact agreement owing to remittances in transit, suspense items, etc. A reconcilement of the book balance with the report should, however, be in evidence.

The importance of verifying the balances purporting to be due from agents cannot be better emphasized than by referring to a case which received wide attention in the newspapers a few years ago. The treasurer of a constituent company of one of the largest systems in the country confessed to having embezzled over $500,000. While a full explanation of the manner in which the funds were abstracted and the defalcation concealed for a period of years was never made public, it was stated in general terms that the treasurer had tampered with the agents' accounts. It would certainly seem that if the internal audit of the agents' accounts had been intelligently and faithfully conducted, the theft could not have been concealed for any considerable length of time. Had the accounts been periodically audited by professional accountants, the embezzlement would in all likelihood either never have begun or would have been detected before the amount had reached large proportions.

With reference to depreciation charges, it may be stated that the Interstate Commerce Commission has made them compulsory for equipment, but not for track or structures. It is still optional with the railroad management whether or not any depreciation at all shall be charged for accruing renewals or obsolesence of track and structures.

While the railroad audit includes many other points, some of them of extreme importance, they are not sufficiently different from those obtaining in other lines of business to call for special treatment at this time.

Valuable papers on steam railroad accounts were presented by Professor Henry C. Adams (connected with the Interstate Commerce Commission) and Arthur W. Teele, C. P. A., to the Atlantic City convention of the American Association of Public Accountants. They are to be found in the Association's 1908 "Year Book."

The following extract from an article in a financial paper summarizes a number of the important points to be covered in auditing railroad accounts:

> No one doubts that the Baltimore and Ohio of to-day is a magnificent property. But that is all the more reason why it should seem very strange that some of those who are still in the board should apparently have forgotten the experience of sixteen years ago. Early in September of 1896, despite the profit and loss surplus of $23,737,000 then existing, Stephen Little was employed to go over the old Baltimore and Ohio's books. Before the end of that month the announcement that a receiver had been appointed for the company came like a bolt out of the blue. In his report Mr. Little gave the following causes for the Baltimore and Ohio's trouble:
>
> 1. The inflation or overstatement of net income.
> 2. The mischarge of worn-out equipment to profit and loss.
> 3. The capitalization of charges to income.
> 4. The capitalization of so-called improvements and betterments of leased lines.
> 5. The payment of unearned dividends.
> 6. The understatement of liabilities, etc.

SHIPPING COMPANIES

Previous to 1911 there was no recognized uniform classification of accounts for shipping companies. The Interstate Commerce Commission now provides very comprehensive classifications of accounts for carriers by water under its jurisdiction.

Shipping-company accounts do not differ materially from those used in ordinary commercial undertakings. However, there are some points in connection with shipping accounts which are of interest. It is customary to arrange them so that the income and expenses of each trip can be stated separately. To each voyage, therefore, its fair share of shore expenses must be allocated besides a proportion of such expenses applying directly to specific vessels, but which cover periods longer than a single voyage. The ascertainment of such amounts often involves considerable detail.

Some shipping companies do business entirely with vessels chartered from their owners. The many forms of these hire-agreements, or "charter-parties," as they are called, make it imperative that the auditor should carefully examine such agreements as may still be in force at the time of the audit.

The auditor should ascertain that all revenues from freight traffic and passenger service have been accounted for, also all moneys due from the government for mail service and from express companies; that all maintenance expenses have been charged as such, and not included in the cost of vessels; that proper provision has been made for depreciation; that all liabilities have been provided for, also any unearned income; that returns of insurance premiums due on account of the "laying up" of any vessel have been obtained.

The Interstate Commerce Commission regulations distinctly require that provisions for depreciation of vessels shall be made. In many cases in the past it was customary not to make provision for depreciation. This was especially so with owners of single ships.

Another custom which has become quite general is that of a company's providing its own insurance fund instead of placing all its insurance with underwriting companies. In such cases the amounts which would be paid to the insurance companies are set aside and a fund created to take care of losses and damages. It is advisable that these amounts should be segregated from other funds and invested in securities which have a ready market. All repairs and replacements which were the result of perils of the sea and the vessels' proportion of general averages would be paid from this fund.

It is quite obvious that only such companies as own a large number of vessels, and can consequently distribute the risk, are really warranted in carrying any part of their own insurance. Even in such cases it is universally recognized that at least a part of each risk should be placed with outside underwriters.

Even when the risk is well distributed, it sometimes happens that the total loss of a large vessel in excess of the outside insurance carried will be greater than the amount accumulated in the company's own insurance fund. In such cases the question arises whether it is proper to carry the debit balance of the insurance fund into the balance sheet as an asset. It is sometimes argued that this is legitimate, especially if the amount is not so large as to preclude the possibility of its being eliminated by future credits within a reasonably short period of time. Such an argument is fallacious, however, as the overdraft on the insurance fund has absolutely no value at the date of the balance sheet and in no way benefits future operations, which would be the only justification for entering among the assets an item which has no present value. If it is desired to preserve the identity of the insurance fund, even though it has been exhausted, the proper procedure would be to show the debit balance thereof in the balance sheet as a distinct item, but deducting it "in short" from the surplus or profit and loss account with an appropriate explanation.

ELECTRIC RAILWAYS

One of the earliest attempts by an unofficial organization to secure the adoption of a uniform system of accounts for any industry was made in 1898, when a committee of the Street Railway Accountants' Association of America (now known as the American Electric Railway Accountants' Association) prepared a standard classification of accounts for street railways. Many street railway companies adopted this classification, and it was also prescribed by the railroad commissioners of a number of States for use in preparing reports submitted by railways under their jurisdiction.

Several years ago the Interstate Commerce Commission

issued a more elaborate classification. As this classification was devised in consultation with the Railway Accountants' Association, and has since also been made the basis of classifications promulgated by State commissions, it is largely taking the place of the earlier classification, which had done good service. It should be borne in mind that, excepting in those States in which commissions having authority to prescribe accounting systems for public utilities have adopted the Interstate Commerce Commission's classification, adoption of the latter's classification is obligatory only on such railways as do an interstate business.

Even in those classifications which differ from that of the Interstate Commerce Commission, it will be found that the differences are more frequently in details than in any essentials. The grouping of the detailed accounts is well nigh universal into the general classes of

Maintenance: Way and Structures.
Equipment.
Conducting Transportation:
Power.
Operation of Cars.
General and Miscellaneous.

The auditor will naturally familiarize himself with the classification in use before beginning his audit.

The revenue of an electric railway is largely on a cash basis, the principal exceptions being sales of tickets to city departments or the Post Office Department or isolated cases of very large ticket users having recognized financial standing, advertising in cars, sales of scrap and other old material, and, in the case of railways carrying freight, accounts with large shippers having good credit. Traffic sheets are made up for each day showing the different runs and the amount of cash fares, tickets, and passes turned in by each conductor. The totals of these sheets should be traced into the cash book. The traffic sheets themselves should be tested by comparing therewith conductors' reports for days in different parts of the period under review. A further test, which is of a reciprocal nature, is to compare the names of conductors on the pay roll with the names on the traffic sheets to see that some amount is entered on the latter for each conductor appearing on the pay roll. While this comparison does not establish the correctness of the amounts entered on the traffic sheets, it would result in the detection of the total omission of the receipts of any conductor. On the other hand, it would reveal any padding of the pay roll as far as conductors are concerned. Indirectly, it also places a check on the number of motormen on the pay roll, as these two classes of carmen should, of course, be in a proper proportion to each other. Traffic receipts should be in evidence for every day in the year.

Receipts from ticket sales can frequently be verified in total by reference to the serial numbers of the first and last tickets sold during the period. Complications in the shape of tickets in the hands of conductors at beginning and end of the period will sometimes be encountered, but these will usually not interfere with verifying the ticket sales, at least approximately.

The earnings from advertising in cars and waiting-rooms are to be verified. Usually this is not a difficult matter. More often than not, a contract for the entire advertising space is made with an agency for a fixed sum per annum. Under such circumstances the verification of the income from this source is exceedingly simple.

Miscellaneous receipts from sales of scrap and similar sources will need to receive careful attention. As they are received at irregular times, failure to account for them could more easily escape attention than in the case of regular traffic receipts. All receipts of whatsoever nature should be deposited in bank. No railway with a well-devised accounting system permits payments to be made from traffic or other receipts.

The treatment of ticket sales in the accounts should receive attention. Theoretically the proceeds of tickets sold may properly be included among the traffic earnings only when the tickets have been collected. Until that time they should appear to the credit of an unearned or deferred income account, which is to be included among the liabilities in stating the balance sheets. As the tickets are sold, the receipts therefrom are credited to the liability account referred to, and at regular intervals, say, monthly, transfers are made therefrom to the credit of earnings for the value of the tickets collected.

In cases where the ticket sales form a very small proportion of the total traffic receipts, the outstanding tickets would be a negligible quantity and no great harm will be done if tickets are treated as earnings when sold. With many companies, however, the outstanding tickets aggregate large amounts, and it is certainly not correct accounting to include among the earnings cash received for service which has not yet been rendered to the company's patrons. Attention is also called to the fact that inaccuracies in the gross earnings, due to the inclusion therein of ticket sales before the tickets have been used, are greatest for some time after forms of tickets or methods of selling them have been changed or when special tickets are sold for a limited period.

As is naturally to be expected, the most important single feature of the audit of the expenditures is the verification of the apportionment between capital and income. This is frequently a most difficult matter, owing to the fact that the nature of many of the expenditures is identical, whether they be for extensions or for maintenance, i. e., they will be for materials and labor, and the items on their face do not indicate conclusively in which category they properly fall.

If a system of recording construction and equipment costs is in use, the auditor will be able to satisfy himself as to the propriety of the construction charges much more readily than when such records are lacking. Unfortunately many companies—probably a majority—do not have such records. The keeping of them does not, as a rule, entail an undue amount of work, and, where not already in use, the auditor should recommend their installation. The essentials are that a separate account, usually in a subsidiary ledger, be opened for each distinctive piece of construction work undertaken and for each addition made to the equipment. All construction charges should find their way into this ledger. In the general ledger the expenditures, storeroom charges, etc., would be debited to a controlling account called, say, Construction in Progress. As a specific piece of construction work is completed, the total shown in the account therefor in the subsidiary ledger would be transferred by journal entry from the Construction in Progress account to the appropriate account or accounts in the classification of construction accounts in the general books. Under this plan the entries for charges to construction accounts show what they are really for and what additions to the company's roadway, structures, or equipment have really been made. The total of the expenditures made on uncompleted construction work appears on the general ledger in the Construction in Progress account, and the details may be referred to in the construction cost ledger.

Where construction records have not been kept, the auditor will find it necessary to consult with the company's engineer and use such other means as are available to get definite information as to just what has been accomplished by the expenditures charged to capital accounts. Having supplemented in this way the data furnished by the books, he will then have to decide whether the company was warranted in charging the expenditures against capital rather than against earnings.

Depreciation of plant—or, if the word "depreciation" has an unpleasant sound, the term "accruing renewals and replacements" may be substituted—is a most important subject in connection with electric railways. Up to a few years ago railway operators, and especially promoters, would not admit that there was any necessity whatever for the inclusion of depreciation charges in the operating accounts. Their stock argument was that the franchises increased in value more rapidly than the physical property deteriorated, and consequently there was no depreciation in the property as a whole. The fact that the increase in franchise values would not produce funds wherewith to make replacements when they were finally needed was ignored. Since the repeated puncturing of this fallacy by the bankruptcy of companies which proceeded on such an unsound basis, railway operators have reluctantly come to admit the necessity for taking account of depreciation, until at the present time practically all engineers of high standing consider it as an item of operating expense. It is a satisfaction that the correctness of a principle for which at one time almost no one but accountants contended has at last been recognized. In cases where companies have not made any allowance for accruing depreciation, the auditor is not warranted in giving a certificate unless it contains a qualification plainly calling attention to the omission of depreciation allowances.

So-called reconstruction expenditures, when no depreciation reserve has been provided against which they can be charged, sometimes present a perplexing problem. Frequently they are the result of the omission over a period of years to make renewals as they are needed, and thus, when extensive expenditures for the rehabilitation of the property are finally imperative, they really represent an accumulation of long-deferred maintenance charges. It is manifestly unfair to charge the entire amount of the expenditures against the operations of the particular year in which they happen to be made. On the other hand, if they are but accumulated maintenance charges, the mere size thereof does not justify capitalizing them. Then, too, the problem is usually complicated by the fact that the expenditures usually result in some increase in the carrying capacity of the road. The worn-out rolling stock is replaced with larger units, heavier rails are laid, and power-plant equipment of increased capacity is installed.

The proper treatment of reconstruction charges is to charge to capital such part thereof as represents an increased value in the reconstructed part of the property over the original cost of the property replaced; such part of the expenditure as represents a fair or normal annual maintenance charge should be debited to operating; and such part as represents the making good of neglected maintenance applying to prior years should be treated as a special charge against profit and loss.

When such reconstruction expenditures are made by a company after the purchase of a dilapidated property, it is assumed that in fixing the purchase price allowance was made for the expenditures required to be made to place the property in good operating condition. Consequently, under such circumstances the entire amount of the reconstruction expenditures are considered to be a proper capital charge. It is to be borne in mind that especially under such circumstances it is essential that depreciation allowances be included in the accounts. Otherwise, with the abnormally low maintenance expenditures which will naturally follow during the first few years after extensive reconstruction, the showing of net earnings will be misleading.

It should be borne in mind that there is danger in capitalizing charges for betterments which do not increase earnings nor decrease operating expenses. On the other hand, in view of rate regulation it is not safe to wipe off all such expenditures. The situation can perhaps best be met by capitalizing the charges and segregating a liberal proportion of the surplus to prevent the payment of unwarranted dividends.

The liability for unsettled damages to persons and property always needs to be thoroughly investigated. In practically all cases some suits will be found to be under way or threatened, and in addition, consideration should be given to all accidents for which releases have not yet been obtained, even though suit has not been entered. Large companies have a special claim department, from which the desired information can be obtained, and for smaller companies a letter from the company's attorney should be obtained stating all unadjusted claims and the probable cost of settlement.

Many companies create an accident reserve by crediting to such an account and charging to operating expenses a certain percentage of the gross earnings. Payments in settlement of claims are charged against the reserve. This plan is preferable to that of charging accident payments directly to operating expenses, as it equalizes the charge to successive fiscal periods and, if the charge is ample, creates a reserve for those claims which are unsettled at the end of each period. The plan must be intelligently used. Some companies use too low a percentage and carry the resulting debit balance in the reserve account along from one period to another as a deferred charge to operations. Obviously, payments for accidents occurring in one period are not of the slightest benefit to the operations of a future period, and if a debit balance develops in an accident reserve account, it should be forthwith written off. Such a condition is sometimes due to an unusually serious and costly accident, which is not likely to occur again soon, and it may not be necessary to raise the percentage of gross earnings credited to the accident reserve. As already stated, however, the overdraft in the reserve account should be immediately written off, as it is not an asset in any sense of the word.

The extensive development of the interurban electric railway field during the past decade has resulted in conditions which in some respects are perhaps even more analogous to those of steam railroads than to those of the city electric railway. With considerable mileage, a large freight and express business, graduated rates of fare for passenger traffic, etc., an efficient auditing department as a part of the company's organization is a necessity. This department will naturally audit the details of the company's operations, and the professional auditor's duty with respect to this part of the work will ordinarily be limited to such tests and investigation as will satisfy him that the prescribed system is being followed and that the client's interests are safeguarded in every way possible.

TAXICAB COMPANIES

In auditing a taxicab company, the procedure would be much the same as for an ordinary manufacturing company, excepting the verification of its chief source of income—the charges for service rendered.

The taxicabs, as the name indicates, are equipped with taximeters. These show both the total mileage and the revenue miles, i. e., the mileage run during the time the cab is carrying passengers.

Most companies keep what is called a master's sheet or some record showing the car number, the time out and in, and the reading of the meter, both as to revenue and total miles. When the cab leaves the garage, the reading is entered on the sheet, and on its return, the reading is again taken and entered alongside of the first or "out" reading. The difference in the revenue miles reading represents the revenue miles run and has to be accounted for by the driver of the cab, either in cash or by proper evidence of having carried a charge customer. With the larger companies most of the calls originate at some hotel or at a stand where there is a starter employed by the company. It is the starter's duty to determine whether or not the customer has an account, and if so, he signs a ticket which is given to the driver, so that the driver turns in either cash or tickets for all fares. By most companies any shortages are deducted from the drivers' wages.

Each driver is provided with a daily card, which should show the same mileage as the master's sheet, but in addition gives the details of the call. The cash received from this source is entered in a cash-fares column in the cash book and the charges are posted from the tickets to the customers' ledgers, the total being posted through a journal to the general ledger. In some cases these charges are written up on sheets, or a journal, and posted to the ledgers therefrom.

It would not be practicable for the auditor to check the accuracy of all of the entries, but a thorough test should be made for a certain period. The total cash fares and charges should be checked with the drivers' cards. The mileage shown by the drivers' cards should be checked with the master's sheets, and the "out" readings of the mileage should be compared with the "in" readings of the previous day. The latter is important, as it would be an easy matter, if collusion existed, for the starter at the garage to add several miles to the "out" readings or to deduct several miles from the "in" readings, which, if the driver used the same figures on his card, would give him less mileage to account for.

Many companies keep mileage records. Where this is not done, it would be well, in connection with the checking of the master's sheets, to make a list of the mileage, both revenue and total, and compare the ratio of the one to the other for the period investigated. There are many expenses which should vary directly as the mileage. Tires sometimes are rented on a mileage basis. Using the mile as the unit and stating the earnings and expenses per mile, especially when such results can be compared with the results of another period, enables the auditor to uncover many discrepancies.

In the verification of the pay rolls, disbursements, purchases, sundry sales of gasoline and supplies, storage, etc., the procedure should be the same as in any other business.

Depreciation is an important item, but it should be borne in mind that a good taxicab can be renewed in large part, and where tires and motors and other repairs are being charged against operations, a reserve of only fifteen to twenty per cent is sufficient to cover all depreciation in a going concern.

As an illustration of the accounts to be found in a taxicab company, the following form of balance sheet and statement of earnings and expenses is presented:

THE TAXICAB COMPANY

STATEMENT OF EARNINGS AND EXPENSES

For the Month of June, 1912, and for the Six Months ended June 30, 1912

Earnings	Month of June, 1912	Six Months Ended June 30, 1912
Motor Car Earnings	....	....
Miscellaneous Earnings	....	....
	....	....
Deductions:		
Refunds and Allowances	....	....
Net Earnings	....	....
Expenses		
Vehicle Operation	....	....
Garage Operation	....	....
Maintenance	....	....
Rent and Insurance	....	....
Taximeters	....	....
Hired Equipment	....	....
Licenses	....	....
Commissions	....	....
Free Riding	....	....
General Expenses	....	....
	....	....
Reserves:		
Motor Cars	....	....
Equipment	....	....
Repair Stock	....	....
Injuries and Damages	....	....
Bad Debts	....	....
Chauffeurs' Clothing	....	....
Total Expenses	....	....
Current Operating Profit:		
Motor Department	....	....
Additions to Income:		
Interest on Deposits	....	....
Discounts Earned	....	....
Total Income	....	....
Deductions from Income:		
Interest on Bonds	....	....
Interest on Notes	....	....
Discount on Bonds	....	....
Organization Expenses	....	....
Total Deductions	....	....
Net Profit	....	....

THE TAXICAB COMPANY

COMPARATIVE BALANCE SHEET, AS AT DECEMBER 31, 1912, AND 1911

Assets	1912 Dec. 31	1911 Dec. 31
Cash:		
In Bank		
Cashier (Receipts not deposited)		
Petty Cash Funds		
Accounts and Notes Receivable:		
Customers		
Sundry Accounts		
Notes Receivable		
Chauffeurs' Accounts		
Inventory, Supplies, etc.		
Deposits:		
John Jones Co.		
William Smith Co.		
Deferred Charges:		
Commissions prepaid		
Insurance do		
Licenses do		
Rent do		
Taxes do		
Building Repairs and Alterations Rented Premises		
Plant:		
Motor Cabs		
Equipment:		
Garage Equipment		
Shop Machinery and Tools		
Office Furniture and Fixtures		
Stand Equipment		
Motor Cab Accessories		
Chauffeurs' Clothing		
Good Will		
Total Assets		

Liabilities—Capital	1912 Dec. 31	1911 Dec. 31
Notes and Accounts Payable:		
Notes Payable		
Sundry Vendors		
Employees' Deposits		
Unclaimed Wages		
Accrued Items:		
Pay Rolls		
Interest Payable on Notes		
Do do Bonds		
Commissions		
Taxes		
Rent		
Sundry Expenses		
Coupons Outstanding		
First Mortgage on Equipment		
Reserves:		
Depreciation on Motor Cabs		
Do Garage Equipment		
Do Shop Machinery and Tools		
Do Office Furniture and Fixtures		
Do Stand Equipment		
Do Repair Stock		
Doubtful Accounts		
Cab Liability (Damages)		
Capital Stock:		
Common		
Preferred		
Surplus		
Total Liabilities, Capital, and Surplus		

DETAILS OF STATEMENT OF EARNINGS AND EXPENSES

For the month of June, 1912, and for the six months ended June 30, 1912

	Month of June, 1912	Six Months Ended June 30, 1912
Vehicle Operation:		
Salaries, Operating Office	....	....
Chauffeurs Wages	....	....
Starters' Wages	....	....
Gasoline	....	....
Lubricants	....	....
Tires	....	....
	....	....
Garage Operation:		
Salaries, Garage Office	....	....
Wages, Garage	....	....
Light, Heat, and Power	....	....
Garage Supplies	....	....
	....	....
Maintenance:		
Body Repairs, Labor	....	....
Do Materials	....	....
Chassis Repairs, Labor	....	....
Do Materials	....	....
Damages Collected from Chauffeurs	....	....
Stock Room Wages	....	....
Motor Car Accessories	....	....
Chauffeurs' Clothing	....	....
Repairs to Equipment	....	....
	....	....
Rent and Insurance:		
Rent:		
Rent Proportion	....	....
Repairs do	....	....
Taxes do	....	....
Insurance on Buildings	....	....
Total Rent	....	....
Insurance other than on buildings	....	....
	....	....

DETAILS OF STATEMENT OF EARNINGS AND EXPENSES—Continued

	Month of June, 1912	Six Months Ended June 30, 1912
General Expenses:		
Salaries of Officers	....	....
Do General Office	....	....
Telephone	....	....
Office Expense	....	....
Stationery	....	....
Postage	....	....
Advertising	....	....
Freight and Expressage	....	....
Miscellaneous	....	....
	....	....

Results per Unit

	Month of June, 1912	Six Months Ended June 30, 1912
Cabs Used	....	....
Live Miles run	....	....
Dead Miles run	....	....
Total Miles run	....	....
Percentage of Live mileage	....	....
Miles run per cab for period	....	....
Drivers' Wages per live mile	....	....
Gasoline per gross mile	....	....
Lubricants do do	....	....
Tires do do	....	....
Chassis Repairs do	....	....
Garage Wages per cab used	....	....
Garage Supplies do	....	....
Body Repairs do	....	....
Net Revenue per live mile	....	....
Total Expenses per live mile	....	....
Do Reserve do do	....	....
Total Cost per live mile	....	....
Current Profit per live mile	....	....

ELECTRIC LIGHT AND POWER COMPANIES

Classifications of accounts for electric light and power companies have been prescribed by a number of States. The Interstate Commerce Commission has also issued a classification for use by the electric companies in the District of Columbia, which are under its jurisdiction. This classification is quite similar to that issued by the New York Public Service Commissions.

The accounting systems of public service corporations of different kinds have much in common. The elements of income from service rendered to the public, the cost of performing such service (made up in turn of the cost of maintaining the physical property and the direct cost of performing the service), and the almost continuous expansion of the plant to keep pace with the growth of the community, are alike met with in the case of street railways, electric light and power companies, gas corporations, water works and telephone companies. Consequently much of what is said under each of these classes of companies applies, sometimes with very slight modification, to all classes. The remarks under the general heading of public service corporations are also to be considered in connection with any one class of such corporations.

Conditions differ somewhat, however, between the various classes. For instance, while the earnings of an urban street railway accrue largely in cash from day to day, the earnings of an electric light and power company are based on monthly charges to consumers who have anywhere from five days to a month in which to make payment, and comparatively little of the revenue is on a cash sale basis.

The consumers' register is the initial record of the gross earnings from electric current sold. This record is usually so designed that it contains not only the original charge to the consumer, but collections and credits for abatements are also posted thereto, and it is in reality a ledger of consumers' accounts, and is in fact called the consumers' ledger in many offices.

Two forms of consumers' register are widely used. One is a wide columnar book, usually with one or two short leaves, with a group of columns for each month, there being separate columns for balances, charges, cash, and credits under each month. One or more lines are allotted to each customer's name or to a location; the months progress horizontally across the page. The respective totals of balances, charges, cash, and credits (rebates, allowances, etc.) which appear in the controlling accounts receivable or consumers' account in the general ledger are ascertained (for charges) or proven (for cash collections, credits, and balances) by footing the column set apart for each.

The other form of ledger has but one consumer's account on a page. This also is a book of original entry as far as the charges are concerned. The totals of charges made, collections posted, etc., are ascertained by scheduling on the adding machine items of a given class from all the consumers' accounts. The advantages claimed for the latter form are that it eliminates the necessity for carrying forward, or to a recapitulation, the totals of hundreds of pages, that a new register does not need to be written up anew each year (as companies of even moderate size will have some thousands of names, this is no small task), and that it permits of a more convenient-sized book than the cumbersome columnar record. The individual account form, as the last-mentioned of the two forms described may be termed, is like a sharp tool. In the hands of a competent workman, it is very useful, but in the hands of any other, its use may produce any but satisfactory results.

The meter-reader's books or cards are the data from which the charges are made in the consumers' register. In the case of flat rates the contract is the basis of the memorandum of the charge to be made monthly, which is noted in the register. The best forms of registers provide columns for showing meter readings. In the wide columnar register, however, the readings are not entered for lack of space. While the auditor is not usually expected to go back of the charges in the consumers' register, it is well for him to avoid getting into a rut by occasionally comparing some of the entries in the meter-reader's books with the register, also seeing that there are no consumers recorded in the meter-reader's books for whom there are no accounts in the register. The monthly totals of charges for current, cash collected, etc., per the consumers' register, will, of course, need to be compared with the entries therefor in the general books.

Sales of appliances, such as electrical irons, stoves, motors, high efficiency lamps, etc., have become a large item in the business of many companies. The profit thereon is usually small. The method of recording such sales should be carefully examined, as the misappropriation of the proceeds of such sales could be more easily concealed than the theft of ordinary collections for the consumption of current. Sales of appliances are frequently made on the installment plan. The accounts receivable for uncollected balances will necessarily require thorough scrutiny. The net profit only from sales of appliances should be included among the gross earnings in stating the company's operations.

The audit of the expenditures involves no features which are not common to practically all public utilities. The distinction between capital and revenue is of first importance. The remarks made on this subject under the head of electric railways are also very pertinent to electric light and power companies.

An unusually low ratio of operating expenses to gross earnings should be the subject of investigation. In the absence of unusual operating advantages, it is frequently due to insufficient expenditures for maintenance, which will sooner or later result in a rundown property.

In the case of machinery which has a tendency to become obsolete as quickly as electrical equipment does, depreciation allowances should be very liberal.

GAS COMPANIES

In many respects the audit of a gas company will be similar to that of an electric light and power company, which has already been considered. Sales of gas are, however, almost invariably made on a metered basis, whereas flat rates for electricity furnished have been and are yet, although to a lesser extent than formerly, quite common.

An item of importance is the sale of residuals, particularly in the case of companies manufacturing coal gas; the residuals recovered in the manufacture of water gas are less in both quantity and value. The quantities of residuals recovered in different fiscal periods should be compared with the quantities of materials "charged," i. e., placed in the retorts, and explanation of variations in the ratio of one to the other should be sought. The system of recording and reporting sales of residuals should also be investigated, so as to be certain that failure to report deliveries to customers will not escape detection.

Another important item of income which needs to be verified is the sale of appliances. With the largely increased use of gas for cooking and heating purposes which has come about in recent years, and the energetic endeavors of the gas companies to encourage such use to the utmost, it has become customary for the company to sell stoves and other appliances on the installment plan, the payments covering a period of one to two years. The business handled in the appliance department is frequently very large, the company not only selling the appliances, but also installing them. All this means that if no loss is to be sustained, careless methods must be avoided and suitable records be kept of the transactions in connection with the sales of appliances and fittings and the diligent prosecution of the collection of the accounts or installments as they fall due. It is preferable to take into the statement of operations only the net profit or loss on sales of appliances, rather than to include the sales among the gross earnings and the cost among the operating expenses.

There are no unusual features involved in the verification of the expenditures. For the ordinary operation of the plant the wages do not usually fluctuate very much. The quantity of coal carbonized, i. e., used in making gas, should within certain limits bear a definite ratio to the quantity of gas produced.

Depreciation of plant is an especially important consideration in the case of gas companies. Some parts of the plant, particularly the retorts or benches, need to be renewed at comparatively short intervals. Hence full provision should be made for such accruing renewals.

At the 1902 Annual Meeting of the American Gas Light Association, a committee appointed for the purpose of devising a uniform system of accounts for gas works submitted a report on "Classification of Operating Expense Accounts; Classification of Betterments on Property Accounts; Forms of Monthly Journal Entries and Rules for Closing." This furnished a working basis for the classifications of accounts for gas companies which have since been issued by the Public Service Commissions of the State of New York and the Interstate Commerce Commission.

WATER COMPANIES

The audit of water companies is very similar to that of gas and electric companies. In many companies a very large part of the charges to consumers is based on contracts for fixed annual rates. These rates are based on a certain charge for each kind of plumbing fixture. The use of water meters is, however, increasing, especially by private companies as distinguished from municipally owned water works. Charges to consumers based on meter readings are naturally treated in the same manner as in the case of gas and electric companies.

Flat rate charges to consumers are most often made quarterly, though in some few cases they are made monthly, and in still other instances semiannually, and—particularly in the case of municipalities—annually. In contradistinction from metered charges, flat rates are ordinarily payable in advance, and it is important to see that in closing the accounts such part of the flat charges as have not yet been earned are treated as a liability, being carried forward as deferred or unearned income.

The consumers' ledger accounts are usually arranged by location, and as most cities and towns are supplied by a single system, the accounts of buildings for which no water rent is charged should be examined to see that the water was off during the entire period. The dates on which the water is turned on or off are usually noted directly on the consumers' ledger.

In addition to vacancies, attention should be given to arrearages and uncollectible accounts. The bad debts should be very small in the case of a well-managed water company. Unpaid water rents due a municipality are, in some States, a lien on the real estate where the water was used.

Municipal ownership of water works is far more general than is the case with any other class of public utilities. Probably less attention has been given to the systematic regulation of water companies by the States than of other public service corporations. This may possibly be due to the fact that so many water works are municipally owned and operated. On the other hand, it is to be noted that there has been much litigation in attempts to regulate the rates charged by water companies. Much of this litigation has been the result of hasty and ill-considered efforts, superinduced by the heat of political campaigns.

None of the State public service commissions have prescribed uniform classifications of accounts for water companies. The New England Water Works Association has for years, however, had a form for uniform reports which has been used by a considerable number of publicly and privately owned water works. In recent years the American Water Works Association has given considerable study to the subject of uniform accounts for water works, and in 1907 the United States Bureau of the Census began a study of the subject. As the result of a conference held at Washington in 1911, at which representatives of the Census Bureau, American Association of Public Accountants, American Water Works Association, New England Water Works Association, and others were present, a suggested scheme of accounts, together with comprehensive instructions for its use, was published by the Census Bureau. The pamphlet, bearing the title "Uniform Accounts for Systems of Water Supply," may be had on application to the Bureau of the Census, Washington, D. C. The scheme of accounts has been so arranged as to make it sufficiently feasible to permit of its adaptation to the accounting needs of both the largest and the smallest water works.

TELEPHONE COMPANIES

A telephone company's main product is service. To a large extent the expense of operation varies but little with fluctuations in the volume of business done.

The largest single item of expense is that of salaries and wages. In the largest company this amounts to about fifty per cent of the total income. Next is supplies, rent, etc., i. e., ordinary operating expense outside of labor.

The disposition of the gross revenue of the Bell System for the year of 1911, as reported by the company, was as follows:

Salaries and Wages	50%
Materials, Rents, Traveling, etc.	20%
Taxes	5%
Interest and Dividends	19%
Surplus	6%
	100%

In many States some form of jurisdiction over telephone

companies has been given the local Public Service Commission. On January 1, 1912, there were twenty-eight States whose Commissions had been given power to regulate rates and service. This fact plays an important part in the *modus operandi* of the auditor.

The assets of a telephone company consist of its telephone plant, its contracts and licenses, supplies and tools, accounts receivable, cash and investments. Its liabilities consist of its outstanding bonded indebtedness, accounts and notes payable, and the contingent liability based upon the numerous contracts with subscribers and others.

The income is derived mainly from local telephone traffic, long-distance tolls, and revenue from investments. There is often other income in the shape of rental derived from property owned or leased, the sale of scrap supplies, the charges for private lines and special temporary installations, and income derived from advertisements in the directories.

The telephone plant is subdivided into numerous accounts, including Buildings, Central Office Equipment, Wire Plant, Construction and Equipment, Substation Equipment, General Office Equipment, Stores Department Equipment, Utility Equipment, etc.

The toll (long distance) and exchange (local) business must be kept separate, and all expenses and income properly apportioned.

Taxes constitute an important item of expense, and should be watched closely. The auditor should see that some adequate means of verifying tax bills, and providing for taxes payable, but unpaid, is in force.

The directories furnish opportunities for considerable peculations if not watched closely. The auditor conducting a thorough audit of a telephone company cannot consistently certify to the accuracy of the income without examining into the management of the directory.

The proper provision for depreciation, for the creation of a sinking fund and an amortization reserve, when necessary, are questions that must be settled in each case according to the rules laid down by the local commission, if one exists, otherwise approved accounting principles should be observed.

The commercial department has charge of public pay stations, and to that account are chargeable the salaries and commissions paid at public pay stations, the cost of labor and other expenses incurred in collecting from such stations, the cost of advertising, and other expenses relating to this branch of the service. The credit to the account consists of the toll received from public pay stations.

The subscribers' ledger records the revenue of the company, and should be kept with great care. It is in the form of a journal ledger, i. e., the original charges are made in this book and the totals thus shown are transferred to the general books. The book is ruled so that it will last for one year without rewriting the names. Short leaves may be used to reduce the size of the book. The columns are headed as follows:

Telephone Number.
Name.
Location.
Date Installed.
Kind of Service.
Rate per Month.
Date Transferred or Discontinued.

Each month's headings follow:

Balance.
Rental.
Toll and Messenger.
Total Debit.
Date Paid.
Amount Paid.
Rental.
Toll and Messenger.
Rebate.

The toll and messenger charges should be divided at the end of the month, as well as the rebate for poor service and the bad debts written off. Two colors of ink are usually employed to mark the distinction in the items.

Depreciation: The Railroad Commission of Wisconsin has issued a textbook on a system of accounting for telephone companies which should be consulted by those interested in telephone accounting. Depreciation is covered by the following instructions:

Depreciation Reserve: This account shows the balance set aside for depreciation available for the replacing and rebuilding of the plant. There is a certain wear and tear taking place in a plant which cannot be made good by ordinary current repair, and it is against this that the reserve for depreciation is made. The reserve should be made at such a rate as will entirely wipe out the asset over the period of its probable life. It has been held that in a moderately large exchange an allowance of seven per cent per annum is sufficient to take care of all depreciations, but in a small exchange an allowance of from eight to ten per cent should be made. If depreciation is not taken care of by means of a reserve fund, then the cost of renewing or reconstructing must be charged to operating expense as that work is done, which has the effect of not providing proper comparisons of one year with another. The years in which little reconstruction work is done show profits in excess of the actual profit, since no provision has been made for the depreciation or deterioration of the plant which actually took place during these years, and, on the other hand, the years in which a great amount of reconstruction work is required to be done show profits greatly short of the actual profits, since the depreciation and deterioration of the plant which took place in earning the profits shown in previous years has been burdened on to them. It is thus to show the accurate result of the operations that this account is established, and its operation is as follows:

At the close of each month this account is credited and *Account No. 76* debited with one-twelfth of the yearly amount of depreciation, which is based upon a fixed percentage of the amount invested in the plant.

This account now being set up so that it will exactly represent the amount of the investment in the plant when the plant has been worn out, it is proper to charge against it the net cost of such renewals, replacements, and extraordinary repairs as will increase the life of the plant. The net cost of any such item is arrived at as follows:

The original cost of labor and material in the part replaced,
The cost of removing same,
Less the scrap value of the parts removed,

this amount being charged to *Depreciation Reserve Account No. 42* and credited to the relative accounts as explained under *Account No. 6.* The cost of the new work is charged directly to the appropriate plant account.

Such ordinary current repairs as do not necessarily increase the life of the plant should be charged to *Maintenance.*

The depreciation account is not designed to take care of such contingencies as extraordinary destruction by storms, and the cost of repairing such damages is chargeable as follows:

All charges in connection with repairing the damage may be charged to *Account No. 31* and the scrap value of all salvage will be credited to this account.

When completed, an inventory of the actual value of the new line should be made, together with the original value of the line rebuilt.

Then *Account No. 31* should be debited with the amount by which the original value exceeds the rebuilt value and *Plant Account* credited, or if the rebuilt value is greater than the original value, then *Plant Account* should be debited and *Account No. 31* credited with the amount of the increase.

An examination should then be made of the *Depreciation Reserve Account* and such sum as may have been set aside as depreciation on the line rebuilt, after deducting any amounts which may have been charged to *Depreciation Reserve Account* for renewals on the rebuilt line, should be charged to *Depreciation Reserve Account* and credited to *Account No. 31*.

When this has been done, *Account No. 31* will show the exact loss from the storm and this amount can then be charged off to *Account No. 77*, either in one sum or in equal monthly installments, covering such period as may be decided upon.

CHAPTER XXVI

SPECIAL POINTS IN DIFFERENT CLASSES OF AUDITS

(Continued)

MUNICIPAL

BEFORE outlining the procedure which an auditor should follow in auditing the accounts of a municipality, it will be well to outline briefly the methods by which cities are financed and to say a word about municipal organization.

Preparation of Budget: A time-honored custom of municipalities and other governmental bodies is that no money can be spent for any purpose whatsoever unless the expenditure has been first authorized. This means that revenues or other funds must be appropriated for specific purposes by the proper authorities. The method of authorizing expenditures and appropriating funds is usually provided for in the city's charter or by State laws. The usual procedure in appropriating revenues is somewhat as follows: Some time before the beginning of the fiscal year the mayor or chief financial officer requests the head of each department, bureau, or office to prepare a detailed estimate of the amounts of money that he will require to meet the expenditure of his department for the ensuing year. These estimates are usually collated by the chief financial officer. In some cities they are examined by comparison with departmental records, as they should be, but in most cases they are not. The financial officer also prepares an estimate of the revenues from sources other than general taxes that will probably be received during the ensuing year, basing the estimate on the experience of previous years. These estimates of expenditures and revenues which constitute what is coming to be called the "tentative budget" are then submitted to the council, board of commissioners, or other authorizing body for action.

Fixing the Tax Rate: After the amount which is to be authorized for expenditure has been determined upon, the amount of estimated revenues is deducted therefrom in order to ascertain what amount must be raised by general taxation. This amount, divided by the total assessed valuation of property, gives the tax rate.

Authorization of Expenditures: These facts having been determined, they are embodied in an ordinance, usually called the budget ordinance or appropriation bill, which is voted by the appropriating body. The charters of most cities provide that the ordinance shall be approved by the mayor.

The funds thus appropriated usually provide only for meeting the current operating and maintenance expenses of the city. Funds for permanent improvements and other property which has a continuing value are generally raised by selling bonds which in most cases run for a long term of years. These bond issues must be authorized by the appropriating body, and sometimes action by the State Legislature is necessary. Funds so raised must also be appropriated for specific purposes.

All amounts appropriated are represented by accounts in the books of account and all amounts payable therefrom are charged to them. The auditor should have a copy of the city charter at hand, and before proceeding with the audit should acquaint himself with the provisions relating to finances and accounts.

Business Departments of a City: All cities except the very small ones have a finance department and a treasury department, which together handle the general financial business of the city as a whole. The most important of these is the finance department. This is, or should be, the central office of financial and accounting control. The official in charge is sometimes called comptroller, sometimes auditor. In commission cities he is called the commissioner of finance, and in the very small cities the functions of the office are performed by the city clerk. He keeps all the general accounts of the city, audits all claims against the city for payment, and performs such other duties pertaining to the finances of the city as may be specified in the city charter. He is usually an elected officer.

The treasurer is sometimes elected, but more frequently he is appointed by the mayor or the council. He is custodian of the city funds, receives all revenues, and pays all claims against the city on the order or warrant of the chief financial officer. His accounts should be under the accounting control of the finance officer, although in some instances this control exists in name only. In very small municipalities the treasurer frequently keeps all of the books.

The various operating departments are managed by officers, usually called either commissioners or directors, appointed in most cities by the mayor. Those common to nearly all cities are the health, public safety, public works, and public charities departments. There are frequently departments for other functions according to circumstances. The bulk of expenditures is incurred by these departments. Usually each has its own purchasing agent, although a few cities have central purchasing departments. Most cities endeavor to make their purchases chiefly by letting contracts, though in practice it is found necessary to make many purchases in the open market.

Invoices and pay rolls are usually prepared for payment on vouchers which are certified by department heads and their subordinates and submitted to the financial officer for audit and payment.

Sources of Revenue: The chief sources of revenue of cities are the general taxes levied annually on the taxable real and personal property within the city. There are many other sources of revenue, among which may be mentioned the following:

Water rates.
Excise taxes and liquor licenses.
Franchises.
Licenses.
Permits.
Privileges.
Rents.
Market fees.
Market rents.
Tolls.
Fees.
Court fines and penalties.
Court costs and fees.
Sale of old material.
Interest.

Control of Receipts and Expenditures: The general theory of control over city revenue is that for all moneys paid into the city treasury there shall be an independent report made by the collecting office to the financial officer from which he can build up a record of cash receipts for the purpose of establishing a controlling account against the treasurer. The means of control over cash payments made by the treasurer originate with the financial officer, since it is only upon the order or warrant of the latter that the treasurer can pay out money. The treasurer's cash account can be reconciled with the comptroller's cash account by taking account of the warrants not yet paid by the treasurer's cheques. In many cases, however, the treasurer draws cheques on the same day on which the warrants are drawn, so that his cash account is, or should be, always in agreement with the financial officer's account.

Few cities have adopted methods by which control may be established over the amount of revenues that should accrue. This can be done absolutely only by the use of controlled financial stationery[1] issued to collecting offices by the chief financial officer. This stationery should be so manufactured as to be difficult to imitate, and should be numbered and charged to the collecting agents, who must account for it either in money or unused forms.

A system should provide for daily and monthly reports of collection, the daily reports to the financial officer to be accompanied by skeleton carbon copies prepared at the time the original document is issued. At the same time daily reports of collections are made to the treasurer, who, after making the necessary entries in his books, acknowledges the receipt of the cash on the reports and transmits them to the finance officer. The latter audits the treasurer's reports by means of the collecting agents' reports and the carbon copies above referred to, thus establishing a current control over the accuracy and completeness of revenue returns.

The accounting methods of most municipalities are crude and archaic, few of them having kept pace with the modern improvements in accounting practice. Their bookkeeping consists mainly of accounts showing the condition of appropriation accounts and the inflow and outgo of cash. Accounts on the basis

[1]This is similar in form to the money orders used by the Post Office Department. The cutting of the dollars and cents on the margin controls the amount to be accounted for by the receiving clerk. The unused portion of each piece of stationery is preserved as a voucher.

of revenue accrued and expenses incurred are the exception, and accounts showing assets such as taxes and other revenue receivable, stores, equipment, and other permanent properties, are either not understood or considered wholly superfluous by all but a few cities.

Periodical Examinations: The following extract from "Short Talks on Municipal Accounting and Reporting," issued by the Metz Fund, August 15, 1912, is of interest:

As a means of insuring continuous conformity to the authorized procedure, it is a good plan to have the accounts audited and the procedure inspected periodically, once or twice a year, by a competent representative of the comptroller's office, or, if necessary, by an outside accountant. In addition to establishing the integrity of the accounts (if they are correct), such an inspection will determine not only whether the procedure is being scrupulously followed, but will afford the examining accountant an opportunity to suggest modifications or improvements which may be needed as conditions change with the lapse of time.

In this relation it may be of interest to quote from a letter received by the Metz Fund from the comptroller of a large New England city. He writes: "We are having an audit conducted in this city of the comptroller's records and of other department records in so far as they relate to the comptroller's records. Some criticism has arisen as to the need of such a step, some maintaining that it is an audit of the auditor and that there should be no need for such a proceeding. While I do not expect you to decide a controversy, yet I consider that a talk on such a subject would be of interest to citizens and officials throughout the country."

It is true that many persons not concerned with the active management of business do not see the necessity of an independent audit made by an outsider. But the experience of thousands of enterprises has so conclusively demonstrated the wisdom of such a procedure that the subject is no longer debatable. A large proportion of well-conducted private concerns, even though their regular office staff includes an auditor or a comptroller, have periodical examinations of their accounts made by professional auditors, and the proportion is constantly increasing. They have learned that the moral effect of an audit on the office staff is salutary; that many a man who, if left to his own devices, might misappropriate funds and falsify the accounts to conceal the misappropriation, would absolutely be deterred from so doing if he knew that an audit of the accounts would be made which would mean exposure. Even the employee who does not have the handling of funds will do his work better if he knows that he may be criticised by an outsider.

The inside auditor, from too close contact, loses his ability as well as his disposition to criticise, hence the outside auditor is needed to supply this deficiency. The professional accountant, moreover, by reason of his contact with the affairs and problems of many widely different concerns, is in a position to make valuable suggestions as to the accounting methods, organization, and business policies of his client, and such service has frequently bridged the gap between failure and success. The need for independent audits is even greater in public business, where tenures of office are frequently of short duration and where there are not the same influences at work which make for strict accountability in private business. There is no reason why systematic audits of municipal accounts should not be made by a properly equipped State department.

Audit of Revenue: The auditor should carefully examine the method of control over revenues, and if it is adequate in principle, he should make tests to satisfy himself that all the revenue to which the city is entitled has been accounted for. If the method of internal check does not sufficiently safeguard the city's interests, his judgment must be guided by circumstances. He must adopt such a procedure as will be necessary to satisfy himself that the cash turned in is the amount collected, and that the amount collected is the amount to which the city is entitled.

Taxes: As general taxes constitute the major portion of the revenues, he should pay particular attention to the method of accounting for them. He should ascertain whether the uncollected taxes recorded on the tax rolls agree with the summary or controlling account in the general ledger. He should see that abatements made are authorized and should make tests to ascertain that the proper amount of interest and penalties has been collected on past-due taxes. He should notice whether alterations have been made in tax assessments in the tax roll and should make sure that all alterations are authorized.

The laws of most States provide that when taxes are in arrears a certain length of time, the tax liens (in some cases the property itself) shall be sold by the city to indemnify it for the taxes unpaid. The auditor should make a note of all taxes in arrears in respect of which the city has not availed itself of its prerogative thus to indemnify itself.

Assessments: Assessments due the city for improvements, such as sewers, grading and paving streets, etc., benefiting particular properties, should also receive attention. In most cases the city undertakes these improvements, financing them by borrowing on public improvement or assessment bonds and then assessing the property benefited to recover the amount spent. Frequently the city bears a percentage of the cost. The auditor should look into the condition of assessments levied to see that they are accounted for in cash or accounts due, and whether the conditions attaching to the assessments are being complied with, such as the payment of principal within a stated period, interest, penalties, etc.

Rents and Franchises: The auditor should see that rents for all properties of which the city is lessor are accounted for and that the income from all franchises granted by the city has been accounted for.

Audit of Outstanding Accounts: The general theory of verifying accounts receivable by sending confirmatory statements to debtors may properly be applied in the audit of municipal accounts. Such a plan would be particularly useful in verifying unpaid taxes, and in many cases would probably be fruitful of results, although there will probably be somewhat more difficulty in reaching persons so indebted than ordinary trade debtors.

Audit of Expenditures: The method of internal audit of claims against the city should be carefully inspected. All vouchers should be approved by the heads of departments in which they originate and should be certified by the subordinates who have knowledge of the facts as to delivery of goods or performance of services, quality, prices, correctness of calculations, etc. If vouchers are by law required to be approved by the council or a council committee, the auditor should see that this rule has been complied with. Payments of an unusual character, such as judgments, damage claims, etc., should be carefully scrutinized. Particular attention should be paid to pay-roll vouchers to see that they are not "padded." Usually the salaries and number of incumbents of all positions other than those of laborers are fixed by the council. Tests may be made by reference to the council's resolutions relating to these matters. Payments of bonds and bond interest should be carefully scrutinized and audited by reference to canceled coupons and bonds, or, in the case of interest on registered bonds, to the record of bonds outstanding.

Tests of prices paid for supplies, particularly those used in large quantities, such as coal, forage, etc., will often reveal improper methods of administration. For example, it will sometimes be found that one department buys coal at one price and that another department pays the same contractor considerably more for the same kind of coal at the same season of the year. The charters or ordinances of most cities fix the maximum amount which may be purchased on open order, requiring that purchases exceeding this limit be made by public letting of contracts. This rule is frequently violated by "splitting" orders among favored dealers, keeping each order within the lawful limit, the result of which is that the city pays very much higher prices than it would have to pay if it obtained competitive bids.

Since expenditures can be made only from appropriated funds, the auditor should see that claims have been charged to the proper appropriation accounts. He should report all appropriations which have been overdrawn.

Sinking Funds: The adequacy of sinking fund provisions should have careful consideration. It is astonishing how many cities fail to lay aside regularly money which will accumulate and be sufficient and available to pay off bond obligations at maturity. In order that the burdens growing out of the acquirement of properties of a more or less permanent character may be to some extent distributed over a period of years, cities finance these acquisitions by issuing long-term bonds, the plan being to raise by taxation and set aside each year in a sinking fund an amount which, with interest accretions, will be sufficient to retire the bonds at maturity. Rarely are these yearly sinking fund installments computed correctly; indeed, in some instances they are not raised at all.

In some States the amounts which cities are required to pay into sinking funds yearly are fixed by law, a certain percentage of the total issue of bonds being specified, while the charters of some cities provide that revenues from certain sources shall be turned into the sinking fund. Sometimes this causes the sinking funds to be in excess of requirements, which means that taxpayers are bearing a heavier burden than is necessary. Sinking fund requirements should be computed on the basis of actuarial tables, and a reserve should be built up by additions each year, which will at all times show what should be in the sinking funds to date. The auditor should ascertain whether the amounts in the sinking funds in cash and securities equal the actuarial reserve. If there is a deficit he should call particular attention to the fact.

Financial Statements: The financial condition of a municipality is more easily understood if its transactions are summarized according to the several groups into which they naturally fall and financial statements prepared accordingly.

The accounts growing out of the raising of current revenues and the incurring of liabilities to meet current operating and maintenance expenses constitute the general account, or the general fund, as it is frequently called. At the end of the fiscal period these transactions are reflected in a balance sheet of the general account and a statement of revenues and expenses. The assets and liabilities of the general account may thus be related to a statement of revenues and expenses as in any private business. The principal items of assets are cash, taxes, and miscellaneous revenues receivable, stores, work in progress, and prepaid expenses. The principal liabilities are invoices and pay rolls payable, vouchers and warrants payable, and temporary loans made in anticipation of the collection of taxes and other revenues.

The second natural division or group has to do with the permanent properties and equipment of a city, construction and improvements in progress, including assessments levied against property owners who are benefited by improvements. The liabilities relating to this group are invoices and pay rolls payable, assessment or special improvement bonds, and funded debt. These constitute the capital account balance sheet.

The third natural division has to do with the funds and properties held in trust by the city, such as intestate estates, bequests, security deposits, pension funds, etc. The condition of these trusts is shown in a trust fund balance sheet.

The fourth group comprises the appropriation fund accounts, which are set forth in a fund balance sheet. These show the condition of appropriated funds and the contingent liabilities of the city on contracts and open orders, the latter being charges or encumbrances against appropriated funds which have not yet become actual liabilities. Opposed to these items are shown the resources, present and prospective, which are looked to for the liquidation of the liabilities.

These several detail balance sheets are brought together in a summary consolidated balance sheet in order to give in a single statement a complete view of the city's finances.

GENERAL ACCOUNT BALANCE SHEET

(Exhibit 2, page 472.)

Accounts Receivable—Unpaid Taxes: This is supported by the uncollected items in the tax rolls, or tax duplicate, as it is sometimes called. Provision for uncollectible taxes should be made currently by including in the annual budget of expenses a percentage of the tax levy sufficient to cover the estimated loss in collection. The product of taxes levied in the year will thus be sufficient to meet all expenses authorized for the year.

Miscellaneous Revenues Receivable: This account is supported by the revenues receivable ledger and includes various uncollected charges.

Due From Other Funds: This account is charged with cash temporarily loaned to the capital account or to trust funds. It is credited when cash is returned or when cash is borrowed from these funds.

Stores (which should be supported by stores ledgers): Are shown in the general account balance sheet and not in the capital account balance sheet, since in the main they are used for meeting current operating and maintenance expenses. If any stores are used for construction purposes, a charge for them is made to the capital account the same as if cash were advanced.

The reserve for stores among the liabilities is merely a device to keep them from being represented in the surplus. Stores and other prepaid items are not available for meeting contingent liabilities which may exist or which may be incurred against appropriated funds, and hence, to find the balance of assets available for further appropriation, they are excluded from the surplus.

Temporary Loans in Anticipation of Taxes: Many cities are obliged to borrow money for short periods pending the collection of taxes and other revenues. In consequence, temporary loans are made which are a lien against these revenues. They should be paid off when the collections are made.

CAPITAL ACCOUNT BALANCE SHEET

(Exhibit 4, page 473.)

Cash: Is held exclusively for meeting liabilities incurred in the acquisition of property having a continuing value, such as lands, buildings, equipment, and improvements. It is obtained by issuing long-term bonds and by the collection of assessments.

Assessments Receivable: Are amounts due from property owners whose property has been benefited by local improvements, such as the paving of streets, the building of new sewers, etc. They are frequently made payable in installments. This item is supported by individual accounts in the assessment rolls or assessment ledger.

Local Improvements in Progress: Represent current expenditures for grading and paving new streets, building sewers, etc., the cost thereof being assessable against property deemed benefited when the improvements are completed, at which time this account is credited and assessments receivable debited. Coincident with this entry, permanent improvements account is charged and capital account surplus is credited. It frequently happens that the city is obliged to stand some portion of the cost of the improvements. This is the case when city property is benefited by them or when the city at the outset agrees to bear a percentage of the cost. When the city's share is determined, long-term bonds are usually issued to meet it. At the time permanent improvements account is charged as noted above, capital surplus is credited for the amount assessed against taxpayers only, local improvements in progress being credited with the amount to be borne by the city.

Other Accounts: When among the assets, will be readily understood by their titles. These items should be supported by detail ledgers showing the various individual properties owned by the city.

The rule in regard to depreciation of assets may be applied in municipal accounts as in the accounts of private concerns, with one exception. The best authorities suggest that instead of creating a depreciation reserve by a mere bookkeeping entry, the depreciation charges should be included in the annual budget of expenses and the cash raised and invested in a fund. At the end of the period estimated to be the life of the property this fund would contain an amount sufficient to replace it, and the property would thus be automatically perpetuated.

The argument advanced against this practice is that it entails a double charge against taxpayers, namely, the annual depreciation charge and the annual sinking fund installments provided for the retirement of the bonds sold to purchase the properties. In some cases at least, it is a question whether, when a public work has outlived its usefulness and an entire reconstruction is in order, there should not be a new issue of bonds for the rebuilding. In this way the cost of the improvement may be spread over its life, and each generation of taxpayers made to bear the burden of the improvements it enjoys by a single charge for the annual sinking fund installments. As a matter of actual practice, however, depreciation of municipal properties is seldom provided for.

Assessment or Special Improvement Bonds: Represent the bonds issued to finance assessable improvements. They are shown under a separate head so that they may be contrasted with assessments receivable which are available for meeting them.

Bonded Debt: Instead of showing sinking fund cash and investments among the assets of the capital account, they are shown as a deduction from bonded debt. This admits of stating them in a supplementary statement (sinking fund balance sheet, Exhibit 5, page 473) in relation to the *reserve required to meet bonded debt at maturity.* As has been previously pointed out, the most important fact to be set forth in connection with sinking funds is the amount that should be on hand in cash and investments at any given date. This can be done only by building up a reserve on an actuarial basis, adding to it each year an amount equivalent to the amount of cash that should be provided each year, which, accumulated to the maturity date of the bonds, plus interest accretions, will yield an amount equal to the amount of bonds to be paid off. If an amount of cash commensurate with the yearly reserve (allowing for interest accretions) is not provided each year, the inadequacy of the sinking funds will be disclosed by the excess of the reserve account. In other words, there will be a deficit in the sinking funds.

TRUST FUND BALANCE SHEET

(Exhibit 8, page 474.)

Cash, Securities, and Investments: Are supported by detail ledger accounts showing how the trust funds are invested. The assets are not necessarily ear-marked according to the several trusts represented, though they may be.

Invoices Payable, Vouchers and Pay Rolls Payable, Warrants Payable: Are the current liabilities of the trust accounts. The number of separate general ledger accounts to be kept will depend somewhat upon the precise methods employed for handling transactions.

Reserve for Public and Private Trusts: Under this head are summarized the various trusts assumed by the city. Each individual trust is represented by an account, and if there are many of them, as is usually the case in large cities, these accounts should be carried in a subsidiary trust fund ledger.

CURRENT OPERATION AND SURPLUS ACCOUNT

(Exhibit 3, page 472.)

As an adjunct of the general account balance sheet it is necessary to show (1) the revenues and expenses for the fiscal period, and (2) the present condition of the surplus of the general account. Revenues should be summarized according to sources, and expenses according to purposes. For the latter, it is suggested that the functional classification adopted by the United States Census Bureau be employed. This classification divides the expenditures of a city under the following significant headings, viz., general government, protection to persons and property, conservation of health, sanitation, highways, charities, correction, education, recreation, interest, and miscellaneous.

The financial statements thus far discussed represent what may be called the proprietary relations of a city, that is, what the city owns and what it owes and the results of current operation. These statements are in every respect analogous to those employed in private business. We shall now discuss the statements that show the funding relations of a city, namely, those which have to do with the restrictions placed upon public officers in the expenditure of funds. There are two main categories of funds—those derived from taxation and those obtained from the sale of long-term bonds. A statement of the former is an adjunct of the general account balance sheet, whereas a statement of the latter is an adjunct of the capital account balance sheet.

FUND BALANCE SHEET—GENERAL ACCOUNT

(Exhibit 6, page 474.)

An analysis of the items appearing on the credit side of this statement will facilitate the understanding of it. When the appropriating body authorizes the amounts which may be expended (budget), it is necessary to establish accounts in the books so that officers may know at any time the amount of authorized funds available for expenditure and so that they may know when they have reached the limit of expenditure. An entry is therefore made in the general ledger crediting *appropriations* or *authorizations to incur liabilities* for the amount authorized. Detailed accounts showing the various purposes of expenditure are opened in a subsidiary ledger. Under the rules of double-entry bookkeeping some account must be charged, and since the appropriations are predicated upon revenues which are expected to accrue, an account is established on the debit side entitled *estimated revenues from taxes and miscellaneous receipts needed to meet budget authorizations.* This gives not only a proper equation, but lays the foundation for currently obtaining two distinct items of information, as will presently be shown.

Some accountants attempt to treat appropriations as liabilities and include them among the liabilities in the balance sheet. This is obviously improper, since the act of appropriating money for expenditures does not make the city a debtor. The argument in favor of treating appropriations as a liability is, that while a mere appropriation is not a liability, yet if taxes have been levied to provide for payment of the municipality's expenses for a whole year and the uncollected part of such levy is included in its entirety among the assets, the omission from the liabilities of the appropriations for which the levy was made shows a surplus which is likely to mislead (at least during the early part of the year) as to the municipality's financial condition. It is quite feasible, however, by means of the fund balance sheet to show the exact condition of affairs without thus doing violence to the accepted meaning of terms.

When contracts are awarded and orders are issued, contingent liabilities are created and appropriations are encumbered. These must be recognized in any statement of a city's financial condition. The details relating to unencumbered appropriations and contingent liabilities on contracts and orders are shown by the appropriation ledger over which these general ledger accounts operate as a control. The details of contracts in the appropriation ledger are further supported by the contract ledger.

In order to maintain a distinct accounting action within the fund group of accounts, it is necessary to introduce two other debit accounts, namely, *available balance* and *unapplied balance.* In doing this, valuable information is currently produced which otherwise could not be obtained without analysis. The *unapplied balance* is identical with cash less demand liabilities shown in the general account balance sheet, and as such it shows what amount of cash is available for meeting contingent liabilities on contracts and orders already incurred, or to be incurred, against available appropriations. It appears only in the general ledger and is not supported by subsidiary accounts. *Available balance* is identical with accounts receivable in the assets. It is built up by credits to the account *estimated revenues from taxes and miscellaneous receipts needed to meet budget authorizations.* It is likewise not supported by subsidiary accounts. Action in both of these accounts is produced by entries secondary or collateral to those which affect assets, liabilities, revenues, and expenses. For example, when cash is received in payment of taxes, *cash* is debited and *taxes receivable* is credited. At the time this entry is made a secondary entry must be made in the fund group of accounts debiting *unapplied balance* and crediting *available balance.*

The item on the credit side entitled *reserve for retirement of loans in anticipation of collection of taxes* represents the item in the general account balance sheet entitled *temporary loans in anticipation of taxes.* It is not supported by any subsidiary accounts.

For further information regarding the bookkeeping procedure relating to the treatment of these accounts, the reader is referred to *"Handbook of Municipal Accounting,"* prepared by the Metz Fund for Promoting Efficient Municipal Accounting and Reporting.

FUND BALANCE SHEET—CAPITAL ACCOUNT

(Exhibit 7, page 474.)

A similar group of accounts is kept to show the condition of funds raised by issuing bonds, and the condition of these funds is shown in a fund balance sheet of the capital account (Exhibit 7). One of the items on the credit side of this statement needs to be explained, namely, *reserve for retirement of assessment bonds.* As assessments are collected *assessments receivable* is credited and cash is debited. At the same time a secondary entry must be made in the fund accounts debiting *unapplied balance* and crediting this reserve. The latter serves to show the cash that should be held available for paying off the assessment bonds by which the assessable improvements were financed.

SUMMARY CONSOLIDATED BALANCE SHEET

(Exhibit 1, page 471.)

We come now to the *summary consolidated balance sheet,* which comprises the several detail balance sheets and fund statements already described and gives in a single statement a comprehensive view of a city's financial condition. It is in two sections, the first dealing with assets, liabilities, and surplus, the second section showing estimated revenues, appropriations, and reserves. It will be noted that the accounts *available balance* and *unapplied balance* are eliminated from this consolidated balance sheet, the assets, which they represent in a detached statement, taking their place. In the second section the excess of assets is added to the balance of *estimated revenues from taxes and miscellaneous receipts* for the reason that appropriations which were predicated on such estimated revenues are stated against them. As any balance of the estimated revenues not accrued (or collected) at the end of the fiscal year will have to be provided for in the following year, it must be regarded as at least a potential asset. The excess of assets and estimated revenues over liabilities, appropriations, and reserves is the amount which is available for further appropriations; in other words, the free surplus.

Exhibit 1

SUMMARY CONSOLIDATED BALANCE SHEET

As at......................191..

Showing Assets, Liabilities, Estimated Revenues, Appropriations, and Reserves

	General Account For Details See Exhibit No. 2	Capital Account For Details See Exhibit No. 4	Sinking Funds For Details See Exhibit No 5	Trust Funds For Details See Exhibit No. 8	Total
Assets					
Cash	$............	$............	$............	$............	$............
Accounts Due to City	....	....	....	....	....
Investments (City Loans)	....	....	....	....	....
Securities Owned	....	....	....	....	....
Lands, Buildings, Equipment, and Other Permanent Improvements	....	....	....	....	....
Due from Other Funds	....	....	....	....	....
Stores, Work in Progress, Prepaid Expenses, etc.	....	....	....	....	....
Total Assets	$............	$............	$............	$............	$............
Liabilities					
Invoices Payable	$............	$............	$............	$............	$............
Vouchers and Pay Rolls Payable	....	....	....	....	....
Warrants Payable	....	....	....	....	....
Bonded Debt	....	....	....	....	....
Due to Other Funds	....	....	....	....	....
Reserve for Stores, Work in Progress, Prepaid Expenses, etc.	....	....	....	....	....
Total Liabilities and Reserves	$............	$............	$............	$............	$............
Excess of Assets Over Liabilities and Reserves	$............	$............	$............	$............	$............
Estimated Revenues, Appropriations, and Reserves					
Estimated Revenues from Taxes and Miscellaneous Sources, as per Exhibit 6–1	$............	$............	$............	$............	$............
Excess of Assets Over Liabilities and Reserves as Above.	....	....	....	....	....
Total	$............	$............	$............	$............	$............
Less Appropriations and Reserves:					
Unencumbered Balances	....	....	....	....	....
Reserves (See Exhibits 5, 6, 7, 8)	....	....	....	....	....
Total	$............	$............	$............	$............	$............
Excess of Assets and Estimated Revenues Over Liabilities, Appropriations, and Reserves	$............	$............	$............	$............	$............

MUNICIPAL ACCOUNTS

Exhibit 2

BALANCE SHEET—GENERAL ACCOUNT

As at.....................191..

Assets

	Current Year	Prior Years	Total	
Cash—General Account				$.........
Accounts Due to the City:				
From Unpaid Taxes:				
Real Property Tax	$.........	$.........	$.........	
Personal Property Tax	....	....	....	
			$.........	
From Miscellaneous Revenues Receivable:				
Excises			....	
Licenses			....	
Fines			....	
Fees			....	
Permits			....	
Total			$.........	
Less Reserve for Loss			....	....
Due from Other Funds				....
Other Assets:				
Stores			$.........	
Work in Progress			....	
Prepaid Expenses and Advances			....	....
Total Assets				$.........
Deficit (Excess of Liabilities)				....
Total Assets and Deficit, General Account				

Liabilities

Invoices Payable		$.........
Vouchers and Pay Rolls Payable		....
Warrants Payable		....
Accrued Interest		....
Temporary Loans in Anticipation of Taxes		....
Due to Other Funds		....
Total Liabilities		$.........
* Reserve for Stores, Work in Progress. Prepaid Expenses and Advances		....
Surplus:		
Excess of Cash Over Immediate Demands for Cash	$.........	
Excess of Other Assets Over Temporary Loans and Reserves	....	
Total Surplus, as per Surplus Account Below		....
Total Liabilities and Surplus, General Account		

Exhibit 3

CURRENT OPERATIONS AND SURPLUS OR DEFICIT ACCOUNTS, YEAR ENDED.................191..

Expenses:	
Expenses (In detail according to functions or purposes)	$.........
Excess of Revenues Over Expenses	....
Total	....
Deficit from Prior Years	....
Charges Against Surplus:	
Excess of Expenses Over Revenues Year Ended 191...from above	....
Surplus December 31, 191..., as per Balance Sheet, General Account	....
Total	

Revenues:	
Revenues (In detail according to sources)	$.........
Excess of Expenses Over Revenues	....
Total	....
Surplus frcm prior years	....
Credits to Surplus:	
Excess of Revenues Over Expenses Year Ended 191... from above	....
Deficit December 31, 191...., as per Balance Sheet, General Account	....
Total	

MUNICIPAL ACCOUNTS

Exhibit 4

BALANCE SHEET—CAPITAL ACCOUNT

As at .... 191..

Permanent Funds, Properties, and Improvements

Assets

Cash, Capital Account		$
Assessments Receivable		
Local Improvements in Progress		
Construction in Progress		
Lands, Buildings, Equipment, and Other Permanent Improvements		
Municipal Utilities		
Due from Other Funds		
Total Assets, Capital Account		

Liabilities

Invoices Payable		$
Vouchers and Pay Rolls Payable		
Warrants Payable		
Assessment or Special Improvement Bonds		
BONDED DEBT	$	
Less Sinking Funds Applicable as per Statement Below		
Net Bonded Debt		
Due to Other Funds		
Total Liabilities		
SURPLUS:		
Excess of Cash Over Immediate Demands for Cash	$	
Excess of Properties and Other Assets Over Bonded Debt and Other Liabilities		
Total Surplus		
Total Liabilities and Surplus, Capital Account		

Exhibit 5

Sinking Fund Assets, Liabilities, and Reserves

Cash	$
Investments (City Loans)	
Securities	
Total Assets	

Vouchers Payable	$
Reserve Required to Meet Bonded Debt at Maturity	
Free Surplus	
Total Liabilities, Reserves, and Surplus	

MUNICIPAL ACCOUNTS

Exhibit 6

FUND BALANCE SHEET—GENERAL ACCOUNT

As at..............................191

Debits		Credits		
Estimated Revenues from Taxes and Miscellaneous Receipts Needed to Meet Budget Authorizations	$.........	Appropriation Accounts (Unexpended Balances)		$........
Available Balance (Accounts Receivable)	....	Unencumbered Balances	$.........	
Unapplied (Net Cash) Balance (Excess of cash over immediate demands for cash)	....	Reserve for Contracts (unfilled contracts)	....	
		Reserve for Open Market Orders (unfilled orders)	....	
		Reserve for Retirement of Loans in Anticipation of Collection of Taxes		....
Total Debit Balances		Total Credit Balances		

Exhibit 7

FUND BALANCE SHEET—LOAN FUNDS (CAPITAL ACCOUNT)

As at..............................191

Debits		Credits		
Loans Authorized and Unissued	$.........	Unexpended Balances of Authorization		$........
Unapplied (Net Cash) Balance	....	Unencumbered Balances	$.........	
		Reserve for Contracts (unfilled contracts)	....	
		Reserve for Open Market Orders (unfilled orders)	....	
		Reserve for Retirement of Assessment Bonds		....
Total Debit Balances		Total Credit Balances		

Exhibit 8

BALANCE SHEET—TRUST FUNDS

As at..............................191

Assets		Liabilities		
Cash	$.........	Invoices Payable		$........
Securities and Properties	....	Vouchers and Pay Rolls Payable		....
		Warrants Payable		....
		Reserve for Public and Private Trusts:		
		Intestate Estates	$.........	
		Pension Funds	....	
		Unclaimed Moneys	....	
		Bequests and Legacies	....	....
Total Assets		Total Liabilities and Reserves		

CHAPTER XXVII

SPECIAL POINTS IN DIFFERENT CLASSES OF AUDITS (Continued)

EXECUTORS AND TRUSTEES

An audit of the accounts of executors or trustees properly begins with a careful reading of the will or deed of trust, as the provisions of these documents will have an important bearing on the actions of the executors or trustees as reflected in their accounts. While the apportionment of receipts and payments between capital and income should always receive attention in the auditing of trusts, it becomes extremely important under some wills and trust deeds.

Having examined the documents from which the trustees derive their power, the auditor should next compare a certified copy of the inventory of the estate, which was filed with a court of probate, with the trustees' books, to see that all the assets scheduled in the inventory have been entered in the books and at the appraised values. Should the trust have already been in existence for a considerable time and the audit not go back to its inception, it is desirable that the examination start with the date with which the most recent account approved by the court closed.

The income from securities should be verified in detail. This can usually be very satisfactorily done; even if the securities are not listed on a stock exchange, information as to dividends or interest paid thereon can in almost all cases be obtained without much difficulty. Overdue interest on mortgages should be investigated.

When examining the securities, which work is an important feature of the audit, the auditor should see that they are registered in the names of all the trustees, if there are more than one.

If real estate has been committed to the care of the trustees, or if the will gives the executors the custody and disposition of the testator's real estate, the rentals therefrom will need to be verified and taxes and other realty expenses vouched.

Vouchers should be submitted to the auditor for all payments. In verifying the correctness of the credits taken by the executors or trustees, the commissions paid or claimed should be carefully scrutinized. Their arithmetical correctness can usually be verified in total, but it is also important to see that the basis on which they were calculated is a proper one. Particularly must duplications of commissions be guarded against. If an executor becomes trustee of an estate after being discharged as executor, he will receive but one commission on the principal of the estate. Furthermore, a commission is not ordinarily allowed on changes of investments, though it is usually allowed on the net increase, if any, in the principal caused by such changes. The average rates of commission allowed executors and trustees of decedents' estates are two and one-half or three per cent on the principal and five per cent on the income handled, but rates vary, and in some States a sliding scale of commissions is in force. In the case of large estates, however, a different rate or a fixed amount of compensation is sometimes named in the will (frequently, no doubt, in pursuance of an agreement between the executor to be and the testator during the latter's lifetime), and by accepting the trust the executor binds himself to limit his commission in accordance with the stipulation in the will. Presumably, however, if the executor declined to serve and no one could be found who would be willing to accept the trust for the stipulated compensation, the probate court could appoint an administrator who would not be bound by this stipulation of the will, but would be allowed the ordinary rate of commission.

In a complete audit of the accounts of a trust estate, the investments made by the trustees should also be reviewed from the standpoint of whether they were legitimate at the time they were made. The character of investments which are legal for trust funds vary in different States; generally they are first mortgages on real estate, Government (Federal, State, county, and municipal) bonds, and the first mortgage bonds of railroads having an established dividend record.

The importance of a correct apportionment of all receipts and payments between principal and income has already been mentioned. In this connection it should be borne in mind that interest and rents accrued to the date of the testator's decease are part of the *corpus* or principal of the estate; that profits realized or losses sustained on the liquidation of legitimate investments are added to or deducted from the principal; that expenses during the period of the executorship are paid out of principal and not from income, excepting expenses connected with improved real estate which are chargeable against the income derived therefrom; that losses on unauthorized or illegal investments are chargeable to the trustees personally with such interest (usually at the rate of six per cent per annum without compounding) as may be directed by the court; that a trustee is similarly chargeable with interest on funds actively applied to his own use or indirectly so applied by merging them with his own funds, even though he may have balances on deposit to his personal credit in excess of the trust funds for which he is responsible; that, even when investments of a wasting nature are specifically authorized, or form the original principal of the estate, a life tenant does not necessarily receive the entire gross income. When the instrument creating the trust provides that the life tenant and the remainderman shall benefit equally from such investments, it is usual to treat such part of the receipts from the investment as equals, say, five per cent on the appraised value of the investment at the time the trust was created as income for the life tenant and to capitalize the amount received in excess thereof.

The terms of the will or trust deed may, however, modify any of the foregoing rules, and hence the importance of the auditor studying carefully the conditions of the trust.

With regard to premiums paid on securities purchased by the estate, the usual rule is that they come out of the principal of the estate. Discounts on bonds purchased inure to the benefit of the principal. As probably the great majority of investments which are legal for trust funds sell at a premium rather than at a discount, one does not offset the other. From an accounting standpoint, premiums paid on bonds purchased should be amortized over the life of the bonds, and a portion of each interest payment retained to refund the premium advanced from the principal of the estate, and only the actual income yield on the investment paid over to the life tenant. The accountant must, however, in this, as in all matters pertaining to trust estates, be guided by the rules laid down by the court, which are not uniform in the different states. It is to be hoped that the courts will in time give effect to a more logical treatment of premiums on bonds than they have in the past.

The division or partition of an estate is frequently quite a complex proceeding. An estate is sometimes left in trust for the children of a family, each to receive his or her respective share of the principal on attaining a specified age. Until such time each beneficiary receives only his or her share of the income. As the specified event would not occur simultaneously in the case of all the beneficiaries, they would not all become entitled to their respective shares at the same time. As soon, however, as any one became entitled to receive his share, he could demand it without having to wait for such time as all the heirs could receive their respective shares of the principal, and, excepting by consent, the estate would have to be forthwith divided. Should the estate consist of securities which are readily divisible, no serious difficulty is encountered, as the beneficiary may then be given his proportion of each of the estate's investments. Should the estate, however, consist of real estate or other nondivisible assets, resort must be had to some other method of determining the beneficiary's share and delivering it to him.

Were all the beneficiaries of age, a mutual agreement could be made, but if any one of the beneficiaries is a minor, he or she cannot give binding consent to such an agreement. The only course left open is to apply to the courts for an order to "partition" the estate; the final order of the court confirming the share determined to be payable to the beneficiary entitled to the partition will be a protection to all parties interested. The payment of his share to the retiring beneficiary forthwith terminates his interest in the estate, and he is not concerned in any fluctuations in the value of the trust investments which may subsequently take place. Such fluctuations would affect only the remaining beneficiaries, for whose benefit the balance of the estate would be administered.

A principle of law which should not be overlooked is that no beneficiary who is under age has power to consent to any changes in the terms of a trust.

EDUCATIONAL INSTITUTIONS

As the greater portion of the income of educational institutions is usually derived from tuition fees, dormitory rents, and board, any failure of the records to control adequately the collection of such income should be reported, and detailed tests should be made (if these records are kept by single entry) to ascertain that all such income is being received and accounted for. Particular attention should be given to cases where no tuition fees, or fees at reduced rates, are received, to ascertain that proper authority therefor has been granted. The collection of extra charges for diplomas, special examinations, laboratory or school supplies, etc., should be given careful attention.

The examination of securities and the verification of the income therefrom are important. The records should show clearly the total amounts of all special funds, the invested and uninvested portion thereof, and, in addition, should enable the auditor to ascertain that the income therefrom has been applied to the purpose designated by the donors.

The annual report will be of material assistance to the auditor in the verification of income from tuition and donations, as the names of students and donors (and the nature and amount of donations) are usually detailed therein. If the report is not published until after the audit, it is desirable for the auditor to verify the proof sheets of the annual report prior to the final printing thereof.

The accounts of most educational institutions are kept only on a cash basis, and uncollected income and outstanding liabilities are usually ignored in stating their financial operations. It would be well for the auditor to recommend changes in the accounting records which will enable accurate statements of operations, as well as of assets and liabilities, to be prepared periodically. These statements will be valuable to the executive officers and trustees and should form part of the annual report.

CHARITABLE ORGANIZATIONS

This class of institutions includes hospitals, asylums, orphanages, relief societies, and all organizations whose aim is to relieve suffering and distress. That respect in which the accounts of charitable organizations especially differ from ordinary commercial accounts is the receipt of voluntary subscriptions and contributions. The receipts or acknowledgments sent to contributors should be consecutively numbered, and preferably so designed that a carbon copy will remain on file. Entries should be found in the cash book for all donations appearing on the copies of acknowledgments to contributors. The only practical way of insuring an accounting for all contributions received is to include in the annual report a list showing both the names of contributors and the amounts of their donations; then if any donations have not been accounted for, the donors may call attention to the omission thereof from the published list.

In hospitals, asylums, and like institutions considerable income is received from pay patients. This should be thoroughly verified. Keeping a controlling account in the general ledger for the patients' accounts will aid materially in verifying the correctness of the income from patients.

Patients' accounts are similar in theory to those of hotel guests. There is a patients' register in which are recorded the arrival and departure of patients, and the books can be so arranged as to permit of a conclusive audit.

Another item of income is from appropriations made by the State. These are sometimes in round sums and in other cases are based on the number of patients cared for at a fixed amount per patient.

In some States the accounts of charitable institutions receiving State aid are subject to audit by representatives of a State bureau. These official audits are usually restricted to an inquiry into the expenditure of the State appropriation and do not embrace the verification of other items of income and expenditure. Some States also prescribe a classification of expenses which institutions receiving State aid must follow, but these classifications have not as a rule been planned with the thoroughness characteristic of the classifications prescribed for public service corporations.

In the great majority of cases the accounts of charitable institutions are kept on a purely cash basis. The need for keeping and stating the accounts on a true income and expense basis so that actual results of operations may be seen is just as great in the case of charitable institutions as in business houses. As every accountant knows, a cash statement does not necessarily show the real cost of conducting an institution, and a large deficit may be accruing of which the published reports give no intimation.

In auditing the disbursements, the actual cost of operation should be ascertained as closely as feasible and the per capita cost determined. This will furnish data for comparison with the operations of other institutions of like nature; such comparisons make for increased efficiency.

The use made of trust funds devised to an institution for specific purposes should receive the auditor's attention. If the income from the funds is not being applied to the objects designated by the donors, or if the principal of funds has been encroached upon, when only the income was to have been used, it is clearly the auditor's duty to call attention to the matter.

The comptroller of the city of New York requires charitable institutions which receive public aid to keep uniform accounts, and to submit to him periodical reports, using the following forms:

COMPARATIVE BALANCE SHEET AND SUMMARY OF INCOME AND EXPENSES

Of.................................

For Six Months Periods Ending.................. 19....

BALANCE SHEET	Six Months Ended....	Six Months Ended....	Increase	Decrease
ASSETS				
Cash on hand and in bank	....	....	....	....
Due from City of New York	....	....	....	....
Other accounts receivable	....	....	....	....
Investments	....	....	....	....
Accrued income on investments	....	....	....	....
Inventory of supplies	....	....	....	....
Special funds	....	....	....	....
Real estate and buildings, donated	....	....	....	....
Real estate and buildings, purchased	....	....	....	....
Equipment	....	....	....	....
Prepaid items	....	....	....	....
Total Assets	....	....	....	....
LIABILITIES				
Accounts payable	....	....	....	....
Loans payable	....	....	....	....
Accrued items	....	....	....	....
Mortgages payable	....	....	....	....
Bonds outstanding..........due..........	....	....	....	....
Total Liabilities	....	....	....	....
Excess of Assets Over Liabilities	....	....	....	....
SURPLUS AND RESERVES				
Surplus at beginning	....	....	....	....
Income	....	....	....	....
Total	....	....	....	....
Less:				
Maintenance expenses	....	....	....	....
Non-maintenance expenses	....	....	....	....
Total	....	....	....	....
Surplus at end	....	....	....	....
Reserves for special funds	....	....	....	....
Surplus and Reserves	....	....	....	....

STATEMENT OF INCOME AND EXPENSES

	Six Months Ended....	Six Months Ended....	Increase	Decrease
INCOME				
New York City for maintenance	....	....	....	....
New York City for education	....	....	....	....
Donations, gifts, etc., for general purposes	....	....	....	....
Donations, gifts, etc., for special "	....	....	....	....
Collections	....	....	....	....
Fairs, entertainments, etc.	....	....	....	....
Sales of manufactured products	....	....	....	....
Legacies, bequests, etc.—general	....	....	....	....
" " " —special	....	....	....	....
Income on investments	....	....	....	....
Interest on trust funds	....	....	....	....
Rents	....	....	....	....
Miscellaneous	....	....	....	....
Total Income	....	....	....	....
EXPENSES				
MAINTENANCE EXPENSES:				
Repairs and renewals to plant and equipment	....	....	....	....
" " " " furniture and fixtures	....	....	....	....
Foodstuffs	....	....	....	....
Supplies—general	....	....	....	....
Clothes	....	....	....	....
Linen and bedding	....	....	....	....
Fuel	....	....	....	....
Light	....	....	....	....
Salaries and wages	....	....	....	....
Forage and care of animals	....	....	....	....
Telephone	....	....	....	....
Printing, stationery, and advertising	....	....	....	....
Postage, telegrams, magazines, and newspapers	....	....	....	....
Professional services	....	....	....	....
Miscellaneous	....	....	....	....
Expenses boarded-out children	....	....	....	....
Board of children	....	....	....	....
Salaries	....	....	....	....
Traveling expenses	....	....	....	....
Clothes	....	....	....	....
Professional services	....	....	....	....
Miscellaneous	....	....	....	....
Total Maintenance Expenses	....	....	....	....
NON-MAINTENANCE EXPENSES:				
Interest on mortgage	....	....	....	....
Interest on loans	....	....	....	....
Rent	....	....	....	....
Insurance	....	....	....	....
Taxes	....	....	....	....
Total Non-Maintenance Expenses	....	....	....	....
Total Expenses	....	....	....	....
Weekly cost	....	....	....	....
Excess of income over expenses	....	....	....	....
Surplus brought forward	....	....	....	....
Surplus	....	....	....	....

CHURCHES

In the majority of cases the audit of church accounts is unsatisfactory to the auditor. One reason is that the church treasurer frequently is not only the custodian of all the church funds, but is tacitly empowered to disburse the same at will. There is usually a total lack of effective internal supervision. At times large sums pass through a treasurer's hands without any proper check being kept upon his dealings.

It is the auditor's duty to check whatever he can, and at the same time to urge upon his clients, judiciously but impressively, the necessity for ordinary commercial caution. He should see that all receipts are deposited in bank, and if a balance appears to be on hand that also should be deposited. This is preferable to an actual count of cash, as in the latter case the church official might exhibit his own funds without any intention of having them reach the church's bank account. A certificate from the bank direct to the auditor should be obtained, this certificate indicating the balance in bank belonging to the church at a stated time.

In some churches a collection register is kept in which are entered the collections as made, the aggregate amount subsequently being transferred to a cash book. The entries in the collection register should, if possible, be verified and initialed by some one other than the church treasurer. Special collections should be vouched for in a similar manner. Where pews are rented, the pew-rent register should be compared with the cash book. If special funds have been devised to the church, the securities held for such funds should be examined. Vouchers should be in evidence for all payments; these are to be compared with the minutes of that board or committee of the church whose duty it is to supervise its finances.

In at least one denomination the sentiment has been expressed that the accounts of a church whose treasurer handles moneys in excess of a stated amount annually should be audited by a Certified Public Accountant. When this sentiment becomes general we shall see a decided improvement in the manner of keeping church accounts, as well as added safety in the use and care of church funds.

CLUBS

In auditing clubs, particular attention should be given to the collection of income, and it will frequently be found that improvements can be made in this feature of their accounting systems. Since the members are the club's proprietors, their cooperation can usually be obtained, if necessary, in safeguarding the clubs from being defrauded by their employees or others.

Members should be requested to pay by cheque to the order of the club for all dues, house, restaurant, and other charges. Where peculations have occurred they have usually been from currency receipts, as the chance of detection is comparatively small if there is no adequate system of check on those handling the currency.

Consecutively numbered receipt forms, charge slips, and bills should be used wherever practicable, as the office copies thereof are valuable for auditing purposes.

The collection of dues can usually be verified by examination of the membership register. If necessary, the latter can, in turn, be verified by comparing it with the membership record at the close of the preceding audit and examining the minutes for names of new members and of those resigned, suspended, or expelled.

Wherever feasible, registers should be used as a basis for room charges. A good additional check thereon, which is valuable for auditing purposes, is to have the housekeeper make a daily record in a suitably ruled bound book of occupancies and vacancies of rentable rooms. Consecutively numbered daily reports to the office should form the basis of other house charges.

Members' signatures are usually required on orders received in the restaurant and bar. In some clubs where it is the practice to return such orders to the members monthly upon payment of their accounts, duplicate orders are obtained by the use of carbon sheets. If these orders are filed chronologically, they may be used in connection with the verification of the deliveries from stock of wines and liquors. If members can be induced to use consecutively numbered ticket books, to be paid for either in advance or charged for in total, the bookkeeping will be entirely eliminated (in the first instance) or materially reduced (in the second) from that necessary when each order must be charged to the personal account of some member.

There usually are, or ought to be, in hotels and clubs, miscellaneous receipts from the sale of bones, fat, and other like sources. The practice, which still exists in some clubs, of allowing the chef to retain the proceeds from the sale of kitchen refuse, should be discouraged, as the pay roll should show the entire compensation of all employees. Under the best of conditions it is difficult to be certain that all such receipts have been accounted for, and comparisons should be made of the receipts during the period audited with similar previous periods, and, in instances where no such receipts are recorded, investigation as to the disposal of the offal and scrap should be made.

Care should be taken to ascertain that proper allowance has been made for depreciation of china, glass, silverware, linen, and other furnishings. Either of two methods for doing this may be used: charge original cost of furnishings to asset accounts and all renewals to expense accounts, or reappraise the entire stock at least once annually. Many clubrooms are from time to time lavishly redecorated and refurnished, and it would be well, instead of charging the entire usually heavy costs of this nature to one year's operations, to distribute the expenditures equally over a period of several years.

It is important that all expenses be properly apportioned among the various activities of the club so that it may be definitely known whether those departments which are in the nature of business activities are in fact yielding sufficient revenue to defray all the expenses (including a proportion of the general expenses) properly chargeable to such activities. Otherwise it may be that departments which are supposed to be self-supporting, and which may on the face of the figures appear to be so, are, if all expenses chargeable thereto are taken into consideration, operating at a loss, which is being made up out of members' dues.

ARCHITECTS

The accounts of architects are not usually so voluminous as to preclude making a detailed audit. Owing to the fact that men who are professionally very able do not always have a keen business sense it is important that the auditor exert every means to safeguard the financial affairs of his client and protect him from loss.

All payments should be carefully scrutinized. This is particularly necessary because some of the expenditures will be recoverable from clients and the auditor should see to it that all such payments have been duly charged to accounts with the clients.

A very important part of the audit is the verification of the commissions and fees charged to clients. Fees of specified amount are sometimes agreed upon, or are charged in the case of preliminary work (such as sketches, etc.) done in cases where the proposed undertaking is abandoned. Usually, however, the architect's compensation is based on an agreed percentage on the cost of the building and its equipment where the latter comes under the architect's supervision. This makes it necessary for the architect to keep a record of contracts let and payments made thereon. The auditor should refer to this record as a means of verifying the charges to clients. Such a record of contracts is, of course, also a necessary part of an architect's records for the purpose of having a basis on which to issue certificates of the amounts which are to be paid by the owners for work done by contractors.

As there is almost invariably considerable work unfinished at the end of a fiscal period, a basis of valuing it must be found. The author's experience is that a quite satisfactory basis is the amount of contracts let, a part of the agreed rate of commission being taken up on the amount of all contracts awarded and the remaining part of the commission on the amount of payments made on the contracts. There will be some engagements on which the work has not yet advanced to the point of awarding construction contracts. Valuations of such work will be made by the architect himself, frequently in round sums, and the auditor should see to it that the estimated valuations are, if anything, ultra-conservative. When the work is only in the preliminary stage there is frequently a possibility of the project being abandoned or indefinitely postponed, and in such cases the architect is not always able to secure remuneration commensurate with the work actually done.

DOCTORS

The absence of a uniform system of bookkeeping on the part of medical men, and their failure, in most instances, to realize the value or desirability of keeping accurate accounts with patients, renders it difficult in the space here available to offer definite useful hints as to the method of audit. Assuming, however, that there is a patients' ledger, it may be suggested that to go behind the charges therein is not necessary. In fact, in many instances it would not be possible to do so, as the charges may or may not represent a stated number of visits, as frequently a lump sum is charged for a case.

The auditor should endeavor to introduce some efficient system of recording visits so that the client may have before him all the facts when making his charges. It would be especially satisfactory for purposes of subsequent reference if this record gave in the case of a family the particular name of the patient visited, though the ledger account might appear in the name of the family head.

All credits on the patients' ledger should be carefully checked by the auditor in order that all moneys credited to patients may be properly accounted for. Any allowances that have been made should be particularly noted. Many practitioners employ one or more assistants who are authorized to receive money. Where this is so, the importance of following ordinary commercial precautions against fraud is apparent.

Occasionally payments are made on account of patients for medicines, consultation fees, or other objects. It is important that the auditor determine that such charges have been charged up and duly collected. Where practitioners supply their patients with medicines and drugs it is necessary that the accounts of druggists, etc., should be carefully checked, and at balancing time an allowance will have to be made for the value of drugs in stock.

Horses and carriages or automobiles that are the property of the practitioner should be depreciated at the rate of fifteen to thirty per cent per annum. If these are rented it is equally important to include cost of hire to the date of balancing, or, in case of payment in advance, to carry a proportionate part forward as a deferred asset.

LAWYERS

The nature of a lawyer's work, together with a general tendency on the part of professional men toward laxity along bookkeeping lines, makes a complete, detailed audit a necessity if it is to be effective.

A difficulty which frequently confronts an auditor going over a lawyer's books is that they are the stock forms sold by law stationers. These are designed with a view to saving time rather than for any other purpose.

An important requirement is to make certain that the amount included in the balance sheet for outstanding charges represents the actual sum included in bills to clients. Every item of costs charged a client might profitably be compared with a copy of the bill rendered to make sure that all amounts chargeable have been properly debited. Care should be taken to note amounts that may have been paid on account.

A not uncommon practice among lawyers is a failure to distinguish between personal funds and those of a client. This very condition emphasizes the necessity and importance of proper accounts being kept by those attorneys who wish to avoid any possible reflection upon their manner of dealing with moneys intrusted to them by clients. This separation of money materially simplifies the keeping of accounts. Each large estate should have its own bank account and separate books, entirely independent of the books of the firm.

A "Clients' Accounts" in the cash book should show all money received in trust for clients, and if there is but one bank account, it would be advisable to recommend separate columns, that the "clients'" accounts may be distinct from the "general" bank account.

It is a common occurrence for a practitioner to make payments on behalf of a client who may not have a credit balance upon the books. It is especially desirable, therefore, that provision be made for charges to be so entered that reference to any account will reflect its true condition and lead to its settlement.

An important advantage in keeping large estates quite separate from the general accounts is that the cost of keeping them, and of having them audited, may then frequently be charged, together with other costs, against the estate. It will be possible, also, to submit these accounts to clients or their representatives without disclosing any other transaction. If they be so examined at regular intervals, it may not be necessary to have them also audited by the lawyer's auditors. In this way a further saving of expense may be effected.

CONTRACTORS

The accounts of contracting companies, erectors, builders, engineers, and others engaged mostly in work carried out under contract may be included under this caption.

In nearly every instance separate accounts are kept for the cost of each contract, or, if the work under one contract is very large, for each of several sections of a contract, which are later combined when each part is completed. Obviously, the value of such a system of cost accounts to the client depends upon the efficiency with which it is carried out. The auditor should examine it carefully to ascertain that it is based upon good accounting theory and that the results shown are in harmony with those shown on the general books.

The system of preparing the pay roll and of accounting for materials purchased and handled through the storeroom should be carefully investigated to ascertain that all reasonable safeguards against fraud and loss are provided. Wages should be paid by office employees not connected with the preparation of the pay roll.

The value of work done on uncompleted contracts is shown on the balance sheet under the head of "Uncompleted Contracts" or "Work in Progress." The auditor should request a certified schedule of the expenditures on each of the contracts included in this account. The schedule may readily be verified in cases where correct cost accounts have been kept, but in other instances the auditor may be obliged to accept the schedule upon the certificate of the engineers, superintendents, or other proper officials, after investigating unusual items and satisfying himself that every effort has been made to prepare the schedule correctly.

As a matter of fact, there is almost always some check on

the amount of work completed. As the work progresses under the supervision of architects or engineers, certificates are secured from them testifying to the quantity and quality of work done and authorizing partial payments on account.

The auditor may not see these certificates unless he asks for them. Contractors are usually more optimistic about the proportion completed than is the architect (unless the two are working together against the owner), so that his estimate as to the part completed at a given time should be verified in every possible way.

The cash receipts are also a clue to the amounts certified to. The stipulated payments are on a basis of ninety per cent of the work completed, sometimes more and sometimes less. The contracts themselves, which must always be open to the inspection of the auditor, and which should be called for, will indicate the percentage reserved until after completion and acceptance.

It is important to note whether or not any profit has been taken on uncompleted contracts. The profit on each contract to any date can readily be ascertained in instances where cost accounts have been kept by preparing a memorandum profit and loss account and making the following entries therein:

Debit: All Direct Contract Costs.
Depreciation of Plant used on Contract Work.
Credit: Value of Work Certified to Date.
Value of Work Done, but not yet Certified.
Stores and Materials Charged to Contract, but still Unused.

The net credit balance of such a profit and loss account will represent the estimated profit to date; a net debit balance will represent the loss to date.

If a contract is nearly completed, the estimated profit upon completion may be ascertained by deducting from the contract price the combined cost of work to date and the estimated cost of completion.

The most conservative method is to ignore entirely profits which may have accrued on uncompleted contracts. It could, however, hardly be claimed to be improper to take at least some part of the profit on the work already done on, say, a large building contract extending over several fiscal periods, provided the percentage of the work completed has been estimated on a conservative basis and a liberal allowance has been made for contingencies. Whenever such profits are taken, it is the auditor's duty to satisfy himself that they have been conservatively calculated. The accounts should show clearly the amounts of estimated profits, if any, taken on uncompleted contracts, and the auditor should show them separately in his statements and also call attention thereto in his report, if deemed necessary.

Monthly statements should be requested from subcontractors, as they may have large claims for work in excess of that called for by their contracts, but for which credits do not appear on the client's books. It may even be found that the client has billed this extra work to the customer, and that credit therefor is entered in the contract account.

At times subcontractors may do extra work under an agreement with the general contractor providing for compensation only in the event of collection therefor by the general contractor from the customer; changes in specifications after subcontracts have been let also furnish grounds for subcontractors' claims. Sufficient reserve must be made to cover the probable amount to be paid on such claims prior to carrying the gross profit from the contract account to profit and loss.

REAL ESTATE

In auditing the accounts of a client engaged in buying, holding, renting, and selling real estate the leases should be examined, and, in the case of office or loft buildings, should be compared with loft plans, and all the rentals accounted for. Actual inspection should be made of properties, or rentable portions thereof, which are recorded on the books as vacant at the time the audit is begun.

Prepaid rents, or security deposited by tenants, should be clearly shown, and changes in the latter during the audit period carefully investigated. Balances due for unpaid rentals, power, alterations, etc., can be verified by correspondence.

All expenses should be vouched and comparisons of the income and expenses of each property and of administration should be made with periods prior to that under review. Extraordinary expenditures for alterations should be called to the attention of the proprietors to ascertain if the tenants should perhaps have been charged therewith.

If properties are managed by the client as agent of other owners, the contracts with the latter should be examined and the collection of the commissions verified. Balances due to or by owners may be verified by sending statements to the latter and requesting confirmation thereof.

Care should be taken to ascertain that proper allowance has been made for accrued taxes, interest on mortgages and ground rents. The mortgage interest paid during a full year is a good check on the principal of the mortgages, in addition to which the amount of the latter, as well as the payments on account thereof during the audit period, can be further verified by correspondence with the mortgagees.

Prepaid insurance premiums should be verified by calculation. The charges to land, buildings, and equipment accounts should be examined to ascertain that they are all for additional land and construction work or improvements.

Accounts covering bonuses which may have been paid for leases purchased, or the cost of improvements on leased ground which will revert to the owners of the latter at the expiration of the ground rent leases, should be reduced at regular intervals.

Settlement records may be used in connection with the verification of sales of real estate.

In the case of undertakings involving the development of large tracts and the sale of lots therefrom, care should be taken to ascertain (if any profits are calculated prior to the disposal of the entire tract) that the costs of the lots sold have been calculated on a conservative basis.

The following illustration of fraud discovered in the accounts of a real estate agency will be of interest: Rent collections were entered in detail in a cash receipt book, footings made each day, and the total deposited to the company's bank account. The footings were verified by the treasurer and agreed with the amounts credited in the pass books each day. After this verification, the cashier entered additional items covering amounts which he had taken, in order that the collector, who checked up the receipts, would see that all items had been collected. These additional items were not, however, included in the totals. The cashier retained currency and cheques in his drawer, which he juggled in order to make up the exact amount of the items he was supposed to be depositing.

The main cash book or cash journal (the total of the day's entries being journalized) included all of the items entered in the cash receipt book, and fraudulent footings were made to agree with the bank accounts.

All items were eventually posted in the ledger to the credit of the various owners and the footings and balances, when inked in, were as they should have been had there been no defalcation. The postings were always from two to four months in arrears, and, in order to prepare a trial balance, postings and footings were falsified. Some months later these errors were corrected as stated above.

The deficiency was partly concealed by depositing to the company's credit cheques drawn to the order of clients which had been properly charged to their accounts, but the cheques were never sent to the clients.

The above-described fraud was practiced for about seven years, and a total of some $26,000 obtained before the omission of an entry for one item of receipt was questioned by the collector and this led to the discovery of the fraud.

LAND AND DEVELOPMENT COMPANIES

The operations of a typical land development company embrace the purchase of a tract of land, the platting of it into streets and lots, the grading and paving of the streets, the laying of sewers and water mains, the laying of sidewalks and curbs, the placing of telephone and light poles, and the selling of the improved lots. Oftentimes there are other features of the plan, such as the building of houses for purchasers, the extension of railway or other transportation facilities to reach the property, and possibly the temporary operation of one or more industries.

There are many fine points involved in the proper distinction between expenses and additions to property. Unlike a railroad, the entire cost and expenses up to the time the property is ready to be marketed cannot be charged against the property. Only such part of the expense as really adds to the value of the property, such as the grading and paving of streets, the cost of the water and sewer installation, etc., is a proper addition to the capital account. Administrative expenses and any preliminary selling expenses, such as advance advertising, publicity work, printing, and the preparation of maps, must be segregated and shown on the balance sheet as deferred charges to future operations until such time as revenue begins to come in.

The books peculiar to the business are these:

"Real Estate Lot Ledger."
"Construction Ledger."
"Improved Real Estate Cost Ledger."
"Improved Real Estate Operating Ledger."

In the Lot Ledger the lots are carried at cost. Unimproved tracts should be represented by an account with the *tract* until such time as the tract is divided into lots, then the total cost of the tract and improvements is spread over the number of lots, the *tract* account is credited with the full amount, and an account is opened with each lot. The basis of division of cost is not the number of lots in the tract, but the relative value of each to the whole, depending upon location, size, etc.

The Construction Ledger contains only the cost of buildings and the carrying charges thereon, and does not include the cost of land. Upon the completion of the building the cost of the same and the cost of the lot are transferred from their respective ledgers to an account in the Improved Real Estate Cost Ledger representing the building and lot complete.

The details of the operation of the property are thereafter carried in the Improved Real Estate Operating Ledger, from which the credit or debit balance is carried at the end of the fiscal period to proper profit and loss accounts.

Following are some of the points that should be covered in the audit of a going concern engaged in the development and sale of land:

Analyze the property account from the beginning of the development, noting the nature of the charges against this account.

Ascertain if there is any record of the prices at which the lots are to be sold and compare selling prices therewith. If no such record exists, see that the sales contracts are approved by one of the principals before being binding upon the client.

Obtain from the client the basis for the distribution of expenses between properties in case more than one property is being handled. Then see to it that the proper distribution is made for every expense incurred. The distribution is usually made on the stub of the cheque or directly in the cash book. There is no reason why the cheque stub cannot be dispensed with, and the cheques entered and distributed directly in the cash book.

Compare a considerable number of the cashier's contract cards with the ledger, testing the correctness of the interest calculations.

Compare contracts entered into during the period under review with the ledgers as to terms, name and address of purchaser, etc.

Compare the payments to salesmen for commissions with the card record of contracts and with the ledgers, noting especially that commissions have been charged back on canceled contracts.

Compare the sales of lots with map (retained by the auditor), noting on the map the price obtained and investigating wide fluctuations.

Compare open items in the "lot book" with the lots unsold at the end of the period per the map.

See contract terms regarding taxes, interest, etc.

Send out verifications of accounts to all customers.

HOTELS

The auditor should analyze the earnings and expense accounts, if necessary, and prepare statements of the financial results in each department, which should be carefully gone over with the proprietors. Such departments as show unsatisfactory returns should be especially investigated to the extent of verifying the detail work for a part of the audit period. Hotels at summer resorts usually have more departments than do city hotels. Frequently the operations of the former include drug stores, various amusements and excursions for guests, all of which are sources of additional income. Stock accounts of cigars, wines, liquors, etc., should be carefully examined in the event of the results being unsatisfactory in departments where they are handled.

The auditor should satisfy himself that all receipts are accounted for, that expense payments are either covered by vouchers or properly approved pay rolls, and that such as have been made on behalf of guests have been charged to their accounts and collected. The subsidiary guests' and purchase ledgers should be proven with the balances in their controlling accounts, and all of the entries in the general ledger should be thoroughly checked.

Careful attention should be given to the question of depreciation of furnishings, such as china, glass, cutlery, silver, linens, etc. These may be reappraised at periods when statements are prepared or depreciated at such times at adequate rates. Another good method is to credit regularly a reserve account and charge against the profit and loss account amounts sufficient to cover the estimated actual renewals and depreciation over a period of years, and then to charge all renewals to this reserve account.

RESTAURANTS

The accounts of restaurants are somewhat similar to those used in hotels and clubs, although, by reason of restaurants having fewer departments, the records are not so complex. It is a difficult matter to safeguard the proprietor against all possible fraud and to discover if any has been perpetrated. The auditor should, however, carefully investigate the manner of serving meals and collecting therefor, and should ascertain that the earnings and expense accounts in the general ledger are so classified that the proprietor can form an opinion as to the efficiency of the management.

In some restaurants the waiters do not issue checks to guests, the checks being issued by a checker at the kitchen door, who scrutinizes the food or drinks served, and who also charges the waiter's account on a columnar checking sheet, which is used as a check at the end of the meal periods against both the waiters and the cashier.

ADVERTISING AGENCIES

It is important for the auditor of an advertising agency to ascertain that the accounting system in use embraces a good internal check on the actual advertising done, on the credits to publishers therefor, and on the charges to the clients for the advertising and commissions, and that the system is actually being carried out in practice.

A good system will provide for the charges to the clients (for the advertising and commissions), the credits to the publishers (for the value of space occupied in their periodicals), and credit to the agency's commission account to be made in one entry from the same original data. If a "space" account is carried in the agency's general ledger and is used as the medium through which the charges to the clients and the credits to the publishers are made, the auditor should ascertain that the balance therein consists of the aggregate value of specific advertising not yet charged to the clients, but credited to the publishers, and of specific advertising not yet credited to the publishers, but charged to the clients.

The contracts of the agency with the publishers of periodicals and with the clients should be examined, and the rates for advertising and commissions should be compared with the agency's records to ascertain that the credits to the publishers for space and the charges to the clients for advertising and commissions are being correctly made.

THEATERS

The auditor of theatrical accounts must at once recognize the fact that a cash system alone prevails and that all persons connected with the financial part of the management necessarily handle this currency. It is a matter of regret that managers cannot be induced to make payments by cheque more generally, but up to the present representations and arguments presenting the advantages of such a system have not been favorably received. However, the practice is increasing gradually, and in time, it is to be hoped, may become general.

While nearly all receipts are in currency, it is not usual for the auditor to be expected to verify such receipts; this is a function for the treasurer, who is considered sufficiently responsible for a service that demands integrity, but no great technical knowledge or unusual ability.

The methods followed in keeping theater accounts are as follows: About half an hour after the beginning of each performance the treasurer of the theater counts his unsold coupon tickets, making up a "rough" statement of the cash which should be on hand; to this he adds the proceeds of sales of "hard tickets" (general admission and exchange), and then submits this statement to the treasurer of the company. The two treasurers then count the tickets contained in the doortenders' boxes, which, except in stormy weather, agree very closely with the rough statement. Following the count the theater treasurer makes out a final statement, which is signed by both treasurers.

A "settlement sheet" is made up at the end of each week by the theater treasurer showing the gross receipts and the share of same due to the theater. Any additional earnings are added thereto, and after deducting the salaries and petty expenses, the treasurer pays the remainder in currency to the manager. The latter usually pays all advertising, bill-posting, light, etc., about Tuesday of each week to cover the previous week. In some theaters the treasurer pays all bills and settles with the manager for the profit or loss shown by the weekly statements only, but this is not a common practice.

The treasurer of the theater also prepares a complete weekly statement for the company treasurer and settles therefor. After making these two settlements he would have on hand only the receipts of the "advance ticket" sales, which latter, as elsewhere considered, should be verified.

It is well to remember that the object of theater bookkeeping is to show the result of each week's business in a manner that will determine which attraction pays best. Such items as annual license fee, rent, repairs, etc., should, therefore, be apportioned weekly on a basis of a season of thirty or thirty-five weeks.

The procedure in an audit of theater accounts should be somewhat as follows:

Deduct the number of coupon tickets on hand from the total capacity of the house; find how many "hard tickets" were furnished the treasurer at the beginning of season, deduct number on hand at time of balancing, and the remainder should be accounted for in cash. The total result should then agree with the cash and vouchers in the hands of the treasurer.

It is necessary to see that all nightly statements of the period under review are signed by the treasurers of the companies. A check on the proper division of receipts may be had by examination of the contracts. These will also enable the auditor to know that the proper shares of extras have been collected from companies. He should also inquire into the manner of preparing pay rolls, in connection with which reference to an attendance book will be necessary. This book records the names of persons entering the premises by the stage door before a performance, and from it fines for absence or lateness are determined.

As both the treasurer and his assistant have access to the

same cash, it will readily be seen that a difficulty obtains in dividing this responsibility; and a similar difficulty arises in connection with the weekly payments to the manager. After making settlement with him, the cash remaining represents the advance ticket sales, which needs to be verified at the time. However, managers seldom count a large number of tickets, and just here more than one defalcation has been covered up or carried along by using advance sales to conceal shortages.

Strip tickets used largely by "vaudeville" or "continuous performance" houses are, of course, easily counted.

THEATRICAL COMPANIES

A treasurer's cash book is the basis of the accounts of a theatrical company; it should be balanced weekly, at least. From it several accounts as here classified (known as "Production" accounts) are built up. These include:

Preliminary Expenses: Incurred during rehearsals, such as salaries of manager, musical director, and orchestra, hall rent, typewriting parts, etc.

Properties: Including almost everything used in the stage representation other than scenery, costumes, or electrical apparatus, such as furniture, draperies, animals (either papier mâché or alive), flowers, etc. Perishable articles should, of course, be absorbed in current expenses and not charged to properties.

Costumes: Covering clothing, shoes, wigs, etc.

Electrical Apparatus: In this item are included calcium lights and special devices. If the electrical equipment is rented instead of being owned, the rental is chargeable to current expenses.

Scenery: The work of building and painting is usually done under contract. The scenery may be built by one firm and painted by different artists. A difficult landscape would probably be done by a high-priced artist, but the painting of a simple interior would be done by a cheaper man.

Vouchers representing expenditures for the foregoing items should be examined. In addition, an audit would include the verification of receipts by comparing them with the nightly statements signed by the house treasurer; and also seeing that the fines imposed by the stage manager are accounted for. The company's earnings statement is made up weekly to agree with the theater accounts.

Owing to the uncertainty of the outcome of theatrical productions, definite rules for the treatment of depreciation cannot be stated. The whole cost of an unsuccessful production should be written off forthwith; on the contrary, the copyright of a successful play does not depreciate rapidly in value. In New York the total cost of production is written off against the first year's business. This is obviously the safest practice.

CHAPTER XXVIII

INVESTIGATIONS

PART of the work of the professional auditor is designated, not as an audit, but as an investigation. There is here an actual distinction, just as the work of the accountant may be differentiated from that of an auditor.

For the purposes of this book, audits and investigations are separated only as to the special points to be observed in the latter, it being assumed that in many investigations a complete detailed audit will be required, and that in others a balance sheet audit is essential.

Investigations are usually undertaken in connection with the sale of a business to a corporation or other purchaser for the purpose of obtaining special information relative to finances or general affairs, or with respect to alleged fraudulent transactions, or into the profits derived from the manufacture of infringing articles, etc.

A curious feature connected with investigations, which rarely arises with respect to audits, is the attempt on the part of disreputable promoters, or of those with no reputation at all, to retain the services of reputable auditors. Usually the enterprise to be investigated lacks books of account and promises little in this respect for the future, or a company has been formed with a large capital stock on one side, and mining claims or some equally uncertain asset on the other. A certificate is desired for publication, or for private exhibition to prospective investors.

In the hands of an honest man, an auditor's certificate in the ordinary form might be unobjectionable, but if the certificate is in the possession of an unscrupulous promoter, it may be represented to be an unqualified indorsement of the enterprise and its promoters, and there are enough ignorant investors to believe these or stronger statements. The wise auditor will never permit his certificate to be so used, for a single mistake of this kind in sizing up a client may mean the loss of one's reputation. Successful auditors can take no chances at all in this respect; they must be more particular about their clients than a bank is about its customers.

The various classes of investigations and the special features of each will be discussed in the following order:

I. Upon the sale or purchase of a business.
II. To ascertain information required by:
(*a*) Creditors, prospective creditors, or stockholders.
(*b*) Parties to litigation or disputes.
III. Investigation of suspected fraud.

SCOPE OF THE WORK

Instructions From Clients: The title of this chapter may convey the impression that the work to be done is more or less restricted in its scope, and that the auditor who undertakes an investigation for a special purpose may expect to receive special instructions, differing from the circumstances under which he would be willing to make an audit. It is not claimed that an auditor would insist on proceeding with any professional work, including audits, which appeared to be even remotely in opposition to his clients' wishes. He could withdraw, and this would be the only proper course if he found himself unable to comply with the directions of those for whom his work was intended.

As a member of a profession with high ideals, he can insist, or in the exercise of his full prerogatives he can demand, that instructions outlining the scope of his work, or the form of his certificate and report, shall accord with honorable motives and straightforward dealing. Otherwise, he cannot proceed without forfeiture of his self-respect.

If the instructions are incomplete and the auditor fails to interpret them broadly, so as to include all of the results which are called for by the nature of the case, he should not attempt to excuse his deficient results by falling back on his instructions. Therefore, at the commencement of an investigation it is most important that specific instructions be issued by the client, or prepared by the auditor and confirmed by the client.

Working Papers to be Preserved: Following up his instructions from the client, the auditor will issue special directions to his own staff. The remarks on working papers (page 77) apply with full force, and, in addition, special care must be taken to preserve all data bearing on the adjustment of the accounts. In few investigations will the auditor's report show accounts and amounts as they appear on the books. Even if net results are not altered, an analysis will have been made resulting in a different arrangement and presentation.

It is of the utmost importance that working sheets be prepared and retained which will show in absolute detail the reconciliation of the original book figures with those appearing in the final report. Neglect of this precaution may subsequently result in censure for neglect, coupled with the necessity of duplicate work, for which a charge cannot, or should not, be made.

In some cases the working papers of an audit have to be referred to after the report is submitted, but in nearly all investigations, questions arise after the work is completed which require reference to the data compiled during the progress of the work.

Detail Which May Be Omitted: If "investigation" were simply another name for an audit, this chapter would not have been written.

In general it may be stated that as an investigation is *not* an audit, but an inquiry into specific matters, the routine requirements of an audit as outlined in this book may be omitted. Later on, the features which must *not* be omitted will be discussed.

Previous Audits: It has also been mentioned that in an ordinary engagement the auditor will often find himself to be the first professional auditor who has been consulted. But with investigations, which are frequently called for in connection with consolidations of prosperous enterprises, it will be found that many of the latter have had their accounts audited. If the auditor can secure the reports of such examinations, he will have a basis upon which to determine what use he can make thereof. Obviously this basis will depend on the standing of the other auditors and the nature of their reports.

If access to previous reports cannot be had, the auditor should secure permission to consult with the previous auditors for the purpose of securing any information possible. If this is not feasible, he will have to proceed as if the accounts had never been audited.

Where Assets are Appraised: It is becoming fairly general in an investigation to employ appraisers as well as auditors. The former must take the responsibility for physical valuations of fixed assets items, and while this is of great assistance to the auditor, he should never incorporate their valuations in his accounts without considering their relation to the profit and loss account. The auditor should steadfastly maintain that he cannot state the net profits of a business irrespective of an examination of the assets and liabilities. If the book assets must be adjusted to an appraisal, the profit and loss account may require adjustment also. The word "may" is used advisedly, as some appraisal companies are inclined to overvalue physical assets. It is pleasing to proprietors (which may explain why it is done), but it does not always afford a reasonable basis for a writing up of book values and a consequent adjustment of the profits.

On the other hand, in view of this tendency, any insufficiency of assets shown by an appraisal should be reflected in the profit and loss account.

Definite Report Wanted: In order that there may be no misunderstanding, it should be understood that the author does not advocate submitting suggestions and criticisms based on mere hearsay, or on incomplete information. The point to be emphasized is that *all* facts pertinent to the inquiry are permissible and may be of more value than a mass of figures.

Certain adjustments are necessary in practically all investigations, but the auditor must be firm in arranging the results and in wording his report, or it may be found that the final conclusions are far from representing a well-thought-out opinion of the standing of the business.

Auditors have been very properly warned that if there is nothing definite for them to report, they should not be led into stating that if the expectations of the promoter are realized his estimates of the profits are correct.

Handling Books and Records: Before making a single mark of any description in a record which is the property of another, the auditor should ask himself the question: "Is there any possibility of these records being falsified, and might it embarrass me later if it were shown that I had made marks herein?" In every case the question should act as a reminder that if marks are warranted they should be small, neat, and so made as to be readily and positively identified on any subsequent occasion.

If fraud is suspected, it is always desirable, and sometimes necessary, that no marks at all should be made. In such a case the entries which are falsified should be rewritten on loose sheets, paged the same as the original records, and the correct amounts shown in an adjoining column. This will permit a summary of the fictitious entries being made up at any time.

False Entries Sometimes Forgeries: The entry of an incorrect amount in a book of record, if made with intent to defraud, is forgery, and therefore a serious crime.

Frequently false entries are found in books which indicate that the one responsible therefor has misappropriated an equivalent sum of money, but it may be difficult to produce satisfactory evidence as to when and how the defaulter actually took the cash.

It is well known that a verdict of guilty is difficult to secure from a jury when the evidence consists largely of complicated and manipulated accounts. The defaulter's plea that his books were unfortunately mixed up, but that he never stole anything, appeals to the sympathy of the average man. If it can be shown conclusively, however, that certain entries are fraudulent on their face, it may be possible to prove a charge of forgery. An auditor should always be familiar with the law of his own State on this subject.

Books as Evidence: Aside from the question of fraud, it is always desirable that books and records be kept neatly and accurately, and that they be complete and coördinate. In other words, there can be no possible argument against accurate and creditable books of account, but serious loss may result from inaccurate and incomplete records. In the course of time a considerable number of business enterprises are compelled to engage in litigation, either as plaintiffs or defendants, in which the books of account must be produced and offered in evidence, and many cases are lost through lack of evidence on some vital point on account of insufficient or discreditable data.

The auditor will have many opportunities of dealing with

the wrong kind of books, which experiences will serve as examples when he tells his clients what not to do.

Loose-Leaf Records: It was formerly held that loose-leaf records were not proper and sufficient evidence, by reason of the supposed danger of substitution, but business custom and convenience forced a change, so that to-day these records, when bearing on their face all the signs of regularity, are admitted without question.

The chief point to bear in mind in any event is the effect on a jury. Carelessly kept bound books may have an adverse effect, while neatly kept loose-leaf records, in binders, may impress the jury as containing complete and dependable records of the transactions in question.

Erasures: The matter of erasures is one to which the auditor should give some attention. It directly affects the neat-looking pages which some bookkeepers love, but it may be laid down as a general rule that an incorrect figure ruled out, and with the correct amount inserted above, always stands for itself, while an erasure or alteration is sometimes hard to understand. If it should develop at some later day that the altered figure is one required to base an action or defense upon, the position of the clerk responsible therefor is not an enviable one.

The one great factor is accuracy, and to this beauty must, if there is need, be subordinated.

Original Records Necessary: The foregoing remarks lead up to a consideration of the value of records which are merely transcripts of others, or to which the entries in other books have been posted.

In England it is customary to keep certain original records in more or less "rough" form, and subsequently transfer the entries to "fair" books. In such a case the moment it is shown that a certain book is merely a copy of another, and was written subsequently, it loses most of its value and the original record is called for. If destroyed, the entire case might be lost.

This possibility contains a twofold lesson: it emphasizes the desirability of making all original records part of the double entry system of accounts without rewriting, and in addition insures the preservation of records which may be called for when least expected.

(1) UPON THE SALE OR PURCHASE OF A BUSINESS

The professional auditor is now being consulted frequently by the man who wishes to sell as well as the man who wishes to buy. The former realizes that the services of an independent auditor are of the utmost value to him in stating the ramifications of his business so clearly that he will not omit any favorable aspects in dealing with a prospective purchaser. Likewise, the buyer feels that he cannot afford to depend on the representations of the seller nor on his own judgment. One may pay too high a price and the other may sell at too low a price unless the professional auditor passes upon the proposition.

It is generally recognized by leading accountants that when an auditor represents a prospective purchaser, much that is necessary in an ordinary audit may be omitted. It is safe and legitimate to assume that the seller will not underestimate his profits, nor his assets, and that he will not overstate his liabilities.

Briefly stated, if the auditor finds actual net earnings and assets equaling the representations, and no more liabilities than are claimed, he need not spend unnecessary time on an inspection of the expense vouchers and similar work.

The chief points of difference which may arise between an investigation of this kind and an audit, are the following:

(*a*) Something more than figures are wanted.
(*b*) Period covered.
(*c*) Analysis of earnings and expenses.
(*d*) Future requirements and economies.
(*e*) System of accounts.
(*f*) Elimination of unusual items.
(*g*) Adjustments and qualifications.
(*h*) Errors in the books.
(*i*) Investigation on behalf of a retiring partner when the business is being sold to a continuing partner.
(*j*) Investigation for those in charge of reorganizations.

(a) Something More Than Figures Wanted: The prospective purchaser of a business wants to know as much of its past history as a man does of his prospective bride. He usually contemplates joining fortunes for an indefinite period, and his associations must represent more than mere financial gain. Who is better equipped to pass on the enterprise from almost every point of view than an experienced auditor?

Most accountants feel that their full duty has been discharged when they submit a balance sheet and a profit and loss statement, together with such comments thereon as modify the figures submitted. Outside of these figures, they will not go, on the theory that to do so would mean a departure from facts into the realm of theory.

Nothing could be more inconsistent! The figures shown are, with very few exceptions, estimates only. The stock-in-trade is always worth something more or less than the inventory valuation. The fixed assets vary in value to such an extent that book valuations are usually shown because actual values are unknown. The accounts receivable are valued on past experience, which may be deceptive. There may be contingent liabilities of large amount unknown and not provided for. Therefore, certain conclusions as to the conduct of the business, the trend of prices, and other general information may be compiled by the auditor and reported upon with about as much dependability as the accounts.

What does a prospective purchaser want? It is not enough that the report of the auditor, the appraiser, or the engineer show that the assets, as represented, are in existence or that the earnings equal the guaranteed estimates. It is of quite as much importance to be assured that the management as it existed at the time of the examination was all that could be desired. Assets are sometimes accumulated and earnings realized through cumulative circumstances which are no longer a factor, or under the administration of men no longer connected with the enterprise.

In the United States, new industries or special and ingenious processes may have been responsible for large profits which subsequently become reduced through the natural economic law of competition and imitation. Capital flows to unusually profitable enterprises as surely as water finds its level.

Suppose the business under investigation has shown unusual profits up to the date of the last balance sheet. Is the auditor charged with the duty of forecasting a probable change? Perhaps not, but many enterprises have failed to maintain past profits, although the latter have been actual, and the auditor's certificates thereto true in all respects. In some cases bankruptcy has resulted within a year after the flotation of a stock or bond issue, due entirely to a drop in gross profits caused by competition, the removal of tariff protection, compulsory reduction in rates by public authority or private demand, or reckless or fraudulent practices.

The auditor is not and would not be held responsible for losses arising out of these contingencies, but if the downward movement were starting during the course of his examination, should he not convey his impressions to his client? It may be said that a prospective purchaser should think of these things himself. Perhaps he should, but he doesn't.

The author has followed this line of suggestion more or less for some years, and has found that the comments are well received and always appreciated, even though his advice may not always be followed.

An auditor who expects to perform a considerable amount of investigating in the course of his practice will find it very useful to compile statistics of various businesses. This may seem to be a formidable undertaking, but it may not be. It so happens that the proprietors of a business will hear that a certain auditor has just completed an examination of the books of some one in the same line as themselves. They feel that he has acquired special knowledge relative to methods, etc., which may be beneficial to them. It should be remarked in passing that only in the rarest cases has an auditor been asked to reveal any confidential information which he has secured from a competitor.

But the auditor may for his own information compile statistics as to what a certain kind of business should earn, and what its expenses and costs should be. Without revealing the source of his information, he may be able to offer constructive suggestions or in the case of a purchase or sale, or other investigation, he may be able to comment more intelligently on the accounts than if he were dependent entirely on the data compiled in each particular case.

There is another line of investigation which is not often reflected in a report: are the accounts to which the auditor will certify, prepared directly from the current books of account, or are they the result of special compilation? If the latter, is the actual state of the books an indication of neglect or ignorance? Have the proprietors kept themselves informed as to the results of operations through monthly or other frequent periodical statements, or have they waited for definite results until the end of their fiscal year, when an inventory is taken?

Have they, therefore, been dependent entirely upon intuitive knowledge, which is possessed more or less (chiefly less) by executives who scorn theory and accounts, and who boast of the value of practical experience? Are the departments coördinated, or do they run independently to such an extent that one does not know what the other is doing? Is it a fact that certain departments are a law unto themselves, that they run along and write up copious records which are never used by those to whom they might be supposed to be of value?

All of these queries and many more might be answered offhand by an auditor who had completed an investigation into assets, liabilities, and earnings, but he could not properly report thereon unless he had been in contact with every department of the business. Having this information, why should he not report thereon verbally or in writing?

All these suggestions have a bearing on the two thoughts which are uppermost in the mind of a prospective purchaser, viz., "Taking everything into consideration, is the business a desirable acquisition?" and "How much is it worth?" The auditor may not wish to give a definite answer to either question, but he can furnish figures and other information which will be of the utmost interest.

(b) Period Covered: As stated at the commencement of this chapter, the auditor should require definite instructions before starting an investigation. These instructions usually specify the period to be covered. As a prospective purchaser wishes to know absolutely all that is possible about the past, it is usual to verify the earnings for as many years back as time will permit. Three years would be a minimum, while ten years would not be too long a period for those who expect to make a permanent investment.

As will be pointed out later, it is not necessary to audit the accounts in the usual sense. An analysis is all that is required. Therefore, it is very little more work to cover six years than three, unless, of course, the records for past years are incomplete or inaccurate. The longer the period, the more accurately will the trend of the business be shown. Most enterprises have good and poor years, and the respective recurrence of these is of great interest.

In no event should the results of two or more years be lumped. A big year and a small year might make a satisfactory average, but few wish to invest in a business where the small year is the last. Therefore, each year must be shown separately, and averages never used unless the actual results of the last year or two are substantially above the average.

The auditor must not fail to inspect the results between the date of the balance sheet and the time of the examination. The most recent month should be compared with the same month for previous years, and if an unfavorable result is shown, the fact should be reported.

(c) Analysis of Earnings and Expenses: Gross Earnings: In an audit it is always important to verify the gross earnings. In many investigations the prospective purchaser is greatly interested therein and is almost indifferent with respect to the net. He says that with his own appraisement of the physical property, and a personal knowledge of local conditions, he requires nothing additional except an accurate statement of the gross receipts or earnings of the enterprise in order to determine upon the price he is willing to pay for the property. The reason is that an experienced executive knows, or thinks he knows, the proper ratio of operating expenses which will be incurred under proper management, and it is of little moment to him how much the old management has expended.

This procedure is followed in connection with the sale of public utility companies oftener than with any other class. The sales or output of these companies is, of course, more nearly constant and dependable than with trading or manufacturing enterprises. But capable men in nearly all lines are found willing to invest in a business with which they are familiar, and if reasonably assured of a minimum of gross earnings, will undertake to guarantee a maximum of operating cost, irrespective of what the previous owner may have done.

Recently a large and unsuccessful taxicab company was purchased by a competitor who was willing to guarantee a satisfactory profit on the purchase price if operated separately, and an additional saving if consolidated with his own company. He had managed a business with exactly the same problems as those of his competitor, and had been able to produce a large profit out of smaller gross earnings. He knew the competitor's shortcomings without seeing an analysis of its expenses.

This illustrates the importance of a thorough understanding of the client's viewpoint before commencing an investigation. If a purchaser is chiefly interested in gross earnings, the auditor will take great care to state them properly, looking carefully into the sources of revenue, comparing one period with another, and noting any deductions therefrom in the shape of discounts, returns, allowances, etc. The latter should be deducted from the gross earnings and not included among the expenses. He will then state the expenses and costs as shown by the books and make such verification only as may be required.

Net Earnings: On the other hand, if a prospective purchaser does not have any preconceived ideas as to the proper relation between gross and net earnings, the auditor will make his examination exhaustive enough to enable him to prepare and submit full and complete analyses of expenses as well as earnings.

The comparative statements of earnings will afford profitable data relating to the progress of the enterprise. Of all businesses in which a purchaser is interested, the one with a stable earning power and small but sure earnings is preferred to the one which fluctuates violently. Many business men manufacturing a novelty, or working under patents, have an unusually prosperous year due to lack of competition or some similar cause. They immediately talk of incorporating or reincorporating on the basis of the one year's earnings, and commence to spend money as if it were an annuity instead of the returns from an exceptional year.

The auditor who is consulted in such a case will do his client a kindness if he will point out the wisdom of waiting until he can show a good three or five-year average before he is justified in considering his business as on a stable basis, and one in which others will care to invest.

Fluctuations must be noted and explained. Gross earnings depend largely on general business conditions, but costs and expenses do not, as a rule, vary to the same extent.

It is necessary to obtain an analysis of the accounts and be able to report the various stages from gross earnings to net profits. In a trading business, for instance, the following form of statement brings out the information which a prospective purchaser requires:

A B COMPANY

Comparative Statement of EARNINGS AND EXPENSES for 3 years ended May 31, 1913

	Years Ended					
	1913 May 31	Per Cent	1912 May 31	Per Cent	1911 May 31	Per Cent
Gross Sales:	....	......	....	......	....	......
Less Allowances and Returns	....	......	....	......	....	......
Net Sales	....	......	....	......	....	......
Inventory, beginning of period	....	......	....	......	....	......
Purchases, net	....	......	....	......	....	......
Less Inventory end of period	....	......	....	......	....	......
Cost of Sales	....	......	....	......	....	......
Gross Profit	....	......	....	......	....	......
Ratio to Sales	....	......	....	......	....	......
Ratio to Cost	....	......	....	......	....	......
Selling Expenses:						
Salesmen's Salaries	....	......	....	......	....	......
Salesmen's Expenses	....	......	....	......	....	......
Commissions	....	......	....	......	....	......
Advertising	....	......	....	......	....	......
Catalogs	....	......	....	......	....	......
Delivery Expenses	....	......	....	......	....	......
Total Selling Expenses	....	......	....	......	....	......
Ratio to Sales	....	......	....	......	....	......
Administration and General Expenses:						
Executive Salaries	....	......	....	......	....	......
Office Salaries	....	......	....	......	....	......
Office Expenses	....	......	....	......	....	......
Stationery and Office Supplies	....	......	....	......	....	......
Telephone and Telegraph	....	......	....	......	....	......
Postage	....	......	....	......	....	......
Traveling Expenses	....	......	....	......	....	......
Legal Expenses	....	......	....	......	....	......
Rent	....	......	....	......	....	......
Insurance	....	......	....	......	....	......
Light, Heat, and Power	....	......	....	......	....	......
Building Repairs, and Maintenance	....	......	....	......	....	......
Depreciation on Furniture and Fixtures	....	......	....	......	....	......
Miscellaneous	....	......	....	......	....	......
Total Administration and General Expenses	....	......	....	......	....	......
Ratio to Sales	....	......	....	......	....	......
Total Expenses	....	......	....	......	....	......
Net Earnings	....	......	....	......	....	......
Deductions: Interest on Loans, etc.	....	......	....	......	....	......
Net Profit	....	......	....	......	....	......

It will be noted that the percentages shown are gross profit to sales, gross profit to cost, selling expenses to sales, administration and other expenses to sales. As an investigation implies a comparison of two or more years, these percentages are of more value, relatively, than the amounts. The net profit for each year being shown, the next most important thing is to know how it was made. If the sales were about the same for two successive years, the variation in the percentages of expenses would be most interesting, and to a prospective purchaser it might be a deciding factor to learn that while the selling expenses increased, the administration expenses decreased.

Verification of Sales: It will be assumed that all sales except of recent date will be verified otherwise than through the sales records. That is, after being charged to the personal accounts of customers, if overdue they will be handled as doubtful accounts.

As it is customary to accept recent sales as collectible, it is necessary for the auditor to satisfy himself that they are bona fide and not manipulated to produce a good showing just before the date of the balance sheet.

The more common forms of manipulation are:

(1) Inclusion of goods sent on consignment and approval as completed sales. This practice may result from ignorance, rather than fraudulent intent.

(2) Sales or earnings may have been unduly inflated by charging out wholly fictitious quantities and amounts. Where the earnings arise from cash sales, the amount by which the earnings are to be increased is arbitrarily added to the daily receipts. At least one instance is known of the improper increase of street railway fares by a promoter who planned ahead to sell out. He knew that the purchase price would be calculated on a certain number of times the net profit realized, or be based on the gross earnings of the most recent period.

It will be seen that if the good will of a property were to be sold on a basis of four times the average net earnings for the last two years, any method of increasing such earnings would at least double the cost thereof, i. e., the addition to cash sales of each $100 would be divided by two to get the average for two years and then multiplied by four to arrive at the purchase price, thus yielding a profit of at least one hundred per cent for the fraudulent practice.

A scheme of this nature must necessarily be planned ahead, which does not apply to most manipulations. This makes it extremely difficult to detect, and no general test can be devised which will surely uncover the fraud. The auditor who keeps constantly before him the possibility of fraud designed to inflate the earnings will have the best chance of discovering it.

Where the legitimate cash sales or receipts are small, no one would be bold enough to inflate them to any considerable extent. Therefore, the most feasible method is to enter among the bona fide sales fictitious names, quantities, and amounts. This fraud will be disclosed to the auditor who investigates the average number of new customers' accounts opened within a given period. Any unusual increase would be worth while looking into in any event. If legitimate, the question of a continuation thereof would be important; if not legitimate, it would be even more important to uncover the irregularity.

If there has been an increase in prices shortly before the date of the balance sheet, the cause thereof should be investigated. Such increases are not always maintained, and it would be unsafe to depend thereon unless the most positive evidence could be secured of the propriety and wisdom of the change.

It may also have been the case that special contracts have been undertaken which have realized large profits, but which may never be repeated. For instance, a small steam railway company reaped the advantage of a military encampment during a considerable part of one summer. The increase over its normal traffic was enormous. Yet a prospective purchaser would have no assurance whatever of a repetition of such earnings.

The period after the closing date up to the time of the investigation must be scanned closely for rebates, allowances, and returns to see if they constitute deductions from prior sales. Likewise, the subsequent sales will be inspected, particularly if suspiciously small, as it might indicate that shipments after the closing date were carried back and charged under false dates.

The Turnover: Authorities differ greatly as to what this term means. The dictionary definitions are: "A completed commercial transaction"; "The money receipts of a business for a given period."

The merchant who speaks of his "turnover" usually refers to his gross sales, but if his answer were analyzed it would be found that his reference was rather to his stock of goods than to the sales value thereof. If he started his fiscal year with a certain inventory, he would endeavor to "turn it over" several times during the year. In this case it would mean the cost of the sales, because his inventory and subsequent purchases are entered at cost, and it is this stock that he is endeavoring to turn over to the greatest possible advantage.

The banker does not look with favor on the borrower whose gross sales are not several times as much as his starting inventory, and it is a fair inference that sales and cost of sales are here used interchangeably.

Uniformity is desirable in accountancy terminology, so the author suggests this definition: The turnover of a merchant or manufacturer represents the number of times his capital in the form of stock in trade is reinvested in stock-in-trade during a given period.

To ascertain the turnover, take the starting inventory, add the purchases or cost of manufactured goods, and deduct the inventory at the end; divide the total by the starting inventory. The result will be the number of times the capital invested in stock in trade has been turned over during the period.

The capital invested in the stock and the physical stock itself may be used synonymously in referring to the "turnover" of a business.

Profits on Fluctuations: Many enterprises using staple raw materials frequently buy their requirements in advance, and in numerous instances have found it more profitable to sell their entire stock on a rapidly advancing market than to operate their mills. This occurs oftener with cotton than with any other commodity, but the practice obtains in other lines, such as grain, pork, copper, etc.

If such profits are actually realized, they should appear as a special item in the current profit and loss account. On the other hand, if the transactions have resulted in a net loss, the most conservative method will be to include the loss in the current accounts, on the theory that an extraordinary profit should not be counted as operating income, but that safety will not permit a loss to be ignored, inasmuch as it will have to be paid out of current earnings.

Decrease in Expenses: The expenses of all classes will be compared for a number of years. If there has been any considerable decrease during the period shortly before the balance-sheet date, a careful analysis should be made to determine the possibility of the omission of liabilities which have been incurred, but the entry and payment thereof postponed.

The auditor must look at all expense payments after the closing of the books; if unduly large, the vouchers should be examined and their dates noted, as some of them may be for expenses incurred prior to the close of the fiscal period.

Advertising and Other Deferred Charges: It will be found that excessive valuations are frequently placed upon the prospective earning power of advertising and other forms of exploitation. In the publishing business, for instance, it has been considered permissible to capitalize the expenses of establishing a magazine. There is no possibility nor expectation of recouping the preliminary expenses out of the earnings of the first year or two. If successful, the early advertising, etc., will have been justified and should be charged against the years which reap the benefit.

In practice, however, the result is not ideal. Many periodicals have incurred large preliminary expenses, capitalized same, and have never been able to charge off any part thereof against earnings. Other publications which have shown a loss in their early years because no deferred charges were carried over have realized large enough profits in subsequent years to recoup all the preliminary expenses.

It is a difficult matter to settle at best, but is doubly hard for a prospective purchaser. The best advice to give is to suggest that if the business has been running for some time, all such charges, unless very recent, should have been absorbed, and that if too recent to forecast the result, the purchase of the prospective profits arising therefrom is a pure gamble, modified perhaps by evidence, if available, of what similar advertising expenditure has produced in the past.

Leases: If the concern under investigation does not own the land and buildings within which its business is transacted, the matter of the lease and renewals thereof is of the utmost importance. It is safe to estimate that out of one hundred leases for a long term, or which provide for extensions, more than seventy-five per cent call for a higher rental during the later years than at the beginning of the term. Where the renewal rate is not fixed, it usually is to be based on an appraisal, and, in perhaps every case, it is contemplated by owner and lessee that the future rental to be fixed on such appraisal will be higher as a result thereof.

Therefore, the prospective purchaser must ascertain definitely whether he can retain the same premises for a reasonable time if he so decides, and whether the prospects for an increased business or other equivalents will compensate for the increased expense if a long lease is desired. Conversely a prospective purchaser may not be willing to buy the business unless it can be removed economically to a new location. In such a case a long lease might in itself prevent the consummation of the deal.

Strange as it may seem, prospective purchasers do not always think of these matters during the early stages of negotiations. The auditor should ascertain the precise state of affairs with respect to the lease before he enters upon an investigation of earnings, the result of which has no interest for a purchaser who may not have known that a long lease on an ascending scale could not be disposed of.

In other cases, a purchaser may be negotiating for several properties with the intention of consolidating them. It may be part of his plans to unite them all in one place. Obviously the terms of the leases, if any, are of extreme importance.

Sometimes mergers are effected, and plants consolidated, leaving certain plants idle. If the plans of the promoters contemplate leasing the idle plants at a remunerative rate, or leave out of consideration the continuation of the payment of rentals which cannot be evaded, a serious difference between estimated and actual profits might ensue.

In conclusion, it cannot be stated too strongly that the location of a business may determine its success or failure, and any facts or opinions relative thereto which the auditor can furnish will be of the greatest interest to his client.

Inventories: In an investigation for a prospective purchaser the question of inventories is one of the most important. Little need be added to the discussion on this subject on pages 107-112 except that the distinction must be especially noted between valuations properly incident to a going business and those which apply in case of a purchase.

Naturally and properly the purchaser wishes to buy as cheaply as possible, and the seller desires to realize as high a price as he can secure. But in representing one or the other, the auditor cannot allow any such considerations to affect his mind in arriving at the earnings. The latter should be the same, whether prepared for a vendor or a vendee.

Inventories vitally affect the profit and loss account and the good will of a business rests upon the profits realized. The result is that inventories actually fix or materially control the purchase price of the business, because the overstatement of an inventory results in an overstatement of profits.

An auditor need not, and, as a matter of fact he cannot, be entirely indifferent to the interests of his client. If he represents a purchaser, it is almost certain that the seller will have stated the inventories at the highest possible price, so that he need not be particularly concerned about not doing justice to him.

The experienced auditor will prepare a report the accuracy of which he can maintain before conflicting interests if misunderstandings arise, as is often the case when commercial enterprises change hands.

Other Factors Which Affect Earnings: Inasmuch as all of the items of assets and liabilities, as well as all sources of income and every class of expenses, enter into the final adjustment of the profit and loss account, the auditor should not pass finally upon the amount of net profit or net loss, to which he will certify, unless he has covered, or intentionally left untouched, all of the procedure required in a balance-sheet audit. The practitioner who does not have his own program for an investigation is, therefore, referred to the chapters of this book describing a balance-sheet audit.

(d) Future Requirements and Economies: An Auditor Should Not Prophesy: The author has taken the position that an auditor is bound to furnish to his client all of the information bearing on the investigation or audit which he believes to be reliable and relevant, and that he is by no means limited to the figures which any intelligent bookkeeper might compile.

But it must be understood most positively that it is never

permissible for an auditor, as such, to certify to future earnings or future results. An auditor can express his opinion as to the effect particular transactions will have if applied to a future date. For instance, an auditor would be justified in stating that if a million dollars of bonds were sold at par the bank account would be increased by the same amount. But an auditor would not be justified in stating over his signature that if a million dollars of bonds were sold at par and invested in the business, savings would result sufficient to net an additional profit. This would be pure surmise, for unexpected losses or expenses might more than offset the savings, or the additional capital might be lost entirely through errors of judgment in its expenditure.

Business men and financiers frequently ask their auditors to calculate the effect certain changes will have on the results of operations. For instance, an auditor will be asked to prepare a statement showing the probable outcome if gross sales are doubled, with no proportionate increase in fixed charges. This is proper, profitable, and pleasing work for a public accountant, and he should welcome the engagement, but it must be distinctly understood, before the work commences and after it is finished, that his work is performed in the capacity of an accountant and not that of an auditor. He should refrain from submitting his estimates on paper which bears his name at the top or the bottom, otherwise there is a risk of the figures being put forth as if they were certified to.

Great pressure is sometimes brought to bear on auditors to have them certify to what are in reality only estimates. It is an astonishing fact that certificates have been issued which are so worded that the untrained mind reads therein that the auditor is satisfied that if certain additional capital is raised, or something of that kind, there will be sufficient earnings to pay a large return thereon. The auditor who lends his name to such near-fraud should be expelled from any accounting body to which he may belong.

There are a number of matters which affect the future upon which an auditor may and should give his opinion, and he may and should discuss the relation which such matters have to the past, but in no case should these be grouped in such a way that there can be read into the opinion a conclusion as to the future net profit or net loss of an enterprise. The author believes that this is the best test to apply when in doubt as to how far an auditor should go in furnishing information.

Insufficient Capital: For instance, a business may have had insufficient working capital, and discounts may not have been taken advantage of. A prospective purchaser may ask that a report be compiled which will assume adequate cash capital. An analysis of past purchases may definitely fix the saving which would have been made, but the point at issue is whether or not a like saving can be realized in the future.

If an auditor is asked to prepare a statement setting forth the past results and then stating that in his opinion the following period will produce a given result, assuming the saving of discounts, he is going far beyond his province. But if in his opinion the discounts will continue, or some equivalent thereof, there can be no valid objection to his stating in a certificate that assuming ample capital and upon the same volume of business there will be one item of saving, mentioning the amount.

There may be other undue expenses or losses due to insufficient capital, but most of the arguments advanced as to what would have been accomplished are fallacies.

Naturally a prospective purchaser wants to know wherein economies can be effected or profits increased, and evidence may be available to prove the truth of the representations made. The most common claim is that the output has been too small, and that additional facilities would have meant greatly increased profits. Output, however, must be sold to produce a profit, and it is always easier to talk about a big increase in sales than to secure actual orders. Men who are partially successful frequently overestimate the buying capacity for what they sell. The market may readily consume all that is offered, but if the offerings were to double, the sales price of the whole might be reduced to an unprofitable basis.

Large capital is by no means a guarantee of financial success, and any investigation into the capital required for a particular business, the effect of a lack of it in the past, and the possible returns therefrom in the future, calls for more acumen and general business knowledge than most men possess. Nevertheless, there are times when an auditor can be of substantial value in such an investigation, and there can be no objection to his placing at the disposal of his client the benefit of his experience, but for his own sake he must not permit the publication of a certificate which can be directly or indirectly interpreted as a statement of future results.

Comments on future requirements should always be accompanied by a statement as to the average net capital employed in the old business. This will afford an opportunity for a prospective purchaser to arrange for additional capital if the old is inadequate.

Economies Exaggerated: One has but to read some of the glowing prospectuses issued a few years ago to appreciate the difference between expectation and realization. Fortunately not much of the responsibility for the failure of many large enterprises can be traced to auditors, but a part of the blame might not be improperly placed on their shoulders.

It has been stated in these pages that an accountant should be available to make calculations and compile data, for which others would take the responsibility. This is true, but no public accountant should ever work in the capacity of a clerk. He may assist in the preparation of a statement which purports to show the economies to be effected by a merger of two or more concerns, but if, through ignorance or lack of experience, estimates are made which the accountant knows cannot be fulfilled, he should not hesitate to express his convictions, and if it appears that facts are to be ignored and the public deceived, he had better withdraw in order to avoid any possible connection with the enterprise.

Almost without exception promoters have, or seem to have, visions of two or more plants being conducted on about the same expense ratio as the most economical of those merged. Economies in all departments are prophesied, and, as a matter of fact, many are possible and are effected. But they are sorely needed to offset the extraordinary expenses and extravagances which seem to be a necessary element in the promotion and establishment of all such consolidations.

To start with, vast sums are paid in cash or securities to promoters, attorneys, and insiders. Then engineers and accountants must receive large fees, although far less in proportion than those paid the lawyers.

The bankers, lawyers, anl others who become members of the board would not think of attending a board meeting at the dingy business offices of one of the old concerns, so a large and expensive suite of offices is secured "downtown." With expensive offices go expensive clerks, and so on down the line. How many poorly paid clerks and others must be dismissed at the works to pay a fractional part of the new and additional expenses which were not referred to in the prospectus?

If anyone thinks this description is an exaggeration, let him examine a few of the popular consolidations of about ten years ago.

Former Owners' Attitude: Except in rare cases the business which changes hands or consolidates with others has been prosperous. It is conceded that the personal element is the most important factor in business life, so that if the personal attention of the former proprietor is not available after the sale takes place, it is absolutely essential that an equivalent be found, or the success of former years will not be duplicated.

This is another of the matters with which an auditor is not usually concerned, but no one has a better opportunity to observe the relative position of each person responsible for the former prosperity than the auditor who investigates the finances of the business for a series of years. If the examination makes it apparent that one or more of the proprietors, managers, or other officials were dominant in its affairs, there can be no reasonable objection to this fact being communicated to the prospective purchaser.

Many men think that ordinary ability, coupled with plenty of money, can win success in almost any line of business, but this is not true, as may be proved beyond a doubt by examining for a while the bankruptcy announcements. Many concerns which start in business with ample capital fail because they are not properly managed. Other concerns with less capital, doing precisely the same kind of business, during the same period of time, will realize large profits.

One of the most striking instances is that of the wholesale grocery business. Here conditions are nearly equal. The same kinds of goods are bought and sold. The same customers are available to all, yet in the same city one concern will earn large profits, while another doing a large business will not earn a dollar of net profit. It is due to the personnel of the management, and where successful executives can be retained, an auditor will not be exceeding his duty if he comments on the matter.

Competition: Some business men wish to expand, or consolidate, or do something else that sounds big just as soon as they have had one big year. It usually happens that the extraordinary profits earned have been due to a monopoly of a certain kind of product. Now economic laws will adjust an inordinate profit by stimulating competition. Publicity which follows a sale or the publication of earnings will, of course, spread the knowledge of large profits.

An exception may be noted in the case of patented articles, where the continuance of a monopoly is protected by law. But where there are no patents of vital importance, the question of competition must be seriously considered.

Another element which affects competition is the personal attention referred to in the preceding section. If the business deals in any goods which are dependent upon the taste of the public, it must be borne in mind that the public is very fickle.

Popular demand may be increased by advertising or maintained more or less by fair dealing and courteous treatment, but no one can foretell what the future will develop in the way of competition, and for this reason a prospective purchaser must think deeply before he commits himself to a proposition, which, to yield a satisfactory return upon the purchase price, will have to continue to earn so large a gross profit that there is an endeavor to keep the facts secret.

How long an economic law can be arrested is for the purchaser to decide.

(e) System of Accounts: Criticisms Should Be Postponed: In special investigations such as here discussed, the auditor should never express an opinion as to the condition of the accounts, except in a confidential report to the prospective purchaser. During the course of the work he must accept things as he finds them, and in order to secure the sympathy or coöperation of the office staff, he must be careful to praise anything which deserves praise, and refrain as much as possible from criticizing accounts or methods which cannot be approved.

When the purchase is consummated and the auditor is requested to submit suggestions and criticisms, then his working papers should disclose full information available for use.

Condition of Accounts an Index to Proprietors: There are some particularly shrewd bankers who make frequent purchases of properties, and in other cases furnish capital, who consider that an auditor's report on the condition of the accounts reflects very accurately the kind of men who have been running the business.

If profits have been large and no accounts worthy of the name have been kept, it is apparent that these men have depended upon their own ability to earn money, and as this cannot be sold and transferred very readily it is not a safe plan to continue such incomplete records.

Preparation for New System: Therefore, in their contracts the bankers sometimes insert stipulations along the following lines:

(1) That within sixty days after the formation of the new company, public accountants satisfactory to the purchasers shall be employed to devise and install a modern system of accounts for the company which will permit of full and accurate reports of its operations and its financial condition being made at least monthly. (In many cases this provision is objected to, but bankers are anxious to have the accounts reorganized wherever dependable results are not readily available, and therefore hesitate to finance a company whose accounts are unsatisfactory.)

(2) That said accountants shall be furnished all requisite information and facilities for carrying into effect such changes as may be necessary, and that the officers and employees of said new company shall coöperate with the accountants in the installation and completion of the new system within a reasonable time, which in no event shall exceed twelve months from the date hereof.

(3) That the reports contemplated by said proposed new system shall be delivered each month to the board of directors of the new company, one copy thereof to remain on file with the secretary of the company, subject to the inspection of any mem-

ber of the board, and one copy thereof to be mailed each month to the purchasers, as long as the (preferred) stock is not retired.

(4) That in the event of accountants being employed for the purposes heretofore stated, then the said accountants shall be retained to audit the accounts of the new company at least annually. If the system in use is satisfactory and accountants are not required immediately, they shall in any event be retained to audit the accounts at least annually; copies of their report to be delivered and filed as set forth in paragraph (3).

(5) If vendors do not name accountants satisfactory to purchasers, the latter may nominate and the vendors agree to employ the accountants so nominated by the purchasers and to carry out all of the provisions referring to accountants with the same effect as if said accountants were appointed by the vendors.

CHAPTER XXIX

INVESTIGATIONS (Continued)

ON SALE OR PURCHASE OF A BUSINESS (Continued)

(f) Elimination of Unusual Items: Earnings: A purchaser profits from future business only. Large special profits may have been made in the past, but his interest lies in the possible profits of the future. Necessarily these are based largely on past experience, but if there are items which probably will not appear under subsequent conditions, they must be eliminated from that part of the report upon which his opinion whether or not to buy will be formed.

Income From Assets Not Taken Over: The auditor, in order to make an intelligent report, must have a copy of the purchase contract or option. In many cases there are items which appear on the books which are not included in the purchase price and which are to be retained by the vendor. It is important to ascertain whether any income from assets of this nature has been included in the current earnings.

Interest on Deposits: If the bank balances have been normal, any interest thereon should not be eliminated unless it is known that the future bank accounts are not to bear interest. Many trust companies carry active business accounts and allow interest, but are not in as good a position to extend loans as National and State banks.

Some firms carry many hundreds of thousands of dollars on deposit all the time, earning, perhaps, two or two and a half per cent, just because they always want to be ready for an emergency. It is not likely that anyone buying such a business would contemplate the same practice.

Sale of Assets: The analysis of earnings will disclose whether anything has been included which represents profit on the sale of a portion of the capital assets. For instance, an old building or some land may be sold at an advance over the book value. This is clearly an extraordinary profit and must not be included among the earnings.

The author was called upon to verify the earnings of a concern and found that among the current earnings were profits on the purchase and sale of the company's own preferred stock.

Appreciation of Assets: It is a common error to assume that an appreciation in the value of land can offset the depreciation of plant.

If a statement of earnings has been prepared from the books, and an appraisal shows that the assets are equal to the book value, but that the land has appreciated in value $100,000 while the machinery has depreciated $100,000, then the amount of appreciation must be eliminated and treated as an extraordinary earning and the depreciation included among the expenses and deducted from earnings.

Insurance Profit: Where a fire has occurred, it may be found that the books show that a profit has been realized. This usually occurs where book values have been written down to be conservative, but the insurance has been left undisturbed. As the assured is entitled to recover the sound or replaceable value of his property, he may be collecting for obsolete or abandoned machinery, etc. In such case, as the prospective purchaser, in order to be conservative, will follow the same system of charging off, and cannot depend on a fire, the apparent profit cannot be included among the current earnings.

Damages for Change of Grade, etc.: Other extraordinary receipts may arise out of damages collected from compulsory change of grade, a portion of the premises being condemned for municipal or public utility use, etc. These are all unusual items and are not apt to recur in the same business, so they cannot be included among current earnings.

Expenses: There may have been special losses or expenses which the prospective purchaser can, or thinks he can, guard against. These, too, must be separately stated.

Excessive Reserves: Just as some men decline to allow for known losses, such as bad debts, depreciation, etc., others insist on writing off all of their furniture and fixtures and create excessive reserves for other wasting assets.

Since the passage of the Federal Corporation Tax Law, some corporations have entered excessive depreciation in their books. Upon a sale they would hardly admit that such charges were proper deductions from profits, and if the auditor finds that they are excessive, he will adjust the accounts accordingly.

The auditor will endeavor to have the reserves represent actual depreciation or prospective losses. When they go beyond this they are in reality part of the surplus and to be so treated.

Defalcations: It is to be assumed that a prospective purchaser wise enough to employ a professional auditor to investigate the business he expects to buy, will, if he acquires the business, bond all employees and have the accounts audited periodically thereafter, so that any past loss through defalcation can be eliminated from the expenses.

Auditors should impress upon new executives the value of surety bonds for all employees. Many employers who have postponed action for many years never do get around to it, but a new proprietor can insist on this matter without offending any sensitive employee. Failure to observe this precaution has entailed enormous losses to some concerns.

Fire and Other Losses Not Insured: Likewise, the purchaser will carry an ample line of all kinds of insurance, so that if there has been a fire loss not fully covered, or if an employee has been injured and no liability insurance has been carried, or if plate-glass windows be broken, etc., etc., the losses so sustained can be eliminated from the current expenses—which should include, however, a sum equal to the premiums on such insurance as if it had been carried.

Another form of protection which prudent business men carry is "profit" insurance. This covers loss of the estimated profit which might have been earned had no fire occurred. The rate is about the same as for fire insurance, which in most manufacturing plants is extremely low.

It cannot be held, however, that an auditor can certify that the earnings of a certain business would have been a given sum if a fire had not occurred. If profit insurance had been carried, and the face of the policies collected, there could be no objection to stating the source of such receipts, but even then an auditor could not include the income so derived among current earnings.

Actions at Law: Where any considerable expenditure has been made by reason of a verdict or compromise arising out of a suit on contract or infringement, etc., it might be that part of such payment would be properly included among the current expenses, but that a part would be applicable to prior periods. The auditor must deal with such items on their own merits.

(g) **Adjustments and Qualifications: Partners' Salaries:** In stating the accounts of a business in connection with a sale, it is customary to eliminate from the expenses the amount charged on the books as partners' salaries. This may be misleading, particularly when the earnings are shown in support of an issue of bonds or preferred stock. For instance, the statement may be made that the net earnings of a partnership have averaged $48,000 per annum, this being four times the interest on an issue of $200,000 six per cent preferred stock. In arriving at the net profit, custom decrees that the partners' compensation may be omitted. It is true that unless mention is made of the amount it would be difficult for anyone without a knowledge of the facts to form an opinion on the matter. Partners frequently pay themselves large periodical sums carried on the books as salaries. Many others credit themselves with about the equivalent of the salary of a manager or good salesman, while in many cases no salary at all is allowed for.

In the case mentioned it may be expected that after the corporation is formed, the officers (former partners) will insist on salaries unless they have stipulated that none will be voted or drawn. Such a stipulation is rare, so that it would not be unusual in a corporation of this size for salaries of $15,000 to $25,000 to be voted to the new officers. This becomes a charge to earnings, and thereby reduces the amount available for dividends on the preferred stock. In other words, the future net earnings will be largely diminished, perhaps half, through the change of name from "partners' withdrawals" (not an expense) to "officers' salaries" (an expense). Therefore a charge should be inserted for *management salaries*. In cases of financing there is frequently some contract provision fixing the amount so to be paid. In any event an intelligent estimate can and should be made.

An auditor is never justified in signing a certificate omitting partners' compensation, unless the fact is clearly stated, and any reference to the bearing past earnings have on a bond or stock issue is qualified by this omission.

Contracts: If a business is of such a nature that contracts for purchases or sales to be received or delivered in the future are the custom, it will not be sufficient to stop with the results of the last fiscal period unless the effect of the contracts outstanding at that time be considered.

For instance, contracts may have been entered into for raw materials at a high figure, and at the time of the examination the market may be much lower. The inventory may have been priced at the lower price, but it is not usual to anticipate a loss on purchase contracts not represented by deliveries.

If the contracts cannot be canceled, with the consequence that the new period is saddled with the necessity of buying materials at an inflated price, the auditor will have to adjust the accounts accordingly. It may be that the prospective purchaser has full knowledge of the unfavorable agreements, but the auditor must not assume this. If it is stated that unfavorable contracts for purchases or sales can be canceled, something more than the word of an interested party will be necessary to convince the auditor.

Taxes: While considering adjustments, the subject of taxes must be considered. It is becoming popular to levy taxes on whatever person or thing will stand it. In many localities real estate taxes are increasing steadily from year to year. At the time of the examination, if an assessment has been made for the following year, the auditor should inspect it and compare the amount payable thereunder with the previous year. As there may be an increase in the valuation as well as the rate, the increased taxes may be a sufficiently large factor to force a somewhat lower price from the seller.

Royalties: Where royalties have been paid under a license, and the financing provides for the purchase of the patents or copyrights, it may be permissible to eliminate from expenses the amounts paid in the past, so far as the possibilities of the future are concerned. But it may be unsafe to make the adjustment unless every detail of the acquisition of the patents is available and it is found that a clear saving will result. Verbal statements of this nature, relied on by auditors, have led to unfortunate experiences in the past.

The adjustment must include a periodical allowance for the extinguishment of the price paid for the patent or copyright.

Orders of Public Service Commissions: In making investigations of public service corporations operating within the jurisdiction of a public service commission, the auditor should not fail to make a thorough inquiry into the question of whether any orders issued by the commission have not yet been complied with by the corporation whose accounts are the subject of examination. Compliance with such orders might require the expenditure of considerable sums of money—perhaps for purposes which will not result in a corresponding increase of revenue; instead of an increase in revenue, there may be only an increased expense for maintaining or operating appliances required to be installed. If the prospective purchaser had knowledge of the matter, he would be in a position to protect himself when conducting negotiations with the seller. In the absence of such knowledge, however, he would receive a severe shock on being required, after concluding the purchase, to make the entirely unexpected expenditures necessitated by the orders issued before his coming into possession of the property.

(h) Errors in the Books: As heretofore stated, an investigation is an audit for a special purpose. If the special purpose is the location of errors, then the auditor will proceed as in a regular audit and nothing additional need be said. But in other classes of investigations, the question frequently arises as to how far the auditor should, or must, go in order to satisfy himself that the accounts are correct.

For instance, in an inquiry into earnings, it is necessary that he should be satisfied that the income is at least as much as the aggregate to which he certifies. But suppose part of the income which should have been included has never been carried into the books, having been misappropriated, or lost through carelessness or neglect?

As to this, the opinions of professional accountants differ. Some say that in investigating the profits of a business with reference to a sale, an accountant is not expected to check the books and entries for the purpose of detecting falsifications, there being a marked difference between an audit and an investigation with a view to profits, that some defalcations could not be discovered without verifying footings, postings, and vouchers, and that clients do not desire, and are unwilling to pay for, a detailed audit. On the other hand, it is contended that an auditor is not justified in certifying to a balance sheet and profit and loss account unless an audit has been made.

In the author's opinion, the test of what should be done depends upon the nature of the result to be attained. If an auditor is requested to examine the accounts of a business for a period of years, to state and certify to the net earnings realized and to the financial condition as of a certain date, then it is proper to restrict oneself to the actual work necessary, and additional work is superfluous. If income or assets have been omitted, and the omission could not have been detected unless a complete audit were made, nevertheless the auditor has fulfilled his duty. If expenses or liabilities have been omitted, the auditor cannot be excused even if a detailed audit were necessary to discover the omissions.

No examination along the lines indicated could be considered as complete in any event unless intelligent analyses were made of the various income and expense accounts. Usually these analyses will disclose fraud or errors of principle if they exist.

The final test of the sufficiency of the examination lies in the skill with which the work has been handled. If the auditor has brought to bear all of the care and skill which might reasonably be demanded of an experienced practitioner, then he cannot be held morally or professionally responsible for well concealed errors or omissions, but it must be remembered that the degree of care and skill called for is much greater than is expected or legally demanded from an inexperienced person or one who does not hold himself out as a professional auditor.

(i) Investigation on Behalf of a Retiring Partner When the Business is Being Sold to a Continuing Partner: When the retirement of a partner is caused by his death or by physical disability, a "continuing" partner may also be a "liquidating" partner. In such case the continuing partner is charged with a greater degree of responsibility than that to which the purchaser of a business under other circumstances would be held. The continuing partner is in the best position to protect his own interests, and the auditor's connection with the liquidation of the old firm will most frequently be as representative of the retiring partner.

The auditor will need to do all the work which is usually included in an investigation made for an intending purchaser, but there are, in addition, certain other phases of the situation which should receive consideration, and it is these of which mention will be made. It is only equitable that the assets should be valued on the basis of a going concern, and it is clearly the duty of the auditor to see that they are not undervalued. It would be most satisfactory to have independent appraisers employed to value such assets as plant and stock in trade, due consideration being given both to the circumstances of the case and the rights of each of the partners. Frequently, however, this is not done, and the business is liquidated by the continuing partner, who himself values the various assets. While specific rules to be followed can hardly be laid down, it should be observed that in cases of doubt as to values the absent partner should have the benefit thereof. This is only fair, as the surviving or continuing partner is in a position to secure what he believes to be his rights, whereas the retiring partner, through death or absence, is not in the same position to urge the consideration of his rights. It is an established rule of law that a liquidating partner must not take advantage of his position, and this of itself is sufficient reason for his deciding all doubtful cases in favor of the absent partner.

Accounts receivable and any other choses in action should be "worked out." The continuing partner is not entitled to any commission for his own services in this connection, though he should be reimbursed for the actual expenses incurred for clerical work entailed thereby. Discounts and other allowances credited to customers upon settlement of the outstanding accounts should be carefully scrutinized. Goods returned by customers subsequent to the date of dissolution would ordinarily be taken into the stock of the new business, and, unless particular attention is given to this class of transactions, the charge which should be made to the new business and credited to the liquidation of the old might very easily be overlooked. Unless the total amount involved is very small indeed, all credits to old customers other than for cash should be analyzed. Those which are for goods returned can then be made the subject of further investigation.

The valuation of the stock on hand is likely to present considerable difficulty. The usual rule of valuing the stock at "market or cost, whichever is lower," does not necessarily apply in such a case. The liquidating partner is under obligation to secure the largest return for all the assets of the business, and he has a right to sell the stock to himself, which he is in effect doing, only if he is willing to pay as much, or more, for it than could have been secured from anyone else. This is not to be construed as meaning what could have been secured at a forced sale.

The fairest valuation would probably be the cost of duplicating the stock as of the date of dissolution, due allowance being made for obsolete or imperfect stock. If the inventory includes only staple goods, little difficulty will be encountered in ascertaining the present cost of duplicating them. If the goods, however, have been made to special order, or are otherwise difficult to value, estimates could be secured from manufacturers for making similar articles or the actual sales of the goods in the inventory could be traced and the customary rates of gross profit applied to estimate the cost. These matters should be covered by an agreement. In drawing such agreements the auditor should be consulted.

If it be agreed to value the stock on the basis of cost, it is to be remembered that this would include not only the original purchase price of the goods, but also freight, cartage, and any other direct charges for handling and placing the goods in stock. It is sometimes urged that the term "cost" in such a case should include interest from the date of purchase to the date of the inventory. This does not seem logical, however, inasmuch as, if market prices were still the same as at the date the goods were bought, the fact that the goods had been in stock a number of months would not add to their value. On the contrary, the longer the goods had been on hand the greater the probability of their already being, or becoming at an early date, unsalable.

Profits realized or losses sustained on the completion of contracts made prior to the dissolution of the partnership are to be apportioned between the retiring and continuing partners. Inasmuch as the retiring partner shared in the expenses of securing the contracts and participated in the risk of undertaking them, it is only fair that he should participate in the profits derived therefrom. On the other hand, he should also help to bear the burden of any losses sustained in carrying out contracts which were made prior to the dissolution of the partnership. There is no reason why the continuing partner should be called on to bear the burden alone, unless a specific agreement is reached under which the continuing partner takes over the contracts at specific values and assumes all further risk in connection with their completion. To do this it would, of course, be necessary to secure the consent of all other parties to the contracts, so that the retiring partner or his estate be released from all liability for the execution of the contracts.

Usually the most equitable method of valuing machinery and fixtures would seem to be cost less proper depreciation allowances. If this differs materially from the cost of reproduction at the present time (also making allowance in this case for accrued depreciation), the valuation will probably have to be made the subject of compromise between the parties.

While the correctness of the balance sheet is of preëminent importance in an investigation such as the one under consideration, the correctness of the income account is likewise of importance if the good will is to be valued on the basis of past earnings. It is also necessary to review the expenses entering into the income account for a period prior to the date of dissolution so as to see that no prepaid expenses which would apply subsequent to the date of dissolution have been absorbed by the old business. The retiring partner will, in due course, be debited with his proportion of all expenses chargeable to the old firm, even though they may not have appeared among the liabilities stated on the books at the time of his retirement. Prepaid expenses applying to the new business would not, however, be so likely to be brought into the liquidation account if they were absorbed in the operations of the old firm.

There are still other questions, such as partners' salaries and interest on partners' accounts, which will need to be carefully considered in the light of the partnership agreement.

(j) Investigation for Those in Charge of Reorganizations: There is an increasing demand for the services of accountants in connection with reorganizations. The special features of such examinations are admirably expressed by A. Lowes Dickinson,

C. P. A., in his paper "Accounting Practice and Procedure," which appears in the American Association Year Book for 1908:

The consideration of a plan for the reorganization of a property which has been reduced to a condition of insolvency requires a full and accurate knowledge of all the existing conditions with regard to the property and its past and probable future earning capacity. The elements to be investigated and determined will, therefore, be as follows:

(1) The sources and nature of the gross earnings and the prospects of any increase therein without further expenditures for development.

(2) The cost of operation, with particular reference to the effect thereon of bad management or bad organization, and to the possibility of remedying these conditions; and the proportion which the cost of operation has borne and may be expected to bear to the gross earnings.

(3) A comparison of the gross and net earnings and capitalization of the property, with some actual or desirable standard, so as to determine the proportion which one should bear to the other if the reorganization is to prove successful.

(4) Hence to arrive at the total interest-bearing and dividend-paying capital, which the reorganized property will stand on some fixed interest basis.

(5) The rank of the different classes of obligations having regard to the property pledged as security therefor; the margin of security; the rate of interest; the date of maturity; the equivalent par value on the basis of the standard rate of interest adopted for all classes; and, if practicable, the extent to which the properties specifically mortgaged show sufficient earnings to meet interest on the indebtedness secured thereon. This class of information will probably require a report from an engineer or other expert on the value and the condition of the physical property.

(6) Following upon the determination of these factors, a consideration of the various separately mortgaged divisions of the property, with a view to determining whether any should be abandoned to the bondholders, rather than be included in a reorganization. And here it is important to observe that the contribution of any specific piece of property to the general organization is not necessarily measured by its ability by itself to earn interest on the obligations secured thereon. Numerous other factors will enter into a consideration of this point, and it may easily appear that a property earning little or nothing toward payment of its obligations is sufficiently valuable to the organization, as a whole, to be retained, if possible.

(7) Another important factor is the amount of new money required to be introduced for the purpose of paying off the floating debt and rehabilitating the property, and the best method of raising such money, whether by the issue of new prior lien securities ranking in front of or on an equality with those issued in exchange for existing mortgages, or by assessments on junior classes of securities. In the latter case it is im-

portant that sufficient inducement be given to the junior classes, in the proportion of new securities issued for old, to induce them to pay these assessments; while for the assessments themselves, the securities issued should represent the par value of the cash paid in on some reasonable market valuation.

(2) INVESTIGATION FOR CREDITORS, ETC.

Auditors are frequently called upon to make examinations the scope of which is practically limited to certain accounts about which the most complete detail is required. For instance, a manufacturer may desire to extend a large line of credit to a jobber or merchant, and before doing so wants to know the latter's capacity for handling his line, as well as to know that his financial condition and method of doing business are satisfactory.

Investigation on Behalf of a Present or Prospective Creditor: Examinations along these lines may be divided into two general classes:

For bankers or note brokers who propose to loan on the promissory notes of the borrower, or for bankers who propose to bring out bond or preferred stock issues.

For individuals or business concerns who propose to make advances for various purposes, or who have extended or who expect to extend credit on open account.

In the main, the points to be observed have been discussed in the chapters on the conduct of a balance-sheet audit, but there are certain special precautions which may, with propriety, be enlarged upon at this time.

(a) Examinations for Bankers

Extension of Business: The most important line of examination, after ascertaining the assets and liabilities and analyzing the profit and loss account, is an inquiry into the plans for the future which have been adopted or which are under consideration. The average business man is not content with a stationary business. He wishes to expand for the purpose of increasing his profits, decreasing his expense ratio, and perhaps the most compelling of all reasons is his ambition to outstrip his competitors.

If his floating debt has been burdensome, he may have been

obliged to keep within certain bounds as to capacity and production, but the moment he is financed it seems almost inevitable that new liabilities are incurred sufficient to use up the additional supply of credit almost before it is available.

Accountants do not always feel concerned with this phase of business life, but as the lender should have some means of determining the use to which his money is to be put other than that supplied or promised by the borrower, he naturally looks to the professional auditor. True, he has looked in vain in many cases, and this may explain the reason why so many banks, bankers, and financiers have secured the services of men who can secure and impart the information required, irrespective of the fact of whether or not they have the degree of Certified Public Accountant.

Collateral v. Integrity: Which is better, to loan money to a dishonest man on ample security, or to a perfectly honest man who wishes to borrow on his own name and who cannot furnish collateral? The former may seem to be more advisable, but there are disadvantages in doing any business whatever with a man who cannot be trusted.

Therefore, no matter how good the collateral may be, the banker wants more information, and the auditor may be able to furnish it. Facts relative to previous business experiences, possible failures or embarrassments caused by speculation, etc., will be secured from the mercantile agencies, but inside information relative to the personnel of the organization can be furnished by the auditor.

Experience has demonstrated that where partners quarrel, or where one does all the work, trouble will follow. Large concerns, solvent so far as finances go, have been placed in the hands of receivers because of internal dissensions. A banker does not want to make a loan which may be paid off eventually by a receiver, even if the assets are double the liabilities.

Then one or more departments of the business may be weak. The sales force may be highly organized and efficient, but if the manufacturing department is poorly managed, or is not coördinated with the sales department, the results will not be satisfactory.

If no criticism is justified and a man's honesty is unquestioned, a banker may prefer the risk to the apparent safety of a loan secured by collateral. It has been said that "a crooked borrower is always a wise window-dresser," and this observation may be enlarged to remind the banker that crooked borrowers when negotiating a loan sometimes offer collateral to which they do not have title.

Future Business: During the progress of any audit which comprehends a balance sheet, there should be available full data with respect to future business and the means whereby it is proposed to finance it.

Schedules of orders booked, the time estimated to complete same, the cost of the raw materials, labor, and other manufacturing expenses, the time within which the proceeds of sales will mature, the dates by which the liabilities for purchase will have to be discharged, and many other factors are all to be compiled and put into readable and dependable form.

If funds are to be furnished to meet pressing obligations, and if any increase in the business means the tying up of additional cash for a considerable period, then there may be a hesitancy about supplying the needs unless a stipulation is furnished that additional business will not be sought until the funds with which to finance it are in sight. The auditor who can secure information of this nature may be helpful to the banker and even more so to the borrower, for it is of no permanent advantage to the latter to be tided over one period of stringency merely to be plunged into another and more serious situation.

Bank Loans to be Repaid: The auditor must bear in mind that the banker whom he represents in these investigations is considering the investment of deposits which are chiefly payable on demand, therefore he is not contemplating the making of a permanent loan, but one which will be repaid within a comparatively short period of time. If a banker were looking purely for security, he would invest a large portion of his funds in real estate mortgages. The security might be better than commercial paper, but the maturities would be from one to three years, and hence entirely unsuitable for his purposes.

If the auditor ascertains that the prospective borrower does not expect to "clean up" at least once a year, he should so report to his client.

(b) Investigation for Purely Credit Purposes

The credit manager of a business concern or the representative of a capitalist who contemplates extending credit to a prospective borrower or debtor must proceed along somewhat different lines than the professional auditor, whose duty is to report upon actual conditions, and upon whom the responsibility is not laid of having to determine immediate action, based more on the estimated outcome of the future than on present financial strength.

For instance, an auditor might ascertain and report that a certain man had cash on hand of $100,000 and no debts. He would have no further responsibility thereafter, unless it were shown subsequently that there were undisclosed liabilities. We will assume, however, that the facts were as reported.

The credit manager might have an entirely different task before him. He should use the same means to ascertain that the $100,000 was actually on hand and free from liens, and that there were no liabilities, but his work would then, in a sense, be merely beginning. He should ascertain the past and present moral and business reputation of the man; he should have an accurate and complete history of his business career; he should question him in detail as to what he intends to do with the money; whether his proposed business venture calls for a capital of more than $100,000, and so on.

It has been said that the credit manager must always look out for three essential elements in passing on a credit basis, viz., character, capital, and capacity, three "C's," and therefore easily remembered.

The author feels that there are so many points of contact between a professional auditor and a credit manager that this opportunity should be taken to discuss the similarities of their work, with a view to standardizing as much of it as possible.

It is not contended that the auditor should attempt all the manifold duties of the credit manager, nor that the latter should burden himself with the technical knowledge required to make a detailed audit. It is, however, urged, without fear of contradiction, that an auditor would be able to render better service to his clients if he could acquire some of the instincts of the successful credit manager and keep constantly before him, when making investigations involving proposed credits or investments, many of the requirements which the science of credits has found to be essential. Likewise, who will deny that the credit manager could perform his work more easily and scientifically if he were conversant with the principles, and could take advantage of the experience, underlying the practice of professional auditing?

During the six months ended June 30, 1912, there were 8,317 business failures throughout the United States with liabilities of $108,012,223, and resulting in losses to creditors of at least $50,000,000, and the number of failures is steadily increasing. In a very large proportion of these cases credit could not be secured if the debtor were obliged to submit his books to an examination by a professional auditor.

Is it unreasonable to suppose that the general use of auditors to verify the accounts of concerns seeking credit would save ten per cent of this annual loss of over $100,000,000? If a saving of over ten millions of dollars could be effected by the expenditure of, say, one million, would it not be worth while to attempt to save another ten per cent or more by compulsory audits of all concerns seeking credit?

Unscientific Methods: Such methods affect business success quite as much as anything else. The auditor may find a satisfactory surplus of assets, but if carelessness or incompetence exists in the accounting and other departments, a day of reckoning will surely arrive.

Signs of carelessness or incompetence may be found in lax collection methods. More than one failure has resulted from a policy of allowing collections to take care of themselves.

The precise procedure followed should be ascertained and reduced to writing. The "follow-up" system must be examined very carefully. It may be that the system is good, but that it is not being followed. Then the relation between the departments must be looked into. Coördination here is absolutely essential to success. Sometimes a credit department will claim that the salesmen are so anxious to sell that a considerable part of the business must be refused. This brings up the question of coördination among the various departments of a business. If it is lacking, one of the elements of failure is present.

An investigation into the methods of doing business thus becomes a necessity where one is looking into the future probabilities of success or failure. Almost anyone can sell goods, but to insure financial success they must be sold at a price which will yield a satisfactory profit and to customers who will pay. Here again the methods of the prospective debtor are all-important, and the representative of the lender or creditor not only has the right to know whether or not scientific methods are in force, but it is his positive duty to ascertain whether or not such is the case.

Lack of Capital: It is said that more failures result from lack of capital than from any other cause. It may seem superfluous to state that it is better to do a small but safe and profitable business than to attempt to trade beyond the limits of capital employed; but this overstretching is going on all the time. It is a point on which the auditor and credit manager can secure accurate information from the balance sheet, but this must be supplemented by an inquiry into plans for extensions to plant, commitments for large purchases for future delivery, and similar negotiations.

Credit Risks: The passion of a salesman is to sell; the dread of a credit manager is to pass a credit which will produce a loss. Between the two may lie the secret of a successful business and large profits. The burden is upon the credit manager, and he cannot escape it by turning down every order about which any doubt exists.

The conclusions upon which he will base his final decision in any case are dependent upon so many different circumstances that they cannot be enumerated here, but it may be mentioned that the margin between the cost and selling price of an article is one of the most important factors to be considered when the question of the acceptance or rejection of an order is to be settled. If the gross profit is large, it is obvious that more risk may be taken than where the margin of profit is too small to admit of any material amount being set aside for bad debts.

In some lines the gross profit is so large that it would be more economical to sell everybody than to maintain a credit department; in others it is equally unnecessary to maintain such a department, because all goods must be shipped sight draft against bill of lading. The point seems obvious, yet many accountants and credit managers do not differentiate between the rules to be observed, which makes their general advice of little or no value.

Insurance: A professional auditor does not always inquire into the sufficiency of insurance of all descriptions, but it is believed that the successful credit manager has this constantly in mind. Auditors now see the importance of this line of inquiry, and among certain firms it is an integral part of the audit program.

Fire insurance is only one of the lines which should be investigated. If the personality of a partner or an employee is of great value, life insurance might be desirable. Except in a very few lines of business, such as railway or taxicab, a reasonable amount of liability insurance, both public and employers', should always be carried.

Profit insurance is frequently as important as fire insurance, especially where a seasonal business is conducted, and large preliminary expenses, such as advertising, are incurred, and where a total loss would result if a factory were to be destroyed.

Errors of Principle: It is not enough that a concern's financial statement shall look well, for sometimes actual conditions are concealed through errors in bookkeeping. This state of things exists in more cases than is generally known.

For instance, in a contracting business the bookkeeper, in closing the accounts, closed all of the credit balances in individual contract accounts to profit and loss. He did not realize that all of them were not completed and that a considerable liability existed in respect of the cost of completion. His balance sheet showed a much better financial position than the concern deserved, but the bookkeeper maintained that it was correct until he was shown how inaccurate it was.

Errors may be honestly made, and yet they will bring ruin on a concern unless discovered and rectified. Failure to provide for depreciation is the most common dereliction, and excessive charges to asset accounts is a close second. The auditor is always on the lookout for such errors, whether intentional or unintentional, but few credit managers realize the importance of ascertaining whether or not the books of a prospective debtor have been regularly examined by a public accountant.

Fraud: Under this class the auditor will find far too many examples. The bankruptcy courts are full of cases in which creditors have been grossly deceived. Many of these are so flagrant that it seems impossible that the debtor should have been able to incur such large debts, yet the fact is obvious that credit managers by the hundred and business concerns by the thousand extended credit to these bankrupts to an aggregate of tens of millions of dollars. The schedules of the bankrupts' debts speak for themselves. The most surprising feature of the whole situation is that in many cases the most cursory examination of the bankrupts' books would have revealed to the trained auditor that gross fraud was being practiced. A more intimate relationship between professional auditors and credit managers would prove to the latter that the auditor can be of inestimable service in many ways.

Character: Last but not least is the element of character. In modern business it is almost concealed, owing to the impossibility of continuing the personal relations between bankers and borrowers. The modern borrower's balance sheet may be submitted to hundreds of bankers. But the author would not like to see the audit program of the auditor or credit manager omit all consideration of character.

The banker has to consider primarily the present ability of the borrower to repay the loan, but further than this his business foresight will make it possible for the banker to size up his man and determine whether there is not some inherent lack of character in him, either moral or executive, which may at some future time make the risk more hazardous than if he were entirely normal.

Some unprincipled business men pay all of their debts, but many are found in the bankruptcy courts being relieved of their obligations, and subsequent success does not incline them to pay the debts thus discharged.

The honest man may fail honestly, but if he can he will pay in time, and we may be thankful that there are many such. Therefore let the auditor and the credit manager study human nature and analyze the conditions presented to them not only from the financial standpoint but from a moral point of view as well.

(c) Investigation in Patent Litigation

An investigation to ascertain profits realized in the manufacture of patented articles, where infringement of patent rights is claimed, and the claim is sustained, or when an examination is ordered pending a decision, presents several novel features, as compared with an ordinary statement of profits.

It is not intended to discuss the matter from a legal point of view, and it may be that the principles hereinafter set forth might not be upheld by the courts in some jurisdictions. It is the author's experience, however, that most of these cases are settled out of court owing to the enormous expenses involved in the taking of testimony before masters, who are usually appointed where matters of account are involved.

The following procedure, therefore, may be taken as the result of actual practice, following negotiations which usually involve concessions on both sides, rather than settled rules laid down in judicial decisions.

General Accounting Principles Do Not Govern: The preliminary conferences in a matter of this sort naturally bring out opinions which differ radically. The injured party will claim everything that can be imagined, and the defendant will produce a statement which shows that the manufacture of the infringing article has been attended with ruinous losses. From the beginning it is a question of gradually drawing the lines closer, until each has stripped his case of redundant matters and the issue is joined.

It will be found that ordinary accounting principles do not form the basis of the claim nor of the defense. The following are exceptions to accepted practice:

There would seem to be no excuse whatever for apportioning any part of the general expenses as a part of the cost of the business. The infringers would have had these expenses to pay in any event in order to carry on their legitimate business.

If the principal business of the defendants consists of manufacturing or dealing in infringing articles, then it may be proper to include a certain part of the general expenses, but items of a questionable nature should not be included.

As defendants are not supposed to have pushed the sale of

the article, it hardly seems proper that any credit should be claimed for special exhibitions.

Where the same kind of materials are legitimately used in the manufacture of other goods handled by the defendants, and the purchases are not earmarked at the time for any particular department, it would seem improper that credit should be allowed for any materials not clearly identified as having been used in the infringing product.

Based on similar accountings, the defendants are not entitled to place a scrap valuation upon materials remaining on hand when they were compelled to stop the sale of the article, but they could be compelled to scrap the articles on hand at that time, and would not be entitled to any credit whatever for the entire cost of the manufacture of said stock.

It does not seem conceivable that the defendants would be permitted to make a profit out of their wrong-doing, and this would be the result if general expenses and similar items were included, as the tendency would be to reduce the expenses of conducting their legitimate business. If they have been ordered to account for the profit made by them in the manufacture and sale of articles, the court will undoubtedly hold that the word "profit" as here used means the difference between the proceeds from the sale of an article and the prime cost (that is, labor and material) of such sales, and that the cost of goods on hand at the end of the period should not be treated as an item of cost for which credit can be claimed.

(3) FRAUD

Following the discovery of a defalcation may be heard expressions of surprise, based on the fact that the defaulter was a trusted employee. It does not seem to occur to most people that, generally speaking, no one but a trusted employee has an opportunity to defraud others. Many trusted employees prove recreant to their trust every year, therefore mere business prudence demands some form of supervision over all those who have a chance to appropriate to their own use the property of others.

In the preceding chapters an attempt has been made to outline the procedure required in audits of various natures, but the procedure there referred to was not intended to cover those cases where a particular person is under suspicion or where a particular form of fraud is suspected, or has been discovered, and where it is important to locate the guilty party or parties without delay.

Then, again, it may be that an audit has been made along usual lines without developing anything wrong; but it is found that an employee is living beyond his means, or is constantly seen in bad company, so that a special investigation becomes desirable. The point immediately arises as to whether there are any special checks, or verifications, which are not usually resorted to in an ordinary audit, but which might be useful when applied to specific cases.

Possibilities to be Studied: In all cases where suspicion exists the quickest way to locate fraud is to ascertain definitely the opportunities which are normally open to the person suspected, and the possible chances which may not be usually open to such person, but of which he may have taken advantage.

For instance, the treasurer of a company may be known to be spending more than his income, and an inquiry is ordered. If the business is at all large, it is obviously not worth while to commence the investigation in the same way as a general audit, but the wise course would be to look into the matters under the personal charge of that officer. Any securities supposed to be in his hands should be called for, and the method of handling cash transactions should be inquired into. If he has always insisted on opening the mail, it may be that customers' accounts have been tampered with; if he has assumed personal charge of the periodical reconciliation of the bank's pass books with the bank balance, it may be that funds have been withdrawn from the bank and not reported.

If the gross profit is unexpectedly small, it may be that stock is being stolen or that fictitious purchases appear in the books.

Extent of Fraud: Frequently the professional auditor is not called in until the defalcation has been disclosed and his services are desired to fix the total. In such a case experience is invaluable, for the position of the auditor may be a most difficult one. The defaulter usually is called upon to give, or proffers, his assistance, and professes to be most anxious to help get at the whole truth. He will state the total amount as positively not exceeding a certain total, and his employer is apt to believe him and to doubt the auditor, whose experience warrants him in stating that thieves rarely tell the truth, and that defaulters hardly ever know the extent of their own fraud, and when they do know will understate it materially in the hope that their attempts at concealment may be at least partially successful.

There is only one safe rule, and that is to calculate every possible source of income open to the defaulter, the maximum amount of such income, and the longest time possible during which the fraud may have been going on.

Records are often destroyed and many sources of income cannot be traced subsequently; therefore it is never wise to take the word of a defaulter for the amount of his theft.

Attitude Toward a Defaulter: Whenever possible the defaulter should be required to attend and assist the auditor. This does not mean that his word is to be taken blindly or that he is to be left alone with the books, but he can do no harm, and in countless cases his presence has been of the greatest assistance.

Here the experience and skill of the auditor have full play. By the exercise of tact he may persuade the criminal to disclose many things which the closest examination of the records would not reveal. A clue is often as valuable as a complete disclosure, and it rarely happens that a trained auditor spends any considerable time with a defaulter without discovering directly or incidentally the system employed and other valuable information.

No one knows so well as professional auditors how small a proportion of these crimes are made public, but defaulters themselves seem to feel intuitively that if they promise to tell all they know and to make restitution, all will be forgiven and forgotten. Unfortunately, from the standpoint of example this is often too true, but even though it is true there can be no objection to an auditor pointing out to the defaulter the fact that if he lies to him (the auditor), it will aggravate his possible punishment. If an examination is likely to result in litigation, the auditor must pay particular attention to any admissions or statements by the suspected party.

The chairman of a board of water commissioners kept a cash book showing his receipts and disbursements. When the balance was ascertained by auditors appointed by the municipality, the chairman was informed of the amount shown by the book to be due from him, the correctness of which he did not dispute. On being asked if he could explain the balance against him, he said he could not, and being then told that it would have to be reported to the authorities, he replied: "Well, you will just have to report it." When he refused to pay subsequently and suit was brought, the court held that this was sufficient evidence upon which to recover the balance.

This supports the principle of law that the statement of an account need not be confined to the original parties. The auditor may have an exceptional chance to secure an admission, and if there is any likelihood of its being used later, he should reduce it to writing at once. This record may be useful in refreshing his memory.

The Millwall Dock Case: This is one of the English cases usually cited to illustrate fraudulent methods of manipulating accounts. The managing director instructed the superintendent to overstate accrued charges for storage and for advances made for account of customers. There were 200 ledgers and 12,000 open accounts. The open items were taken off on sheets, certified by superintendent, chief clerk at docks and ledger clerk, and the summary was signed by the managing director.

Rates were excessive, but calculations were correct, and the auditors verified the footings and calculations. Outstandings grew from $110,000 in 1870 to $1,150,000 in 1898. Of the latter amount $1,000,000 was fictitious. For most of the period, the managing director received a fixed salary, and thus did not participate directly in the fraud, except that he kept his job.

The auditors could have discovered the manipulation at any time if they had footed every other page, instead of every page, of the sheets on which the outstandings were listed, and spent the time thus saved in testing the accuracy of the charges as transferred to the sheets. Or a subsequent test to ascertain whether the accrued charges at the former audit were realized would have disclosed the system of fraud. One hour thus spent would have been sufficient to reveal the fraud, as the charges were uniformly excessive.

The Bank of Liverpool Case: This is another celebrated English case.

The ledger clerk forged the signature of a depositor to a cheque and stated that the payee was his mother. He had the cheque cashed and did not charge it to the account of the depositor whose name he forged when it came in at balancing time, but debited some other account, reversing the entry next day.

When pass books of those with whose accounts he tampered came in while auditors were there, he secured the books and forged the audit clerk's initials therein. The bank inspector saw the initials and did not verify the settlements.

While the internal audit may here be blamed, yet the case illustrates the possibilities of fraud when a dishonest clerk concentrates his energies upon thinking out a scheme to outwit those who are engrossed in the routine work of a large enterprise.

CHAPTER XXX

HOLDING COMPANIES

Consolidated Balance Sheets and Profit and Loss Statements: In the face of the Sherman Act, business combinations are being formed daily. They may be in flagrant or in reasonable restraint of trade, or they may deal with concerns operating solely within the boundaries of a single State and thus escape Federal prosecution and be subject to State regulation only if buying or selling necessities.

Politicians and friends of the "plain people" may cry aloud that competition must and shall be preserved, but the real fact is that business men will compete up to a certain point only, and any law which prohibits competitors who are losing money from coming to an understanding or consolidating is doomed to ultimate failure. Auditors will therefore be called upon more and more to investigate proposed consolidations and to advise with respect to their accounts after mergers have been effected. It is not intended to discuss the economic features of holding companies. Any one interested in this phase of the subject is referred to the paper by William M. Lybrand, C. P. A., which appears in the Year Book of the American Association of Public Accountants for 1908.

Balance Sheet: The usual statement of assets and liabilities published by a holding company is wholly devoid of the information an investor or stockholder seeks. On one side appears a huge sum opposite the caption, "Securities of Subsidiary Companies." Then there will be another item representing advances (usually huge also) to subsidiaries; there may be a little cash, but other assets are scarce.

Nor is the lack of information found in connection with the so-called "trusts" only. There are a great many combinations of small concerns, and with these the failure to render intelligent accounts is quite as marked as is the case with larger enterprises.

The chief criticism leveled against these formal statements is that in the absence of data relative to the quick assets and liabilities of the subsidiaries, no opinion can be formed as to whether the concern as a whole is properly financed or whether there is absolute need of additional working capital to prevent bankruptcy.

The balance sheets of some holding companies show among the assets the *net* assets of the subsidiaries. That is, from the accounts receivable and inventories will be deducted the accounts payable, the resulting balance being shown as an asset. This is obviously wrong. The trade debts may be out of proportion to the assets and may be overdue and pressing.

Strong pressure is sometimes brought to bear on an auditor to induce him to prepare the balance sheet of a holding company so that it will indicate a stronger financial position than actually exists. The best answer to such a request is a positive declaration on the part of the auditor that proper accounting procedure requires a certain form of balance sheet and that there will be no deviation therefrom.

Form of Balance Sheet: As just stated, the form of the balance sheet is of great importance. Mr. Lybrand, in the paper heretofore mentioned, covers this point:

It is now very generally recognized, however, that the submission of the balance sheet of the holding company only does not furnish the owners of the company with the information as to its real financial position to which they may justly consider themselves entitled.

The holding company was, as heretofore stated, organized for the purpose of acquiring the capital stocks of affiliated companies, and thus effecting a combination which would bear the test of adverse legal scrutiny. While each company under this scheme retains its corporate identity, and is in the eyes of the law a separate corporation, yet there is a virtual consolidation of ownership, the results of which can be properly expressed in a statement of their accounts only by consolidating the balance sheets of all the companies into one balance sheet, eliminating therefrom the intercompany stocks, bonds, and accounts which indicate the relation of one company to another and not to the public.

A consolidated balance sheet, therefore, is intended to reflect the financial position of the whole group of affiliated companies, considered as one undertaking. In a typical balance sheet of this character, the following grouping and arrangement of the assets and liabilities has been adopted:

ASSETS:	LIABILITIES:
Property Account.	Capital Stock of Holding Corporation.
Deferred Charges to Operation.	Capital Stocks of Subsidiary Companies not owned by Holding Corporation.
Investments.	Bonded Indebtedness.
Sinking and Reserve Fund Assets.	Current Liabilities.
Current Assets.	Sinking and Reserve Funds.
	Surplus.

When a holding company purchases the capital stock of another company, the price paid for this capital stock presumably represents the holding company's estimate of the value of the equity in the subsidiary company's assets. This price may be greater than the combined capital stock and surplus account of the subsidiary company, in which event the difference must be assumed to denote the value of the subsidiary company's good will, or other assets, not appearing on its balance sheet, otherwise, if they were included there, the cost of the capital stock to the holding company would be exactly equal to the combined capital and surplus of the subsidiary company. On the other hand, if the price paid by the holding company, for the capital stock of the subsidiary company, is less than the combined capital and surplus, the difference must be assumed to express the amount at which the assets of the subsidiary company are overvalued on its books.

In consolidating the "Property" accounts of the subsidiary companies (their property accounts including good will, trade marks, franchises, etc., as well as tangible property), the total must, therefore, be increased or reduced by as much as the cost of the capital stocks of the respective subsidiary companies, as at the date of their purchase by the holding company exceeds or falls below their combined capital and surplus account.

It might seem at first thought that the surplus accounts of the subsidiary companies should not be applied as stated in the foregoing paragraph, but that they, together with the surplus accrued subsequent to the purchase by the holding company, should be combined and their aggregate entered on the consolidated balance sheet as the surplus of the whole undertaking. The fallacy of this statement has been proven in various ways. Perhaps the most simple and direct argument is somewhat along the following lines: the surplus of a corporation, generally speaking, represents the balance of earnings which have accumulated from its operations, and which have not been paid out to the stockholders, applied in immediate reduction of valuation of assets or reserved for the ultimate replacement thereof. As a surplus can accrue only during the operating of a company, it is fairly obvious that the holding corporation prior to its organization cannot have earned such a fund, and that therefore it would be entitled to merge into its consolidated surplus account only the balances of profits accumulated by the subsidiary companies during the period of their ownership by the holding corporation.

Further, as the amount paid by the holding company for the capital stock of a subsidiary company represents the holding company's estimate of the equity in the subsidiary company, and as that equity is presumed to be represented by its capital stock and surplus account, it follows that in the process of consolidating, the capital stocks of the subsidiary company in the holding company's books will be eliminated, as will be the capital stock and surplus account on the subsidiary company's books. The surplus account being thus absorbed, cannot, of course, appear again as a surplus in the consolidated balance sheet.

It will be noted from the foregoing that all intercompany accounts are eliminated, thus exhibiting the debts due from the public and to the public. Any other form of balance sheet which includes as assets accounts due by one company to another, and as liabilities accounts due from one company to another, is misleading and useless for the purpose of disclosing what will be realized from the quick assets and the amounts which will have to be paid.

Accounts Receivable: Where advances have been made to subsidiary companies by the holding company itself, the aggregate thereof will appear among the assets of the holding company, but the auditor should never permit the item to be stated in such a manner as to sustain a belief on the part of any outsider that the receivables are due from debtors other than subsidiary companies.

Quoting again from Mr. Lybrand:

Frequently other large items of assets are advances made to the subsidiary companies for which the latter may have issued their notes in favor of the parent company. Such advances are usually made to provide for extensions or additions to the plants of the subsidiary companies after they have been acquired by the holding company, or they may have been made for the purpose of furnishing additional funds to purchase larger stocks of materials, to carry contracts requiring considerable time to complete, or for any other legitimate business purpose. If the moneys advanced have been for the purpose of adding to the plants of the subsidiary companies, it may be that these loans will subsequently be funded by the subsidiary companies through the medium of mortgage bonds, which, if sold to the public, will enable the subsidiary companies to discharge their debts to the parent company. Or possibly, if the whole of the authorized stock of the subsidiary company is not outstanding, a further amount may be issued and delivered to the parent company in settlement of the advances, thus changing the form of the asset on the holding company's books from an account receivable to a security ownership. It is improbable that such a course would be pursued except in very special instances, as the holding company would doubtless prefer to appear as a creditor of the subsidiary company rather than as an owner of more shares of its capital stock, because, if the subsidiary company were unprofitable and it became necessary to wind it up, the holding company would claim, with the other creditors, its proportion of the realizations from the subsidiary company's assets. Such a position, we believe, would be assumed by the holding company in the absence of direct ruling to the contrary, but serious doubt has been cast recently on the ability of a holding company to sustain such a contention where it is the owner of the entire capital stock issue of the underlying company.

Advances made by a parent company to its subsidiary companies are not always represented in the latter by tangible property. Such advances may have been made to recoup the subsidiary company for losses sustained by it in operating. The advances appearing on the books of the parent company would, under such conditions, be nominal assets only, and as such in a balance sheet of the holding company they should be offset by a reserve sufficient to provide for the whole or such part of them as may be represented by losses.

Profit and Loss Account: Certain holding companies continue to show as gross earnings only such dividends as have been received during the period from the subsidiary companies. Such practice merits the strongest censure. The author has heard it contended that inasmuch as the only legal method which a corporation has of distributing profits is by means of dividends, it would be most improper for a holding company to take credit for part or all of the earnings of a subsidiary company which had not been so distributed. This sounds well in theory, but in practice it is the argument of dishonest men. Almost invariably the sole reason for taking advantage of this technicality is that one or more of the subsidiaries has incurred a net loss in excess of the aggregate profits of all of the companies, and the management of the holding company, wishing to conceal such loss, seeks by subterfuge to justify the action.

An auditor cannot be too positive on this point. Wherever a holding company owns and controls one or more subsidiaries, the profits or losses of the subsidiaries must be stated for the same period as that of the holding company and consolidated. Any other method may lead to gross abuse.

The directors of a holding company, the sole income of which was the dividends of subsidiaries, could withhold dividends from prosperous companies while they were accumulating the stock of the holding company, and would be lavish with such dividends whenever they desired to sell their holding company stock. This is not mere supposition on the part of the author. Holding company profit and loss accounts are made up in the manner indicated, and inexperienced professional auditors are sometimes induced to certify to their accuracy, being misled by the apparent legality of the procedure.

As experienced and reputable auditors invariably decline to permit their names to be connected with a form of statement which is dishonest in fact if not in theory, this caution as to the profit and loss account of holding companies should be taken advantage of by an auditor who may have the matter presented to him for the first time.

Ernest Reckitt, C. P. A., relates the following incident:

> I have in mind a case where I was called in to make, as I supposed, an audit of the books not only of the "Holding Company," but also of those of the subsidiary companies, and was amazed to find that it was proposed to have me audit only the "Holding Company's" books. Upon explaining that I could give no certificate on such audit, the most specious arguments were advanced and the president of the company attempted to use the full force of his strong personality to persuade me to defer to his wishes, which naturally only made me suspect still more the motives which actuated him. Finally, and with great reluctance, they handed me the books of the subsidiary companies, and I found out that two of the companies had made losses aggregating over $200,000, no part of which losses had been taken care of on the books of the "Holding Company," though they had been careful to bring on to the books of the "Holding Company" the profits made by other subsidiary companies. One year later, the "Holding Company" and most of the subsidiary companies were in bankruptcy, as they deserved to be.

The author was called upon several years ago to audit the accounts of a holding company in a large Southern city, and of all of its subsidiaries. The latter included enterprises of different kinds, but as the holding company owned practically all of the stock of each underlying company, it was necessary to consolidate the operations of the entire group in order to show its exact net earnings. Unfortunately, several of the concerns were not profitable, and the consolidated profit and loss account was not a document to be proud of.

One of the subsidiaries, however, was quite prosperous, and its net earnings in themselves were sufficient to pay interest and dividends on the holding company's bonded debt and capital stock, but the losses of the other companies seriously depleted the funds of the holding company and rendered dividends impossible.

A short time afterwards, the president of the company appeared in New York with a large block of the holding company's bonds for sale. He submitted to the bankers, not the auditors' report, but a statement showing the earnings of the profitable subsidiary and ignoring so far as possible the existence of the other companies, and the bonds sold readily.

Quoting Mr. Lybrand on the matter of the preparation of the profit and loss account:

> Most of the comment that is applicable to the consolidated balance sheet is pertinent to the consolidated profit and loss account. In the consolidated profit and loss account transfer of profits from subsidiary companies to the holding company through the medium of dividends will be ignored, and the earnings, expenses, and charges of the several companies will be combined and stated as though the corporation were one enterprise.
>
> In the consolidated statement, therefore, will appear the entire gross earnings of the group of affiliated companies. Such gross earnings will represent cumulatively the operations of the several underlying companies, i. e., merchandise transformed into a marketable condition by one company and transferred to a second company for further manipulation and sale in a different form would appear in the gross earnings of each company and their aggregate in the consolidated profit and loss account. While on the surface it would seem that there is a duplication of gross earnings under this method, it is probably the only practical way in which to state them where there is a large number of companies with very many manufacturing processes.
>
> Again, as the property account of the various subsidiary companies are consolidated in the balance sheet, it would seem that the gross operations of those companies should likewise be aggregated in order to show the relation of the volume of business to the property investment.
>
> From such gross earnings will be deducted the entire operating costs incurred in producing those earnings, the balance resulting being then subject to the addition of income of a miscellaneous nature, and the deduction of expenses which are not applicable directly to the manufacturing and producing operations.
>
> In stating the consolidated income and profit and loss account there will probably be some difference of opinion as to the point at which charges

other than for ordinary operating should rest, in order that the current net earnings of the undertaking may be shown.

It is fairly clear that from the gross earnings must first be deducted the costs in labor, materials, and operating expenses incurred in producing those earnings, in order that a—let us call it manufacturing—profit may be shown. It is true that in an industrial enterprise, which includes mining, land and water transportation, as well as many forms of manufacturing, such an expression is in a sense a misnomer, but as the mining and transportation are really tributary to the manufacturing, the title might stand. It is true also that there are so many different kinds of products, with varying rates of profits included in the gross earnings that comparatively little use can be made of the figures as a basis of comparison from year to year. Nevertheless, as it is impossible in a condensed statement to show the volume and profit of each line of business, the aggregate figures will give the stockholder some information as to the total business, and, in a rough way, the rate of profit thereon for comparison with preceding periods.

From the gross profit so ascertained would be deducted the administrative, selling, and general expenses, virtually common to the whole enterprise, and chargeable against the operations as a whole. The resulting balance will be subject to adjustments because of extraordinary items relating to operating, but which cannot be included fairly in the current operating costs; and by income from investments other than those representing the holding company's ownership of the subsidiary companies.

The balance then carried forward from the current profit and loss to the income or general profit and loss account will be reduced by reason of reserves for depreciation, replacement, sinking fund requirements, etc., which are properly appropriated out of current earnings. Logically, such items should be deducted before the balance of current profits is struck, because the depreciation and replacement reserve at least are charges directly connected with operating, but as heretofore remarked, depreciation statistics are not sufficiently accurate, and the practice of reserving for depreciation is not yet common enough to justify the inclusion of such charges with the ordinary operating costs. Further, if they are stated separately, attention is drawn to the fact that reserve for depreciation has been made and to the amount of that provision.

The balance of profits, after deducting the foregoing reserves, shows the position of the earnings with respect to the interest payable on the debt of the subsidiary and holding companies. It may be held that interest on bonds of subsidiary companies (being a lien which must be deducted by the subsidiary company from its earnings before it can appropriate the remainder to the holding company) should be applied before the balance of current earnings is shown. It is suggested, however, that it is preferable to embrace all of the interest on the funded debt of the companies in one group, in order that the total thereof may appear; also because the bonded debt of the subsidiary companies may change by reason of new securities of the holding company being issued in lieu thereof, or it may be reduced through the operation of the sinking funds, in either of which events the interest charge would be lessened and a comparison of operating profits from year to year disturbed.

After the deduction of interest on the bonded debt, the balance remaining represents the profits available for dividends.

Partial Ownership of Subsidiaries: The foregoing remarks apply where the holding company owns all of the stock of the subsidiary companies, but in those cases where the holding company owns part only of the stock, some adjustment of the consolidated profit and loss account may be necessary.

Where a profit is shown, the amount to be included as the share of the holding company is the proportion the stock owned by the holding company bears to the total capital outstanding. It must be assumed that the minority stockholders will eventually receive through dividends their share of the profits.

Where a loss is shown, and where losses form the chronic condition of the subsidiary, it may as well be recognized that the holding company will have to assume all of it. This, of course, applies only to those cases where a subsidiary company is so largely owned by the holding company that the minority interest cannot be depended upon to advance its share of the funds necessary to take care of the loss.

The holding company may carry these advances as an asset, but the auditor will place such a value upon these items as the facts warrant, and it is reasonably certain that the final result will be to include all of the loss in the consolidated profit and loss account, although something less than one hundred per cent of the stock of the subsidiary is owned.

Comparative Statements: Where the accounts of several subsidiaries, operating along substantially the same lines, are examined, one very important object is to endeavor so to state the accounts that the results are reduced to a uniform basis. Many adjustments may be necessary to take care of local conditions, etc., but no form of presentation is clearer or more valuable.

Where comparative costs are feasible, it is important to ascertain the amount of the plant investment, as it may be that the costs as reported do not include depreciation nor interest. The latter is usually omitted from costs on the ground that it is a profit on capital employed and therefore cannot be an element of cost. Admitting this, "without prejudice," it might nevertheless serve to conceal actual lack of ability on the part of the manager of one factory as compared with another. One might keep twice as much capital tied up in raw materials and goods in process as the other, and where units of costs are stated in fractions of a cent, the interest on the excessive capital employed might be sufficient to prove the superiority of one manager over another.

CHAPTER XXXI

INTEREST

THE professional auditor should be thoroughly acquainted with the various methods of calculating interest. There is a remarkable lack of uniformity among business houses, and even banks, on the subject. The audit clerk who verifies interest collections or interest payments feels relieved if his own calculation agrees within a few dollars with the amount received or paid and lets it go at that.

As the "few dollars" multiplied a number of times will aggregate a considerable sum, it is important that the auditor familiarize himself with, and require his clerks to learn, the laws and customs governing interest, so that when a test is made it will be done intelligently, and if the amount received is insufficient or the amount paid is excessive, a report may be made thereon with confidence in the correctness of the criticism.

The three factors entering into the calculation of interest are principal, rate, and time.

Principal: Is simply the amount on which interest is to be calculated. There are two methods of reckoning principal. In bank discount the principal is regarded as the entire face of the note. For example, the bank discount on a note for $1,000 payable at one year at six per cent would be $60, and the proceeds paid to the customer would be $940. It will be noted that here the customer has the use of only $940 for one year, and yet he pays interest for the use of $1,000 for one year. The actual principal on which interest should be chargeable is only $940. The fictitious principal, on which interest actually is charged, is $1,000. The true principal in such case is found by the following proposition:

$$1.06 : 1.00 :: \$1{,}000 : X$$

which gives a present value of $943.40 for X

In spite of the foregoing facts, it is now thoroughly well settled by universal usage that this system of bank discount will be permitted by the courts, even though it does actually effectuate usury.

The right is expressly given to national banks by U. S. Rev. Stats. Sec. 5197, now Sec. 5197 of the U. S. Compiled Statutes.

The right is also given to New York Banks by Section 74 of the Banking Law of that State.

But the practice of anticipating the interest in this fashion has been held not to authorize the charging of interest on the anticipated interest in case such interest is not paid at the date of the execution of the note.

In the case of First National Bank v. Davis, 108 Ill. 633 (Sup. Ct. Ill., 1884), a note was given for $8,000 at one year at ten per cent. It was renewed at maturity. The renewal note, instead of being for $8,800, was for $8,880, made up as follows: $8,000 principal, $800 anticipated interest, and, as the bank did not receive the $800 anticipated interest on the date of execution of the renewal, but merely took the debtor's promise to pay the $800 at one year, the bank added 10 per cent of this $800 (or $80) to the face of the renewal note, making it total $8,880, as stated. The court held this to be usury.

The question of principal also occurs where payments are made on an old account which is drawing interest. Under such circumstances the debtor sometimes claims that all payments should apply on account of principal; but unless there is a clear and specific agreement that they shall be so applied, the rule is well settled that such payments are applicable in the first instance to all arrears of interest before any application can be made on account of principal.

The question of principal is also involved in cases dealing with compounded interest. It has been held that interest may be added to and become a part of principal at stated times and under certain conditions, and the question of whether or not this is permissible will sometimes determine whether or not the transaction is usurious or otherwise. This is a point upon which an auditor is frequently required to pass.

Loan accounts and book accounts between interrelated enterprises sometimes run along for years without a final settlement. When a statement is desired upon which a settlement may be based, there is always a temptation to state the transactions in as short rests or periods as possible, the interest being calculated and included in each balance carried forward. This results in compounding the interest, is illegal, and should never be permitted by the auditor.

It may be a hardship to the lender, as compound interest would be legal and proper in such a case if the accounts had been written up properly at the time, interest actually entered in the books, and statements prepared therefrom and submitted to the borrower or debtor. If not objected to at the time nor within a reasonable time thereafter, the transaction would have the legal effect of an account stated, and each new starting balance, although including interest calculated at shorter intervals than a year, being acquiesced in, would be binding.

In the absence of special custom or agreement, however, interest should not be compounded.

Rate of Interest: This rarely or never admits of dispute except in those cases where a note, contract, bond, or other obligation is made in one jurisdiction, to be paid or performed in another jurisdiction without specifying the rate of interest, and the legal rate of interest in the two jurisdictions is different. Then the question sometimes arises whether the rate at the place of making the note or the rate at the place of payment is to govern.

A similar question arises where one rate of interest is the legal rate at the time of making the note, contract, or bond, and another legal rate is in force when the obligation falls due.

In the absence of an intention to the contrary shown by express stipulation or otherwise, the rate of interest is to be regulated by the law as it existed at the time and place of making the contract, and not by the law existing when the debt falls due or when the remedy is sought. (8 Cyc. 310.)

It is well settled, however, that the parties may contract for the legal rate in either place and the contract will govern.

Time: The time which interest is to run gives rise to a wide diversity of practice.

There is an underlying principle which is of very general, although not absolutely universal, application, and it is this, that if the first day of the interest period is included in the computation, then the last day shall be excluded; and if the first day is excluded, then the last day is included. The parties can, if they will, contract otherwise. (See Blanchard v. Hilliard, 11 Mass. 85.)

Custom in Banks and Trust Companies: In Kirkbride & Sterrett's "The Modern Trust Company" (page 84), the rule is stated to be: "In computing interest on loans, the actual number of days is taken. If the day on which the loan was made is included, the day of payment is not counted."

It is more or less common, however, for banks to count both the first and last days when the interest is *payable to themselves.* This custom will not override the common law rule unless the parties expressly agree to it. The bank that figures time thus at the full legal rate of interest in the State of Vermont is guilty of usury, but not *corrupt* usury. Bank of Burlington v. Durkee, 1 Vt. 399. The bank that does this same thing in the State of Virginia is not guilty of usury at all. Crump v. Trytitle, 5 Leigh 251 (Court of Appeals of Virginia, 1834).

In the Crump case, last cited, the court even held that it was proper for the bank to charge interest not only on the first and last day of the original note, but also on the first and last day of successive renewal notes, the result being that the bank received double interest on every day that a renewal was executed. Many banks follow that custom, although some banks are content with charging the first and last day on the original note, and not on the renewal note.

The legal fiction of the common law was that a day is indivisible, and therefore even if a customer received his discount money just before closing on the date of his note, and paid it immediately after opening on the date of maturity, he would still, in strict contemplation of law, have had the use of that money all of both the terminal days, and on that fiction the decision in the Crump case was undoubtedly sound law. Whether it was equitable or not is another question.

Where banks, however, have to *pay interest,* instead of receive it, they apply a widely different rule.

First: They quite generally credit interest on deposits only the day after deposit, on the theory that most deposits are made by cheque and it takes one day on an average to collect through the clearing house.

Second: Some banks provide that deposits made between the

second and the fifteenth of the month shall draw interest from the fifteenth; and that deposits made between the sixteenth and the first of the following month shall draw interest from the latter date.

Assuming a uniform volume of deposits for each day of the month, this arrangement is advantageous to the bank as against its depositors in the ratio of 2 to 1.

Third: Savings banks quite generally provide that deposits made between the first and fifth day of the month shall draw interest from the first, while deposits made after the fifth shall draw interest from the first day of the following month.

Assuming a uniform volume of deposits for each day of the month, this arrangement is to the advantage of the bank as against its depositors in the ratio of 5 to 1.

Fourth: Some banks allow interest on savings accounts only by full calendar months.

Fifth: Some banks provide that if the depositor makes a withdrawal during any semiannual interest period, he thereby loses all interest which may have accrued thereon since the last interest date.

This rule works largely to the profit of the banks and to the loss of the depositors.

As to how far an auditor may wish to criticize these rules is a question for individual determination. The fact is, however, that most business men know nothing about the customs with respect to interest. They can negotiate for a low rate of interest on loans or a high rate on deposits, but they do not know that their bank may have established arbitrary interest rules which yield them a greater profit than other banks exact. It may therefore be proper for the auditor to examine into the whole matter and report thereon to the client.

Custom Among Business Houses: Business and commercial houses as a rule count only the first or last day, but not both, when they figure interest.

Custom Among Stock Brokers: Stock brokers settle purchases the day following the sale, and they debit the customer's account on the day of settlement. In charging monthly interest to the customer, the broker includes both the day of settlement and the last day of the month. The broker justifies this by showing that he, in turn, is compelled to pay interest on his loan to the bank in like manner by including both the terminal days of the period in his calculation.

The stock broker, by rendering accounts monthly and calculating interest for the same period, compounds the interest monthly.

New York Clearing House: In its official announcements, the New York Clearing House includes the first day only and excludes the last day.

The Treasury Department of the United States: In the Treasury Department it is provided that:

> Only one of the two days of date and due date of an obligation is taken into account in stating the time for which interest is to be calculated.

The Unit Period: Interest, either expressly or impliedly, is at such a rate "per annum."

Where the interest runs for one month, quarterly, or semi-annually, the proportion is one-twelfth, one-fourth, or one-half of a year.

A month is held to be one-twelfth of the year, no matter whether the month have twenty-eight, twenty-nine, thirty, or thirty-one days.

Both of the foregoing rules are in force universally and are sanctioned by the rules of the United States Treasury Department.

Where the interest runs, however, for so many days, there is a sharp diversity of opinion as to whether a calendar year of 365 days (366 days for a leap year) or an artificial year of 360 days is the proper unit of calculation.

The New York Clearing House calculates interest on the basis of 360 days to a year. For instance, the interest on $1,000 from January 1, 1912, to March 12, 1912, at 4 per cent per annum was officially calculated as $7.89. This represented 71 days on a 360-day-to-the-year basis.

It has also been held by the courts that the artificial year of 360 days is a proper basis. State Bank of North Carolina v. Cowan, 8 Leigh 238 (Court of Appeals of Virginia, 1837).

But the better rule, at least in modern times, would seem to be that the calendar year of 365 days is the proper basis.

N. Y. Firemen Ins. Co. v. Ely, 2 Cowen 705 (Supreme Court of New York, 1824), held that taking interest on the basis of 360 days to the year was usury.

Chap. 148 of the Acts of Massachusetts of 1909, approved March 6, 1909, entitled, "An Act Relative to the Computation of Interest on Bonds and Notes in Dealings with the Commonwealth," makes the year of 365 days the standard for all loans to or by the Commonwealth.

After many vicissitudes, the State of New York now has in force the following (Sec. 58 of the General Construction Law of New York):

> "The term years in a statute, contract, or any public or private instrument, means 365 days, but the added day of a leap year and the day immediately preceding shall, for the purpose of such computation, be counted as one day . . . the term year means twelve months, the term half year, six months, and the term quarter of a year, three months."

The rules of the Treasury Department of the United States Government are as follows:

> In calculating interest for a fractional period, the time is the true fraction of that period. For an annual rate, the time is the exact number of days for which the interest runs divided by the number of days in the year, 365 or 366; for a semiannual or quarterly period, it is the number of days for which the interest runs divided by the number of days in the particular half year or quarter year.
>
> Unless the unit period is a month, the month does not enter into interest computations, only days and the full unit period being considered.

The rule just enunciated is somewhat at variance with the rule generally obtaining on bonds or mortgages where the interest accrues regularly, as for example, quarterly or semiannually. There, when interest is computed for a part of such quarterly or semiannual period, it is the usual custom to state the time in months and days rather than entirely in days. In such a calculation the number of full months from the initial date to the same numbered day of the month next preceding the final date should first be ascertained, and then the odd days to the final date.

When we figure these odd days, there are two ways of making the computation.

First: They may be taken at so many thirtieths of a month (on the 360-day basis).

Second: They may be taken as so many twenty-eighths, twenty-ninths, thirtieths, or thirty-firsts, according to the month in which they fall.

Third: They may be taken as so many three hundred and sixty-fifths of a year.

It is not assumed by any means that the foregoing discussion covers the question of interest at all exhaustively, but the author hopes that the customs and decisions reviewed will enable a student or practitioner to substantiate any criticisms which he may deem proper to make during the progress of an audit.

CHAPTER XXXII

THE LIABILITIES OF AUDITORS

Legal Responsibility: In my opinion the quickest way to weed out the incompetent men who now hold themselves out as public accountants would be to make them understand the civil responsibility of a professional accountant. Naturally, an unreliable, incompetent man cares nothing about his moral responsibility, and so long as he knows that American courts have never laid down specific rules regulating the duties or obligations of public accountants, he probably feels safe from any legal responsibility. One sure and very desirable result of the weeding out process would be the raising of the professional standard, for a few irresponsible men can offset the good work of ten times their number.

As is well known, there are numerous English decisions dealing with the rights and liabilities of professional auditors. In view, however, of the total number of accountants in practice and the number of years the decisions cover, the number does not seem at all appalling. While the fact that we have no reported decisions speaks well for the integrity and good judgment of our accountants, yet it is felt that occasions have arisen where a test case would have been made had it not been known that any judgment involving money damages which might have been rendered would have been worthless so far as the possibility of collection was concerned.

It is unfortunate that anyone should be permitted to practice as a public accountant who, in case of gross negligence or malpractice, has so little financial responsibility that a judgment against him would be worthless, and who, moreover, is beyond the legal reach of his fellow practitioners, who at present have no opportunity to prefer charges against one who is neither a member of a State society nor certified by a State board.

The absence of decided cases, however, does not alter the

principle of law that anyone who holds himself out to be skillful in any trade or profession, and who is negligent in the performance of what he undertakes, becomes responsible in damages for such failure. This civil responsibility is settled and cannot be debated, but it should not be passed over lightly and should be emphasized on all occasions. The measure of legal responsibility, however, is much too low for a conscientious accountant. The law requires of him only the skill of an ordinary skillful accountant; the law gives him the privilege of assuming the accuracy of many things unless he has definite suspicions to the contrary, and, as already stated, the law never requires one to measure up to the standard of the most skillful in the same profession or trade. In this respect accountants are to be congratulated, for it is common knowledge that the majority of professional accountants in the United States seek to do more for their clients than the law requires, and every year witnesses a more general desire to advance the quality of services rendered.

It is earnestly hoped that further progress will be made in this direction. Since the wish for high standards is general, let each individual accountant do his part toward maintaining them. Public opinion should be aroused so that unqualified practitioners will gradually cease to practice, and in their place a united certified body will control all accountancy matters—not because the law grants them exclusive privileges, but by reason of the fact that they can be depended upon at all times and under all circumstances, while the others cannot.*

As heretofore stated, the State and Federal courts of the United States appear to be barren of any decisions upon this important question.

On the other hand, both the common and statute law of Great Britain are prolific in decisions and enactments, prescribing with a good deal of exactness the precise nature of the liabilities which an auditor may conceivably incur while in the exercise of the multifarious activities incident to his profession.

It is highly probable that in the event of any litigation of importance occurring here and involving that question, the courts of America will look to the English cases as affording, if not

*The author wrote the foregoing article for the Journal of Accountancy several years ago.

binding precedents, at least valuable guides to the considerations and principles of law applicable in such case.

For this reason a brief résumé of some of the more important English cases is in order. A number of English cases which appear to turn entirely upon the peculiar enactments of certain British statutes, and which therefore would be of little or no value as precedents or analogies in American courts, are omitted.

As to the Exact Status of an "Auditor" in England: It should be noted that the term "auditor" as used in England is not the precise analogue of the term "auditor" as used in America. This is explained by the official recognition given to auditors by the English Companies Act.

The English courts make a sharp distinction between an "auditor" and an "accountant":

In Herbert Alfred Burleigh v. Ingram Clark, Lim., Chancery Division, Apl. 2, 1901 (Acct. L. R., 1901, p. 651), it was held that an accountant has a lien on such books as he has actually worked upon, in respect of his proper remuneration for work upon those books only.

An auditor, who merely does work in respect of the books, has no such lien.

Wilde and others v. Cape and Dalgleish, decided by the Queen's Bench Division, May 27, 1897 ("The Accountant," Eng., June 5, 1897), rested on the following question:

> "Did the accountant contract and agree to act as a simple accountant, and merely to see that the books are brought to a correct balance, taking the entries and balance in the books as correct; or, on the other hand, did the accountant contract and agree to act as an auditor and make a cash audit, and check receipts and payments, and examine the cash and bank book, and be responsible for the accuracy of the cash transactions?"

The English "auditor" has certain statutory rights, powers, duties, and obligations in connection with English corporations. These rights, powers, duties, and obligations are not discussed here with any fullness, as the present work relates only to American accountancy. Briefly stated, the "auditor" is required under the English statutes to present his certificate to the stockholders at their annual meetings, and is liable in connection with that certificate under certain circumstances which will be briefly touched on in some of the following cases.

As to the Lien of an Auditor: It seems that an auditor has no lien for his fees on the books which he has examined, such, for example, as an attorney has upon papers of a client in the State of New York. Therefore, it seems even if an auditor has not been paid his fees, he is, nevertheless, bound to surrender the books and papers to his client on demand. See Burleigh v. Clark, *supra.*

As to the Rights of an Auditor Who is Retained by the Year and Dismissed During the Year: In such case the auditor is entitled to his full year's pay. See Homan v. Quilter; City of London Court, February 27, 1908 (Acct. L. R. 1908, p. 25), which decided that an auditor employed at an annual fee and dismissed during the currency of a year is entitled to a full year's fee.

As to the Criminal Liability of an Auditor for Corruptly and Knowingly Certifying Falsely: Happily, the high standard of the profession in America has left this question a moot one up to the present time. Such a case, however, has arisen in England, and the courts of that country did not shrink from the unpleasant duty thereby cast upon them. See Dumbell's Banking Co., Lim.: Special Court at Douglas, Isle of Man, November 5 to 14, 1900 (Acct. L. R. 1900, p. 181).

In this case two chartered accountants were convicted and sentenced under a local statute for issuing false balance sheets, knowing them to be false, and with intent to deceive, although it was not shown that the accountants received any benefit therefrom other than the audit fees received by them. The correspondence between the directors and auditors showed, however, that the latter were aware of the unsatisfactory financial condition of the bank, but they did not disclose the true state of affairs to the stockholders.

It is believed that the criminal statutes of America would result in a similar conviction and sentence, if the occasion should ever arise.

AS TO THE CIVIL LIABILITY OF AN AUDITOR WHO IS NEGLIGENT IN THE PREPARATION OF HIS REPORT AND LIKE MATTERS

(1) In General: The following discussion in the select committee of the House of Lords, appointed in 1896 to inquire into the Company Law amendment may prove of interest, as indicating the views of some very high English authorities. Mr. Frederick Whinney, F. C. A., was before the committee, and the proceedings, as officially reported, follow:

Passing to clause 29, which deals with the appointment of auditors, he suggested the addition of words to the effect that, unless it was otherwise provided by the articles of association, one of the auditors, or the auditor, if there was only one, should be a professional accountant and should not necessarily be a shareholder. In support of that proposition he pointed out that joint-stock enterprise had grown very largely of late years, and he maintained that very few balance sheets could be audited properly except by a professional accountant. He went on to suggest the insertion in the bill of a provision that no auditor other than the retiring auditor should be appointed at a general meeting unless notice had been sent out to the shareholders with the notice of the meeting. That, he said, was brought forward with the object of preventing the question of the auditor being "rushed," as was sometimes the case at present. The bill provided that there should be a balance sheet containing all details—technically, what was known as the trial balance. It was scarcely necessary to provide for that by legislation, because a balance sheet could not be made out unless the details were given. As to the duties of auditors, the bill proposed that they should use reasonable diligence with the view of ascertaining that the books of the company had been properly kept and recorded correctly the financial and trading transactions of the company. The latter part of the section he did not object to, but he thought the words "properly kept" should be omitted. "Properly kept" was a vague term, and the section would be quite sufficient to meet the difficulty without its insertion. It would be the duty of the auditors to say that the books had not been properly kept if that was the case.

The bill cast upon auditors the duty of checking the balance sheet, including the amount of debts due to the company after making a proper deduction for debts considered to be bad or doubtful. It would be impossible for the auditors to do that in the case of large companies where the debtors numbered, say, one thousand. In the case of banks, for instance, where the number of debtors was very large, it was found necessary to keep an aggregate account of debtors, showing the total amount due to the company by its debtors. The auditors would have to take that account, and schedules would be prepared, and, if necessary, would be tested afterwards. The duty should not be thrown upon auditors of checking every balance. In one case he might mention the debtors numbered 750,000. (Laughter.) It should be sufficient if they gave a certificate to the effect that they had used all reasonable care and diligence in ascertaining that the balance sheet was true.

LORD DAVEY: "I should like to ask whether you conceive it to be the proper duty of an auditor to say not only whether the books are properly kept, but to go into questions behind the books and say whether the assets are properly valued?" A. "I do not know that I can give a better definition of the duties of the auditor than that laid down by Lord Justice Lindley. He said that it was the duty of an auditor to be honest, to exercise all reasonable care and skill to ascertain that which he certifies is true, and to exercise all reasonable care and skill in ascertaining the truth."

LORD FARRER: "That is all very well; but what is the truth which he is to ascertain?" LORD DAVEY: "Yes; that is it. Can he, for instance, when the properties are valued at a certain sum in the books, and on the face of the books are properly valued, can it be his duty, not being a valuer, to go into the question of value and say that the directors have put too high a value on the real estate?" A. "No, I do not think so. It would be giving the auditor a different position from that which it was contemplated he should have, namely, that he should examine the accounts of the directors and see whether they are correct. Anything calculated to arouse his suspicion he ought, of course, to look into."

LORD FARRER: "After all, the responsibility lies with the directors?" A. "Not altogether with the directors. There are the managers of the company."

LORD FARRER: "Do you wish to place the auditor in the position of an administrator, who is to check the directors in their management of the company?" A. "Certainly not."

LORD DAVEY: "Is not the sounder principle this: that the auditor is bound to know everything the books tell him, to have all the suspicions that the books suggest, and to make all the inferences to what he finds in the books would lead him?" A. "I think that would cover the whole of his duty. I think it is his duty not to certify a balance sheet until he believes it to be true, and he has taken all reasonable care that it is so. He is bound to see that the balance sheet is brought before the shareholders in such a form that they themselves can exercise their judgment upon it."

The next suggestion he had to make was that the pains and penalties of auditors should be modified. At present the auditor was supposed to be responsible if dividends were paid out of capital. LORD DAVEY: "Is he? I never knew it." THE LORD CHANCELLOR: "Putting aside fraudulent connivance, what do you suppose to be the responsibility of an auditor?" THE WITNESS: "That if dividends have been paid out of capital, assuming, of course, that the company is wound up, the directors and auditors are responsible for the amount of the dividends so paid, subject to the Statute of Limitations in favor of the auditors." LORD DAVEY: "Where do you find that?" THE LORD CHANCELLOR: "I am not aware of any such law. I am not aware of any case in which the innocent mistake of a director has been held to be the subject for an action." THE WITNESS: "There was a case before Mr. Justice Stirling." LORD DAVEY: "There, there was fraudulent connivance." THE WITNESS: "I think there was not connivance, but that the auditor himself was ignorant." THE LORD CHANCELLOR: "To me it is a startling suggestion that for an innocent mistake an auditor should be liable."

(2) Cases Where the Auditor Was Held Not Liable: In re Kingston Cotton Mill Co., 2 Ch. Div. 279 (Court of Appeal, May 19, 1896), the court said:

"I come now to the real question in this controversy, and that is, whether the appellants have been guilty of any breach of duty to the company. To decide this question it is necessary to consider (1) what their duty was; (2) how they performed it, and in what respects (if any) they failed to perform it. . . . I protest against the notion that an auditor is bound to be suspicious, as distinguished from being reasonably careful. To substitute the one expression for the other may easily lead to serious error. I pass now to consider the complaint made against the auditors in this particular case. The complaint is that they failed to detect certain frauds. There is no charge of dishonesty on the part of the auditors. They did not certify or pass anything which they did not honestly believe to be true. It is said, however, that they were culpably careless. The circumstances are as follows: For several years frauds were committed by the manager, who, in order to bolster up the company and make it appear flourishing when it was the reverse, deliberately exaggerated both the quantities and values of the cotton and yarn in the company's mills. He did this at the ends of the years 1890, 1891, 1892, and 1893. There was no book or account (except the stock journal, to which I will refer presently) showing the quantity or value of the cotton or yarn in the mill at any one time. It would not be easy to keep such a book. Nor is it wanted for ordinary purposes. There is considerable waste (twenty or twenty-five per cent on the average) in the manufacture of yarn from cotton, and the market prices of both cotton and yarn are subject to great fluctuations. The balance sheets of each year contained on the assets side entries of the values of the stock-in-trade at the end of the year, and those entries were stated to be 'as per manager's certificate.'

"There were also in the balance sheets entries on the opposite side of the values of the stock-in-trade at the beginning of the year. The quantities did not appear in either case. The auditors took the entry of the stock-in-trade at the beginning of the year from the last preceding balance sheet, and they took the values of the stock-in-trade at the end of the year from the stock journal. The book contained a series of accounts under various heads purporting to show the quantities and values of the company's stock-in-trade at the end of each year, and a summary of all the accounts, showing the total value of such stock-in-trade. The summary was signed by the manager, and the value, as shown by it, was adopted by the auditors and was inserted as an asset in the balance sheet, but 'as per manager's certificate.' The summary always corresponded with the accounts summarized, and the auditors ascertained that this was the case. But they did not examine further into the accuracy of the accounts summarized. The auditors did not profess to guarantee the correctness of this item. They assumed no responsibility for it. They took the item from the manager, and the entry in the balance sheet showed that they did so. I confess I cannot see that their omission to check his returns was a breach of their duty to the company.

"It is no part of an auditor's duty to take stock. No one contends that it is. He must rely on other people for details of the stock-in-trade in hand. In the case of a cotton mill, he must rely on some skilled person for the materials necessary to enable him to enter the stock-in-trade at its proper value in the balance sheet. In this case the auditors relied on the manager. He was a man of high character and of unquestioned competence. He was trusted by every one who knew him. The learned judge has held that the directors are not to be blamed for trusting him. The auditors had no suspicion that he was not to be trusted to give accurate information as to the stock-in-trade in hand, and they trusted him accordingly in that matter.

"But it is said they ought not to have done so, and for this reason: The stock journal showed the quantities—that is, the weight in pounds—of the cotton and yarn at the end of each year. Other books showed the quantities of cotton bought during the year and the quantities of yarn sold during the year. If these books had been compared by the auditors they would have found that the quantity of cotton and yarn in hand at the end of the year ought to be much less than the quantity shown in the stock journal, and so much less that the value of the cotton and yarn entered in the stock journal could not be right, or, at all events, was so abnormally large as to excite suspicion and demand further inquiry. This is the view taken by the learned judge. But, although it is no doubt true that such a process might have been gone through, and that, if gone through, the fraud would have been discovered, can it be truly said that the auditors were wanting in reasonable care in not thinking it necessary to test the managing director's returns? I cannot bring myself to think they were, nor do I think that any jury of business men would take a different view.

"It is not sufficient to say that the frauds must have been detected if the entries in the books had been put together in a way which never occurred to anyone before suspicion was aroused. The question is whether, no suspicion of anything wrong being entertained, there was a want of reasonable care on the part of the auditors in relying on the returns made by a competent and trusted expert relating to matters on which information from such a person was essential. I cannot think there was. The manager had no apparent conflict between his interest and his duty. His position was not similar to that of a cashier who has to account for the cash which he receives, and whose own account of his receipts and payments could not be reasonably taken by an auditor without further inquiry.

"It is the duty of an auditor to bring to bear on the work he has to perform that skill, care, and caution which a reasonably competent, careful, and cautious auditor would use. What is reasonable care, skill, and caution must depend on the particular circumstances of each case. An auditor is not bound to be a detective, or, as was said, to approach his work with suspicion, or with a foregone conclusion that there is something wrong. He is a watchdog, but not a bloodhound. He is justified in believing tried servants of the company in whom confidence is placed by the company. He is entitled to assume that they are honest and to rely upon their representations, provided he takes reasonable care. If there is anything calculated to excite suspicion, he should probe it to the bottom, but in the absence of anything of that kind he is only bound to be reasonably cautious and careful. . . . The duties of auditors must not be rendered too onerous. Their work is responsible and laborious, and the remuneration moderate. I should be sorry to see the liability of auditors extend any further than In re The London and General Bank. Indeed, I assented to that decision only on account of the inconsistency of the statement made to the directors with the balance sheet certified by the auditors and presented to the shareholders. This satisfied my mind that the auditors deliberately concealed that from the shareholders which they had communicated to the directors. It would be difficult to say this was not a breach of duty. Auditors must not be made liable for not tracking out ingenious and carefully laid schemes of fraud when there is nothing to arouse their suspicion, and when those frauds are perpetrated by tried servants of the company and are undetected for years by the directors. So to hold would make the position of an auditor intolerable."

In Maynards, Lim. v. Maynards and others; Chancery Division, January 16, 1900 (Acct. L. R., 1900, p. 24), it was held that where auditors act honestly and are honestly satisfied of the correctness of their report, they are not to be held liable.

In Short & Compton v. Brackett; Colchester County Court, May 6, 1904 (Acct. L. R., 1904, p. 85):

An accountant making an investigation of accounts for an incoming partner is entitled to assume that the books are correct, the accountant not having been instructed to audit, but merely to make up the account from the books.

The Liverpool & Wigan Supply Association, Lim.; Liverpool Court of Bankruptcy, June 14, 1907 (Acct. L. R., 1907, p. 4). The court said:

"In this case I think that the auditor was negligent as an auditor in the sense that he relied on statements made to him by the directors, and did not put in his certificate the fact that he was relying on the statements of the directors. The auditor did not disclose that there was no cash book, and, if it were material in this case to say so, I think the auditor ought to have disclosed it. I don't think he ought to have accepted the statements of a director as to the taking of stock, and the balance sheets should have shown the position of the company on the dates they purport to show the position. But none of these acts appear to me to have diminished the assets of the company as such."

Held, therefore, that the auditor was not liable.

(3) Cases Where the Auditor Has Been Held Liable: Leeds Estate Building & Investment Society, Lim. v. Shepherd, L. R., 36 Ch. Div. 787 (August 9, 1887).

Dividends had been paid out of capital and the auditor had passed the account.

Held that it was the duty of the auditor in verifying the accounts of the company not to confine himself to verifying the arithmetical accuracy of the balance sheet, but to inquire into its special accuracy and to ascertain if it contained the particulars specified in the articles of association and was properly drawn up to contain a true and accurate representation of the company's affairs.

"In each of these years, L. (the auditor) certified that the accounts were a true copy of those shown in the books of the company. That certificate would naturally be understood to mean that the books of the company showed (taking, for example, the certificate for the year 1879) that, on April 30, 1879, the company was entitled to 'moneys lent' to the amount of approximately £150,000. This was not in accordance with the fact; the accounts, in this respect, did not truly represent the state of the company's affairs, and it was a breach of duty upon L.'s part to certify as he did with reference to them. The payment of the dividends, directors' fees, and bonuses to the manager actually paid in those years appears to be the natural and immediate consequence of such breach of duty; and I hold L. liable for damages to the amount of the money so paid."

In re London & General Bank, 2 Ch. Div. 673 (1895).

An auditor who is dissatisfied with the accounts of a company must plainly draw attention to the grounds of his dissatisfaction in his certificate.

The court said:

"It is not part of an auditor's duty to give advice either to directors or shareholders as to what they ought to do. An auditor has nothing to do with the prudence or imprudence of making loans with or without security. It is nothing to him whether the business of a company is being conducted prudently or imprudently, profitably or unprofitably. It is nothing to him whether dividends are properly or improperly declared, provided he discharged his own duty to the shareholders. His business is to ascertain and state the true financial position of the company at the time of the audit, and his duty is confined to that. But then comes the question: How is he to ascertain such position? The answer is: By examining the books of the company. But he does not discharge his duty by doing this without inquiry and without taking any trouble to see that the books of the company themselves show the company's true position. He must take reasonable care to ascertain that they do. Unless he does this, his duty will be worse than a farce. Assuming the books to be so kept as to show the true position of the company, the auditor has to frame a balance sheet showing that position according to the books, and to certify that the balance sheet presented is correct in that sense. But his first duty is to examine the books, not merely for the purpose of ascertaining what they do show, but also for the purpose of satisfying himself that they show the true financial position of the company. This is quite in accordance with the decision of Mr. Justice Stirling in the Leeds' Estate Company v. Shepherd, in 36 Chancery Division, page 802. An auditor, however, is not bound to do more than exercise reasonable care and skill in making inquiries and investigations. He is not an insurer; he does not guarantee that the books do correctly show the true position of the company's affairs; he does not guarantee that his balance sheet is accurate according to the books of the company. If he did, he would be responsible for an error on his part, even if he were himself deceived, without any want of reasonable care on his part, say, by the fraudulent concealment of the book from him. His obligation is not so onerous as this.

"Such I take to be the duty of the auditor: he must be honest—that is, he must not certify what he does not believe to be true, and he must take reasonable care and skill before he believes that what he certifies is true.

"What is reasonable care in any particular case must depend upon the circumstances of that case. Where there is nothing to excite suspicion, very little inquiry will be reasonable and sufficient; and in practice, I believe, business men select a few cases haphazard, see that they are right, and assume that others like them are correct also. Where suspicion is aroused more care is obviously necessary, but still an auditor is not bound to exercise more than reasonable care and skill even in a case of suspicion, and he is perfectly justified in acting on the opinion of an expert where special knowledge is required.

"Mr. Theobald's evidence satisfied me that he took the same view as myself of his duty in investigating the company's books and preparing his balance sheet. He did not content himself with making his balance sheet from the books without troubling himself about the truth of what they showed. He checked the cash, examined vouchers for payments, saw that the bills and securities entered in the books were correct, took reasonable care to ascertain their value, and in one case obtained a solicitor's opinion on the validity of an equitable charge. I see no trace whatever of any failure by him in the performance of this part of his duty.

"The balance sheet and certificate of February, 1892, that is, for the year 1891, was accompanied by a report to the directors of the bank. Taking the balance sheet, the certificate, and report together, Mr. Theobald stated to the directors the true financial position of the bank, and if this report had been laid before the shareholders, Mr. Theobald would have completely discharged his duty to them. Unfortunately, however, this report was not laid before the shareholders, and it becomes necessary to consider the legal consequences to Mr. Theobald of this circumstance.

"A person whose duty it is to convey information to others does not discharge that duty by simply giving them so much information as is calculated to induce them, or some of them, to ask for more. Information and means of information are by no means equivalent terms. Still, there may be circumstances under which information given in the shape of a printed document circulated amongst a large body of shareholders would, by its consequent publicity, be very injurious to their interests, and in such a case I am not prepared to say that an auditor would fail to discharge his duty, if, instead of publishing his report in such a way as to insure publicity, he made a confidential report to the shareholders and invited their attention to it, and told them where they could see it. The auditor is to make a report to the shareholders, but the mode of doing so, and the form of the report, are not prescribed. If, therefore, Mr. Theobald had laid before the shareholders the balance sheet and the profit and loss account accompanied by a certificate in the form in which he had prepared it, he would, perhaps, have done enough, under the peculiar circumstances of the case. I feel, however, the great danger of acting on such a principle, and in order not to be misunderstood, I will add that an auditor who gives shareholders means of information instead of information in respect of a company's financial position does so at his peril, and runs the very serious risk of being held, judicially, to have failed to discharge his duty.

"In this case I have no hesitation in saying that Mr. Theobald did fail to discharge his duty to the shareholders in certifying and laying before them the balance sheet of February, 1892, without any reference to the report which he laid before the directors, and with no other warning than is conveyed by the words, 'The value of the assets as shown on the balance sheets is dependent upon realization.' The most important asset on that balance sheet is put down as 'Loans to customers and other securities, £346,975,' and on those a full and detailed report was made to the directors, showing the very unsatisfactory state of these loans and securities, and it is impossible to read the oral evidence, the report of Mr. Balfour and Mr. Brock, dated December 22, 1891, and the report of the auditor to the directors of February 3, 1892, without coming to the conclusion that the entry of that large sum as a good asset without explanation was justifiable. It is a mere truism to say that the value of loans and securities depends upon their realization. We are told that a statement to that effect is so unusual that the mere presence of those words is enough to excite suspicion. But, as already stated, the duty of an auditor is to convey information, not to arouse inquiry, and although an auditor might infer from an unusual statement that something was seriously wrong, it by no means follows that ordinary people would have their suspicions aroused by a similar statement if, as in this case, its language expresses no more than any ordinary person would infer without it.

"But Mr. Theobald relies on the fact that he was induced to omit from his certificate all reference to the report which he made to the directors, because Mr. Balfour, the chairman, promised to mention such report in his speech to the shareholders, and he did so. But although Mr. Balfour twice alluded to the report, he did so in such a way as to avoid attracting attention to it. The second time he mentioned it was after a dividend had been declared, and when a motion to reappoint the auditors was before the meeting. The truth is that not a word was said to convey to the shareholders the substance of the information contained in the report, or to induce them to ask any question about it. The balance sheet and the profit and loss account were true and correct in this sense, that they were in accordance with the books. But they were, nevertheless, entirely misleading, and misrepresented the real position of the company. Under these circumstances, I am compelled to hold that Mr. Theobald failed to discharge his duty to the shareholders with respect to the balance sheet and certificate of February, 1892. Possibly he did not realize the extent of his duty to the shareholders as distinguished from the directors, and he, unfortunately, consented to leave the chairman to explain the true state of the company to the shareholders instead of doing so himself. The fact, however, remains, and cannot be got over, that the balance sheet and certificate of February, 1892, did not show the true position of the company at the end of 1891, and that was owing to the omission by the auditor to lay before the shareholders material information which he had obtained in the course of his employment as auditor of the company, and to which he called the attention of the directors.

"The real truth is that the assets of the bank were put down in the balance sheet at far too high a figure, and this entry, though not misleading if explained (as it was to the directors), was seriously misleading in the absence of explanation."

Irish Woolen Company, Lim. v. Tyson and others, decided by the Irish Court of Appeal, January 20, 1900 (Acct. L. R., 1900, p. 13).

The accounts of a company had been falsified and dividends improperly paid out of capital in consequence. The auditor was held responsible on the ground that the falsifications might have been discovered by the exercise of reasonable care and skill from an inspection of the books themselves.

"An accountant with a large business is not supposed to do everything himself. The auditor is bound to give reasonable care and skill, but this can also be exercised by his deputy. I do not think there is anything to be gained by considering in the abstract the duties of an auditor of a joint stock company. He is entitled to see the company's books and the materials for their books, and also to ask for explanations. But he is not called on to seek for knowledge outside the company, or to communicate with customers or creditors. He is not an insurer against fraud or error; and if fraud is alleged it must be shown with precision the acts of negligence for which he is said to be responsible. Nine balance sheets were prepared, and the figures on some represent the aggregate amount of many items, but I propose to deal only with matters that have been referred to during the hearing. There are three sets of figures with which I will deal: (1) stock-in-trade; (2) sundry debtors; (3) sundry creditors on the liability side of the balance sheet. Taking these in order . . . There was certainly no duty cast on the auditor to take stock. What he did was to have the calculations checked in his office, and this was done with proper care. Mr. Kevans said he was particularly careful as to the deduction for discount, and, as far as I could gather, the universal rate of ten per cent seems reasonable. Moreover, an auditor has nothing to do with the terms upon which the company, or a trader, buys or sells. . . . As to the provision for the 'bad debts,' if there is any one thing upon which an auditor is dependent upon the officers, it is the writing off, or the making of a prospective allowance for, bad debts. He has no personal knowledge of the customers, and Mr. Kevans seems to have taken particular attention in reference to this. (See questions 2,125 to 2,127 in the evidence.) He said 'he had some special knowledge on the subject, that he saw all ascertained bad debts duly written off, and that there was a fund amounting to £500 as a provision therefor.' For the foregoing reasons there is no ground for alleging negligence against Mr. Kevans on the 'assets side' of the balance sheet. . . . Now, dealing with 'sundry creditors'; here, evidently, there is a fraud, and a curious thing is that no one seemed to have derived any benefit from the fraud."

Dealing with the invoices, the learned judge detailed the practice in connection with the statements of accounts being laid before the meetings, and said:

"The ledger was used for the purchases made and for the payments on account thereof. If, then, all this were rightly done, it would be easy for the auditor to ascertain the amounts due to the creditors, but, unfortunately, the books were not correctly kept. The creditors' accounts in the ledger did not show all the goods purchased up to the time for the audit, nor could the auditor discover the omissions on account of many of the invoices being either 'suppressed' or not put into the book until a later date—a process described as 'carrying over.' There is some doubt as to whether the deficiency arose from the suppression or the carrying over, but my impression is that the whole of it comes within the last-mentioned class, for at the end of 1894 we find they amounted to £4,095. Mr. Peter White is now dead, and he should not be condemned unheard, but it is difficult to believe that this system was not within his own knowledge. As chief promoter, he was no doubt anxious to see that the company was successful. Crawford, who was the secretary, appears to have continued the process. It seems strange that a system of fraud so long continued, and for so extensive a period, was never detected by the auditor. Once or twice he noticed something, and the explanation that was given was 'that the goods were not taken into stock.' The question is, Was it negligent not to have seen this? There is no doubt that both the suppression and carrying over of invoices would have been detected if the auditor had called for the creditors' statements of accounts upon which payment was ordered and compared them with the ledger. I should have thought this was part of the auditor's duty for many reasons; but all the accountants examined, except Mr. Southworth, stated that this course is never taken unless there is something to arouse suspicion. Mr. Pixley, the eminent London accountant, says it could not well be done except in the case of a very small concern. In the face of such evidence I should not leave myself at liberty to hold that Mr. Kevans' assistants were guilty of negligence in not looking at these statements of account if they were engaged in an ordinary audit. Little time is allowed for doing so; but in this case there was this system of monthly checking. From the time that Crawford was accountant in 1890, the accounts of the company were completely in his hands. Now, White, for the two years following, may have given general directions, but he was often away in America for months at a time, and it is clear that the monthly audit was instituted for the purpose of seeing that he (Crawford) would do his work regularly and honestly. I am unable to conceive how, if there was nothing wrong about this monthly checking, it did not lead at an early period to the detection of the frauds in this ledger. Mr. Kevans ought to have found out, by the accounts, the payments that were made—and no better means could be adopted than that of a comparison with the statements of accounts. It ought to have been done in some way, and, if it had, detection would have been certain. I do not base my decision on this alone; apart altogether from the statements of account and the monthly check, I do not understand how the carrying over of the invoices could have escaped detection by the accountant, who should have used due care and skill, and who was not a mere machine. The invoices carried over were ultimately posted to the ledger. If they were posted to their true dates, it would be at once apparent that they were not entered in at the proper time. If they were posted under false dates, why was this not detected when the ledger accounts were checked with the invoices? And when no invoices came into the books, it is admitted that this ought to have excited suspicion. For these reasons I am of opinion that if due care and skill had been exercised, the carrying over and suppression of invoices would have been discovered, and the auditor is liable for any damage the company may have sustained from the understatement of liabilities in the balance sheet due to this cause since January 4, 1892. I consider that not only are Mr. Kevans and his assistants not free from blame for this, but also for the mechanical way the audit was carried out.

"As regards the measure of the duty of a gentleman employed as Mr. Kevans was in this case, the result is the same, as it occurs to me, in all cases in which professional skill is employed, except one, the peculiar instance of a barrister. The measure of duty is the bringing of reasonable care and skill to the performance of the business directed to be done, having regard, first to the contract of employment, then to the character of the business itself, to the remuneration of the defendant, and to all the other circumstances of the case. In strict rule, however, the measure of the duty is to be ascertained by applying to all the circumstances of the case the best consideration, so as to ascertain what ought to have been done under the circumstances. . . . I think the fairest way to deal with Mr. Kevans in this case is to treat him as being charged with having failed to find just cause of suspicion on the face of these books, which if found, would have imposed on him the duty of pursuing his suspicion until he found whether it was or was not well founded. . . . The English cases have established that the auditor is entitled, in the absence of the elements of suspicion, to assume that the books are honestly kept, and that, therefore, unless on the face of a presumably honest book something appears to excite his suspicion, he is not guilty of negligence, whatever other people might be in their departments, if he does not discover that something was wrong. . . .

"I cannot conceive any more clear or glaring grounds of suspicion than to discover in the account of a single customer items amounting to £600 having got into the books after the trial balance is struck under dates going back two months prior to the period of the ascertaining of the trial balance. . . . It appears to me that the moment I come to the conclusion that that was on the face of it a suspicious mode of dealing with Hill & Son's figures, I am bound to show how it would be corrected. . . . That it would then have been necessary to call for the creditors' statements of account, and at that moment they would have disclosed on the face of them not merely those postdated items, but the suppressed invoices also; and at the instant that this discovery was made, there is an absolute conviction of something wrong forced upon the mind of the auditor. It, therefore, occurs to me that, upon these two branches, all that is required, both to show the negligence, to arouse suspicion, and to supply the means of putting a stop to the frauds, is to be found on the face of the books, and for all I have said I have no foundation except what is upon the face of that book (creditors' ledger)."

Astrachan Steamship Co., Ltd. and others v. Harmood Banner & Son ("Liverpool Mercury" of March 2 and 3, 1900; also Spicer & Pegler "Practical Auditing," p. 410).

Action for alleged negligence in failing to detect defalcations. The case was finally settled in favor of the plaintiff.

London Oil Storage Co., Lim. v. Seear, Hasluck & Co., King's Bench Division, June 1, 1904 (Acct. L. R., XXXI, p. 1).

The auditor took no steps to verify the existence of petty cash as stated in the balance sheet. The balance sheet showed £796 petty cash, whereas only £30 was actually in the cash box, the bookkeeper having embezzled the difference. The court left it for the jury to find as matter of fact, whether or not the auditor's failure to verify this balance was negligent under the circumstances. The court charged the jury in part as follows:

"The auditor most undoubtedly does undertake very considerable responsibilities, and is liable for the proper discharge of his duties, and if by neglect of his duties, or by want of reasonable care, he neglects his duty, and damage is caused to the company as such, he is responsible for that damage. I will not adopt any fanciful expression which may be quoted from any particular judgment, but he has got to bring to bear upon those duties reasonable and watchful care, he has got to discharge those duties remembering that the company look to him to protect their interests. He is not, however, supposed to be a man constantly going about suspecting other people of doing wrong, and that is the only respect in which, I think, Mr. Bankes in his most able speech pressed the matter a little too high. While Mr. Hasluck has by the exercise of due and reasonable care to see that all the officials of the company are doing their duty properly in so far as the accounts are concerned, he is not bound to assume when he comes to do his duty that he is dealing with fraudulent and dishonest people; and there comes in the most important consideration from one point of view—perhaps more important than the other, though I do not think of such substantial weight in the matter—if circumstances of suspicion arise it is the duty of the auditor, in so far as those circumstances relate to the financial position of the company, to probe them to the bottom."

The jury brought in a verdict for the plaintiff for five guineas with the further statement that they considered the directors had been guilty of gross negligence.

Smith v. Sheard, Liverpool Assizes, May 11, 1906 (Accountant, L. R., 1906, p. 65).

The plaintiff's cashier had embezzled about £700, and the plaintiff thereupon sued the auditor, on the ground that the auditor should have detected the embezzlement. The defendant alleged that he had never been retained to make a complete audit, but that the only work he undertook was the stating of accounts between the partners.

The case was tried before a special jury, which found for the plaintiff.

(4) Periodical Audits: Martin v. Isitt, decided before Lord Chief Justice Russell, in the Queen's Bench Division, March 3 and 4, 1898 (Acct. L. R., 1898, p. 41).

James Martin & Sons sued Isitt & Co., chartered accountants, alleging that as auditors they were negligent in failing to check the cash book and the bank pass book, and that thereby a clerk was able to embezzle £612.

The defendants had been retained to make monthly audits. They claimed, however, that they had been unable to conduct their work properly, owing to the tardiness of plaintiff's bookkeepers in giving them definite information on questioned items, whereby they were kept about six months behind in their audit. A trial of the case was begun, but the defendants settled during the course of the trial.

(5) No Expedient Can Overcome the Obligation of the Auditor to Make Full Disclosure to the Stockholders: Newton v. Birmingham Small Arms Company, Lim., Chancery Division, June 27, 1906 (22 Times, L. R., p. 664).

The Birmingham Small Arms Company, Ltd., passed a resolution purporting to prevent the auditors appointed by the shareholders from disclosing any information to the shareholders or otherwise touching the "internal reserve fund" of the company. An injunction to restrain the company from acting on this special resolution was granted.

The court held that the shareholders were clearly entitled to this information, and that the auditors could not lawfully withhold the information.

(6) As to the Liability of an Auditor for Libel: Lawless v. Anglo-Egyptian Cotton & Oil Co. Lim. (4 Q. B. 262).

When the alleged libel is true in point of fact, and is published by the auditor in good faith and without malice, and in the *bona fide* discharge of his duty, it would, no doubt, be held to be privileged.

Summary

Based upon the foregoing decisions and upon the principles of the common law in force in the United States, the professional auditor's legal duties and liabilities may be summarized as follows:

(1) Anyone who holds himself out as skilled in a profession is charged with a higher degree of responsibility than one who is inexperienced and who does not seek professional work. Acting in a professional capacity, an auditor must do more than ascertain the mere arithmetical accuracy of the accounts. If the

accounts do not represent the true financial position of the undertaking under examination, and if that fact is apparent or can reasonably be deduced from the face of the accounts themselves, then the auditor is under a legal obligation to discover and disclose the true state of affairs.

(2) The auditor, however, is not an insurer unless he assumes such a position. If he uses reasonable care—the care of an ordinarily skillful auditor, under the circumstances of the case—no legal responsibility is incurred by him.

(3) Reasonable care has been stated by the courts to depend upon the circumstances of each case. Where there is no reasonable ground for suspicion of fraud, it is not necessary to take as many precautions as are requisite where the auditor is led to believe that irregularities exist.

(4) Ordinarily what is known as a test audit is sufficient, but in every case there must be a careful survey of the assets, the liabilities, the income, and the expenses, in order that the auditor may satisfy himself that the assets and the income are accounted for, and that the liabilities and expenses are properly supported. The auditor need not verify every item, but he must not omit any part of an audit which the custom of the profession decrees should be covered.

(5) The experience of other practitioners and access to recognized authorities on the subject being available, a defense of ignorance as to what is required in an audit will not save an auditor from responsibility for failure to follow settled rules of practice.

(6) The general rule of the common law, that all men are considered honest until proved dishonest, may be observed by an auditor with respect to the staff of the client; but he is charged with an exceptional degree of diligence in recognizing indications of dishonesty on the part of those who occupy responsible positions.

(7) An auditor's relation to his client is in the highest degree confidential, and he has no legal right to communicate with third parties (debtors or creditors) unless he secures permission to do so. If his position as auditor becomes incompatible with honesty, he may withdraw at any time, but he is not at liberty to disclose to outsiders the cause of his withdrawal.

(8) In communicating with his client, however, the auditor is bound to disclose information, of whatever nature it may be, which is of value to the client, and any suppression of material facts is at his own risk.

(9) In the event of loss through an auditor's negligence, the client may recover damages against him. The measure of damages is the amount which the client or other interested party has lost as a legal consequence of the auditor's failure to properly perform his duty.

OFFICIAL LEGAL OPINION ON DUTIES AND LIABILITIES OF AUDITORS

When the English Companies Act, 1907, was passed, the Council of the Institute of Chartered Accountants in England and Wales obtained the joint opinion of eminent counsel on the clauses particularly affecting auditors. That opinion was as follows:

(1) In our opinion the auditor's report to be made pursuant to paragraph (2) of section 19 of the Companies Act, 1907, should, in cases where the auditors have no special comments to make, run as follows:

> "Report of the auditors to the shareholders of Limited.
>
> "We have audited the balance sheet of the Limited, dated the day of , and (here identify it as: 'above set forth' or 'within contained,' or 'a copy of which is annexed hereto and initialed by us,' or 'a copy of which has been initialed by us').
>
> "We have obtained all the information and explanations we have required.
>
> "In our opinion such balance sheet is properly drawn up so as to exhibit a true and correct view of the state of the company's affairs according to the best of our information and the explanations given us, and as shown by the books of the company."

We consider that the report should identify very clearly the particular balance sheet to which it refers, so that there may be no room for after-dispute or confusion, and no danger that by mistake or otherwise the balance sheet submitted to the shareholders, though bearing the proper date, should not be the one actually referred to in the report.

Perhaps the surest mode of identification is to write the report at the foot or indorse it on the balance sheet to be submitted, for by these means the two documents are made inseparable; or, in other words, the report runs with the balance sheet. But, as above appears, there are alternatives open. In any case, the auditors should keep a copy of the balance sheet they audit, and place a memorandum of identity thereon, so that if the question arises, they may be able to testify certainly as to the matter.

(2) Under the section, the auditors' report is to be attached to the balance sheet or referred to at the foot thereof. In the former case we consider that the attachment should be effected either by printing the two documents continuously on the same sheet of paper or by fastening the report to the balance sheet. We consider that the best mode of attachment is that the report should be written or printed at the foot of the balance sheet, or indorsed thereon.

(3) If the report is not attached to the balance sheet, there should at the foot of the balance sheet be words referring to the report, e. g., "the report to the shareholders of Messrs. , the company's auditors, on the above balance sheet, is dated the day of and is open to inspection."

In our opinion it is for the directors to make the reference and settle the form thereof, and not for the auditors.

(4) In our opinion the act does not impose on the auditors the duty of seeing that the report is attached to the balance sheet, or referred to at the foot thereof. This duty, we consider, is imposed on the company and its directors.

(5) It appears to us that it is not the duty of the auditors to see that the balance sheet is signed by the required number of directors. Subsection (3) of section 19 clearly contemplates that the balance sheet is to be issued after the report has been made, for a copy is to be attached or referred to. As to cases in which there are no officers called directors, the balance sheet should be signed by the manager or other person occupying the position of director, for section 30 of the Act of 1900, with which the Act of 1907 is to be read (see section 52), provides that the term "Directors" includes any person occupying the position of director, by whatever name called.

(6) In our opinion it is not the duty of the auditors to supply to shareholders, when requested, copies of the balance sheet and their report, or to furnish information to individual shareholders.

(7) In our opinion the statement in the form of a balance sheet referred to in section 21 of the Act of 1907 is a document to be submitted by the directors to the auditors for audit. The document must contain, as the section requires, a summary of the company's capital, liabilities, and assets, giving such particulars as would disclose the general nature of such liabilities and assets, and how the value of the fixed assets has been arrived at, but it is not necessary to include in it a statement of profit or loss.

We consider that in many cases the last-audited balance sheet will be sufficient statement in the form of a balance sheet; but where the balance sheet does not state how the value of the fixed assets has been arrived at, it would, in order to comply with the section, have to be supplemented by a note or memorandum stating how the value of such assets was arrived at.

Where the balance sheet, whether supplemented as aforesaid, or otherwise, is adopted for the purposes of the section as a statement in the form of a balance sheet, it should, in our opinion, be accompanied by a copy of the report of the auditors on such balance sheet; and if it is so supplemented, the auditors should certify that, according to the best of their information, the method specified in the supplementary note or memorandum has been adopted.

We consider, however, that it is open to the directors to frame the statement "in the form of a balance sheet" referred to in section 21 in more general terms than the balance sheet, provided that it complies with the requirements of the section; but in such case the statement must be audited by the company's auditors, and the result of the audit should be certified at the foot of the statement.

(8) As to the general duties of the auditors, under section 19 of the Act of 1907, we consider that they should perform these duties with due regard to the provisions of the company's Articles of Association, in so far as those Articles are consistent with the Acts, and that they should call for all such information and explanations as they consider requisite to enable them to make the report to the shareholders contemplated by the section. They should not have the least hesitation in reporting fully as to any unsatisfactory features in the position.

Lastly, we do not consider that the auditor's duties are limited to a comparison of the figures in the balance sheet and those in the books. No doubt he has to examine the books, but, as Lord Justice Lindley said In re The London & General Bank (1895, 2 Ch. 683), "he does not discharge his duty by doing this without inquiry and without taking any trouble to see that the books themselves show the company's true position. He must take reasonable care to ascertain that they do so."

The duties of the auditor are defined by the Companies (Consolidation) Act, 1908, as follows:

Section 113.—(2) The auditors shall make a report to the shareholders on the accounts examined by them, and on every balance sheet laid before the company in general meeting during their tenure of office, and the report shall state

(*a*) Whether or not they have obtained all the information and explanations they have required; and,

(*b*) Whether, in their opinion, the balance sheet referred to in the report is properly drawn up so as to exhibit a true and correct view of the state of the company's affairs according to the best of their information and the explanations given to them, and as shown by the books of the company.

CHAPTER XXXIII

THE LIABILITIES OF DIRECTORS

IT may be thought that the duties and responsibilities of an auditor are onerous enough without injecting into a treatise of this nature an intimation that a professional auditor is charged with looking after the directors of a corporation as well as its officers and clerks.

Such is rarely the case, however, because most of the directors in the United States who direct and who perform acts which require review are officers as well, and the auditor examines their transactions as such and not in their capacity as directors.

Board-Minutes Inspection: Nevertheless, the auditor may find in reading the minutes of the proceedings of the board of directors or of an executive or other committee that one or more directors have been intrusted with negotiations to purchase property or with similar commissions. In such cases the auditor should verify the transaction along the usual lines.

Compensation of Directors: Directors usually receive an attendance fee ranging from five to fifty dollars, and so long as there is nothing in the by-laws to prevent, the auditor can accept as authority therefor a resolution which has been regularly adopted. The minutes should record the names of all directors present at each meeting, which will serve as a check on the amount disbursed for this purpose. Compensation in excess of the attendance fee is rarely paid to a director who is not an officer.

If any sum is voted to one or more directors, the auditor should ascertain whether the by-laws permit the payment, and whether the action was taken at a full board meeting or whether any were absent who might have objected. If any director who is benefited votes for the resolution, or if his presence is necessary to make a quorum, the action is voidable and may be attacked. All such transactions should be reported to and ratified by the annual meeting of stockholders. If no such action has been taken by the stockholders, the auditor should mention the fact in his report.

It has been held by the courts that officers are not entitled to compensation simply because they occupy office and perform the duties incident thereto. Their salaries should be fixed before election as directors, if possible. If this is not feasible, the amounts paid to the directors in compensation for their services should be reported to the annual meeting and be formally approved by the stockholders.

As a practical matter, where the officers and directors own all or nearly all of the stock and are acting in good faith, it is not necessary to report salaries nor other matters of detail to the stockholders' meeting.

Directors May Inspect Books: It is not generally known that a director has an absolute right to inspect the books and papers of a corporation of which he is a director. There are a great many men who represent minority interests on a board and who are almost totally ignored in the management of the company. Information with respect to finances or earnings is rarely furnished to them, and is then handed out as if there were no obligation to do so.

Auditors are frequently consulted by directors who state that they have tried to secure information without success. The auditor should advise them that their legal right to full access to the books is unquestioned, and that they may be accompanied by a professional auditor if they require assistance. Directors are charged with a knowledge of what is going on, and if they fail to keep informed, they may be held jointly responsible for the acts of others. In all cases, therefore, where they have any doubt as to what is going on, it is nothing more than simple business prudence to employ an auditor who will ascertain exact conditions.

Legal Liabilities of Directors: The auditor's consideration of the possible legal liabilities of directors need not extend beyond matters connected with the accounts, but wherever accounting questions are involved, the auditor's familiarity therewith should be unquestioned. In the American Malting case, decided in New York in 1904, the court discussed the relation and duties of directors to the accounts. The decision is of sufficient interest to warrant its reproduction in full:

ARCHIBALD A. HUTCHINSON and VICTOR K. MCELHENY, JR., on Behalf of Themselves and All Other Stockholders of the American Malting Co., Similarly Situated, *Plaintiffs*,

v.

ALEXANDER M. CURTISS and THE AMERICAN MALTING CO., *Defendants.*

(SUPREME COURT, NEW YORK SPECIAL TERM, DECEMBER, 1904.)

The statutes of this State allow the recovery, from directors of a foreign corporation, of dividends unauthorized by the laws under which such corporation is organized. It is the foreign statute that makes the dividends unauthorized, but the recovery is to be had under the New York statute.

No dividends can be made except from "surplus or net profits."

Contracts entered into by a corporation for future deliveries of a product not yet made by it, from raw material not yet purchased, cannot be taken as assets in figuring said surplus or net profits. Dividends cannot be made on a mere hope or expectation of profits.

Where raw material is bought by weight, and after manufacture is increased in weight and value, the corporation is entitled to treat it as an asset at its increased value.

A director who is not present when an unauthorized dividend is declared is not liable under the statute, even though he is present at a subsequent meeting when the minutes of the former meeting are ratified.

A director, sued for unauthorized dividends, cannot be credited with the profits which subsequently accrued under a change of management.

A director is not liable for commissions paid on the sale of bonds of a corporation which had made unauthorized dividends in the absence of proof of fraud and conspiracy for the defendant's personal benefit; such loss is included in the loss caused by the illegal dividends which defendant must pay.

Action against director for making unauthorized dividends.

CLARKE, *J.:*

The American Malting Company was organized under the laws of New Jersey, September 28, 1897. It began business on October 11, 1897. On October 15, 1897, it filed a copy of its charter in the office of the Secretary of State of New York to enable it to do business in this State, and received the usual certificate for that purpose. The principal office of the company was situated in the city of New York, at No. 80 Broadway, from its organization until the fall of 1899, and since then it has been situated continuously at East River and Sixty-third Street, New York City. The company has had no plant or property in New Jersey. It has kept no bank account there. It had merely a formal, statutory office in that State. Its capital stock is $30,000,000, divided into 300,000 shares of $100 each, of which 144,400 shares of preferred stock and 145,000 shares of common stock have been issued. The preferred stock is seven per cent cumulative, having a preference as to dividends only. The company is engaged in the manufacture and sale of malt. Its stock was issued to promoters for twenty-one malting establishments, situated in various parts of the United States, on which they had acquired options, and for $2,080,000 cash working capital. No stock-in-trade was, however, acquired by the issue of stock. As soon as the organization was effected the company was compelled to purchase from the vendors of the various malting plants their stocks of barley and malt, for which the company issued its obligations, amounting to upward of $1,600,000. A little over two months after the company began business, and on December 20, 1897, the board of directors declared a dividend of one and three-fourths per cent to preferred stockholders, payable January 15, 1898. This amounted to $219,450. Thereafter a dividend at the same rate was declared and made payable at each of the following dates: April 15, 1898, $219,450; July 15, 1898, $219,450; October 15, 1898, $219,450; January 15, 1899, $219,450; April 15, 1899, $252,700; July 15, 1899, $252,700; October 15, 1899, $252,700. In all $1,855,350. Barely two weeks after the payment of the dividend of October 15, 1899, and on November 2, 1899, the minutes of the board of directors disclosed its serious financial condition as reported to said board, viz., its outstanding obligations amounted to $2,800,000 in notes; that the officers were unable to negotiate further temporary loans; that the company needed additional working capital, and that the board authorized the sale of $4,000,000 mortgage bonds of the company. Said bonds, six per cent fifteen-year gold mortgage bonds, were subsequently disposed of at a discount of $400,000. This is an action brought by plaintiffs as stockholders on behalf of themselves and all other stockholders similarly situated against the defendant Curtiss as director of the company to compel him to account for and pay to the company the amount of the dividends declared and paid as not having been paid out of the profits, but out of the capital. The board of directors having upon demand refused or neglected to bring suit in the name of the company, it was joined as a party defendant. At first the company put in a defense, but subsequently, its management having changed, it obtained leave to file an amended answer admitting the allegations of the complaint and joining in the prayer of the plaintiffs for the relief demanded. In a similar action against another of the directors the complaint was dismissed upon the trial. Upon appeal the Appellate Division reversed that judgment. *Hutchinson v. Stadler,* 85 App. Div. 428. That case settled the law for this court to this extent; that an action could be maintained in the courts of this State against a director of a New Jersey corporation to recover the amount of dividends declared in violation of the laws of that State. Two opinions were handed down, in which the learned justices arrived at the conclusion that the action could be maintained upon different grounds. With each of these opinions a justice concurred. The fifth learned justice concurred in the result. I cite this division of opinion because this court is now called upon to apply the law, as laid down with this practical embarrassment, that while it was the unanimous decision that the action could be maintained, yet the difference in the grounds therefor means a difference of hundreds of thousands of dollars in the judgment I am about to order. As I interpret it that case holds this court has jurisdiction because section twenty-three of the Stock Corporation Law of this State provides: "The directors of a stock corporation shall not make dividends, except from the surplus profits arising from the business of such corporation; nor divide, withdraw, or in any way pay to the stockholders, or any of them, any part of the capital of such corporation, or reduce its capital stock, except as authorized by law. In case of any violation of the provisions of this section, the directors under whose administration the same may have happened, except those who may have caused their dissent therefrom to be entered at large upon the minutes of such directors at the time, or were not present when the same happened, shall jointly and severally be liable to such corporation and to the creditors thereof to the full amount of the capital of such corporation so divided, withdrawn, paid out, or reduced"; and because section thirty of the General Corporation Law of New Jersey provides: "No corporation shall make dividends, except from the surplus or net profits arising from its business, nor divide, withdraw, or in any way pay to the stockholders, or any of them, any part of its capital stock, or reduce its capital stock, except according to this act, and in case of any violation of the provisions of this section the directors under whose administration the same may happen shall be jointly and severally liable at any time within six years after paying such dividends to the corporation and to its creditors in the event of its dissolution or insolvency to the full amount of the dividend made or capital stock so divided, withdrawn, paid out, or reduced, with interest on the same from the time such liability accrued; provided that any director who may have been absent when the same was done, or who may have dissented from the act or resolution by which the same was done, may exonerate himself from such liability by causing his dissent to be entered at large on the minutes of the directors at the time the same was done, or forthwith after he shall have notice of the same, and by causing a true copy of said dissent to be published within two weeks after the same shall have been so entered in a newspaper published in the county where the corporation has its principal office"; and because section sixty of the Stock Corporation Law of this State provides: "Except as otherwise provided in this chapter the officers, directors, and stockholders of a foreign stock corporation transacting business in this State, except moneyed and railroad corporations, shall be liable under the provisions of this chapter, in the same manner and to the same extent as the officers, directors, and stockholders of a domestic corporation for: 1. The making of unauthorized dividends . . . Such liabilities may be enforced in the courts of this State in the same manner as similar liabilities imposed by law upon the officers, directors, and stockholders of domestic corporations." That is, by virtue of the statutes, this State allows the recovery of dividends unauthorized by the State of New Jersey from directors of a New Jersey corporation in the same manner and to the same extent as the directors of a domestic corporation. That is, it is the New Jersey statute which makes the dividend unauthorized, but the recovery is to be had according to the New York statute. What, then, is unauthorized? "No corporation shall make dividends except from the surplus or net profits arising from its business." Net profits are defined in the Century Dictionary as "what remains as the clear gain of any business after deducting the capital invested in the business, the expenses incurred in its management, and the losses sustained by its operation." And the controlling question of fact is, were these dividends paid from "net profits"?

The twenty-one branches, located in many places and in different States, which were actually engaged in the business of manufacturing the malt from the barley, sent in to the general office in New York daily, weekly, and monthly statements in great detail of their business. From these statements branch books were made, and from these a general set of books was prepared. All of the books and papers from the general office, which were used in the accounting department, were produced in court, identified, and marked in evidence. The defendant objects to the summaries made up from these books, and from any and all conclusions of fact to be drawn from said books and said summaries upon the ground that concededly the contracts and the contract books were not produced and were not considered. It was in evidence that malt was always oversold, that contracts for future deliveries, running over many months, were entered into, and the claim is that such contracts were required to be taken into consideration when it came to be determined whether any particular dividend was warranted or not. Such claim, in my opinion, is unfounded. The law is that "No corporation shall make dividends except from the surplus or net profits." These contracts were to deliver at a future time a product not yet made from raw material, not yet purchased, with the aid of labor not yet expended. The price agreed to be paid at that future time had to cover all the possible contingencies of the market in the meanwhile, and might show a profit, and ran the chance of showing a loss. When the sales actually took place they were entered in the books. But to calculate months in advance on the results of the future transactions, and on such calculations to declare dividends, was to base such dividends on paper profits—hoped for profits, future profits—and not upon the surplus or net profits required by law. It does not seem to me that you can "divide," that is, make a dividend of a hope based on an expectation of a future delivery at a favorable price of what is not yet in existence, under the statute. So the objection to the books upon that ground is of no weight. From the books certain statements were made up for the aid of the court upon different theories and in different ways. One set of statements was testified to be exactly what the books showed, without the change of a figure. These exhibits are known as 10 P, 10 Q. As to these statements I do not understand that there is any controversy as to the accuracy of the figures. A second statement, known as 10 R, 10 S, is identical with the foregoing, with the elimination of one entry, which, as a matter of fact, was eliminated by the company itself some months after its entry. There was entered on the books on December 31, 1898, an item of $388,063.36 of the anticipated or estimated future profits on contracts for future deliveries running over many months. This entry, for the reasons stated in regard to the contracts for future deliveries, was unjustifiable. The company subsequently removed this entry. The actual transactions, that is, the deliveries of the malt called for by the contracts and the receipts in payment therefor being reported from time to time as they occurred, resulting in double credits, the cancellation or reversal of the entry was absolutely required. On the other hand, I find against the plaintiffs in regard to their contention as to the increase account. Barley is bought by the bushel of forty-eight pounds. Malt, the manufactured article made from barley by steeping, is dealt in by the bushel of thirty-four pounds. The process of manufacture produces about fifteen per cent more of malt by the bushel than the barley measures from which it is produced. The amount of this fifteen per cent excess is reported from each of the manufactories month by month as increase. Of course, this increase has a value, as it is sold as malt at malt prices. For the purpose of inventory the company has ascribed to it the value of the barley. This, plaintiffs claim, is error, because that amount has already once been charged to malt account, and they say this increase should have no value ascribed to it until sold and delivered, when its proceeds go into the books as cash. But it certainly is an asset of the company, and as an asset at inventory periods, or when it is necessary to ascertain the actual condition of the company, it must be valued in some way. As it has always been the custom in the malting business to treat it as treated by this company, I am unwilling to disregard that custom. The accounts upon which I based my conclusions treated it as this company did. I find that at the time of the declaration and payment of the third dividend, July, 1898, a deficit was caused thereby of $142,774.59, and from that time to the end of the period under consideration none of the dividends were paid out of net profits, but all were paid out of capital. But it appears that defendant Curtiss was not present at the meeting on February 28, 1899, when the dividend paid April 15, 1899, was authorized. Under the New York statute—under which we are proceeding—a director who was not present when the dividend was declared is not liable. The approval of the minutes at the following June meeting, at which he was present, was only the authentication of the proof of what had happened at the previous meeting. He is, therefore, not to be held liable for that dividend. He is liable, in my judgment, as follows: For dividends paid July 15, 1898, to the extent of $142,774.59; October 15, 1898, $219,450; January 15, 1899, $219,450; July 15, 1899, $252,700; October 15, 1899, $252,700—$1,087,074.59, with interest thereon from the several dates of payment. As the highest court of New Jersey, interpreting the law of the State under which this company was incorporated, held, "for the full protection of the company the liability of the directors must be absolute" (*Appleton v. Am. Malting Co.*), I find against the defendant upon his claim that the accrued profits of the company, made under a changed management, can be credited in his favor against his liability. It is claimed that this is a harsh law. If it were, such complaint should be made to the Legislature, and not to the court. It does not seem to me that in these days of great corporations and of combinations into one of many corporations it is asking too much of directors, fiduciary officers as they are, that they should obey the law of their incorporation, and not bring their companies to the verge of bankruptcy and ruin by the payment of quarterly dividends on preferred stock out of capital instead of net earnings. As to the second cause of action: While the allegations are profuse as to a "willful, fraudulent, and illegal conspiracy," the proof failed to establish that there was any such conspiracy for defendant's personal benefit. The cases establishing the cause of action pointed at in these allegations have been where directors have diverted to themselves for their own benefit the property of the company. The damage here flowed out of the making of the dividends, if any there was. It was alleged that the company had to issue bonds, and that the commissions, discounts, and interest thereon amount to $650,000, which, as a waste of its funds, the plaintiff seeks to recover. But as I find that this flowed as a damage only from the declaration and payment of the dividends, I am persuaded by the language of Mr. Justice Hatch in *Hutchinson v. Stadler, supra,* that it does not under the facts of this case constitute a separate cause of action. He says: "In point of fact the statute of the State of New Jersey upon this subject, as well as our own, does little more than lay down a rule of damage to be enforced against directors for breach of duty. At common law a recovery could be had for the waste, but the extent of the recovery would depend upon the damage sustained by the corporation and be the subject of proof. The statute measures the loss sustained, which is usually the correct amount, and authorizes a recovery therefrom of the individuals who produced that result." It seems to me that any other theory would result in turning the amount recovered for illegal dividends into a penalty. The Court of Errors and Appeals of New Jersey, in this very matter, as well as our Appellate Division, have held: "The liability imposed by the statute is not penal in its character. Its sole purpose is not to punish, but to provide for the making of compensation by wrongdoers for the injury sustained by their wrongful act." This alleged loss must, therefore, be held to have been included in that for which the defendant is required to make compensation by paying into the company an amount equal to the illegal dividends.

CHAPTER XXXIV

FEDERAL EXCISE TAX ON CORPORATIONS

Of all the various methods and schemes of taxation enacted by the Federal Congress or by State Legislatures, there is none which is of more importance to the auditor than that portion of the Payne-Aldrich tariff act which relates to the taxation of corporations based upon net income in excess of $5,000.

To all intents and purposes this is an income tax, and, although it has been declared constitutional by the Supreme Court of the United States, it is very generally admitted that to describe it as other than an income tax is a legal fiction.

Income taxation has been known in Great Britain since the close of the eighteenth century, and in many other countries the principle has been applied with at least fairly satisfactory results; but there is in America a deep-rooted antipathy to the idea of taxing incomes, and this receives constitutional indorsement by clause four of Article I, section 11 of the National Constitution, which is as follows:

No capitation or other direct tax shall be laid, unless in proportion to the census or enumeration hereinbefore directed to be taken.

At the time of the War of 1812 an income tax was proposed, but was rejected by Congress. During the Civil War, however, an income tax was imposed and continued in force until 1872. The Wilson tariff bill, passed in 1894, contained provision for a tax of two per cent on incomes in excess of $4,000, but this was declared unconstitutional by the Supreme Court, and no serious effort was made to secure the passage of an income tax between that time and 1909, when the Payne-Aldrich bill became law.

The evasion of the constitutional disability which characterized the corporation tax found so much favor in certain quarters that a bill was introduced in the second session of the sixty-second Congress by the leader of the majority, the Hon. Oscar W. Underwood, to extend the provisions of the corporation tax law to include the income or profits of firms, copartnerships, and individuals. Although this bill did not become law, it was largely supported in the House of Representatives and serves as an illustration of the ease with which a legal fiction may be used to evade a constitutional limitation. (See text of bill, p. 632.)

Sooner or later it is believed that the necessary number of State Legislatures will ratify the proposal to amend the Federal Constitution so that income taxation may be permitted under its true name, but until that has been done the Federal corporation tax section of the Payne-Aldrich tariff law remains the chief center of interest to the auditor of corporations upon which the tax falls.

The full text of the law (section 38 of the tariff act, approved August 5, 1909) follows:

Sec. 38. That every corporation, joint stock company or association, organized for profit and having a capital stock represented by shares, and every insurance company now or hereafter organized under the laws of the United States or of any State or Territory of the United States, or under the Acts of Congress applicable to Alaska or the District of Columbia, or now or hereafter organized under the laws of any foreign country and engaged in business in any State or Territory of the United States or in Alaska or in the District of Columbia, shall be subject to pay annually a special excise tax with respect to the carrying on or doing business by such corporation, joint stock company or association, or insurance company, equivalent to one per centum upon the entire net income over and above five thousand dollars received by it from all sources during such year, exclusive of amounts received by it as dividends upon stock of other corporations, joint stock companies or associations, or insurance companies, subject to the tax hereby imposed; or if organized under the laws of any foreign country, upon the amount of net income over and above five thousand dollars received by it from business transacted and capital invested within the United States and its Territories, Alaska, and the District of Columbia during such year, exclusive of amounts so received by it as dividends upon stock of other corporations, joint stock companies, or associations, or insurance companies, subject to the tax hereby imposed: *Provided, however,* That nothing in this section contained shall apply to labor, agricultural or horticultural organizations, or to fraternal beneficiary societies, orders, or associations operating under the lodge system, and providing for the payment of life, sick, accident, and other benefits to the members of such societies, orders, or associations, and dependents of such members, nor to domestic building and loan associations, organized and operated exclusively for the mutual benefit of their members, nor to any

***The marginal notes are here inserted for the convenience of the reader; they are not an integral part of the law.**

corporation or association organized and operated exclusively for religious, charitable, or educational purposes, no part of the net income of which inures to the benefit of any private stockholder or individual.

Second. Such net income shall be ascertained by deducting from the gross amount of the income of such corporation, joint stock company or association, or insurance company, received within the year from all sources:

1st. All the ordinary and necessary expenses actually paid within the year out of income in the maintenance and operation of its business and properties, including all charges, such as rentals or franchise payments, required to be made as a condition to the continued use or possession of property.

2nd. All losses actually sustained within the year and not compensated by insurance or otherwise, including a reasonable allowance for depreciation of property, if any, and in the case of insurance companies the sums other than dividends, paid within the year on policy and annuity contracts and the net addition, if any, required by law to be made within the year to reserve funds.

3rd. Interest actually paid within the year on its bonded or other indebtedness to an amount of such bonded and other indebtedness not exceeding the paid-up capital stock of such corporation, joint stock company or association, or insurance company, outstanding at the close of the year, and in the case of a bank, banking association, or trust company, all interest actually paid by it within the year on deposits.

4th. All sums paid within the year for taxes imposed under the authority of the United States or of any State or Territory thereof, or imposed by the government of any foreign country as a condition to carrying on business therein.

5th. All amounts received by it within the year as dividends upon stock of other corporations, joint stock companies or associations, or insurance companies, subject to the tax hereby imposed:

Provided, That in the case of a corporation, joint stock company, or association, or insurance company, organized under the laws of a foreign country, such net income shall be ascertained by deducting from the gross amount of its income received within the year from business transacted and capital invested within the United States and any of its Territories, Alaska, and the District of Columbia:

1st. All the ordinary and necessary expenses actually paid within the year out of earnings in the maintenance and operation of its business and property within the United States and its Territories, Alaska, and the District of Columbia, including all charges such as rentals or franchise payments required to be made as a condition to the continued use or possession of property.

2nd. All losses actually sustained within the year in business conducted by it within the United States or its Territories, Alaska, or the District of Columbia not compensated by insurance or otherwise, including a reasonable allowance for depreciation of property, if any, and in the case of insurance companies the sums other than dividends, paid within the year on policy and annuity contracts and the net addition, if any, required by law to be made within the year to reserve funds.

3rd. Interest actually paid within the year on its bonded or other indebtedness to an amount of such bonded and other indebtedness, not exceeding the proportion of its paid-up capital stock outstanding at the close of the year which the gross amount of its income for the year from business transacted and capital invested within the United States and any of its Territories, Alaska, and the District of Columbia bears to the gross amount of its income derived from all sources within and without the United States.

4th. The sums paid by it within the year for taxes imposed under the authority of the United States or of any State or Territory thereof.

5th. All amounts received by it within the year as dividends upon stock of other corporations, joint stock companies or associations, and insurance companies, subject to the tax hereby imposed. In the case of assessment insurance companies, the actual deposit of sums with State or Territorial officers, pursuant to law, as additions to guaranty or reserve funds shall be treated as being payments required by law to reserve funds.

Third. There shall be deducted from the amount of the net income of each of such corporations, joint stock companies or associations, or insurance companies, ascertained as provided in the foregoing paragraphs of this section, the sum of five thousand dollars, and said tax shall be computed upon the remainder of said net income of such corporation, joint stock company or association, or insurance company, for the year ending December thirty-first, nineteen hundred and nine, and for each calendar year thereafter; and on or before the first day of March, nineteen hundred and ten, and the first day of March in each year thereafter, a true and accurate return, under oath or affirmation of its president, vice-president, or other principal officer, and its treasurer or assistant treasurer, shall be made by each of the corporations, joint stock companies or associations, and insurance companies, subject to the tax imposed by this section, to the Collector of Internal Revenue for the district in which such corporation, joint stock company or association, or insurance company, has its principal place of business, or, in the case of a corporation, joint stock company or association, or insurance company, organized under the laws of a foreign country, in the place where its principal business is carried on within the United States, in such form as the Commissioner of Internal Revenue, with the approval of the Secretary of the Treasury, shall prescribe, setting forth:

1st. The total amount of the paid-up capital stock of such corporation, joint stock company or association, or insurance company, outstanding at the close of the year.

2nd. The total amount of the bonded and other indebtedness of such corporation, joint stock company or association, or insurance company, at the close of the year.

3rd. The gross amount of the income of such corporation, joint stock company or association, or insurance company, received during such year from all sources, and if organized under the laws of a foreign country, the gross amount of its income received within the year from business transacted and capital invested within the United States and any of its Territories, Alaska, and the District of Columbia; also the amount received by such corporation, joint stock company or association, or insurance company, within the year by way of dividends upon stock of other corporations, joint stock companies or associations, or insurance companies, subject to the tax imposed by this section.

4th. The total amount of all the ordinary and necessary expenses actually paid out of earnings in the maintenance and operation of the business and properties of such corporation, joint stock company or association, or insurance company, within the year, stating separately all charges such as rentals or franchise payments required to be made as a condition to the continued use or possession of property, and if organized under the laws of a foreign country, the amount so paid in the maintenance and operation of its business within the United States and its Territories, Alaska, and the District of Columbia.

5th. The total amount of all losses actually sustained during the year and not compensated by insurance or otherwise, stating separately any amounts allowed for depreciation of property, and in the case of insurance companies, the sums other than dividends, paid within the year on policy and annuity contracts and the net addition, if any, required by law to be made within the year to reserve funds; and in the case of a corporation, joint stock company or association, or insurance company, organized under the laws of a foreign country, all losses actually sustained by it during the year in business conducted by it within the United States or its Territories, Alaska, and the District of Columbia, not compensated by insurance or otherwise, stating separately any amounts allowed for depreciation of property, and in the case of insurance companies the sums other than dividends, paid within the year on policy and annuity contracts and the net addition, if any, required by law to be made within the year to reserve fund.

6th. The amount of interest actually paid within the year on its bonded or other indebtedness to an amount of such bonded and other indebtedness not exceeding the paid-up capital stock of such corporation, joint stock company or association, or insurance company, outstanding at the close of the year, and in the case of a bank, banking association, or trust company, stating separately all interest paid by it within the year on deposits; or in case of a corporation, joint stock company or association, or insurance company, organized under the laws of a foreign country, interest so paid on its bonded or other indebtedness to an amount of such bonded and other indebtedness not exceeding the proportion of its paid-up capital stock outstanding at the close of the year, which the gross amount of its income for the year from business transacted and capital invested within the United States and any of its Territories, Alaska, and the District of Columbia, bears to the gross amount of its income derived from all sources within and without the United States.

7th. The amount paid by it within the year for taxes imposed under the authority of the United States or any State or Territory thereof, and separately the amount so paid by it for taxes imposed by the government of any foreign country as a condition to carrying on business therein.

8th. The net income of such corporation, joint stock company or association, or insurance company, after making the deductions in this section authorized. All such returns shall, as received, be transmitted forthwith by the collector to the Commissioner of Internal Revenue.

Fourth. Whenever evidence shall be produced before the Commissioner of Internal Revenue which, in the opinion of the Commissioner, justifies the belief that the return made by any corporation, joint stock company or association, or insurance company, is incorrect, or whenever any collector shall report to the Commissioner of Internal Revenue that any corporation, joint stock company or association, or insurance company, has failed to make a return as required by law, the Commissioner of Internal Revenue may require from the corporation, joint stock company or association, or insurance company making such return, such further information with reference to its capital, income, losses, and expenditures as he may deem expedient; and the Commissioner of Internal Revenue, for the purpose of ascertaining the correctness of such return or for the purpose of making a return where none has been made, is hereby authorized, by any regularly appointed revenue agent specially designated by him for that purpose, to examine any books and papers bearing upon the matters required to be included in the return of such corporation, joint stock company or association, or insurance company, and to require the attendance of any officer or employee of such corporation, joint stock company or association, or insurance company, and to take his testimony with reference to the matter required by law to be included in such return, with power to administer oaths to such person or persons; and the Commissioner of Internal Revenue may also invoke the aid of any court of the United States having jurisdiction to require the attendance of such officers or employees and the production of such books and papers. Upon the information so acquired, the Commissioner of Internal Revenue may amend any return or make a return where none has been made. All proceedings taken by the Commissioner of Internal Revenue under the provisions of this section shall be subject to the approval of the Secretary of the Treasury.

Fifth. All returns shall be retained by the Commissioner of Internal Revenue, who shall make assessments thereon; and in case of any return made with false or fraudulent intent, he shall add one hundred per centum of such tax, and in case of a refusal or neglect to make a return or to verify the same as aforesaid, he shall add fifty per centum of such tax. In case of neglect occasioned by the sickness or absence of an officer of such corporation, joint stock company or association, or insurance company, required to make said return, or for other sufficient reason, the collector may allow such further time for making and delivering such return as he may deem necessary, not exceeding thirty days. The amount so added to the tax shall be collected at the same time and in the same manner as the tax originally assessed unless the refusal, neglect, or falsity is discovered after the date for payment of said taxes, in which case the amount so added shall be paid by the delinquent corporation, joint stock company, or association, or insurance company, immediately upon notice given by the collector. All assessments shall be made, and the several corporations, joint stock companies or associations, or insurance companies, shall be notified of the amount for which they are respectively liable on or before the first day of June of each successive year, and said assessments shall be paid on or before the thirtieth day of June, except in cases of refusal or neglect to make such return, and in cases of false or fraudulent returns, in which cases the Commissioner of Internal Revenue shall, upon the discovery thereof, at any time within three years after said return is due, make a return upon information obtained as above provided for, and the assessment made by the Commissioner of Internal Revenue thereon shall be paid by such corporation, joint stock company or association, or insurance company, immediately upon notification of the amount of such assessment; and to any sum or sums due and unpaid after the thirtieth day of June in any year, and for ten days after notice and demand thereof by the collector, there shall be added the sum of five per centum on the amount of tax unpaid and interest at the rate of one per centum per month upon said tax from the time the same becomes due.

Sixth. When the assessment shall be made, as provided in this section, the returns, together with any corrections thereof which may have been made by the Commissioner, shall be filed in the office of the Commissioner of Internal Revenue and shall constitute public records and be open to inspection as such.

Seventh. It shall be unlawful for any collector, deputy collector, agent, clerk, or other officer or employee of the United States to divulge or make known in any manner whatever not provided by law to any person any information obtained by him in the discharge of his official duty, or to divulge or make known in any manner not provided by law any document received, evidence taken, or report made under this section except upon the special direction of the President; and any offense against the foregoing provision shall be a misdemeanor and be punished by a fine not exceeding one thousand dollars, or by imprisonment not exceeding one year, or both, at the discretion of the court.

Eighth. If any of the corporations, joint stock companies or associations, or insurance companies, aforesaid, shall refuse or neglect to make a return at the time or times hereinbefore specified in each year, or shall render a false or fraudulent return, such corporation, joint stock company or association, or insurance company, shall be liable to a penalty of not less than one thousand dollars and not exceeding ten thousand dollars.

Any person authorized by law to make, render, sign, or verify any return, who makes any false or fraudulent return, or statement, with intent to defeat or evade the assessment required by this section to be made, shall be guilty of a misdemeanor, and shall be fined not exceeding one thousand dollars or be imprisoned not exceeding one year, or both, at the discretion of the court, with the costs of prosecution.

All laws relating to the collection, remission, and refund of internal revenue taxes, so far as applicable to and not inconsistent with the provisions of this section, are hereby extended and made applicable to the tax imposed by this section.

Jurisdiction is hereby conferred upon the circuit and district courts of the United States for the district within which any person summoned under this section to appear to testify or to produce books, as aforesaid, shall reside, to compel such attendance, production of books, and testimony by appropriate process.

As soon as the text of the bill was made known some of the leading accounting firms, recognizing the impracticability of the bill as drafted, prepared a letter which was sent to each member of Congress and to the Attorney General. Although the letter and resultant correspondence have previously been published, it is necessary to a clear understanding of the case that they should be given here. The letter was signed by twelve accounting firms in New York.

NEW YORK CITY, July 8, 1909.

DEAR SIR:

On reading the text of the proposed corporation tax law, as reported in the *Commercial and Financial Chronicle* of July 3, 1909, we have formed the opinion that some of its provisions are absolutely impossible of application, and others violate all the accepted principles of sound accounting.

Under the third clause it is provided "that there shall be deducted from the amount of the net income of each of such corporations, . . . ascertained as provided in the foregoing paragraphs of this section, the sum of $5,000, and said tax shall be computed upon the remainder of said net income of such corporation . . . for the year ending December 31, 1909, and for each year thereafter, and on or before the 1st day of March, 1910, and the 1st day of March of each year thereafter, a true and accurate return under oath or affirmation of its president," etc., etc.

In connection with this clause we would call attention to the fact that, as you are no doubt aware, the fiscal year of a number of corporations is not, and for business reasons cannot be, the calendar year, and consequently, having in mind that in such cases an inventory was not taken at the beginning of the calendar year 1909, it is and will be quite impossible for any business, corporation, or institution, whose fiscal year does not terminate with the calendar year, to make a true return of its profits as required by the proposed law.

Under clause 1 the tax is to be charged upon the "entire net income," and the net income is to be "ascertained by deducting from the gross amount of the income . . . from all sources,"

(1) "Expenses actually paid,"

(2) "Losses actually sustained,"

(3) "Interest actually paid,"
in each case "within the year." The words "actually paid" convey, and it is to be presumed are intended to convey, actual disbursements out of the treasury.

The proper deductions should be:

(1) Expenses actually incurred because the payment is not necessarily made in the year in which the expense is incurred;

(2) Losses actually ascertained because losses may be incurred and the amount not be ascertained until a subsequent period;

(3) Interest actually accrued because interest is never paid until the end of the period during which it accrues, and the interest accrued is the proper charge against income.

In clause 1 the bill refers to "net income received"; in clause 2 it refers to "gross income" without the addition of word "received"; in clause 3, paragraph 3, it refers to "gross income received." There is here a complete confusion between income and income received, which can only lead to endless complication.

Two methods may be adopted for taxation purposes, either

(1) To tax the difference between actual cash receipts on revenue account and actual cash payments on revenue account, which difference will seldom if ever represent the profits of a manufacturing concern; or

(2) To tax profits made up in the ordinary commercial way, namely, to ascertain the gross income earned, whether received or not, and to deduct therefrom—

1. Expenses actually incurred during the year, whether paid or not;
2. Losses actually ascertained and written off during the year whenever incurred;
3. Interest accrued during the year, whether paid or not;
4. A reasonable allowance for depreciation of property; and
5. Taxes.

As accountants actively engaged in the audit and examination of a number of varied businesses and enterprises, we unhesitatingly say that the law as framed is absolutely impossible of application, and would suggest that in the said clauses 1, 2, and 3 of paragraph 2, the words "actually paid" and "actually sustained" be changed to read "actually incurred" and "actually ascertained," and that the third clause be changed to read so that the return will be based on the last completed fiscal year prior to December 31st in cases where the fiscal year of a corporation is not the calendar year.

Yours very truly,

(Signed by twelve firms of accountants.)

The Attorney General replied as follows:

WASHINGTON, D. C., July 12, 1909.

GENTLEMEN:

I am in receipt of the letter signed by your firm and a number of others with respect to the proposed corporation tax law, in which you advise me that you have formed the opinion that some of its provisions are absolutely mpossible of application and others violate all the accepted principles of sound accounting.

You first call my attention to the fact that "the fiscal year of a number of corporations is not, and for business reasons cannot be, the calendar year, and consequently, having in mind that in such cases an inventory was not taken at the beginning of the calendar year 1909, it is and will be quite impossible for any business, corporation or institution, whose fiscal year does not terminate with the calendar year, to make a true return of its profits as required by the proposed law."

I beg to call your attention, in the first place, to the fact that the proposed law does not impose a tax upon "profits," but upon "the entire net income over and above five thousand dollars received by" the corporation, joint stock company or association, or insurance company, subject to the law, from "all sources during such year." It has been the uniform practice of the Government in framing revenue bills to require the tax to be paid as of a fixed date, and, so far as I have been able to ascertain, in every instance the tax is imposed for the calendar year ending December 31st. Such was the income tax law of 1894. It may be inconvenient, but it is certainly not impossible for any corporation which keeps just and true books of account to make up a return such as that required by the proposed law, particularly as the return requires statements of actual receipts and payments, and not, as you recommend in your communication, of expenses "incurred," interest "accrued," and losses "ascertained."

2. You next object that the proposed law authorizes the deductions of "expenses actually paid," and you contend that this should be changed to read "expenses actually incurred." The bill was purposely framed to deal with receipts and disbursements made within the year for which the tax was to be imposed, and the words "actually paid" were employed advisedly. The same may be said with respect to losses actually sustained and interest actually paid. The theory of the framers of the bill in this respect differs from that which you advocate.

3. You then object that in Clause 1 the bill refers to "net income received"; in Clause 2 it refers to "gross income" without the addition of the word "received"; and in Clause 3, Paragraph 3, it refers to "gross income received," and you comment: "There is here a complete confusion between income and income received, which can only lead to endless complication."

I cannot agree that there is any confusion whatever in this respect. "Gross income" in Clause 2 obviously and necessarily means "gross income received." The tax is imposed by Clause 1 upon the entire net income above five thousand dollars received from all sources during the year. By Clause 2 "such net income" is to be ascertained by deducting from the gross amount of the income from all sources the specified items; and if anybody could question whether that meant "gross income received," his doubt would be removed by the provisions in Paragraph 3 of Clause 3.

Your further statement that "as accountants actively engaged in the audit and examination of a number of varied businesses and enterprises, we unhesitatingly say that the law as framed is absolutely impossible of application," causes me very great surprise. My personal acquaintance with you and a number of the other signers of the letter leads me to the belief that you have underestimated your capacity. Certainly the statement of objections made in your letter is entirely insufficient to support the conclusion which you express.

I am, respectfully yours,
(Signed) GEORGE W. WICKERSHAM,
Attorney General.

The following reply, stating in more detail the reasons why the law as framed was impossible of application, was sent to the Attorney General:

NEW YORK, July 21, 1909.

DEAR SIR:

We have to acknowledge receipt of your letter of July 12th, replying to ours of July 8th.

Our only object in addressing you was to be of assistance in a matter of practical accounting which enters into the proposed law, as to which we believe that our experience specially qualifies us to speak. We have purposely refrained from any reference to the policy involved in the law, with which we, as accountants, are not concerned.

The views expressed in your letter of the 12th instant would seem to indicate that you have not fully appreciated the difficulties which will be met with in carrying into effect the provisions of the proposed law as amplified and explained in your letter; and we therefore feel that, in justice to ourselves, we must refer at greater length to some matters which were only briefly touched upon in our letter of July 8th.

We are glad to have your clear expression as to the intention of the law to deal with Receipts and Disbursements only (presumably on Income Account) and not with Income Earned (or Profits) and Expenditures Incurred. Under these circumstances it would seem better to use the term "Receipts on Income Account" and "Disbursements on Income Account" rather than "Income" and "Expense," as the latter terms are more commonly defined and used in relation to Income Earned and Expenses Incurred. In any case, if in Clause 2 "Gross Income" means, as you state it is intended to mean, "Gross Income Received," it would certainly be better to say so and thus remove any possible ambiguity.

We note that you refer to the precedent of the Income Tax Law of 1894. We believe that this law was declared unconstitutional before there had been time to experience the difficulties and uncertainties which any attempt to enforce it, if drawn on the lines of the present bill, would have involved. In this connection we may perhaps point to the precedent of the English Income Tax Law, which has stood the test of over half a century. In this case the tax is on Profits, which in this country are frequently termed "Net Income"; and the accounts of corporations prepared in the regular course of business for their respective fiscal years are and always have been accepted as the basis of taxation, subject to minor provisions as to rates of depreciation, interest deductions, etc.

Our main criticism of the bill in its present form is that in the large majority of cases it will be impossible of application for the year 1909, as explained in our previous letter, and very difficult and expensive, if not altogether impossible, in subsequent years.

Railroads perhaps require the simplest form of accounting obtaining among business corporations. These accounts are kept in a form prescribed by the Interstate Commerce Commission, and severe penalties can be inflicted for any departure from those forms. They must be kept on a basis not of Receipts and Disbursements, but of Earnings, whether collected in cash or not, and of Expenses, whether paid or not, which in both cases accrue during the fiscal year closing on June 30th, the outstanding Income and Expense items uncollected and unpaid running into very large figures and frequently varying considerably in amount between one year and another. While it would be possible to prepare also an account of Receipts and Disbursements, this would involve a great deal of extra work in the compilation of special data and would raise most difficult questions as to the proper distribution between Capital and Income of large payments for stores, the ultimate use of which is not and cannot be known at the time of payment.

Turning now from this, which is perhaps the most simple case, to that of a large manufacturing concern producing all kinds of finished products out of purchases of ore and other raw materials, an accurate or even approximate statement of Cash Receipts and Disbursements on Income Account is a practical impossibility at any time. Cash Receipts arising from sales of products can be ascertained without much difficulty beyond requiring considerable extra work. But no system of accounting can give even approximately "the ordinary and necessary expenses actually paid within the year out of Income in the maintenance and operation of its business and properties." Such expenses presumably must include the cost of the goods sold. Into this cost, and following it through all the intricate accounting which has been found to be necessary, are raw materials actually used in manufacture, labor expended, and innumerable items of expense which are taken into costs as they accrue, quite irrespective of the date of payment. Very large inventories are carried of materials and supplies which are purchased at one period, paid for at another, and used at all sorts of times, in all sorts of quantities, and for all sorts of purposes, mainly for manufacture into products for sale, but to a large extent for additions to or extensions of the plant. Such as are used for the latter purpose are not, as we understand the proposed law, a proper deduction from Gross Income, and yet long before they are used all identity between the materials themselves and the disbursements made for them has been lost. There is, in our opinion, no method by which any such statement as that called for in the proposed law can be prepared short of an entirely independent and separate set of books, designed to follow each bill paid through to the ultimate destination of the materials or services covered thereby, thus duplicating the present cost of the Accounting Department and serving no useful purpose whatever. Even if such method were adopted, it is very doubtful if it would produce the results required with even approximate accuracy.

Without unduly burdening this letter, it is impossible to go into further details here; but the facts must, in the opinion of any one familiar with the operations and accounts of a complicated modern manufacturing concern, fully justify the conclusions which we expressed in our letter of July 8th, and which we now emphatically indorse. Whether the proposed method is physically impossible, or merely, as you state, "inconvenient," it will, we think, be generally conceded that it is in the general interest of the effective administration of laws relating to taxes that they should involve as little inconvenience as possible upon those required to make returns thereunder. The basis for arriving at the amount liable to taxation suggested in our former letter would have the advantage of simplicity, and if the tax is to be a permanent institution, its efficient operation would be greatly facilitated by conformity with regular accounting methods.

We have felt it our duty to protest strongly against the wording of the proposed bill upon the grounds set forth, but our object is to help, and not to hinder. If you think any good purpose would be served by our appearing before you and discussing this matter fully with a view of arriving at a satisfactory solution, which we are satisfied can be done, we shall be pleased to hold ourselves at your disposal for this purpose.

Regretting our inability to in any way modify the conclusions already expressed, We are, Dear Sir,

Yours very truly,

(Signed by eleven firms of accountants.)

The Attorney General's reply to the second letter of the accountants was as follows:

WASHINGTON, D. C., July 22, 1909.

DEAR SIRS:

I have a letter dated the 21st instant, signed by yourself and a number of other firms of accountants, in response to my letter of July 12th, replying to your former letter of July 8th. In your last letter you set forth in somewhat more detail the following proposition:

"But no system of accounting can give even approximately 'the ordinary and necessary expenses actually paid within the year out of income in the maintenance and operation of its business and properties.'"

I think the bare statement of that proposition would be received with very great incredulity by most minds. Certainly, I am quite unable to assent to it. However, it is now too late to attempt to recast the corporation tax amendment bill on the basis of such proposition.

Respectfully yours,

(Signed) GEORGE W. WICKERSHAM,

Attorney General.

A glance at the text of the law as it stands on the statute books will show that in spite of the protest of the accountants, who in this case were the men best qualified to judge of the workability of the law, the bill was allowed to pass in its awkward and unworkable form. Those interested in the subject should compare the law with the accountants' letters and the Treasury explanations. It will be found that the position of the accountants was fully confirmed although no recognition of this fact has been made. The Treasury Department practically rewrote the law, thus proving its impracticability. Out of this have resulted some interesting incidents. Where litigation is resorted to, the court follows the law—not the interpretation thereof by the Treasury. Probably nine-tenths of the returns would, or could be altered if the law were followed instead of the prescribed forms.

For some time after the passage of the act the Treasury Department, which was intrusted with the collection of the tax, and the Attorney General's department, which was responsible for the wording of the law, were unable to agree as to the method of collection, the exemptions to be allowed, and the calculation of net profits.

While things were in this chaotic condition in the Government offices, corporations were equally undecided as to what returns were desired and what amount of taxes each would be called upon to pay. Shortly after the passage of the act, however, the Treasury Department issued an explanation of the law and the regulations which would be laid down for its administration. The text of this explanation follows.

Corporation Excise Tax

PREPARATION OF BLANKS AND REGULATIONS

In the preparation of blanks and regulations for the administration of the Corporation Excise Tax, provided for in section 38 of the tariff act of August 5, 1909, the first question was to ascertain the real intent of the law. After ascertaining the real intent of the law, the problem was then to so prepare the forms and regulations as to carry out that intent and at the same time avoid, as far as consistent, unnecessary and unreasonable interference with ordinary practices of business. The standard adopted in making the regulations was that they should be fair, just, and reasonable to the taxpaying corporations as well as to the Government.

A study of the act discloses clearly that the intent of the law is as follows:

1. That the law is a revenue measure and should be construed liberally for the purpose of producing revenue for the Government.

2. That the real intent of the law is to collect a tax of 1 per cent on the *net income,* less $5,000, of the individual corporation, joint stock company, or association, liable to the tax.

In order to clearly understand the intent of the law a few primary definitions are essential:

NET INCOME

The term "net income" as used in this law means not only net profits arising from the operation of the principal business of the corporation, but all items of income received from other sources, such as investments, holdings in other companies, and businesses, etc. The expression "net income" is used because there can be no question as to its embracing amounts of income received from these outside sources, whereas there might be some question as to whether or not such items would be included in the expression "net profits" or "net earnings."

GROSS INCOME

In the same manner the term "gross income" includes gross profits, the expression being used because there can be no question but what it embraces all items of income received by any corporation from any source, while there might be some question as to whether "gross profits" or "gross earnings" would embrace such items.

A great amount of adverse criticism of this law is due to misapprehension of the proper definitions of these terms. The opinion was advanced that because "gross income" was not "gross profits" it must be "gross receipts," and that, in the same way, because "net income" was not "net profits," it meant "net receipts." An examination of the law, however, will show that if gross income meant gross receipts, the statutory deductions therefrom would not leave net receipts, but would leave merely an arbitrary sum. It also appeared from calculations that if these interpretations were given to the law from mercantile and manufacturing companies alone, the amount of tax received would be many times the sum which was estimated to be collected from all corporations, joint stock companies, and associations of whatever nature.

It is clear, therefore, that the purpose of the law was not to put a tax on receipts, but a tax on profits; and that the terms "gross income" and "net income" are used because, while they are practically indentical with "gross profits" and "net profits," they are yet more embrasive and consequently permit a more comprehensive administration of the law.

The law requires that the return from every corporation, joint stock company, and association liable to the tax shall show the "gross amount of the income . . . received during the year from all sources," and authorizes certain deductions such as "ordinary and necessary expenses actually paid out of earnings in the business and property of such corporations . . . within the year; all losses sustained during the year; amount of interest actually paid within the year; amount paid by it within the year for taxes; amount received within the year as dividends upon stock of other corporations liable to this tax, etc."

Very careful consideration has been given to these expressions in order to determine what evidence shall be required in order to determine what items are to be considered as "income" in calculating "gross income," and what items should be allowed as deductions under the language of the law. An impression has obtained in some quarters that no item should be considered in making up the account of the corporation, either as income or a deduction, unless its receipt or disbursement was evidenced by an actual cash transaction. It was owing to this interpretation placed on the law that a great number of accountants throughout the country declared that the law was impossible of administration, and if their interpretation of the law had been correct, there would indeed have been the most serious difficulty.

Upon first reading the law and studying the authorities relating to the language used, it would appear that the words admit of no interpretation other than that an item must have been evidenced by the actual disbursement of cash, or something of equal value, before it could be considered in making up the account of a corporation. It is interesting to note, however, that all definitions and decisions regarding the expression "actually paid," consider the matter from the standpoint of debtor and creditor, and not from the standpoint of the individual himself, or in this case, from within a corporation concerned solely with its own accounts from which alone the law requires this return for taxation to be made, and not taking into consideration the standpoint of the debtor.

It is clear that to hold that the phrase "actually paid within the year" requires evidence of actual disbursement in cash during the year would prohibit anything like accurate returns being made by any corporation, and would render it impossible to carry out what is the main purpose of the law, because to subtract from the gross income the deductions specified in the statute, calculated on a cash basis, would give net income, on which the tax is to be measured, only when the entire business transacted by the corporation is done in cash and the transactions are completed every day. It is not believed that there is any such corporation in existence. The return predicated on gross income received in cash and deductions represented by cash transactions, will vary from the real net income somewhat in proportion as the business transacted by the corporation varies from the absolutely cash basis.

This is viewing the matter in its simplest aspect. When we contemplate the complications and intricacies of the business affairs of a great corporation, with its many dealings with other corporations and individuals which are never settled in cash, but are settled on somewhat the clearing-house plan; its many advances of funds and long-deferred statements of accounts, purchases of supplies and materials at one time, which are mixed with supplies and materials already on hand and those purchased at other times, and which are used and disbursed without any relation to their time of purchase, any attempt to follow each of these transactions out into the cashbook and to settle the accounts of such complicated actions of a corporation on the cashbook instead of on the ledger would result in inextricable confusion, uncertainty, and inaccuracy, and the friction occasioned the business world by such an attempt would be a very serious proposition.

Relating to statutory deductions, the regulation is to the effect that the deductions authorized shall include all expense items under the various heads acknowledged as liabilities by the corporation making the return and entered as such on its books from January 1 to December 31 of the year for which return is made. It will appear, therefore, that the return is to be made up from the ledger and not the cash book, and that entry on the ledger from January 1 to December 31 of the year for which return is made is the evidence which will determine whether or not an item is to be taken account of in making the return.

It is believed that this interpretation furnishes a practical working method by which the amount of income subject to the tax can be fairly and justly determined in every case.

Of course, in administering a law applying to so many taxpayers (lists prepared by collectors show something over 400,000 corporations which will have to make returns) some of the returns will be inaccurate. The causes of inaccuracy will be two: First, honest error; Second, willful intent to defraud the Government of revenue. If an honest error is made in calculating the return for one year, it will be corrected if possible, and even if not corrected in one year, it would more than probably correct itself later. Where fraudulent purpose is discovered, vigorous prosecution will follow. This bureau feels that in dealing with the incorporated business of the country it is dealing, in the main, with honest men. However, the regulations are drawn sufficiently rigid to restrain anyone who does not measure up to this standard.

The regulations do not call for specific methods of keeping accounts or any particular method of bookkeeping; the requirement is simply that the transaction be so recorded that accurate returns can be made therefrom and verified when necessary.

In many corporations, mercantile and manufacturing particularly, an inventory, or its equivalent, is essential at the close of each calendar year. The law specifically states that the tax shall be collected for the calendar year, and no return for any other period can be accepted. Provision is, however, made for preparing returns for the present year, when no inventory or equivalent was taken at close of last calendar year. Provision is made for a method of fairly determining amount of loss and depreciation claimed; also for a fair adjustment of profit or loss in case of sale of capital assets acquired prior to January 1, 1909; also for properly accounting for materials and supplies, etc.

Great numbers of communications have been received relative to the publicity clause. While there is apparently some inconsistency between the two paragraphs of the law relating to making public the information received, the language of the law relating to filing returns for record and public inspection is so clear that the Bureau of Internal Revenue has no discretion whatever in the matter.

The forms and regulations will go to the collector of each district, who will send copies of the blanks and a copy of the regulations to every corporation whose name and address the collector has been able to secure. Failure to receive the blanks or any notice relative thereto will not excuse a corporation from making the return required by law, nor will it relieve it from penalties for failure so to do. If copies of blanks and regulations are not received on or about January 1, application should be made to the collector in whose district the principal office of the corporation is located, so that the return can be in the hands of the collector by the time required in the statute.

The regulations issued by the Commissioner of Internal Revenue are as follows:

REGULATIONS

Relative to

Excise Tax on Corporations, Joint Stock Companies, Associations and Insurance Companies.

Imposed by authority of Section 38, Act of August 5, 1909.

ARTICLE I

The attention of collectors and others is specially called to the fact that the tax imposed by this section of the law applies to all corporations, joint stock companies, associations, or insurance companies described (except those specifically exempted), without reference to the kind of business carried on, and that the tax is to be computed upon the NET INCOME of such corporations, joint stock companies, associations, and insurance companies, which shall be calculated by subtracting from the gross income received from all sources during the year certain deductions specifically set forth in the statute.

Every corporation, joint stock company, association, or insurance company not specifically enumerated as exempt shall make the return required by law, whether it may have net income liable to tax or not.

In the case of corporations, joint stock companies, associations, or insurance companies organized under the authority of the United States or any State or Territory thereof, including Alaska and District of Columbia, such net income relates not only to the business carried on within the confines of the United States, but to income received from business transacted in any foreign country as well. In case of corporations, joint stock companies, and associations organized under the authority of foreign countries, the terms "Gross income," "Net income," and "Authorized deductions" relate only to business transacted within the United States or any State or Territory thereof.

ARTICLE II.—*Gross Income*

The following definitions and rules are given for determining the gross income of the various classes of corporations:

1 A. *Banks and other financial institutions.*—Gross income consists of the gross revenue derived from the operation and management of the business and property of the corporation making the return, together with all amounts of income (including dividends received on stock of other corporations, joint stock companies, associations, and insurance companies subject to this tax) derived from all other sources, as shown by the entries on its books from January 1 to December 31 of the year for which return is made.

1 B. *Insurance companies.*—Same as 1 A above.

2. *Transportation companies.*—Same as 1 A above.

3. *Manufacturing companies.*—Gross income received during the year from all sources will consist of the total amount, ascertained through an accounting, that shows the difference between the price received for the goods as sold and the cost of such goods as manufactured. The cost of goods manufactured shall be ascertained by an addition of a charge to the account of the cost of goods as manufactured during the year of the sum of the inventory at beginning of the year and a credit to the account of the sum of the inventory at the end of the year. To this amount should be added all items of income received during the year from other sources, including dividends received on stock of other corporations, joint stock companies, associations, and insurance companies subject to this tax. In the determination of the cost of goods manufactured and sold as above such cost shall comprehend all charges for maintenance and operation of manufacturing plant, but shall not embrace allowances for depreciation of property nor for losses sustained which are to be taken account of in ascertaining the net income subject to tax under the proper heading in the authorized deductions.

4. *Mercantile companies.*—Gross amount of income received during the year from all sources consists of the total amount ascertained through inventory, or its equivalent, which shows the difference between the price received for goods sold and the cost of goods purchased during the year, with an addition of a charge to the account of the sum of the inventory at beginning of the year and a credit to the account of the sum of the inventory at the end of the year. To this amount should be added all items of income received during the year from other sources inclusive of dividends received on stock of other corporations, joint stock companies, associations, and insurance companies subject to this tax. In determining this amount no account shall be taken of allowances for depreciation of property, nor for losses sustained which are to be taken account of in ascertaining the net income subject to tax under the proper heading in the authorized deductions.

5. *Miscellaneous.*—Gross income consists of the gross revenue derived from the operation and management of the business and property

of the corporation making the return, together with all amounts of income (including dividends received on stock of other corporations, joint stock companies, associations, and insurance companies subject to this tax) derived from all other sources as shown by the entries on the books from January 1 to December 31 of the year for which return is made.

It will be noted from these definitions that gross income is practically the same as gross profits, the only difference being that gross income is more inclusive, embracing as it does not only gross profits of the corporation, joint stock company and association itself, but also all amounts of income received from other sources. It is immaterial whether any item of gross income is evidenced by cash receipts during the year or in such other manner as to entitle it to proper entry on the books of the corporation from January 1 to December 31 for the year in which return is made.

Sale of capital assets.—In ascertaining income derived from the sale of capital assets, if the assets were acquired subsequent to January 1, 1909, the difference between the selling price and the buying price shall constitute an item of gross income to be added to or subtracted from gross income according to whether the selling price was greater or less than the buying price. If the capital assets were acquired prior to January 1, 1909, the amount of increment or depreciation representing the difference between the selling and buying price is to be adjusted so as to fairly determine the proportion of the loss or gain arising subsequent to January 1, 1909, and which proportion shall be deducted from or added to the gross income for the year in which the sale was made. But for the purpose of determining the selling price, as provided in this section, there shall be added to the price actually realized on sale any amount which has already been set aside and deducted from gross income by way of depreciation as defined in article 4, and has not been paid out in making good such depreciation on the property sold.

Where a corporation is engaged in carrying on more than one class of business, gross income derived from the different classes of business shall be ascertained according to the definitions above, applicable thereto.

Article III.—*Net Income*

"Net income shall be ascertained by deducting from the gross amount of the income of such corporation, joint stock company or association, or insurance company, received within the year from all sources, (first) all the ordinary and necessary expenses actually paid within the year out of income in the maintenance and operation of its business and properties, including all charges such as rentals or franchise payments required to be made as a condition to the continued use or possession of property; (second) all losses actually sustained within the year and not compensated by insurance or otherwise, including a reasonable allowance for depreciation of property, if any, and in the case of insurance companies the sums other than dividends, paid within the year on policy and annuity contracts and the net addition, if any, required by law to be made within the year to reserve funds; (third) interest actually paid within the year on its bonded or other indebtedness to an amount of such bonded and other indebtedness not exceeding the paid-up capital stock of such corporation, joint stock company or association, or insurance company, outstanding at the close of the year, and in the case of a bank, banking association, or trust company, all interest actually paid by it within the year on deposits." In case of corporations, joint stock companies, and associations organized under the laws of a foreign country, "the proportion of its paid-up capital stock outstanding at the close of the year which the gross amount of its income for the year from business transacted and capital invested within the United States and any of its Territories, Alaska, and the District of Columbia, bears to the gross amount of its income derived from all sources within and without the United States; (fourth) all sums paid by it within the year for taxes imposed under the authority of the United States or of any State or Territory thereof, or imposed by the government of any foreign country as a condition to carrying on business therein; (fifth) all amounts received by it within the year as dividend upon stock of other corporations, joint stock companies or associations, or insurance companies, subject to the tax hereby imposed."

The section further provides:

That in the case of a corporation, joint stock company, or association, or insurance company, organized under the laws of a foreign country, such net income shall be ascertained (by making like deductions) from the gross amount of its income received within the year from business transacted and its capital invested within the United States and any of its Territories, Alaska, and the District of Columbia.

Also that:

In the case of assessment insurance companies the actual deposit of sums with state or territorial officers, pursuant to law, as additions to guaranty or reserve fund, shall be treated as being payments required by law to reserve fund.

Also (third paragraph) that:

There shall be deducted from the amount of the net income of each of such corporations, joint stock companies, or associations, or insurance companies, ascertained as provided in the foregoing paragraphs of this section, the sum of five thousand dollars.

The net income, therefore, is the remainder of the gross income after making the specified deductions.

Article IV.—*Deductions*

The specified deductions actually paid within the year, set forth in the statute and as described in Article III preceding, shall include all proper items of expenses and charges under the respective heads as designated. The amount returned for ordinary and necessary expenses actually paid within the year out of income in maintenance and operation of the business and properties of the corporation should not, however, embrace allowances for depreciation of fixed property which are otherwise to be taken account of under the proper heading in the authorized deductions, nor expenses paid within the year and charged to such allowances for depreciation credited in the current year or in previous years. In ascertaining expenses proper to be included in the deductions to be made under this article, corporations carrying materials and supplies on hand for use should include in such expenses the charges for materials and supplies only to the amount that the same are actually disbursed and used in operation and maintenance during the year for which the return is made.

It is immaterial whether the deductions are evidenced by actual disbursements in cash, or whether evidenced in such other way as to be properly acknowledged by the corporate officers and so entered on the books as to constitute a liability against the assets of the corporation, joint stock company, association, or insurance company making the return.

Losses.—The deduction for losses must be in respect of losses actually sustained during the year and not compensated by insurance or otherwise. It must be based upon the difference between the cost value and salvage value of the property or assets, including in the latter value such amount, if any, as has in the current or previous years been set aside and deducted from gross income by way of depreciation as defined in the following section and not been paid out in making good such depreciation.

Depreciation.—The deduction for depreciation should be the estimated amount of the loss, accrued during the year to which the return relates, in the value of the property in respect of which such deduction is claimed that arises from exhaustion, wear and tear, or obsolescence out of the uses to which the property is put, and which loss has not been made good by payments for ordinary maintenance and repairs deducted under the heading of expenses of maintenance and operation or in the ascertainment of gross income. This estimate should be formed upon the assumed life of the property, its cost value, and its use. Expenses paid in any one year in making good exhaustion, wear and tear, or obsolescence in respect of which any deduction for depreciation is claimed, must not be included in the deduction for expense of maintenance and operation of the property or in the ascertainment of gross income, but must be made out of accumulative allowances deducted for depreciation in current and previous years.

ARTICLE V.—*Inventories*

It will be noted that an inventory or its equivalent of materials, supplies, and merchandise on hand for use or sale at the close of each calendar year is essential in the case of certain corporations in order to determine the gross income, and in case of other corporations to determine their expenses of operation. Where such inventory or its equivalent was not taken at the close of the year 1908, a supplemental statement showing such inventory approximately must be submitted with the return on the regular form. Such supplemental statement shall be verified under oath by the treasurer or principal financial officer in submitting the same.

Where any item under any of the deductions is of an unusual nature, a special explanatory note referring to such item shall be made and attached to the form at the appropriate place and made a part thereof by proper reference.

Paragraph 3 of said section 38 also provides:

And said tax shall be computed upon the remainder of said net income of such corporation, joint stock company or association, or insurance company, for the year ending December thirty-first, nineteen hundred and nine, and for each calendar year thereafter; and on or before the first day of March, nineteen hundred and ten, and the first day of March in each year thereafter, a true and accurate return under oath or affirmation of its president, vice-president, or other principal officer, and its treasurer or assistant treasurer, shall be made by each of the corporations, joint stock companies or associations, and insurance companies, subject to the tax imposed by this section, to the collector of internal revenue for the district in which such corporation, joint stock company or association, or insurance company, has its principal place of business, or, in the case of a corporation, joint stock company or association, or insurance company, organized under the laws of a foreign country, in the place where its principal business is carried on within the United States, in such form as the Commissioner of Internal Revenue, with the approval of the Secretary of the Treasury, shall prescribe.

Each return so made is required to set forth:

(*a*) The total amount of the paid-up capital stock of such corporations, joint stock companies or associations, or insurance companies, outstanding at the close of the year;

(*b*) The total amount of bonded and other indebtedness of such corporation, joint stock company or association, or insurance company, at the close of the year;

(*c*) The gross amount of the income of such corporation, joint stock company or association, or insurance company, received during the year from all sources, and if organized under the laws of a foreign country, the gross amount of its income received within the year from business transacted and capital invested within the United States and any of its Territories, Alaska, and the District of Columbia.

Such returns are also required to set forth the items claimed as deductions (Article IV), also the net income after such deductions have been made.

Article VI

Under the authority conferred by this act forms of returns have been prescribed, in which the various items specified in the law are to be stated.

Blank forms of this return will be mailed to collectors and should be furnished to every corporation, not expressly excepted, on or before January 1, 1910, and on or before January 1 of each year thereafter. Failure on the part of any corporation, joint stock company, association, or insurance company liable to this tax to receive a blank form will not excuse it from making the return required by law, or relieve it from any penalties for failure to make the return in the prescribed time. Corporations not supplied with the proper forms for making the return should make application therefor to the collector of internal revenue in whose district is located its principal place of business. Each corporation should carefully prepare its return so as to fully and clearly set forth the data therein called for.

Bookkeeping.—No particular system of bookkeeping or accounting will be required by the Department. However, the business transacted by corporations, joint stock companies, associations, or insurance companies must be so recorded that each and every item therein set forth may be readily verified by an examination of the books and accounts, where such examination is deemed necessary.

Calendar year.—As the law specifically provides that the tax imposed shall be computed on the net income during each "*calendar* year" returns of income based on any period other than the calendar year cannot be accepted.

Corporations organized during the year or going into liquidation during the year should nevertheless render a sworn return on the prescribed form.

ROYAL E. CABELL, *Commissioner.*

Approved:

FRANKLIN MACVEAGH,
Secretary of the Treasury.

Since the date of the explanation given above, the Treasury Department has been called upon to render decisions on various questions not fully elucidated before. These decisions have been gathered in a synopsis issued by the Commissioner of Internal Revenue under date of December 5, 1911, of which the text is given below, with the exception of paragraphs 83-94, inclusive, and 96 to the end, which are quoted earlier in this volume in Chapter XXII, "The Corporation Tax Law and Depreciation."

Classes of Corporations, etc., Subject to Tax

1. The tax imposed by the act applies to all corporations, joint stock companies, and associations, and every insurance company except those specifically exempted, without reference to the kind of business carried on.

2. Every corporation, etc., not specifically enumerated as exempt shall make the return required by law, although its net income during the year may not have exceeded $5,000. (Opinion Attorney-General, January 24, 1910.)

3. Corporations claiming special exemption should nevertheless make return (in blank, if desired), accompanied by a statement setting forth the ground on which exemption is claimed. Failure to receive blanks upon which to make return is no excuse for delinquency in making return, as there is no duty imposed upon the Government to furnish corporations with such blanks.

4. Charitable institutions supported by voluntary contributions or State appropriations are held to be exempt from the payment of the special excise tax on corporations, but should file a return in blank as provided in paragraph 3 hereof.

5. Corporations, etc., organized during the year or going into liquidation during the year should nevertheless render a sworn return on the prescribed form. The tax imposed, however, does not apply to corporations which went out of existence prior to the passage of the act (August 5, 1909).

6. Where company has dissolved and the required return is not made by its officers, such return will be prepared by Commissioner. (T. D., 1736.)

7. Where corporation has gone into bankruptcy, returns in such cases to be made by trustee in bankruptcy.

8. Railroad companies operating leased or purchased lines to include all receipts derived therefrom, and if bonded indebtedness has been assumed, may deduct interest thereon to an amount not exceeding its own paid-up capital stock. If such subsidiary companies receive income in the way of rentals, etc., return to be also made by such companies.

9. Corporations, etc., organized under the authority of the United States or any State or Territory thereof, or Alaska, or the District of Columbia, to include in their returns not only the income derived from the business carried on within the confines of the United States, but income received from business transacted in any foreign country as well.

10. Corporations having branch or subsidiary companies to include in their returns the income of all such companies when no distinction is made in operating and accounting by reason of the separate incorporation of such subsidiary companies; otherwise a return by each corporation should be made.

11. Foreign companies having several branch offices in the United States should each designate one of such branches as its principal office and should also designate the proper officers to make the required return.

12. Where a consolidation of two or more corporations has been effected during the year, and each or any such corporation subsequent to such consolidation collects prior existing debts, each such corporation should make separate return and include therein all such collected debts, as also all income received during the year prior to the date of consolidation.

13. "Principal place of business" is held to mean the principal office where the company keeps its books, from which the required return is to be prepared, and not necessarily the place where the operating plant is located.

14. As the law specifically provides that the tax imposed shall be computed on the net income during each calendar year, returns of income based on any period other than the calendar year cannot be accepted.

15. Full amount of stock, as represented by the par value of the shares issued, to be regarded as the paid-up capital stock, except when such stock is assessable on account of deferred payments, in which case the

amount actually paid on such shares will constitute the actual paid-up capital stock of the corporation.

16. Capital stock held to include both preferred and common stock.

17. Surplus and undivided profits not to be included in capital stock.

18. Holding companies known as "voting trusts," receiving only dividends on stock held, and having no capital stock, etc., not liable.

19. Mutual savings banks having no capital stock not liable to tax imposed. (Opinion Attorney-General, February 14, 1910.)

20. Coöperative dairies not issuing stock and allowing patrons dividends based on butter fat in milk furnished not liable.

21. Foreign steamship companies having no office in the United States, whose vessels only occasionally touch at ports in the United States, not regarded as doing business in this country within the meaning of the statute.

22. Companies organized in Porto Rico and not engaged in business in the United States not subject to tax.

23. Corporations owning sugar or other plantations and disposing of the products thereof not entitled to exemption as agricultural organizations.

24. Corporations organized to sell provisions, etc., to stockholders and others not exempted.

25. Corporations organized for the purpose of holding real estate to make return of income derived from the property so held.

26. Corporations going into liquidation during any tax period may, at the time of such liquidation, prepare a "final return" covering the business done during the fractional part of the year during which they were engaged in business, and immediately file the same with the collector of the district in which the corporation has its principal place of business.

27. Corporations organized for the purpose of insuring against death, or injury by accident, or against damage to property by hail, storm, or lightning, however maintained, are held to be insurance companies, and unless they may be properly classed as "fraternal beneficiary organizations operating under the lodge system," must make returns of annual net income. (T. D., 1738.)

28. Corporations engaged in agricultural or horticultural pursuits for profit are liable under the law to make returns and to pay the special excise tax thereby shown to be due. Agricultural and horticultural associations specifically enumerated as exempt are held to be such associations as county fairs or like organizations, not themselves engaged in such pursuits, but which, by means of awards, etc., are intended to encourage better production, and no part of whose net income inures to the benefit of any private stockholder or individual. (T. D., 1737.)

29. Fruit growers' associations whose purpose is to promote the mutual benefit of their members in growing, harvesting, and marketing their products, and which are not organized for profit and have no capital stock represented by shares, and whose income is derived wholly from membership fees, dues, and assessments to meet necessary expenses, are not liable.

30. Corporations engaged in growing fruits, vegetables, and the like products for profit, and distributing such profits among their members on the basis of the capital invested, are liable and must make returns and pay taxes, if any are found to be due. (T. D., 1737.)

31. Associations or trusts voluntarily formed by parties at interest and not organized "under the laws of the United States or of any State or Territory thereof, or of the laws applicable to the District of Columbia or Alaska," are not corporations within the meaning and intent of the law, and are not liable. (United States Supreme Court opinion in Amory Eliot v. James G. Freeman, et al., No. 448.)

32. National banks do not come within any of the exemptions named in the act.

33. "Agricultural organizations" held not to come within the statutory exemption, unless their chief object is the promotion or advancement of agricultural interest, and no part of the net income inures to the benefit of their stockholders.

34. Mutual Hall Association regarded as an insurance company and not as an agricultural association, and therefore liable to tax.

35. Exemption in favor of fraternal beneficiary associations does not apply to mutual fire insurance companies.

36. Limited partnerships, if organized for profit and having a capital stock represented by shares, although no "certificates of stock" are issued, are liable to the tax imposed. (Opinion Attorney-General, February 14, 1910.)

37. Interest received on Government bonds to be included in gross income. (Opinion Attorney-General, January 13, 1910.)

38. Returns should be signed and verified by two of the officers designated in the law. Signing of one person holding two such offices not permitted. Agents for foreign steamship companies may sign the required returns if so authorized by their companies.

39. Returns not required to have corporate seal affixed.

40. Returns filed with deputy collector regarded as having been filed with collector.

41. No form of protest prescribed. Any form of protest sufficient if filed before payment of tax. Right of protest not to be denied.

Inventories, Accounts, etc.

42. Where an inventory or its equivalent was not taken at the close of the year 1908, a supplemental statement showing such inventory approximately must be submitted with the return on the regular form. Such supplemental statement shall be verified under oath by the treasurer or principal financial officer submitting the same. (T. D., 1578.)

43. Profits realized on sale of real estate during the year, also increase in value of unsold property, if taken up on the books of the corporation, to be included in income.

44. Cost of manufactured articles, or articles in process of manufacture, held to include original cost of materials used, plus cost of labor, etc.

45. Mortgaged real estate should be inventoried at its full value and amount of mortgage reported as indebtedness.

46. Receipts from sale of patent rights to be included in income.

47. No particular system of bookkeeping or accounting will be required by the department. However, the business transacted by corporations, etc., must be so recorded that each and every item therein set forth may be readily verified by an examination of the books and accounts where such examination is deemed necessary.

48. Any increase in the value of the capital assets, as determined by a physical revaluation and taken cognizance of by the corporation in book entries, is gain, and must be accounted for as income for the year in which such increase is so recognized and recorded.

Deductions, Expenses, etc.

49. It is immaterial whether the deductions are evidenced by actual disbursements in cash or whether evidenced in such other way as to be properly acknowledged by the corporate officers and so entered on the books as to constitute a liability against the assets of the corporation, etc., making the return.

50. Mortgage indebtedness on real estate, if assumed by the corporation acquiring such real estate, to be included in the indebtedness of the corporation. But if not so assumed and remains only as a lien on the property, interest paid thereon may be deducted as a charge "made as a condition to the continued use or possession of the property." (Opinion Attorney-General, February 21, 1910.)

51. Cost of erecting building, if included in lease under which property is held by company, is a proper deduction, to be prorated according to time fixed by lease.

52. General expenses, such as coal, ship stores, etc., of foreign steamship companies, to be prorated as provided in act for interest deductions.

53. Amount received by nursery companies from sales of trees, etc., less amount expended for seedlings and young trees, to be included in gross income. Amount expended for labor, salesmen, etc., to be deducted as expenses.

54. Commissions allowed salesmen, paid in stock, may be deducted as expense if so charged on books.

55. Sales of stock and bonds are regarded as sales of capital assets and should be so accounted for. (Art. II, Reg. 31.) But proceeds derived from sale of bonds used in defraying ordinary and necessary expenses are a proper deduction in determining the company's net income.

56. Stock issued in payment of property purchased represents capital investments and notes issued during the year represent indebtedness. Corporate funds applied to the payment of outstanding notes not a proper deduction in ascertaining net income.

57. Amounts expended in additions and betterments which constitute an increase in capital investment not a proper deduction.

58. Dividends received by corporations on stock of other corporations whose net income does not exceed $5,000 is nevertheless a proper deduction under the law. (Opinion Attorney-General, January 24, 1910.)

59. Dividends received on stock of foreign corporations not subject to tax not a proper deduction.

60. Dividends paid employees in lieu of wages not proper deduction as expenses.

61. Royalties on patent rights to be reported as income. Allowance for depreciation of patents expiring during year, however, will be allowed.

62. In the case of lands bought prior to January 1, 1909, and sold during any subsequent year, the profits arising from such sale, if no accounting of increased value of land was made in returns for previous years, should be prorated in accordance with the number of years the land was held by the corporation and the number of years the law was in effect.

63. Banks paying taxes assessed against their stockholders because of their ownership of the shares of stock issued by such bank cannot deduct the amount of tax so paid in making their return for the special excise tax on corporations.

64. Amounts paid for pensions to retired employees, or to their families or others dependent upon them, or on account of injuries received by employees, are proper deductions as "ordinary and necessary expenses"; gifts or gratuities to employees in the service of a corporation are not properly deductible in ascertaining net income. Donations made for purposes connected with the operation of the property, when limited to charitable institutions, hospitals, or educational institutions, conducted for the benefit of its employees, or their dependents, shall be proper as a deduction under the same head.

65. Where allowances on account of salaries are deemed excessive and for the purpose of evading the tax due, investigation will be made, and if the facts warrant, prosecution will follow.

66. Interest paid on time deposits and deposits subject to check constitutes a proper deduction from the amount of gross income during the year.

67. Interest on portions of bonded or other indebtedness bearing different rates of interest may be deducted from gross income during the year, provided the aggregate amount of such indebtedness does not exceed the paid-up capital stock of the corporation.

68. Interest paid during the year on notes given prior to January 1, 1909, to be prorated. But interest on notes given in 1909, and payable subsequent to December, 1909, unless charged on the company's books, is not a proper deduction from the income of that year.

69. Interest, taxes, or other items allowable as deductions, accruing prior to January 1, 1909, are not allowable deductions from the gross income of years subsequent thereto.

70. Unearned premiums set aside by insurance companies as reserve

not to be included as income until earned, unless the same shall be entered on the ledger as income during the year in which received.

71. Funds set aside by company for insuring their own property not a proper deduction.

72. As the tax imposed is measured by and is not a tax upon the net receipts of corporations, etc., interest received during the year on Government bonds is not a proper deduction from such income in determining the amount of tax due. (Opinion Attorney-General, T. D., 1583.)

73. State, county, or municipal taxes paid during the year a proper deduction in ascertaining the net income of corporations.

74. Import duties or taxes, if included in arriving at cost of goods, are not deductible under the head of taxes paid during the year.

75. Bad debts, if so charged off the company's books during the year, are proper deductions. But such debts, if subsequently collected, must be treated as income.

76. The net addition to reserves of insurance companies, required by law, may be based on the highest amount of reserves required by any State in which the insurance company does business. (T. D., 1727.)

77. Reserves for taxes cannot be allowed, as the law specifically provides that only such sums as *are paid* within the year for taxes can be deducted. (T. D., 1727.)

78. Where a corporation or insurance company holds bonds which were purchased at a rate above par, and a proportionate deduction of the value of such bonds is made on its books each year so that the book value shall be the redemption value of the bonds when they become due and payable, the return of annual net income may show the depreciation on account of amortization of such bonds. (T. D., 1727.)

79. Dividends declared by insurance companies are not deductible from gross income under the guise of rebates or otherwise, and such dividends, when applied to the payment of renewal premiums, or to shorten the endowment or premium-paying period, or applied to purchase paid-up additions and annuities, must be considered and accounted for as income.

80. Railroad or other corporations which have leased their properties in consideration of a rental equivalent to a certain rate of interest on its outstanding capital stock and the interest on the bonded indebtedness, and such rental is paid by the lessee directly to the stock and bondholders, should, nevertheless, make a return of annual net income showing the rental so paid as having been received by the corporation.

81. Salaries paid to an officer who is a stockholder, to constitute an allowable deduction, must be a reasonable and fair compensation for the services rendered, regardless of the amount of stock which such officer may hold, and must have been authorized by the board of directors and made a matter of record on the minute books of the corporation.

82. "Good Will" represents the value attached to a business over and above the value of the physical property, and is such an entirely intangible asset that no claim for depreciation in connection therewith can be allowed.

Publicity

95. A person who as trustee or in any other fiduciary relation has the ownership or possessory right to stock in a corporation is a stockholder in such corporation within the equity of the rule set down in Treasury Decision No. 1665, governing the publicity of returns. (Opinion Attorney-General, December 27, 1910.)

Few decisions have been rendered since the date of the synopsis above given. Among the decisions since rendered was one to the effect that "Dividends declared by Insurance Companies are the dividends referred to in section 38, act of August 5, 1909, as not being deductible from gross income, and when such dividends are applied to the payment of renewal premiums to shorten the endowment or premium-paying period, to purchase paid-up additions and annuities, etc., they must be included and accounted for as income."

Two special decisions relative to the rate of depletion of deposits and the return of cash investments to corporations with respect to natural gas and petroleum properties have been rendered. These two decisions are numbered T. D. 1,754 and 1,755, respectively.

One of the most undesirable features of the corporation tax law is that it requires all corporations, irrespective of their convenience or preëxisting fiscal arrangements, to make their returns and inventories as of December 31st of each year. With the object of securing relief from the burden which is thus unnecessarily put upon the shoulders of the tax payer, the American Association of Public Accountants has been waging a campaign to secure the passage of an amending bill which will permit returns to be made as of the end of each individual fiscal year. Many of the leading commercial and industrial bodies of the country have indorsed the proposal and various bills have been introduced in the House of Representatives and the Senate with the object of bringing about the much-needed reform.

The Treasury Department itself, which for a long time was opposed to the adoption of the fiscal year instead of the calendar year, has now been converted, and at a hearing before the Ways and Means Committee of the House on January 10, 1912, the Commissioner of Internal Revenue stated that it was the opinion of the Treasury Department that the law should be changed.

PARTNERSHIP AND INDIVIDUAL EXCISE TAX

The following is the text of the bill introduced in the last session of Congress, which extends the excise tax on net profits to firms and individuals. Congress adjourned August 26, 1912, without enacting the bill into law, but the same or a somewhat similar measure may confidently be expected to become law within the near future.

AN ACT

To extend the special excise tax now levied with respect to doing business by corporations, to persons, and to provide revenue for the Government by levying a special excise tax with respect to doing business by individuals and copartnerships.

Be it enacted by the Senate and House of Representatives of the United States of America in Congress assembled, That every person, firm, or copartnership residing in the United States, any Territory thereof, or in Alaska or the District of Columbia, shall be subject to pay annually a special excise tax with respect to the carrying on or doing business by such person equivalent to one per centum upon the entire net income over and above five thousand dollars received by such person from all sources during each year; or, if a nonresident, such nonresident person shall likewise be subject to pay annually a special excise tax with respect to the carrying on or doing business by such person equivalent to one per centum upon the amount of net income over and above five thousand dollars received by such person from business transacted and capital invested within the United States and its Territories, Alaska, and the District of Columbia during each year. The term "business," as herein used, is and shall be held to embrace everything about which a person can be employed, and all activities which occupy the time, attention, and labor of persons for the purpose of a livelihood or profit. The word "person" wherever used in this Act shall be held to include natural persons or individuals and firms or copartnerships.

SEC. 2. That the term "business" as herein used is and shall also be held to embrace the act or acts of holding, receiving, caring for and disbursing, either personally or through agents, the returns or profits of investments of capital of whatever kind; and every person, firm, or copartnership residing as aforesaid holding the bonds, debentures, or other evidence of indebtedness of any corporation or association organized under the laws of either the United States or of any State, Territory, or District of the United States, or doing business therein, shall, upon the carrying on or doing business by such person either personally or by agent, in respect to the income therefrom as aforesaid, and upon the right to hold, possess, manage, and control the principal and to collect the interest or other income of said bonds or other evidence of indebtedness, be subject to pay annually a special excise tax equivalent to one per centum upon the annual interest or income payable upon said bonds or other evidence of indebtedness: *Provided,* That said tax shall not be paid upon the interest or income derived from said bonds or other evidences of indebtedness when the same is otherwise paid under the provisions of this Act by the person holding or owning the same: *And provided further,* That said tax shall not be paid by the holder or owner of said bonds or other evidence of indebtedness except to the extent that the said interest or income from the same shall when added to the other net income of said holder or owner for the year exceed the net income of five thousand dollars received by such person from all sources during each year.

SEC. 3. That in computing incomes the necessary expenses actually incurred in carrying on any business, not including personal, living, or family expenses, shall be deducted, and also all interest paid within the year by such person on existing indebtedness; and all national, State, county, school, and municipal taxes, not including those assessed against local benefits, paid within the year shall be deducted from the gains, profits, or income of the person who has actually paid the same, whether such person be owner, tenant, or mortgagor; also losses actually sustained during the year, incurred in trade or arising from fires, storms, or shipwreck, and not compensated for by insurance or otherwise, and debts ascertained to be worthless: *Provided,* That no deduction shall be made for any amount paid out for new buildings, permanent improvements, or betterments, made to increase the value of any property or estate: *Provided further,* That only one deduction of five thousand dollars shall be made from the aggregate income of all the members of any family composed of one or both parents and one or more minor children, or husband and wife; that guardians shall be allowed to make a deduction in favor of each and every ward, except that in case where two or more wards are comprised in one family and have joint property interests the aggregate deduction in their favor shall not exceed five thousand dollars: *And provided further,* That in cases where the salary or other compensation paid to any person in the employment or service of the United States shall not exceed the rate of five thousand dollars per annum, or shall be by fees, or uncertain or irregular in the amount or in the time during which the same shall have accrued or been earned, such salary or other compensation shall be included in estimating the annual gains, profits, or income of the person to whom the same shall have been paid, and shall include that portion of any income or salary upon which a tax has not been paid by the employer, fiduciary, or other person, where the employer, fiduciary, or other person is required by law to pay on the excess over five thousand dollars: *And provided further,* That in computing the income of any person there shall not be included the amount received from any corporation, joint stock company or association, or insurance company as dividends upon the stock of such corporation, joint stock company or association, or insurance company, if the special excise tax of one per centum now imposed by law has been paid by such corporation, joint stock company or association, or insurance company: *And provided further,* That in computing the income of any person there shall not be included the amount received from any firm or copartnership, if the special excise tax of one per centum imposed by this Act has been paid upon such amount by such firm or copartnership: *And provided further,* That nothing in this Act contained shall apply to labor, agricultural or horticultural organizations, or to fraternal beneficiary societies, orders, or associations operating under the lodge system and providing for the payment of life, sick, accident, and other benefits to the members of such societies, orders, and associations and dependents of such members, nor to domestic building and loan associations organized and operated exclusively for the mutual benefit of their members, nor to any corporation or association organized and operated exclusively for religious, charitable, or educational purposes no part of the net income of which inures to the benefit of any private stockholder or individual.

SEC. 4. That there shall be deducted from the amount of the net income of each of such persons, ascertained as provided herein, the sum of five thousand dollars, and said tax shall be computed upon the remainder of said net income of such person for the year ending December thirty-first, nineteen hundred and twelve, and for each calendar year thereafter; and on or before the first day of March, nineteen hundred and thirteen, and the first day of March in each year thereafter, a true and accurate return, under oath or affirmation, shall be made by each person of lawful age, subject to the tax imposed by this Act, to the collector of internal revenue for the district in which such person resides or has his principal place of business, or, in the case of a person residing in a foreign country, in the place where his principal business is carried on within the United States, in such form as the Commissioner of Internal Revenue, with the approval of the Secretary of the Treasury, shall prescribe, setting forth specifically the gross amount of income from all separate sources and from the total thereof, deducting the aggregate items or expenses and allowance herein authorized, and likewise returning the amount of income, gains, and profits of any minor or person for whom they act, but persons having less than four thousand five hundred dollars net income are not required to make such report; and the collector or deputy collector shall require every list or return to be verified by the oath or affirmation of the party rendering it, and may increase the amount of any list or return if he has reason to believe that the same is understated: *Provided,* That no such increase shall be made except after due notice to such party and upon proof of the amount understated; and in case such person having a taxable income shall neglect or refuse to make and render such list and return, or shall render a willfully false or fraudulent list or return, it shall be the duty of the collector or deputy collector to make such list according to the best information he can obtain, by the examination of such person or any other evidence, and to add fifty per centum as a penalty to the amount of the tax due on such list in all cases of willful neglect or refusal to make and render a list or return; and in all cases of a willfully false or fraudulent list or return having been rendered, to add one hundred per centum as a penalty to the amount of tax ascertained to be due, the tax and the additions thereto as a penalty to be assessed and collected in the manner provided for in other cases of willful neglect or refusal to render a list or return, or of rendering a false or fraudulent return: *Provided further,* That any person in his or her behalf, or as such employer, or fiduciary, shall be permitted to declare, under oath or affirmation, the form and manner of which shall be prescribed by the Commissioner of Internal Revenue, with the approval of the Secretary of the Treasury, that he, she, or his or her ward, employee, or beneficiary was not possessed of an income of five thousand dollars, or may declare that he, she, or his or her ward, employee, or beneficiary has been assessed and has paid a special excise tax elsewhere for the same year, under authority of the United States, measured by all his or her income, gains, or profits, and upon all the income, gains, or profits for which he or she is liable as such employer or fiduciary, as prescribed by this law; and if the collector or deputy collector shall be satisfied of the truth of the declaration, such person shall thereupon be exempt from excise tax in the said district for that year; or if the list or return of any person shall have been increased by the collector or deputy collector, such person may be permitted to prove the amount liable to be assessed; but such proof shall not be considered as conclusive of the facts, and no deductions claimed in such cases shall be made or allowed until approved by the collector or deputy collector. Any person feeling aggrieved by the decision of the deputy collector, in such cases may appeal to the collector of the district, and his decision thereon, unless reversed by the Commissioner of Internal Revenue, shall be final. If dissatisfied with the decision of the collector, such person may submit the case, with all the papers, to the Commissioner of Internal Revenue for his decision, and may furnish the testimony of witnesses to prove any relevant facts, having served notice to that effect upon the Commissioner of Internal Revenue, as herein prescribed.

Such notice shall state the time and place at which and the officer before whom the testimony will be taken; the name, age, residence, and business of the proposed witness, with the questions to be propounded to the witness, or a brief statement of the substance of the testimony he is expected to give: *And provided further,* That the Government may at the same time and place take testimony upon like notice to rebut the testimony of the witnesses examined by the person taxed.

The notice shall be delivered or mailed to the Commissioner of Internal Revenue a sufficient number of days previous to the day fixed for taking testimony, to allow him, after its receipt, at least five days, exclusive of the period required for mail communication with the place at which the testimony is to be taken, in which to give, should he so desire, instructions as to the cross-examination of the proposed witness.

Whenever practicable the affidavit or deposition shall be taken before a collector or deputy collector of internal revenue, in which case reasonable notice shall be given to the collector or deputy collector of the time fixed for taking the deposition or affidavit.

SEC. 5. That all assessments shall be made and all persons shall be notified of the amount for which they are respectively liable on or before the first day of June of each successive year, and said assessments shall be paid on or before the thirtieth day of June, except in cases of refusal or neglect to make such return, and in cases of false or fraudulent returns, in which cases the Commissioner of Internal Revenue shall, upon the discovery thereof, at any time within three years after said return is due, make a return upon information obtained as above provided for, and the assessment made by the Commissioner of Internal Revenue thereon shall be paid by such person or persons immediately upon notification of the amount of such assessment; and to any sum or sums due and unpaid after the thirtieth day of June in any year, and for ten days after notice and demand thereof by the collector, there shall be added the sum of five per centum on the amount of tax unpaid, and interest at the rate of one per centum per month upon said tax from the time the same becomes due.

SEC. 6. That it shall be the duty of all paymasters and all disbursing officers under the Government of the United States, or persons in the employ thereof, when making any payment to any officers or persons as aforesaid, whose compensation is determined by a fixed salary, or upon settling or adjusting the accounts of such officers or persons, to deduct and withhold the aforesaid tax of one per centum, and the pay rolls, receipts, or accounts of officers or persons paying such tax as aforesaid shall be made to exhibit the fact of such payment. And it shall be the duty of the accounting officers of the Treasury Department, when auditing the accounts of any paymaster or disbursing officer, or any officer withholding his salary from moneys received by him, or when settling or adjusting the accounts of any such officers, to require evidence that the taxes mentioned in this Act have been deducted and paid over to the Treasurer of the United States or other officer authorized to receive the same. Every person, firm, or corporation who pays to any officer, employee, or other person a salary or compensation, interest, or other accrued profits, exceeding five thousand dollars for a taxable year, every lessee or mortgagor of real or personal property who pays to the lessor or mortgagee interest or compensation exceeding five thousand dollars for a taxable year, and every trustee, executor, administrator, conservator, agent, or receiver, employing any person or paying any person business earnings, within the meaning of this Act, exceeding five thousand dollars for any taxable year, computed on the basis herein prescribed, shall make and render a return as provided herein to the collector or a deputy collector of his district, and shall deduct and withhold the tax herein imposed, and shall pay on said return the tax of one per centum per annum as required by this Act: *Provided*, That any officer, employee, or other person for whom return has been made and the tax paid, as aforesaid, shall not be required to make a return unless such person has other net income, but only one deduction of five thousand dollars shall be made in the case of any such officer or employee: *Provided further,* That salaries paid to State, county, or municipal officers shall be exempt from the special excise tax herein levied: *And provided further,* That interest upon the bonds or other obligations of a State or any political subdivision thereof and also the proceeds of life insurance policies paid upon the death of the person insured shall not be included in computing the net income of a person subject to the tax herein imposed: *And provided further,* That all property or its value passing by will or by intestate laws or transferred by deed or gift made or intended to take effect in possession after the death of the grantor, donor, testator, or ancestor shall be exempt from the operation of this law.

SEC. 7. That if any person, corporation, company, or association liable to make the return or pay the tax aforesaid shall refuse or neglect to make a return at the time or times hereinbefore specified in each year, or shall render a false or fraudulent return, such person shall be liable to a penalty of not less than fifty dollars and not exceeding five hundred dollars. Any person, corporation, company, or association required by law to make, render, sign, or verify any return who makes any false or fraudulent return or statement with intent to defeat or evade the assessment required by this Act to be made shall be guilty of a misdemeanor and shall be fined not exceeding one thousand dollars or be imprisoned not exceeding one year, or both, at the discretion of the court, with the costs of prosecution.

SEC. 8. That it shall be the duty of every collector of internal revenue to whom payment of any tax is made, under the provisions of this Act, to give to the person making such payment a full written or printed receipt expressing the amount paid and the particular account for which such payment was made; and whenever such payment is made such collector shall, if required, give a separate receipt for each tax paid by any debtor on account of payments made or to be made by him to separate creditors in such form that such debtor can conveniently produce the same separately to his several creditors in satisfaction of their respective demands to the amounts specified in such receipts; and such receipts shall be sufficient evidence in favor of such debtor to justify him in withholding the amount therein expressed from his next payment to his creditor; but such creditor may, upon giving to his debtor a full written receipt, acknowledging the payment to him of whatever sum may be actually paid, and accepting the amount of tax paid as aforesaid (specifying the same) as a further satisfaction of the debt to that amount, require the surrender to him of such collector's receipt.

SEC. 9. That jurisdiction is hereby conferred upon the district courts of the United States for the district within which any person summoned under this Act to appear to testify or to produce books shall reside, to compel such attendance, production of books, and testimony by appropriate process.

SEC. 10. That all administrative, special, and general provisions of law, including the laws in relation to the assessment, remission, collection, and refund of internal revenue taxes not heretofore specifically repealed and not inconsistent with the provisions of this Act, are hereby extended and made applicable to all the provisions of this Act and to the tax herein imposed.

SEC. 11. That the Act entitled "An Act to promote reciprocal trade relations with the Dominion of Canada, and for other purposes," approved July twenty-sixth, nineteen hundred and eleven, be, and is hereby, repealed: *Provided,* That from and after the passage of this Act the duty on chemical wood pulp shall be one-twelfth of one per cent per pound, dry weight, if unbleached, and one-eighth of one per cent per pound if bleached, and the duty on printing paper as described in paragraph four hundred and nine of the Act approved August fifth, nineteen hundred and nine, shall be one-tenth of one cent per pound if valued at not above three cents per pound, two-tenths of one cent per pound if valued above three cents and not above five cents per pound, and seven and one-half per centum ad valorem if valued above five cents per pound.

Passed the House of Representatives March 19, 1912.

Attest: SOUTH TRIMBLE,
Clerk.

Passed the Senate with amendments July 26, 1912.

CHAPTER XXXV

CERTIFIED PUBLIC ACCOUNTANT LAWS AND EXAMINATIONS

THE first Certified Public Accountant law was enacted by the Legislature of the State of New York in 1896. Three years later Pennsylvania followed, and in 1900 Maryland passed its law. Since that time there has been a steady increase in the number of States having C. P. A. laws, and in nearly every State in the Union efforts have been made to secure the passage of this necessary legislation.

The objections which have been raised by legislators have been the arguments common to the ultraconservative, and in those cases in which bills have not passed their failure has generally been due to an unwillingness on the part of legislators to be convinced rather than to any lack of convincing argument.

To-day there are twenty-three States having on their statute books laws providing for the regulation of professional accountants. In the following list the names of these States and the year in which each law was enacted are given.

1896 New York
1899 Pennsylvania
1900 Maryland
1901 California
1903 Washington
1903 Illinois
1904 New Jersey
1905 Michigan
1905 Florida
1906 Rhode Island
1907 Utah
1907 Colorado
1907 Connecticut
1908 Ohio
1908 Louisiana
1908 Georgia
1909 Massachusetts
1909 Missouri
1909 Minnesota
1909 Montana
1909 Nebraska
1910 Virginia
1911 West Virginia

Among the States in which efforts are being made to secure similar laws may be mentioned Alabama, Kentucky, Kansas, North Carolina, Oklahoma, Oregon, Tennessee, Texas, and Wisconsin.

The vast majority of State laws specify that applicants for the degree of C. P. A. shall pass examinations in "theory of accounts," "practical accounting," "auditing," and "commercial law," and these topics are specifically mentioned in the model law presented at the 1907 Annual Meeting of the American Association of Public Accountants by the then committee on legislation. Exceptions to the rule are found in the case of New York, Pennsylvania, Maryland, New Jersey, and Massachusetts.

In Pennsylvania the examinations are grouped under two general headings, viz., "commercial law" and "general accounting." In the latter are included "theory of accounts," "practical accounting," and "auditing." This grouping of subjects has much in its favor, as it simplifies the work of the examiner, renders coördination of questions possible, and is less confusing to the candidate.

In New York and Illinois it has been recognized from the beginning that there should be an educational qualification. In New York the candidate, before taking the examination, must possess a high grade in the regents' system of qualifications. Indeed, throughout the country it is becoming more and more the conviction that the public accountant must have a broader general education and a more scientific preparation than was expected a few years ago. The work of the accountant covers to-day a vastly wider field than that of his predecessors in the latter part of the last century, and it may be said, generally speaking, that the wider the accountant's general knowledge, the greater will be his efficiency in the profession which he has undertaken.

Another question which has been raised, and on which there is a wide divergence of opinion, is the requirement of a certain amount of professional experience before the candidate is examined. This experience may take the form of simple bookkeeping or it may involve the service in the office of a public accountant for one year or two or three, as the case may be, but it is becoming increasingly felt that some degree of experience is of great importance before the candidate applies for his degree as a Certified Public Accountant. As the profession grows in importance the requirement of experience will, and should be, strengthened.

In the following pages are given recent examination papers

in auditing prepared by the accountancy boards of a number of representatives States. In cases in which there is no separate paper on auditing and the subject is dealt with in the course of a paper such as that on general accounting, the entire paper is given, so that readers may form their own opinions as to the desirability of the grouping of subjects and of treating these subjects separately.

University of the State of New York

THIRTY-THIRD ACCOUNTANT EXAMINATION

AUDITING

Wednesday, June 26, 1912—1.15 to 4.15 P. M. only

Answer 10 *questions, but no more, selecting at least two questions from each group. Each complete answer will receive* 10 *credits. Papers entitled to* 75 *or more credits will be accepted.*

GROUP I

1. If you were sent to make the first audit of a concern, what are the steps you would take?

2. What condition of office organization, above all others, leads to fraud and defalcation by bookkeepers and cashiers? Support your opinion.

3. In making an audit of a concern doing a mercantile business, what would you require to enable you to certify to the correctness of the inventory of merchandise that they had prepared?

4. What means would you employ to verify the usual cash receipts of the average social club?

5. Give at length your views on the "ethics" of accountancy.

GROUP II

6. Assuming that you are a Certified Public Accountant and employed as auditor by a corporation, state what you would consider it your duty to do in order to safeguard your clients regarding the fire insurance that they carry on their stock of merchandise.

7. A foreign agent of a life insurance company sends monthly the following data: a report showing his receipts and disbursements, with dates; vouchers supporting the disbursements; list of overdue premiums; a statement of his daily cash balances in bank, supported by a certificate from his bank as to his closing balances. How would you audit his report?

8. A company has acquired, at $90 per share, 100 shares of its own

capital stock, of the par value of $100 per share. Its balance sheet shows treasury stock $9,000. Is this correct? If so, why? If not, state how you would adjust the books.

9. Describe briefly the way you carried out an audit which you planned and conducted personally.

10. In auditing the books of a corporation capitalized at $250,000 you find that three years previously they acquired the business of a copartnership included in which was an asset called good will valued at that time at $25,000, since which the same has not been written down. The average profits of the corporation for three years have been nine per cent on the capitalization. How would you treat the item good will? Give reasons.

Group III

11. What steps would you take to audit the Notes Receivable Purchased and the Notes Receivable on Commission held by a commercial paper house, to satisfy yourself that there had been no fraud by substitution?

12. The cashier of a concern is at the same time its bookkeeper. During his absence on vacation slight irregularities are discovered and you are engaged to audit his books. He returns on the day you begin your audit and admits a defalcation of $5,000. Knowing that his receipts were supposed to be deposited daily in the bank, state the steps that you would take to ascertain the truth of his admission.

13. The result of your count of the "cash on hand" at a large agency on January 1, 1912, discloses:

Bills		$1,979
Coin		484.19
Cash items supported by properly signed vouchers:		
January 14, 1908—Subagent Jones	$200	
July 20, 1909—Subagent Thomas	140	
August 20, 1909—Subagent Vincent	75	
September 30, 1910—Subagent Nelson	230	645
Cash balance as per general ledger		$3,108.19

Does this count complete your duty as an auditor? If you consider that further steps are necessary state what you would do.

14. What instructions would you give to a junior accountant to whom you had intrusted the audit of the account Investment in Bonds and Mortgages appearing on the books of a trust company?

15. You find that a concern whose books you are auditing has capitalized the amount of royalties that it would have had to pay on the sales of a three years' period if it had not owned the patents. On the increase of surplus thus obtained the directors have declared a stock dividend. Would you consider yourself called on to criticize the action of the directors? If so, state what would be the character of your criticism.

Pennsylvania State Board of Public Accountants

Examination Questions

GENERAL ACCOUNTING

Monday, November 20, 1911, 9 a. m. to 1 p. m.

1. Describe fully any business enterprise for the purpose of giving comprehensive information to a possible purchaser who is not very familiar with the property or any phase of its organization, operations, or financial condition or requirements, and who would expect, in case of purchase, to use this information to have the business managed to the best advantage.

2. Outline a system of accounting for a stock broker's office, including provision for the daily balancing of all securities.

Monday, November 20, 1911, 2 p. m. to 5 p. m.

3. Describe fully the usual accounting system employed in a national bank in one of the larger cities, with deposits of $15,000,000 and upwards.

Explain fully how to make a thorough examination and verification of each of the following:

Cash, cash items, and exchanges.
Loans of all classes.
Collaterals.
Securities owned.
Deposits.
Earnings.

4. The Borough of Exeter decides to pave and curb Main and Broad Streets, on the former of which is located the town hall and on the latter the town high school. State concisely the usual method employed to finance the expenditures involved in these improvements, and what accounts or records would be required in connection therewith.

Tuesday, November 21, 1911, 9 a. m. to 1 p. m.

5. The books of the Mapes & Manning Company, manufacturers of and dealers in farm implements, show for the past five years net profits as follows:

1906	$177,000
1907	143,000
1908	206,000
1909	16,000
1910	98,000

You are instructed by a banking syndicate to examine the accounts of the company and report upon the profits during the above period. In the course of your examination you ascertain the following facts:

Current liabilities were not taken into the accounts, as follows:

January 1, 1906	for	New Buildings	$42,000
		Accrued Wages	5,300
December, 31, 1906		Repair Charges	2,600
		Accrued Wages	2,900
December 31, 1908		Merchandise Invoices	6,800
		Current Expenses	5,400
December 31, 1910		Accrued Wages	3,200
		Materials and Supplies	4,600
		Shop Equipment	8,400

At December 31, 1910, the company engaged two real estate experts to appraise its land and buildings. The lower of the two showed a present value of $587,000, and this valuation was adopted by the Board of Directors, who instructed the bookkeeper to charge Real Estate Account and credit Profit and Loss at the above date with the difference between the foregoing amount and the book figures of $560,000.

A mortgage of $200,000, bearing 5 per cent remained upon the property during the whole of the period under review, and interest on this mortgage was charged before arriving at the book profits.

Satisfactory provision was made in each year for depreciation of buildings, machinery, etc.

Revise the profits for each year in accordance with the facts disclosed by your examination, and draft the form of certificate you would be prepared to give thereon to the bankers for prospectus purposes.

Assuming that after submitting this certificate to your clients they prefer instead to publish a certificate showing the average profits for the five-year period, what position would you take and what form of certificate would you be willing to sign?

6. A manufacturing concern is required to carry a six months' supply of a certain kind of raw material, and, as the material is not of the kind that can be purchased every day, they must purchase it at any time it is offered to them. For this reason the prices fluctuate sometimes very considerably. When they purchase this material, they pay cash for same and have the material shipped in as wanted. What method would you use in arriving at the cost of this raw material used during any one month in manufacturing?

Tuesday, November 21, 1911, 2 P. M. to 5 P. M.

7. A textile mill, employing some 700 hands, operates five departments, with a superintendent or head foreman in each. About 500 hands are paid upon a piecework basis, 50 on a part piecework and part day rate, according to the duties assigned to them from day to day; 100 are on a straight

day-rate basis, while the remainder are paid weekly salaries, but no overtime. Describe clearly and concisely the methods you would recommend for assembling and recording the data entering into the weekly pay roll. Also state how you would have the pay roll prepared and the wages, as shown thereon, paid to the hands, having in view both economy in the clerical work and the securing of proper safeguards against frauds.

8. (*a*) How should advancements which appear in the Inventory and Appraisement of a decedent's estate be treated by the Executors in distributing the Principal to the heirs?

(*b*) In the absence of instructions in the will, what disposition should be made of sale of "rights" or "warrants" by an Executor?

(*c*) An Executor of an estate in Pennsylvania forecloses a mortgage owned by the Estate, and title is taken to the property, the property remaining in the Estate at the time of filing his account. How should the transaction appear in his account?

WEDNESDAY, NOVEMBER 22, 1911, 9 A. M. TO 1 P. M.

9. A. B., desiring to incorporate his business, secures a charter under the laws of the Commonwealth of Pennsylvania on December 28, 1910, the A. B. Company being organized for the purpose of manufacturing chemicals and for the sale of the products of such manufacture. The capital stock of the company consists of 3,000 shares, of the par value of $100 each, the subscribers being as follows:

A. B.	2,996 shares
C. D.	1 share
E. F.	1 "
G. H.	1 "
J. K.	1 "
	3,000 shares

A. B. advances from his own funds the minimum amount of cash capital required by law. The balance of the subscription is to be paid for in Formulæ, Trade Marks, and Patents belonging to A. B. to the amount of $150,000, and a sufficient amount of the tangible assets of A. B.'s business, a Balance Sheet of which at January 1, 1911, is as follows:

Assets:		
Real Estate	$25,000	
Machinery	30.000	
Fixtures	15,600	
		$70,600
Inventories:		
Manufactured Product	15,220	
Materials	28,650	
Coal	572	
Prepaid Insurance	1,856	
		46,298

chasers, also during the same year 300 plots were sold on the installment plan as outlined in the foregoing.

Expenses not subject to inference from the foregoing:

Administration	$2,500
Salaries	5,000
Advertising	5,000
Taxes accrued, not paid	2,500

Prepare a Balance Sheet at December 31, 1908, and a Profit and Loss Account for the year ended on that date.

WEDNESDAY, NOVEMBER 22, 1911, 2 P. M. TO 5 P. M.

11. In a given trade, goods are purchased on terms of 5 per cent discount for cash in ten days, or net thirty days. In certifying a Balance Sheet in this trade, how would you deal with the question of this discount in stating the value of the inventory of merchandise on hand? Give your reasons for the treatment you would advocate.

12. You are retained to make an examination of the accounts of a hardware manufacturing company, and prepare a Balance Sheet and a Statement of its Earnings for the past ten years, the examination to be of sufficient scope to enable you to issue a certificate to the Balance Sheet and also to give the assurance that the Statement of Earnings presented is substantially correct.

Give an outline of your audit procedure, showing to what extent you would carry your examination in respect to the several classes of assets and liabilities, and if it were stated to you that depreciation of the plant and equipment had been provided for through the inclusion in the manufacturing cost of expenditures for new additions and betterments, what method would you take to ascertain the extent of such provision?

University of Illinois

EXAMINATION FOR CERTIFICATE AS CERTIFIED PUBLIC ACCOUNTANT

CHICAGO, ILL., MAY 28, 29, AND 31, 1912

AUDITING

WEDNESDAY, MAY 29, 1.30 TO 4.30 P. M.

The general intelligence with which the questions are answered will be considered in the marking, as well as the technical accuracy of each answer.

CURRENT ASSETS:			
Inventories—			
Raw Materials		$170,000	
Finished Stock at Selling Prices, less Discount 5 per cent		100,000	
Consignments (Selling Value)		50,000	
Supplies (Estimated)		200,000	
		$520,000	
Accounts and Bills Receivable, including Advances to Employees		125,000	
Stocks in Treasury (Unissued)—			
Preferred	$150,000		
Common	137,225		
		$287,225	
Investments in Subsidiary Companies		225,500	
Cash and Miscellaneous Items		50,500	
			$1,208,225
			$2,308,225

LIABILITIES

CAPITAL STOCK:		
Preferred Stock		$500,000
Common Stock		750,000
Bonds and Bankers' Loans		575,000
CURRENT LIABILITIES:		
Accounts Payable	$ 15,225	
Other Indebtedness	231,000	
Accrued Items	2,000	
		248,225
RESERVES:		
For Depreciation	$50,000	
Less—Renewal Expenditures written off	65,000	
Balance (Debit)	$15,000	
For Bad Debts	20,000	
Other Contingencies	5,000	
		10,000
Surplus (less Dividends Paid) including appreciation in Real Estate and other Capital Assets and Profit on Inventorying Raw Materials at Market Prices		225,000
		$2,308,225

(17½ Credits.)

6. You find in the course of an annual examination as of December 31, the following:

(1) A credit balance in the Cash Account of.................... $625.00

(2) In the Credit Ledger a debit balance for Cash charged to Davis & Co., on July 31 for.................... 375.00

(3) In the Debit Ledger a credit balance for Cash paid by Jones & Co., on December 31.................... 250.00

(4) A debit balance also in the Debit Ledger to Winslow & Co.:

July 1, Mdse...............	$ 50.00	Aug. 20, cash and discount...	$ 50.00
Aug. 3, Mdse...............	60.00	Oct. 3 " " ...	75.00
Sept. 15, Mdse...............	75.00	Dec. 1 " " ...	100.00
Oct. 10, Mdse...............	100.00	Dec. 31, Balance...........	60.00
	$285.00		$285.00

December 31, Balance $60.00.

What would be your view of each of these items?

(7½ Credits.)

7. In auditing the accounts of a Corporation, you find that the Company has utilized its own Materials and Labor in the construction of extensive additions to its plant, and that it has charged up such work at regular trade prices sufficient to yield to it a substantial Profit, which has been credited to Profit and Loss Account. Do you see any objection to this course? Explain fully the theory upon which your answer is based.

(10 Credits.)

8. A Company insures the life of its Manager for its own benefit in the sum of $50,000, the annual premium being $1,250. Explain the method you would adopt of treating the disbursement at the annual accounting during the period the policy was in force.

(10 Credits.)

Answer Any Two of the following Five Questions:

9. (*a*) In auditing the Disbursements of a Company, what books and documents would you call for; what would be your exact procedure, and to what points would you pay particular attention?

(*b*) Under what conditions would indorsed checks be regarded as ADEQUATE VOUCHERS?

(10 Credits.)

10. How far is an Auditor entitled to probe into matters beyond the term which he is instructed to audit, and for what purposes should he do so?

(10 Credits.)

11. In auditing the accounts of the following, what documents and records would you expect to see other than the regular double entry set of books?

(1) The Trust Estate of a deceased person.

(2) A private Partnership.

(3) A new Company which had not been previously audited.

(4) A Charitable Institution.

(10 Credits.)

12. In the course of audit of an Investment and Brokerage Corporation you find that the Directors have written up the value of some of the securities, which they contend is in harmony with current market values. The accounts show that the dividend proposed to be paid has not been earned unless the increment in value referred to is included as a Profit. What is your view of the proposed procedure of the Directors? If you concur with their proposed action, state your reasons; and if not, state the procedure, as Auditor, you would follow.

(10 Credits.)

13. (*a*) In the accounts of a Wholesale Dry Goods Company, under what, if any, circumstances is it permissible to carry forward to a subsequent period the whole or any portion of the Expenditures for Salesmen's Salaries or Commissions and Traveling Expenses?

(*b*) In the accounts of a Lumber Company owning large tracts of standing Timber, how should the book value of "Stumpage" be disposed of? What do you understand by "Stumpage"?

(10 Credits.)

State of Massachusetts

Fourth Public Accountant Examination

AUDITING

Wednesday, June 5, 1912, 1 p. m. to 5.30 p. m.

Answer questions 39, 40, 41, and 42, and 6 others, but no more.

39. State fully how you would verify the bank account of a concern depositing with six banks and making frequent transfers of funds between them.

40. Of what value in auditing is a unit of production?

41. A client (A. B. Co.) presents you the following statement as of January 1, 1912:

Assets		Liabilities	
Cash	$10,600.27	Notes payable	$20,000.00
Accounts receivable	30,219.73	Accounts payable	30,140.10
Merchandise	39,320.14	Profit and Loss	5,000.04
Machinery	10,000.00	Capital Stock	40,000.00
Loans to directors	5,000.00		
	$95,140.14		$95,140.14

You are required on January 10, 1912, to make sufficient examination and audit to certify the statement for credit purposes.

State fully how, and to what extent, you would verify the different items, and draw formal certificate covering same.

42. A corporation takes from its customers their notes in partial settlement of their accounts. Some of these notes are discounted by the corporation, and with its unlimited indorsement. Notes receivable account is credited with the notes discounted, and interest account is charged with the discount. State (a) your procedure in auditing the notes receivable transactions; (b) how you would ascertain what notes are not matured; and (c) how you would deal with the latter in the certificate of your audit?

43. In auditing the accounts of a tax collector, what should be done to determine if he accounts for the interest on overdue taxes paid?

44. You are auditor of a manufacturing corporation which has been operating five years and which has, amongst other accounts, the following, viz.: Plant account, $700,000; Reserve for Depreciation, $200,000; Surplus, $100,000. The officers ask you to certify a statement embracing the above items in the following form, viz.: "Plant," $700,000; "Surplus and Reserve accounts," $300,000. State (a) whether you approve same and (b) the reasons supporting your answer.

45. How would you audit the accounts of a Tax Collector?

46. The officers and directors of a Massachusetts corporation have executed and submitted to you, for your signature as the auditor chosen under the provisions of the statutes, their Certificate of Condition, April 1, 1912. At the same time, the treasurer asks you to prepare the corporation's "Return" to the Tax Commissioner, April 1, 1912, showing, therein, valuations of the merchandise and accounts receivable which the treasurer claims to be fair cash values, but which are less than the respective amounts included in the Certificate of Condition. State what action you would take (a) regarding the Certificate of Condition; (b) regarding the tax "Return"; and (c) the reasons supporting your answers.

47. To what extent do you deem it necessary to verify the following

in order that you may certify to the correctness of a Profit and Loss statement:

Materials and Supplies.
Goods in Process.
Finished Goods.
Accounts Receivable.

48. Describe a complete audit of the Trust Department of a Trust Company.

49. Your visit as auditor of The Iroquois Bank of Pittsfield happens to be concurrent with that of the examiners from the Bank Commissioner's Office. State in detail what modifications, if any, you would feel justified in making in the scope and thoroughness of your audit.

50. You are instructed to make a report on the earning capacity of a manufacturing plant, as disclosed by its operations during a period of five years. Inventories were taken at the beginning and end of this period, and at yearly intervals between same. What would your procedure be in the examination, and what salient features would you bring out in your report?

51. A corporation has on its books $210,000 of accounts receivable, of which $49,000 are long overdue, and apparently worthless. The inventory of finished goods, taken at contract price, less 5 per cent amounts to $124,000, and from this sum has been deducted $45,000 "to provide for any losses."

How would you deal with this state of affairs in reporting to the Bank Commissioner on the condition of the corporation for savings bank loans?

52. The "system of internal checking" of a savings bank calls for regular observance by the Board of Investment, whether the records of collateral received, and changes thereof, on loans, accord with the votes of the Board. Under these conditions, and in the case of loans on collateral security, state (a) whether you would write to each borrower to send to you the details of the note, together with a list of the collateral deposited therewith; (b) whether you would ascertain the market value of the collateral; (c) what action you would take if you thought that the character of the collateral was inferior, or that the margin was insufficient. State (d) whether you would restrict the extent of your general audit because of a high degree of excellence in the "system of internal checking"; (e) the reasons supporting your answers.

53. A corporation in closing its fiscal year has some 60 items of current liabilities, which it enters on its books as follows:

(Sundry accounts)	$53,827.34	
Accounts payable		$53,827.34

On the first day of the new year, the bookkeeper makes the following entry:

Accounts payable	$53,827.34	
(Sundry accounts)		$53,827.34

How should the auditor deal with this condition?

The State Board of Accountancy of Ohio

AUDITING

FRIDAY, DECEMBER 8, 1911, AT 9 A. M. (TIME ALLOWANCE, THREE HOURS)

1. (*a*) Describe briefly but in detail the several steps you would take in making a complete and detailed audit of the books of account of a manufacturing corporation.

(*b*) Give a list of the books of such a corporation which in a detailed audit the auditor should examine.

2. Under instructions calling for a complete audit and verification of all entries, what supporting data would you require for the following?

(*a*) Purchases.
(*b*) Returned Purchases.
(*c*) Sales.
(*d*) Returned Sales.
(*e*) Cash Receipts.
(*f*) Cash Payments.
(*g*) Journal Entries.

3. In the case of an unexplained absence of a bookkeeper who has entire charge of the accounting for a corporation, state the steps that in your judgment should be taken to determine: first, the actual existing conditions; second, whether or not irregularities had been committed.

4. (*a*) You are called upon to audit the books of account of a concern and discover that for the fiscal year under your inspection it has not shown sufficient profit to justify the payment of any dividends. The manager, in order to make a profit showing, has failed to set up the usual reserves for depreciation of buildings, plants, machinery, tools, etc., nor has he sufficiently allowed for losses in the collection of Accounts Receivable, etc. In making your report of audit, what would you do under the circumstances? Give your reasons therefor fully in such form as you would submit them in your report.

(*b*) In what way, if at all, would you report the fact that a trusted office manager had overdrawn his salary account at various times, in no case more than $300, all of which had been returned before the time of the annual audit? State your reasons fully.

5. State the arrangement of a report in which it is desired to present Balance Sheet with supporting schedules of Accounts Receivable, Accounts Payable, Notes Receivable, Notes Payable, and Profit and Loss Account, together with comments on the extraordinary features of the business.

6. (*a*) How would you account for the proceeds of sales to customers without checking each entry?

(*b*) In passing upon the value shown in the inventory, how should the auditor treat materials costing $10 per unit when the market price is $8 per unit, and when the market price is $12 per unit? State reasons fully.

7. How should the following assets be valued for a balance sheet?

(*a*) Manufactured goods.

(*b*) Raw material.

(*c*) Accounts Receivable.

(*d*) Partially manufactured goods.

(*e*) Notes receivable.

(*f*) Stock, bonds, and similar investments.

(*g*) A building company engaged in construction work under contract has a number of contracts in process of completion. In auditing the accounts of such a company, how would you compute the value of such unfinished contracts as an asset in the Balance Sheet?

8. A firm having several branches maintains an account with each branch in the ledger and charges all such accounts with goods sent the agents for stock. When the inventory of stock is taken, the balance of each branch account is treated as an ordinary Accounts Receivable and is included in the general debts owing to the firm. If you see any objections to this method, say how you would deal with the accounts.

9. Does an auditor's duty in any way extend beyond the careful examination and certifying of the books and accounts submitted to him? Discuss briefly different theories.

10. (*a*) The auditor of an incorporated company which has been accustomed to making investments in interest paying securities, in making his statement to the directors presented a Balance Sheet showing a surplus of $65,000. After discussion, the directors determined that they did not wish to declare a dividend out of this surplus, and gave their auditor the following order:

"Decrease this surplus by investing $50,000 in the 5 per cent bonds of the X Y Z Railroad Company."

Presuming there was an item in the aforesaid Balance Sheet of cash $75,000, what effect will the carrying out of the directors' order have upon the surplus of $65,000?

(*b*) What is an audit? Make a definition.

Minnesota State Board of Accountancy

Examination April 11, 1912

AUDITING

Time Allowed, Six Hours

1. State the purposes of an audit. To what extent should an audit deal with accounting system? With bookkeeping system?

2. Distinguish between the "continuous" and the "completed" audit, stating the advantages and disadvantages of each.

3. Describe the method of verifying cash on hand at the close of the period under review.

4. Discuss "the best method of auditing cash receipts."

5. Discuss "the best method of auditing cash payments."

6. How would you audit a pay roll?

7. What special matters should be investigated in the audit of corporate books?

8. What different considerations govern the valuation for balance sheet purposes of "fixed" and "current" assets?

9. What is the best procedure in verifying the existence and value of land, buildings, stock-in-trade, investments in stocks and bonds, plant and machinery, work-in-progress?

10. Discuss "the proper method of treating discounts, freight, and haulage on goods or equipment purchased," "on goods sold."

11. Discuss "the limitations of an investigation of a business on behalf of a projected purchasing company." To what extent would fraud by employees of the vendor bear upon the subject?

12. In what respects would an investigation of a business on behalf of a retiring or deceased partner differ from one on behalf of a projected purchasing company?

13. Discuss "the extent of the auditor's certification."

14. Discuss "the proper method of presenting the condition and earnings of a holding company which owns from 75 to 100 per cent of the stock of a number of subsidiary corporations."

15. State the special features which pertain to the audit of the books and accounts of a building loan association.

16. State the special features which pertain to the audit of the books and accounts of a street railway company.

17. State the special features which pertain to the audit of the books and accounts of a fire insurance company.

18. A mercantile concern sustains a partial loss by fire. The books are modern, except no cost accounting is incorporated. The end of the fiscal year is December 31, when a physical inventory is taken; the fire occurred in October and was evidently a two-thirds loss, with full insurance. While the adjusters are at work you are called in to satisfy the firm as to their loss, so that they may be prepared for discussion with the insurance companies.

Outline your procedure and state how you arrive at the actual loss.

Utah

Examination April 12, 1912

AUDITING

Time Limit, Three Hours

1. Explain the meaning of good will. When may it properly appear upon the books of a company as a valuable asset? What principal factors should be taken into consideration in placing a valuation on good will?

2. Are stock dividends legitimate at any time? Would you consider it justifiable at any time to pay a dividend with borrowed money? Give reasons for your answers.

3. What are secret or hidden reserves? How may they be created, and what do you think of their propriety?

4. For several years a corporation makes reserves of profits to provide for redemption of bonds and for building extensions. When the bonds are redeemed and the extensions made, what disposition would you make of the reserve accounts?

5. Under what headings would you generally classify the resources and the liabilities in a balance sheet of a manufacturing company?

6. State the steps necessary to verify the cash receipts and payments for a period, including the resultant cash balance.

7. In examining the mortgage loans of a bank, insurance company, or other loan company, what papers and records would you examine, and to what points would you give particular notice?

8. In auditing a corporation, what books and records besides the regular financial account books would you want to examine? In naming any book or record give fully your reasons for calling for it.

9. In what ways may a bookkeeper who is also cashier conceal thefts, his books being kept by double-entry and in balance?

10. In preparing the balance sheet of a business at the close of a year, how should you treat each of the following items: (a) bad and doubtful debts, (b) premiums for fire insurance unexpired, (c) interest paid in advance on notes payable discounted, (d) discount on accounts receivable, (e) discount on accounts payable, (f) depreciation of plant.

INDEX

N

The History of Accounting

An Arno Press Collection

Bennet[t], James [Arlington]. **The American System of Practical Book-Keeping** and Foster, B[enjamin] F[ranklin], **The Origin and Progress of Book-Keeping.** 1842/1852. Two vols. in one

Brief, Richard P., editor. **The Late Nineteenth Century Debate Over Depreciation, Capital and Income.** 1976

Brief, Richard P. **Nineteenth Century Capital Accounting and Business Investment.** 1976

Bruchey, Stuart W[eems]. **Robert Oliver and Mercantile Bookkeeping in the Early Nineteenth Century.** 1976

Church, A[lexander] Hamilton. **Production Factors in Cost Accounting and Works Management.** 1910

Cole, William Morse. **Accounts:** Their Construction and Interpretation for Business Men and Students of Affairs. 1908

Dicksee, Lawrence R[obert]. **Advanced Accounting.** 1903

Dicksee, Lawrence R[obert]. **Auditing:** A Practical Manual for Auditors. 1892

Dicksee, Lawrence R[obert]. **Auditing:** A Practical Manual for Auditors. Authorized American Edition, Edited by Robert H. Montgomery. 1905

Dicksee, Lawrence R[obert]. **Depreciation, Reserves, and Reserve Funds.** 1903

Dicksee, Lawrence R[obert] and Frank Tillyard. **Goodwill and Its Treatment in Accounts.** 1906

Folsom, E[zekiel] G[ilman]. **Folsom's Logical Bookkeeping:** The Logic of Accounts. 1873

Garcke, Emile and J[ohn] M[anger] Fells. **Factory Accounts, Their Principles and Practice.** 1893

Hatfield, Henry Rand. **Modern Accounting:** Its Principles and Some of its Problems. 1916

Kehl, Donald. **Corporate Dividends:** Legal and Accounting Problems Pertaining to Corporate Distributions. 1941

Leake, P[ercy] D[ewe]. **Depreciation and Wasting Assets and Their Treatment in Assessing Annual Profit and Loss.** 1912

Lisle, George. **Accounting in Theory and Practice.** 1900

Matheson, Ewing. **The Depreciation of Factories, Mines and Industrial Undertakings and Their Valuation.** 1893

Montgomery, Robert H. **Auditing Theory and Practice.** 1912

Norton, George Pepler. **Textile Manufacturers' Book-Keeping for the Counting House, Mill and Warehouse.** 1894

Paton, William A[ndrew] and Russell A[lger] Stevenson. **Principles of Accounting.** 1916

Pixley, Francis W[illiam]. **Auditors:** Their Duties and Responsibilities Under the Joint-Stock Companies Acts and the Friendly Societies and Industrial and Provident Societies Acts. 1881

Reiter, Prosper, Jr. **Profits, Dividends and the Law.** 1926

Scott, DR. **Theory of Accounts.** 1925

Scovell, Clinton H. **Interest as a Cost.** 1924

Sells, Elijah Watt. **The Natural Business Year and Thirteen Other Themes.** 1924

Soulé, Geo[rge]. **Soulé's New Science and Practice of Accounts.** 1903

Sprouse, Robert T[homas]. **The Effect of the Concept of the Corporation on Accounting.** 1976

Zeff, Stephen A., editor. **Asset Appreciation, Business Income and Price-Level Accounting: 1918-1935.** 1976